ABOUKHEIR

PENGUIN REFERENCE

Penguin Pocket Rhyming Dictionary

Rosalind Fergusson is a freelance editor and lexicographer with a wide range of reference books to her name, including the *Penguin Dictionary of Proverbs* (1983), the *Penguin Dictionary of Synonyms and Antonyms* (1992), the *Chambers Dictionary of Foreign Words and Phrases* (1995) and the *Cassell Dictionary of English Idioms* (1999). She has also contributed to such titles as the *Oxford-Hachette French Dictionary* (1994), the *Macmillan Guide to English Grammar* (1998), the *Penguin English Dictionary* (2000) and the *Chambers Book of Days* (2004). She lives in Kent and occupies her leisure time with walking, sailing, literature and European travel.

D0582415

PENGUIN POCKET RHYMING DICTIONARY

Rosalind Fergusson

PENGUIN BOOKS

PENGUIN BOOKS

Published by the Penguin Group
Penguin Books Ltd, 80 Strand, London WC2R 0RL, England
Penguin Group (USA) Inc., 375 Hudson Street, New York, New York 10014, USA
Penguin Group (Canada), 90 Eglinton Avenue East, Suite 700, Toronto, Ontario, Canada M4P 2Y3
(a division of Pearson Penguin Canada Inc.)
Penguin Ireland, 25 St Stephen's Green, Dublin 2, Ireland
(a division of Penguin Books Ltd)
Penguin Group (Australia), 250 Camberwell Road, Camberwell, Victoria 3124, Australia
(a division of Pearson Australia Group Pty Ltd)
Penguin Books India Pvt Ltd, 11 Community Centre,
Panchsheel Park, New Delhi – 110 017, India
Penguin Group (NZ), cnr Airborne and Rosedale Roads, Albany,
Auckland 1310, New Zealand (a division of Pearson New Zealand Ltd)
Penguin Books (South Africa) (Pty) Ltd, 24 Sturdee Avenue,
Rosebank 2196, Johannesburg, South Africa

Penguin Books Ltd, Registered Offices: 80 Strand, London WC2R 0RL, England

www.penguin.com

First published 2006
4

Copyright © Market House Books Ltd, 2006

The moral right of the author has been asserted

Set in Stone Sans and ITC Stone Serif
Printed in England by Clays Ltd, St Ives plc

ISBN-13: 978-0-141-02721-0
ISBN-10: 0-141-02721-5

Preface

This pocket edition is an abridged version of the highly successful *Penguin Rhyming Dictionary*, which was first published in 1985.

Milton, in his preface to *Paradise Lost*, complained of the 'troublesome and modern bondage of rhyming...the invention of a barbarous age, to set off wretched matter and lame metre'. Yet many creators of superb matter and lilting metre, both before and since 1668 (when these words were written), have felt it necessary to make their verses rhyme. Some poets have relied on their heads to satisfy their need, others have resorted to rhyming dictionaries. *Walker's Rhyming Dictionary*, for example, has been in continuous publication for 150 years. According to its preface, it has 'been a friend in need to generations of poets and rhymesters from Byron downwards'. But when John Walker, a retired schoolmaster, compiled his *Rhyming Dictionary* in 1775, he had to do so without the benefit of a computer.

Had he had access to modern technology, the main part of his *Rhyming Dictionary*, in which the words are listed in reverse alphabetical order (working from the last letter of each word back to the first), would have been relatively simple to produce from the headword list of any standard dictionary. However, this list alone does not provide the poet seeking a rhyme for, say, *trite*, with any of the perfect rhymes: *sight, indict, Fahrenheit, acolyte*, or *apartheid*. On the other hand, it throws together as if they rhymed those classic examples of English spelling inconsistency: *bough, cough, though, rough*, and *through*.

To compile the *Penguin Rhyming Dictionary*, a list of words together with their phonetic transcriptions was extracted from a standard dictionary data base. The computer was programmed to sort these words, working from the end of the phonetic transcription back to the beginning, into phonetic order. Unsuitable and unrhymable words were then discarded and the remainder of the list was sorted into rhyming groups. The result is that homophones (phonetically identical words of different meaning), such as *sight, cite*, and *site*, are now grouped together, and such rhymes as *stipulation* and *manipulation*, rather than being buried in an alphabetical list of -*ation* words, appear side by side.

With its ability to scan through a complete list of phonetic transcriptions in a matter of minutes, the computer is an incomparably more versatile rhymester than the live poet with his dying brain cells and deteriorating memory. This dictionary offers to the poet the fruits of the computer's labour, providing him or her with all the words that one would expect to find in a standard English dictionary, including a selection of proper names. There is only one condition of entry for a word: that there should be at least one other word that rhymes with it. Because poetry is not only a question of rhymes – and because poets may wish to know what their verses mean – a short gloss is provided for the more obscure words.

RF
2006

Guide to the dictionary

1. To find rhymes for any particular word, first look in the index, which forms roughly the second half of the book.

2. The index will refer the user either to a group number (e.g. **15**) or a subgroup number (e.g. **15.3**) in the first part of the book.

3. Find the word you have looked up in the group or subgroup to which you have been referred. The words closest to this word will be its closest rhymes.

4. If you have been directed to a group rather than to a subgroup, you will find several separate paragraphs under the group heading. The first paragraph contains monosyllabic words, the second paragraph disyllabic words, and so on.
   Example: To find the closest rhymes to **ballet**, look this word up in the index. The reference **2** means that it will be found in the group headed **2**. Because it has two syllables it will be found in the second paragraph. The words that follow it – **Calais**, **palais**, **chalet**, etc. – are its closest rhymes.

5. Note that **ballet** can be made to rhyme, with varying degrees of closeness, with all the words in group **2** and its subgroups. This applies to all the words in all the groups (see note (b), below).

6. Within each paragraph, whether in a main group or in a subgroup, the words given are listed in phonetic order, working from the end of the word to the beginning. The basis of the phonetic order is given on page viii. However, in most cases, paragraphs are short enough for a word to be located by quickly scanning it, rather than by trying to work out its position in the phonetic order.

7. If the index directs you to a subgroup rather than to a group, you will find a list of close rhymes that have been picked out and placed in a subgroup because it would not have been possible to place them next to each other in a main group. (This usually means that some of the words in the subgroup contain different numbers of syllables).
   Example: To find the closest rhymes to **atmosphere**, go as directed by the index to subgroup **6.1**, where all the words ending in -**osphere** are listed – from **biosphere** to **magnetosphere**.

The following points should be noted:

(a) All the words in the lists contained in the first part of the book are included in the alphabetical index in the second part of the book.

(b) The rhyming words are arranged in the numbered groups under one-syllable headings, such as *-ite*, *-ank*, and *-oe*. These headings are broad guides to the final sound of the words in the groups. For example, the *–oe* group contains **potato**, **although**, and **show** as well as **hoe** and **roe**.

(c) Some group headings are followed by a guide to further rhyming possibilities, often in the form of a cross-reference. Unless otherwise stated, these cross-references apply to all the subgroups of both the group in which they appear and the group to which they refer. For example, the cross reference from group **5** to group **16** applies also to the subgroups **5.1** to **5.24** and subgroups **16.1** to **16.406**.

(d) The glosses that follow difficult words are intended as brief guides to their meanings or to the field in which they are used; they do not constitute full dictionary definitions. The italicized labels – *US*, *Scot*, *Austral*, etc. – indicate that the word is an American, Scottish, or Australian synonym, often informal, for the given gloss. Thus (*Welsh mountain*) means 'a Welsh word for mountain'. However, (Welsh mountain) means 'a mountain in Wales'.

Phonetic order

a as in *sat*
ar as in *card, half*
ay as in *day, rail*
e as in *bed*
err as in *err, fern*
air as in *pair, rare*
ee as in *meet, teach*
ear as in *veer, fear*
i as in *win*
ie as in *tie, bite*
ire as in *fire*
o as in *pot*
or as in *form, talk*
oor as in *moor*
oy as in *boy, coil*
oe as in *toe, boat*
ow as in *town, foul*

our as in *hour*
u as in *mug*
oo as in *foot*
ue as in *true, tool*
er as in *water and other unstressed vowel sounds*
b as in *big*
k as in *kite, car*
ch as in *chip*
d as in *day*
f as in *fall, phone*
g as in *gate*
j as in *job, page*
h as in *hat*
l as in *lean*
m as in *mope*

n as in *neat*
ng as in *sing*
p as in *pearl*
qu as in *quick*
r as in *ripe*
s as in *soon*
sh as in *sheep, nation*
zh as in *treasure*
t as in *team*
th as in *thing*
dh as in *bathe*
v as in *vase*
w as in *wool*
x as in *box, works*
y as in *yoke*
z as in *zoo, reason*

Dictionary

1 -ar

are, ah, bar, baa, car, scar, char, dah (sound in Morse code), fa, far, gar (freshwater fish), jar, ha, haar (North Sea fog), lah, blah (silly talk), mar, ma, knar (knot in wood), parr, par, pa, spar, spa, Kwa (language group), Ra, bra, Kra (isthmus of Thailand), Fra (title of Italian monk), Saar (European river), shah, ta, tar, tahr (goatlike mammal), star, var (unit of power), moire, schwa (unstressed vowel sound), tsar.

aa (volcanic rock), baba, Sabah (Malaysian state), durbar (native ruler's court), drawbar (metal bar on tractor), crowbar, towbar, Pooh-Bah, subah (province in Mogul empire), Akbar (Mogul emperor of India), rollbar, unbar, Dunbar, disbar, crossbar, kasbah, fracas, markka (Finnish currency), taka (Bangladeshi currency), Neckar (German river), trocar (surgical instrument), sidecar, railcar, Shankar, streetcar, boxcar (US closed railway van), cha-cha, kwacha (Zambian currency), Dada, radar, sirdar, Gondar (Ethiopian city), sofar (marine location system), shofar (ancient Jewish horn), afar, solfa, gaga, Degas, Hagar (Old Testament character), durgah (tomb of Muslim saint), nougat, Elgar, kanga (African woman's cotton garment), ajar, nightjar, Lehár, Doha (capital of Qatar), Zohar (Jewish mystical work), hoo-ha, nullah (Indian stream or drain), moolah (*Slang* money), kiblah (direction of Mecca), dobla (medieval Spanish coin), éclat (brilliant success), verglas (thin film of ice), hoopla, Omagh, grandma, dinar, thenar (palm of the hand), Donar (Germanic god), sonar, faux pas, papa, culpa (act of neglect), oompah, grandpa, COSPAR (Committee on Space Research), feldspar, Berar (region of India), Kura (Asian river), hurrah, Accra, Stranraer, paisa (Indian coin), pulsar, orgeat (drink made from barley), Qatar, ta-ta, guitar, sitar, hectare, kantar (unit of weight), qintar (Albanian coin), daystar (the sun), lodestar (star used in navigation), Telstar, sunstar (starfish), earthstar (woodland fungus), navar (aircraft-navigation system), Avar (former European people), halvah (Middle Eastern sweet), boulevard, boudoir, couloir (mountain gully), armoire, memoir, Renoir, mirepoix (mixture of sautéed vegetables), octroi (duty on goods), bourgeois, patois, Magyar, quasar, Isar (European river), bizarre, Mizar (multiple star), beaux-arts, hussar.

antiar (Javan tree), caviar, Cantuar. (of Canterbury), handlebar, turbocar, judo-ka (judo expert), Halakah (traditional Jewish literature), motorcar, advocaat, la-di-da, deodar (Himalayan cedar), tah-sildar (Indian tax collector), havildar (Indian noncommissioned officer), zamindar (Indian landowner), Kandahar (Afghan city), Omaha, Tsushima (Japanese islands), seminar, Achernar (star), jaçana (long-legged

bird), grandpapa, Peckinpah, fluorspar, Amen-Ra (Egyptian sun-god), registrar, commissar, Manisa (Turkish city), collapsar (black hole), Aisha (favourite wife of Mohammed), langue de chat, Parashah (reading in synagogue), coup d'état, pietà, Bogotá, Janata (Indian political party), avatar (manifestation of Hindu deity), superstar, colcothar (jeweller's rouge), bolivar (Venezuelan currency), cultivar (cultivated plant), chihuahua, pesewa (Ghanaian coin), Aduwa (Ethiopian town), peau de soie (silk or rayon fabric), escritoire.
Mauna Kea (extinct Hawaiian volcano), justiciar (medieval king's deputy), Mauna Loa (active Hawaiian volcano), Kathiawar (large Indian peninsula), petit bourgeois.

1.1
debar, millibar (unit of atmospheric pressure), Zanzibar.

1.2
Calabar (Nigerian port), Malabar (Indian coastal region), coolabah, cinnabar (chief ore of mercury), isobar.

1.3
doodah, Üsküdar (Turkish town).

1.4
cigar, Chandigarh (Indian city), budgerigar.

1.5
aha, ha-ha, brouhaha.

1.6
Bihar (Indian state), Cooch Behar (Indian city), pakeha (non-Maori).

1.7
à la, fa-la, Lala (Indian form of address), tra-la, Haleakala (Hawaiian volcano).

1.8
zila (Indian administrative district), Shangri-la.

1.9
galah (Australian cockatoo), escolar (spiny-finned fish), Agartala (Indian city).

1.10
Armagh, Hama (Syrian city), Toyama (Japanese city).

1.11
cymar (woman's short jacket), Waldemar (Danish king), Kohima (Indian city).

1.12
mama, Shema (basic Jewish doctrine), jacamar (tropical bird), Palomar (Californian mountain observatory), Beach-la-Mar (Pacific trading language), grandmama, Panama.

1.13
hoorah, tempura (Japanese food).

1.14
mara (South American rodent), Pará (Brazilian state), Tambora (Indonesian volcano), baccarat, agora (Israeli coin), Aymara (South American Indian people).

1.15
Navarre, baklava (rich cake), samovar (Russian tea urn).

1.16
peignoir, rouge et noir (card game).

1.17
abattoir, repertoire, conservatoire.

1.18
devoirs (compliments), reservoir.

1.19
bazaar, alcazar (Moorish palace in Spain), Balthazar, kala-azar (tropical disease).

2 -ay
eh, ay, bay, bey (Turkish form of address), Kay, cay (low island or bank), day, dey, fay, fey, gay, jay, hey, hay, hae (*Scot* have), lay, clay, flay, gley (bluish-grey soil), play, splay, slay, sleigh, May, may, neigh, nay, née, nae (*Scot* no), Neagh (Northern Irish lake), pay, Spey, spay, re, ray, bray, brae, cray (*Austral* crayfish), dray, fray, Frey (Norse god), frae (*Scot* from), grey, Gray, spray, tray, trey, stray, say, Tay, tay (*Irish* tea), stay, they, weigh, whey, way, ngwee (Zambian coin), sway, yea.

plié (ballet posture), mouillé (phonetics term), foyer, abbé, Torbay, cube (tropical palate), sickbay, Bombay, bombé (having projecting swollen shape), rosebay (type of rhododendron), parquet, Les Cayes (Haitian port), okay, croquet, tokay (small lizard), bouquet, Biscay, risqué, heyday, Mayday, payday, bidet, Friday, workday, weekday, midday, halfday, someday, Mande (language group), Monday, sundae, Sunday, noonday, washday, birthday, Thursday, Tuesday, doomsday, café, parfait (frozen dessert), au fait, Hofei (Chinese city), buffet, margay (catlike mammal), reggae, nosegay, deejay, ballet, Calais, palais, chalet, Male (capital of the Maldives), vale (farewell), waylay, melee, Pelé, relay, Islay, au lait, olé, piolet (type of ice-axe), coulee (flow of molten lava), bouclé, pipeclay, soufflé, reflet (lustre), agley (Scot awry), inlay, unlay (untwist), replay, foreplay, wordplay, swordplay, endplay, screenplay, gunplay, display, misplay (play badly), horseplay, mislay, bobsleigh, outlay, lamé, Niamey (capital of Niger), gourmet, dismay, nene (Hawaiian goose), fine (musical term), chiné (mottled), mornay, pince-nez, frappé, épée, prepay, repay, Taipei (capital of Taiwan), Hopeh (Chinese province), coupé, Hupeh (Chinese province), Nupe (Nigerian people), toupee, Gaspé (peninsula in Quebec), jaspé (variegated), strathspey (Scottish reel), parkway, walkway, beret, ciré, Shiré (African river), foray, moray, Fauré, Kure (Japanese port), hooray, chambray (fine woven cloth), hombre (US man), defray, affray (noisy fight or disturbance), passé, Tigré (Ethiopian province), in re (in the matter of), sunray, stingray, cy pres (legal term), respray, betray, portray, entrée, distrait, astray, ashtray, Vouvray (dry white wine), x-ray, essay, per se, lycée, plissé, hearsay, assay, gainsay, unsay, soothsay, cliché, broché (woven with raised design), crochet, bouchée (vol-au-vent), touché, dragée, Roget, projet (draft of proposed treaty), congé, satai (spiced barbecued meat), pâté, jeté, mainstay, outstay, backstay (nautical term), jackstay (nautical term), Cathay, pavé (paved surface), névé (mass of ice), survey, corvée (forced labour), duvet, purvey, chevet (part of church), inveigh, convey, airway, fairway, stairway, leeway, freeway, seaway, clearway, doorway, Norway, throughway (US motorway), subway, hatchway, archway, headway, Medway, speedway, skidway (US platform for logs), midway, tideway (strong tidal current), Broadway, roadway, halfway, railway, Solway, Galway, hallway, tramway, someway, Anhwei (Chinese province), Conway, runway, gangway, slipway, shipway (shipbuilding structure), paceway (Austral racecourse), Kweisui (Chinese town), gateway, outweigh, footway (pedestrian path), beltway (US ring road), pathway, driveway, causeway, soignée, passepied (17th-century minuet), blasé, Laotze (ancient Chinese philosopher).

holiday, everyday, unbirthday, Wednesday, coryphée (leading ballet dancer), merengue (Caribbean dance), popinjay, cassoulet, underclay, cor anglais, teleplay, underplay, interplay, overplay, animé, consommé, résumé, Dubonnet (Trademark), cloisonné (type of enamel work), Hogmanay, Massenet (French composer), underpay, overpay, Kol Nidre (Jewish prayer), émigré, Castlereagh (British statesman), divorcé, fiancé, Colonsay (Hebridean island), recherché, écorché (anatomical figure), ricochet, negligee, protégé, Fabergé, décolleté, overstay, naiveté, Milky Way, alleyway, anyway, taxiway, Camagüey (Cuban city), cableway, Hemingway, expressway (US urban motorway), sommelier, atelier, Parmentier (cookery term).

Marinduque (Philippine island), Hiroshige (Japanese artist), Tenzing Norgay, companionway (stairway on ship), ukiyoe (school of Japanese painting).

2.1

Rainier, Fourier, dossier, métier, boulevardier, Du Maurier, couturier, Olivier.

2.2

Douai (French city), roué, Niue (Pacific island).

2.3

Benue (Nigerian state), tatouay (large armadillo), habitué.

2.4

obey, mangabey (monkey), disobey, Iskander Bey (Albanian patriot).

2.5

flambé, harambee (East African work chant).

2.6

piqué, appliqué.

2.7

decay, tourniquet, sobriquet, communiqué.

2.8

today, workaday, Faraday, Saturday, yesterday, alackaday.

2.9

Santa Fe, auto-da-fé (ceremony of Spanish Inquisition), Morgan le Fay.

2.10

Haringey, Fotheringhay.

2.11

belay (make secure), delay, gilet (bodice resembling waistcoat), Millais, relay, roundelay (medieval dance), virelay (old French poem).

2.12

allay, Malay, Pelée (volcano in Martinique), Rabelais, Mandalay (Burmese city), Charollais (breed of cattle), underlay, beaujolais, interlay, overlay, cabriolet.

2.13

roble (oak tree), paso doble.

2.14

carnet, KaNgwane (South African homeland).

2.15

matinée, ratiné (coarse cloth), in nomine (musical term).

2.16

barré (guitar-playing procedure), Le Carré.

2.17

mare (plain on moon's surface), moiré, soiree, Whangarei (New Zealand port).

2.18

bourrée, purée, de jure (according to law).

2.19

array, cabaret, disarray, Monterey (Californian city), Monterrey (Mexican city).

2.20

assay, chassé (ballet step), bio-assay (biology term), immunoassay (immunology technique).

2.21

Ruse (Bulgarian city), repoussé (raised design), retroussé.

2.22

cachet, sachet, attaché, papier-mâché.

2.23

maté (tree cultivated for caffeine), écarté (card game), Hakodate (Japanese port).

2.24

sauté, Obote, cenote (natural well in limestone), chayote (tropical climbing plant), chicalote (type of poppy).

2.25

velouté, kachang puteh (Malaysian roasted nuts).

2.26

byway, highway, superhighway (*US* fast dual carriageway).

2.27

noway, Ogooué (African river).

2.28

aweigh, away, flyaway, throwaway, stowaway, breakaway, takeaway, hideaway, foldaway, Alloway, Galloway, mulloway (Australian fish), Stornoway, caraway, faraway, straightaway, waterway, motorway, cutaway, counterweigh, castaway, Hathaway, overweigh.

2.29

ridgeway, carriageway, steerageway (nautical term), passageway.

2.30

Bizet, frisé (fabric with long nap), Champs Élysées.

2.31

rosé, San Jose (Californian city), exposé.

3 -err

err, Ur, burr, bur, birr (make whirring sound), cur, Kerr, chirr (make shrill sound), fur, fir, her, blur, slur, myrrh, knur (knot in tree trunk), per, purr, spur, br'er, sir, shirr, stir, were, whirr, 'twere.

voyeur, recur, occur, incur, concur, coiffeur, defer, refer, prefer, infer, confer, transfer, demur, Hotspur, larkspur, cockspur (type of grass), masseur, chasseur, douceur (a tip or bribe), deter, hauteur, inter, bestir, astir, aver, priedieu, milieu, seigneur, poseur.

butterbur (flowering plant), cocklebur (coarse weed), underfur, connoisseur, force majeure, voyageur (Canadian woodsman), rapporteur (person who prepares report), disinter, raconteur, Richelieu, écraseur (surgical cutting device).

entrepreneur, carillonneur (bell-ringer).

3.1

saboteur, littérateur (professional writer), restaurateur.

4 -air

air, heir, e'er, Ayr, ere, bare, bear, care, scare, chair, dare, fare, fair, hair, hare, lair, blare, Clare, flair, flare, glare, glair (egg-white), mare, mayor, Khmer (former Cambodian civilization), ne'er, snare, pear, pare, pair, spare, quare (*Irish* remarkable), square, rare, prayer, share, tear, tare, stair, stare, there, their, they're, vair (medieval fur trimming), wear, ware, where, swear.

tuyère (nozzle in blast-furnace), howe'er, forebear, forbear, Flaubert, threadbare, Rambert, highchair, wheelchair, armchair, pushchair, midair, Kildare, Mayfair, warfare, fieldfare, welfare, fanfare, unfair, funfair, mohair, horsehair, éclair, declare, Sinclair, commère (female compere), nightmare, plein-air (art term), whene'er, Bonaire (West Indian island), ensnare, au pair,

ampere, impair, compere, compare, despair, foursquare (firmly), headsquare, where'er, confrère, corsair, torchère (stand for holding candelabrum), ploughshare, parterre (formally-patterned garden), Altair (star), Voltaire, Basse-Terre (West Indian island), Astaire, Lothair (German king), trouvère (medieval French poet), seaware (large seaweed), nowhere, neckwear, hardware, stemware (stemmed glasses), firmware (computer term), somewhere, treenware (wooden utensils), tinware, stoneware, glassware, forswear (reject with determination), elsewhere, unswear (retract), sportswear, nightwear, footwear, software, liveware (personnel working with computers), menswear, Gruyère, meunière (cookery term), Robespierre, misère.

overbear, Medicare (*US* health insurance programme), aftercare, Aberdare, nom de guerre, maidenhair (tropical fern), De la Mare, doctrinaire (theoretical and impractical), abampere, portecochere (covered entrance for vehicles), solitaire, Finisterre (Spanish headland), tableware, kitchenware, ironware, earthenware, ovenware, basaltware (black stoneware), chargé d'affaires.

4.1

premiere, derrière (buttocks), portière (curtain hung in doorway), rivière, jardinière, boutonniere (flowers worn in buttonhole), son et lumière.

4.2

carfare (*US* bus fare), savoir-faire.

4.3

affair, thoroughfare, chemin de fer.

4.4

bêche-de-mer (marine organism), coco de mer (palm tree), Weston-super-Mare.

4.5

debonair, questionnaire, legionnaire, billionaire, millionaire, concessionaire, commissionaire, multimillionaire.

4.6

repair, prepare, disrepair.

4.7

beware, anywhere, everywhere.

4.8

aware, underwear, Delaware, well-aware, chinaware, unaware, otherwhere, silverware.

4.9

knitwear, agateware (ceramic ware resembling agate), graniteware (enamel-coated iron vessels).

5 -ee [see also 16]

be, bee, quay, key, ski, Dee, fee, ghee (clarified butter), gie (*Scot* give), gee, he, lea, Leigh, lee, ley (line of prehistoric track), flea, flee, glee, plea, mi, me, knee, pea, pee, re, Brie, bree (*Scot* thin soup), Cree, scree, dree (*Scot* endure), free, spree, tree, three, see, sea, Hsi (Chinese river), she, tee, te, tea, thee, wee, we, twee, Twi (Negroid people), ye, zee (*US* zed).

drawee, cooee, bawbee (former Scottish coin), Frisbee (*Trademark*), ackee (tropical fruit tree), Bacchae (priestesses of Bacchus), Torquay, trochee (metrical foot), latchkey, turnkey, passkey, Volsci (ancient Latin people), ashkey, lychee, Kochi (Japanese port), Chaldee, grandee, standee (person who stands), vendee, spondee, Dundee, fundi (East African mechanic), thuggee (practices of Indian thugs), burgee (ship's identification flag), gee-gee, squeegee, ogee (architectural moulding), Fuji, algae, Belgae (ancient Celtic people), pongee (silk fabric), mallee (shrubby eucalyptus tree), bailee, Orly, Thule, Eastleigh, thermae (ancient Roman public baths), gimme, Cannae (ancient Italian city), Pawnee, Shawnee, donee (receiver of gift), townee, whangee (bamboo grass), rappee (English snuff), tapis (tapestry or carpet), tepee, cowpea (tropical climbing plant), rupee, Tupi (South American Indian people), yippee, chickpea, boree (Australian acacia tree), Horae (Roman goddesses), Puri (Indian port), decree, machree (*Irish* my dear), carefree, grigri (African talisman), agree, Capri, esprit, shoetree, gumtree, crosstree (nautical term), farci (stuffed), Parsee (member of religious sect), precis, emcee (master of ceremonies), Shansi (Chinese province), Kiangsi (Chinese province), sightsee, Clichy (industrial Parisian

suburb), specie, chichi, buckshee, banshee, shoji (Japanese rice-paper screen), bougie (catheter), settee, coatee, goatee, suttee (Hindu custom), bootee, tutee, draftee, Santee (US river), grantee, mustee (person of mixed parentage), trustee, peewee, ennui, étui.

employee, diploë (bone in skull), Meroë (ancient Sudanese city), honeybee, bumblebee, heitiki (Maori neck ornament), Waikiki, Cherokee, après-ski, hydroski (hydrofoil on seaplane), debauchee, Tweedledee, Sekondi (Ghanaian port), refugee, takahe (New Zealand bird), appellee (accused person), parolee, internee, Mycenae, calipee (edible part of turtle), Principe (island west of Africa), cap-a-pie (from head to foot), conferee (conference participant), disagree, saddletree (frame of saddle), whiffletree (crossbar in harness), trestletree (ship's timber), axletree (carriage axle), Sadducee, fricassee, undersea, oversee, Marshalsea (former English court), licensee, garnishee (legal term), repartee, allottee, deportee, legatee (recipient of legacy), manatee (whale-like mammal), devotee, inductee (US military conscript), appointee, El Misti (Peruvian volcano), peccavi, vis-à-vis, eau de vie, ratatouille, fedayee (Arab commando), bourgeoisie, devisee (legal term), jalousie, Zuider Zee, chimpanzee.

evacuee, interviewee, Wu-lu-mu-ch'i (Chinese city), chincherinchee (South African plant), fiddle-de-dee, satyagrahi (exponent of nonviolent resistance), recognizee (legal term).

5.1

lei, payee, Danaë (Greek mythological character), Pompeii.

5.2

torii (gateway to Japanese temple), reliquiae (fossil remains), facetiae (witty sayings), minutiae, exuviae (layers of shed skin), amicus curiae (legal adviser to court).

5.3

marquee, maquis (Mediterranean shrubby vegetation), raki (strong aromatic drink), bidarkee (Eskimo canoe).

5.4

chickadee (small songbird), Pasargadae (ancient Persian city).

5.5

pledgee, Himeji (Japanese city).

5.6

gidgee (small acacia tree), mortgagee, obligee (creditor), perigee.

5.7

agee (*Scot* awry), apogee.

5.8

pili (Philippine tree), jubilee, Galilee, galilee (medieval church porch), Rosie Lee.

5.9

alee, Tralee, libellee, fleur-de-lis, Omphale (Greek mythological queen), shiralee (*Austral* swagman's bundle), Peterlee, Trincomalee (Sri Lankan port), Thermopylae.

5.10

bouquet garni, maharani, Liliuokalani (queen of Hawaiian islands).

5.11

trainee, distrainee (legal term), detainee.

5.12

jinni (Muslim mythological spirit), nominee, examinee, Mnemosyne (Greek goddess), Euphrosyne (Greek goddess).

5.13

Chinee, assignee (legal term), consignee.

5.14

Guarani (Paraguayan currency), Kootenay (US river), alienee (legal term), abandonee (legal term).

5.15

kepi, escapee.

5.16

topee, épopée (epic poem).

5.17

Marie, sirree, jamboree, referee, transferee, dungaree, kedgeree, gaucherie, chinoiserie.

5.18

degree, pedigree, filigree, mistigris (joker in poker game).

5.19

lessee, addressee.

5.20

promisee, Tennessee, Pharisee, felo de se (person who commits suicide).

5.21

foresee, endorsee, divorcee.

5.22

remittee, Hippolyte (queen of the Amazons).

5.23

amputee, distributee (legal term).

5.24

guarantee, warrantee, absentee, patentee, covenantee.

6 -eer

ear, bier, beer, cheer, deer, dear, fear, sphere, gear, jeer, here, hear, leer, Lear, Leah, clear, mere, smear, near, sneer, peer, pier, spear, queer, rear, sear, sere, sheer, shear, tear, tier, steer, veer, weir, Wear, we're, year.

Aïr (region in the Sahara), Zaïre, Meir, fakir, Bashkir (Mongoloid people), voir dire (legal term), nadir, reindeer, endear, mandir (Hindu temple), ensphere, headgear, footgear, Aegir (Norse god), Tangier, cohere, adhere, menhir, inhere, mishear, unclear, emir, Vermeer, Thirlmere, Grasmere, besmear, Kashmir, cashmere, Izmir (Turkish port), compeer (person of equal status), Shakespeare, eyrir (Icelandic coin), career, Fenrir (Norse mythological wolf), uprear, Asir (region of Saudi Arabia), Landseer, sincere, cashier, Ayrshire, Cheshire, Berkshire, Yorkshire, Shropshire, Hampshire, Wiltshire, Flintshire, wheatear (small songbird), frontier, austere, Goodyear, vizier.

Aboukir, belvedere, bombardier, Agadir, brigadier, balladeer, grenadier, commandeer, interfere, hemisphere, barysphere (central portion of earth), bathysphere, overhear, chandelier, cameleer, fusilier, bandoleer (soldier's shoulder belt), gondolier, gasolier (fitting for gaslights), pistoleer (soldier armed with pistol), cavalier, chanticleer, Tirich Mir (Pakistani mountain), insincere, Derbyshire, Denbighshire, Lancashire, Radnorshire, Leicestershire, Gloucestershire, Worcestershire, Warwickshire, Brecknockshire, Pembrokeshire, Staffordshire, Bedfordshire, Hertfordshire, Oxfordshire, Cambridgeshire, Monmouthshire, racketeer, rocketeer (rocket engineer), musketeer, profiteer, gadgeteer (lover of gadgetry), muleteer, pamphleteer, sonneteer, puppeteer, corsetier, gazetteer, volunteer, oversteer.

Diyarbakir (Turkish city), Buckinghamshire, Nottinghamshire.

isodiaphere (type of atomic nucleus), Merionethshire.

6.1

biosphere, ecosphere, atmosphere, troposphere (lowest atmospheric layer), aerosphere (earth's entire atmosphere), centrosphere (central part of earth), mesosphere (atmospheric layer), stratosphere, lithosphere (earth's crust), exosphere (highest atmospheric layer), ionosphere, ozonosphere (region of stratosphere), magnetosphere.

6.2

Vladimir, epimere (part of embryo), cassimere (woollen cloth), kerseymere (woollen cloth).

6.3

amir (former ruler of Afghanistan), Windermere, Buttermere, blastomere (embryonic cell), Rothermere (British newspaper magnate), actinomere (biology term).

6.4

veneer, engineer, domineer, scrutineer, mutineer, mountaineer, carabineer (soldier armed with carbine).

6.5

pioneer, buccaneer, chiffonier (tall chest of drawers), sloganeer, cannoneer, auctioneer, souvenir, electioneer.

6.6

appear, reappear, diapir (geological fold), disappear.

6.7

cuirassier (16th-century mounted soldier), xerosere (ecology term), adipocere (waxy substance from corpses).

6.8

Breconshire, Lincolnshire, Huntingdonshire, Cardiganshire, Northamptonshire, Carmarthenshire, Caernarvonshire.

6.9

privateer, charioteer.

6.10

megathere (extinct sloth), dinothere (extinct elephant-like mammal), isothere (line on map), chalicothere (extinct horse-like mammal), uintathere (extinct rhinoceros-like mammal).

6.11

revers, revere, severe, Bedivere, Guinevere, persevere, Guadalquivir (Spanish river).

7 -ie

I, ay, aye, eye, bye, buy, by, Skye, sky, die, dye, fie, guy, hi, high, hie (hurry), lie, lye (alkaline solution), Bligh, fly, ply, sly, my, nigh, pie, pi, spy, wry, rye, cry, scry (divine by crystal-gazing), dry, fry, pry, spry, try, sigh, shy, tie, Thai, sty, thigh, thy, vie, why, Wye.

shiai (judo contest), aye-aye, kowhai (New Zealand tree), rabbi, thereby, whereby, hereby, nearby, flyby (flight past), Dubai, goodbye, Sakai (Japanese port), cockeye (squinting eye), rocaille (decorative rock work), sockeye, Tokay (Hungarian sweet wine), buckeye (US tree), pinkeye (acute conjunctivitis), bronchi, deadeye (nautical term), redeye, Sendai (Japanese city), hi-fi, sci-fi, gilgai (*Austral* natural water hole), nilgai (Indian antelope), magi, fungi, Weihai (Chinese port), Shanghai, shanghai, ally, Eli, walleye (divergent squint), mayfly, firefly, blowfly, shoofly, blackfly, gadfly, sandfly, gallfly, greenfly, horsefly, housefly, botfly, imply, comply, Katmai (Alaskan volcano), Panay (Philippine island), Menai, mooneye (US freshwater fish), Brunei, Sinai, porkpie, magpie, espy, decry, descry, retry, Kasai (African river), Masai (African people), Pasay (Philippine city), Versailles, nisi, loci, bonsai, workshy, cockshy (target in throwing games), shuteye, necktie, recti (straight muscles), hogtie (US tie limbs together), untie, pigsty, Levi (Old Testament character), oxeye, cocci (bacteria), banzai (Japanese patriotic cheer).

Haggai (Old Testament prophet), alibi, syllabi, lullaby, passer-by, overdye, argufy, satisfy, ultrahigh, jai alai (Spanish game), butterfly, overfly, damselfly, dragonfly, haeremai (Maori expression of welcome), Iceni (ancient British tribe), goldeneye (diving duck), Philippi, occupy, counterspy, samurai, Madurai (Indian city), prophesy, lex loci (law of the place), Hokusai, Paraguay, Uruguay, tiger's-eye.

locus standi (legal term), dissatisfy, preoccupy, decree nisi.

certiorari (legal term), corpus delicti (facts constituting an offence), dramatis personae.

7.1

radii, bindi-eye (Australian plant), nuclei, genii, Helvetii (Celtic tribe), pons Varolii (nerve fibres in brain).

7.2

Mackay, Malachi.

7.3

defy, deify, reify (make real), speechify, preachify, Frenchify, ladyfy, edify, modify, codify, dandify, jellify, stellify (change into a star), vilify, nullify, uglify, amplify, simplify, ramify, mummify, tumefy (swell up), unify, cockneyfy, magnify, damnify (injure), typify, stupefy, liquefy, aerify (change into a gas), scarify, rarefy, horrify, torrefy (dry with intense heat), scorify (refine by smelting), glorify, purify, metrify (translate into poetic metre), petrify, vitrify, nitrify (treat with nitrogen), putrefy, countrify, basify (make basic), casefy (become cheese-like), specify, versify,

ossify, crucify, calcify, falsify, Nazify, certify, prettify, citify, fortify, mortify, notify, brutify (brutalize), beautify, sanctify, stultify, quantify, testify, mystify, justify, vivify (bring to life).

syllabify, alkalify, exemplify, saponify (change into soap), personify, reunify, indemnify, solemnify, transmogrify, electrify, diversify, intensify, denazify, identify, demystify, revivify, detoxify, oversimplify.

7.3.1

rigidify, solidify, humidify, lapidify (change into stone), acidify, dehumidify.

7.3.2

jollify, mollify, qualify, disqualify.

7.3.3

dignify, lignify (make woody), signify, presignify.

7.3.4

clarify, saccharify (convert into sugar).

7.3.5

terrify, verify, esterify (chemistry term).

7.3.6

gasify, classify, pacify, declassify.

7.3.7

dulcify (sweeten), demulsify (separate an emulsion), emulsify.

7.3.8

ratify, gratify, stratify, beatify.

7.3.9

rectify, objectify (represent concretely), subjectify (interpret subjectively).

7.4

assegai (sharp light spear), anthropophagi (cannibals).

7.5

belie, quillai (South American tree), rely, villi (finger-like projections), morbilli (measles), locus sigilli (position of document seal).

7.6

July, vox populi, lapis lazuli.

7.7

ally, alkali, underlie, Lorelei, overlie, antalkali.

7.8

reply, multiply.

7.9

apply, supply, misapply.

7.10

deny, Gemini, anno Domini.

7.11

sori (spore-producing structures), tori (*plural of* torus), a priori, a fortiori, memento mori, a posteriori.

7.12

awry, serail (harem), Terai (Indian marshland), caravanserai.

7.13

Mira Ceti (star), arbor vitae (coniferous tree), aqua vitae, curriculum vitae.

8 -ire [see also **17.4**]

ire, byre, dire, fire, gyre (circular movement), hire, lyre, mire, pyre, spire, quire, choir, squire, sire, shire, tire, Tyre, tyre, wire.

sapphire, backfire, wildfire, hellfire, shellfire, camphire (henna), samphire (Eurasian plant), bonfire, gunfire, misfire, crossfire, spitfire, bemire, admire, quagmire, pismire (*Dialect* ant), vampire, empire, umpire, respire, transpire, inspire, conspire, expire, acquire, inquire, enquire, esquire, satire, retire, attire, saltire (heraldic term), entire, haywire, rewire, tripwire, desire.

retrofire (firing of retrorocket), retrochoir (space behind cathedral altar), Molly Maguire (Irish secret society member).

8.1

afire, melaphyre (type of basalt), granophyre (granitic rock), lamprophyre (igneous rock).

8.2

aspire, perspire, suspire (to sigh), acrospire (botany term).

8.3

require, antechoir (part of church).

9 -or

or, oar, ore, o'er, awe, boar, bore, caw, corps, core, score, chore, door, daw (jackdaw), four, for, fore, gore, jaw, hoar, whore, haw, lore, law, lor (exclamation of dismay), claw, flaw, floor, more, maw, nor, gnaw, snore, paw, pore, pour, spore, squaw, roar, raw, braw (*Scot* excellent), craw, draw, drawer, straw, soar, saw, sore, shore, Shaw, pshaw, tor, tore, taw (large marble), store, thaw, Thor, Waugh, war, wore, swore, yaw, your, yore.

forbore, Gabor, smoothbore, markhor (Himalayan goat), décor, encore, threescore, fourscore, stridor (high-pitched breathing sound), moidore (former Portuguese coin), sudor (sweat), jackdaw, bandore (16th-century stringed instrument), landau, vendor, indoor, condor, outdoor, ephor (ancient Greek magistrate), therefore, wherefore, guffaw, Roquefort, Balfour, rigor (medical term), gewgaw (showy trinket), nylghau (Indian antelope), pledgor, lockjaw, heehaw, Hawhaw, Johore (Malaysian state), Lahore (Pakistani city), abhor, bylaw, folklore, dewclaw, Danelaw, deplore, implore, explore, coleslaw, outlaw, claymore (two-edged sword), Seymour, Timor, Broadmoor, ignore, rapport, forepaw, pawpaw, Cawnpore (Indian city), downpour, southpaw, furor, withdraw, uproar, bedstraw, lessor, Esau, seesaw, eyesore, Mysore, foresaw, Warsaw, tussore (Indian silk), bedsore, handsaw, jigsaw, whipsaw (saw with flexible blade), footsore, seashore, foreshore, ashore, bashaw (important person), kickshaw (worthless trinket), rickshaw, Bradshaw, offshore, scrimshaw (shell or ivory carving), inshore, onshore, longshore, Utah, lector (university lecturer), Choctaw (American Indian people), cantor (leading singer in synagogue), grantor, Nestor (Greek mythological character), restore, drugstore, prewar, postwar, hacksaw, bucksaw (woodcutting saw), Luxor (Egyptian town), señor, signor.

hellebore (poisonous plant), usquebaugh (Irish liqueur), Maribor (Slovenian city), underscore, battledore (former racket game), theretofore, heretofore, underfloor, son-in-law, Barrymore, Baltimore, Aviemore, Mount Rushmore, Tengri Nor (Chinese salt lake), assignor (legal term), Elsinore, nullipore (red seaweed), madrepore (coral), Singapore, archespore (spore-making cell), overawe, overdraw, windlestraw (*Dialect* dried grass stalks), promisor, Arkansas, wappenshaw (gathering of Scottish clansmen), alongshore, Wichita, Ouachita (US river), legator (person making bequest), Minotaur, guarantor, warrantor, patentor, man-of-war.

daughter-in-law, sister-in-law, father-in-law, mother-in-law, brother-in-law, imperator, caveat emptor.

9.1

Dior, Melchior, Gwalior (Indian city), excelsior, Confiteor (Catholic prayer).

9.2

macaw, albacore (variety of tunny), esprit de corps, anemochore (botany term).

9.3

louis d'or (former French coin), humidor (humid tobacco-storing container), cuspidor (spittoon), corridor, stevedore, Corregidor (Philippine island), lobster thermidor.

9.4

adore, picador, commodore, Ecuador, Labrador, comprador (agent of foreign enterprise), matador, Salvador, toreador, conquistador, El Salvador, San Salvador.

9.5

before, petit four, hereinbefore.

9.6

afore, semaphore, ctenophore (marine invertebrate), pinafore, carrefour, sporophore (spore-bearing organ), photophore (light-producing organ), siphonophore (marine invertebrate), ommatophore (eye-bearing stalk), gametophore (plant part).

9.7

Tagore (Indian poet), Chandernagore (Indian port).

9.8

galore, Vellore (Indian town), Bangalore, Mangalore (Indian port).

9.9

hackamore (*US* rope halter), sycamore, sophomore, sagamore (American Indian chief), mattamore (subterranean storehouse), furthermore, evermore, nevermore, forevermore.

9.10

diaspore (mineral), zoospore, endospore, megaspore (botany term), microspore (botany term).

9.11

Chickasaw (American Indian people), stegosaur, dinosaur, pterosaur, vavasor (baron's vassal), plesiosaur, ichthyosaur, megalosaur, tyrannosaur.

9.12

mentor, centaur, stentor (loud-voiced person).

9.13

herbivore, carnivore, omnivore, insectivore.

10 -oor

boor, Boer, dour, lur (Bronze Age musical horn), Moore, Moor, moor, poor, spoor, Ruhr, sure, tour, you're, cure, lure, Muir, pure.

Niebuhr (German historian), tambour, pandour (18th-century Croatian soldier), Darfur (Sudanese province), Uigur (Mongoloid people), langur (monkey), adjure, abjure, conjure, velours, Namur (Belgian province), Sedgemoor, unmoor, Dartmoor, Exmoor, Nippur (ancient Babylonian city), Nagpur (Indian city), Kanpur (Indian city), parure (set of jewels), hachure (lines drawn for shading), brochure, assure, cocksure, unsure, detour, contour, procure, obscure, ordure (excrement), bordure (outer edge of shield), endure, immure, demure, tenure, inure, conure (small parrot), manure, purpure (heraldic purple), guipure, impure, couture, gravure (method of printing).

troubadour, pompadour (18th-century women's hairstyle), Kohinoor, Nishapur (birthplace of Omar Khayyám),

Jamshedpur (Indian city), Jabalpur (Indian city), Bhagalpur (Indian city), commissure (tissue linking two organs), embouchure, reassure, plat du jour, dasyure (small marsupial), clair-obscure (art term), Réaumur, confiture (fruit preserve), prefecture, calenture (mild tropical fever), cynosure (centre of attraction).

Chota Nagpur (East Indian plateau), Kuala Lumpur, photogravure, rotogravure.

10.1

amour (love affair), Amur (Asian river), paramour.

10.2

ensure, insure, reinsure, coinsure.

10.3

liqueur, secure, pedicure, manicure, sinecure, epicure, insecure.

10.4

allure, colure (circle on celestial sphere), velure, craquelure (cracks on old paintings), cannelure (groove around bullet).

10.5

mature, armature (moving electrical part), premature, immature, overture, caricature, magistrature.

11 -oy

boy, buoy, coy, Fowey, joy, hoy (freight barge), cloy, ploy, poi (Hawaiian food), Roy, Troy, soy, toy.

dayboy, playboy, choirboy, hautboy (strawberry), doughboy (boiled dumpling), lowboy (US table with drawers), cowboy, ploughboy, linkboy (torch carrier in streets), pageboy, bellboy, callboy, smallboy (steward's assistant), tallboy, schoolboy, tomboy, houseboy, footboy (boy servant), liftboy, postboy, decoy, Khoikhoi (language group), McCoy, enjoy, ahoy, alloy, deploy, employ, Amoy (Chinese port), Hanoi, annoy, charpoy, sepoy (Indian soldier), teapoy (table with tripod base), Rob Roy, viceroy, destroy, Tolstoy, travois (American Indian sled), savoy, Savoy, envoy, renvoi (legal term), convoy, borzoi.

maccaboy (rose-scented snuff), paperboy, attaboy, stableboy, didicoy (type of gypsy), overjoy, permalloy (iron–nickel alloy), redeploy, Illinois, Iroquois, corduroy.

hobbledehoy, paduasoy (silk fabric).

11.1

alloy, kumbaloi (worry beads), hoi polloi, saveloy.

12 -oe

owe, oh, beau, bow, dough, doe, doh, foe, go, Joe, ho, hoe, lo, low, blow, flow, floe, glow, slow, sloe, mow, mo (*short for* moment), mot (witty remark), know, no, snow, Poe, po (chamber pot), Po (Italian river), row, roe, crow, fro, grow, pro, throw, sew, sow, so, soh, show, toe, tow, stow, though, whoa, woe, Vaud (region of Switzerland), zo (Tibetan cattle).

Rouault (French artist), duo, Abo (*short for* Aborigine), jabot, Garbo, oboe, hobo, bubo (a swelling), elbow, flambeau (torch), mambo (dance), crambo (word game), combo, rainbow, longbow, crossbow, oxbow (curved lake), psycho, Tycho (crater on moon), bucko (*Irish* young fellow), stucco, milko (*Austral* milkman), wilco, salchow (ice-skating jump), Glencoe, plonko (*Austral* alcoholic), bronco, Moscow, gaucho, poncho, shadow, eddo (Asian plant), meadow, Bordeaux, dildo, rondeau (poem), rondo (musical work), Sappho, Defoe, UFO, nympho, info, ergo, Virgo, doggo, forego, sorgo (fodder crop), bongo, Congo, drongo (tropical bird), outgo, Glasgow, banjo, heigh-ho, coho (Pacific salmon), Soho, halo, Gwelo (Zimbabwean town), furlough, Lilo (*Trademark*), silo, Shiloh, rouleau, tableau, pueblo, deathblow, airflow, inflow, outflow, whitlow, Oslo, Hounslow, ammo, demo, memo, trumeau (architectural term), Sumo (Japanese wrestling), Malmö, lino, rhino, wino, mono, tonneau, foreknow, dunno, Gounod (French composer), Juno, capo (guitar attachment), chapeau (hat), hippo, hypo, typo, tempo, burrow, furrow, scarecrow, Velcro (*Trademark*), escrow (legal term), hydro, Afro, aggro, outgrow, hedgerow,

Monroe, repro, metro, retro, de trop (superfluous), Cointreau, intro, Castro, bistro, maestro, Jethro, peso, verso, torso, whoso (whoever), Rousseau, trousseau, CUSO (Canadian voluntary service organization), Tussaud, also, fatso, scherzo, schizo, sideshow, peepshow, ditto, Shinto (Japanese religion), tiptoe, bestow, gusto, although, bravo, servo, Provo, galvo (*short for galvanometer*), salvo, Volvo (*Trademark*), Oyo (Nigerian state), yo-yo, Tokyo, ouzo, muso (*Austral* musician).

Bilbao, cacao, sirocco, Morocco, Monaco, touraco (African bird), fiasco, Tabasco, gazpacho, quebracho (South American tree), foreshadow, aboideau (Canadian dyke), tournedos, commando, tally-ho, bibelot (trinket), Fontainebleau, overflow, Alamo, dynamo, piano, volcano, Huguenot, Llandudno, Limpopo, status quo, quid pro quo, Diderot (French philosopher), bordereau (insurance invoice), Cicero, allegro, overgrow, semipro, in vitro, overthrow, Curaçao, oversew, so-and-so, calypso, concerto, undertow, hammertoe, de facto, tick-tack-toe (*US* noughts and crosses), mistletoe, octavo (book size), proviso.

continuo (musical term), La Rochefoucauld (French writer), Acapulco, overshadow, fortepiano (type of piano), Avogadro (Italian physicist).

12.1

KO, Mayo (Irish county), carabao (water buffalo), Galileo, Bulawayo (Zimbabwean city).

12.2

Leo, Cleo, Rio, trio, con brio (musical term), absente reo (legal term).

12.3

radio, audio, rodeo, studio, cameo, Romeo, Borneo, Scipio (Roman general), Scorpio, stereo, cheerio, curio, embryo, nuncio (papal representative), patio.

Pinocchio, capriccio (lively musical work), adagio, solfeggio (musical term), arpeggio, seraglio (harem), intaglio (engraving), Ontario, etaerio (class of fruit), Ajaccio, pistachio, mustachio.

braggadocio (boasting), oratorio, ex officio.

12.3.1

video, presidio (Spanish military establishment).

12.3.2

billyo, punctilio (strict etiquette).

12.3.3

olio (miscellany), folio, polio, portfolio, imbroglio (confused situation).

12.3.4

Roneo (*Trademark*), Antonio.

12.3.5

Rosario (Argentine port), scenario, Lothario (libertine), impresario.

12.3.6

ratio, fellatio.

12.4

Io (satellite of Jupiter), ngaio (New Zealand tree), noyau (nut liqueur), Ohio.

12.5

Ibo (African people), placebo, gazebo, Essequibo (South American river).

12.6

bimbo, limbo, akimbo.

12.7

umbo (small hump), gumbo (thick stew), jumbo, Colombo, mumbo jumbo.

12.8

squacco (European heron), shako, whacko (*Slang* exclamation of delight), tobacco.

12.9

echo, dekko, gecko, re-echo, Art Deco, El Greco.

12.10

chico (US shrub), Nikko (Japanese town), picot, pekoe, beccafico (European songbird), Puerto Rico.

12.11

tricot (knitted fabric), medico, calico, coquelicot (corn poppy), haricot,

Jericho, portico, Mexico, magnifico, simpatico (pleasant), politico.

12.12

cocoa, loco, smoko (*Austral* teabreak), poco (musical term), rococo, con fuoco (musical term), Orinoco.

12.13

flamenco, Lysenko (Russian geneticist), Timoshenko (Russian general).

12.14

fresco, Enesco (Rumanian musician), UNESCO, alfresco, Ionesco (French dramatist).

12.15

disco, Frisco (*short for* San Francisco), cisco (fish), Morisco (Spanish Moor), San Francisco.

12.16

mikado, Barnardo, bravado, avocado, El Dorado, Colorado, desperado, muscovado (raw sugar), amontillado, aficionado, incommunicado.

12.17

dado, Toledo, tornado, strappado (form of torture), bastinado (form of torture), carbonado (industrial diamond).

12.18

lido, speedo, credo, libido, Toledo, torpedo, tuxedo.

12.19

widow, aikido (Japanese self-defence system), comedo (blackhead), do-si-do, Bushido (code of the samurai).

12.20

Dido, Hokkaido.

12.21

dodo, Jodo (Buddhist sect), Komodo (East Indian island), Quasimodo.

12.22

judo, ludo, Trudeau, pseudo, escudo (Portuguese currency), testudo (Roman military manoeuvre).

12.23

bandeau (headband), Brando, Orlando, glissando (musical term), sforzando (musical term), ritardando, San Fernando, rallentando.

12.24

kendo (Japanese sport), crescendo, innuendo, diminuendo (musical term).

12.25

window, tamarindo (tamarind).

12.26

argot, Argo, cargo, largo, embargo, Chicago, virago, farrago (hotchpotch), botargo (fish roe), Santiago.

12.27

sago, Tobago, lumbago, plumbago (graphite), imago (adult insect), San Diego, Winnebago (US lake), solidago (plant genus).

12.28

ego, gigot (leg of mutton), Vigo (Spanish port), amigo, Montego, superego, alter ego.

12.29

chigoe (tropical flea), Bendigo (Australian city), indigo, vertigo, Abednego.

12.30

Sligo, serpigo (skin disease), prurigo (skin disease), lentigo (freckle), intertrigo (chafed skin), impetigo.

12.31

logo, Togo (African republic), à gogo.

12.32

Hugo, colugo (flying lemur), aerugo (verdigris), lanugo (covering of fine hair).

12.33

ago, undergo, sapsago (Swiss cheese), archipelago.

12.34

NALGO, hidalgo (Spanish nobleman).

12.35

mango, quango, tango, fandango, Durango (Mexican state), contango (stock exchange term).

12.36

bingo, dingo, jingo, lingo, gringo, flamingo, Santo Domingo (capital of Dominican Republic).

12.37

Idaho, Navaho, Arapaho.

12.38

aloe, callow, fallow, hallow, mallow, sallow, shallow, tallow, marshmallow.

12.39

Carlow (Irish county), Harlow, Marlowe, Monte Carlo.

12.40

bellow, cello, fellow, jello (*US* jelly), hello, mellow, yellow, bordello, bedfellow, Longfellow, morello, Martello, Othello, Novello, Punchinello (clown), saltarello (Italian dance), violoncello.

12.41

kilo, Iloilo (Philippine port).

12.42

below, billow, pillow, willow, furbelow, pomelo (grapefruit), tupelo (tree), Murillo (Spanish painter), peccadillo (trivial misdemeanour), armadillo, cigarillo, Michelangelo.

12.43

follow, hollow, wallow, swallow, Apollo.

12.44

bolo (a knife), kolo (Serbian folk dance), Jolo (Philippine island), polo, solo, criollo (type of cocoa), palolo (marine worm), Marco Polo.

12.45

hallo, cembalo (harpsichord), cymbalo (dulcimer), piccolo, pedalo (pedal boat), buffalo, brigalow (Australian acacia tree), gigolo, bungalow, tangelo (tangerine–grapefruit hybrid), tremolo, bummalo (Bombay duck), cattalo (breed of cattle), diabolo (game with spinning top).

12.46

aglow, afterglow, counterglow (glow in sky).

12.47

Imo (Nigerian state), primo, supremo.

12.48

Eskimo, ultimo (last month), proximo (next month), Geronimo, centesimo (monetary unit), fortissimo, bravissimo, pianissimo, generalissimo.

12.49

Como, Nkomo, homo, duomo (cathedral), major-domo.

12.50

machismo, verismo (type of opera), gran turismo.

12.51

Arno (Italian river), Kano (Nigerian state), Carnot (French physicist), llano (South American grassland), guano, Meccano (*Trademark*), soprano, Cinzano, San Stefano (Turkish village), oregano.

12.52

meno (musical term), tenno (Japanese emperor), steno (*US* shorthand typist), Renault (*Trademark*), ripieno (musical term).

12.53

journo (*Austral* journalist), Pernod (*Trademark*), inferno.

12.54

beano, keno (US game of chance), chino (cotton twill cloth), fino (dry sherry), leno (fabric weave), Reno, vino, albino, bambino, amino, merino, neutrino (elementary particle in physics), casino, Latino (*US* Latin American), Trevino, maraschino, cappuccino, Borodino (Napoleonic battle site), palomino, Filipino, San Marino (European republic), andantino (musical term), Valentino, San Bernardino (Californian city).

12.55

minnow, winnow, domino, Maginot.

12.56

kimono, kakemono (Japanese wall hanging).

12.57

Apo (Philippine mountain), da capo (musical term), Gestapo.

12.58
depot, Aleppo (Syrian city).

12.59
kakapo (parrot), apropos, malapropos.

12.60
arrow, barrow, farrow, Jarrow, Harrow, harrow, marrow, narrow, sparrow, tarot, yarrow, handbarrow, wheelbarrow, restharrow (woody plant).

12.61
claro (cigar), taro (Asian plant), Pissarro (French painter), Pizarro (conqueror of Peru), Kilimanjaro.

12.62
Pharaoh, faro (card game), ranchero (*US* rancher), bolero, torero (bullfighter), Herero (African people), sombrero, cruzeiro (Brazilian currency), caballero (Spanish gentleman), banderillero (bullfighter's assistant).

12.63
hero, Nero, Pierrot (French pantomime clown), zero, Pinero (English dramatist), subzero, antihero, superhero, Rio de Janeiro.

12.64
Biro (*Trademark*), Cairo, giro, tyro (novice), autogiro (aircraft).

12.65
borrow, morrow, sorrow, tomorrow.

12.66
Douro (Spanish–Portuguese river), Truro, bureau, maduro (cigar), Politburo, chiaroscuro (art term).

12.67
Negro, Montenegro.

12.68
basso (bass singer), Picasso, sargasso (seaweed), El Paso (Texan city).

12.69
gesso (white plaster), expresso.

12.70
so-so, maestoso (musical term), grandioso (musical term), mafioso (member of the Mafia), virtuoso,

oloroso (sherry), doloroso (musical term), amoroso.

12.71
mezzo (musical term), Arezzo (Italian city), intermezzo.

12.72
bateau (flat-bottomed boat), gateau, plateau, chateau, mulatto, annatto (tropical tree).

12.73
dato (Philippine chief), rubato (musical term), spiccato (musical term), Waikato (New Zealand river), staccato, legato, tomato, esparto, vibrato, castrato, pizzicato, obbligato (musical term), moderato, inamorato (lover).

12.74
Cato, jato (jet-assisted takeoff), Plato, NATO, potato.

12.75
ghetto, zucchetto (skullcap), stiletto, palmetto (small tropical palm tree), libretto, falsetto, amoretto (cupid), vaporetto (Venetian steamboat), Tintoretto, lazaretto (ship's locker), allegretto.

12.76
Quito (capital of Ecuador), Leto (mother of Apollo), Pitot (French physicist), Tito, veto, coquito (palm tree), mosquito, graffito, bonito (small marine fish), magneto, Negrito (member of Asian people), Hirohito, sanbenito (garment worn by heretics), incognito.

12.77
Otto, Giotto, lotto, blotto, motto, potto (short-tailed mammal), grotto, Watteau, risotto.

12.78
auto, quarto, Oporto.

12.79
koto (Japanese musical instrument), photo, Kyoto (Japanese city), con moto (musical term), in toto, telephoto.

12.80
couteau (a knife), Pluto, Maputo (capital of Mozambique), prosciutto (Italian cured ham), sostenuto (musical term).

12.81

recto, perfecto (cigar).

12.82

alto, Rialto, contralto.

12.83

canto, manteau (a cloak), panto, portmanteau, Taranto (Italian port), Esperanto, Espíritu Santo (Pacific island).

12.84

lento, cento (type of poem), memento, pimento, Sorrento, pentimento (art term), Sacramento, Risorgimento (Italian political movement), divertimento (musical work).

12.85

conto (Portuguese currency), pronto, Toronto.

12.86

presto, manifesto.

13 -ow

ow, bow, bough, cow, scow (boat), chow, ciao (Italian greeting), dhow (Arab sailing boat), how, Lao (Asian people), plough, Slough, slough (bog), mow (grimace), now, pow, row, brow, Frau, prow, sow, sough (make sighing sound), thou, vow, wow.

meow, Cracow, Foochow (Chinese port), Soochow (Chinese city), Changchow (Chinese city), Hangchow (Chinese port), Moldau, endow, know-how, somehow, pilau, allow, snow-plough, Mau Mau, eyebrow, highbrow, lowbrow, hausfrau, kowtow, Paotow (Chinese city), avow, bow-wow, pow-wow.

disendow, anyhow, disallow, middle-brow, disavow.

14 -our

our, hour, bower, cower, scour, dower (widow's inheritance), Gower, lour (look menacing), flour, flower, glower, power, sour, shower, tower.

embower, Glendower (Welsh chieftain), deflower, safflower, Mayflower, wall-flower, cornflower, cornflour, sun-flower, moonflower (night-blooming plant), willpower, empower, manpower, horsepower, watchtower, devour.

Eisenhower, gillyflower, cauliflower, passionflower, hydropower, superpower, overpower.

15 -oo

ooh, boo, coo, coup, chew, do, goo, Jew, who, loo, blue, blew, clue, clew (ball of yarn), flu, flew, flue, glue, slew, moo, gnu, pooh, rue, roux, roo (*Austral* kangaroo), brew, crew, Crewe, cru (wine-producing region), screw, drew, grew, sprue (tropical disease), shrew, true, strew, through, threw, Sioux, sue, sou (coin), shoe, shoo, choux (type of pastry), too, to, two, woo, ewe, you, yew, queue, cue, Kew, kyu (judo grade), skew, due, dew, few, phew, hue, hew, lieu, mew, smew (diving duck), knew, new, pew, spew, stew, thew (muscle), view, zoo.

zebu (type of ox), bamboo, cuckoo, Manchu (Chinese dynasty), eschew (avoid), hairdo, redo, Urdu, kudu (African antelope), hoodoo, voodoo, Hindu, undo, outdo, snafu, Corfu, kung fu, ragout (stew), juju, boohoo, Wuhu (Chinese port), yoo-hoo, yahoo, igloo, canoe, Vishnu (Hindu god), coypu, hoopoe, pooh-pooh, shampoo, Nehru, guru, Hebrew, ecru (yellowish-grey colour), aircrew, accrue, wood-screw, thumbscrew, unscrew, corkscrew, withdrew, Andrew, Renfrew, untrue, bestrew, construe, lasso, shih-tzu (breed of dog), fichu (scarf), cashew, cachou (type of sweet), snowshoe, gumshoe, Honshu, horseshoe, bijou, battue (hunting term), tattoo, thereto, where-to, hereto, Hutu (African people), tutu, Bantu, Mantoux (French physician), into, onto, unto, bayou (marshy stream), debut, imbue (instil), fescue (a grass), rescue, miscue, askew, subdue, mildew, fondue, undue, sundew, cur-few, argue, ague, value, curlew, purlieu (outlying area), emu, menu, venue, non-U, foreknew, anew, issue, tissue, pursue, ensue, statue, virtue, Matthew, nephew, purview (scope), preview, revue, review, Jesu.

caribou, bunraku (Japanese puppet theatre), Katmandu, derring-do, Dien Bien Phu (Vietnamese battle site),

kinkajou, ballyhoo, misconstrue, overthrew, jujitsu, overshoe, acajou,
Lissajous (French physicist), passe-
partout, cockatoo, thitherto, hitherto,
Timbuktu, thereinto, whereinto, hereinto, rendezvous, IOU, barbecue,
curlicue (decorative curl), autocue,
feverfew, Montague, clerihew (humorous verse), devalue, revalue, ingénue
(naive girl), impromptu, interview,
overview.

Machu Picchu (ruined city of Incas),
Mogadishu (capital of Somali Republic),
tu-whit tu-whoo, undervalue,
Bartholomew, cock-a-doodle-doo.

15.1

taboo, peekaboo, bugaboo (source of
fear), marabou (African stork),
marabout (Muslim holy man).

15.2

teledu (Asian badger), billet-doux (love
letter), didgeridoo.

15.3

ado, to-do, amadou (fungal tinder),
well-to-do, overdo.

15.4

Lulu, Sulu (Philippine archipelago),
Zulu, Honolulu.

15.5

halloo, trou-de-loup (pit dug for
defence), toodle-oo, ormolu (gilt deco-
ration), Port-Salut (French cheese),
Peterloo, Waterloo, Tuvalu (group of
Pacific islands), hullabaloo, Kinabalu
(Malaysian mountain).

15.6

Karoo (South African plateau), Peru,
jackeroo (*Austral* trainee sheep-station
manager), buckaroo (*US* cowboy), wanderoo (Indian monkey), kangaroo, wallaroo (large kangaroo), Timaru (New
Zealand port), Brian Boru (medieval
Irish king).

15.7

bedew (cover with dew), honeydew,
residue.

15.8

adieu, overdue.

15.9

renew, sinew, detinue (legal term),
retinue, continue, avenue, revenue,
discontinue.

15.10

bazoo (*US* mouth), kazoo, razoo (*Austral*
coin), Kalamazoo.

16 -y [This is the unstressed syllable at
the end of such words as *baby*, *charity*,
and *autonomy*. Rhymes dependent on
this syllable alone are unsatisfactory
and should be avoided. Further rhymes
for **16.112–16.209** may be created by
adding -*ly* to appropriate adjectives. See
also **5**.]

rugby, busby, Grimsby, Trotsky, hardly,
homely, scarcely, costly, lively, paisley,
acme, pygmy, chimney, chutney,
scampi, debris, laundry, foundry,
sundry, belfry, angry, hungry, paltry,
poultry, sultry, pastry, Chelsea, Nazi,
safety, ninety, empty, sixty, earthy,
lengthy, filthy, swarthy, ivy, envy,
clumsy, Swansea.

panoply, calumny, industry, bankruptcy, dynasty.

16.1

ai (three-toed sloth), Bahai (member of
religious group), Lanai (Hawaiian
island), Molokai (Hawaiian island).

16.2

Hawaii, Mordecai (Old Testament character).

16.3

doughy, joey, blowy, Chloe, snowy,
showy, shadowy, billowy, willowy.

16.4

chewy, phooey, gooey, hooey, louis,
Louis, bluey (*Austral* blanket or bun-
dle), gluey, screwy, dewy, Dewey,
Drambuie (*Trademark*), Rapa Nui (Easter
Island).

16.5

abbey, cabby, scabby, gabby (talkative),
flabby, crabby, shabby, tabby,
Newtonabbey.

16.6

Babi (Persian religious heretic), Derby,
Mugabe, Punjabi, Wahhabi (member of

Muslim sect), kohlrabi, Abu Dhabi, Hammurabi (ancient Babylonian king).

16.7

baby, gaby (simpleton), maybe, cry-baby, bushbaby.

16.8

plebby, webby, Entebbe.

16.9

Kirkby, herby.

16.10

Phoebe, Hebe (Greek goddess), freebie, Galibi (American Indian people).

16.11

bobby, dobby (loom attachment), hobby, lobby.

16.12

obi, Kobe (Japanese port), dhobi, goby, Gobi, Toby, adobe, Nairobi, Okeechobee (lake in Florida).

16.13

chubby, hubby, clubby (sociable), scrubby, grubby, shrubby, tubby, stubby.

16.14

booby, jube (gallery in church), looby (foolish person), ruby.

16.15

wallaby, Araby, sassaby (African antelope).

16.16

Philby, trilby, astilbe (flowering plant).

16.17

Djambi (Indonesian port), namby-pamby.

16.18

Tshombe (African statesman), zombie.

16.19

baccy, lackey, tacky, wacky.

16.20

khaki, kaki (Asian fruit tree), charqui (dried meat), parky, saki (monkey), sake (Japanese liquor), Saki (Scottish author).

thearchy (government by gods), malarkey (nonsense), menarche (first occurrence of menstruation), gynarchy (government by women), eparchy, Iraqi, squirearchy, autarchy (unrestricted rule), autarky (economic self-sufficiency).

matriarchy, patriarchy, oligarchy, hierarchy, Nagasaki, Kawasaki, sukiyaki, teriyaki (Japanese cookery term).

16.21

laky (reddish), flaky, snaky, quaky, shaky, headachy.

16.22

checky (heraldic term), recce, Shimonoseki (Japanese port).

16.23

jerky, murky, perky, quirky, turkey, Turkey, Albuquerque.

16.24

cheeky, leaky, cliquey, sneaky, peaky, squeaky, creaky, freaky, streaky, cock-a-leekie.

16.25

dicky, hickey (gadget), quickie, tricky, sticky, garlicky, gimmicky, panicky, finicky.

16.26

spiky, crikey, psyche, Tyche (Greek goddess).

16.27

cocky, jockey, hockey, gnocchi, rocky, stocky, outjockey (outwit by deception), jabberwocky.

16.28

chalky, Gorky, gawky, porky, pawky (*Scot* having dry wit), talkie, stalky, Milwaukee, walkie-talkie.

16.29

Loki (Norse god), smoky, poky, croaky, karaoke, hokey cokey, okey-dokey.

16.30

ducky, lucky, clucky, plucky, mucky, yukky, unlucky, Kentucky.

16.31

bookie, cookie, hooky, rookie, Gurmukhi (Punjabi script).

16.32
kooky, fluky, spooky, kabuki (Japanese drama), Saluki, bouzouki.

16.33
anarchy, monarchy, schipperke (breed of dog), synecdoche (figure of speech), sciamachy (fight with imaginary enemy), theomachy (battle among the gods), logomachy (argument about words), tauromachy (bullfighting), Andromache, gigantomachy (battle fought by giants).

16.34
milky, silky.

16.35
bulky, sulky.

16.36
hanky, lanky, manky, cranky, swanky, hanky-panky, Killiecrankie (Scottish battle site).

16.37
inky, kinky, dinky, slinky, pinkie, Malinke (African people), Helsinki.

16.38
donkey, wonky.

16.39
chunky, funky, junkie, flunky, monkey, spunky.

16.40
pesky, kromesky (type of croquette).

16.41
risky, frisky, whisky.

16.42
dusky, husky, musky, Russky.

16.43
Dostoevsky, Alexander Nevski (Russian prince).

16.44
Tchaikovsky, Stokowski (US conductor), Malinowski (Polish anthropologist).

16.45
Nijinsky, kolinsky (Asian mink).

16.46
catchy, snatchy (disconnected), patchy, scratchy, Apache.

16.47
starchy, hibachi (portable brazier), Karachi, vivace, mariachi (Mexican street musicians).

16.48
sketchy, stretchy, tetchy.

16.49
itchy, bitchy, pitchy.

16.50
botchy, blotchy, veloce (musical term), sotto voce, viva voce.

16.51
Bauchi (Nigerian state), grouchy.

16.52
duchy, touchy, archduchy.

16.53
duce, Baluchi (Muslim people), penuche (coarse Mexican sugar), Vespucci, Mizoguchi (Japanese film director).

16.54
Ranchi (Indian city), Comanche.

16.55
paunchy, raunchy.

16.56
bunchy, punchy, crunchy.

16.57
baddie, caddie, caddy, daddy, laddie, Paddy, paddy, sugar daddy, finnan haddie.

16.58
cadi (Muslim judge), hardy, Mahdi (Sudanese military leader), mardy (*Dialect* spoilt or irritable), tardy, foolhardy.

16.59
lady, shady, charlady, milady, landlady, maravedi (Spanish coin).

16.60
eddy, heady, neddy, ready, thready, steady, already, unready, unsteady.

16.61
birdie, sturdy, wordy, Makurdi (Nigerian port), hurdy-gurdy.

16.62

beady, needy, speedy, reedy, greedy, seedy, weedy, tweedy.

16.63

biddy, kiddy, giddy, midi, Zebedee, perfidy, raggedy, tragedy, remedy, comedy, Kennedy, subsidy, accidie (apathy), chickabiddy (term of endearment), tragicomedy.

16.64

bridie (*Scot* meat pie), tidy, vide, untidy, mala fide, bona fide.

16.65

body, Noddy, shoddy, toddy, wadi (watercourse), embody, dogsbody, anybody, everybody, antibody, busybody, underbody, disembody, Irrawaddy (Burmese river).

16.66

bawdy, gaudy, Geordie, lordy (exclamation of surprise).

16.67

Cody, toady, petalody (botany term), polypody (type of fern).

16.68

dowdy, howdy, cloudy, rowdy, Saudi, pandowdy (*US* fruit pie), howtowdie (Scottish chicken dish).

16.69

buddy, bloody, muddy, nuddy, ruddy, study, fuddy-duddy, understudy.

16.70

goody, woody, goody-goody.

16.71

Judy, moody, broody, camoodi (anaconda).

16.72

nobody, Lombardy, somebody, Picardy, malady, melody, psalmody, threnody (ode of lamentation), hymnody, jeopardy, parody, prosody, rhapsody, bastardy, custody, chiropody.

16.73

alcalde (Spanish mayor), Vivaldi, Fittipaldi (Brazilian motor-racing driver).

16.74

wieldy, unwieldy.

16.75

Grimaldi, Garibaldi, garibaldi.

16.76

oldie, mouldy.

16.77

Andy, bandy, candy, dandy, Gandhi, handy, randy, brandy, sandy, shandy, jaborandi (tropical shrub), onus probandi (burden of proof).

16.78

bendy, trendy, Wendy, effendi (Turkish title of respect).

16.79

bhindi (Indian vegetable), Hindi, Sindhi (inhabitant of Pakistan), shindy, windy, Rawalpindi.

16.80

Fundy (Canadian bay), Lundy, Grundy, salmagundi (mixed salad dish), jaguarundi (feline mammal).

16.81

Burgundy, organdie, Ormandy (US conductor), Normandy.

16.82

daffy, NAAFI, Taffy, taffy (*US* chewy sweet).

16.83

furphy (*Austral* rumour), Murphy, surfie (*Austral* surfer), turfy.

16.84

Ife (Nigerian town), beefy, leafy.

16.85

jiffy, Liffey (Irish river), miffy (easily upset), sniffy (contemptuous), squiffy, salsify.

16.86

coffee, toffee.

16.87

trophy, strophe, Sophie, Sophy (title of Persian kings).

16.88

huffy, fluffy, snuffy (unpleasant), puffy, scruffy, toughie, stuffy, dandruffy.

16.89

goofy, Sufi (member of Muslim sect), Newfie (inhabitant of Newfoundland).

16.90

atrophy, pansophy (universal knowledge), telegraphy, calligraphy, epigraphy (study of ancient inscriptions), stratigraphy (study of geological history), hypertrophy, catastrophe, monostrophe (type of poem), apostrophe, radiotelegraphy.

16.90.1

tenorrhaphy (surgical repair of tendons), herniorrhaphy (surgical repair of hernia), staphylorrhaphy (repair of cleft palate).

16.90.2

biography, cacography (bad handwriting or spelling), zincography, discography, stylography (engraving with stylus), xylography (printing from wooden blocks), holography, tomography (x-ray technique), filmography, seismography, cosmography, pornography, typography, topography, cerography (engraving on waxed plate), xerography, micrography, hydrography (mapping oceans and rivers), reprography, petrography (classification of rocks), cartography, glyptography (engraving gemstones), cryptography (study of codes), lithography, orthography.

lexicography, selenography (mapping moon's surface), iconography.

autobiography, palaeontography (description of fossils).

16.90.2.1

geography, cardiography, radiography, hagiography, palaeography (study of ancient handwriting), bibliography, choreography, biogeography, zoogeography, historiography, electrocardiography.

16.90.2.2

pyelography (x-ray examination of kidneys), metallography (branch of metallurgy), dactylography (study of fingerprints), crystallography, encephalography.

16.90.2.3

demography, anemography (recording wind measurements).

16.90.2.4

planography (printing from flat surface), stenography, uranography (mapping of stars), oceanography.

16.90.2.5

dittography (unintentional repetition), hyetography (study of rainfall distribution).

16.90.2.6

photography, chromatography (chemistry term), telephotography, astrophotography, cinematography.

16.90.3

dystrophy, epistrophe (rhetorical device), antistrophe (section of choral ode).

16.90.4

theosophy (religious or philosophical system), philosophy, anthroposophy (mystical doctrine).

16.91

baggy, jaggy (jagged), flaggy (limp), quaggy (marshy), ragi (cereal grass), craggy, scraggy, shaggy.

16.92

leggy, dreggy (full of dregs).

16.93

piggy, ciggy, twiggy.

16.94

boggy, doggy, foggy, froggy, groggy, soggy, demagogy.

16.95

corgi, porgy (Atlantic fish).

16.96

bogey, bogie (wheels on railway coach), dogie (*US* motherless calf), fogy, yogi, judogi (judo costume).

16.97

buggy, muggy, shuggy (*Dialect* fairground swing).

16.98

boogie, boogie-woogie.

16.99

romaji (alphabet for transliterating Japanese), argy-bargy.

16.100

cagey, stagy (theatrical).

16.101

edgy, fledgy (feathered).

16.102

clergy, theurgy (divine intervention), zymurgy (study of fermentation processes), micrurgy (microscopic technique), dramaturgy.

16.103

widgie (*Austral* unruly young woman), prodigy, effigy, elegy, strategy, syzygy (position of celestial body), Murrumbidgee (Australian river), apophyge (architectural term).

16.104

bodgie (*Austral* unruly young man), dodgy, splodgy, podgy, stodgy, pedagogy (teaching principles and practice).

16.105

orgy, Georgie.

16.106

anagoge (allegorical interpretation), apagoge (logic term), paragoge (linguistics term), isagoge (academic introduction to topic).

16.107

budgie, smudgy, pudgy.

16.108

eulogy, energy, synergy, liturgy, lethargy.

16.108.1

geophagy (eating soil), theophagy (sacramental eating of god), omophagy (eating raw food), anthropophagy (cannibalism).

16.108.2

allergy, mammalogy (study of mammals), analogy, tetralogy (four related literary works), metallurgy, genealogy, mineralogy.

16.108.3

trilogy, brachylogy (concise style), antilogy (contradiction in terms).

16.108.4

ology, symbology, ecology, oncology, conchology (study of shells), graphology, psephology (study of elections), nephology (study of clouds), morphology, ufology, hoplology (study of weapons), pomology (fruit cultivation), homology, nomology (science of law), seismology, cosmology, oenology (study of wine), menology (ecclesiastical calendar), penology (punishment of crime), rhinology, Sinology (study of Chinese), technology, hymnology, ethnology, virology, hierology (sacred literature), orology (mapping mountain relief), horology, urology, neurology, necrology (list of dead people), hydrology, dendrology (study of trees), petrology (study of rocks), metrology (study of measurement units), gastrology, astrology, misology (hatred of reasoning), nosology (classification of diseases), scatology, tautology, otology, proctology, histology, Christology, pathology, anthology, sexology, doxology.

methodology, angelology, enzymology, entomology, ophthalmology, iconology, immunology, herpetology (study of reptiles), Scientology (religious cult).

geomorphology, palaeethnology (study of prehistoric man), dialectology, psychopathology, neuropathology.

16.108.4.1

geology, rheology (branch of physics), theology.

archaeology, radiology, ideology, ophiology (study of snakes), hagiology (writings about saints), teleology, speleology, craniology, Mariology, embryology, glaciology, sociology, aetiology (study of causes), deltiology (collecting picture postcards), ichthyology, phraseology, physiology.

astrogeology, venereology, soteriology (doctrine of salvation), bacteriology, ecclesiology (study of Christian Church).

epidemiology, phytosociology (study of plant communities).

16.108.4.2

biology, myology (study of muscle diseases), bryology (study of mosses), cryobiology, psychobiology, microbiology, radiobiology, sociobiology.

16.108.4.3

oology (study of bird's eggs), zoology, protozoology (study of protozoans), palaeozoology (study of fossil animals).

16.108.4.4

trichology (study of hair), codicology (study of manuscripts), myrmecology (study of ants), gynaecology, lexicology (study of vocabulary), toxicology, musicology.

16.108.4.5

phycology (study of algae), mycology (study of fungi), psychology, parapsychology, metapsychology.

16.108.4.6

cacology (bad choice of words), malacology (study of molluscs), pharmacology.

16.108.4.7

pharyngology, laryngology, otolaryngology.

16.108.4.8

philology, syphilology, dactylology (manual sign language), vexillology (study of flags).

16.108.4.9

anemology (study of winds), etymology, epistemology (theory of knowledge).

16.108.4.10

phenology (study of recurring phenomena), phrenology, palynology (study of pollen), selenology (study of the moon), terminology, criminology, phenomenology.

16.108.4.11

phonology, chronology, volcanology, demonology, campanology, oceanology, dendrochronology.

16.108.4.12

apology, topology, escapology, anthropology.

16.108.4.13

acarology (study of mites), futurology, numerology (divination by numbers), martyrology, meteorology, gastroenterology.

16.108.4.14

phytology (botany), cytology, sitology (study of nutrition), parasitology.

16.108.4.15

eschatology (branch of theology), dermatology, haematology, thaumatology (study of miracles), rheumatology, pneumatology (branch of theology), erotology, geratology, teratology (study of monsters), symptomatology.

16.108.4.15.1

climatology, primatology (branch of zoology), microclimatology, palaeoclimatology (study of past climates).

16.108.4.16

ontology (philosophy term), deontology (branch of ethics), gerontology, palaeontology.

16.108.4.17

cryptology (study of codes), Egyptology.

16.108.4.18

lithology (study of rocks), mythology, ornithology.

16.109

mangy, rangy.

16.110

dingy, mingy, stingy, lozengy (heraldic term).

16.111

scungy (*Austral* miserable), gungy, spongy.

16.112

alley, bally, dally, galley, Halley, pally, rally, sally, Sally, challis (lightweight fabric), tally, valley, tomalley (lobster's liver as food), reveille, teocalli (truncated Aztec pyramid), dilly-dally, shillyshally, peelie-wally (*Scot* looking unwell).

16.113

Bali, barley, Kali (Hindu goddess), Charlie, Dali, Mali, parley, quale (essential quality), Somali (African people), tamale (Mexican food), finale, Umtali (Zimbabwean city), triticale (wheat–rye hybrid), Mexicali (Mexican city).

16.114

Bailey, bailey, bailie (*Scot* municipal magistrate), ceilidh, scaly, daily, gaily, Old Bailey, Israeli, Disraeli, ukulele, jus naturale (Roman natural law).

16.115

belly, Kelly, Delhi, deli, jelly, smelly, nelly, Shelley, telly, Leadbelly, potbelly, Grappelli, underbelly, vermicelli, tagliatelle, Machiavelli.

16.116

early, Burghley, burly, curly, girlie, hurley (stick used in hurling), pearly, surly, hurly-burly.

16.117

barely, fairly, squarely, rarely.

16.118

Ely, Healey, Lely (Dutch portrait painter), mealy (powdery), freely, Greeley (US political leader), steely, stele (upright stone slab), wheelie, Swahili, sapele, Ismaili (follower of Aga Khan), Matabele (African people), campanile (bell tower), jus civile (Roman civil law).

16.119

dearly, merely, nearly, really, yearly, sincerely, biyearly.

16.120

billy, Chile, chilly, chilli, filly, gillie (*Scot* huntsman's attendant), hilly, lily, frilly, Scilly, silly, Tilly.

Cybele (Phrygian goddess), hillbilly, readily, steadily, bodily, Caerphilly, family, simile, homily, merrily, verily, Sicily, Chantilly.

cantabile, rockabilly (type of rock music), Piccadilly, piccalilli, subfamily, facsimile, willy-nilly, lilly-pilly

(Australian tree), willy-willy (*Austral* cyclone or duststorm).

superfamily (biological classification), sal volatile.

16.120.1

primarily, ordinarily, necessarily, momentarily.

16.121

phyle (ancient Greek tribe), highly, Riley, wily, corpus vile (worthless object of experiment), heterostyly (botany term).

16.122

collie, dolly, folly, golly, jolly, holly, lolly, Molly, Polly, poly, brolly, trolley, volley, wally, wolly (*Dialect* pickled cucumber), loblolly (US pine tree), Barbirolli.

16.123

Chorley, Morley, squally, Crawley, sorely, Warley (English town), Macaulay, Bengali, Nepali, creepy-crawly.

16.124

poorly, surely, purely, Kalgoorlie (Australian city).

16.125

oily, doily, roily (cloudy or muddy).

16.126 [see also 16.164]

coley, goalie, holy, holey, lowly, slowly, aïoli (garlic mayonnaise), unholy, ravioli, guacamole, roly-poly.

16.127

hourly, sourly.

16.128

cully (*Slang* pal), gully, mulley (having no horns), sully.

16.129

bully, fully, pulley, woolly, patchouli (tree yielding fragrant oil), fearfully, awfully, dreadfully, hopefully, frightfully.

16.130

coolie, schoolie (*Austral* schoolteacher), Julie, truly, duly, newly, Grand Coulee (US dam), unruly, unduly, douroucouli (monkey).

16.131
neighbourly, Kimberley (South African city), Stromboli (island with active volcano), broccoli, rascally, Wycherley (English dramatist), orderly, elderly, soldierly, gingerly, scholarly, formerly, normally, mannerly, finally, signally, equally, thoroughly, Thessaly, cicely (aromatic plant), partially, specially, leisurely, Italy, quarterly, utterly, masterly, westerly, easterly, systole, sisterly, fatherly, northerly, motherly, brotherly, southerly, gravelly, Beverly, Tivoli, overly, miserly.

usually, hyperbole, melancholy, disorderly, anomaly, unmannerly, naturally, generally, literally, severally, especially, officially, initially, diastole, northwesterly, southwesterly, northeasterly, southeasterly.

materially, macrocephaly (abnormal largeness of skull), microcephaly (abnormal smallness of skull), hydrocephaly, universally, incidentally.

16.131.1
virtually, actually, effectually, eventually.

16.131.2
beggarly, splenomegaly (abnormal enlargement of spleen), acromegaly (chronic disease), cardiomegaly (abnormal enlargement of heart).

16.131.3
marginally, originally.

16.131.4
personally, occasionally.

16.131.5
Tripoli, Gallipoli.

16.131.6
properly, monopoly, oligopoly (economics term), Trichinopoly (Indian city).

16.131.7
latterly, philately.

16.132
drably, chablis.

16.133
pebbly, trebly.

16.134
ghibli (hot North African wind), glibly, scribbly.

16.135
knobbly, wobbly.

16.136
bubbly, doubly, stubbly.

16.137 [further rhymes may be derived from **228.16**]
probably, terribly, horribly, passably, possibly, presumably.

16.138
trembly, Wembley, assembly, subassembly.

16.139
humbly, crumbly, grumbly.

16.140
darkly, clerkly, Berkeley.

16.141
meekly, treacly, weakly, weekly, biweekly, triweekly.

16.142 [further rhymes may be derived from **228.23**]
quickly, prickly, sickly, thickly, radically, tragically, publicly, typically, basically, drastically, physically, specifically, strategically, emphatically, dramatically, diametrically.

16.143
likely, unlikely.

16.144
blankly, frankly.

16.145
Hinckley (English town), wrinkly, crinkly.

16.146
badly, gladly, madly, Bradley, sadly.

16.147
deadly, medley.

16.148 [further rhymes may be created by adding -ly to the past participle of appropriate verbs]
fiddly, Ridley (English bishop), tiddly, markedly, fixedly, decidedly, allegedly, ashamedly, concernedly, resignedly,

assuredly, confessedly, repeatedly, admittedly, reportedly, advisedly, supposedly, confusedly, unashamedly, unconcernedly, unadvisedly.

16.148.1
deservedly, reservedly, unreservedly.

16.149
oddly, godly, ungodly.

16.150
lordly, broadly.

16.151
cuddly, Dudley.

16.152
cowardly, niggardly, dastardly, inwardly, outwardly.

16.153
worldly, unworldly, otherworldly.

16.154
friendly, unfriendly.

16.155
kindly, blindly.

16.156
roundly, soundly, profoundly.

16.157
secondly, jocundly.

16.158
chiefly, briefly.

16.159
snuffly, roughly.

16.160
giggly, niggly, wiggly.

16.161
ugli, ugly, smugly.

16.162
googly, Hooghly (Indian river).

16.163
singly, shingly, tingly.

16.164 [see also **16.126**]
wholly, solely.

16.165
gamely, lamely, namely.

16.166
seemly, extremely, unseemly.

16.167
timely, sublimely, untimely.

16.168
comely, glumly.

16.169
manly, Stanley, unmanly, Osmanli (relating to Ottoman Empire).

16.170
gainly, mainly, vainly, ungainly.

16.171
Henley, cleanly, uncleanly.

16.172
keenly, cleanly, queenly.

16.173
only, lonely.

16.174
christianly, maidenly, seamanly, commonly, womanly, humanly, workmanly, matronly, certainly, heavenly, slovenly, uncommonly, gentlemanly.

16.175 [further rhymes may be created by adding -ly to the present participle of appropriate verbs]
kingly, jokingly, seemingly, swimmingly, exceedingly, accordingly, decreasingly, surprisingly.

16.176
wrongly, strongly.

16.177
ripply, triply.

16.178
amply, damply.

16.179
pimply, simply.

16.180
parsley, sparsely.

16.181
bristly, gristly, Sisley (French painter), thistly.

16.182
closely, jocosely, morosely.

16.183
loosely, sprucely, profusely.

16.184
purposely, seriously, previously, obviously.

16.185
fleshly, freshly.

16.186
Attlee, Batley (English town), flatly, rattly.

16.187
Atli (legendary Norse king), Hartley, partly.

16.188
lately, stately.

16.189
fitly, minutely (every minute), alternately, definitely, fortunately, immediately.

16.189.1
ultimately, approximately.

16.190
slightly, knightly, nightly, rightly, sprightly, sightly (attractive), fortnightly, unsightly.

16.191
hotly, motley.

16.192
courtly, portly, shortly.

16.193
minutely (in detail), absolutely.

16.194
compactly, exactly.

16.195
directly, correctly.

16.196
faintly, saintly.

16.197
Bentley, gently, intently.

16.198
urgently, patiently, patently, instantly, constantly, presently, evidently, consequently.

16.199
ghastly, lastly.

16.200
beastly, priestly, Priestley.

16.201
modestly, honestly.

16.202
ghostly, mostly.

16.203
deathly, Llanelli.

16.204
earthly, unearthly.

16.205
monthly, bimonthly, trimonthly.

16.206
actively, positively, effectively, respectively, comparatively.

16.207
lovely, unlovely.

16.208
Lesley, Presley, Wesley.

16.209
drizzly, grisly, grizzly.

16.210
gammy, jammy, hammy, clammy, mammy, ramie (shrub yielding fibre), chamois, tammy, Miami.

16.211
army, barmy, balmy, kami (Japanese divine spirit), smarmy, palmy (prosperous), swami (Hindu title of respect), kirigami (art of paper cutting), salami, tsunami, macramé, pastrami, origami.

16.212
Amy, gamy.

16.213
Emmy (US television award), jemmy, semi.

16.214
Fermi, wormy, taxidermy, diathermy, radiothermy (radiation treatment).

16.215
creamy, dreamy, preemie (*US* premature baby), seamy, steamy, polysemy (having many meanings), monosemy (having only one meaning), Aruwimi (Zaïrese river).

16.216
Jimmy, shimmy, blasphemy, Ptolemy, synonymy, eponymy (derivation from person's name), toponymy, metonymy (figure of speech).

16.217
limy, limey, blimey, slimy, rimy, grimy, stymie, cor blimey.

16.218
dormie (golf term), horme (psychology term), stormy.

16.219
Komi (Finnish people), foamy, homy, loamy, cleome Dahomey, Salome, anomie (lack of social standards), polychromy (multicoloured decoration).

16.220
chummy, dummy, gummy, lumme, plummy, mummy, rummy, Brummie, crummy, crumby, tummy, yummy.

16.221
gloomy, plumy, roomy, rheumy.

16.222
Naomi, alchemy, sodomy, infamy, enemy, gourami, sesame, bosomy, academy, anatomy, epitome.

16.222.1
bigamy, digamy (second marriage), polygamy.

16.222.2
oogamy (type of sexual reproduction), endogamy (marriage within social unit), homogamy (botany term), monogamy, misogamy (hatred of marriage), isogamy (botany term), exogamy (marriage outside social unit), anisogamy (type of sexual reproduction).

16.222.3
bonhomie, economy, agronomy (science of cultivation), gastronomy, astronomy, isonomy (equality before the law), autonomy, taxonomy, Deuteronomy.

16.222.3.1
theonomy (being governed by God), physiognomy.

16.222.4
zootomy (animal dissection), phlebotomy (incision into vein), lobotomy, dichotomy, trichotomy (division into three categories), leucotomy (brain surgery), neurotomy (surgical cutting of nerve), necrotomy (dissection of corpse), microtomy (cutting of thin sections), cystotomy (incision into bladder), lithotomy (removal of bladder stone), varicotomy, pharyngotomy, laryngotomy, tonsillotomy, laparotomy (investigative abdominal surgery).

16.222.4.1
tracheotomy, craniotomy, stereotomy (cutting three-dimensional solids), osteotomy (surgical cutting of bone), ovariotomy.

16.222.5
splenectomy (removal of spleen), nephrectomy (removal of kidney), gastrectomy, vasectomy, mastectomy, cystectomy (removal of bladder), appendectomy, tonsillectomy, pneumonectomy, prostatectomy, appendicectomy.

16.222.5.1
thyroidectomy, adenoidectomy, haemorrhoidectomy.

16.222.5.2
hysterectomy, oophorectomy (removal of ovary).

16.222.6
colostomy, gastrostomy (artificial stomach opening), tracheostomy, ileostomy (abdominal operation).

16.223
Annie, canny, Danny, fanny, nanny, cranny, granny, trannie, kokanee (type of salmon), uncanny, hootenanny.

16.224
ani (tropical bird), barney, blarney, Mani (Persian prophet), rani (Indian queen or princess), Mbabane (capital of

Swaziland), afghani (Afghan currency), Killarney, biriani, frangipani (fragrant shrub), Pakistani, Hindustani, chilli con carne, Azerbaijani (Iranian people).

16.225

rainy, brainy, grainy, veiny, zany, Na-Dene (language group), Dunsany (Irish writer).

16.226

any, benny (*Slang* amphetamine tablet), fenny (marshy), jenny, Jenny, blenny, many, penny, Kilkenny, catchpenny (designed for instant appeal), pinch-penny (miserly), Asantehene (ruler of Ghana).

16.227

Ernie, Bernie, journey, attorney.

16.228

beanie (*US* close-fitting hat), genie, meany, teeny, weeny, Sweeney, bikini, zucchini, Puccini, Houdini, Irene, Rossini, martini, linguini (type of pasta), Cherubini, fettucine, fantoccini (marionettes), Toscanini, scaloppine (thin slices of meat), Mistassini (Canadian lake).

16.228.1

Cellini (Italian sculptor), Fellini, Mussolini, tortellini (type of pasta).

16.229

skinny, finny, guinea, Guinea, hinny, Linnhe (Scottish loch), blini, Pliny, mini, ninny, pinny, spinney, cine, tinny, whinny, dominie (*Scot* school-master), hominy (*US* coarsely-ground maize), satiny, scrutiny, mutiny, destiny, ignominy, piccaninny.

16.229.1

polygyny (having many female partners), aborigine.

16.229.2

progeny, philogyny (fondness for women), phylogeny (evolution of species), homogeny (similarity through common ancestry), monogyny (having one female partner), orogeny (mountain formation), misogyny, ontogeny (development of organism), epeirogeny (formation of continents).

16.229.3

Rimini, postliminy (legal term), niminy-piminy.

16.229.4

larceny, coparceny (joint heirship).

16.230

piny, spiny, briny, sine (without), shiny, tiny, winy, sunshiny.

16.231

bonny, Johnny, Swanee, yonnie (*Austral* a stone).

16.232

corny, horny, brawny, scrawny, tawny, thorny, mulligatawny.

16.233

bony, cony, phoney, pony, crony, Tony, stony, yoni (female genitalia in Hinduism).

Marconi, Bodoni (style of type), spumone (Italian ice cream), Oenone (Greek nymph), Benoni (South African city), padrone (Italian innkeeper), Shoshone (American Indian people), canzone (lyrical song).

cannelloni, chitarrone (large lute), Gaborone (capital of Botswana), macaroni, cicerone (tourist guide), minestrone, rigatoni (type of pasta), panettone (Italian spiced bread), zabaglione.

Antonioni (Italian film director), Sierra Leone.

16.233.1

baloney, polony, abalone, provolone (soft cheese).

16.234

downy, brownie, townie.

16.235

bunny, dunny, funny, honey, money, runny, sunny, sonny, Sunni (branch of orthodox Islam), tunny, baldmoney (aromatic flowering plant).

16.236

loony, Cluny (French town), moony, spoony (foolishly amorous), uni (*short for* university), puny, Sakyamuni (title of Buddha).

16.237

peony, ebony, Albany, balcony, Gascony, Tuscany, Alderney, euphony, symphony, agony, villainy, colony, scammony, Chamonix, Tammany (US Democratic party organization), harmony, Germany, simony, Romany, fourpenny, twopenny, fivepenny, timpani, company, tenpenny, sixpenny, barony, tyranny, irony, atony, rhatany (South American shrub), betony (Eurasian plant), tetany, dittany (aromatic plant), litany, Brittany, gluttony, Antony, Bethany, Saxony, saxony, oniony.

chalcedony, telephony, Persephone, Antigone, disharmony, alimony, ceremony, acrimony, agrimony (flowering plant), matrimony, patrimony, parsimony, sanctimony, antimony, testimony, accompany.

16.237.1

irony (resembling iron), bryony, Hesione (Greek mythological princess), Alcyone (Greek mythological character).

16.237.2

Tiffany, polyphony (musical term), epiphany, antiphony (type of choral singing).

16.237.3

Zoffany (British painter), cacophony, colophony (translucent amber substance), homophony, monophony.

16.237.3.1

theophany (manifestation of deity), radiophony (electronic music), stereophony.

16.237.4

theogony (origin of the gods), mahogany, cosmogony (origin of universe), schizogony (type of asexual reproduction).

16.237.5

felony, miscellany.

16.237.6

lemony, hegemony (domination by one group), anemone, Gethsemane.

16.237.7

botany, cottony, neoteny (zoology term), monotony, palaeobotany (study of fossil plants).

16.238

acne, hackney, Hackney, chloracne (skin disease), Arachne (Greek mythological character).

16.239

cockney, Hockney, Procne (Greek mythological princess).

16.240

kidney, Sydney, Sidney.

16.241

slangy, tangy.

16.242

dinghy, springy, stringy.

16.243

chappie, happy, nappy, snappy, crappy, scrappy, sappy (full of energy), yappy, unhappy, slaphappy.

16.244

harpy, okapi, syncarpy (botany term), parthenocarpy (fruit development without fertilization).

16.245

peppy, cacoepy (bad pronunciation), orthoepy (study of correct pronunciation).

16.246

chirpy, Euterpe (Greek Muse).

16.247

sleepy, creepy, weepy, Praesepe (cluster of stars).

16.248

chippy, dippy (*Slang* crazy), gippy, hippie, lippy (*US* insolent), clippie, slippy, nippy, drippy, zippy, recipe, gossipy, Xanthippe (wife of Socrates), Mississippi.

16.249

stripy, stenotypy (form of shorthand), phonotypy (phonetic transcription of speech), stereotypy.

16.250

copy, kopje (small hill), choppy, floppy, sloppy, poppy, stroppy, soppy, jalopy, microcopy (reduced photographic copy), photocopy.

16.251

dopey, Hopi (American Indian people), ropy, soapy.

16.252

guppy, puppy.

16.253

loopy, droopy, groupie, soupy, NUPE.

16.254

syncope, Agape (Christian love), canopy, canapé, therapy, syrupy, entropy.

calliope (*US* steam-powered organ), apocope (linguistics term), telescopy, Penelope, Parthenope (Greek mythological character), lycanthropy (transformation into wolf), philanthropy, misanthropy.

cryotherapy, psychotherapy, chemotherapy, hypnotherapy, hydrotherapy, phototherapy (medical treatment using light).

radiotherapy, heliotherapy (therapeutic use of sunlight), physiotherapy, immunotherapy, roentgenotherapy (therapeutic use of x-rays).

16.254.1

wicopy (US plant), pericope (passage read in church).

16.254.2

endoscopy, horoscopy, uroscopy (examination of urine), microscopy, spectroscopy (analysis of spectra), stethoscopy, stereoscopy, ophthalmoscopy, ornithoscopy (divination by bird observation).

16.255

impi (Bantu warriors), skimpy, Wimpy (*Trademark*).

16.256

Pompey, swampy.

16.257

bumpy, dumpy, jumpy, humpy (angry or gloomy), lumpy, scrumpy, grumpy, stumpy.

16.258

crispy, wispy.

16.259

colloquy, obloquy (defamatory statement), soliloquy, somniloquy (talking in one's sleep), ventriloquy.

16.260

Barrie, Barry, carry, Gary, harry, Harry, Larry, marry, parry, tarry, miscarry, glengarry (Scottish woollen cap), remarry, intermarry.

16.261

Bari (Italian port), Chari (African river), sari, tarry, starry, safari, Bihari (member of Indian people), curare, Ferrari, Vasari (Italian writer and artist), Cagliari (Sardinian port), zamindari (large Indian agricultural estate), Carbonari (Italian secret political society), Stradivari, charivari.

16.261.1

Pahari (language group), Kalahari, Mata Hari.

16.262

berry, bury, Bury, Kerry, skerry (*Scot* small rocky island), cherry, Derry, ferry, jerry, Jerry, merry, perry, sherry, Terry, very, wherry (type of boat), knobkerrie (South African tribesman's stick), chokecherry (US species of cherry), equerry, beriberi, Pondicherry, Londonderry.

16.263

burry (prickly), furry, firry (abounding in fir trees), blurry.

16.264

aery, airy, Carey, scary, chary, dairy, fairy, hairy, lairy (*Austral* gaudy), glary, Mary, nary (*Dialect* not), prairie, vary, wary, canary, unwary, airy-fairy, Tipperary, cassowary, condottiere (former European mercenary soldier).

16.265

eyrie, eerie, Erie, beery, cheery, deary, leery, bleary, peri, Peary (US arctic explorer), query, dreary, theory, weary, Kashmiri, Guarneri (family of violin-makers), bokmakierie (South African songbird), metatheory (critical study of philosophy).

16.266

daiquiri (iced drink containing rum), Valkyrie, porphyry (type of rock), harakiri.

16.267

fiery, miry, spiry, wiry, expiry, enquiry, inquiry.

16.268

corrie (circular hollow in hillside), lorry, quarry, sorry, whare (Maori hut).

16.269

dory (spiny-finned fish), gory, hoary, lory (small parrot), glory, saury (tropical fish), Tory, storey, story, John Dory (spiny-finned fish), vainglory, outlawry, furore, centaury (Eurasian plant), clerestory (row of church windows), blindstorey (church storey without windows), signori, hunky-dory, con amore, Montessori (Italian educational reformer), cacciatore (Italian cookery term), multistorey, Alpha Centauri, viola d'amore (former stringed instrument).

16.270

jury, Jewry, houri, Drury, Curie, fury, Tandoori, potpourri, Venturi (Italian physicist), Missouri.

16.271

cowry, kauri (New Zealand coniferous tree), dowry, Lowry, Maori.

16.272

curry, scurry, hurry, flurry, slurry, Murray, Surrey, surrey, worry.

16.273

mercury, augury, strangury, penury.

16.274

diary, friary, priory, flowery, floury, showery, brewery, Barbary, Burberry (*Trademark*), turbary (peat-cutting area), bribery, daubery, strawberry, snowberry, crowberry, blubbery, rubbery, shrubbery, blueberry, dewberry, Newbury, hackberry, blackberry, cloudberry, Sudbury, dogberry, bilberry, Tilbury, mulberry, Banbury, cranberry, spiceberry, Shaftesbury, Avebury, Tewkesbury, raspberry, Shrewsbury, gooseberry, Dewsbury, Aylesbury, Salisbury, Bloomsbury, Queensberry, quackery, Thackeray, Zachary, bakery, peccary (pig-like mammal), succory (chicory), cookery, rookery, hatchery, archery, lechery, treachery, witchery, butchery, century, spidery, doddery, powdery, quandary, boundary, thundery, Nagari (type of Indian script), vagary, beggary, Gregory, roguery, sugary, Calgary, forgery, cudgerie (tropical tree), drudgery, soldiery, alary (relating to wings), raillery, hellery (wild behaviour), celery, sealery, Tuileries, coloury (having colour), scullery, foolery, saddlery, chandlery, burglary, jugglery, butlery (butler's room), cutlery, mammary, gramarye (magic), emery, memory, creamery, primary, flummery, mummery, nummary (relating to coins), summary, summery, rosemary, cannery, granary, tannery, stannary (tin mine), swannery, joinery, clownery, gunnery, nunnery, apery (imitative behaviour), papery, drapery, peppery, foppery, coopery (barrel-making), dupery, trumpery, orrery (model of solar system), library, contrary, brasserie, glossary, sorcery, grocery, chancery, tertiary, washery, fishery, luxury, treasury, usury, lingerie, battery, cattery, flattery, artery, Tartary, lottery, pottery, cautery, watery, coterie, notary, rotary, votary, buttery, psaltery (ancient stringed instrument), mastery, blustery, lathery, feathery, leathery, carvery, reverie, every, ovary, Calvary, silvery, Mercury, colliery, misery, rosary.

checkerberry, elderberry, syllabary (list of syllables), chinaberry, Canterbury, huckleberry, whortleberry, loganberry, Glastonbury, boysenberry, serviceberry, grotesquery, debauchery, lapidary (dealer in gemstones), embroidery, prebendary, secondary, legendary, periphery, midwifery, housewifery, menagerie, corollary, tomfoolery,-

exemplary, Montgomery, customary, chicanery (verbal trickery), reliquary, antiquary, arbitrary, patisserie, greengrocery, illusory, adversary, compulsory, secretory, bijouterie (type of jewellery), perfunctory, emunctory (relating to excretory organ), adultery, desultory, effrontery, peremptory, monastery, upholstery, recovery, discovery.

Devanagari (Indian syllabic script), haberdashery, introductory.

jiggery-pokery, noli-me-tangere (warning against touching).

16.274.1

apiary, topiary, vespiary (wasps' nest), farriery, curriery, furriery, bestiary, vestiary (relating to clothes), aviary, breviary, hosiery, subsidiary, stipendiary, incendiary, pecuniary, fiduciary (trustee), intermediary.

16.274.1.1

biliary (relating to bile), miliary (resembling millet seeds), ciliary, nobiliary (relating to the nobility), auxiliary, domiciliary, superciliary (relating to the eyebrow).

16.274.1.2

judiciary, officiary (body of officials), justiciary, beneficiary.

16.274.2

mortuary, actuary, February, January, ossuary (receptacle for human bones), statuary, sanctuary, estuary, textuary (relating to a text), residuary, obituary, voluptuary.

16.274.3

bobbery (pack of hunting dogs), jobbery (corruption in public office), slobbery, snobbery, robbery, corroboree (*Austral* noisy gathering).

16.274.4

chicory, hickory (US nut tree), trickery, formicary (ant hill), Terpsichore (Greek Muse), apothecary.

16.274.5

mockery, rockery, crockery, comstockery (*US* excessive censorship).

16.274.6

goliardery (ribald Latin verse), camaraderie.

16.274.7

dromedary, hebdomadary (weekly).

16.274.8

grindery (place for sharpening tools), bookbindery.

16.274.9

piggery, amphigory (piece of nonsense writing), allegory, vinegary, category.

16.274.10

buggery, snuggery, thuggery, skulduggery.

16.274.11

Hungary, ironmongery.

16.274.12

doggery (surly behaviour), toggery (clothes), pettifoggery, demagoguery.

16.274.13

perjury, surgery, psychosurgery, neurosurgery, cryosurgery.

16.274.14

injury, gingery, orangery.

16.274.15

calorie, gallery, Malory, salary, Valerie, kilocalorie.

16.274.16

Hilary, Hillary, pillory, armillary (relating to bracelets), pupillary, capillary, ancillary, artillery, fritillary, tutelary (serving as guardian), distillery, axillary (relating to the armpit), maxillary (relating to upper jaw), submaxillary (relating to lower jaw).

16.274.17

drollery, cajolery.

16.274.18

formulary (book of prescribed formulas), cartulary (collection of legal records), vocabulary, constabulary.

16.274.19

chancellery, intercalary (inserted in the calendar), epistolary (relating to letters).

16.274.20
armoury, gendarmerie.

16.274.21
spermary (sperm-producing organ), infirmary.

16.274.22
bloomery (type of ironworks), perfumery.

16.274.23
hennery (place for keeping poultry), venery, millenary (one thousand years), decennary (decade).

16.274.24
fernery, ternary, turnery (objects made on lathe), quaternary (consisting of four).

16.274.25
beanery (cheap restaurant), deanery, denary (based on ten), plenary (complete), greenery, scenery, machinery, catenary (type of geometric curve), centenary, duodenary (relating to twelve), bicentenary, tricentenary, quincentenary, quatercentenary.

16.274.26
ordinary, millinery, culinary, seminary, luminary, urinary, parcenary (joint heirship), mercenary, sanguinary, extraordinary, imaginary, disciplinary, preliminary, coparcenary (joint ownership), veterinary, multidisciplinary, interdisciplinary, genitourinary, eleemosynary (dependent on charity).

16.274.27
binary, finery, pinery, quinary (consisting of five), trinary (consisting of three), vinery (place for growing grapes), winery, refinery.

16.274.28
unary (consisting of single element), buffoonery, sublunary (between moon and earth), festoonery.

16.274.29
legionary, pulmonary, coronary, cautionary, dictionary, functionary, visionary, precautionary, reactionary, revolutionary, evolutionary.

16.274.29.1
stationery, stationary, inflationary.

16.274.29.2
cessionary (legal term), discretionary, concessionary.

16.274.29.3
missionary, seditionary, expeditionary.

16.274.29.4
lectionary (book of church readings), confectionery, insurrectionary.

16.274.30
slippery, frippery, polypary (base of coral colony).

16.274.31
empery (dominion), extempore.

16.274.32
numerary (relating to numbers), honorary, funerary, temporary, literary, itinerary, contemporary, supernumerary.

16.274.33
tracery, embracery (attempt to corrupt jury).

16.274.34
pessary, accessory, possessory (relating to possession).

16.274.35
bursary, cursory, nursery, precursory, anniversary.

16.274.36
emissary, commissary, promissory, janissary (Turkish sovereign's personal guard), necessary, rotisserie, unnecessary.

16.274.37
spicery, derisory.

16.274.38
sensory, dispensary, suspensory, incensory (incense-burner), extrasensory.

16.274.39
residentiary (officially resident), penitentiary, obedientiary (holder of monastic office), plenipotentiary.

16.274.40 [some words in **16.274.43** may be pronounced to rhyme with this group]

datary (Catholic official), gyratory, natatory (relating to swimming), condemnatory, celebratory, compensatory, anticipatory.

16.274.40.1

judicatory, applicatory, deprecatory, justificatory.

16.274.40.2

ambulatory (relating to walking), circulatory, adulatory, congratulatory.

16.274.41

jittery, glittery, pituri (Australian shrub).

presbytery, auditory, pellitory (European plant), military, solitary, cemetery, limitary, dormitory, fumitory (European plant), planetary, sanitary, monitory (warning), monetary, unitary, dignitary, feretory (Catholic shrine), territory, transitory.

proprietary, pituitary, hereditary, insanitary, premonitory, depository, repository, suppository, expository, paramilitary.

16.274.42

tributary, salutary, statutory, contributory, executory (not yet effective), noncontributory, interlocutory, circumlocutory.

16.274.43

dietary, placatory, predatory, laudatory (expressing praise), mandatory, prefatory, offertory, purgatory, nugatory (of little value), fumatory (relating to smoking), signatory, damnatory, repertory, vibratory, secretary, migratory, pulsatory, hortatory (urging), lavatory.

educatory, obligatory, consolatory, lacrimatory, reformatory, explanatory, cosignatory, declaratory, preparatory, perspiratory, respiratory, dispensatory, invitatory, salutatory, sternutatory (causing sneezing), conservatory, observatory, accusatory, excusatory.

reverberatory, undersecretary.

16.274.43.1

aleatory (dependent on chance), retaliatory, conciliatory, reconciliatory.

16.274.43.2

amendatory (*US* corrective), recommendatory.

16.274.43.3

rogatory (seeking information), derogatory, interrogatory, supererogatory (superfluous).

16.274.43.4

dilatory (time-wasting), depilatory.

16.274.43.5

amatory, defamatory, declamatory, acclamatory, proclamatory, exclamatory, inflammatory.

16.274.43.6

minatory (threatening), discriminatory, hallucinatory.

16.274.43.7

oratory, laboratory, exploratory.

16.274.44

factory, lactary (relating to milk), olfactory, phylactery (case containing Hebrew texts), refractory, calefactory (giving warmth), satisfactory.

16.274.45

nectary (nectar-secreting structure), rectory, sectary (member of a sect), refectory, trajectory, directory.

16.274.46

victory, valedictory, contradictory.

16.274.47

sedimentary, rudimentary, alimentary, elementary, supplementary, complimentary, complementary, documentary, parliamentary, testamentary (relating to a will), unparliamentary.

16.274.48

sedentary, voluntary, commentary, promontory, momentary, fragmentary, dysentery, inventory, involuntary.

16.274.49

bistoury (long surgical knife), history, mystery, magistery (alchemical substance), prehistory, consistory (diocesan court), protohistory.

16.274.50
slavery, knavery, bravery, savoury, unsavoury, antislavery.

16.274.51
livery, quivery, shivery, delivery, olivary (olive-shaped).

16.274.52
ivory, salivary.

16.274.53
revisory, advisory, supervisory.

16.275
gimmickry, mimicry.

16.276
bawdry (obscene language), Cawdrey (English lexicographer), tawdry.

16.277
balladry, bastardry (*Austral* malicious behaviour), wizardry.

16.278
ribaldry, cuckoldry, heraldry.

16.279
husbandry, legendry.

16.280
orphrey (embroidered border on vestment), gallimaufry (*US* hotchpotch).

16.281
comfrey (Eurasian plant), Humphrey.

16.282
imagery, savagery.

16.283
jewellery, hostelry, cavalry, devilry, revelry, chivalry, rivalry.

16.284
deaconry, falconry, cannonry (artillery), canonry (office of canon), weaponry, heronry (colony of herons), masonry, blazonry, archdeaconry, freemasonry, citizenry.

16.285
poetry, marquetry, parquetry, circuitry, rocketry, coquetry (flirtation), basketry, musketry, gadgetry, toiletry, puppetry, corsetry, telemetry (measurement of distant events), photogrammetry (making measurements from photographs).

16.285.1
symmetry, planimetry (measurement of plane areas), asymmetry, dissymmetry, altimetry, bathymetry (measurement of ocean depth), acidimetry, alkalimetry, dolorimetry (measurement of pain).

16.285.2 [further rhymes may be derived from **17.342.3**]
biometry (statistics applied to biology), zoometry (branch of zoology), psychometry (measurement of mental processes), thermometry, hypsometry (measurement of altitude), photometry, optometry, anemometry (measurement of wind speed), dynamometry (power measurement), anthropometry (measurement of human body).

16.285.2.1
geometry, tacheometry (measurement of distance), craniometry, stereometry (measurement of volume), sociometry (study of social relationships).

16.285.2.2
chronometry, trigonometry.

16.286
bigotry, helotry (serfdom), zealotry (excessive zeal), papeterie (box for papers), barratry (legal term).

16.286.1
psychiatry, podiatry (*US* chiropody), antipsychiatry (psychiatric theory), neuropsychiatry.

16.286.2
zoolatry (worship of animals), bardolatry (excessive admiration for Shakespeare), idolatry, monolatry (worship of one god), necrolatry (worship of the dead), iconolatry, demonolatry.

16.286.2.1
hagiolatry (veneration of saints), heliolatry (sun worship), bibliolatry (excessive devotion to Bible), Mariolatry (veneration of Virgin Mary).

16.287
gantry, pantry.

16.288
entry, gentry, sentry, re-entry, passementerie (decorative trimming).

16.289
wintry, carpentry.

16.290
country, upcountry.

16.291
pedantry, infantry, pageantry, gallantry, tenantry, errantry, Coventry, pleasantry, peasantry.

16.292
vestry, ancestry.

16.293
sophistry, registry, palmistry, chemistry, ministry, tapestry, forestry, artistry, dentistry, baptistry, casuistry, biochemistry.

16.294
dassie (rodent-like mammal), gassy, lassie, glacé, Plassey, Massey, massy (massive), brassie, sassy, chassis, Kumasi (Ghanaian city), Manasseh (Old Testament character), Malagasy (inhabitant of Madagascar), Tallahassee, Haile Selassie.

16.295
farcy (veterinary term), classy, glassy, brassy, grassy, dalasi (Gambian currency), sannyasi (Brahman mendicant), Adivasi (member of Indian people).

16.296
Basie, lacy, racy, Tracy, O'Casey, Sulawesi (Indonesian islands).

16.297
Jesse, messy, Crécy, dressy, in esse (actually existing).

16.298
mercy, Percy, pursy (short-winded), Circe, gramercy, controversy.

16.298.1
reversi (board game), arsy-versy.

16.299
fleecy, Naoise (Irish mythological character), greasy, Tbilisi (Russian city).

16.300
missy, prissy, sissy, prophecy, Gallice (in French), policy, Anglice (in English), pleurisy, secrecy, courtesy, Eurydice,
Chalcidice (Greek peninsula), sub judice, impolicy, discourtesy.

16.300.1
Odyssey, geodesy (measurement of earth), theodicy (branch of theology).

16.301
icy, dicey, spicy, pricey, vice (instead of).

16.302
bossy, lossy (dissipating energy), flossy (*US* showy), glossy, mossy, posse.

16.303
horsy, Glauce (Greek mythological character), saucy.

16.304
mousy, Firdausi (Persian epic poet), housey-housey.

16.305
fussy, hussy, pussy.

16.306
goosy, juicy, Lucy, Senussi (member of Muslim sect), Debussy, acey-deucy (type of backgammon).

16.307
abbacy, embassy, argosy (large merchant ship), legacy, fallacy, jealousy, prelacy (office of prelate), Wallasey, pharmacy, primacy, lunacy, papacy, heresy, piracy, oracy (use of speech), curacy (office of curate), leprosy, fantasy, ecstasy, privacy.

idiocy, celibacy, advocacy, candidacy, delegacy, profligacy, supremacy, diplomacy, contumacy (wilful resistance to authority), Varanasi (Indian city), obstinacy, adequacy, conspiracy, accuracy, magistracy, apostasy.

episcopacy (church government by bishops), inadequacy, inaccuracy, idiosyncrasy.

16.307.1
efficacy, delicacy, intricacy, inefficacy.

16.307.2
intimacy, legitimacy, illegitimacy.

16.307.3
geognosy (study of earth's structure), pharmacognosy (branch of pharmacology).

16.307.4
numeracy, literacy, confederacy, degeneracy, illiteracy.

16.307.5
mobocracy, ochlocracy (mob rule), democracy, nomocracy (government based on law), monocracy, pornocracy (domination by prostitutes), technocracy, hypocrisy, bureaucracy, isocracy (equality of political power), stratocracy (military rule), autocracy, plutocracy, gynaecocracy, hierocracy (government by priests), pantisocracy (community ruled by all), meritocracy, gerontocracy, aristocracy.

16.307.5.1
theocracy (government by deity), theocrasy (mingling of deities), hagiocracy (government by holy men).

16.308
Anglesey, minstrelsy.

16.309
fancy, Nancy, theomancy (divination through an oracle), sciomancy (divination through ghosts), rhabdomancy (water divining), chiromancy (palmistry), pyromancy (divination by fire), necromancy (black magic), hydromancy (divination by water), cartomancy (fortune-telling with cards), ornithomancy (divination from bird behaviour).

16.310
chancy, Jhansi (Indian city).

16.311
wincey (type of cloth), chaplaincy, De Quincey (English essayist), captaincy.

16.312
buoyancy, fluency, truancy, vacancy, piquancy, pudency (modesty or prudishness), infancy, agency, regency, valency, clemency, tenancy, pregnancy, frequency, currency, flagrancy, vagrancy, decency, potency, constancy, solvency, poignancy.

incumbency, presidency, redundancy, exigency, Excellency, inclemency, subtenancy, permanency, malignancy, discrepancy, occupancy, infrequency, delinquency, transparency, complacency, indecency, militancy, hesitancy, expectancy, consultancy, accountancy, consistency, conservancy, insolvency. constituency, eigenfrequency (physics term), belligerency (being at war), itinerancy, inconsistency, electrovalency (chemistry term).

16.312.1
leniency, expediency.

16.312.2
tendency, dependency, ascendancy, superintendency (office of superintendent).

16.312.3
urgency, surgeoncy (office of surgeon), emergency, insurgency, detergency (cleansing power), counterinsurgency.

16.312.4
stringency, contingency.

16.312.5
efficiency, deficiency, proficiency, sufficiency, inefficiency, insufficiency.

16.312.6
blatancy, patency, dilatancy (physics term).

16.313
epilepsy, narcolepsy (medical term), nympholepsy (state of violent emotion), catalepsy (medical term).

16.314
gypsy, tipsy.

16.315
popsy (*Slang* attractive young woman), dropsy, biopsy, autopsy.

16.316
curtsy, Chertsey.

16.317
ritzy, baronetcy.

16.318
footsie, tootsy, Watutsi (member of African people), tootsy-wootsy.

16.319

ashy, flashy, plashy (wet or marshy), splashy, mashie, trashy, Lubumbashi (Zaïrese city).

16.320

marshy, Ustashi (former Yugoslav terrorist organization).

16.321

fleshy, meshy.

16.322

dishy, fishy, rubbishy, maharishi.

16.323

squashy, washy (watery), wishy-washy.

16.324

gushy, slushy, mushy, rushy.

16.325

bushy, cushy, pushy.

16.326

sushi (Japanese food), acouchi (South American rodent).

16.327

batty, catty, scatty, chatty, fatty, natty, patty, ratty, tatty, Scarlatti, chapatti, Hanratty, Togliatti (Russian city), Cincinnati.

16.328

arty, hearty, lathi (Indian policeman's wooden stick), smartie, party, coati, Masbate (Philippine island), nonparty, ex parte (legal term), Astarte (Phoenician goddess), illuminati (enlightened people).

16.328.1

karate, Marathi (Indian language), Gujarati (Indian people), literati (scholarly people).

16.329

eighty, Ate (Greek goddess), Haiti, platy (geology term), slaty, matey, weighty.

16.330

Getty, jetty, petty, sweaty, yeti, confetti, spaghetti, machete, Rossetti, spermaceti (white waxy substance), Donizetti (Italian operatic composer).

16.331

dirty, shirty, thirty.

16.332

Beatty, meaty, peaty, treaty, sweetie, graffiti, Tahiti, entreaty, Papeete (capital of Tahiti), Nefertiti.

16.333

bitty, kitty, ditty, nitty, pity, gritty, smriti (Hindu sacred literature), pretty, city, shitty, witty.

laity, moiety (half), probity, rackety (noisy), crotchety, nudity, crudity, fidgety, nullity, comity (courtesy), committee, enmity, wapiti (large US deer), uppity, self-pity, equity, rarity, varsity, scarcity, paucity, falsity, sanctity, quantity, chastity, velvety, laxity, fixity.

acerbity, improbity, heredity, absurdity, fidelity, credulity, extremity, Yosemite, infirmity, subcommittee, amenity, indemnity, solemnity, inequity, obliquity, iniquity, antiquity, propinquity (nearness), jequirity (tropical climbing plant), entirety, alacrity, integrity, nitty-gritty, necessity, caducity (perishableness), intercity, perplexity, complexity, convexity.

infidelity, incredulity, serendipity, mediocrity.

16.333.1

deity, velleity (weakest level of desire), multeity, haecceity (philosophy term), spontaneity, corporeity, homogeneity, erogeneity, incorporeity.

16.333.2

piety, ubiety (being in particular place), dubiety, impiety, sobriety, propriety, society, satiety, anxiety, inebriety, impropriety.

16.333.2.1

variety, contrariety, notoriety.

16.333.3

congruity, vacuity, acuity, tenuity, annuity, fortuity, fatuity, gratuity, superfluity, incongruity, perspicuity, promiscuity, assiduity, ambiguity, contiguity, perpetuity.

16.333.3.1

ingenuity, continuity, discontinuity.

16.333.4

rickety, pernickety.

16.333.5

quiddity (essential nature), fluidity, morbidity, rigidity, frigidity, solidity, validity, timidity, humidity, cupidity, stupidity, rapidity, liquidity, viridity (greenness), aridity, acridity, lucidity, avidity, invalidity.

16.333.5.1

acidity, placidity, hypoacidity, hyperacidity.

16.333.6

oddity, commodity, incommodity, discommodity (economics term).

16.333.7

fecundity, jocundity, profundity, infecundity.

16.333.8 [further rhymes may be derived from **228**]

locality, rascality, modality, sodality (Catholic religious society), feudality, frugality, molality (chemical concentration), venality, finality, tonality, plurality, neutrality, centrality, natality, vitality, mortality, totality, brutality, fatality, causality, animality, externality, atonality, hospitality, immortality, polytonality, universality, inhospitality.

16.333.8.1

reality, ideality, cordiality, geniality, unreality, partiality, speciality, sociality, bestiality, joviality, congeniality, materiality, impartiality, commerciality, provinciality, territoriality, artificiality, superficiality, extraterritoriality.

16.333.8.1.1

potentiality, confidentiality.

16.333.8.1.2

triviality, conviviality.

16.333.8.2

duality, actuality, punctuality, sensuality, mutuality, sexuality, spirituality, eventuality, individuality, homosexuality, heterosexuality.

16.333.8.3

technicality, topicality, practicality, whimsicality, illogicality, impracticality.

16.333.8.4

regality, legality, prodigality, illegality.

16.333.8.5

formality, normality, informality, abnormality, subnormality.

16.333.8.6

criminality, originality.

16.333.8.7

banality, commonality (commonness), personality, impersonality, conventionality, constitutionality, unconventionality.

16.333.8.7.1

nationality, rationality, irrationality.

16.333.8.8

principality, municipality.

16.333.8.9

morality, liberality, amorality, immorality, generality, temporality, ephemerality.

16.333.8.10

mentality, sentimentality.

16.333.9

agility, fragility, humility, tranquillity, sterility, virility, febrility (feverishness), gracility (slenderness), docility, facility, fertility, motility, utility, futility, gentility, hostility, servility, civility, solubility, puerility, imbecility, infertility, versatility, infantility, incivility.

16.333.9.1

mobility, nobility, immobility.

16.333.9.2 [further rhymes may be derived from **228.16**]

ability, debility, stability, probability, credibility, fallibility, gullibility, inability, capability, disability, possibility, sensibility, notability, suitability, flexibility, instability, permeability, improbability, practicability, availability, desirability, impossibility, responsibility, compatibility, unsuitability, susceptibility, suggestibility, manipulability, incompatibility.

16.333.9.2.1

liability, viability, reliability, unreliability.

16.333.9.2.2
risibility, visibility, divisibility, invisibility.

16.333.9.3
senility, juvenility.

16.333.10
jollity, polity (political organization), quality, equality, frivolity, inequality.

16.333.11
amity, calamity.

16.333.12
dimity (cotton fabric), sublimity, proximity, anonymity, synonymity, unanimity, magnanimity, equanimity, pusillanimity.

16.333.13
deformity, conformity, enormity, uniformity, nonconformity, unconformity.

16.333.14
sanity, vanity, urbanity, profanity, humanity, inanity, insanity, Christianity, inhumanity.

16.333.15
lenity, serenity, obscenity.

16.333.16
modernity, maternity, paternity, quaternity (group of four), fraternity, confraternity (organized group of men).

16.333.16.1
eternity, coeternity (eternal coexistence), taciturnity.

16.333.17
trinity, affinity, infinity, virginity, vicinity, Latinity, divinity, masculinity, femininity, asininity, consanguinity.

16.333.17.1
salinity, alkalinity.

16.333.18
unity, immunity, community, impunity, disunity, importunity, opportunity.

16.333.19
dignity, indignity, malignity, benignity.

16.333.20
charity, clarity, parity, barbarity, vulgarity, molarity (chemical concentration),

polarity, disparity, solidarity, viviparity, oviparity.

16.333.20.1
familiarity, peculiarity, unfamiliarity, multicollinearity (statistics term).

16.333.20.2
hilarity, similarity, capillarity (surface tension), dissimilarity.

16.333.20.3 [further rhymes may be derived from **17.174**]
secularity, jocularity, muscularity, regularity, angularity, singularity, popularity, insularity, irregularity, unpopularity.

16.333.20.3.1
particularity, perpendicularity.

16.333.21
ferity (wildness), verity, celerity (speed), temerity, asperity, prosperity, sincerity, austerity, posterity, dexterity, severity, insincerity, ambidexterity.

16.333.22
priority, majority, minority, sonority, sorority, authority, seniority, inferiority, superiority.

16.333.23
purity, security, obscurity, impurity, futurity, maturity, insecurity, immaturity.

16.333.24
celebrity, muliebrity (womanhood).

16.333.25
audacity, mordacity, mendacity, sagacity, tenacity, pugnacity, opacity, loquacity, veracity, voracity, vivacity, pertinacity, inveracity.

16.333.25.1
capacity, rapacity, incapacity.

16.333.26
diversity, perversity, adversity, university.

16.333.27
cecity (blindness), obesity.

16.333.28
felicity, publicity, duplicity, simplicity, complicity, tonicity, sphericity, lubricity (lewdness), toxicity, infelicity,

catholicity, Catholicity, atomicity, historicity (historical authenticity), eccentricity, concentricity, electricity, authenticity, domesticity, alcoholicity, thermoelectricity, hydroelectricity, photoelectricity.

16.333.28.1

triplicity (group of three), multiplicity.

16.333.28.2

plasticity, elasticity, inelasticity, homoscedasticity (statistics term), heteroscedasticity (statistics term).

16.333.29

nicety, benedicite (blessing).

16.333.30

verbosity, viscosity, velocity, callosity, pomposity, porosity, atrocity, monstrosity, nebulosity, animosity, tenebrosity, reciprocity.

16.333.30.1

grandiosity, curiosity, preciosity (affectation), speciosity, religiosity (extreme piety), incuriosity.

16.333.30.2

virtuosity, strenuosity, sinuosity, tortuosity, impetuosity.

16.333.30.3

precocity, bellicosity, varicosity.

16.333.30.4

vinosity (distinctive quality of wine), luminosity, voluminosity.

16.333.30.5

ferocity, tuberosity, generosity.

16.333.31

density, immensity, propensity, intensity, extensity (psychology term).

16.333.32

entity, identity, nonentity.

16.333.33

cavity, gravity, suavity, concavity, depravity.

16.333.34

levity, brevity, longevity.

16.333.35

privity (relationship recognized by law), declivity (downward slope), acclivity (upward slope), proclivity, captivity, festivity, expressivity, creativity, permittivity (electrical property), sensitivity, objectivity, subjectivity, selectivity, collectivity, reflectivity, receptivity, resistivity (electrical property).

16.333.35.1

nativity, negativity, relativity.

16.333.35.2

activity, reactivity, inactivity, hyperactivity, radioactivity.

16.333.35.3

productivity, conductivity, reluctivity (physics term), superconductivity.

16.334

Blighty, flighty, mighty, nightie, almighty, Venite (95th psalm), Aphrodite, Amphitrite (Greek goddess), pendente lite (legal term).

16.335

Scottie, dotty, hottie (*Austral* hot-water bottle), zloty, knotty, snotty, potty, spotty, Menotti (Italian composer), manicotti (large stuffed noodles).

16.336

dorty (*Scot* sullen or haughty), forte, forty, haughty, naughty, sporty, sortie, shortie, warty, pianoforte.

16.337

surety, Trimurti (three Hindu gods).

16.338

dacoity (armed robbery), hoity-toity.

16.339

dhoti (Indian man's long loincloth), floaty, roti (type of unleavened bread), throaty, peyote (cactus), coyote, Don Quixote.

16.340

doughty, grouty.

16.341

butty, cutty, smutty, nutty, putty, puttee (cloth wound around leg), rutty (full of ruts).

16.342

footy, sooty, tutti (musical term), bobotie (South African curried dish), deputy.

16.343

booty, cootie (*US* body louse), snooty, fruity, beauty, cutie, duty, Djibouti (African republic), agouti, tutti-frutti.

16.344

gaiety, liberty, puberty, Hecate (Greek goddess), maggoty, property, champerty (legal term), carroty, poverty, chocolaty, Amravati (Indian town), Ross and Cromarty.

16.345

crafty, draughty.

16.346

hefty, lefty.

16.347

fifty, nifty, thrifty, shifty, swiftie (*Austral* a trick).

16.348

lofty, softy, toplofty (haughty).

16.349

mufti, Mufti (Muslim legal adviser), tufty.

16.350

guilty, silty.

16.351

faulty, malty, salty.

16.352

fealty, realty, cruelty, faculty, penalty, mayoralty, specialty, subtlety, shrievalty (office of sheriff), novelty, casualty, difficulty, commonalty (ordinary people), personalty (personal property), admiralty, severalty (state of being separate).

16.352.1

loyalty, royalty, disloyalty, viceroyalty.

16.353

anti, ante, scanty, Dante, Fanti (Ghanaian people), shanty, Zante (Greek island), chianti, andante, infante (Spanish prince), Ashanti (region of Ghana), Alicante, vigilante, Ypsilanti (Greek revolutionary), dia-

manté, Rosinante (worn-out old horse), dilettante, concertante (musical term), pococurante (indifferent).

16.354

dainty, painty.

16.355

kente (brightly-coloured African cloth), plenty, twenty, aplenty, lentamente (musical term), cognoscenti (connoisseurs).

16.356

flinty, minty, shinty (form of hockey), teosinte (Central American grass).

16.357

Monty, monte (gambling card game), Brontë.

16.358

jaunty, flaunty (ostentatious).

16.359

bounty, county, Mountie.

16.360

frumenty (sweetened spiced porridge), guaranty, warranty, certainty, seventy, sovereignty, suzerainty, uncertainty.

16.361

Asti, pasty, hyponasty (growth of plant part), photonasty (plant's response to light), pederasty.

16.361.1

neoplasty (surgical repair of tissue), anaplasty (plastic surgery), rhinoplasty (plastic surgery of nose), autoplasty (transplantation from own body), osteoplasty (bone grafting), heteroplasty (transplantation from another body), dermatoplasty (skin grafting), keratoplasty (plastic surgery of cornea).

16.362

nasty, vasty, contrasty (having sharp contrast).

16.363

hasty, pasty, tasty.

16.364

chesty, testy, Tibesti (African mountain range).

16.365
thirsty, bloodthirsty.

16.366
misty, Christie, twisty, modesty, majesty, honesty, amnesty, touristy, sacristy, travesty, immodesty, lese-majesty, dishonesty, Corpus Christi.

16.367
frosty, Anticosti (Canadian island).

16.368
busty, dusty, fusty, gusty, lusty, musty, rusty, crusty, trusty.

16.369
breathy, abernethy.

16.370
pithy, stichomythy (dialogue in Greek drama).

16.371
bothy (*Scot* small shelter), mothy, frothy.

16.372
couthie (*Scot* friendly), toothy.

16.373
Timothy, apathy, empathy, sympathy, telepathy, antipathy.

16.373.1
psychopathy, allopathy, neuropathy (disease of nervous system), hydropathy (water cure), naturopathy.

16.373.1.1
theopathy (religious emotion after meditation), idiopathy (disease of unknown cause), homeopathy, osteopathy.

16.374
healthy, stealthy, wealthy, unhealthy.

16.375
worthy, airworthy, seaworthy, road-worthy, blameworthy, unworthy, note-worthy, trustworthy, praiseworthy, newsworthy, Galsworthy.

16.376
smithy, prithee, stithy (*Dialect* a forge), withy (willow tree).

16.377
navvy, savvy.

16.378
ave, jarvey (coachman), Harvey, grave (musical term), Mohave (American Indian people).

16.379
cavy, cave, Davy, slavey (female servant), navy, gravy, wavy, agave (tropical plant).

16.380
bevy, bevvy (*Dialect* alcoholic drink), chevy, heavy, levee, levy, replevy (legal term).

16.381
curvy, scurvy, nervy, topsy-turvy.

16.382
bivvy (*Slang* small tent), skivvy, chivy, divvy (*short for* dividend), Livy, privy, civvy (*Slang* civilian), tantivy (at full speed), divi-divi (tropical tree).

16.383
covey, lovey, lovey-dovey.

16.384
movie, groovy.

16.385
Muscovy, anchovy, Pahlavi (Middle Persian language).

16.386
maxi, braxy (disease of sheep), taxi, waxy, epitaxy (growth on crystal), anthotaxy (flower arrangement on stem).

16.387
sexy, apoplexy.

16.388
dixie (large metal pot), Dixie (southern states of USA), nixie (female water sprite), pixie, tricksy (mischievous).

16.389
doxy (opinion or doctrine), foxy, moxie (*US* courage), proxy, epoxy, orthodoxy, heterodoxy.

16.390
galaxy, metagalaxy (the universe).

16.391

jazzy, snazzy.

16.392

carzey, ghazi (Muslim fighter against unbelievers), Swazi (African people), Benghazi (Libyan port), Nastase, kamikaze, Ashkenazi.

16.393

daisy, hazy, lazy, mazy (perplexing), crazy, Bel Paese (creamy Italian cheese), upsy-daisy.

16.394

kersey (woollen cloth), jersey, Jersey, Mersey.

16.395

easy, cheesy, sleazy, queasy, breezy, wheezy, Zambezi, speakeasy, pachisi (Indian board game), uneasy.

16.396

busy, dizzy, fizzy, frizzy, tizzy, poesy, tin lizzie, busy Lizzie.

16.397

gauzy, mawsie (*Scot* woollen jersey), Gagauzi (Russian language).

16.398

Boise (US city), noisy, cramoisy (crimson).

16.399

cosy, dozy, Lozi (Zambian language), mosey, nosy, posy, rosy, prosy.

16.400

lousy, blowzy (slovenly), drowsy, frowzy (shabby), Dalhousie (British statesman).

16.401

fuzzy, muzzy.

16.402

boozy, choosy, floozy, woozy, newsy, Pusey (English ecclesiastic), Brancusi, Watusi (member of African people).

16.403

flimsy, slimsy (*US* frail), whimsy.

16.404

gansey (*Dialect* pullover), pansy, tansy (flowering plant).

16.405

frenzy, Mackenzie.

16.406

Kinsey (US zoologist), quinsy.

17 -er [This is the unstressed syllable at the end of such words as *grocer* and *ancestor*. Rhymes dependent on this syllable alone are unsatisfactory and should be avoided. Further rhymes may be created by adding *-er* to appropriate adjectives and verbs.]

chamber, vodka, polka, Oscar, butcher, scripture, rupture, sculpture, pasture, moisture, Buddha, pilfer, sulphur, Edgar, soldier, chandler, handler, burglar, stapler, sampler, dogma, asthma, Wagner, partner, cobra, extra, pizza, fuchsia, tonsure, azure, sculptor, Ulster, hamster, monster, gangster, youngster, ether, author, premier, Kenya, junior, Windsor, sepulchre.

17.1

layer, player, payer, Freya (Norse goddess), stayer, Malaya, bricklayer, platelayer (railway-track layer), ratepayer, taxpayer, soothsayer, purveyor, surveyor, conveyor, Eritrea (Ethiopian province).

17.2

skier, rhea, Rhea, ria, seer.

Euboea (Greek island), Achaea (region of Greece), trachea, Medea (Greek mythological princess), idea, Judaea, Hygeia (Greek goddess), Crimea, spiraea, chorea, sangria, sightseer, tortilla (Mexican pancake), Hosea.

Kampuchea, ratafia, Tanzania, Nicosia, panacea, overseer, Boadicea, galatea (strong cotton fabric), barathea.

Laodicea, Arimathea.

17.2.1

Cassiopeia, pharmacopoeia (list of drugs), prosopopoeia (figure of speech), onomatopoeia.

17.2.2

Korea, Maria, sharia (Islamic doctrines), diarrhoea, pyorrhoea (discharge of pus), leucorrhoea (vaginal discharge), banderilla (bullfighter's assistant), logorrhoea (excessive talkativeness), gonorrhoea, pizzeria, trattoria, Caesarea, Tia Maria (*Trademark*), amenorrhoea, dysmenorrhoea, spermatorrhoea.

17.3

Nubia, clarkia, branchia (aquatic animal's gill), bronchia (bronchial tubes), breccia (type of rock), India, morphia, collier, cochlea, trochlea (anatomy term), nuclear, buddleia, Anglia, denier, daphnia, Bosnia, Napier, rapier, sepia, copier, croupier, barrier, carrier, farrier, garrya (ornamental shrub), harrier, aria, Zaria (Nigerian city), terrier, quarrier (quarryman), warrior, carrier, furrier, spurrier (spur maker), Bactria (ancient Asian country), Istria (peninsula in Adriatic Sea), Austria, Mercia, meteor, cottier (Irish smallholder), courtier, Ostia, Parthia, Scythia, clothier, clavier, salvia, banksia (Australian shrub), nausea, zoysia (type of grass).

euphorbia (flowering plant), Colombia, Columbia, Slovakia, Walachia, Cambodia, Hollandia (Indonesian port), Thuringia (region of Germany), saintpaulia (African violet), East Anglia, costumier, arrhythmia, petunia, insignia, insomnia, Olympia, Calabria (region of Italy), eupepsia (good digestion), dyspepsia, eclampsia (toxic condition during pregnancy), rickettsia (pathogenic microorganism), strelitzia (African plant), opuntia (prickly pear), poinsettia, forsythia, anoxia (lack of oxygen), tillandsia (tropical plant).

Appalachia, Philadelphia, multinuclear, thermonuclear, mononuclear, photocopier, Alexandria, hypochondria, Cappadocia (ancient Asian region), polydipsia (excessive thirst), preeclampsia (toxic condition during pregnancy), Yugoslavia, Andalusia.

Czechoslovakia, intelligentsia, macula lutea (spot on retina), gynaecomastia (abnormal male breast development), anacoluthia (lack of grammatical sequence).

17.3.1

labia, Swabia (former German duchy), Arabia, Bessarabia (region of Russia).

17.3.2

Serbia, suburbia, ytterbia (chemical compound), exurbia (*US* region outside suburbs).

17.3.3

Libya, tibia, Namibia.

17.3.4

obeah (type of witchcraft), cobia (game fish), phobia, zoophobia, Francophobia, algophobia (fear of pain), ochlophobia (fear of crowds), Anglophobia, xenophobia, aquaphobia, aerophobia, acrophobia, necrophobia, hydrophobia, astraphobia (fear of thunderstorms), claustrophobia, photophobia, nyctophobia (fear of night), Germanophobia, agoraphobia, triskaidekaphobia (fear of number thirteen).

17.3.5

Gambia, Zambia, Senegambia (region of Africa).

17.3.6

gaillardia (flowering plant), La Guardia (US politician), tachycardia (abnormally rapid heartbeat), bradycardia (abnormally slow heartbeat), megalocardia (abnormal enlargement of heart).

17.3.7

stadia, Arcadia, Acadia (Maritime Provinces of Canada).

17.3.8

media, redia (parasitic larva), acedia (apathy), multimedia, cyclopedia, hypnopaedia, encyclopedia.

17.3.9

Lydia, Numidia (ancient African country).

17.3.10

Mafia, raffia, tafia (West Indian rum), dysgraphia (impaired writing ability), paragraphia (psychiatric term).

17.3.11

Sofia, dystrophia.

17.3.12 [see also **17.146**]

aphagia (inability to swallow), dysphagia (difficulty in swallowing), polyphagia (abnormal desire to eat), aerophagia (spasmodic swallowing of air), menorrhagia (excessive bleeding during menstruation).

17.3.13 [see also **17.149**]

diplegia, aquilegia, hemiplegia, quadriplegia, paraplegia, aqua regia (metal-dissolving corrosive mixture).

17.3.14 [see also **17.150**]

Phrygia, steatopygia (excessively fat buttocks).

17.3.15

cambogia (gum resin), apologia.

17.3.16

myalgia (muscular pain), analgia (inability to feel pain), neuralgia, nephralgia, gastralgia, arthralgia, otalgia (earache), nostalgia, coxalgia (pain in hip joint), cardialgia, cephalalgia (headache), odontalgia (toothache).

17.3.17

Somalia, Charlotte Amalie (capital of Virgin Islands).

17.3.18 [see also **17.433**]

dahlia, galea (helmet-shaped structure), vedalia (Australian ladybird), Westphalia, regalia, Australia, azalea, Lupercalia (Roman fertility festival), echolalia (psychiatric term), glossolalia (gift of tongues), marginalia (marginal notes), penetralia (innermost parts), genitalia.

17.3.18.1

bacchanalia, Saturnalia (ancient Roman festival), paraphernalia.

17.3.19

Saint Helier, hotelier, psychedelia.

17.3.20

Elia, lobelia, Rumelia (part of Ottoman empire), camellia, stapelia (cactus-like plant), Karelia (region of Russia), phocomelia (congenital deformity of limbs).

17.3.21

cilia, Pamphylia (ancient Asian region), familiar, Cecilia, conciliar (of ecclesiastical councils), Brasília, sensibilia, unfamiliar, juvenilia, bougainvillea.

17.3.21.1

memorabilia, imponderabilia.

17.3.21.2

zoophilia, paedophilia, Anglophilia, haemophilia, necrophilia, coprophilia (abnormal interest in faeces), Germanophilia, ailurophilia (liking for cats).

17.3.22

foliar (relating to leaves), Grolier (denoting decorative bookbinding style), Mongolia, magnolia, melancholia, Anatolia (Asian part of Turkey).

17.3.23

Julia, dulia (veneration for saints), abulia (loss of willpower), peculiar, hyperdulia (veneration for Virgin Mary).

17.3.24

lamia (monster in classical mythology), zamia (tropical plant), macadamia (Australian tree), Mesopotamia.

17.3.25

Urmia (Iranian lake), hypothermia, hyperthermia.

17.3.26

pyaemia (blood poisoning), leukaemia, ischaemia (inadequate blood supply), Bohemia, anaemia, uraemia, sapraemia (blood poisoning), academia, septicaemia, hypoglycaemia (insufficient blood sugar), hyperglycaemia (excessive blood sugar).

17.3.26.1

toxaemia, anoxaemia (oxygen deficiency in blood).

17.3.27

skimmia (ornamental shrub), bulimia.

17.3.28

kalmia (evergreen shrub), ophthalmia (inflammation of the eye), xerophthalmia (eye disease).

17.3.29 [see also **17.434**]

pannier (large basket), Hispania, Britannia.

17.3.30
Sarnia (Canadian port), Goiânia (Brazilian city), Titania, Oceania (Pacific islands), Christiania.

17.3.31
mania, Rainier, Albania, Rumania, leishmania (pathogenic protozoan), Tasmania, Campania (region of Italy), Lithuania, Araucania (region of Chile), miscellanea, Pomerania (region of Europe), collectanea (miscellany), Transylvania, Pennsylvania.

17.3.31.1
theomania (religious mania), nymphomania, phagomania (compulsive desire to eat), egomania, Anglomania, monomania, pyromania, dipsomania, kleptomania, bibliomania, decalcomania (process of transferring designs), megalomania, balletomania, erotomania (abnormally strong sexual desire).

17.3.31.2
Mauritania, Ruritania, Lusitania, Tripolitania (part of Libya).

17.3.32
hernia, vernier (measuring scale), Hibernia.

17.3.33 [see also **17.435**]
taenia (ancient Greek headband), xenia (botany term), gardenia, Armenia, Ruthenia (region of Russia), asthenia, Slovenia, catamenia (menstruation), leucopenia (insufficient white blood cells), hebephrenia (form of schizophrenia), schizophrenia, sarracenia (insectivorous plant), myasthenia (muscular weakness), neurasthenia (nervous breakdown).

17.3.34
linear, tinea (fungal skin disease), zinnia (flowering plant), robinia (tree genus), Sardinia, Virginia, bilinear, trilinear, collinear (on same straight line), actinia (sea anemone), Bithynia (ancient Asian country), vaccinia (cowpox), gloxinia, rectilinear, curvilinear, interlinear, Abyssinia.

17.3.35
cornea, salicornia (salt-marsh plant), California.

17.3.36
Ionia, zirconia (chemical compound), Snowdonia, aphonia (loss of voice), dysphonia (speech impairment), begonia, mahonia (evergreen shrub), pneumonia, ammonia, claytonia (succulent plant), Livonia, Slavonia, Caledonia, Macedonia, Babylonia, eudemonia (happiness), myotonia (lack of muscle tone), catatonia (form of schizophrenia), bronchopneumonia.

17.3.36.1
pogonia (orchid), Paphlagonia (ancient Roman province), Patagonia.

17.3.36.2
valonia (acorns used in tanning), escallonia (ornamental shrub), Cephalonia (Greek island), Catalonia.

17.3.37
myopia, diplopia (double vision), photopia (eye's adaptation to light), Utopia, dystopia (worst possible place), presbyopia, Ethiopia, cornucopia, asthenopia (eyestrain).

17.3.37.1
nyctalopia (night blindness), hemeralopia (day blindness).

17.3.37.2
tritanopia (blue blindness), protanopia (red blindness), deuteranopia (green blindness).

17.3.37.3
scotopia (adjustment for night vision), heterotopia (displacement of body part).

17.3.38
area, Caria (ancient Asian region), varia (collection of literary works), Icaria (Greek island), cercaria (larva of parasitic flatworm), Bulgaria, Dzungaria (region of China), filaria (parasitic roundworm), Samaria, Bavaria, araucaria (coniferous tree), cineraria, persicaria (red-stemmed plant), urticaria, Carpentaria (Australian gulf).

17.3.38.1
malaria, talaria (winged sandals), calceolaria.

17.3.39

feria (Catholic non-feast day), ceria (chemical compound), Iberia, Liberia, Siberia, inferior, Egeria (female adviser), Nigeria, Algeria, superior, bacteria, ulterior, anterior, interior, hysteria, wisteria, posterior, exterior, diphtheria, cafeteria, echeveria (tropical plant), sansevieria (cultivated plant).

17.3.40

Syria, Styria (province of Austria), porphyria (hereditary metabolic disease), Illyria, Assyria.

17.3.41

scoria (mass of lava), Gloria, gloria, thoria (chemical compound), euphoria, dysphoria (uneasy feeling), peloria (botany term), Pretoria, Vitória (Brazilian port), Victoria, Astoria, phantasmagoria.

17.3.42

courier, urea, curia, Manchuria, Etruria, Liguria (region of Italy), anuria (suppression of urine production), dysuria (painful urination), polyuria (excessive urine production), haematuria, phenylketonuria (congenital metabolic disorder).

17.3.42.1

albuminuria (urine containing albumin), haemoglobinuria (urine containing haemoglobin).

17.3.42.2

Masuria (region of Poland), glycosuria (excess sugar in urine).

17.3.43

Cambria (Latin name for Wales), Salambria (Greek river).

17.3.44

Umbria (mountainous region of Italy), Cumbria, Northumbria.

17.3.45

Andrea, calandria (part of heat-exchanger).

17.3.46

cassia (tropical plant), glacier, brassiere, Circassia (region of Russia).

17.3.47

mahseer (Indian fish), tarsier, intarsia (mosaic of inlaid wood).

17.3.48

fancier, financier, estancia (Spanish-American ranch).

17.3.49 [see also **17.326**]

indicia (distinguishing markings), comitia (Roman legislative assembly), Phoenicia, notitia (register of ecclesiastical districts), adventitia (body organ's external covering).

17.3.50

Numantia (ancient Spanish city), tradescantia, bona vacantia (unclaimed goods).

17.3.51

lithia (chemical compound), Pythia (Greek mythological priestess), stichomythia (dialogue in Greek drama).

17.3.52

Cynthia, Carinthia (Austrian province).

17.3.53 [see also **17.436**]

Xavier (Spanish saint), Moldavia, Moravia, Belgravia, Octavia, Scandinavia.

17.3.54

trivia, Olivia, Bolivia.

17.3.55

fovea (anatomy term), Segovia, synovia (lubricating fluid in joint), Monrovia (capital of Liberia).

17.3.56

apraxia (disorder of nervous system), ataxia (lack of muscular coordination), ataraxia (peace of mind), echopraxia (psychiatric term).

17.3.57

cachexia (weakened condition), alexia (word blindness), dyslexia, anorexia.

17.3.58

ixia (flowering plant), asphyxia.

17.3.59 [see also **17.332**]

glazier, brazier, grazier, Caucasia, aphasia (disorder of nervous system), dysphasia (impaired coordination of speech), aplasia (congenital absence of organ), dysplasia (abnormal development of organ), fantasia, Anastasia, Australasia, euthanasia, achondroplasia (skeletal disorder), antonomasia (rhetorical device).

17.3.60 [see also **17.334**]

framboesia (tropical disease), Silesia (central European region), ecclesia (church congregation), amnesia, aesthesia (normal sensitivity), analgesia, Indonesia, hypermnesia (unusually good memory), telaesthesia (paranormal perception), thermaesthesia (sensitivity to temperature), anaesthesia, kinaesthesia (sensitivity to movement), cryptaesthesia (extrasensory perception).

17.3.61

Tunisia, Dionysia (ancient Greek festivals).

17.3.62 [see also **17.335**]

osier, hosier, crosier (bishop's crook), ambrosia, afrormosia (hard teak-like wood).

17.4 [see also **8**]

ayah, buyer, dyer, liar, flyer, maya (Hindu concept), Maia (Greek mythological character), briar, crier, dryer, fryer, friar, prior, stria, via.

Aglaia (Greek goddess), inlier (geology term), supplier, outlier (geology term), papaya, Uriah, greenbrier, sweetbrier, Messiah, Josiah, Isaiah.

Surabaya (Indonesian port), Zedekiah, Hezekiah, Obadiah, lammergeier (rare vulture), jambalaya (Creole savoury dish), multiplier, Nehemiah, Jeremiah, Zephaniah, occupier, Araguaia (Brazilian river).

peripeteia (abrupt turn of events), photomultiplier (device measuring electromagnetic radiation).

17.4.1

modifier, qualifier, amplifier, magnifier, purifier, pacifier, rectifier, quantifier, humidifier, disqualifier, preamplifier, intensifier, dehumidifier.

17.4.2

pariah, Zachariah, Zechariah, Black Maria.

17.5 [see also **17.430**]

oyer (13th-century assize), coir (coconut fibre), Goya, hoya (Australasian plant), soya, employer, sequoia (giant redwood tree), destroyer, paranoia.

17.6

boa, koa (Hawaian tree), goer, goa (Tibetan gazelle), Goa (district of India), lower, blower, mower, moa, Noah, rower, grower, sower, stoa.

Iowa, jerboa, Balboa (port on Panama Canal), widower, playgoer, churchgoer, racegoer, Alloa, follower, aloha, glassblower, Samoa, genoa, Genoa, borrower.

Shenandoah, concertgoer, Krakatoa, Mies van der Rohe (US architect).

17.7

Padua, Joshua, vacua (*plural of* vacuum), rescuer, valuer, Capua (Italian town), Papua, decidua (membrane lining pregnant uterus).

17.7.1

jaguar, Nicaragua.

17.7.2

mantua (loose gown), Mantua (Italian city), Gargantua.

17.8

doer, brewer, sewer, ewer, skewer, skua, Dewar, viewer, wrongdoer, pursuer, reviewer, evildoer, tamandua (tree-living mammal), Porirua (New Zealand city), Rotorua, interviewer.

17.9

Abba, dabber (printers' ink pad), jabber, blabber, crabber (crab fisherman).

17.10

arbour, barber, harbour, Saba (West Indian island), casaba (melon), Ali Baba, Orizaba (Mexican city).

17.11

caber, labour, neighbour, sabre, tabor (small drum), Weber (German composer), belabour (thrash severely).

17.12

Berber, Djerba (Tunisian island), Thurber (US humorist).

17.13

Sheba, amoeba, Kariba (dam on Zambezi river), Beersheba (Israeli town), Bathsheba, entamoeba (parasitic amoeba).

17.14

bibber (drinker), fibber, gibber, calibre, Excalibur.

17.15

Khyber, fibre, briber, scriber (pointed tool), Tiber, copaiba (yellowish resin), subscriber.

17.16

cobber, jobber, clobber, slobber, robber, stockjobber (stock exchange dealer).

17.17

dauber, Micawber, absorber, Catawba (American Indian people).

17.18

lobar, sober, October, araroba (Brazilian tree), Manitoba.

17.19

lubber (clumsy person), blubber, rubber, scrubber, grubber (heavy hoe), landlubber.

17.20

goober (peanut), Luba (African people), Cuba, scuba, Nuba (Sudanese people), tuber, tuba, Aruba (West Indian island), simarouba (tropical tree).

17.21

Aqaba (port of Jordan), cordoba (Nicaraguan currency), dagoba (Buddhist shrine), jellaba (hooded cloak), Annaba (Algerian port), mastaba (pyramid prototype), Addis Ababa.

17.22

Elba, Melba.

17.23

amber, camber, clamber, mamba, samba, caramba (Asian tree), liquidambar (yellow balsam), viola da gamba.

17.24

ember, Bemba (African people), member, Pemba (Tanzanian island), remember, nonmember, dismember, December, September, November.

17.25

limber, timber, marimba.

17.26

ombre (card game), sombre, Zomba (Malawi city).

17.27

umber, cumber (to hinder), Humber, lumbar, lumber, clumber (type of spaniel), slumber, number, rumba, cucumber, encumber, Columba, outnumber, disencumber.

17.28

backer, Dakar (capital of Senegal), Dacca (capital of Bangladesh), lacquer, slacker, smacker, knacker, packer, cracker, tracker, stacker, hijacker, Malacca (Malaysian state), alpaca, maraca, firecracker, nutcracker, attacker, greywacke (dark rock), bushwhacker (*Austral* travelling woodlander).

17.29

barker, kaka (New Zealand parrot), charkha (Indian spinning wheel), marker, parka, Parker, sifaka (Madagascan mammal), Osaka (Japanese port), moussaka, Lusaka (capital of Zambia), nosyparker, koulibiaca (Russian fish pie), Hamilcar Barca (Carthaginian general).

17.30

acre, baker, faker, maker, nacre (mother-of-pearl), Quaker, breaker, saker (large falcon), shaker, taker, weka (New Zealand bird).

cloaca, haymaker, shoemaker, Jamaica, clockmaker, bookmaker, matchmaker, watchmaker, pacemaker, dressmaker, peacemaker, tiebreaker, jawbreaker, lawbreaker, backbreaker, strikebreaker, icebreaker, housebreaker, heartbreaker, moonraker (square sail), boneshaker, caretaker, wiseacre, stavesacre (Eurasian plant).

moneymaker, merrymaker, boilermaker, troublemaker, undertaker.

17.31

chequer, checker, Mecca, pecker, wrecker, trekker, Rebecca, exchequer, woodpecker, oxpecker (African starling), Voortrekker (Afrikaner settler), Rijeka (Croatian port), double-decker.

17.32

burka (Muslim garment), Gurkha, circa, shirker, worker, tear-jerker, outworker, mazurka, wonder-worker.

17.33

beaker, speaker, squeaker, streaker, seeker, sika (Japanese deer), theca (biology term), Guernica, loudspeaker, eureka, Dominica, Costa Rica, Tanganyika, Judaica (Jewish literature), bibliotheca (library), Cyrenaica (region of Libya).

17.34

bicker, kicker, dicker (US to barter), liquor, clicker, flicker, slicker, nicker, snicker, picker, ticker, sticker, vicar, wicker, whicker (whinny).

Baedeker (travel guidebook), Boudicca (Latin name of Boadicea), trafficker, silica, replica, bootlicker, arnica (plant genus), Seneca, picnicker, areca (Asian palm), Africa, paprika, brassica (vegetable genus), Jessica, vesica (bladder), Corsica, Utica (ancient African city), swastika.

angelica, basilica (Roman building), nux vomica (tree yielding poisonous seeds), amphitricha (bacteria), erotica, exotica, Antarctica, materia medica (study of drugs).

17.34.1

Monica, moniker, Salonika (Greek port), harmonica, japonica (Japanese quince), Veronica, santonica (Oriental plant).

17.34.2

Erica, America.

17.34.3

Attica, sciatica, hepatica (woodland plant).

17.35

duiker (African antelope), hiker, plica (anatomical fold), Micah, mica, pica, pika (burrowing mammal), striker,

hitchhiker, Formica (*Trademark*), myrica (medicinal root bark), lorica (protective shell), balalaika.

17.36

ocker (*Austral* boorish person), cocker, chocker (*Austral* full up), docker, Fokker, locker, blocker, mocha, knocker, quokka (small wallaby), rocker, soccer, shocker, stocker, Knickerbocker (*US* New Yorker).

17.37

corker, hawker, porker, talker, stalker, walker, yorker (cricket term), Minorca, deerstalker, jaywalker, sleepwalker, shopwalker, streetwalker, Majorca, kwashiorkor (protein deficiency).

17.38

ochre, coca (Andean shrub), choker, joker, smoker, poker, broker, croaker (tropical fish), nonsmoker, stockbroker, pawnbroker, Asoka (Indian emperor), mediocre, tapioca, carioca (Brazilian dance).

17.39

chukker (polo term), fucker, mucker (*Slang* friend), pukka, pucker, trucker, succour, sucker, tucker, yucca, felucca (Mediterranean boat), seersucker, bloodsucker, sapsucker (US woodpecker), goatsucker (*US* nightjar), motherfucker, honeysucker (nectar-feeding bird).

17.40

cooker, hooker, hookah, looker, onlooker.

17.41

lucre, snooker, euchre (US card game), palooka (*US* clumsy person), verruca, bazooka, involucre (botany term), Juan de Fuca (US–Canadian strait).

17.42

abaca (Philippine plant), stomacher (decorative piece of material), Hanukkah (Jewish festival), spinnaker, massacre, Whitaker, Ithaca, Karnataka (Indian state).

17.43

anchor, banker, canker, hanker, flanker, spanker, rancour, ranker, chancre, tanker, tanka (Japanese verse), Sri Lanka, barranca (*US* ravine), Casablanca, lingua franca (common language).

17.44
Inca, Dinka (Sudanese people), blinker, clinker, drinker, sinker, tinker, stinker, thinker, winker, Treblinka (Nazi concentration camp), headshrinker, stotinka (Bulgarian coin), freethinker.

17.45
conquer, conker, tonka (tree yielding fragrant seeds), Dzongka (Asian language).

17.46
bunker, punka (palm-leaf fan), Junker (Prussian landowner), mossbunker (US fish), spelunker (cave explorer).

17.47
lascar (East Indian sailor), Alaska, marasca (European cherry tree), Nebraska, Athabaska (Canadian lake), Madagascar.

17.48
risker, frisker, whisker.

17.49
busker, Musca (constellation), tusker.

17.50
catcher, dacha (Russian country house), stature, Thatcher, thatcher, viscacha (South American rodent), backscratcher, oystercatcher, baby-snatcher, body-snatcher, cradle-snatcher.

17.51
archer, marcher, departure.

17.52
nature, denature, legislature.

17.53
lecher, Fletcher, stretcher.

17.54
lurcher, nurture, searcher, researcher, gutta-percha (rubbery substance).

17.55
feature, Nietzsche (German philosopher), creature, preacher, teacher, schoolteacher.

17.56
pitcher, twitcher, forfeiture, garniture (decoration), furniture, miniature, signature, portraiture, expenditure, discomfiture, literature, temperature, investiture, primogeniture (legal term).

17.57
botcher, boccia (Italian bowls game), watcher, topnotcher.

17.58
scorcher, torture.

17.59
cloture (closure in US Senate), poacher, panocha (coarse sugar).

17.60
sloucher, voucher.

17.61
suture, future, cachucha (Spanish dance).

17.62
cubature (cubic contents), arcature (small arcade), ligature, filature (silk-spinning), tablature (form of musical notation), aperture, quadrature (maths term), curvature, judicature, musculature, nomenclature.

17.63
fracture, contracture, manufacture.

17.64
lecture, conjecture, architecture.

17.65
picture, stricture.

17.66
structure, substructure, superstructure, infrastructure.

17.67
cincture (surround), tincture.

17.68
juncture, puncture, conjuncture, venipuncture (puncturing of a vein), acupuncture.

17.69
culture, multure (miller's fee), vulture, sepulture (burial), viniculture, sericulture (silkworm rearing), agriculture, viticulture (grape cultivation), horticul-

ture, monoculture (single-crop cultivation), counterculture (alternative social culture), arboriculture.

17.70

bencher (a judge), denture, trencher (wooden platter), venture, debenture, backbencher, indenture, adventure, peradventure, misadventure.

17.71

lyncher, clincher, flincher, wincher.

17.72

capture, rapture, recapture, enrapture.

17.73

gesture, vesture (garment).

17.74

posture, imposture.

17.75

texture, contexture (weaving).

17.76

fixture, mixture, affixture, admixture, intermixture.

17.77

adder, ladder, bladder, madder, stepladder.

17.78

ardour, cadre (nucleus of trained personnel), Garda (Italian lake), larder, RADA, cicada, Haggadah (part of Jewish literature), armada, retarder, Nevada, enchilada (Mexican food), autostrada (Italian motorway).

17.78.1

panada (thick sauce), Granada (Spanish city), promenader.

17.79

aider, Ada, raider, grader (earth-levelling machine), trader, Seder (Jewish ceremonial meal), Veda (Hindu scriptures), wader, Grenada, crusader, Bethsaida (Israeli town), Rig-Veda (Hindu poetry), invader, alameda (US tree-lined promenade), Ayurveda (Hindu medical treatise).

17.80

Edda (Old Norse poems), bedder (college servant), kheda (elephant enclo-

sure), Cheddar, header, spreader, shredder, shedder (animal that moults), tedder, Vedda (Sri Lankan people), homesteader.

17.81

girder, herder, murder, purdah.

17.82

feeder, leader, Leda (Greek mythological character), bleeder, pleader, reader, breeder, Breda (Dutch city), cedar, seeder, cheerleader, ringleader, stockbreeder, proofreader, lip-reader, interpleader (legal term), olla podrida (Spanish stew).

17.83

bidder, Jidda (Saudi Arabian port), whydah (African weaverbird), Saida (Lebanese port), Florida, reseda (Mediterranean plant), Cressida, consider, Andromeda, reconsider, spina bifida, asafoetida (foul-smelling resin), primigravida (obstetrics term), multigravida (obstetrics term), camera lucida (microscope attachment).

17.84

eider, Ida, guider, glider, slider, spider, rider, cider, Oneida (US lake), joyrider, nightrider, outrider, decider, insider, outsider, divider.

17.85

dodder, fodder, plodder.

17.86

order, boarder, border, hoarder, Lauder (Scottish singer), warder, suborder, recorder, marauder, disorder.

17.87

moider (*Dialect* to bother), embroider.

17.88

odour, Oder (European river), coda, coder, loader, soda, decoder, encoder, pagoda, Baroda (Indian state), Fashoda (Sudanese town).

17.89

chowder (thick clam soup), Gouda, howdah (seat on elephant), powder, gunpowder.

17.90

udder, chuddar (Indian shawl), judder, rudder, shudder.

17.91

Judah, brooder, Tudor, Barbuda (West Indian island), mouthbrooder (African fish), intruder, Bermuda, draught-excluder, barracuda.

17.92

gelada (African baboon), Canada, forwarder, ambassador.

17.93

elder, welder.

17.94

fielder, shielder, wielder.

17.95

builder, guilder, Hilda, tilde (phonetic symbol), shipbuilder, Saint Kilda (Hebridean island), Matilda, bewilder.

17.96

alder, Balder (Norse god).

17.97

older, boulder, folder, holder, moulder, smoulder, polder, solder, shoulder, shareholder, freeholder, beholder, stockholder, stadholder (Dutch chief magistrate), smallholder, gasholder, leaseholder, householder.

17.98

candour, dander, gander, panda, pander, sander, Luanda (capital of Angola), Rwanda (African republic), Buganda (Ugandan state), Uganda, backhander, right-hander, left-hander, philander, solander (botanical specimen box), outlander (stranger), germander (flowering plant), pomander, Menander (Greek dramatist), expander, Miranda, Lysander, goosander (type of duck), dittander (small plant), bystander, propaganda, gerrymander, calamander (hard wood), salamander, Anaximander (Greek philosopher).

17.98.1

Leander (Greek mythological character), meander, oleander, coriander.

17.98.2

veranda, jacaranda (tropical tree), memoranda.

17.99

Lahnda (Pakistani language), slander, commander, Alexander.

17.100

remainder, attainder (former legal term).

17.101

bender, fender, gender, lender, blender, splendour, slender, mender, spender, render, sender, tender, vendor, weekender, defender, offender, agenda, engender, suspender, surrender, bartender, pretender, attender, extender, hacienda, moneylender.

17.102

hinder, Pindar (Greek poet), cinder, tinder, calendar, calender (machine for smoothing cloth), cylinder, provender (feed for livestock).

17.103

binder, finder, hinder (at the rear), minder, grinder, winder, bookbinder, viewfinder, rangefinder, pathfinder, reminder, rewinder, sidewinder.

17.104

Fonda, Honda (*Trademark*), ponder, squander, Rhondda, wander, yonder, Golconda (ruined Indian town), transponder (radio transmitter–receiver), anaconda.

17.105

launder, maunder (behave aimlessly).

17.106

joinder (legal term), rejoinder, nonjoinder (legal term), misjoinder (legal term).

17.107

bounder, founder, flounder, rounder, sounder.

17.108

under, chunder, blunder, plunder, sunder, thunder, wonder, thereunder, hereunder, asunder, rotunda (circular domed building), floribunda (cultivated rosebush), barramunda (Australian fish).

17.109
seconder, islander, Highlander, colander, Jullundur (Indian city), woodlander, Greenlander, Laplander, lavender, New Zealander.

17.110
chaffer (haggle), gaffer, Jaffa, Staffa.

17.111
chafer (beetle), wafer, cockchafer.

17.112
heifer, zephyr.

17.113
ephah (Hebrew unit of measure), FIFA, reefer, Recife (Brazilian port), synalepha (linguistics term).

17.114
differ, conifer, aquifer (water-containing rock), thurifer (incense carrier), Lucifer, crucifer (family of plants), Potiphar (biblical character), rotifer (minute aquatic animal), Apocrypha.

17.115
Haifa (Israeli port), hypha (part of fungus), lifer, cipher, decipher, encipher.

17.116
offer, Offa (king of Mercia), coffer, scoffer, proffer.

17.117
Ophir (biblical region), gopher, goffer (to crimp), loafer, sofa, chauffeur.

17.118
buffer, duffer, luffa (tropical climbing plant), bluffer, snuffer, puffer, suffer, chufa (tropical sedge).

17.119
loofah, woofer (loudspeaker), tufa (soft rock).

17.120
agrapha (unrecorded sayings of Christ), metaphor, Christopher, telegrapher, philosopher, Pseudepigrapha (Jewish writings).

17.120.1 [further rhymes may be derived from **16.90.2**]
biographer, stenographer, photographer, radiographer, Hagiographa (section of Old Testament), choreographer, historiographer.

17.121
alpha, pedalfer (lime-deficient soil), alfalfa, Wadi Halfa (Sudanese town).

17.122
camphor, chamfer.

17.123
dagger, gagger, Jagger, nagger, quagga (extinct horse), bragger, saggar (fireproof box for pottery), stagger, swagger, carpetbagger.

17.124
aga (Turkish title), laager (African camp), lager, raga (Indian musical term), saga.

17.125
agar, eagre (tidal bore), jaeger, telega (Russian four-wheeled cart), rutabaga (*US* swede).

17.126
egger (moth), beggar, bootlegger.

17.127
burger, burgher, turgor (biology term), virga (meteorology term), beefburger, hamburger, Limburger (strong white cheese).

17.128
eager, meagre, Riga (Russian port), Vega (bright star), bodega (Spanish wine shop), beleaguer, quadriga (chariot), Antigua.

17.129
chigger (mite larva), digger, figure, jigger, snigger, rigour, rigger, trigger, vigour, prefigure, disfigure, transfigure, omega, vinegar, Honegger (French composer), outrigger.

17.130
Eiger, Geiger, liger (lion–tiger hybrid), saiga (Asian antelope), tiger, canaigre (US dock plant), Auriga (constellation).

17.131

Dogger, jogger, logger, wagga (*Austral* blanket), pettifogger, Wagga Wagga (Australian city).

17.132

auger (boring tool), augur (predict), sauger (US fish), massasauga (US venomous snake), Mississauga (Canadian town).

17.133

ogre, toga, yoga, Saratoga, Ticonderoga (US battle site).

17.134

bugger, lugger (small boat), slugger (*US* hard-hitting person), mugger, nuggar (Egyptian sailing boat), rugger, Srinagar (Indian city), huggermugger.

17.135

sugar, Yuga (Hindu age of mankind).

17.136

cougar, Luger, Kruger (Boer statesman), beluga (large sturgeon), sastruga (ridge on snowfield), Chattanooga.

17.137

realgar (rare mineral), Trafalgar.

17.138

Olga, brolga (Australian bird), Volga.

17.139

mulga (Australian acacia), vulgar.

17.140 [see also **17.245**]

anger, Bangor, languor, clangour, panga (African knife), Tanga (Tanzanian port), Kananga (city in Zaïre), Zamboanga (Philippine port).

17.141 [see also **17.246**]

finger, linger, forefinger, fishfinger, malinger, syringa (flowering shrub), churinga (Aboriginal sacred amulet), cotinga (tropical bird), alcheringa (Aboriginal mythical golden age).

17.142

conger, conga, Tonga, Tsonga (African people), Alba Longa (city of ancient Latium), Rarotonga (Pacific island).

17.143

hunger, munga (*Austral* food), scaremonger, whoremonger, warmonger, fishmonger, costermonger, scandalmonger, ironmonger.

17.144

agger (Roman earthwork), badger, cadger.

17.145

charger, Djaja (Indonesian mountain), rajah, enlarger, turbocharger, supercharger, maharajah.

17.146 [see also **17.3.12**]

gauger (customs officer), major, stager (experienced person), wager, teenager.

17.147

ledger, dredger, Saint Leger.

17.148

merger, perjure, verger, verdure.

17.149 [see also **17.3.13**]

Ouija, procedure, supersedure.

17.150 [see also **17.3.14**]

voyager, mortgagor, packager, veliger (larva of mollusc), villager, armiger (heraldic term), manager, cottager, integer, vintager (grape harvester).

17.151

Niger, Elijah.

17.152

bodger, codger, dodger, loggia, lodger, Roger.

17.153

Borgia, forger, gorger, Georgia.

17.154

dowager, tanager (US songbird), onager (Iranian wild ass), sockdologer (*US* decisive blow), astrologer.

17.155

grandeur, phalanger (arboreal marsupial).

17.156

danger, manger, ranger, stranger, endanger, arranger, hydrangea, bushranger (person living in bush), moneychanger.

17.157

injure, ginger, Jinja (Ugandan town), harbinger, wharfinger (wharf manager), challenger, Salinger (US writer), derringer (US pistol), porringer (small dish), Massinger (English dramatist), passenger, messenger, Kissinger, scavenger.

17.158

lounger, scrounger.

17.159

conjure, blunger (large vat), plunger, sponger.

17.160

Allah, Bala (Welsh lake), calla (African plant), pallor, valour, Whyalla (Australian port), Valhalla, cavalla (tropical fish), Caracalla (Roman emperor).

17.161

gala, challah (Jewish plaited loaf), haler (Czech coin), Mahler, parlour, thaler (silver coin), nyala (African antelope), koala, cabbala (ancient Jewish tradition), Kampala, impala, Marsala, Uppsala (Swedish city).

17.161.1

kamala (East Indian tree), Guatemala.

17.162

alar (relating to wings), bailor, baler, scalar, scaler, jailer, mailer, kwela (South African beat music), trailer, sailor, tailor, Taylor, whaler, Akela, loud-hailer, inhaler, shillelagh, blackmailer, wholesaler, retailer, Venezuela.

17.163

Keller, feller, fellah (Arab peasant), Heller, Pella (ancient Greek city), speller, seller, cellar, teller, stellar, dweller.

paella, Viyella (*Trademark*), rubella, bierkeller, lamella (thin layer), canella (West Indian spice), Capella (bright star), propeller, umbrella, bonsela (African gift), saltcellar, novella, rosella (Australian parrot).

Rockefeller, villanella (Neapolitan song), salmonella, citronella (Asian grass), fustanella (Greek man's white skirt), Cinderella, mozzarella, varicella (chickenpox), vorticella (small animal), storyteller, fortune-teller, tarantella.

17.163.1

glabella (medical term), clarabella (organ stop), Isabella.

17.163.2

patella, panatella.

17.164

curler, pearler (pearl-fishing boat), purler (headlong fall).

17.165

chela (claw), dealer, feeler, healer, kneeler, peeler, spieler (*US* glib talker), sealer, Sheila, vealer (veal calf), velar (linguistics term), wheeler, tequila, candela (unit of luminous intensity), weigela (Asian shrub), Philomela (Greek mythological princess).

17.166

killer, filler, miller, pillar, squilla (shrimp), thriller, Scylla (Greek sea nymph), Schiller, tiller, villa.

weedkiller, painkiller, chinchilla, spine-chiller, cedilla, megillah (Hebrew scroll), mamilla, similar, Aquila (constellation), Priscilla, Attila, flotilla, mantilla (Spanish scarf), scintilla, distiller, Anguilla (West Indian island), axilla (armpit), maxilla (upper jawbone).

granadilla (passion-flower), sapodilla (tropical evergreen tree), drosophila (fruit fly), gypsophila (Mediterranean plant), dissimilar, verisimilar (likely to be true).

17.166.1

manilla, Manila (Philippine port), vanilla, manzanilla (very dry sherry).

17.166.2

papilla (small protuberance), caterpillar.

17.166.3

barilla (salty plant extract), guerrilla, gorilla, zorilla (African mammal), cascarilla (West Indian shrub), camarilla (Spanish cabal), sarsaparilla.

17.167

filar (relating to thread), hyla (tree frog), miler, tiler, Tyler, strobila (body of tapeworm), Delilah, compiler, astylar (architectural term), Rottweiler.

17.168

olla (Spanish cooking pot), collar, choler (anger), scholar, dollar, dolour (grief), holler, squalor, wallah, corolla, Eurodollar, petrodollar, ayatollah.

17.169

caller, faller (*Austral* lumberjack), mauler, brawler, crawler, trawler, footballer, mandorla (art term).

17.170

oiler, boiler, spoiler, broiler.

17.171

bowler, bola (South-American Indian weapon), cola, coaler (coal transporter), Ndola (Zambian city), Lola, molar, polar, roller, stroller, solar, tola (Indian weight), Zola (French novelist).

payola (*US* bribe), viola, tombola, Angola, Gongola (Nigerian state), potholer, premolar, bipolar, transpolar, roadroller, steamroller, controller, scagliola (imitation marble).

Carniola (region of Slovenia), Moviola (*Trademark*), Coca-Cola (*Trademark*), Pianola (*Trademark*), Hispaniola (West Indian island), Gorgonzola.

17.172

Fowler (English grammarian), howler, growler, prowler, bobowler (*Dialect* large moth).

17.173

colour, mullah (Muslim religious leader), Sulla (Roman dictator), discolour, medulla, Technicolor (*Trademark*), watercolour, nulla-nulla (Aboriginal wooden club), Gujranwala (Pakistani city).

17.174

bulla (seal on papal bull), fuller.

ampulla (flask), ferula (Mediterranean plant), spirula (tropical mollusc), gastrula (animal embryo), nebula, globular, tubular, vascular, oscular (relating to the mouth), modular, nodular, glandular, scrofula, regular, jugular, angular, singular, cellular, stellular (resembling small stars), primula, formula, nummu-lar (coin-shaped), scapula, scapular (part of monastic habit), Ursula, consular, spatula, blastula (animal embryo), fistula, Vistula (Polish river), pustular, uvula, valvular.

carbuncular, avuncular, calendula (flowering plant), irregular, Caligula, triangular, rectangular, manipular (relating to manipulation), discipular, tarantula, equiangular.

17.174.1

tabular, incunabula (book printed before 1500).

17.174.2

fibula, mandibular, vestibular.

17.174.3

facula (bright area on sun), macula, vernacular, oracular, spectacular, tentacular, sustentacular (supporting).

17.174.4

fecula (plant starch extract), specular (having mirror-like properties), secular, nubecula (small galaxy), molecular, Vulpecula (constellation).

17.174.5

furcula (fork-like organ), circular, tubercular, semicircular.

17.174.6

orbicular (circular), corbicula (bee's pollen carrier), pedicular (infested with lice), vehicular, follicular, vermicular (worm-like), funicular, auricula (cultivated alpine primrose), ventricular, articular, particular, lenticular (lens-shaped), navicular (boat-shaped), appendicular, perpendicular, extracurricular.

17.174.7

ocular, jocular, locular (biology term), binocular, monocular.

17.174.8

muscular, crepuscular, corpuscular, neuromuscular, intramuscular.

17.174.9

annular, cannula (small surgical tube), planula (larval form), granular, campanula.

17.174.10
copula (type of verb), scopula (spider's tuft of hair), popular, unpopular.

17.174.11
insula, insular, peninsula, peninsular.

17.174.12
situla (Iron Age container), titular, capitular (relating to cathedral chapter).

17.175
cooler, Fula (African people), gular (relating to the throat), hula (Hawaiian dance), ruler, Beulah, Lobengula (Matabele king).

17.176
jeweller, dueller, labeller, falbala (gathered frill), bachelor, modeller, gondola, pergola, signaller, cupola, gospeller, quarreller, chancellor, councillor, counsellor, hosteller, traveller, leveller, reveller, shoveler (duck).

rubeola (measles), alveolar (anatomy term), roseola (red rash), parabola, hyperbola, amygdala (almond-shaped body part), teetotaller, epistoler, Methuselah.

17.176.1
dialler, viola (flowering plant), variola (smallpox).

17.176.2
tricolour, Agricola.

17.176.3
victualler, hospitaller.

17.177
dabbler, gabbler.

17.178
cobbler, gobbler.

17.179
gambler, rambler, scrambler.

17.180
bumbler, fumbler, mumbler, grumbler, tumbler.

17.181
tickler, stickler, chronicler.

17.182
sprinkler, twinkler.

17.183
Adler, paddler, saddler.

17.184
meddler, medlar (fruit), pedlar.

17.185
curdler, hurdler.

17.186
fiddler, tiddler.

17.187
idler, sidler, bridler.

17.188
coddler, toddler, waddler, mollycoddler.

17.189
kindler, swindler.

17.190
riffler (a file), whiffler.

17.191
muffler, ruffler, shuffler.

17.192
haggler, straggler.

17.193
juggler, smuggler, struggler.

17.194
angler, wrangler, strangler.

17.195
Doppler (Austrian physicist), poplar.

17.196
Templar, exemplar (a model).

17.197
nestler, wrestler.

17.198
ostler, jostler.

17.199
bustler, hustler, rustler.

17.200
battler, rattler, prattler, tattler.

17.201
Hitler, whittler.

17.202
butler, cutler, sutler (former army provisions merchant).

17.203
antler, dismantler.

17.204
guzzler, muzzler, puzzler.

17.205
dammar (resin), gamma (Greek letter), hammer, clamour, glamour, mamma (breast), crammer, grammar, shammer, stammer, yammer, windjammer, sledge-hammer, enamour, programmer, Alabama, yellowhammer.

17.206
armour, amah (Eastern nurse), karma (destiny), charmer, dharma (Hindu custom), farmer, llama, lama (Tibetan priest), Parma, Rama (Hindu mythological hero), Brahma (Hindu god), drama, Zama (ancient African city), embalmer, pyjama, Manama (capital of Bahrain), Dalai Lama, diorama (small three-dimensional scene), cyclorama (picture around cylindrical room), panorama, Cinerama (*Trademark*), psychodrama, melodrama, Vasco da Gama.

17.207
squama (scale), framer, tamer, disclaimer, Macías Nguema (Guinean island).

17.208
emmer (variety of wheat), gemma (plant reproductive structure), hemmer, lemma (logic term), tremor, stemma (family tree), dilemma, maremma (marshy maritime region), neurolemma (nerve-fibre sheath), analemma (type of sundial).

17.209
Burma, derma (deep inner skin layer), murmur, Sturmer (eating apple), leucoderma (unpigmented area of skin), scleroderma (skin disease), xeroderma (abnormally dry skin), terra firma.

17.210
bema (Athenian speaker's platform), schema, schemer, femur, lemur, Lima, reamer (steel tool), creamer, screamer, dreamer, prima, streamer, steamer.
oedema, redeemer, blasphemer, day-dreamer, blastema (biology term).

seriema (South American bird), empyema (accumulation of pus), myxoedema (disease of thyroid gland), Iwo Jima (Pacific island), treponema (bacterium), emphysema, Hiroshima, erythema (red patches on skin), exanthema (a rash).

17.211
skimmer, dimmer, glimmer, slimmer, krimmer (Crimean lambswool), trimmer, simmer, shimmer, swimmer.
polymer, anima, enema, minima (*plural of* minimum), cinema, lorimer, dulcimer, Fatima, Mortimer, ultima (final syllable of word), nonswimmer, maxima (*plural of* maximum), eczema, Proxima (star).
sclerenchyma (supporting plant tissue), parenchyma (soft plant tissue).
Alma-Tadema (painter), Quinquagesima, Quadragesima, Sexagesima, Septuagesima.

17.212
dimer (chemistry term), lima (US bean), climber, primer, trimer (chemistry term), timer, old-timer, full-timer, part-timer, Oppenheimer, Maritimer (inhabitant of Canadian Maritimes), autotimer.

17.213
bomber, comma, homa (sacred plant).

17.214
ormer (edible mollusc), korma (Indian food), dormer, former, Norma, trauma, warmer, reformer, performer, informer, transformer, bedwarmer.

17.215
omer (ancient Hebrew measure), coma, comber, Homer, homer, roamer, soma, stoma (mouthlike part), vomer (thin flat bone).
glioma (tumour), myoma (muscle tumour), sarcoma, glaucoma, trachoma (eye disease), Tacoma (Washington port), beachcomber, diploma, misnomer, aroma, fibroma (fibrous tumour), scotoma (blind spot), xanthoma (yellowish nodule on skin).
osteoma (bone tumour), Oklahoma, papilloma (tumour), myeloma (tumour of bone marrow), adenoma (glandular

tumour), carcinoma, haematoma (tumour of clotted blood).

17.216
bummer, gumma (syphilitic tumour), plumber, mummer, rummer (drinking glass), drummer, summer, newcomer, latecomer, midsummer.

17.217
boomer, bloomer, rumour, Nkrumah, Sumer (region of Babylon), humour, puma, tumour, satsuma, perfumer, consumer, mazuma (*US* money), empyreuma (burning smell), Montezuma (Aztec emperor).

17.218
agama (small lizard), isomer (chemistry term), gossamer, Latimer, tautomer (chemistry term), Gautama (early name of Buddha), customer, elastomer (rubbery material), anathema.

17.218.1
monomer (chemistry term), gastronomer, astronomer.

17.219
chacma (baboon), drachma.

17.220
agma (phonetic symbol), magma, syntagma (linguistics term).

17.221
smegma, bregma (part of skull).

17.222
sigma (Greek letter), stigma, enigma, sterigma (botany term).

17.223
plasma, miasma, chiasma (biology term).

17.224
melisma (musical term), charisma.

17.225
Anna, banner, canner, scanner, Hannah, lanner (large falcon), planner, manner, manor, manna, spanner, tanner, Diana, Guyana (South American republic), goanna (Australian monitor lizard), bandanna, alannah (Irish term of endearment), Fermanagh, Montana, Havana, Savannah (US port), savanna

(open grassland), hosanna, Susanna, Susquehanna (US river), ipecacuanha (purgative drug).

17.225.1
Indiana, Pollyanna, Louisiana.

17.226
ana (anecdotes about a person), kana (Japanese syllabic writing), Ghana, garner, tana (Madagascan lemur), varna (Hindu caste), bwana, Tswana (African people).

Tucana (constellation), gymkhana, Fergana (region of Asia), banana, piranha, Tirana (capital of Albania), sultana, nirvana, Tijuana, Botswana, iguana, Ljubljana (capital of Slovenia).

ikebana (Japanese flower-arranging), katakana (Japanese syllabic writing), hiragana (Japanese syllabic writing), vox humana, Weimaraner (breed of dog), Lippizaner (breed of horse), Rosh Hashanah (Jewish New Year), marijuana, Mahayana (school of Buddhism), Hinayana (early form of Buddhism), Tell el Amarna (Egyptian ruins).

17.226.1
liana, Ludhiana (Indian city), Juliana, dulciana (organ stop), poinciana (tropical tree), Australiana, Shakespeareana, Victoriana.

17.226.2
Afrikaner, Americana.

17.227
Cana (biblical town), Gaynor, gainer, planar, planer, drainer, trainer, strainer, arcana (tarot cards), Ndjamena (capital of Chad), campaigner, restrainer, detainer, retainer, lantana (tropical shrub), container, sustainer, abstainer, cantilena (musical term), Magdalena (Colombian river), entertainer.

17.228
Jenner (English physician), henna, penna (large feather), senna, tenner, tenor, sienna, Siena, Vienna, duenna, Gehenna (place of torment), antenna, Ravenna (Italian city), Avicenna (Arab philosopher), countertenor.

17.229

earner, burner, learner, Smyrna, turner, cisterna (space containing body fluid), afterburner.

17.230

Lena, cleaner, Nina, Tina, vena (vein), wiener (*US* smoked sausage), weaner (newly weaned animal), Zena.

hyena, verbena, kachina (American Indian spirit), Medina (Saudi Arabian city), saphena (leg vein), congener (member of category), tahina (sesame-seed paste), euglena (microscopic fresh-water organism), demeanour, subpoena, tsarina, Messina, piscina (basin in Catholic church), retsina, catena (connected series), cantina (Spanish bar), sestina (Italian verse form), Christina, Athena, novena (Catholic devotion), convener.

karabiner (clip used in mountaineering), amphisbaena (worm lizard), Pasadena, Saint Helena, semolina, Messalina, misdemeanour, Wilhelmina, Agrippina, signorina, orchestrina (musical instrument), scarlatina, sonatina, concertina, cavatina (musical composition), Argentina.

Herzegovina, Quezon y Molina (first Philippine president).

17.230.1

arena, Carina (constellation), farina (flour), marina, ocarina, ballerina.

17.231

inner, skinner, dinner, finner (whale), Minna (Nigerian city), pinna (biology term), spinner, sinner, Cinna (Roman aristocrat), thinner, winner, tachina (bristly fly), Kitchener, beginner, Eleanor, milliner, mariner, foreigner, parcener (coheir), Porsena (legendary Etruscan king), platina (platinum alloy), patina, retina, breadwinner, determiner, phenomena, Proserpina (Roman goddess), submariner.

17.231.1

lamina, stamina, examiner.

17.232

China, china, diner, Dinah, liner, miner, mynah, minor, shiner.

trichina (parasitic roundworm), refiner, Aegina (Greek island), Regina, vagina, angina, airliner, eyeliner, salina (salt lake), recliner, headliner, freightliner, jetliner, consignor, moonshiner (*US* whisky smuggler), diviner, designer. Indochina, Carolina.

casuarina (Australian tree), globigerina (microscopic animal).

17.233

honour, Donna, goner, gonna, wanna, O'Connor, dishonour.

17.233.1

Madonna, belladonna, prima donna.

17.234

corner, fauna, mourner, sauna, avifauna (birds of particular region).

17.235

joiner, amboyna (Indonesian tree), Amboina (Indonesian island).

17.236

owner, boner, donor, Jonah, loner, moaner, Mona, krone, toner, Iona, cinchona (quinine-producing tree bark), landowner, Bellona (Roman war goddess), Pamplona (Spanish city), Cremona, Pomona (Roman goddess), shipowner, corona, Verona, persona, Daytona, Altona (German port), Barcelona, Arizona.

17.237

scunner (*Scot* aversion), gunner, runner, Sunna (Islamic law), stunner, oner (something outstanding), forerunner, Corunna (Spanish port), roadrunner, gunrunner, outrunner, frontrunner.

17.238

schooner, lunar, Luna (Roman moon goddess), Poona, crooner, pruner, sooner, tuna, tuner, Kaduna (Nigerian state), cislunar (between earth and moon), koruna (Czech currency), vicuna, lacuna (gap), Fortuna (Roman goddess), semilunar, circumlunar, honeymooner.

17.239

baconer (type of pig), reckoner, thickener, falconer, questioner, Londoner, stiffener, softener, wagoner, Helena, almoner, commoner, sharpener, opener, coroner, fastener, freshener, pensioner, sweetener, lightener, whitener, Westerner, Easterner, strengthener, Northerner, Southerner, taverner, governor, prisoner, poisoner.

confectioner, redemptioner (early emigrant to America), Ecbatana (ancient Iranian city).

executioner, paralipomena (supplementary writings).

17.239.1

stationer, probationer, vacationer.

17.239.2

conditioner, commissioner, parishioner, petitioner, practitioner, exhibitioner (scholarship student).

17.240

Gardiner, gardener, hardener, pardner.

17.241

Pydna (ancient Macedonian town), echidna.

17.242

Jumna (Indian river), alumna (female graduate), columnar.

17.243

Mishnah (Jewish precepts), Krishna, Ramakrishna (Hindu religious reformer).

17.244

Etna, Gretna.

17.245 [see also 17.140]

banger, ganger (foreman of labour gang), hangar, hanger, clanger, cliffhanger, straphanger, Selangor (Malaysian state), Tauranga (New Zealand port), paperhanger, Doppelgänger.

17.246 [see also 17.141]

clinger, pinger, ringer, wringer, springer, stringer, singer, stinger, winger, swinger, humdinger, gunslinger, klipspringer (small African antelope), minnesinger (medieval German minstrel), Meistersinger (German poet or musician).

17.247

kappa (Greek letter), dapper, clapper, flapper, napper, snapper, wrapper, rapper, grappa, trapper, sapper, schappe (silk yarn or fabric), kidnapper, Harappa (Pakistani city), whippersnapper, Phi Beta Kappa (US academic society).

17.248

scarper, Harper, sharper, tapa (paper mulberry bark), cardsharper.

17.249

caper, neper (unit in physics), paper, scraper, draper, shaper, tapir, taper, vapour, flypaper, sandpaper, endpaper, wallpaper, notepaper, newspaper, skyscraper.

17.250

leper, pepper, stepper.

17.251

chirper, Sherpa, usurper.

17.252

keeper, sleeper, nipa (palm tree), Dnieper (Russian river), peeper, reaper, creeper, weeper, sweeper, beekeeper, doorkeeper, storekeeper, book-keeper, goalkeeper, gamekeeper, timekeeper, innkeeper, shopkeeper, housekeeper, gatekeeper, minesweeper, Arequipa (Peruvian city), wicketkeeper.

17.253

kipper, skipper, chipper, dipper, clipper, flipper, slipper, nipper, ripper, tripper, stripper, shipper, tipper, zipper, mudskipper (tropical coastal fish), calliper, juniper, Agrippa (Roman general), daytripper, worshipper.

17.254

sniper, piper, viper, wiper, sandpiper (bird).

17.255

copper, chopper, Joppa, hopper, popper, cropper, dropper, proper, shopper, topper, stopper, whopper, treehopper (insect), clodhopper, froghopper (small leaping insect), grasshopper, sharecropper (US tenant farmer), eavesdropper, improper, gobstopper, teenybopper.

17.256

scorper (fine chisel), pauper, torpor.

17.257

coper (horse dealer), groper, sopor (abnormally deep sleep), toper, L-dopa (natural body substance), landloper (*Scot* vagrant), Europa (satellite of Jupiter), NATSOPA, methyldopa (a drug), interloper.

17.258

upper, cuppa, scupper, crupper (saddle strap), supper.

17.259

Cooper, cooper (barrel-maker), looper (moth larva), blooper (*US* blunder), snooper, grouper (tropical fish), trouper, trooper, super, whooper (white swan), pupa, stupor, mosstrooper (border country raider), peasouper, super-duper.

17.260

walloper (*Austral* policeman), hanaper (wickerwork basket), developer.

17.261

camper, scamper, damper, hamper, pamper, tamper, Tampa (Florida resort).

17.262

temper, distemper.

17.263

crimper, shrimper, simper, whimper.

17.264

bumper, dumper, jumper, lumper (*US* stevedore), plumper, show-jumper, buckjumper (*Austral* untamed horse).

17.265

asper (Turkish coin), Caspar (one of the Magi), jasper.

17.266

crisper, whisper.

17.267

ROSPA (accident prevention society), prosper.

17.268

Ara (constellation), Harar (Ethiopian city), Nara (Japanese city), cascara, mascara, Bukhara (Russian city), Sahara, Amhara (Ethiopian province), Damara (African people), Carrara (Italian town), Ferrara, Guevara, gurdwara (Sikh place of worship), capybara, caracara (bird of prey), Connemara, tuatara.

17.268.1

tiara, Honiara (capital of Solomon Islands).

17.269

error, terror, naira (Nigerian currency), Kagera (African river), busera (Ugandan alcoholic drink).

17.270

stirrer, preferrer, conferrer.

17.271

Eire, bearer, Sarah, wearer, sierra, torch-bearer, trainbearer, cupbearer, mace-bearer, caldera (volcanic crater), wayfarer, seafarer, declarer, Dun Laoghaire, repairer, Riviera, pintadera (Neolithic decorative stamp), habanera (Cuban dance), demerara, cordillera.

17.272

era, hearer, Hera, lira, sclera (outer covering of eyeball), sera (*plural of* serum), Madeira, chimera (hybrid monster), lempira (Honduran currency), sheepshearer, hetaera (female prostitute), Cythera (Greek island), Gezira (region of Sudan), Hegira (flight of Mohammed), phylloxera (insect that attacks vines).

17.273

mirror, Pyrrha (Greek mythological character), sirrah, wirra (Irish exclamation of sorrow).

17.274

hirer, Lyra, tayra (arboreal mammal), wirer, Stagira (ancient Macedonian city), admirer, palmyra (tropical palm), enquirer, spirogyra (freshwater alga).

17.275

horror, begorra, Camorra (Neapolitan secret society), Gomorrah, Illawarra (Australian coastal district).

17.276

aura, borer, bora (violent north wind), Cora, corer, scorer, Dora, Laura, flora, Flora, Morar (Scottish loch), Nora, snorer, schnorrer (*US* professional beggar), pourer.

woodborer (beetle larva), bombora (submerged reef), fedora (brimmed hat), Andorra, Pandora, angora, explorer, menorah (Jewish ceremonial candelabrum), aurora, Masora (Hebrew bible text), restorer, signora.

Bora Bora (Pacific island), Tuscarora (American Indian people).

17.277

juror, Jura, pleura (membrane enveloping lungs), crura (leglike structures), surah (twill fabric), tourer, tamboura (Indian musical instrument), Madura (Indonesian island), nonjuror, insurer, procurer, bravura, caesura, El Mansura (Egyptian city), tessitura (musical term), angostura, acciaccatura (musical term), appoggiatura (musical term), coloratura, Bonaventura (Italian saint), camera obscura (optical device).

17.278

borough, durra (cereal grass), thorough, demurrer (objection), kookaburra.

17.279

Scarborough, labourer, Deborah, Berbera (Somalian port), Loughborough, Marlborough, Flamborough, slumberer, Canberra, Farnborough, Gainsborough, Greensboro (US city), Ankara, conqueror, torturer, lecturer, murderer, borderer, solderer, wanderer, plunderer, sufferer, amphora, agora (ancient Greek marketplace), perjurer, conjurer, cholera, camera, stammerer, armourer, Marmara (Turkish inland sea), Woomera, genera (*plural of* genus), corpora (*plural of* corpus), emperor, Klemperer (orchestral conductor), tempera (painting medium), whisperer, tessera (square mosaic tile), sorcerer, treasurer, usurer, chatterer, flatterer, caterer, slaughterer, stutterer, fruiterer, poulterer, plasterer, plethora, cithara (stringed instrument).

Peterborough, Attenborough, Edinburgh, adventurer, philanderer, anaphora (rhetorical device), mandragora (narcotic plant), malingerer, in camera, nullipara (obstetrics term), multipara (obstetrics term), Diaspora (Jews' dispersion from Palestine), adulterer, upholsterer, deliverer, discoverer.

17.279.1

remora (marine fish), ephemera.

17.279.2

Sisera (biblical character), viscera (large internal body organs), chelicera (spider's claw), lonicera (honeysuckle).

17.280

Aldabra (Indian Ocean islands), abracadabra.

17.281

sabra (Israeli-born Jew), macabre.

17.282

zebra, cause célèbre (famous lawsuit).

17.283

Libra, algebra, vertebra.

17.284

timbre, Alhambra, Anambra (Nigerian state).

17.285

umbra, penumbra.

17.286

Phaedra (wife of Theseus), ex cathedra (with authority).

17.287

Alexandra, double entendre.

17.288

tundra, Ramachandra (Hindu mythological character).

17.289

Niagara, podagra (gout), pellagra (vitamin deficiency disease).

17.290

opera, copra (dried coconut kernel).

17.291

quatre (playing card), Cleopatra.

17.292

Chartres, Sumatra, Sinatra.

17.293

Petra (ancient Jordanian city), tetra (tropical fish), et cetera.

17.294

sutra (Sanskrit sayings), Brahmaputra (Asian river), Kamasutra.

17.295

spectra, Electra.

17.296

mantra, Tantra (Sanskrit sacred books).

17.297

orchestra, aspidistra.

17.298

Assur (Assyrian god), gasser, NASA, Mombasa, Makasar (Indonesian port), antimacassar.

17.299

chaser, facer, mesa (tableland), macer (macebearer), pacer, spacer, racer, bracer, tracer, Hargeisa (Somalian city), steeplechaser.

17.300

lesser, dresser, Odessa, professor, confessor, hairdresser, aggressor, depressor, oppressor, compressor, processor, assessor, successor, possessor, predecessor, microprocessor.

17.301

bursar, bursa, cursor, mercer, purser, precursor, vice versa.

17.302

kisser, purchaser, officer, Orissa (Indian state), Larisa (Greek city), vibrissa (whisker), abscissa (maths term), mantissa (maths term), artificer (skilled craftsman).

17.303

slicer, Neisse (German–Polish river), ricer (US sieve), de-icer.

17.304

Ossa (Greek mountain), dosser, fossa (anatomical depression), glossa (tongue), Canossa (Italian castle), Saragossa (Spanish city), Barbarossa (Holy Roman Emperor).

17.305

courser, Chaucer, Horsa (leader of Jutes), saucer.

17.306

grocer, mucosa (mucous membrane), mimosa, Formosa, greengrocer, Via Dolorosa (road to Calvary), anorexia nervosa.

17.307

douser, Hausa (African people).

17.308

Susa (ancient Iranian city), Teucer (Greek mythological character), anchusa (Eurasian plant), reducer, seducer, producer, transducer, Appaloosa (US breed of horse), babirusa.

17.309

trespasser, canvasser.

17.310

balsa, waltzer.

17.311

ulcer, Tulsa.

17.312

cancer, Cancer, merganser (marine diving duck).

17.313

answer, dancer, lancer, enhancer.

17.314

fencer, Mensa, Spencer, censor, sensor, censer (incense burner), tensor (tensing muscle), condenser, dispenser, extensor (extending muscle).

17.315

mincer, pincer, rinser.

17.316

sponsor, responser (radio receiver).

17.317

bouncer, denouncer, announcer.

17.318

balancer, silencer, sequencer (electronic device), encumbrancer (legal term).

17.319

matza (Jewish biscuit), tazza (wine cup), piazza.

17.320

bitser (Austral mongrel dog), Switzer (Swiss), howitzer, Pulitzer, tsaritsa (wife of tsar), Amritsar (Indian city).

17.321

Asher, dasher (plunger in a churn), flasher, masher, smasher, pasha (Turkish title), rasher, thrasher (US songbird), tamasha (Indian entertainment), gate-crasher, haberdasher.

17.322

Asia, fascia, geisha, Croatia, acacia, Ilesha (Nigerian town), Galatia, Dalmatia, Laurasia (hypothetical prehistoric land mass), Eurasia, ex gratia, osteomalacia (bone disease).

17.323

flesher (*Scot* butcher), fresher, pressure, tressure (heraldic term), thresher, refresher.

17.324

Persia, inertia.

17.325

Esher, Rhodesia, godetia, Belisha, Portlaoise (Irish town), Venetia (region of ancient Italy), magnesia, aubrietia (trailing plant), montbretia (African plant), Ossetia (region of Russia), Lutetia (ancient name for Paris), Helvetia (Latin name for Switzerland), alopecia.

17.326 [see also 17.3.49]

fisher, fissure, wisher, Frobisher, kingfisher, militia, polisher, publisher, varnisher, furnisher, finisher, Britisher, well-wisher, extinguisher.

17.327

cosher, quassia (tropical tree), washer, dishwasher.

17.328

kosher, scotia (architectural moulding), Boeotia (region of ancient Greece), Nova Scotia.

17.329

usher, gusher, blusher, Russia, crusher, Prussia.

17.330

censure, dementia (mental deterioration), amentia (congenital mental deficiency).

17.331

affenpinscher (breed of dog), Doberman pinscher.

17.332 [see also 17.3.59]

erasure, embrasure.

17.333

leisure, pleasure, measure, treasure, displeasure, commeasure (be the same as), admeasure (share out), countermeasure.

17.334 [see also 17.3.60]

freesia, seizure, nemesia (cultivated plant), Polynesia, Melanesia, Micronesia, Austronesia.

17.335 [see also 17.3.62]

closure, foreclosure, enclosure, disclosure, composure, exposure, discomposure, underexposure, overexposure.

17.336

attar (oil used in perfume), batter, scatter, chatter, hatter, latter, clatter, flatter, platter, splatter, matter, smatter, natter, patter, spatter, ratter, satyr, shatter, tatter, regatta, bespatter, Kenyatta, antimatter, pitter-patter.

17.337

barter, Carter, charter, darter (aquatic tropical bird), garter, martyr, Sparta, strata, sartor (tailor), tartar, Tartar, starter, Djakarta (capital of Indonesia), toccata, Siddhartha (personal name of Buddha), sonata, errata, pro rata, cassata (ice cream), cantata, nonstarter, Magna Carta, alma mater, Stabat Mater (Latin hymn).

17.337.1

chipolata, taramasalata (fish-roe paté).

17.337.2

Maratha (Indian people), desiderata, inamorata.

17.338

eta (Japanese outcast), cater, skater, data, gaiter, hater, later, plater, slater, mater, pater, crater, freighter, frater (friar), grater, traitor, tater, stator (stationary part of machine), waiter.
debater, Mercator, dilator, collator, translator, equator, curator, vibrator, peseta, pulsator, rotator, scrutator (examiner), spectator, dictator, testator, dumbwaiter.
incubator, educator, liquidator, percolator, escalator, legislator, lacrimator (substance causing tear flow), imprimatur (church licence to publish), dura mater (membrane enclosing brain), aspirator,

procurator, perpetrator, illustrator, demonstrator, crux ansata (symbolic cross), commutator, sternutator (substance causing sneezing), commentator, excavator, conservator (custodian).

attenuator, continuator, vasodilator, administrator, totalizator (betting system).

17.338.1
creator, gladiator, radiator, mediator, aviator, delineator (tailor's pattern), negotiator, annunciator (location indicator).

17.338.2
indicator, trafficator (car indicator), applicator, duplicator, lubricator, desiccator (drying apparatus), adjudicator, vinificator (wine-making apparatus), scarificator (surgical instrument), purificator (Communion cloth).

17.338.3
negator (electronic circuit), alligator, navigator, investigator.

17.338.4
propagator, corrugator (brow-wrinkling muscle), interrogator.

17.338.5
relator (legal term), oscillator, ventilator, scintillator (physics term), invigilator, defibrillator (medical apparatus).

17.338.6
tabulator, speculator, calculator, modulator, regulator, simulator, stimulator, insulator, perambulator, articulator, accumulator.

17.338.7
terminator, supinator (muscle of forearm), buccinator (muscle in cheek), coordinator, exterminator, discriminator, denominator.

17.338.8
detonator, alternator, resonator, impersonator.

17.338.9
narrator, liberator, decorator, moderator, numerator, generator, separator, operator, respirator, collaborator, refrigerator, accelerator, enumerator (person taking census), incinerator.

17.338.10
agitator, imitator, resuscitator.

17.338.11
levator (raising muscle), elevator, activator, cultivator.

17.339
better, debtor, fetter, feta (Greek cheese), getter, letter, Quetta (Pakistani city), setter, tetter (skin eruption), sweater.

Gambetta (French statesman), vendetta, unfetter, go-getter, muleta (matador's small cape), Valletta (capital of Malta), newsletter, biretta (clerical cap), bonesetter, typesetter, pacesetter, jetsetter, mozzetta (clerical cape), Rosetta.

arietta (short aria), carburettor, operetta, sinfonietta (short symphony).

17.340
skirter (*Austral* fleece trimmer), hurter (protective object), stertor (laborious noisy breathing), Alberta, frankfurter, Lacerta (constellation), inverter (electrical circuit), converter, Bizerte (Tunisian port), deserter.

17.341
eater, beater, beta, chaeta (small bristle on worm), cheetah, fetor (offensive smell), heater, litre, meter, metre, peter, Peter, rhetor (teacher of rhetoric), praetor (Roman magistrate), seta (small bristle), teeter, theta, tweeter (loudspeaker).

eggbeater (*US* helicopter), windcheater, beefeater, veleta, Demeter (Greek goddess), Machmeter, ammeter, repeater, saltpetre, ureter, excreta, amrita (Hindu ambrosia), masseter (cheek muscle), two-seater, partita (musical composition), anteater.

honey-eater (small songbird), millilitre, centilitre, millimetre, centimetre, taximeter, nanometre, kilometre, señorita, margarita (cocktail), Bhagavad-Gita (sacred Hindu text).

17.342
bitter, skitter (scamper), fitter, jitter, hitter, litter, flitter, glitter, knitter, pitta

(flat Greek bread), quitter, critter, fritter, sitter, titter, witter, twitter.

rabbiter, arbiter, embitter, presbyter, cricketer, traditor (early Christian betrayer), auditor, taffeta, outfitter, Sagitta (constellation), aglitter, transmitter, janitor, genitor (biological father), monitor, chapiter (upper part of column), Jupiter, trumpeter, heritor, bedsitter, catheter, servitor, Exeter.

inhibitor, exhibitor, counterfeiter, Hippolyta (Greek mythological queen), diameter, parameter, voltameter, pentameter, hexameter, telemeter (distance measurer), progenitor, per capita, accipiter (hawk), non sequitur, inheritor, interpreter, capacitor, solicitor, competitor, primogenitor.

17.342.1

editor, creditor, subeditor.

17.342.2

emitter, remitter, scimitar, planimeter (plane-area measurer), dosimeter (radiation measurer), pulsimeter, densimeter, altimeter, acidimeter, alkalimeter.

17.342.2.1

perimeter, saccharimeter (sugar-concentration measurer), calorimeter, polarimeter (light-polarization measurer), solarimeter (solar-radiation measurer), colorimeter.

17.342.3

cryometer (low-temperature thermometer), tachometer, viscometer, pedometer, speedometer, odometer, mileometer, coulometer, cyclometer, clinometer, monometer (verse line), swingometer, aerometer, pyrometer, spirometer (lung-capacity measurer), micrometer, hydrometer, hygrometer (humidity measurer), nitrometer, gasometer, optometer, Comptometer (*Trademark*), bathometer.

anemometer (wind-speed measurer), salinometer, inclinometer (aircraft instrument), actinometer (sun-radiation measurer), tellurometer (surveying instrument), magnetometer, densitometer, sensitometer, refractometer, piezometer (pressure measurer), alcoholometer.

17.342.3.1

rheometer (blood-flow measurer), geometer (person who studies geometry), tacheometer (surveying instrument), radiometer, audiometer, craniometer, goniometer (angle measurer), variometer, tensiometer, potentiometer.

17.342.3.2

thermometer, dynamometer (power measurer).

17.342.3.3

tonometer, phonometer (sound-intensity measurer), manometer (instrument for comparing pressures), chronometer (nautical timepiece), galvanometer (electric-current measurer).

17.342.3.4

barometer, interferometer, decelerometer, accelerometer.

17.342.3.5

spectrometer (spectrum producer and measurer), electrometer (electrical-potential measurer).

17.342.4

visitor, inquisitor.

17.342.5

prepositor (prefect), depositor, compositor, expositor (person who expounds), ovipositor (insect's egg-laying organ).

17.343

fighter, lighter, blighter, mitre, nitre, writer, titre, bullfighter, gunfighter, prizefighter, Gauleiter (German governor under Hitler), moonlighter, lamplighter, igniter, songwriter, typewriter, scriptwriter, ghostwriter, amanita (genus of fungi), telewriter, copywriter, underwriter.

17.344

otter, cotter, gotta, jotter, blotter, plotter, potter, spotter, squatter, rotter, trotter, totter, swatter, ricotta (soft white cheese), pelota (Spanish ball game), globetrotter, terra cotta.

17.345

daughter, slaughter, mortar, snorter, porter, quarter, sorter, water.

aorta, goddaughter, granddaughter, stepdaughter, manslaughter, ripsnorter, reporter, supporter, colporteur (book pedlar), importer, transporter, exporter, backwater, breakwater, forequarter, hindquarter, shearwater, firewater (whisky), Bridgwater, freshwater, dishwater, saltwater, Ullswater, kicksorter (physics apparatus).
underwater, Derwentwater.

17.346

Oita (Japanese city), goitre, loiter, Reuter, reconnoitre.

17.347

boater, Kota (Indian city), scoter, bloater, floater, motor, quota, rota, rotor, voter, iota, biota (biology term), Dakota, promoter, sapota (tropical fruit), nonvoter, locomotor (relating to locomotion), dynamotor (current-converting machine), Minnesota.

17.348

outer, scouter, doubter, pouter (domestic pigeon), router (cutting tool).

17.349

utter, butter, cutter, scutter (scurry), gutter, clutter, flutter, splutter, mutter, nutter, putter, sputter, shutter, stutter, rebutter (legal term), abutter (owner of adjoining property), woodcutter, leafcutter (South American ant), Calcutta, stonecutter, daisycutter (cricket term).

17.350

first-footer, six-footer, shot-putter, coadjutor (bishop's assistant), contributor, distributor, executor, prolocutor (Anglican Church official), interlocutor.

17.351

scooter, hooter, looter, fluter, fruiter, suitor, neuter, pewter, tutor, freebooter, accoutre, peashooter, sharpshooter, commuter, computer, barracouta (predatory fish), troubleshooter, persecutor, prosecutor, collocutor (person making conversation), Abeokuta (Nigerian town).

17.352

theatre, predator, comforter, balata (tropical tree), Galata (Turkish port), amateur, stigmata, senator, orator, waratah (Australian shrub), idolater, automata (*plural of* automaton), Antipater (Macedonian general), comparator (comparing device), conspirator, amphitheatre, Mahabharata (Indian poem).

17.352.1

dieter, rioter, proprietor.

17.353

actor, factor, tractor, reactor, varactor (electronic device), refractor, retractor, protractor, contractor, extractor, contactor (type of switch), malefactor, benefactor, chiropractor, subcontractor, azotobacter (bacterium).

17.354

hector, nectar, spectre, rector, recta (*plural of* rectum), sector, vector, effector (nerve ending), defector, ejector, dejecta (solid body waste), projector, injector, elector, collector, selector, reflector, connector, respecter, prospector, inspector, erector, director, bisector, detector, protector, convector.

17.355

dicta (*plural of* dictum), lictor (Roman official), victor, predictor, character, constrictor, vasoconstrictor (substance constricting blood vessels).

17.356

okta (meteorological unit), doctor, proctor.

17.357

adductor (type of muscle), inductor (electrical component), conductor, destructor (furnace for burning refuse), instructor, nonconductor, semiconductor.

17.358

after, laughter, rafter, grafter, wafter (fan), thereafter, hereafter.

17.359

snifter, drifter, shoplifter, weightlifter, CARIFTA (Caribbean Free Trade Area).

17.360

kofta (Indian meatballs), lofter (golf club), crofter, softa (Muslim student).

17.361

kelter (condition), delta, smelter, spelter (impure zinc), shelter, Shelta (Irish tinkers' secret language), welter, swelter, helter-skelter.

17.362

filter, philtre (love potion), milter (sexually mature male fish).

17.363

alter, altar, falter, halter, Malta, palter (be insincere), salter, psalter, defaulter, Gibraltar.

17.364

bolter (*Austral* outsider in race), coulter (plough blade), Volta (Italian physicist).

17.365

antre (cavern), banter, canter, plantar, manta (large ray fish), Granta (River Cam), Santa, Tanta (Egyptian city), decanter, trochanter (projection on femur), Vedanta (Hindu school of philosophy), infanta, Atlanta, instanter (without delay), levanter (Mediterranean easterly wind), almucantar (astronomy term), tam-o'-shanter.

17.366

chanter, planter.

17.367

fainter, painter.

17.368

enter, renter, centre, tenter (cloth-stretching frame), venter (belly), scienter (wilfully), magenta, polenta (Italian porridge), tormentor, assentor, placenta, Jobcentre, concentre, preventer (nautical term), inventor, accentor (small songbird), succentor (cathedral cleric), presenter, hypocentre (area below nuclear explosion), impedimenta.

17.368.1

dissenter, precentor (cathedral cleric), epicentre (area above earthquake origin), barycentre (centre of mass).

17.369

linter (fibre-stripping machine), splinter, Pinter (English dramatist), pinta (skin disease), printer, sprinter, sinter (deposit from hot springs), winter, carpenter, midwinter, teleprinter, overwinter (spend the winter).

17.370

saunter, taunter.

17.371

jointer (tool for pointing wall), pointer, appointor (legal term).

17.372

counter, encounter.

17.373

chunter (mutter), junta, hunter, punter, grunter, shunter, pothunter (prize-seeking competitor), marabunta (West Indian wasp).

17.374

captor, chapter, raptor (bird of prey), adapter.

17.375

sceptre, septa (*plural of* septum), receptor, preceptor (teacher), interceptor (fighter aircraft), proprioceptor (nerve ending).

17.376

anaglypta, lex non scripta (unwritten law).

17.377

copter (*short for* helicopter), dioptre, helicopter, ornithopter (aircraft with flapping wings).

17.378

tempter, pre-emptor, attempter.

17.379

aster, Astor, pasta, Rasta, raster, piastre (South Vietnamese currency), Jocasta (mother of Oedipus), cadaster (property register), pilaster (rectangular column in wall), canasta, oleaster (flowering shrub), Zoroaster (Persian prophet), poetaster (inferior poet), cotoneaster, Antofagasta (Chilean port).

17.380

castor, caster, plaster, master, pastor, forecaster, broadcaster, newscaster, paymaster, choirmaster, taskmaster, headmaster, bandmaster, grandmaster, schoolmaster, ringmaster, housemaster, scoutmaster, postmaster, toastmaster, quizmaster, disaster, alabaster, quartermaster, stationmaster.

17.381

slaister (*Scot* confused mess), taster, shirtwaister.

17.382

Esther, ester, Chester, fester, jester, Leicester, pester, tester, Vesta, wester (to move towards west).

podesta (Italian magistrate), egesta (body waste), digester, ingesta (food taken by mouth), celesta (keyboard instrument), molester, semester, trimester, sequester, arrester, ancestor, protester, Avesta (Zoroastrian scriptures), investor, sou'wester, Cirencester.

17.382.1

fiesta, siesta, polyester.

17.383

Easter, keister (*US* buttocks), leister (pronged fishing spear), Dniester (Russian river), quaestor (Roman magistrate), autopista (Spanish motorway).

17.384

bistre (drawing pigment), Lister, blister, clyster (enema), glister, Mr, mister, sister, vista, twister, xyster (surgical file).

Chichester, Rochester, Dorchester, Colchester, Manchester, Winchester, register, ballista (ancient catapult), banister, canister, ganister (sedimentary rock), barrister, thyristor (electronic component), chorister, forester, varistor (electronic component), stepsister, harvester, resistor, transistor, deregister.

17.384.1

minister, sinister, administer, maladminister.

17.385

costa (a rib), foster, hosta (Oriental plant), Gloucester, roster, zoster (shingles), impostor, defroster, paternoster.

17.386

oyster, cloister, roister.

17.387

coaster, poster, throwster (yarn spinner), toaster, four-poster, billposter.

17.388

buster, Custer, duster, lustre, bluster, cluster, fluster, muster, thruster (rocket engine), Worcester, blockbuster, Augusta, lacklustre, lincrusta (embossed wallpaper), filibuster, broncobuster, knuckle-duster, Famagusta (Cypriot port).

17.389

booster, rooster.

17.390

Lancaster, Doncaster, baluster, canaster (dried tobacco leaves).

17.391

lobster, mobster.

17.392

bolster, holster, pollster (person who conducts polls), upholster.

17.393

deemster (Manx magistrate), teamster.

17.394

minster, spinster, Westminster, Axminster, Kidderminster.

17.395

Munster, punster.

17.396

hipster, quipster, tipster.

17.397

Arthur, Martha.

17.398

aphtha (small ulceration), naphtha (chemical compound).

17.399

anther, panther, pyracantha (ornamental shrub).

17.400

gather, blather, forgather (assemble), ingather.

17.401

father, farther, lather, slather (large quantity), rather, forefather, godfather, grandfather, stepfather.

17.402

feather, heather, leather, nether, tether, whether, weather, wether (castrated male sheep), together, bellwether (leader of flock), altogether.

17.403

further, murther (murder).

17.404

breather, bequeather.

17.405

dither, hither, slither, thither, whither, wither, swither (*Scot* hesitate), zither.

17.406

either, neither.

17.407

bother, pother (commotion).

17.408

other, mother, smother, brother, god-mother, grandmother, stepmother, another, stepbrother.

17.409

carver, kava (Polynesian shrub), Java, larva, lava, laver (seaweed), Drava (European river), guava, palaver, Delmarva (US peninsula), Morava (European river), cassava (tropical plant), ottava (octave), Balaclava, Bratislava (capital of Slovakia), Costa Brava, piassava (South American palm tree).

17.410

deva (Hindu–Buddhist god), favour, haver (dither), laver (baptismal font), claver (*Scot* to gossip), flavour, slaver, quaver, raver, savour, saver, shaver, waiver, waver, cadaver, disfavour, engraver, vena cava (large vein), clish-maclaver (*Scot* gossip), semiquaver.

17.411

ever, clever, never, sever, however, who-ever, whichever, endeavour, whomever, whenever, wherever, forever, whatever, howsoever, whatsoever.

17.412

fervour, Nerva (Roman emperor), serv-er, conferva (freshwater alga), Minerva, timeserver, observer.

17.413

beaver, diva, fever, lever, cleaver, Neva (Russian river), Siva (Hindu god), viva (long live!), weaver, weever (marine fish), believer, Geneva, retriever, deceiv-er, receiver, transceiver (radio transmit-ter–receiver), unbeliever, cantilever, underachiever.

17.414

giver, liver, flivver (cheap old car), sliv-er, quiver, river, shiver, lawgiver, gingi-va (gum), deliver, Oliver, miniver (fur on ceremonial robes), Nineveh, vetiver (tall Asian grass).

17.415

skiver, diver, fiver, driver, Saiva (Hindu worshipper), viva (oral examination), Godiva, saliva, co-driver, screwdriver, survivor, conjunctiva.

17.416

bovver, hover, windhover (*Dialect* kestrel).

17.417

ova, over, Dover, clover, nova, rover, drover, trover (legal term).

flyover, Markova, walkover, Andover, changeover, Jehovah, pullover, Pavlova, Hanover, ars nova (14th-century music style), hangover, wrapover, slipover, stopover, moreover, Passover, crossover, flashover (electric discharge), pushover, leftover.

supernova, Casanova, bossa nova.

17.418

cover, lover, glover, plover, recover, uncover, discover, undercover, redis-cover.

17.419

Hoover (*Trademark*), louvre, mover, Suva (capital of Fiji), Vancouver, remover, manoeuvre, outmanoeuvre, Lietuva.

17.420

salvor (person salvaging boats), salver, quacksalver (quack doctor).

17.421

elver, selva (dense equatorial forest).

17.422

silver, sylva (trees of particular region), quicksilver.

17.423

volva (botany term), revolver.

17.424

culver, vulva.

17.425

Oshawa (Canadian city), Ottawa, pip-sissewa (evergreen plant).

17.426

flexor, plexor (medical hammer), indexer.

17.427

fixer, mixer, nixer (*Dialect* spare-time job), elixir.

17.428

boxer, coxa (hip bone or joint), moxa (Oriental medicinal plant substance), bobbysoxer, chionodoxa (Eurasian plant).

17.429

coaxer, hoaxer.

17.430 [see also **17.5**]

lawyer, sawyer.

17.431

bowyer (maker of archery bows), Nagoya (Japanese city), kabaragoya (large monitor lizard).

17.432

thuja (coniferous tree), alleluia.

17.433 [see also **17.3.18**]

failure, derailleur (bicycle gear-changing device).

17.434 [see also **17.3.29**]

Nyanja (African people), lasagne.

17.435 [see also **17.3.33**]

senior, Tigrinya (Ethiopian language), Monsignor.

17.436 [see also **17.3.53**]

paviour (material for paving), saviour, behaviour, misbehaviour.

17.437

lazar (leper), Belshazzar (biblical character), Salmanazar (large wine bottle).

17.438

Gaza, plaza, Kinshasa (capital of Zaïre).

17.439

laser, blazer, maser (microwave laser), razor, Fraser, stargazer, chalaza, trail-blazer, eraser.

17.440

geezer, geyser, Pisa, squeezer, freezer, Caesar, teaser, visa, Theresa, Mona Lisa, Ebenezer.

17.441

Kaiser, miser, riser, visor, incisor, devisor (legal term), divisor, adviser, liquidizer, stabilizer, tranquillizer, steril-izer, fertilizer, dialyser, equalizer, neu-tralizer, totalizer, Breathalyzer (*Trademark*), atomizer, organizer, wom-anizer, moisturizer, synthesizer, exercis-er, appetizer, advertiser, sympathizer, supervisor.

17.441.1

coryza (head cold), mycorrhiza (botany term), tenderizer, vaporizer, pasteurizer, coleorhiza (grass root sheath).

17.442

dozer (*short for* bulldozer), closer, poser, Rosa, bulldozer, Mendoza (Argentine city), Spinoza, composer, sub rosa (in secret), proposer, mariposa (flowering plant), decomposer (organism causing decay).

17.443

bowser (fuel tanker), dowser (water diviner), Mauser, mouser, browser, wowser (*Austral* puritanical person), carouser.

17.444

boozer, loser, bruiser, cruiser, Sousa, user, accuser, medusa (jellyfish), dif-fuser, infuser (tea-making device), misuser, Lampedusa (Mediterranean island), arethusa (US orchid).

17.445

panzer, kwanza (Angolan currency), stanza, organza, bonanza, extravaganza.

17.446

cleanser, credenza (small sideboard), cadenza, influenza.

18 -ab

cab, scab, dab, fab, gab, jab, lab, blab, flab, slab, Mab (fairy queen), nab, crab, drab, grab, tab, stab.

Joab (biblical character), Moab (biblical kingdom), kebab, vocab, prefab, confab, Ahab, Skylab, lablab (African bean plant), Chenab (Himalayan river), mihrab (niche in mosque), Cantab.

baobab (African tree), pedicab (Asian passenger-carrying tricycle), minicab.

19 -arb

barb, garb, Saab (*Trademark*), rhubarb, bicarb, Punjab, nawab (Muslim prince), inqilab (revolution in India).

20 -abe

babe, astrolabe (former astronomers' instrument).

21 -eb

ebb, deb, bleb (a blister), pleb, neb (*Dialect* projecting part), reb (*US* Confederate soldier), web, cubeb (Asian climbing plant), Deneb (star), Zagreb, cobweb.

22 -erb

kerb, curb, herb, blurb, Serb, verb, suburb, cowherb (flowering plant), potherb (plant used in cooking), superb, perturb, disturb, proverb, adverb, willowherb.

23 -ebe

Beeb, glebe, grebe, ephebe (ancient Greek youth), sungrebe (aquatic bird).

24 -ib

bib, dib, fib, jib, lib, glib, nib, snib (*Scot* door fastening), squib, rib, crib, sib (kin), sahib, ad-lib, Carib (American Indian people), sparerib, midrib (leaf vein), memsahib, Sennacherib (Assyrian king).

25 -ibe

kibe (chilblain), gibe, bribe, scribe, tribe, imbibe, describe, prescribe, proscribe, ascribe, subscribe, transcribe, inscribe, circumscribe, diatribe.

26 -ob

bob, cob, fob, gob, job, hob, lob, blob, glob, slob, mob, nob, knob, snob, squab (young pigeon), rob, throb, sob, swab, yob, nabob (rich person), skibob (vehicle running on skis), corncob, kincob (Indian silk fabric), demob, hobnob, thingumabob.

27 -orb

orb, daub, sorb (tree), bedaub, absorb, adsorb, chemisorb (chemistry term).

28 -obe

daube (meat stew), Job, lobe, globe, robe, probe, strobe, aerobe (organism needing oxygen), microbe, wardrobe, enrobe, disrobe, bathrobe, Francophobe, Anglophobe, Negrophobe, Russophobe, xenophobe (fearer of strangers), Germanophobe, ailurophobe (fearer of cats).

29 -ub

cub, chub, dub, hub, blub, club, slub, nub, snub, pub, rub, scrub, drub (to beat), grub, shrub, sub, tub, stub, hubbub, nightclub, washtub, bathtub, syllabub, Beelzebub.

30 -ube

boob, rube (*US* country bumpkin), cube, tube, jujube, flashcube, Danube, teletube (*short for* television tube).

31 -'b

Jacob, Arab, carob, scarab, cherub, Maghreb (northwest Africa).

32 -ack

back, jack, Jack, hack, lack, lac (resin), black, clack, claque (hired applauders), flak, plaque, slack, mac, smack, knack, snack, pack, quack, rack, wrack (seaweed), crack, track, sac, sack, shack, tack, stack, vac, whack, thwack, yak.

kayak, chiack (*Austral* to tease), Dyak (Malaysian people), greyback (hooded crow), bareback, dieback (tree disease), tieback (curtain fastening), zwieback (toasted rusk), drawback, throwback, kickback, hatchback, switchback, hunchback, hardback, feedback, halfback, hogback (narrow ridge), tailback, shellback (experienced sailor), fullback, comeback, greenback, slingback, humpback, leaseback (property transaction), horseback, flashback, splashback, outback, cutback, ack-ack, skyjack, hijack, blackjack, smokejack (spit-turning device), flapjack, slapjack (card game), skipjack, muntjac (small Asian deer), kulak (Russian peasant), alack, shellac, shoeblack, lampblack (form of carbon), bootblack, Senlac (Battle of Hastings site), Tarmac (*Trademark*), sumach (shrub), Micmac (American Indian people), knickknack, gopak (Russian dance), mudpack, calpac (brimless hat), woolpack, unpack, hayrack, Dirac (English physicist), rickrack, gimcrack, wisecrack, Shadrach, backtrack, sidetrack, soundtrack, racetrack, Barsac (sweet French wine), Cossack, corsac (Asian fox), mailsack, woolsack, ransack, knapsack, hopsack, Meshach, Dvořák, Cuttack (Indian city), ticktack (bookmakers' sign language), hardtack (hard biscuit), thumbtack, haystack, smokestack, Slovak, bushwhack (travel through woods), rucksack, galyak (fur), Cognac, Muzak (*Trademark*), Balzac, Anzac.

Kerouac (US writer), bivouac, piggyback, stickleback, ipecac (purgative drug), amberjack (Atlantic fish), lumberjack, crackerjack, natterjack (toad), applejack (apple brandy), steeplejack, Cadillac (*Trademark*), almanac, Sassenach, Pasternak (Russian writer), amphibrach (metrical foot), bric-a-brac, ovisac (egg sac), Gay-Lussac (French scientist), cul-de-sac, haversack, paddywhack (a smack), Armagnac.

biofeedback (medical term), diamondback (US terrapin), Aniakchak (Alaskan volcanic crater), tacamahac (resinous gum), Czechoslovak.

32.1

cardiac, Kodiak (large bear), zodiac, coeliac (of the abdomen), umiak (Eskimo boat), maniac, Syriac (former Syrian dialect), Pontiac (Indian chief), demoniac (like a demon), simoniac (person who practises simony), ammoniac (gum resin), insomniac, celeriac (vegetable), amnesiac, nymphomaniac, egomaniac, pyromaniac, dipsomaniac, kleptomaniac, hypochondriac, aphrodisiac, Dionysiac (relating to Dionysus), megalomaniac.

32.1.1

ileac (relating to the ileum), iliac (relating to the ilium), sacroiliac (joint of pelvis), haemophiliac.

32.2

aback, pickaback, huckaback (coarse fabric), leatherback (turtle), paperback, quarterback, razorback (whale).

32.3

Bacharach, bladderwrack (seaweed), sandarac (tree yielding resin), Skagerrak, tamarack (US larch), anorak, sazerac (US cocktail), azedarach (bark of chinaberry tree).

32.4

attack, nunatak (isolated rock peak), counterattack.

33 -ark

ark, arc, bark, Bach, barque (sailing ship), dark, dhak, hark, lark, clerk, Clark, Vlach (medieval European people), Mark, mark, marc (remnants of pressed fruit), marque (brand of car), nark, park, spark, quark, Sark, shark, stark.

debark (disembark), embark, tanbark (bark producing tannin), soapbark (South American tree), macaque, skylark, salesclerk, mudlark, woodlark, seamark, earmark, nomarch (ancient Egyptian administrator), pockmark, bookmark, trademark, tidemark, landmark, hallmark, Denmark, Finnmark (Norwegian county), pressmark (code on library book), sitzmark (skiing term), platemark (hallmark), footmark, postmark, birthmark, Bismarck, ethnarch (ruler of province), eparch (Orthodox Church bishop), toparch (ruler of small state), ballpark, Arak (Iranian town), Iraq, Petrarch, tetrarch, Pesach (Passover), Rorschach, landshark (land profiteer), Plutarch, Landtag (German legislative assembly), futhark (phonetic alphabet), aardvark, exarch (head of Orthodox Church).

paperbark (Australian tree), disembark, Offenbach, oligarch, meadowlark, fingermark, monomark (identification mark on goods), watermark, hierarch, ectosarc (ectoplasm of amoeba).

33.1

matriarch, patriarch, gymnasiarch (Greek education magistrate), heresiarch (leader of heretical movement).

33.2

remark, remarque (mark on engraved plate), telemark (skiing term), polemarch (ancient Greek official).

34 -ake

ache, bake, cake, fake, hake, lake, Blake, flake, slake, make, snake, spake, quake, rake, brake, break, crake (bird), drake, strake (metal part of wheel), sake, sheik, shake, take, steak, stake, wake.

hardbake (almond toffee), clambake, backache, teacake, seedcake, beefcake, pancake, queencake, cupcake, shortcake, oatcake, fruitcake, cheesecake, headache, Hoylake, snowflake, remake, unmake, opaque, seaquake (earthquake on seabed), lyke-wake (night vigil over corpse), moonquake (moon tremor), earthquake, earache, daybreak, firebreak, wordbreak, handbrake, windbreak, jailbreak, heartbreak, outbreak.

 muckrake, corncrake, firedrake (firebreathing dragon), sheldrake, mandrake, forsake, namesake, keepsake, handshake, heartache, partake, retake, betake, intake, uptake, mistake, beefsteak, sweepstake, toothache, awake.

stomachache, griddlecake, rattlesnake, parabrake (aircraft parachute), undertake, overtake, wapentake (former county subdivision), kittiwake, radiopaque (impervious to radiation).

35 -eck

beck, keck (retch), Czech, check, cheque, deck, heck, Lech (European river), lek (Albanian currency), cleck (*Dialect* gossip), fleck, neck, sneck (*Dialect* latch), peck, spec, speck, wreck, rec (*short for* recreation), trek, sec.

Purbeck, rebec (former stringed instrument), Seebeck (German physicist), xebec (Mediterranean sailing ship), Quebec, Warbeck (pretender to English throne), Brubeck (US jazz musician), pinchbeck (imitation gold), Baalbek (Lebanese town), crombec (African songbird), Steinbeck, Kazbek (Russian volcano), háček (phonetic symbol), raincheck, crosscheck, bedeck, foredeck, cromlech (prehistoric stone structure), fartlek (sports term), fennec, wryneck (woodpecker), crew-neck, breakneck, redneck, roughneck, rollneck, gooseneck (nautical term), OPEC, kopeck (Russian coin), henpeck, flyspeck (small speck), varec (seaweed), tenrec (small mammal), shipwreck, parsec (unit of astronomical distance), Toltec (American Indian people), Mixtec (American Indian people), Aztec.

overcheck, quarterdeck, afterdeck, rubberneck, turtleneck, bottleneck, Chiang Kai-shek, discotheque, Zapotec (American Indian people), Tehuantepec (region of Mexico).

36 -erk

erk, irk, berk, Burke, kirk, dirk, jerk, lurk, murk (gloomy darkness), smirk, perk, quirk, cirque (semicircular depression in mountains), shirk, Turk, stirk (heifer), work.

hauberk (long coat of mail), Selkirk, Falkirk, brickwork, clockwork, rework, firework, wirework, patchwork, coachwork, spadework, roadwork, woodwork, fieldwork, groundwork, legwork, bridgework (small dental plate), framework, teamwork, timework, homework, stonework, glasswork, casework, guesswork, presswork (operation of printing press), piecework, housework, brushwork, artwork, network, fretwork, brightwork (metal car trimmings), outwork, footwork, breastwork, earthwork, waxwork, berserk.

Atatürk (Turkish general), bodywork, handiwork, fancywork, timberwork, wickerwork, wonderwork (miracle), paperwork, counterwork, overwork, needlework, metalwork, ironwork, openwork, trelliswork, basketwork.

37 -eek

eke, beak, cheek, geek, leak, leek, bleak, clique, sleek, meek, sneak, pique, peke, peek, peak, speak, squeak, reek, wreak, creek, creak, freak, Greek, shriek, streak, seek, Sikh, chic, teak, week, weak, tweak.

caïque (boat), grosbeak (bird), Belleek (delicate porcelain), oblique, houseleek (a plant), unique, technique, forepeak (nautical term), bespeak, newspeak, pipsqueak, tugrik (Mongolian currency), cacique (American Indian chief), pratique (permission to use port), critique, boutique, antique, triptyque (permission to import vehicle), mystique, midweek, bezique, physique.

stickybeak (*Austral* inquisitive person), Mozambique, Martinique, ortanique (orange–tangerine hybrid), Chesapeake, fenugreek, hide-and-seek.

38 -ick [further rhymes may be created by removing -al from some adjectives in 228.23]

kick, chick, Dick, hic, hick, lick, click, flick, slick, Mick, nick, snick, pick, quick, rick, brick, crick, prick, trick, sick, sic, tick, tic, stick, thick, Wick, wick.

spruik (*Austral* speak in public), Bewick (English wood engraver), rhombic, Turkic (language group), psychic, sidekick, dabchick, Dardic (language group), Vedic (relating to Hindu scriptures), medic, medick (a plant), Nordic, dik-dik (small African antelope), Indic (language group), syndic (business agent), asdic (echo sounder), Kufic (early Arabic script), Delphic, georgic (poem about rural life), garlic, Gaelic, cowlick, niblick, public, cyclic, suslik (Eurasian ground squirrel), shashlik (kebab), bootlick, formic (relating to ants), gnomic (relating to aphorisms), bromic (containing bromine), chromic (containing chromium), seismic, cosmic, runic, Munich, Punic, tunic, picnic, strychnic (relating to strychnine), Chetnik (Serbian nationalist), beatnik, sputnik, ethnic, epic, unpick, aspic, toothpick, baric (relating to atmospheric pressure), hayrick, xeric (growing in dry conditions), fabric, airbrick, firebrick, rubric, Kubrick (US film director),

redbrick, cambric, quadric (maths term), baldric (sash for carrying sword), Ugric (language group), Cymric (Welsh language), cupric (containing copper), pinprick, citric, vitric (relating to glass), nitric, gastric, carsick, basic, airsick, seasick, homesick, brainsick, heartsick, lovesick, deictic (logic term), Celtic, Baltic, haptic (relating to touch), caustic, fustic (tree yielding yellow dye), rustic, crabstick, matchstick, swordstick, maulstick (artist's hand-steadying stick), drumstick, broomstick, greenstick, nonstick, unstick, chapstick (*US* lip salve), slapstick, dipstick, lipstick, ethic, Gothic, Sothic (relating to Sirius), Slavic, Narvik (Norwegian port), pelvic, Lerwick (Scottish town), Brunswick, Keswick, physic, music.

syllabic, amoebic, acerbic, Arabic, alembic, anarchic, druidic, bromidic (dull), acidic, fatidic (prophetic), malefic, benefic, lethargic, neuralgic, nephralgic, gastralgic, arthralgic, nostalgic, catholic, Catholic, republic, ophthalmic, orgasmic, arsenic, Dubrovnik, Olympic, epeiric (relating to continental drift), oneiric (relating to dreams), Frederick, bishopric, undertrick (bridge term), gastrotrich (minute aquatic animal), overtrick (bridge term), electric, dioptric, silicic (containing silicon), Tungusic (language group), forensic, intrinsic, extrinsic, cathartic (purgative), acoustic, monostich (single-line poem), tetrastich (four-line poem), pentastich (five-line poem), hexastich (six-line poem), fiddlestick, candlestick, helminthic (relating to parasitic worms), Reykjavik, bailiwick, candlewick, dyslexic.

orthorhombic (crystallography term), demagogic, cataclysmic, microcosmic, polytechnic, pyrotechnic (relating to fireworks), archbishopric, dielectric (physics term), geodesic (maths term), anthelmintic (substance destroying intestinal worms), anacoustic (soundless), ataraxic (calming), analgesic, metaphysic.

polysyllabic, monosyllabic, turbo-electric, thermoelectric (physics term), hydroelectric, photoelectric, onomatopoeic.

38.1

laic, archaic, trochaic (verse form), Judaic, Altaic (language group), voltaic, prosaic, mosaic, formulaic, Ptolemaic, Aramaic, Pharisaic, deoxyribonucleic.

38.1.1

Hebraic, algebraic.

38.2

stoic, echoic, heroic, anechoic, Eozoic, Neozoic, Cenozoic, Mesozoic, entozoic (living inside an animal), cryptozoic (living in dark places), Palaeozoic.

38.3

phobic, strobic (spinning), aerobic (requiring oxygen), xenophobic (afraid of foreigners), acrophobic (afraid of heights), necrophobic (afraid of death), hydrophobic, claustrophobic, anaerobic (not requiring oxygen), agoraphobic.

38.4

cubic, pubic, cherubic.

38.5

iambic (metrical foot), galliambic (verse metre), dithyrambic (passionately eloquent).

38.6

Bacchic, Noachic (relating to Noah), stomachic.

38.7

Chadic (language group), dyadic (twofold), dryadic, nomadic, tornadic, faradic (physics term), sporadic.

38.8

comedic (relating to comedy), logaoedic (verse form), orthopaedic, encyclopedic.

38.9

iodic (containing iodine), melodic, psalmodic, spasmodic, synodic, parodic, rhapsodic, periodic, episodic, aperiodic (at irregular intervals), antispasmodic.

38.10

scandic (containing the element scandium), Icelandic.

38.11

[further rhymes may be derived from **16.90.2** and **158.1**]

graphic, traffic, Sapphic (verse form), edaphic (relating to soil), seraphic, telegraphic, epigraphic, pornographic, photographic, epitaphic.

38.12

deific (godlike), morbific (causing disease), prolific, omnific, horrific, febrific (causing fever), specific, Pacific, pacific, calcific (forming lime), conspecific (within the same species), transpacific, beatific, scientific, hieroglyphic, unscientific.

38.12.1

terrific, sudorific (causing sweating), calorific (relating to heat), colorific (relating to colour), honorific, vaporific (producing vapour), soporific.

38.13

trophic (relating to nutrition), strophic (poetry term), eutrophic (ecology term), atrophic, autotrophic (biology term), apostrophic, catastrophic, philosophic.

38.14

Orphic (mysterious), geomorphic (concerning the earth's surface), endomorphic (having heavy build), monomorphic (having only one form), mesomorphic (having muscular build), metamorphic, protomorphic (primitive), ectomorphic (having thin build), theriomorphic (depicted in animal form), anthropomorphic (depicted in human form), heteromorphic (having different forms).

38.15

magic, tragic, pelagic (relating to open sea), haemorrhagic, anthropophagic (cannibalistic), archipelagic.

38.16

allergic, anergic (lacking energy), lysergic (type of acid), endoergic (energy-absorbing), exoergic (energy-emitting), metallurgic, cholinergic (biology term), adrenergic (biology term).

38.17

strategic, hemiplegic, quadriplegic, paraplegic.

38.18

logic, choplogic, pedagogic, hypnagogic (psychology term).

38.19

Alec, phallic, Gallic, salic (having high silica content), vocalic (relating to a vowel), alkalic (having high alkali content), medallic, cephalic (relating to the head), Uralic (language group), smart aleck, encephalic (relating to the brain), intervocalic (between vowels).

38.19.1

italic, metallic, bimetallic, nonmetallic, genitalic.

38.20

relic, telic (purposeful), Goidelic (language group), angelic, Gadhelic (Gaelic language), psychedelic, philatelic.

38.21

killick (small stone anchor), idyllic, Menelik (Abyssinian emperor), vanillic (relating to vanilla), Cyrillic, acrylic, dactylic (metrical foot), ethylic, methylic, basilic (vein in arm), lyophilic (chemistry term), cryophilic (thriving at low temperatures), zoophilic (fond of animals), haemophilic, thermophilic (thriving in warm conditions), hydrophilic (chemistry term).

38.22

colic, rollick, frolic, Aeolic (ancient Greek dialect), carbolic, ecbolic (inducing labour or abortion), embolic, symbolic, bucolic, Mongolic, systolic, vitriolic, diabolic, anabolic, hyperbolic, parabolic, catabolic, metabolic, melancholic, hypergolic (spontaneously flammable), alcoholic, diastolic, apostolic.

38.23

aulic (relating to royal court), hydraulic.

38.24

gamic (biology term), agamic (biology term), Islamic, dynamic, ceramic, balsamic, potamic (relating to rivers), panoramic, thermodynamic, aerodynamic.

38.25

alchemic, pandemic, endemic, polemic, Moslemic, totemic, systemic, epidemic, academic.

38.26

spermic, endermic (absorbed through skin), taxidermic, hypodermic, diathermic (medical term), endothermic (chemistry term), photothermic (of light and heat), exothermic (chemistry term).

38.27

haemic (relating to blood), anaemic, phonemic (relating to speech sounds), racemic (chemistry term), epistemic (relating to knowledge).

38.28

gimmick, mimic, acronymic, metronymic (relating to maternal name), patronymic.

38.29

comic, syndromic, atomic, entomic (relating to insects), pentomic (dividing into five groups), tragicomic, diatomic (containing two atoms), triatomic (containing three atoms), subatomic, physiognomic, intra-atomic, interatomic.

38.29.1

economic, metronomic, astronomic, gastronomic, autonomic (occurring involuntarily), taxonomic, uneconomic, socioeconomic.

38.30

rhythmic, eurhythmic (having pleasing rhythm), logarithmic.

38.31

manic, panic, tannic, stannic (containing tin), mechanic, volcanic, organic, Brahmanic, Germanic, tympanic, Hispanic, uranic (containing uranium), Britannic, titanic, satanic, tetanic, sultanic, galvanic, inorganic, aldermanic, talismanic, aeromechanic.

38.31.1

messianic (relating to the Messiah), oceanic, suboceanic, transoceanic.

38.32

genic (relating to a gene), splenic (relating to the spleen), phrenic (relating to the diaphragm), sthenic (energetic and strong), sphenic (wedge-shaped), eugenic, Hellenic, asthenic (weak), telegenic (looking good on television), oxygenic, schizophrenic, Saracenic, callisthenic.

38.32.1

myogenic (muscle-forming), psychogenic, oncogenic (tumour-forming), allergenic, chromogenic (colour-producing), pyrogenic (heat-producing), neurogenic (of nervous origin), androgenic, oestrogenic, allergenic, phytogenic (obtained from plants), photogenic, lactogenic, cryptogenic (of unknown origin), pathogenic, toxicogenic, immunogenic, audiogenic (caused by sound), cariogenic (producing tooth decay), erotogenic (erogenous), teratogenic (causing fetal deformity).

38.32.1.1

carcinogenic, hallucinogenic.

38.33

scenic, hygienic, irenic (conciliatory), axenic (uncontaminated).

38.34

Finnic (language group), clinic, cynic, rabbinic, albinic, Brahminic, Dominic, actinic (denoting type of radiation), succinic (relating to amber), kinnikinnick (mixture for smoking), polyclinic (general hospital), histaminic, nicotinic.

38.35

conic, phonic, clonic (medical term), chronic, sonic, tonic.

ionic, Ionic, bionic, thionic (relating to sulphur), carbonic, bubonic, iconic, laconic, draconic, sardonic, euphonic, symphonic, colonic, cyclonic, harmonic, sermonic, demonic, mnemonic, pneumonic, pulmonic, Pharaonic, ironic, Byronic, moronic, subsonic, atonic (unstressed), plutonic (geology term), Teutonic, subtonic (musical note), tectonic, planktonic, Miltonic, Brythonic (language group), pythonic, Slavonic, ozonic.

aniconic (forbidding idol worship), telephonic, polyphonic (musical term), philharmonic, nonharmonic, geoponic (relating to agricultural science), macaronic (type of verse), diachronic (linguistics term), anachronic (out of date), electronic.

anticyclonic, architectonic (relating to architectural qualities), geotectonic (relating to earth's crust), microelectronic.

38.35.1

thermionic (physics term), embryonic, histrionic, avionic, chameleonic, Napoleonic.

38.35.2

aphonic (voiceless), megaphonic, xylophonic, homophonic (having identical pronunciation), monophonic, microphonic, quadraphonic, saxophonic, radiophonic, stereophonic.

38.35.3

ammonic, Solomonic, pathognomonic (indicating a particular disease).

38.35.4

masonic, freemasonic, supersonic, infrasonic (below frequency of sound), ultrasonic.

38.35.5

Platonic, diatonic (musical term), hypotonic (lacking tension), hypertonic (having high tension), isotonic (having equal tension), pentatonic (musical term).

38.36

philippic (speech of bitter denunciation), polytypic (having several different types), monotypic (having only one type), stereotypic.

38.37

tropic, topic, myopic, ectopic, entopic (in normal position), Ethiopic, telescopic, periscopic, isotopic, radioisotopic.

38.37.1 [further rhymes may be

derived from **16.254.2** and **278.1**]
stroboscopic, macroscopic, microscopic, hygroscopic (absorbing moisture from air), orthoscopic (relating to normal vision), stereoscopic, kaleidoscopic.

38.37.2
allotropic (existing in several forms), inotropic (affecting muscle contraction), hydrotropic (growing towards water), phototropic (growing towards light), thixotropic (becoming thinner when stirred).

38.37.3
philanthropic, misanthropic, palaeanthropic (relating to early man), neoanthropic (resembling modern man), therianthropic (part animal, part human).

38.38
baric (relating to atmospheric pressure), daric (ancient Persian coin), Garrick, stearic (relating to suet), barbaric, Pindaric (type of ode), margaric (resembling pearl), Amharic (Ethiopian official language), tartaric, Balearic, centrobaric (of centre of gravity), isobaric.

38.39
Eric, Berwick, derrick, Derek, ferric, cleric, steric (chemistry term), valeric (relating to valerian), Homeric, numeric, mesmeric, generic, glyceric (containing glycerol), enteric, hysteric, hemispheric, atmospheric, stratospheric, polymeric, esoteric, exoteric (comprehensible), alphanumeric, gastroenteric.

38.40
lyric, pyrrhic, vampiric, empiric, satiric, satyric, panegyric (speech of praise).

38.41
choric (relating to a chorus), Doric (architectural term), Warwick, euphoric, camphoric, phosphoric, caloric, folkloric, historic, meteoric, pyrophoric (igniting spontaneously), semaphoric, metaphoric, allegoric, categoric, prehistoric, phantasmagoric.

38.42
auric (containing gold), boric, chloric, hydrochloric.

38.43
Rurik (Scandinavian Viking leader), uric, Zürich, mercuric, sulphuric, telluric (terrestrial).

38.44
agaric, Alaric (king of the Visigoths), choleric, turmeric, limerick, Limerick, rhetoric, maverick, Theodoric (king of the Ostrogoths), climacteric.

38.45
Patrick, iatric (relating to medicine), Kirkpatrick, Downpatrick (Irish town), psychiatric, paediatric, geriatric.

38.46 [further rhymes may be derived from **16.285.2** and **17.342.3**]
metric, dimetric (crystallography term), trimetric (relating to verse line), obstetric, asymmetric, bisymmetric, geometric, diametric, kilometric, barometric, isometric.

38.47
centric, acentric, concentric, eccentric, theocentric (theology term), geocentric (having earth at centre), egocentric, homocentric (having the same centre).

38.48
classic, Liassic, Triassic, thalassic (relating to the sea), thoracic, Jurassic, boracic.

38.49
Attic, attic, batik, phatic (relating to social conversation), static, vatic (relating to a prophet).
sciatic, emphatic, lymphatic, spermatic, haematic, climatic, traumatic, komatik (Eskimo sledge), somatic (relating to the body), pneumatic, rheumatic, magmatic, pragmatic, phlegmatic, dogmatic, dalmatic (tunic-like vestment), asthmatic, Carnatic (region of India), venatic, hepatic, aquatic, erratic, piratic, Socratic, quadratic, ecstatic, sylvatic (growing in a wood).
Eleatic (school of philosophy), pancreatic, Adriatic, mydriatic (causing pupil dilation), Hanseatic, Asiatic, acrobatic, aliphatic (chemistry term), subaquatic, hieratic (relating to priests), operatic, antistatic.
semiaquatic, idiosyncratic.

38.49.1
schematic, thematic, dilemmatic, cinematic, systematic, unsystematic.

38.49.2
chromatic, dramatic, problematic, emblematic, diplomatic, aromatic, achromatic (without colour), dichromatic, trichromatic, programmatic, automatic, symptomatic, idiomatic, axiomatic (self-evident), polychromatic, monochromatic, melodramatic, epigrammatic, diagrammatic, anagrammatic, monogrammatic, psychosomatic, asymptomatic, semiautomatic.

38.49.3
stigmatic, enigmatic, astigmatic, paradigmatic (linguistics term), anastigmatic.

38.49.4
prismatic, schismatic, numismatic, charismatic.

38.49.5
fanatic, morganatic, aplanatic (physics term).

38.49.6 [further rhymes may be derived from **16.307.5**]
democratic, Hippocratic, bureaucratic, autocratic, plutocratic, aristocratic.

38.49.7
geostatic (geology term), haemostatic (stopping blood flow), thermostatic, hypostatic, gyrostatic (concerned with rotating bodies), hydrostatic (physics term), electrostatic.

38.50
metic (ancient Greek alien), thetic (relating to metrical stress).
hebetic (relating to puberty), eidetic (psychology term), syndetic (linguistics term), prophetic, balletic, athletic, hermetic, emetic, mimetic (imitative), cosmetic, magnetic, pyretic (relating to fever), uretic (relating to urine), ascetic, synthetic, aesthetic, prosthetic, Helvetic (Swiss).
asyndetic (without cross references), exegetic (explanatory), homiletic (relating to a sermon), arithmetic, apyretic (without fever), diuretic, dietetic, parenthetic, anaesthetic.
antimagnetic, isomagnetic (having equal magnetic force), antipyretic (preventing fever), diaphoretic (causing perspiration), peripatetic, photosynthetic.
galactopoietic (inducing milk production), electromagnetic.

38.50.1
noetic (relating to the mind), poetic, dianoetic (relating to thought).

38.50.2
diabetic, alphabetic, analphabetic.

38.50.3
energetic, synergetic (acting together), apologetic.

38.50.4
kinetic, genetic, splenetic, frenetic, Venetic (ancient Italian language), telekinetic, hydrokinetic (relating to moving fluids), autokinetic (self-moving), pathogenetic (relating to disease).

38.50.5
phonetic, cybernetic.

38.50.6
bathetic, pathetic, nomothetic (giving laws), apathetic, empathetic, sympathetic, antipathetic, parasympathetic.

38.51
Rhaetic (geology term), cretic (metrical foot), acetic.

38.52
lytic (biology term), clitic (unstressed), critic.
phlebitic, rachitic (having rickets), bronchitic, mephitic (poisonous), graphitic, politic, enclitic (linguistics term), Hamitic (language group), Semitic, Sinitic (language group), granitic, Sanskritic, nephritic (relating to the kidneys), arthritic, Cushitic (language group).
Jesuitic, troglodytic, holophytic (biology term), meningitic, laryngitic, syphilitic, tonsillitic, impolitic, stalagmitic, porphyritic (geology term), diacritic, stalactitic.
hermaphroditic, anti-Semitic, Protosemitic (language group), osteoarthritic.

38.52.1

oolitic, thermolytic (relating to heat loss), analytic, paralytic, hydrolytic (chemistry term), catalytic, electrolytic, sympatholytic (inhibiting nerve impulses), bacteriolytic (destroying bacteria), psychoanalytic.

38.52.2

sybaritic, Ugaritic (extinct Semitic language), Himyaritic (language group), meteoritic.

38.52.3

lymphocytic, parasitic, anthracitic, erythrocytic, semiparasitic.

38.53

glottic (relating to the tongue), chaotic, thrombotic, narcotic, mycotic (relating to fungal infections), psychotic, aphotic (growing without light), demotic (of the common people), zymotic (relating to fermentation), osmotic, nepotic, despotic, sclerotic, erotic, cirrhotic, neurotic, parotic (situated near the ear), necrotic (relating to dead tissue), quixotic, azotic (relating to nitrogen), exotic.

idiotic, symbiotic (mutually dependent), semiotic (relating to symbols), amniotic, patriotic, creosotic, asymptotic.

epizootic (veterinary term), psychoneurotic.

38.53.1

biotic (relating to living organisms), meiotic, antibiotic, macrobiotic (relating to vegetarian diet).

38.53.2

hypnotic, posthypnotic, agrypnotic (relating to insomnia), autohypnotic.

38.54

aortic, astronautic.

38.55

otic (relating to the ear), photic (relating to light), lotic (inhabiting flowing water), rhotic (linguistics term), euphotic (ecology term), periotic (around the ear).

38.56

maieutic (philosophy term), scorbutic, propaedeutic (preparation before further study), hermeneutic (relating to biblical interpretation), therapeutic, antiscorbutic, radiotherapeutic.

38.57

lunatic, heretic, arithmetic.

38.58

lactic, tactic, didactic, galactic, climactic, syntactic, prophylactic, parallactic (relating to parallax), chiropractic, anaphylactic, extragalactic, anticlimactic.

38.59

arctic, Nearctic (zoogeographical term), subarctic, Holarctic (zoogeographical term), Antarctic, subantarctic.

38.60

hectic, smectic (chemistry term), eclectic, dyslectic, orectic (relating to desire), cathectic (psychology term), dialectic, apoplectic.

38.61

systaltic (relating to heartbeat), peristaltic.

38.62

antic, mantic (relating to prophecy), frantic, pedantic, gigantic, Atlantic, semantic, romantic, sycophantic, transatlantic.

38.63

lentic (inhabiting still water), argentic (containing silver), crescentic, authentic.

38.64

Pontic (of the Black Sea), quantic (maths term), deontic (logic term), orthodontic.

38.65

sceptic, peptic, septic, dyspeptic, aseptic, epileptic, analeptic (restorative drug), antiseptic.

38.66

diptych, glyptic (relating to engraving), cryptic, triptych, styptic, elliptic, ecliptic, apocalyptic.

38.67

optic, Coptic (language group), bioptic, panoptic (taking in all viewpoints), synoptic, orthoptic (relating to binocular vision).

38.68

clastic (geology term), plastic, mastic (aromatic resin), spastic, drastic.

bombastic, sarcastic, stochastic (statistics term), elastic, scholastic, aplastic, dynastic, monastic, gymnastic, fantastic.

inelastic, thromboplastic (forming a blood clot), thermoplastic (becoming soft when heated), ceroplastic (relating to wax-modelling), onomastic (relating to proper names), hudibrastic (mockheroic), periphrastic (circumlocutory).

interscholastic, iconoclastic.

38.68.1

orgiastic, ecclesiastic, enthusiastic.

38.69

majestic, telestich (short poem), domestic, agrestic (rural).

38.70 [further rhymes may be derived from **242.35**]

distich (two-line poem), fistic (relating to boxing), mystic, tristich (three-line poem), cystic.

sadistic, sophistic, stylistic, simplistic, hemistich (half line of verse), eristic (logic term), floristic, touristic, heuristic (helping to learn), juristic, patristic (relating to Church Fathers), artistic, autistic, linguistic.

atheistic, egoistic, jingoistic, altruistic, casuistic, masochistic, Hellenistic (relating to Greek civilization), chauvinistic, communistic, narcissistic, inartistic.

evangelistic, relativistic, sadomasochistic.

38.70.1

logistic, phlogistic (relating to inflammation), syllogistic, eulogistic, synergistic (acting together).

38.70.2

ballistic, symbolistic, journalistic, socialistic, fatalistic, novelistic, cannibalistic, nationalistic, rationalistic, nat-uralistic, commercialistic, capitalistic, sensationalistic, individualistic.

38.70.2.1

realistic, idealistic, surrealistic, materialistic.

38.70.3

euphemistic, pessimistic, optimistic.

38.70.4

mechanistic, modernistic, antagonistic, anachronistic, impressionistic.

38.70.5

meristic (biology term), futuristic, aphoristic, humoristic, voyeuristic, characteristic, behaviouristic.

38.70.6

statistic, egotistic, chrematistic (relating to money-making).

38.71

gnostic, agnostic, prognostic, acrostic, diagnostic.

38.72

gnathic (relating to the jaw), spathic (resembling the mineral spar), empathic, telepathic, psychopathic, allopathic, homeopathic, osteopathic, naturopathic.

38.73

lithic (made of stone), ornithic (relating to birds), Eolithic, Neolithic, megalithic, monolithic, Mesolithic, Palaeolithic.

38.74

civic, Bolshevik, Menshevik.

38.75

toxic, hypoxic (relating to oxygen deficiency), radiotoxic.

39 -ike

bike, dyke, hike, like, mike, pike, spike, Reich, shrike, trike, strike, psych, tyke.

Vandyke, Klondike, Thorndike, hitch-hike, hairlike, warlike, alike, snakelike, suchlike, godlike, swordlike, childlike, lifelike, shell-like, dreamlike, manlike, swanlike, unlike, apelike, glasslike, cat-like, antlike, Christlike, ghostlike, van Eyck, garpike (freshwater fish), turn-pike.

motorbike, ladylike, workmanlike, sportsmanlike.

39.1

dislike, businesslike.

40 -ock

och, bock (beer), cock, chock, dock, doc, Jock, hock, lock, lough, loch, bloc, block, clock, flock, schlock (US inferior goods), mock, smock, knock, pock, Spock, rock, roc, brock (badger), crock, frock, sock, shock, stock, wok.

sjambok (heavy whip), Lombok (Indonesian island), steinbok (small antelope), springbok, gemsbok (large antelope), haycock (small pile of hay), Leacock (Canadian humorist), peacock, seacock, gorcock (male red grouse), moorcock, spatchcock, Hitchcock, spitchcock, woodcock, Alcock (British aviator), ball cock, gamecock, Hancock, turncock (water company official), Bangkok, stopcock, Médoc, burdock, Murdoch, Van Gogh, forehock, ad hoc, charlock, Belloc, airlock, Shylock, oarlock, forelock, warlock, Moloch, breechblock (metal block in firearm), roadblock, picklock, o'clock, padlock, deadlock, headlock, wedlock, elflock (tangled lock of hair), daglock (dung-encrusted sheep's wool), hemlock, unlock, gunlock, Matlock, fetlock, wristlock, lovelock (lock of hair), Enoch, kapok, epoch, baroque, pibroch, bedrock, defrock, unfrock, shamrock, windsock, Bartók, ticktock, diestock (screw-cutting tool), nostoc (blue-green alga), Rostock (German port), Vostok (Russian spacecraft), headstock (part of machine tool), bloodstock, tailstock (part of machine tool), drillstock (part of machine tool), linstock, gunstock, whipstock (whip handle), rootstock, livestock.

manioc (tropical plant), Antioch, poppycock, weathercock, monocoque (car or aircraft body), shuttlecock, hollyhock, interlock, antiknock (petrol additive), monadnock (hill of hard rock), aftershock, alpenstock.

41 -ork

auk, orc (whale), balk, cork, Cork, caulk (fill cracks), chalk, fork, gawk (clumsy person), hawk, nork (Austral female

breast), pork, squawk, talk, torque, stalk, stork, walk, York.

uncork, Dundalk (Irish town), hayfork, pitchfork, Mohawk, goshawk, nighthawk, newshawk (US newspaper reporter), cakewalk, shoptalk, crosstalk, leafstalk, beanstalk, jaywalk, sidewalk, boardwalk, sleepwalk, sheepwalk (land for sheep-grazing), ropewalk (narrow rope-making passage), spacewalk, crosswalk (US pedestrian crossing), catwalk.

sparrowhawk, tomahawk.

42 -oke

oak, coke, choke, folk, joke, bloke, cloak, moke, smoke, poke, spoke, broke, croak, stroke, soak, toque, stoke, woke, yoke, yolk.

decoke, workfolk, menfolk, tradesfolk, kinsfolk, slowpoke (US slowcoach), mopoke (Australian owl), bespoke, keystroke, sidestroke, sunstroke, upstroke, heatstroke, breaststroke, backstroke, evoke, revoke, provoke, invoke, convoke, awoke, unyoke.

artichoke, okey-doke, gentlefolk, womenfolk, Roanoke (US island), masterstroke, Basingstoke.

43 -uck

buck, chuck, duck, fuck, guck (slimy substance), luck, cluck, pluck, muck, puck, ruck, cruck (roof timber), truck, struck, suck, shuck, tuck, stuck, yuk.

roebuck, reedbuck (African antelope), jumbuck, woodchuck, shelduck, mukluk (Eskimo's sealskin boot), potluck, amok, Kalmuck (Mongoloid people), dumbstruck, moonstruck, untuck, unstuck.

waterbuck (African antelope), chempaduk (Malaysian fruit tree), mallemuck (sea bird), thunderstruck.

44 -ook

book, cook, hook, look, nook, rook, brook, crook, shook, took.

daybook, boobook (Australian owl), bluebook (British government publication), chequebook, workbook, cookbook, bankbook, sketchbook, studbook, handbook, logbook, chapbook (book of popular ballads), scrapbook, passbook, notebook, textbook, Kirkuk (Iraqi city), billhook, unhook, pothook, boathook, Windhoek (African city), outlook, Pembroke, Innsbruck, forsook, nainsook (soft cotton fabric), partook, betook, mistook.

copybook, storybook, pocketbook, overcook, tenterhook, overlook, inglenook, Volapuk (artificial language), donnybrook (rowdy brawl), Alanbrooke (British field marshal), Bolingbroke, undertook, overtook.

44.1

Tobruk (Libyan port), Beaverbrook.

45 -uke

kook (*US* eccentric person), Luke, fluke, snook, spook, tuque (Canadian knitted cap), stook, duke, nuke, puke, caoutchouc (rubber material), Seljuk (member of Turkish dynasty), Nanook, Chinook, Farouk, peruke (men's wig), rebuke, archduke, Mameluke (military Egyptian ruler), Pentateuch, Heptateuch, Hexateuch, gobbledegook, bashibazouk (19th-century Turkish soldier).

46 -'ck

Newark, Lubbock (Texan city), Southwark, haddock, paddock, shaddock (tropical fruit tree), piddock (mollusc), Norfolk, Suffolk, hillock, lilac, pollack (Atlantic fish), rowlock, bullock, hammock, hummock, stomach, bannock (Scottish cake), Cannock, Lanark, Greenock, jonnock (*Dialect* genuine), monarch, dunnock (hedge sparrow), eunuch, arrack (alcoholic spirit), barrack, carrack, cassock, hassock, tussock, mattock (agricultural tool), buttock, futtock (part of boat), havoc, bulwark, Isaac.

Habakkuk (Old Testament prophet), Potomac, Kilmarnock, coronach (*Scot* dirge), laverock (*Dialect* skylark), Sarawak (Malaysian state).

elegiac, paranoiac.

47 -alk

calque (linguistics term), talc, catafalque (platform for coffin).

48 -elk

elk, spelk (*Dialect* wood splinter), whelk.

49 -ilk

ilk, bilk (thwart), milk, silk, Liebfraumilch, buttermilk.

50 -ulk

bulk, skulk, hulk, sulk.

51 -ank

ankh (symbolic cross), bank, dank, hank, lank, blank, clank, flank, plank, spank, rank, crank, drank, franc, frank, Frank, prank, shrank, sank, shank, tank, stank, thank, wank, swank, yank, Yank.

Clydebank, sandbank, embank, outflank, gangplank, outrank, Cruickshank, redshank (red-stemmed plant), scrimshank (*Slang* shirk work), greenshank (European shore bird), sheepshank.

mountebank, antitank.

52 -ink

ink, kink, skink (tropical lizard), chink, fink, gink, jink, link, blink, clink, slink, mink, pink, rink, brink, drink, prink, shrink, sink, sync, stink, think, wink, twink, zinc.

ratfink, snowblink (luminosity reflected from snow), iceblink (luminosity reflected from ice), Haitink (Dutch conductor), Bentinck (governor-general of India), rethink, unthink, outthink, hoodwink.

bobolink (US songbird), Maeterlinck (Belgian poet), interlink, countersink, doublethink.

53 -onk

conk, conch, gonk, honk, clonk, plonk, cronk (*Austral* unsound), stonk (bombard with artillery), honky-tonk.

54 -unk

bunk, skunk, chunk, dunk, funk, gunk (*Slang* slimy substance), junk, hunk, clunk, flunk, slunk, monk, punk, spunk, drunk, shrunk, trunk, sunk, stunk, debunk, chipmunk, quidnunc (gossipmonger), preshrunk.

55 -ask

Basque, casque (helmet-like structure), hask (*Dialect* dry cough), Monegasque (citizen of Monaco).

56 -arsk
ask, bask, cask, flask, mask, masque, task, unmask, overtask.

57 -esk
desk, burlesque, Moresque (Moorish decoration), grotesque, Junoesque, statuesque, arabesque, Romanesque (architectural style), picaresque, picturesque, sculpturesque, humoresque.

58 -isk
bisque, disc, disk, risk, brisk, frisk, whisk, obelisk, basilisk (tropical lizard), odalisque (female slave), tamarisk (ornamental tree), asterisk.

59 -osk
bosk (small wood), mosque, kiosk, abel-mosk (tropical plant).

60 -usk
Usk (British river), busk, dusk, husk, musk, rusk, brusque, tusk, subfusc (drab), cornhusk.

61 -'sk
mollusc, damask.

62 -atch
batch, catch, hatch, latch, match, natch, snatch, patch, scratch, thatch, crosshatch, nuthatch, unlatch, potlatch (American Indian ceremonial activity), rematch, mismatch, dispatch, cross-patch, detach, attach.

63 -arch
arch, larch, march, March, parch, starch, frogmarch, routemarch, corn-starch, countermarch, overarch.

64 -etch
etch, ketch, sketch, fetch, lech, fletch (fit with a feather), wretch, retch, stretch, vetch, Dolmetsch (British musician), outstretch.

65 -erch
birch, church, lurch, smirch (to soil), perch, search, unchurch (excommunicate), Christchurch, besmirch, pikeperch (freshwater fish), research.

66 -eech
each, beach, beech, leech, leach, bleach, pleach (interlace shoots in hedge), peach, speech, reach, breach, breech, screech, preach, teach, horse-leech, impeach, outreach, beseech, unteach, overreach.

67 -itch
itch, bitch, kitsch, ditch, fitch (polecat), hitch, flitch, niche, snitch, pitch, quitch (type of grass), rich, stitch, which, witch, switch, twitch.

cowitch (tropical climbing plant), Redditch, orache (herbaceous plant), eldritch (unearthly), enrich, ostrich, hemstitch, backstitch, bewitch, Ipswich, Prestwich, Northwich.

overpitch (cricket term), featherstitch, tsarevitch.

Shostakovich, Rostropovich, Mohorovičić (Yugoslav geologist).

68 -otch
botch, scotch, Scotch, blotch, splotch, notch, crotch, watch, swatch, hop-scotch, topnotch, hotchpotch, dogwatch, stopwatch, wristwatch, deathwatch, butterscotch, overwatch.

69 -orch
scorch, nautch (traditional Indian dance), porch, torch, debauch, blow-torch.

70 -oach
coach, loach, poach, roach, broach, brooch, slowcoach, stagecoach, mail-coach, cockroach, encroach, reproach, approach, motorcoach.

71 -ouch
ouch, couch, slouch, pouch, crouch, grouch, vouch, debouch (move into larger space).

72 -utch
Kutch (former Indian state), cutch (resinous substance), Dutch, hutch, clutch, much, crutch, such, touch, declutch, nonesuch (flowering plant), retouch, insomuch, overmuch, inasmuch, forasmuch.

73 -ootch
butch, cootch (hiding place).

74 -ooch
hooch, mooch, smooch, pooch.

75 -elch

belch, squelch.

76 -ilch

filch, milch (milk-yielding), pilch (infant's outer garment), zilch.

77 -ulch

culch (base of oyster bed), gulch, mulch.

78 -anch

blanch, ranch, branch, stanch, carte blanche, disbranch, avalanche, anabranch (stream branching from river).

79 -ench

bench, blench, clench, quench, wrench, drench, French, trench, tench, stench, wench, workbench, retrench, entrench.

80 -inch

inch, finch, lynch, clinch, flinch, Minch (Atlantic channel off Scotland), pinch, squinch (supporting arch in tower), cinch, winch, chaffinch, hawfinch, goldfinch, bullfinch, greenfinch.

81 -ornch

haunch, launch, flaunch (slope around chimney top), paunch, staunch.

82 -unch

bunch, hunch, lunch, munch, punch, brunch, crunch, scrunch, honeybunch.

83 -ad

ad, add, bad, bade, cad, scad (marine fish), Chad, dad, fad, gad, had, lad, clad, glad, plaid, mad, pad, rad (unit of absorbed radiation), brad (small nail), grad (*short for* graduate), trad, sad, shad, tad.

forbade, Akkad (ancient Babylonian city), cycad (tropical plant), caudad (towards the tail), Baghdad, granddad, egad, jihad (Islamic holy war), unclad, nomad, maenad (priestess of Bacchus), kneepad, footpad, Conrad, tetrad (group of four), dorsad (towards the back), octad, pentad, heptad, hexad.

alidad (surveying instrument), Trinidad, aoudad (wild mountain sheep), Galahad, cephalad (towards the head), ironclad, superadd (add as extra), Petrograd, Stalingrad, Leningrad, Upanishad (ancient Hindu sacred book).

83.1

Iliad, chiliad (group of one thousand), Gilead, gwyniad (freshwater fish), oread (Greek mountain nymph), bromeliad (fleshy-leaved plant), Olympiad.

83.2

dyad (maths term), pleiad (talented group of seven), naiad, dryad, triad, Omayyad (caliph), jeremiad (long mournful lamentation), hamadryad (tree nymph).

83.3

gonad (sex organ), monad (philosophy term), trichomonad (microscopic parasitic animal).

84 -ard [also 1 + -ed]

bard, card, chard, guard, hard, lard, nard (aromatic plant), pard, Sade, sard (gemstone), shard, yard.

Liard (Canadian river), liard (former European coin), bombard, Jacquard (fabric with patterned weave), placard, scorecard, filecard, timecard, racecard, discard, postcard, Goddard, blackguard, rearguard, fireguard, Bogarde, Midgard (Norse mythological place), mudguard, safeguard, lifeguard, vanguard, Asgard (home of Norse gods), Utgard (Norse mythological place), coastguard, diehard, blowhard (boastful person), ballade (verse form), mallard, foulard (soft light fabric), poulard (spayed hen), roulade, pomade (perfumed hair oil), canard (rumour or hoax), Barnard, spikenard (aromatic Indian plant), Stoppard, charade, estrade (dais), brassard (identifying armband), glissade (ballet step), façade, Hansard, mansard, petard, retard, ill-starred, noyade (execution by drowning), oeillade (suggestive glance), Riyadh (capital of Saudi Arabia), dooryard (US yard outside door), foreyard (nautical term), brickyard, dockyard, stockyard, junkyard, churchyard, kaleyard (*Scot* vegetable garden), steelyard, farmyard, barnyard, vineyard, boneyard, shipyard, courtyard, graveyard.

milliard (thousand million), Savoyard (native of Savoy), Kierkegaard, avant-garde, Abelard, interlard, communard (member of a commune), promenade, leotard, timberyard, lumberyard, Montagnard (member of mountain people), camelopard (giraffe).

84.1

regard, bodyguard, disregard.

85 -ade [also 2 + *-ed*]

aide, aid, cade (juniper tree), fade, jade, laid, lade (load cargo), blade, glade, maid, made, paid, spade, raid, braid, grade, trade, shade, staid, they'd, wade, suede.

arcade, decade, cockade, blockade, stockade, brocade, alcaide (Spanish castle commander), cascade, inlaid, unlade (unload), barmaid, mermaid, remade, limeade, milkmaid, handmade, self-made, unmade, nursemaid, housemaid, bridesmaid, prepaid, well-paid, unpaid, postpaid, tirade, abrade, upbraid, afraid, Belgrade, downgrade, upgrade, comrade, crusade, cliché'd, eyeshade, sunshade, nightshade, pervade, evade, invade, unweighed, dissuade, persuade.

Medicaid (US health assistance programme), barricade, autocade (US motorcade), motorcade, cavalcade, ambuscade (an ambush), alidade (surveyor's instrument), orangeade, Almohade (former Muslim ruler), Adelaide, fusillade (rapid gunfire), accolade, escalade (scaling walls with ladders), underlaid, marmalade, chambermaid, escapade, underpaid, overpaid, unafraid, overtrade, balustrade, rodomontade (boastful talk).

85.1

brigade, renegade.

85.2

grenade, pasquinade (satire), marinade, serenade, harlequinade.

85.3

carbonate, gasconade (boastful talk), colonnade, esplanade, lemonade, cannonade, cottonade (coarse fabric), gabionade (construction controlling water flow).

85.4

parade, masquerade.

85.5

degrade, tardigrade (minute segmented animal), saltigrade (moving by jumps), centigrade, unguligrade (walking on hooves), digitigrade (walking on toes).

85.6

aggrade (geology term), retrograde, intergrade (biology term).

86 -ed

bed, dead, fed, head, lead, led, fled, sled, Med, sped, red, read, bread, bred, dread, spread, shred, tread, thread, said, shed, ted, stead, wed, zed.

co-ed, seedbed, roadbed, childbed, embed, hotbed, deathbed, sheep-ked (parasitic fly), airhead, stairhead, spearhead, sorehead (US peevish person), warhead, blackhead, blockhead, bulkhead, deadhead, redhead, Godhead, Roundhead, egghead, bighead, nailhead (decorative device), railhead (end of railway), wellhead, drumhead, bonehead, springhead (source of stream), crosshead, sheepshead (Atlantic fish), Gateshead, cathead (nautical term), fathead, flathead (Pacific fish), pithead, Spithead, hothead, pothead (Slang cannabis user), masthead, hogshead, unlead (printing term), misled, Ahmed, premed, biped, moped, beebread (food for bee larvae), purebred, lowbred, shewbread (Old Testament bread), sowbread (European plant), homebred, inbred, unbred, crispbread, crossbred, sweetbread, shortbread, well-read, unread, bespread, bedspread, widespread, outspread, re-tread, packthread, unthread, unsaid, bloodshed, woodshed, oersted (unit in physics), bedstead, roadstead, farmstead, homestead, instead, Dyfed, Enzed (New Zealand).

underfed, overfed, knucklehead (foolish person), bufflehead (diving duck), shovelhead (common shark), Birkenhead, maidenhead, Maidenhead, woodenhead (stupid person), dragon-head (flowering plant), quadruped, infrared, underbred (of impure stock), gingerbread, thoroughbred, Ethelred, aforesaid, watershed, Holinshed, newly-wed, Samoyed.

86.1

abed, flowerbed, slugabed, riverbed.

86.2

behead, Holyhead, sleepyhead, poppy-head.

86.3

bowhead (arctic whale), towhead (blond-haired person), arrowhead.

86.4

skinhead, pinhead, fountainhead.

86.5

ahead, go-ahead, timberhead (nautical term), Leatherhead, dunderhead, thunderhead (anvil-shaped cloud top), figurehead, loggerhead, hammerhead (shark), copperhead (venomous snake), letterhead, overhead.

86.6

aliped (having wing-like limbs), taliped (having a club foot), pinniped (having flipper-like limbs), fissiped (having separate toes).

87 -erd [also 3 + -ed]

bird, Byrd, curd, Kurd (nomadic Turkic people), furred, gird, heard, herd, nerd, surd, turd, third, word.

firebird, lyrebird, snowbird, bluebird, blackbird, jailbird, rainbird, sunbird, songbird, lovebird, potsherd, begird (to surround), cowherd, swineherd, swanherd, unheard, goatherd, absurd, swearword, reword, byword, foreword, catchword, watchword, headword, password, crossword.

ladybird, whirlybird, friarbird, bowerbird, butcherbird, thunderbird, tailorbird, weaverbird, mockingbird, hummingbird, undergird, overheard, undeterred, Mesa Verde (high plateau in Colorado), afterword (postscript), overword (repeated phrase or word).

88 -aird [also 4 + -ed]

Baird, laird, tow-haired, long-haired, short-haired, unaired, unrepaired, unprepared, unimpaired.

89 -eed [also 5 + -ed]

Bede, bead, deed, feed, heed, he'd, lead, lied (type of song), bleed, plead, mead, Mede, knead, need, speed, reed, read, Reid, breed, creed, screed, greed, cede, seed, she'd, steed, weed, we'd, swede, Swede, tweed, Tweed.

indeed, misdeed, handfeed, spoon-feed, fairlead (nautical term), nosebleed, misplead (plead incorrectly), mislead, knock-kneed, stampede, impede, airspeed, Godspeed, groundspeed, inbreed, crossbreed, outbreed, proof-read, Siegfried, agreed, lip-read, misread, sight-read, birdseed, rapeseed, flaxseed, Jamshid (Persian mythological king), Flamsteed (English astronomer), mayweed, seaweed, fireweed, pokeweed, duckweed, milkweed, stinkweed, bindweed, pondweed, ragweed, pigweed, hogweed, knapweed, knotweed, goutweed, accede, exceed, stickseed (plant producing prickly fruits), succeed.

underfeed, winterfeed, overfeed, invalid, interplead (legal term), Ganymede, Runnymede, copyread (US subedit), interbreed, waterweed, silverweed, cottonweed.

Harun al-Rashid (8th-century caliph), Berwick-upon-Tweed.

89.1

millipede, cirripede (marine animal), centipede, velocipede (early type of bicycle).

89.2

recede, precede, secede, aniseed, antecede.

89.3

proceed, supersede, retrocede (give back), intercede.

89.4

linseed, pumpkinseed (US fish).

89.5

concede, cottonseed.

89.6

chickweed, stickweed, colicweed.

89.7

thimbleweed, tumbleweed, bugleweed, pickerelweed.

90 -eerd [also **6** + *-ed*]

eared, beard, fyrd (Anglo-Saxon local militia), weird, greybeard (old man), Bluebeard, Blackbeard (English pirate), goatsbeard (plant with woolly stem), lop-eared.

91 -id [Also **16** + *-ed*. Further rhymes may be created by adding *-ed* to appropriate verbs and nouns.]

id, bid, kid, Kidd (Scottish pirate), skid, did, fid (nautical term), gid (disease of sheep), hid, lid, slid, mid, quid, squid, rid, grid, Sid.

sayyid (Muslim title), rabid, crabbed, turbid, verbid (linguistics term), morbid, outbid, naked, wicked, orchid, crooked, tailskid, wretched, bearded, crowded, hooded, wooded, winded, minded, bonded, fronded, undid, wounded, outdid, aphid, bifid, trifid, jagged, ragged, cragged, dogged, rugged, pongid (type of ape), aged, turgid, algid (chilly), masjid (Arab mosque), eyelid, cichlid (tropical fish), Euclid, skidlid, timid, humid, tumid, desmid (freshwater alga), phasmid (plant-eating insect), learned, honeyed, moneyed, rapid, sapid (having a pleasant taste), vapid, torpid, Cupid, stupid, limpid, vespid (wasplike), cuspid (tooth having one point), liquid, varied, serried, storied, lurid, hurried, hybrid, acrid, sacred, Madrid, kindred, Alfred, hatred, putrid, blessed, cursed, cussed, muscid (type of fly), El Cid, fancied, rancid, gifted, tufted, kilted, stilted, tinted, wonted, hunted, stunted, waisted, frosted, worsted, Hampstead, avid, gravid, David, livid, vivid, ivied, Ovid, bovid, languid, pinguid (fatty or greasy), palsied, frenzied.

half-naked, unheeded, unseeded, katydid, secluded, included, overdid, longwinded, high-minded, like-minded, broad-minded, three-legged, bowlegged, cross-legged, annelid (segmented worm), Ozalid (*Trademark*), Mohammed, unlearned, hominid, cyprinid (freshwater fish), elapid (venomous snake), bicuspid, tricuspid, illiquid, satyrid (type of butterfly), unwearied, unhurried, eupatrid (ancient Greek landowner), accursed, Abbasid (Muslim caliph), assorted, undoubted, sure-footed, club-footed, flat-footed, hydatid (cyst containing tapeworm larva), bigoted, spermatid (immature sperm), propertied, impacted, unbolted, enchanted, unwanted, unwonted, unscripted, adopted, beloved.

disembodied, bloody-minded, narrow-minded, feeble-minded, single-minded, open-minded, prehominid (extinct man-like primate), tertium quid, geometrid (type of moth), ill-assorted, self-inflicted, unrestricted, malimprinted, unadopted, Hemel Hempstead.

unreconstructed, isoniazid (crystalline compound).

91.1

Aeneid, scarabaeid.

91.2

tineid (type of moth), clupeid (type of fish), Nereid (Greek nymph), araneid (spider), saturniid (tropical moth), reduviid (type of bug).

91.3

Clwyd, fluid, druid, semifluid, superfluid (physics term).

91.4

forbid, underbid, carabid (dark-coloured beetle), overbid.

91.5

guarded, unguarded, retarded.

91.6

faded, gadid (marine fish), jaded, braided, unaided, unshaded, colonnaded.

91.7

leaded, wedded, bareheaded, baldheaded, bigheaded, light-headed, unleaded (printing term), muddleheaded, levelheaded.

91.8

misguided, decided, one-sided, lopsided, undecided, undivided.

91.9
corded, sordid, prerecorded, unrewarded.

91.10
loaded, woaded, outmoded, unexploded.

91.11
studied, blue-blooded, cold-blooded, full-blooded, warm-blooded, hot-blooded, unstudied.

91.12
candid, candied, landed, stranded, barehanded, high-handed, forehanded, backhanded, cack-handed, red-handed, right-handed, left-handed, empty-handed, heavy-handed, underhanded, single-handed.

91.13
splendid, commended, intended, undefended, undescended, unattended.

91.14
rounded, unbounded, unfounded, confounded, astounded.

91.15
rigid, Brigid, frigid, nonrigid, semirigid.

91.16
pallid, valid, invalid.

91.17
jellied, gelid, potbellied.

91.18
olid (foul-smelling), squalid, solid, stolid, semisolid.

91.19
amid, pyramid.

91.20
Enid, sciaenid (type of fish), scorpaenid (spiny-finned fish).

91.21
balconied, Sassanid (member of Persian dynasty), oceanid (Greek nymph), Achaemenid (member of Persian dynasty), unaccompanied.

91.22
hackneyed, arachnid.

91.23
tepid, intrepid.

91.24
lipid, insipid, phospholipid.

91.25
arid, married, sparid (tropical fish), subarid, unmarried, semiarid.

91.26
forehead, horrid, florid, torrid.

91.27
acarid (tick or mite), ascarid (parasitic worm), salaried, lepori (mammal of hare family), liveried, ephemerid (mayfly), elaterid (click beetle).

91.28
acid, flaccid, placid, subacid (moderately acid), peracid (type of acid), antacid, oxyacid (acid containing oxygen).

91.29
viscid, bombycid (type of moth), culicid (mosquito), tortricid (small moth), dytiscid (carnivorous aquatic beetle).

91.30
lucid, deuced, mucid (mouldy), pellucid (translucent), Seleucid (member of ancient dynasty).

91.31
capsid (plant-eating bug), therapsid (extinct reptile).

91.32
fatted, matted, dratted, caryatid.

91.33
uncharted, hardhearted, cold-hearted, kind-hearted, half-hearted, whole-hearted, downhearted, light-hearted, stouthearted, softhearted, departed, tenderhearted, chicken-hearted, lion-hearted, brokenhearted.

91.34
dated, fated, plated, truncated, outdated, hydrated (containing water), unabated, educated, calculated, simulated, mentholated, dissipated, constipated, antiquated, celebrated, fenestrated (having windows), elevated, cultivated, dilapidated, self-opinionated, unpremeditated.

91.34.1
foliated, floriated (architectural term), asteriated (crystallography term), unappropriated, unsubstantiated.

91.34.2
infatuated, superannuated.

91.34.3
dedicated, complicated, desiccated, sophisticated, unsophisticated.

91.34.4
variegated, unmitigated.

91.34.5
belated, related, castellated, pixilated (*US* eccentric).

91.34.6
hyphenated, uncoordinated.

91.34.7
serrated, saturated, perforated, unsaturated, unperforated, exaggerated, incorporated, supersaturated (physics term), unadulterated, polyunsaturated.

91.35
fetid, fretted, sweated, indebted, coroneted.

91.36
concerted, perverted, deserted, disconcerted.

91.37
heated, seated, repeated, conceited.

91.38
fitted, knitted, nitid (bright), limited, helmeted, spirited, turreted, quick-witted, halfwitted, dim-witted, sharp-witted, unedited, unlimited, inherited, unmerited, dispirited, high-spirited, multifaceted.

91.39
sighted, whited, delighted, benighted, united, far-sighted, clear-sighted, near-sighted, unsighted, long-sighted, short-sighted, excited, unrequited, uninvited, overexcited.

91.40
dotted, knotted, potted, spotted, unspotted, carotid, parotid, besotted.

91.41
coated, bloated, noted, devoted.

91.42
booted, fluted, reputed, unsuited, undiluted, unpolluted, convoluted, undisputed.

91.43
affected, dejected, collected, unaffected, unreflected, unconnected, unsuspected, unexpected, undirected, undetected.

91.44
malted, salted, vaulted, exalted.

91.45
sainted, unpainted, acquainted, unacquainted.

91.46
rented, scented, demented, lamented, contented, discontented, unprecedented.

91.47
haunted, undaunted.

91.48
jointed, pointed, disjointed, double-jointed, disappointed.

91.49
mounted, uncounted, unmounted.

91.50
talented, unwarranted.

91.51
blasted, flabbergasted.

91.52
crested, vested, buprestid (tropical beetle), undigested, unmolested, double-breasted, unattested.

91.53
listed, tightfisted, unlisted, forested, interested, uninterested, disinterested, unassisted.

91.54
crusted, disgusted, maladjusted.

91.55
fervid, cervid (mammal of deer family), perfervid (extremely ardent).

92 -ide [also 7 + -ed]

eyed, I'd, bide, chide, dyed, guide, hide, Hyde, Clyde, glide, slide, nide (flock of pheasants), snide, pied, ride, bride, pride, stride, side, tied, tide, wide.

carbide (chemical compound), abide, cockeyed, sulphide, confide, misguide, waveguide (electronics term), rawhide, cowhide, horsehide, oxhide, halide (chemical compound), walleyed, bolide (large bright meteor), allied, collide, nuclide (type of atomic nucleus), Strathclyde, applied, landslide, backslide, bromide, popeyed, deride, fluoride, hydride (chemical compound), nitride (chemical compound), outride, well-tried, untried, bestride, astride, Tayside, wayside, quayside, seaside, nearside, fireside, cross-eyed, subside, bedside, broadside, offside, hillside, Tyneside, downside, ringside, stateside, Port Said, outside, Teesside, betide, Hocktide (former British festival), yuletide, peptide, riptide (turbulent water in sea), Twelfthtide (Epiphany), Shrovetide, divide, worldwide, backside, azide (chemical compound), reside, preside.

iodide (chemical compound), disulphide, trisulphide, aldehyde (chemical compound), ophicleide (obsolete wind instrument), actinide (radioactive element), telluride (chemical compound), East Kilbride, anhydride (chemical compound), Ironside, slickenside (polished rock surface), alongside, mercaptide (chemical compound), dipeptide (biochemical compound), Christmastide, subdivide, nationwide.

hydrosulphide, dissatisfied, formaldehyde, benzaldehyde (fragrant oil), polyamide (polymer), preoccupied, unoccupied, Allhallowtide, polypeptide (biochemical compound).

acetaldehyde (colourless volatile liquid), chlorothiazide (drug).

92.1

qualified, dignified, rarefied, countrified, classified, certified, citified, unqualified, undignified, unclassified, unstratified.

92.2

elide, acetylide (chemical compound), acetanilide (crystalline substance).

92.3

sodamide (crystalline substance), thalidomide, sulphonamide, tolbutamide (medicinal compound), sulphanilamide (crystalline substance), nicotinamide (component of vitamin B).

92.4

cyanide, uranide (type of element), arsenide (chemical compound), lanthanide (type of element).

92.5

boride (chemical compound), chloride, dichloride, trichloride, hydrochloride, tetrachloride.

92.6

saccharide (a sugar), glyceride (chemical compound), override, polysaccharide, monosaccharide.

92.7

beside, decide.

deicide, suicide, herbicide, regicide, algicide, fungicide, filicide, silicide (chemical compound), stillicide (legal term), Barmecide (illusory), germicide, spermicide, vermicide, homicide, parricide (killing of parent), matricide, patricide, fratricide, countryside, feticide, pesticide, larvicide, Heaviside, Merseyside.

tyrannicide, bactericide, sororicide, uxoricide, insecticide, infanticide, rodenticide.

92.7.1

miticide (mite-killing substance), parasiticide.

92.8

aside, biocide (chemical for killing organisms), Humberside, ecocide (destruction of natural environment), glycoside (biochemical compound), underside, genocide, waterside, riverside, silverside, nucleoside (biochemical compound), taeniacide (tapeworm-killing substance).

92.9

inside, coincide, Qaboos bin Said (sultan of Oman).

92.10

topside, diopside (type of mineral).

92.11

phosphatide (biochemical compound), Eastertide, nucleotide (biochemical compound), polynucleotide (biochemical compound).

92.12

Whitsuntide, Passiontide, eventide, Ascensiontide.

92.13

provide, Almoravide (member of Islamic people).

92.14

oxide, dioxide, trioxide, monoxide, peroxide, hydroxide.

93 -ired [also **8** + *-ed*]

oilfired, uninspired, unexpired, overtired.

94 -od

odd, bod, cod, god, hod, Lod (Israeli town), clod, plod, mod, nod, pod, quad, quod (*Slang* jail), squad, rod, prod, trod, sod, shod, tod, Todd, wad.

lingcod (Pacific fish), ephod (Old Testament priest's vestment), bipod, tripod, ramrod, Nimrod, pushrod, roughshod, slipshod, tightwad.

Hesiod (ancient Greek poet), ostracod (tiny freshwater animal), demigod, amphipod (aquatic organism), polypod, unipod, goldenrod (yellow-flowered plant).

94.1

decapod, chilopod (crawling invertebrate), tylopod (type of mammal), pteropod (marine mollusc), theropod (dinosaur), sauropod (dinosaur), tetrapod, gastropod, arthropod, chaetopod (type of worm), octopod, hexapod, rhizopod (minute organism), brachiopod (marine invertebrate), branchiopod (freshwater organism), myriapod (crawling invertebrate), cephalopod (marine mollusc), ornithopod (dinosaur).

95 -ord [also **9** + *-ed*]

oared, board, bawd, baud (unit in computer technology), cord, chord, ford, hoard, horde, lord, laud, Maud, broad, fraud, sword, ward, sward, fjord, Njord (Norse god).

keyboard, leeboard (board in ship), freeboard (nautical term), seaboard, scoreboard, floorboard, strawboard (board of compressed straw), backboard, blackboard, blockboard, corkboard, chalkboard (*US* blackboard), buckboard (horse-drawn carriage), duckboard (board covering muddy ground), matchboard, switchboard, cardboard, hardboard, headboard, breadboard, sideboard, surfboard, pegboard, scaleboard (veneer), tailboard, billboard, millboard (strong pasteboard), inboard, signboard, springboard, stringboard (part of staircase), chipboard, clipboard, shipboard, chessboard, dashboard, flashboard (board on dam), splashboard, washboard, dartboard, skateboard, outboard, draughtboard, pasteboard, cheeseboard, record, concord, Concorde, ripcord, whipcord (strong fabric), discord, afford, milord, warlord, landlord, applaud, maraud, abroad, defraud, broadsword, reward, greensward.

shuffleboard, smorgasbord, needlecord, overlord.

95.1

aboard, chequerboard, weatherboard, fingerboard, clapperboard, paperboard (thick cardboard), scraperboard, mortarboard, centreboard (supplementary keel), plasterboard, overboard.

95.2

record, harpsichord, clavichord, misericord.

95.3

accord, monochord (instrument for acoustic analysis), urochord (zoology term), disaccord, notochord (zoology term), octachord (eight-stringed musical instrument).

95.4

award, toward, untoward.

96 -oord [also 10 + -ed]

gourd, Sigurd (Norse mythological hero), assured, insured, self-assured, uninsured, unsecured.

97 -oid [also 11 + -ed]

Boyd, Lloyd, Freud, void.

hyoid (bone at tongue base), pyoid (pus-like), globoid, cuboid, rhomboid, sarcoid (flesh-like), cricoid (cartilage in larynx), trochoid (geometric curve), fucoid (brown seaweed), mucoid, discoid, viscoid, gadoid (type of fish), xiphoid (sword-shaped), typhoid, lymphoid, fungoid, styloid (stylus-like), xyloid (woody), colloid, tabloid, cycloid (circular), haploid (biology term), diploid (biology term), triploid (biology term), sphygmoid (pulse-like), sigmoid (S-shaped), desmoid (firm tumour), ethmoid (bone of the face), lipoid (fatty), choroid (membrane of eyeball), toroid (geometry term), fibroid, scombroid (marine fish), cancroid (cancer-like), chancroid (soft venereal ulcer), android, dendroid (tree-like), Negroid, schizoid, deltoid, dentoid (tooth-like), mastoid, cestoid (ribbon-shaped), histoid (resembling normal tissue), cystoid, lithoid (stone-like), devoid, ovoid, avoid.

scorpioid (scorpion-like), osteoid, ichthyoid, amoeboid, anthracoid, autacoid (natural internal body secretion), Celluloid (*Trademark*), unemployed, echinoid (marine animal), arachnoid (membrane covering brain), polypoid, anthropoid, porphyroid (geology term), sciuroid (squirrel-like), lemuroid, cylindroid, sinusoid (maths term), emulsoid, ellipsoid, parotoid (poison gland on toad), haematoid, rheumatoid, keratoid (horny), teratoid (monster-like), allantoid (sausage-shaped), acanthoid (spiny), trapezoid, Caucasoid.

paratyphoid, underemployed, epileptoid.

97.1

geoid (shape of earth), scarabaeoid.

97.2

percoid (type of fish), cysticercoid (tapeworm larva).

97.3

trichoid (hair-like), helicoid (spiral-shaped), gynaecoid (woman-like), lumbricoid (worm-like), cercopithecoid (monkey), mineralocorticoid (steroid hormone).

97.4

meloid (long-legged beetle), varicelloid (resembling chickenpox).

97.5

phylloid (leaf-like), myeloid (anatomy term), amyloid (starch-like protein), cotyloid (cup-shaped), nautiloid (mollusc), erysipeloid (type of dermatitis).

97.6

hyaloid (transparent), sialoid (saliva-like), alkaloid, mongoloid, unalloyed, coralloid, metalloid (type of element), petaloid, crystalloid, paraboloid (geometric surface), hyperboloid (geometric surface), amygdaloid (volcanic rock).

97.7

sphenoid (wedge-shaped), glenoid (having a shallow cavity), ctenoid (comb-like), scorpaenoid (spiny-finned fish).

97.8

crinoid (marine animal), adenoid, solenoid, hominoid, actinoid (having a radiate form), resinoid, albuminoid, carotenoid (red or yellow pigment).

97.8.1

platinoid (platinum-like), gelatinoid.

97.9

annoyed, melanoid (dark-coloured), humanoid, salmonoid, paranoid.

97.10

spheroid, scleroid (hardened), steroid, theroid (beast-like), hemispheroid, corticosteroid.

97.11

spiroid (spiral), thyroid, parathyroid.

97.12

amberoid (synthetic amber), acaroid (mite- or tick-like), saccharoid, Polaroid (*Trademark*), haemorrhoid, asteroid, meteoroid.

98 -ode [also **12** + *-ed*]

ode, bode, code, goad, lode, load, mode, node, Spode, road, rode, strode, toad, woad.

geode (crystal-lined rock cavity), diode, triode (electronic valve), forebode, abode, decode, encode, postcode, hallowed, payload, reload, freeload, workload, truckload, unload, shipload, implode, explode, cartload, boatload, anode, epode (part of Greek ode), erode, byroad, highroad, corrode, railroad, inroad, cestode, cathode.

unhallowed, overload, wagonload, à la mode, antinode (physics term), hemipode (quail-like bird), antipode (the exact opposite), megapode (ground-living bird), nesselrode (rich frozen pudding), electrode, episode, nematode, trematode (parasitic flatworm), hydathode (water-secreting plant pore).

98.1

commode, incommode, discommode, alamode (light silk).

99 -oud [also **13** + *-ed*]

Oudh (region of India), loud, cloud, crowd, proud, shroud, Stroud, Saud, unbowed, aloud, becloud, enshroud, avowed, well-endowed, overcrowd, ibn-Saud.

99.1

Macleod, thundercloud, overcloud.

100 -ud

bud, cud, scud, dud, blood, flood, mud, spud, rudd (freshwater fish), crud, stud, thud, disbud, rosebud, lifeblood, oxblood (dark reddish-brown colour), m'lud.

101 -ood

could, good, hood, should, stood, would, wood.

Gielgud, boyhood, monkhood, godhood, childhood, selfhood, girlhood, manhood, nunhood, falsehood, knighthood, sainthood, priesthood, monkshood (poisonous plant), Talmud, withstood, Larwood (English cricketer), baywood (light soft wood), Heywood, Sherwood, dyewood (wood yielding dye), plywood, firewood, matchwood, touchwood, hardwood, deadwood, redwood, bogwood (wood preserved in bogs), dogwood (European shrub), logwood (tree yielding red dye), Wedgwood, wormwood, greenwood, brushwood, heartwood (central core of tree), Fleetwood, whitewood, driftwood, softwood, bentwood, Brentwood, rosewood.

babyhood, hardihood, likelihood, livelihood, widowhood, neighbourhood, sisterhood, fatherhood, motherhood, brotherhood, maidenhood, womanhood, adulthood, parenthood, understood, Hollywood, Isherwood, zebrawood (tree yielding striped wood), candlewood (resinous wood), sandalwood, satinwood, misunderstood.

102 -ude [also **15** + *-ed*]

food, Jude, who'd, lewd, mood, snood, rood, rude, brood, crude, prude, shrewd, you'd, dude, feud, hued, nude, pseud.

seafood, wholefood, elude, illude, delude, preclude, seclude, occlude, include, conclude, exclude, protrude, obtrude, intrude, extrude, subdued, prelude, denude, transude, étude, exude.

Safid Rud (Iranian river), unvalued.

102.1

allude, collude, interlude.

102.2

quietude, longitude, solitude, amplitude, plenitude (abundance), magnitude, turpitude (baseness), pulchritude, lassitude, certitude, fortitude, rectitude, sanctitude, altitude, multitude, aptitude, promptitude, servitude, mansuetude (gentleness), consuetude (established custom).

inquietude (restlessness), disquietude (unease), desuetude (state of disuse), similitude, decrepitude, solicitude, vicissitude, incertitude, exactitude, correctitude, ineptitude.

dissimilitude, inexactitude, verisimilitude (appearance of truth).

102.2.1

attitude, latitude, platitude, gratitude, beatitude, ingratitude.

103 -'d [also **17** + -*ed*]

froward (obstinate), coward, Howard, steward, scabbard, tabard, larboard, starboard, cupboard, Hubbard, halberd (spear with axe head), Lombard, chequered, tankard, drunkard, whiskered, Richard, orchard, pochard (diving duck), pilchard, cultured, standard, Stafford, Rockford, Crockford (directory of Anglican clergy), Bradford, Telford, Guildford, Salford, Longford, Stratford, Dartford, Hertford, Hartford, Watford, Wexford, Oxford, Chelmsford, haggard, laggard, staggered, jiggered, niggard, sluggard, ballad, salad, armoured, mannered, Reynard, gurnard (European marine fish), synod, leopard, shepherd, backward, awkward, farad, Herod, hundred, dotard, sceptred, dastard, bastard, plastered, cloistered, bustard, custard, mustard, method, Harvard, fevered, louvred, wayward, leeward, seaward, Edward, headward, sideward, landward, windward, homeward, inward, onward, downward, upward, outward, westward, eastward, northward, southward, galliard (17th-century dance), halyard, billiard, lanyard, Spaniard, hazard, gizzard, lizard, blizzard, wizard, trousered, buzzard.

unnumbered, good-natured, unstructured, substandard, nonstandard, Hereford, Waterford, Rutherford, Muhammad, enamoured, unanswered, untutored, self-centred, Hereward, northwestward, southwestward, northeastward, southeastward, haphazard, butterfingered.

103.1

period, myriad, photoperiod (period of daylight).

103.2

Bedford, Redford, eisteddfod.

103.3

bollard, Lollard, pollard, Bacolod (Philippine town).

103.4

coloured, dullard, varicoloured, particoloured, multicoloured.

103.5

rumoured, good-humoured.

103.6

leisured, measured, treasured, unmeasured.

103.7

uncovered, undiscovered.

103.8

forward, shoreward, henceforward, straightforward.

104 -ebbed

ebbed, webbed, cobwebbed.

105 -erbed [also **22** + -*ed*]

uncurbed, unperturbed, undisturbed.

106 -ogged [also **185** + -*ed*]

fogged (photography term), hogged (nautical term), waterlogged.

107 -inged

stringed, winged, stockinged.

108 -aged [also **193** + -*ed*]

uncaged, engaged, unpaged (having no page numbers), unengaged.

109 -edged [also **194** + -*ed*]

alleged, unfledged, fully-fledged.

110 -idged [also **197** + -*ed*]

privileged, unabridged, disadvantaged, underprivileged.

111 -anged [also **207** + -*ed*]

estranged, prearranged.

112 -aled [also **214** + -*ed*]

veiled, hobnailed, detailed, pigtailed, fan-tailed.

113 -eld [also **215** + -*ed*]

geld, held, meld, weld, Krefeld (German city), Ziegfeld, Danegeld, beheld, upheld, withheld, self-propelled, unparalleled.

114 -erld [also **216** + -*ed*]

world, unfurled, antiworld (world composed of antimatter), underworld, afterworld.

115 -eeld [also **217** + -*ed*]

bield (*Dialect* refuge), field, heeled, shield, Weald, wield, yield.

Sheffield, airfield, Scofield, snowfield, Nuffield, Wakefield, Lichfield, midfield, oilfield, coalfield, Enfield, urnfield

(cemetery of cremation urns), infield,
minefield, cornfield, Springfield,
Masefield, Mansfield, Hatfield, outfield,
well-heeled, windshield, gumshield.

battlefield, Huddersfield, Macclesfield,
Beaconsfield, Sutton Coldfield.

115.1

afield, chesterfield, Chesterfield.

116 -ild [also **218** + *-ed*]

build, skilled, gild, guild, sild, rebuild,
upbuild, unskilled, wergild (price on
man's life), Brunhild (legendary
German queen), self-willed, unwilled,
overbuild, semiskilled.

117 -iled [also **219** + *-ed*]

child, Fylde, mild, wild, Wilde, godchild, grandchild, brainchild, stepchild,
Rothschild, undefiled.

118 -orld [also **221** + *-ed*]

auld, bald, scald, walled, piebald, skewbald, close-hauled (with the sails flat),
Cumbernauld.

119 -oiled [also **222** + *-ed*]

well-oiled, unspoiled, shopsoiled.

120 -oled [also **223** + *-ed*]

old, bold, cold, scold, fold, gold, hold,
mould, sold, told, wold.

kobold (German mythological mischievous spirit), threefold, fourfold,
twofold, blindfold, billfold, tenfold,
enfold, ninefold, unfold, sheepfold,
eightfold, gatefold (folded oversize
page), fivefold, sixfold, freehold, toe-
hold, handhold, stronghold, uphold,
leasehold, household, foothold, with-
hold, remould, Detmold (German city),
unpolled, unsold, threshold, foretold,
untold, Cotswold.

semibold (printing term), manifold,
centrefold, sevenfold, marigold, stran-
glehold, Leopold, Hammarskjöld.

120.1

behold, copyhold (legal term).

121 -uled [also **227** + *-ed*]

Gould, unruled, unschooled, unsched-
uled.

122 -'ld [also **228** + *-ed*]

marbled, fabled, gabled, ribald, freckled, pickled, cuckold, raddled, handled,
brindled, scaffold, Arnold, pimpled,
Harold, titled, Tynwald, chiselled, grizzled, sozzled.

spectacled, unbridled, unruffled,
bedraggled, newfangled, oldfangled,
Macdonald, principled, unequalled,
emerald, untitled, disgruntled, untrav-
elled, dishevelled, unrivalled, bespectacled, unprincipled.

122.1

Gerald, herald, Fitzgerald.

122.2

mettled (brave), unsettled.

123 -armed [also **230** + *-ed*]

armed, becalmed, unharmed, alarmed,
unarmed.

124 -amed [also **231** + *-ed*]

forenamed, unaimed, unnamed,
unframed, ashamed, untamed, unacclaimed, unashamed.

125 -ormed [also **238** + *-ed*]

deformed, reformed, malformed,
unformed, uninformed.

126 -imed [also **236** + *-ed*]

unrhymed, well-timed.

127 -'md [also **242** + *-ed*]

envenomed, accustomed, unfathomed,
unaccustomed.

128 -and [Some *-land* words in **143**
may be pronounced to rhyme with this
group. Also **245** + *-ed*.]

and, band, canned, hand, land, bland,
gland, manned, rand, brand, grand,
strand, Strand, sand, stand.

proband (person in genealogical study),
neckband, headband, sideband (electronics term), armband, disband,
hatband, sweatband, waistband, waveband, noseband (part of bridle), forehand, backhand, offhand, stagehand,
unhand, longhand, shorthand,
unmanned, expand, firebrand,
Streisand, quicksand, suntanned,
headstand, bandstand, handstand,
grandstand, washstand, withstand,

newsstand, kickstand (stand for bicycle), inkstand.

graduand, bellyband (part of harness), saraband, contraband, Samarkand, beforehand, underhand, overhand, behindhand, second-hand, confirmand, Ferdinand, ordinand, ampersand, Kristiansand (Norwegian port), understand.

Witwatersrand (South African region), analysand (person undergoing psychoanalysis), misunderstand.

128.1
radicand (maths term), multiplicand (number multiplied).

129 -arned
darned, demand, remand, command, allemande (musical term), reprimand, countermand.

130 -aned [also **247** + -*ed*]
pained, strained, harebrained, crackbrained, ingrained, close-grained, unstrained, bloodstained, scatterbrained, featherbrained, unrestrained, self-contained.

131 -end
end, bend, fend, lend, blend, mend, penned, spend, rend, friend, trend, send, tend, vend, wend.

unbend, unkenned (*Dialect* unknown), addend (number added to), defend, forfend (protect), offend, pitchblende, hornblende, emend, stipend, upend, append, perpend, impend, misspend, expend, befriend, boyfriend, girlfriend, descend, ascend, godsend, transcend, portend, attend, subtend, intend, contend, distend, Ostend, extend, Southend, Wallsend, Gravesend.

minuend (number subtracted from), dividend, subtrahend (number subtracted), condescend, coextend, Demavend (Iranian volcanic peak), superintend.

131.1
apprehend, reprehend, comprehend, misapprehend.

131.2
amend, commend, recommend, discommend.

131.3
depend, vilipend (treat with contempt).

131.4
suspend, overspend.

131.5
pretend, repetend (repeated digit).

132 -erned [also **249** + -*ed*]
unearned, concerned, unturned, unconcerned.

133 -eened [also **251** + -*ed*]
fiend, archfiend, uncleaned, unscreened.

134 -ind [also **252** + -*ed*]
finned, Sind (region of Pakistan), tinned, wind, thick-skinned, thin-skinned, sequined, rescind, destined, headwind, woodwind, tailwind, whirlwind, downwind, upwind, crosswind, wunderkind (child prodigy), determined, tamarind, undetermined.

135 -ined [also **253** + -*ed*]
bind, kind, find, hind, blind, mind, rind, grind, wind.

cowbind (climbing plant), spellbind, unbind, mankind, unkind, refined, behind, purblind (partly blind), inclined, streamlined, unlined, remind, unsigned, rewind, enwind, unwind.

gavelkind (former land tenure system), womankind, humankind, unrefined, nonaligned, mastermind, undersigned, overwind.

136 -ond
bond, donned, fond, blonde, blond, pond, frond, Fronde, sonde (device for observing atmosphere), wand, Zond (unmanned Russian spacecraft), second, abscond, keeshond, beau monde, millpond, respond, beyond, vagabond, demimonde, Garamond (typeface), correspond, Trebizond (Turkish port).

137 -orned [also **255** + -*ed*]
corned, horned, maund (Asian unit of weight), unmourned, unadorned.

138 -oaned [also **257** + -*ed*]
stoned, rawboned (having bony physique), unboned, unowned, unatoned, unchaperoned.

139 -ound [also **258** + -ed]
bound, found, hound, mound, pound, round, ground, sound, wound, swound (*Dialect* swoon).

rebound, snowbound, abound, strikebound, hidebound, fogbound, spellbound, stormbound, inbound, unbound, brassbound, casebound, icebound, housebound, outbound, westbound, eastbound, earthbound, clothbound, northbound, southbound, redound, profound, dumbfound, confound, greyhound, deerhound, boarhound, horehound (flowering plant), elkhound, bloodhound, wolfhound, staghound, hellhound (fiend), sleuthhound, foxhound, renowned, propound, impound, compound, expound, uncrowned, playground, fairground, foreground, background, stoneground, unsound, astound, unwound, resound.

ironbound (unyielding), ultrasound, series-wound (electrical term).

superabound, merry-go-round.

139.1
around, surround, turnaround.

139.2
aground, underground, overground.

140 -und [also **259** + -ed]
bundh (general strike in India), fund, refund, re-fund, rotund, obtund (deaden), moribund, cummerbund, iracund (easily angered), orotund.

141 -oond
Bund (federation), Lund (Swedish city), dachshund.

142 -ooned [also **260** + -ed]
wound, marooned.

143 -'nd [also **261** + -ed]
viand (type of food), prebend (church stipend), riband (ribbon awarded for achievement), husband, second, fecund, jocund, hardened, ligand (chemistry term), brigand, legend, taloned, garland, Wayland (character in European folklore), island, highland, Thailand, Ireland, Holland, foreland, moorland, lowland, Poland, Roland, Dowland (English musician), clubland, scrubland, parkland, Lakeland, dockland, Auckland, Falkland, midland, woodland, England, farmland, homeland, mainland, Greenland, inland, Finland, Vinland (stretch of US coast), Rhineland, gangland, Langland (English poet), Lapland, upland, grassland, Iceland, marshland, heartland, Shetland, Scotland, Gotland (Swedish island), Portland, Jutland, Rutland, wasteland, Cleveland, Friesland (Dutch province), Queensland, Hammond, almond, gourmand, Lomond, Richmond, Edmund, Redmond, Sigmund, Dortmund, errand, gerund, wizened, thousand.

infecund, rubicund, unquestioned, abandoned, Zululand, Newfoundland, tableland, diamond, Sigismund (Holy Roman Emperor), unopened, reverend, old-fashioned, impassioned, unleavened.

millisecond, nanosecond, microsecond, Sudetenland (region of Czech Republic), aforementioned, undermentioned, well-intentioned.

143.1
eland, hieland (*Scot* Highland), Zealand, New Zealand.

143.2
Disneyland, fairyland, Maryland, Dixieland, Swaziland, Somaliland, Matabeleland.

143.3
Pondoland (region of South Africa), Togoland, Heligoland (North Sea island).

143.4
Oberland, timberland, borderland, Gelderland (Dutch province), Sunderland, wonderland, Westmorland, Switzerland, hinterland, fatherland, motherland, Sutherland, overland, Bechuanaland, Gondwanaland, Nyasaland.

143.4.1
Cumberland, Northumberland.

143.5
conditioned, unconditioned, noncommissioned.

143.6

reasoned, weasand (windpipe), unseasoned.

144 -athed [also **473** + -*ed*]

unscathed, enswathed.

145 -othed [also **478** + -*ed*]

unclothed, betrothed.

146 -aved [also **482** + -*ed*]

unpaved, depraved, unsaved, well-behaved.

147 -erved [also **483** + -*ed*]

reserved, undeserved, unreserved, well-preserved, unobserved.

148 -eeved [also **484** + -*ed*]

leaved, relieved, well-received, unperceived.

149 -ived [also **486** + -*ed*]

deprived, contrived.

150 -ooved [also **490** + -*ed*]

moved, removed, unmoved, approved, unproved, unimproved.

151 -olved [also **493** + -*ed*]

unsolved, involved, resolved, unresolved, undissolved.

152 -azed [also **509** + -*ed*]

crazed, unglazed.

153 -eezed [also **513** + -*ed*]

pleased, well-pleased, diseased.

154 -ized [also **516** + -*ed*]

sized, pearlized, advised, undisguised, civilized, undersized, oversized, ill-advised, unadvised, uncivilized, well-organized, disorganized, unauthorized, uncircumcised.

155 -ozed [also **520** + -*ed*]

closed, composed, unposed, disposed, exposed, undisclosed, indisposed, unexposed, undiagnosed.

155.1

supposed, unopposed.

156 -oozed [also **523** + -*ed*]

used, bruised, accused, bemused, amused, disused.

157 -aff

caff, daff, faff, gaff, gaffe, draff (husks remaining after fermentation), WAAF, piaffe (dressage term), chiffchaff (European warbler), Llandaff, kenaf (jute-like fibre), carafe, riffraff, agraffe (a fastening), bathyscaph, shandygaff.

158 -arf

calf, scarf, chaff, half, laugh, graph, staff, zarf (coffee-cup holder), mooncalf (fool), headscarf, behalf, giraffe, digraph (two-letter sound), trigraph (three-letter sound), distaff, plough-staff, flagstaff, tipstaff, pikestaff, telegraph, polygraph (lie detector), epigraph (opening quotation in book), serigraph (silk-screen print), shadow-graph, epitaph, cenotaph, quarterstaff (former English weapon).

158.1

tachograph, Van de Graaff (US physicist), allograph (signature written for another), stylograph (type of pen), xylograph (wood engraving), holograph (original manuscript), thermograph, homograph, sphygmograph (blood-pressure recorder), seismograph, stenograph, Chinagraph (*Trademark*), monograph, chronograph, barograph, paragraph, spirograph (breathing-movement recorder), macrograph (drawing showing enlarged image), micrograph (picture of microscope image), autograph, photograph, pictograph, pantograph (instrument for scale drawing), cryptograph (code), lithograph.

oscillograph, Addressograph (*Trademark*).

photomicrograph (photograph of microscope image), cinematograph (type of cine-projector), microphotograph (photograph showing reduced image), electroencephalograph.

158.1.1

cardiograph, radiograph, heliograph, Mimeograph (*Trademark*), stereograph (three-dimensional picture), choreograph, spectroheliograph (instrument for photographing sun), electrocardiograph.

158.1.2

phonograph, coronagraph (optical instrument).

158.1.3

spectrograph (instrument for photographing spectrum), electrograph.

159 -afe

chafe, strafe, safe, waif, vouchsafe, unsafe.

160 -eff

eff, deaf, lev (Bulgarian currency), clef, ref, chef, tef (African grass), ASLEF, Brezhnev, UNICEF.

160.1

Kiev, Prokofiev.

161 -erf

kerf (cut made by saw), scurf, serf, surf, turf.

162 -eef

beef, chief, fief (property granted to vassal), leaf, lief, reef, brief, grief, sheaf, thief, naïf, enfeoff (legal term), flyleaf, debrief, massif, motif, interleaf, overleaf, cloverleaf, leitmotiv, apéritif.

162.1

belief, relief, unbelief, disbelief, misbelief (unorthodox belief), bas-relief, demirelief.

162.2

kharif (autumn-harvested crop), Tenerife.

163 -iff

if, biff, kif (marijuana), skiff, cliff, glyph (groove on frieze), miff, niff, sniff, quiff, Rif (Moroccan people), riff (music term), tiff, stiff, whiff.

kerchief, mischief, Cardiff, Aycliffe (English town), Wycliffe (English religious reformer), Radcliffe, Sutcliffe, tariff, midriff, caitiff (cowardly person), plaintiff, pontiff, mastiff, skewwhiff, Joseph.

neckerchief, handkerchief, anaglyph (stereoscopic picture), hieroglyph, petroglyph (prehistoric rock carving), logogriph (word puzzle), hippogriff (Greek mythological monster).

163.1

bailiff, caliph, bumbailiff (debt collector).

163.2

serif, sheriff, sanserif, undersheriff.

164 -ife

fife, Fife, life, knife, rife, strife, wife, highlife, wildlife, half-life, nightlife, jackknife, penknife, loosestrife, midwife, goodwife, alewife (herring-like fish), housewife, fishwife, afterlife, paperknife, pocketknife.

165 -off

off, cough, scoff, doff, quaff, prof, trough, toff, takeoff, Chekhov, Khrushchev, sendoff, brushoff, liftoff, blastoff, Nabokov, whooping cough, Godunov (Russian tsar), stroganoff, Romanov (Russian imperial dynasty), Molotov, Rimsky-Korsakov.

165.1

Ustinov, Rachmaninoff.

166 -orf

orfe, Orff (German composer), corf (wagon used in mines), morph, wharf, dwarf, swarf, Waldorf, Düsseldorf, polymorph, perimorph (mineral enclosing another).

166.1

endomorph, lagomorph (type of mammal), allomorph, mesomorph, isomorph (organism with similar form), ectomorph, rhizomorph (root-like fungal structure), hystricomorph (type of rodent).

167 -oaf

oaf, loaf, limitrophe (near a frontier).

168 -uff

buff, cuff, scuff, chuff, chough, duff, guff, huff, luff (leading edge of sail), bluff, Clough, fluff, slough, muff, snuff, puff, ruff, rough, scruff, gruff, tough, tuff (volcanic rock), stuff.

rebuff, handcuff, earmuff, enough, woodruff (flowering plant), dyestuff, foodstuff, greenstuff, overstuff.

169 -oof

poof, woof.

170 -ufe

goof, hoof, kloof (South African mountain pass), pouffe, spoof, roof, proof, woof.

shadoof, aloof, sunroof, reproof, wearproof, fireproof, shockproof, skidproof, soundproof, shellproof, foolproof, flameproof, stormproof, rainproof, disproof, rustproof, mothproof.

Al Hufuf (Saudi Arabian town), showerproof, weatherproof, shatterproof, waterproof, bulletproof.

171 -'f

ganef (*US* unscrupulous opportunist), daraf (unit in physics), paraph (flourish following a signature), seraph, teraph (Old Testament household god), dandruff.

172 -elf

elf, skelf (*Dialect* wood splinter), pelf (money), self, shelf, Guelph (Italian political faction member), thyself, myself, yourself, herself, himself, oneself, itself.

173 -olf

golf, Rolf, Rudolf, Randolph.

174 -ulf

gulf, engulf.

175 -oolf

wolf, Woolf, Wolfe, werewolf, aardwolf (nocturnal mammal), Cynewulf (Anglo-Saxon poet), Beowulf (Old English epic poem), Fenriswolf (Norse mythological wolf).

176 -imph

lymph, nymph, perilymph (fluid in ear), endolymph (fluid in ear).

177 -umph

bumph, humph, triumph, galumph.

178 -ag

bag, fag, gag, jag, hag, lag, flag, slag, mag, nag, snag, rag, brag, crag, scrag, drag, sag, shag, tag, stag, wag, swag.

debag, fleabag, workbag, feedbag, handbag, sandbag, windbag, ragbag, mailbag, beanbag, gasbag, ratbag, postbag, nosebag, stalag, greylag, Gulag, washrag (*US* face cloth), ragtag (the rabble), chinwag, zigzag.

saddlebag, lallygag (*US* loiter aimlessly), bullyrag (bully with practical jokes), scallywag.

178.1

kitbag, carpetbag.

179 -arg

bagh (Indian garden), darg (*Dialect* day's work), Prague, Reichstag, Bundestag (German legislative assembly).

180 -aig

Haig, Hague, plague, Craig, vague, stravaig (*Dialect* wander aimlessly).

181 -eg

egg, beg, keg, skeg (nautical term), leg, cleg (horsefly), peg, dreg, teg, foreleg, blackleg, dogleg, bootleg, nutmeg, unpeg, Tuareg (member of Berber people), thalweg (geography term), filibeg (Scottish Highlander's kilt), Scanderbeg (Albanian patriot), Winnipeg.

182 -erg

erg, burg (town), berg (*short for* iceberg).

Marburg, Coburg, Newburg, Lindbergh, Strindberg, Bamberg (German town), Hamburg, Limburg, Gomberg (US chemist), homburg, Romberg (US composer), Schoenberg, iceberg, Hapsburg, Vicksburg (American Civil War site), Strasbourg, exergue (inscription on coin).

Magdeburg, Middelburg (Dutch city), Heidelberg, inselberg (isolated rocky hill), Nuremberg, Württemberg, Luxembourg, Oldenburg (German city), Brandenburg, Hindenburg, Mecklenburg (region of Germany), Battenburg, Gutenberg, Gothenburg (Swedish port), Gettysburg, Williamsburg (former capital of Virginia), Drakensberg (African mountain range), Saint Petersburg.

182.1

Louisburg (Canadian fortress), Harrisburg (capital of Pennsylvania), Johannesburg.

182.2

Pittsburgh, Pietermaritzburg (capital of Natal).

183 -eeg

league, Grieg, gigue, colleague, renege, blitzkrieg, sitzkrieg, intrigue, sque-teague (Atlantic fish), fatigue.

184 -ig

big, dig, fig, gig, jig, pig, rig, brig, frig, grig (*Dialect* lively person), prig, sprig, trig, cig, Whig, wig, swig, twig.

shindig, fishgig (pole for impaling fish), rejig (re-equip), pfennig, bushpig (African wild pig), unrig, Danzig (fancy pigeon), Leipzig, earwig, bagwig (18th-century wig), bigwig.

infra dig, caprifig (wild fig), whirligig, guinea pig, thimblerig (game of chance), periwig, Zagazig (Egyptian city), thingumajig.

185 -og

bog, cog, dog, fog, Gog, jog, Hogg, hog, log, clog, flog, glogg (hot alcoholic drink), slog, mog, smog, nog, snog, frog, grog, prog, trog (to stroll), tog.

seadog, firedog, watchdog, bulldog, sundog (small rainbow near horizon), hangdog, sheepdog, hot dog, Magog, goosegog, quahog, hedgehog, prologue, backlog, eclogue, unclog, footslog, eggnog, bullfrog, leapfrog, Hertzog.

underdog, Tagalog, epilogue, antilog, dialogue, duologue, Decalogue, homo-logue, analogue, monologue, apologue (moral fable), catalogue, travelogue, golliwog, polliwog.

185.1

befog, pettifog.

185.2

agog, pedagogue, demagogue, haema-gogue (promoting blood flow), syna-gogue, mystagogue (teacher of mystical doctrines), sialagogue (stimulating saliva flow), galactagogue (inducing milk secretion).

186 -org

Borg, morgue, Swedenborg (Swedish scientist and theologian).

187 -oorg

bourg (French market town), Coorg (former province of India), Cherbourg, faubourg.

188 -oag

rogue, brogue, drogue (funnel-shaped device), vogue, collogue (conspire), pirogue (canoe), prorogue, pishogue (*Irish* sorcery), disembogue (discharge or flow out).

189 -ug

bug, chug, dug, fug, jug, hug, lug, plug, slug, mug, smug, snug, pug, rug, drug, shrug, trug, tug, thug.

debug, firebug (arsonist), bedbug, red-bug (parasitic larva), humbug, earplug, unplug.

jitterbug, litterbug, doodlebug, spittle-bug (leaping insect).

190 -oog

Moog (*Trademark*), fugue.

191 -adge

badge, cadge, fadge (*Dialect* agree), hajj (Muslim pilgrimage to Mecca).

192 -arge

barge, charge, large, marg, marge, sparge (sprinkle), raj, sarge, taj (Muslim's tall cap), surcharge, recharge, discharge, enlarge, undercharge, super-charge, countercharge, overcharge.

193 -age

age, cage, phage (virus that destroys bacteria), gauge, gage (a pledge), page, rage, sage, stage, wage, swage (shaped tool).

birdcage, encage, greengage, engage, teenage, rampage, enrage, outrage, Osage (American Indian people), off-stage, downstage, upstage, backstage, assuage.

disengage, archimage (great magician), interpage, underage, overage, saxifrage, multistage.

193.1

macrophage (cell in animal tissue), bacteriophage (virus that destroys bacteria).

194 -edge

edge, kedge (nautical term), hedge, ledge, fledge, pledge, sledge, dredge, sedge, veg, wedge, allege, frankpledge (medieval tithing system), straightedge (strip used as ruler), featheredge (plank with thin edge).

195 -erge

urge, scourge, dirge, splurge, merge, purge, spurge, serge, surge, verge, emerge, submerge, resurge (rise again), deterge (cleanse), diverge, converge, demiurge (philosophy term), dramaturge, thaumaturge (performer of miracles).

196 -eege

liege, siege, besiege.

197 -idge

midge, ridge, bridge, fridge.

triage (sorting according to priority), buoyage, voyage, flowage, towage, stowage, brewage, sewage, Babbage (English mathematician), cabbage, garbage, Burbage (English actor), herbage (vegetation for grazing), cribbage, package, breakage, leakage, dockage (charge for docking ships), blockage, corkage, linkage, shrinkage, boscage (thicket), adage, wordage, bandage, bondage, poundage, groundage (fee for anchorage), roughage, baggage, mortgage, luggage, mileage, silage, haulage, spoilage, soilage (green fodder), ullage (unfilled part of container), sullage (sewage), Coolidge, damage, rummage, scrummage, plumage, carnage, cranage (use of crane), drainage, dunnage (material for packing cargo), tonnage, seepage, stoppage, peerage, steerage, borage (flowering plant), forage, Norwich, porridge, floorage, storage, moorage, weighbridge, drawbridge, Trowbridge, Stourbridge, abridge, Cambridge, umbrage, Tonbridge, footbridge, Lethbridge (Canadian city), Oxbridge, Uxbridge, suffrage, cartridge, partridge, passage, sausage, dosage, usage, cartage, cottage, pottage, wattage, portage (transport), shortage, footage, voltage, vantage, mintage, vintage, frontage, wastage, vestige, hostage, postage, Carthage, lavage

(medical procedure), ravage, savage, cleavage, lovage, salvage, selvage, language, sandwich, visage.

verbiage, foliage, lineage, appendage, vassalage, assemblage, endamage, orphanage, baronage, patronage, matronage, parsonage, personage, Stevenage, sewerage, harbourage, acreage, vicarage, brokerage, anchorage, pasturage, pilferage, cellarage, Coleridge, haemorrhage, porterage (charge for porter's work), quarterage (quarterly payment), waterage (transportation by ship), fosterage, average, beverage, leverage, coverage, agiotage (business of currency exchange), pilotage, advantage, parentage, envisage.

vagabondage, overdosage, disadvantage, protolanguage (reconstructed extinct language), metalanguage (linguistics term).

197.1

pillage, spillage, grillage (arrangement of beams), tillage, village, pupillage, sacrilege, mucilage, ensilage (process of storing fodder), cartilage, sortilege (divination by drawing lots), tutelage, privilege.

197.2

college, knowledge, foreknowledge, acknowledge.

197.3

image, scrimmage, pilgrimage, afterimage.

197.4

homage, West Bromwich.

197.5

manage, pannage (pasturage for pigs), tannage (process of tanning), mismanage.

197.6

ennage (printing term), empennage (rear part of aircraft).

197.7

spinach, Greenwich, concubinage.

197.8

slippage, equipage (horse-drawn carriage).

197.9
carriage, Harwich, marriage, mis-carriage, remarriage, disparage, under-carriage, intermarriage.

197.10
courage, encourage, discourage, demur-rage (delay of carrier's departure).

197.11
message, presage, expressage (con-veyance by express).

197.12
hermitage, maritage (feudal right), her-itage, baronetage.

197.13
dotage, flotage, anecdotage.

197.14
tentage (tents), ventage (small hole), percentage.

198 -ige
oblige, disoblige.

199 -odge
bodge, dodge, lodge, splodge, modge (*Dialect* to botch), stodge, wodge, dis-lodge, hodgepodge, horologe (time-piece).

200 -orge
forge, gorge, George, regorge (to vomit), engorge, disgorge.

201 -oge
doge, gamboge (gum resin).

202 -ouge
gouge, scrouge (*Dialect* to crowd).

203 -udge
budge, fudge, judge, bludge (*Austral* to scrounge), sludge, smudge, nudge, drudge, grudge, trudge, prejudge, fore-judge, adjudge, misjudge, begrudge.

204 -uge
smoodge (*Austral* smooch), Scrooge, stooge, huge, refuge, deluge, vermifuge (worm-expelling drug), febrifuge (fever-reducing drug), centrifuge, subterfuge.

205 -ulge
bulge, indulge, divulge.

206 -ange
flange, phalange (finger- or toe-bone), Falange (Spanish Fascist movement).

207 -ainge
change, mange, range, grange, strange, exchange, arrange, estrange, inter-change, counterchange, rearrange, disarrange.

207.1
derange, omnirange (radio navigational system).

208 -enge
henge (area with stone circle), Stonehenge, revenge, avenge.

209 -inge
binge, dinge, hinge, cringe, fringe, springe (small snare), singe, tinge, whinge, swinge, twinge, unhinge, challenge, impinge, syringe, orange, infringe, scavenge, lozenge.

210 -ounge
lounge, scrounge.

211 -unge
scunge (*Austral* borrow), gunge, lunge, blunge (ceramics term), plunge, sponge, expunge, muskellunge (US game fish).

212 -al
gal, pal, sal (salt), shall, cabal, decal (transferred design), fallal (showy orna-ment), grand mal, canal, La Salle (Canadian city), Laval (Canadian city), caracal (desert lynx), warrigal (*Austral* dingo), petit mal, falderal (worthless tri-fle), chaparral (dense growth of trees), citronellal (fragrant natural oil), Guadalcanal (Pacific island), Ashurbanipal (Assyrian king).

213 -arl
Basle, Baal, Carl, dal (Indian food), farl (oatmeal cake), marl, gnarl, snarl, rale (medical term), Vaal (South African river), joual (Canadian French dialect), toile, jarl (medieval Scandinavian chieftain). real (former Spanish coin), timbale (dish cooked in mould), locale, house-carl (medieval Danish household ser-vant), Heimdall (Norse god), Ruisdael

(Dutch painter), halal (Muslim custom), unsnarl, Bhopal (Indian city), corral, chorale, morale, Transvaal, riyal (Saudi Arabian currency), khayal (Indian classical vocal music).

Taj Mahal, caporal (strong tobacco), pastorale, Provençal, Nembutal (*Trademark*), Emmenthal, Van der Waal (Dutch chemist).

Escorial (Spanish architectural site), Neanderthal.

213.1

banal, rationale.

214 -ale

ail, ale, bale, bail, kale, scale, dale, fail, faille (soft light fabric), gale, Gael (Gaelic-speaking person), jail, hail, hale, flail, male, mail, nail, snail, pail, pale, quail, rail, Braille, frail, Grail, trail, sail, sale, shale, tale, tail, stale, they'll, veil, vale, wail, whale.

percale (closely-woven fabric), Airedale, Rochdale, Drysdale, Clydesdale, regale, inhale, exhale, e-mail, female, blackmail, treenail (dowel joining planks), doornail, toenail, hobnail, thumbnail, hangnail, impale, derail, guardrail, handrail, taffrail (rail at ship's stern), Sangraal (Holy Grail), contrail (vapour trail from aircraft), staysail, resale, skysail, trysail, wassail, foresail, assail, abseil, wholesale, mainsail, topsail, curtail, detail, retail, hightail, bobtail, cocktail, broadtail (fur from Persian lambs), swordtail (tropical fish), wagtail, pigtail, telltale, fantail, entail, pintail (greyish-brown duck), dovetail, oxtail, foxtail, travail, prevail, avail, unveil, bewail.

Wensleydale, Chippendale, Skelmersdale, Abigail, Fine Gael (Irish political party), martingale (strap in horse's harness), galingale (European plant), nightingale, farthingale (framework worn under skirts), fingernail, monorail, ponytail, swallowtail (type of butterfly), tattletale, cottontail, Ebbw Vale, countervail (act with equal force).

215 -ell

ell, bell, belle, bel, dell, fell, jell, gel, hell, mel (pure form of honey), smell,

knell, spell, quell, cell, sell, shell, tell, well, dwell, swell, yell.

Nowell, barbell, harebell, rebel, doorbell, Nobel, cowbell, bluebell, handbell, dumbbell, Scafell, befell, pell-mell, Parnell, fresnel (unit of frequency), spinel (mineral), Brunel, prunelle (French liqueur), quenelle (meat or fish dumpling), rappel (mountaineer's method of descent), repel, lapel, propel, impel, compel, dispel, misspell, expel, Bakewell, inkwell, morel (edible fungus), Marcel, Purcell, outsell, seashell, eggshell, bombshell, nutshell, artel (Russian cooperative union), cartel, Ravel, Tavel (French rosé wine), farewell, stairwell, speedwell, bridewell (jail), Caldwell, indwell, Cromwell, unwell, excel, Moselle, gazelle.

decibel, Jezebel, Isabel, Zinfandel (Californian wine grape), parallel, calomel (purgative powder), philomel (nightingale), béchamel, organelle (tiny structure inside cell), mangonel (stone-throwing war engine), villanelle (verse form), pimpernel, personnel, fontanelle, aquarelle, chanterelle (edible fungus), pipistrelle, pedicel (flower stalk), photocell, cockleshell, tortoiseshell, brocatelle (heavy brocade), moschatel (small flowering plant), muscatel (rich sweet wine), bagatelle, clientele, caravel (sailing ship), Camberwell, demoiselle (small Eurasian crane).

spirituel (having refined wit), materiel (materials and equipment), eau de Javelle (bleaching solution), mademoiselle.

215.1

cadelle (small beetle), asphodel.

215.2

nacelle (part of aircraft), undersell, carousel, oversell.

215.3

Courtelle (*Trademark*), foretell, immortelle (everlasting flower).

215.4

boatel, hotel, motel, maître d'hôtel.

216 -erl

earl, burl (small lump in wool), curl, skirl (*Dialect* play bagpipes), churl, furl, girl, hurl, merle (*Scot* blackbird), knurl (small ridge), purl, pearl, whirl, swirl, twirl, uncurl, unfurl, showgirl, cowgirl, impearl (adorn with pearls), papergirl, mother-of-pearl.

217 -eel

eel, Biel (Swiss town), keel, Kiel (German port), deal, feel, heel, heal, he'll, leal (*Scot* loyal), meal, kneel, Neil, peel, peal, spiel, squeal, reel, creel, seal, she'll, teal, steel, steal, veal, we'll, wheel, weal (raised mark on skin), zeal.

ordeal, misdeal, congeal, selfheal, all-heal, allele (genetics term), schlemiel (*US* clumsy), inchmeal (inch by inch), wholemeal, piecemeal, sweetmeal, oatmeal, repeal, appeal, kriegspiel (war game), newsreel, unseal, conceal, genteel, Bastille, Castile, reveal, Deauville, freewheel, gearwheel, flywheel, side-wheel (riverboat's paddle-wheel), aiguille (needle-shaped mountain peak), cogwheel, millwheel, pinwheel, cartwheel.

dishabille, Dormobile (*Trademark*), snowmobile, Israfil (archangel in the Koran), cochineal, glockenspiel, imbecile, cockatiel, commonweal, automobile.

217.1

anneal, chenille, eau de nil (pale yellowish-green colour).

217.2

underseal, hydrocele, rectocele, blastocoel (embryology term), haemocoel (invertebrate's body cavity), cystocele, haematocele (blood cyst).

218 -ill

ill, bill, kill, skill, chill, dill, fill, gill, hill, mill, mil (unit of length), nil, pill, spill, quill, squill (Mediterranean plant), rill, brill, krill, drill, frill, grill, grille, shrill, trill, thrill, sill, till, still, will, swill, twill.

playbill, waybill, Erbil (Iraqi city), gerbil, sibyl (ancient Greek prophetess), wrybill, twibill (agricultural implement), bluebill, shoebill, handbill, hornbill, thornbill, spoonbill, waxbill, hawksbill (small tropical turtle), storksbill (flowering plant), cranesbill (flowering plant), Gaitskell, Churchill, idyll,

condyle (rounded projection on bone), refill, fulfil, argil (potter's clay), Virgil, strigil (ancient Roman's body-scraper), vigil, Edgehill, molehill, downhill, dunghill, uphill, foothill, amyl (chemical group), Tamil (member of Asian people), sawmill, De Mille, treadmill, windmill, vinyl, tranquil, jonquil, fibril (small fibre), quadrille, mandrill, tendril, nostril, Bovril (*Trademark*), doorsill, dactyl, dentil (architectural term), lentil, until, pastille, distil, pistil, standstill, instil, ethyl, methyl, chervil, Melville, anvil, Nashville, dullsville, goodwill, pigswill, axil, Brazil.

razorbill, winterkill (kill by frost exposure), overkill, cacodyl (oily poisonous liquid), daffodil, minipill, overspill, escadrille (French aircraft squadron), espadrille, codicil, windowsill, acetyl, tormentil (Eurasian plant), Bougainville (Pacific island), Jacksonville (US port), whippoorwill.

Invercargill, pterodactyl, Merthyr Tydfil.

218.1

sclerophyll (woody evergreen plant), mesophyll (middle layer of leaf), xanthophyll (plant pigment), chlorophyll, neutrophil (white blood cell), eosinophil (white blood cell).

218.2

beryl, Beryl, peril, imperil.

218.3

Seville, Baskerville, vaudeville, Stoke Mandeville.

219 -ile

isle, aisle, I'll, bile, chyle (milky fluid in intestine), kyle (*Scot* narrow strait), file, guile, lisle, mile, smile, Nile, pile, rile, tile, style, stile, vile, Weill (German composer), wile, while.

labile (unstable), stabile (stationary abstract construction), mobile, nubile, aedile, defile, profile, nailfile, misfile, Argyll, beguile, agile, fragile, Carlisle, Carlyle, penile, senile, stockpile, woodpile, compile, sterile, virile, febrile, facile, gracile (gracefully slender), sessile (botany term), docile, fertile, quartile (statistics term), motile, protyle (hypothetical substance), rutile (mineral), futile, fictile (moulded from clay), ductile, pantile, reptile, hairstyle, freestyle, hostile, turnstile, servile, revile, awhile, meanwhile, erstwhile, worthwhile, exile.

immobile, crocodile, camomile, Chari-Nile (language group), juvenile, thermopile (radiant energy detector), puerile, indocile, expansile (able to expand), reconcile, infertile, volatile, versatile, pulsatile (beating rhythmically), inductile (not pliant), mercantile, infantile, peristyle (colonnade surrounding building).

antifebrile, acrylonitrile (colourless liquid).

219.1

zoophile (animal lover), Francophile, paedophile, Anglophile, thermophile (organism thriving in warmth), xenophile (admirer of foreigners), Negrophile, Russophile, audiophile (hi-fi enthusiast), bibliophile, myrmecophile (animal living with ants), Germanophile, ailurophile (cat lover).

219.2

fissile, missile, scissile (capable of being cut), domicile, antimissile, circumscissile (botany term).

219.3

ensile (store in silo), pensile (ornithology term), tensile, prehensile, thermotensile (physics term).

219.4

tractile (ductile), tactile, retractile (able to be withdrawn), protractile (able to be extended), contractile.

219.5

sectile (easily sliced), projectile, erectile.

219.6

Gentile, percentile (statistics term).

219.7

hypostyle (architectural term), urostyle (zoology term), cyclostyle, amphiprostyle (architectural term).

219.8

sextile, textile, bissextile (relating to leap year).

220 -oll

col, doll, dol (unit of pain intensity), loll, moll.

obol, COBOL, glycol (liquid used as antifreeze), argol (deposit in wine vats), Gogol, googol (large number), ALGOL, Algol (bright star), Mongol, Jehol (region of China), enol (chemical compound), phenol (carbolic acid), redpoll (finch), atoll, naphthol (crystalline substance), menthol, AWOL, podzol.

protocol, alcohol, ethanol, methanol, Interpol, cortisol (hormone), creosol (yellow oily liquid), regosol (type of soil), Limassol (Cypriot port), plasmasol (fluid form of protoplasm), parasol, aerosol, girasol (type of opal), entresol (mezzanine floor), lithosol (type of soil), amatol (explosive substance).

220.1

borneol (chemical compound), vitriol, oestriol (hormone), terpineol (chemical compound), urushiol (poisonous liquid).

220.2

Komsomol (Russian youth association), paracetamol.

220.3

quinol (crystalline substance), eugenol (oily liquid), orcinol (crystalline substance), retinol (biochemical compound), allopurinol (synthetic drug).

220.4

glycerol (syrupy liquid), calciferol (vitamin), tocopherol (vitamin), cholesterol, zoosterol (biochemical compound), ergosterol (biochemical compound), sitosterol (extract from soya beans).

221 -orl

awl, all, ball, bawl, caul, call, fall, Gaul, gall, hall, haul, maul, mall, small, pall, Paul, pawl (part of ratchet mechanism), spall (rock splinter), squall, brawl, crawl, scrawl, drawl, sprawl, trawl, thrall, Saul, shawl, tall, stall, wall, waul (wail like a cat), yawl.

hairball, eyeball, highball, fireball, snowball, screwball, blackball, punch-ball, oddball, handball, pinball, baseball, netball, meatball, football, mothball, jackal, catcall, recall, withal, bradawl, holdall, befall, snowfall, land-fall, windfall, rainfall, downfall, catfall (nautical term), pratfall, pitfall, nightfall, shortfall, footfall, windgall (swelling on horse's fetlock), Bengal, guildhall, keelhaul, downhaul (nautical term), town hall, Whitehall, Nepal, appal, Blackwall, enthral, Walsall, fore-stall, thumbstall, install, footstall (base of column), bookstall, sidewall, Cornwall, stonewall.

carryall, Montreal, volleyball, cannon-ball, basketball, wherewithal, waterfall, Senegal, Donegal, overhaul, overall, disenthral, Tattersall, fingerstall, cater-waul.

222 -oil

oil, boil, Boyle, coil, Doyle, foil, noil (short textile fibres), spoil, roil, broil, soil, toil, voile, parboil, gumboil, recoil, uncoil, trefoil, airfoil, cinquefoil (type of plant), milfoil (yarrow), tinfoil, gar-goyle, turmoil, despoil, embroil, sub-soil, topsoil, multifoil (looped design), disembroil, undersoil.

222.1

aerofoil, hydrofoil, quatrefoil (architec-tural ornament), counterfoil, Fianna fail (Irish political party).

223 -ole

bowl, boll, bole, coal, kohl, Cole, skoal (drinking toast), dole, foal, goal, whole, hole, mole, knoll, Pole, pole, poll, role, roll, scroll, droll, prole, troll, stroll, soul, sole, Seoul (capital of South Korea), shoal, toll, stole, thole (wooden peg in boat), vole.

creole, Sheol (abode of the dead), punchbowl, fishbowl, charcoal, clearcole (size for painting walls), bricole (billiards term), indole (crys-talline substance), de Gaulle, cajole, keyhole, kneehole, eyehole, blowhole, hellhole, armhole, manhole, pinhole, peephole, loophole, knothole, pothole, porthole, foxhole, maypole, dipole (pair of electric charges), catchpole (medieval sheriff's officer), tadpole, flagpole, bargepole, ridgepole, Walpole, beanpole, payroll, pyrrole (colourless toxic liquid), Tyrol, bankroll, bedroll, enrol, unroll, patrol, control, turnsole (plant turning towards sun), insole,

console, pistole (former European gold coin), extol.

vacuole, amphibole (type of mineral), rocambole (garlic-like plant), caracole (half turn in dressage), pratincole (swal-low-like bird), cubbyhole, pigeonhole, buttonhole, Seminole (American Indian), multirole, rock-and-roll, decontrol, self-control, thiazole (chemi-cal compound), carbazole (chemical compound), bibliopole (dealer in rare books).

223.1

bronchiole, cariole (horse-drawn cart), dariole (mould used in cookery), oriole, aureole (halo), cabriole, capriole (leap), petiole (leaf stalk), ostiole (small pore), arteriole (subdivision of artery).

223.2

condole, farandole (lively Provençal dance), girandole (ornamental candle-holder).

223.3

parole, barcarole, banderole (long nar-row ship's flag), fumarole (vent in vol-cano), rigmarole, casserole, profiterole.

223.4

rissole, camisole, anisole (colourless fra-grant liquid).

224 -owl

owl, cowl, scowl, foul, fowl, jowl, howl, growl, prowl, yowl, peafowl, befoul, moorfowl, afoul, wildfowl, waterfowl.

225 -ull

cull, scull, skull, dull, gull, Hull, hull, lull, mull, Mull, null, Tull (English agri-culturalist), numbskull, annul, caracul (Persian lamb), Solihull, multihull, dis-annul.

226 -ul [further rhymes may be creat-ed by adding -ful to appropriate nouns]

bull, full, pull, wool.

Kabul (capital of Afghanistan), bulbul (tropical songbird), playful, careful, prayerful, gleeful, earful, cheerful, fear-ful, tearful, eyeful, joyful, rueful, wakeful, tankful, thankful, watchful, dreadful, heedful, needful, handful, mindful, changeful, vengeful, baleful, guileful, bowlful, doleful, soulful, armful, harmful, blameful, shameful, brimful, roomful, manful, skinful, sinful, scornful, mournful, spoonful, tuneful, wrongful, songful, hopeful, helpful, graceful, peaceful, blissful, useful, bashful, wishful, artful, cartful, hurtful, fitful, potful, thoughtful, doubtful, fruitful, tactful, restful, wistful, boastful, faithful, mirthful, wrathful, slothful, mouthful, healthful, stealthful, easeful.

Istanbul, bellyful, merciful, fanciful, pitiful, beautiful, dutiful, plentiful, bountiful, powerful, wonderful, colourful, masterful, flavourful, quiverful, reproachful, regardful, remindful, unmindful, revengeful, thimbleful, needleful, meaningful, worshipful, disgraceful, purposeful, deceitful, pocketful, unfaithful.

226.1
awful, lawful, unlawful.

226.2
woeful, sorrowful.

226.3
skilful, wilful, unskilful.

226.4
baneful, gainful, painful, disdainful.

226.5
stressful, successful.

226.6
forceful, remorseful, resourceful.

226.7
fateful, hateful, plateful, grateful, ungrateful.

226.8
fretful, forgetful, regretful.

226.9
spiteful, rightful, frightful, delightful.

226.10
neglectful, respectful, disrespectful.

226.11
eventful, resentful, uneventful.

226.12
tasteful, wasteful, distasteful.

226.13
lustful, trustful, distrustful.

226.14
ruthful, truthful, toothful (small draught of liquor), youthful, untruthful.

227 -ool
boule (pear-shaped imitation gemstone), Boole (British mathematician), cool, school, fool, ghoul, Goole (English inland port), joule, who'll, pool, Poole, spool, rule, drool, shul (synagogue), tool, stool, yule, you'll, mule, mewl, pule (to whimper), tulle.

babul (type of acacia), Stambul (old part of Istanbul), playschool, deschool, preschool, befool (make a fool of), tomfool, cagoule, Banjul (capital of Gambia), Blackpool, whirlpool, ampoule, cesspool, ferrule (metal cap), ferule (flat cane for punishment), spherule (tiny sphere), misrule, toadstool, faldstool (bishop's backless seat), close-stool, footstool, lobule, globule, tubule, macule, saccule, locule (biology term), floccule (small mass of particles), bascule (type of bridge), schedule, module, nodule, virgule (printing term), cellule, pilule, granule, venule (small vein), papule (small pimple), capsule, noctule (insectivorous bat), pustule, frustule (botany term), ovule, valvule.

supercool, Hartlepool, Pontypool, Liverpool, overrule, vestibule, majuscule, minuscule, gallinule (aquatic bird).

animalcule, hierodule (ancient Greek temple slave).

227.1
spicule (slender pointed structure), ridicule, molecule, fascicule (published instalment of book), graticule (grid), reticule (woman's bag), monticule (small hill).

228 -'l
babble, dabble, gabble, rabble, scrabble, Drabble, grabble (grope about), barbel (European fish), garble, marble, Schnabel (US musician), jebel (hill in Arab country), pebble, rebel, treble, burble, herbal, verbal, feeble, Bible,

libel, tribal, bobble, cobble, gobble, hobble, nobble, squabble, wobble, bauble, corbel, warble, foible, Jubal (biblical character), rouble, bubal (African antelope), tubal, fimble (male hemp plant), nimble, cymbal, symbol, timbal (type of kettledrum), thimble, wimble (hand tool), umbel (type of inflorescence), bumble, scumble (art term), fumble, jumble, humble, mumble, rumble, crumble, grumble, tumble, stumble, faecal, treacle, faucal (anatomy term), snorkel, paucal (linguistics term), ducal, ankle, fankle (*Scot* entangle), rankle, Wankel (German engineer), Gaskell (English writer), pascal (unit of pressure), mascle (heraldic term), rascal, fiscal, hatchel (to comb flax), satchel, Rachel, Mitchell, fardel, hadal (relating to ocean depths), ladle, cradle, heddle (part of loom), medal, meddle, pedal, peddle, treadle, curdle, girdle, hurdle, beadle, needle, wheedle, caudal, dawdle, modal, nodal, yodel, Kendal, Mendel (Austrian botanist), Grendel (legendary man-eating monster), sendel (fine silk fabric), dirndl, fondle, rondel (type of poem), poundal (unit of force), roundel (circular mark or object), bundle, rundle (ladder rung), trundle, baffle, snaffle, raffle, Eiffel, rifle, trifle, stifle, offal, coffle (line of chained slaves), waffle, gargle, burgle, gurgle, ogle, bogle (*Dialect* bogey), mogul, Vogul (member of Siberian people), juggle, smuggle, snuggle, struggle, Mongol, bungle, fungal, jungle, cudgel, angel, dermal, thermal, primal, pommel (part of saddle), pummel, Brummell, carnal, charnel (sepulchral), darnel (type of grass), Chunnel, funnel, gunnel (eel-like fish), gunwale (nautical term), runnel (small stream), tunnel, Bracknell, cracknel, spignel (European plant), signal, hymnal, simnel, grapnel, shrapnel, carpal (wrist bone), carpel (female part of flower), maple, papal, staple, sepal, purple, couple, supple, scruple, cupel (gold-refining vessel), duple, pupil, scalpel, ample, trample, temple, dimple, pimple, crimple (crumple), simple, wimple, rumple, crumple, gospel, rorqual, mayoral, feral (wild), spheral (spherical), squirrel, Cyril, Wirral, gyral (rotating), viral, spiral,

timbrel (tambourine), whimbrel (European curlew), sacral, mandrel (spindle in machine tool), spandrel (architectural term), scoundrel, mongrel, April, petrol, petrel, neutral, spectral, astral, wastrel, cloistral, minstrel, hassle, tassel, vassal, basal, nestle, pestle, wrestle, trestle, Cecil, vessel, Faisal, sisal, dorsal, morsel, plimsoll, cancel, handsel (*Dialect* new year gift), chancel, tinsel, council, counsel, groundsel, Etzel (legendary German king), quetzal (crested bird), pretzel, schnitzel, special, bushel, crucial, nuptial, hurtle, myrtle, turtle, rectal, lintel, pintle (hinge pin), quintal (unit of weight), pastel, coastal, postal, Bethel, lethal, brothel, larval, marvel, navel, naval, serval, hovel, novel, grovel, oval, Lovell, shovel, narwhal (arctic whale), Orwell, lingual, Cromwell, gromwell (flowering plant), Sitwell, Maxwell, Boswell, axle, bezel (surface on cutting tool), easel, diesel, teasel, weasel, chisel, fizzle, mizzle (*Dialect* drizzle), drizzle, frizzle, grizzle, sizzle, swizzle, nozzle, schnozzle (*US* nose), causal, guzzle, muzzle, nuzzle, puzzle, damsel.

enfeeble, ensemble, archducal, Arundel, triumphal, conjugal, Portugal, Tintagel, archangel, caramel, communal, tribunal, autumnal, uncouple, quadruple, octuple, quintuple, septuple, sextuple, catarrhal, deferral, referral, palpebral (relating to the eyelid), cerebral, vertebral, sepulchral, integral, urethral, especial, provincial, palatal, pivotal, betrothal, interval, bilingual, trilingual, sublingual, embezzle, reprisal, devisal (act of devising).

chromosomal, metacarpal, thermocouple, episcopal, Sebastopol (Russian port), equinoctial, multilingual, monolingual.

228.1

bael (Indian tree), Jael (biblical character), Raphael, Ishmael (biblical character), betrayal, portrayal, Israel.

228.2

real, ideal, corneal, surreal, unreal, epigeal (living on soil surface), hypogeal (living below soil surface), pharyngeal, laryngeal, perineal, oesophageal, peritoneal.

228.3

labial (relating to a lip), brachial (relating to the arm), bronchial, radial, prandial, mondial (of the whole world), Belial (demon), cuneal (wedge-shaped), burial, Gabriel, Umbriel (satellite of Uranus), atrial, patrial, uncial (type of capital letter), lacteal (relating to milk), osteal (relating to bone), gavial (Asian crocodile).

proverbial, adverbial, connubial (relating to marriage), Ezekiel, parochial, allodial (former property law term), custodial, postprandial, lymphangial (relating to lymphatic vessel), phalangeal (anatomy term), binomial, trinomial, monomial, biennial, triennial, millennial, perennial, centennial, colloquial, mercurial, industrial, carnassial (type of tooth), popliteal (behind the knee).

myocardial, endocardial, polynomial, entrepreneurial.

228.3.1

medial, predial (relating to land), remedial.

228.3.2

cordial, primordial.

228.3.3

effigial, vestigial, apterygial (zoology term).

228.3.4

filial, familial.

228.3.5

cranial, geranial (chemistry term), intracranial.

228.3.6

genial, menial, venial, congenial.

228.3.7

lineal, pineal, matrilineal, patrilineal.

228.3.8

colonial, baronial, ceremonial, matrimonial, patrimonial, testimonial.

228.3.9

troupial (South American songbird), marsupial.

228.3.10

aerial, Ariel (satellite of Uranus), narial (relating to the nostrils), vicarial, malarial, bursarial, actuarial, estuarial, secretarial, antimalarial.

228.3.11

ferial (relating to weekday), cereal, serial, sidereal, venereal, funereal, imperial, arterial, material, bacterial, ethereal, diphtherial, managerial, immaterial, magisterial, ministerial, monasterial.

228.3.12

oriel, boreal (relating to the north).

arboreal, armorial, marmoreal (relating to marble), memorial, manorial, corporeal, gressorial (adapted for walking), cursorial (adapted for running), fossorial (used for burrowing), scansorial (adapted for climbing), tonsorial, sartorial, tutorial, factorial, pictorial, raptorial (predatory), uxorial.

immemorial, incorporeal, insessorial (adapted for perching), professorial, prefectorial, directorial.

ambassadorial, gladiatorial.

228.3.12.1

editorial, territorial, inquisitorial, extraterritorial.

228.3.12.2

piscatorial (relating to fish), purgatorial, senatorial, equatorial, dictatorial, saltatorial (adapted for jumping), legislatorial, gubernatorial (relating to a governor), subequatorial, conspiratorial, visitatorial (relating to official visitation), accusatorial.

228.3.13

bimestrial (lasting for two months), terrestrial, extraterrestrial.

228.3.14

bestial, celestial.

228.3.15

trivial, quadrivial (having four roads meeting), convivial.

228.3.16

jovial, synovial.

228.3.17
fluvial (relating to a river), pluvial (relating to rain), diluvial (produced by a flood), alluvial.

228.3.18
axial, biaxial, triaxial, coaxial, abaxial (away from the axis), adaxial (facing towards the axis), uniaxial.

228.4
dial, phial, myall (Australian acacia), rial (Iranian currency), trial, sial (part of earth's crust), viol, sundial, denial, espial, retrial, mistrial, self-denial.

228.5
knawel (Eurasian plant), withdrawal.

228.6
loyal, royal, disloyal, pennyroyal (Eurasian plant).

228.7
Noel, bestowal.

228.8
bowel, dowel, Powell, rowel (spiked wheel on spur), trowel, towel, vowel, embowel, avowal, disembowel, semivowel (phonetics term), disavowal.

228.9
menstrual, gradual, Samuel, sensual, casual, visual, usual, virtual, mutual, punctual, textual, sexual.
premenstrual, continual, consensual, unusual, perpetual, accentual (rhythmical), eventual, conventual (relating to a convent), perceptual, conceptual, contextual, asexual, bisexual, transsexual.
pari-mutuel (betting system), unisexual, homosexual.
audiovisual, heterosexual.

228.9.1
residual, individual.

228.9.2
annual, manual, biannual, Emmanuel.

228.9.3
ritual, habitual, spiritual.

228.9.4
actual, factual, tactual (caused by touch), contractual.

228.9.5
effectual, aspectual (linguistics term), ineffectual, intellectual.

228.10
jewel, cruel, crewel, gruel, dual, duel, fuel, newel, bejewel, refuel, renewal.

228.11
Abel, able, Babel, cable, fable, gable, label, sable, table, stable, enable, unable, disable, worktable, timetable, turntable, unstable, disenable.

228.12
kibble, dibble (small garden tool), nibble, quibble, Ribble, scribble, dribble, fribble (fritter away), gribble (small marine animal), Sybil, mandible, cannibal, Hannibal, thurible (container for burning incense), crucible.

228.13
global, noble, ennoble, Grenoble, ignoble.

228.14
bubble, double, nubble (small lump), rubble, trouble, stubble, redouble.

228.15
Hasdrubal (Carthaginian general), soluble, voluble, chasuble, insoluble, resoluble, indissoluble, irresoluble.

228.16 [further rhymes may be created by adding *-able* or *-ible* to appropriate verbs]
playable, payable, probable, peccable (liable to sin), workable, likable, lockable, vocable (vocal sound), bankable, stretchable, touchable, quenchable, readable, affable, laughable, effable, chargeable, legible, changeable, fallible, gullible, tenable, tunable, pregnable, damnable, stoppable, palpable, culpable, equable, arable, parable, sparable (small nail), terrible, horrible, passable, peaceable, possible, forcible, satiable, washable, notable, potable (drinkable), quotable, tractable, printable, constable, Dunstable, lovable, taxable, flexible, feasible, plausible.
unknowable, improbable, implacable, remarkable, impeccable, unspeakable, educable, revocable, detachable, untouchable, degradable, unreadable,

avoidable, refundable, ineffable, illegible, infallible, indelible, redeemable, estimable, conformable, consumable, presumable, fathomable, untenable, amenable, impregnable, unflappable, unstoppable, impalpable, transferable, desirable, adorable, deplorable, execrable, demonstrable, manoeuvrable, irascible, impassable, impossible, reducible, purchasable, expansible, responsible, pronounceable, collapsible, insatiable, compatible, redoubtable, comfortable, vegetable, palatable, retractable, intractable, perfectible, delectable, respectable, expectable, detectable, predictable, unprintable, adaptable, corruptible, attemptable, contemptible, resistible, exhaustible, observable, forgivable, inflexible, erasable, implausible, opposable, disposable.

imperturbable, ineducable, irrevocable, unavoidable, interchangeable, reconcilable, inviolable, irredeemable, inestimable, unfathomable, undesirable, impenetrable, indemonstrable, irreducible, irresponsible, unpronounceable, incompatible, uncomfortable, unpredictable, incorruptible, irresistible, inexhaustible, unforgivable, irresolvable.

biodegradable, irreconcilable.

228.16.1

agreeable, foreseeable, disagreeable, unforeseeable.

228.16.2

malleable, amiable, permeable, expiable, variable, pitiable, dutiable, enviable, impermeable, invariable, unenviable, irremediable, differentiable.

228.16.3

liable, pliable, friable, triable, viable, reliable, deniable, unreliable, undeniable.

228.16.3.1

modifiable, magnifiable, verifiable, classifiable, specifiable, certifiable, notifiable, rectifiable, quantifiable, justifiable, identifiable.

228.16.4

enjoyable, employable, unemployable.

228.16.5

dowable (legal term), allowable.

228.16.6

arguable, valuable, issuable, invaluable.

228.16.7

doable, suable, viewable, renewable.

228.16.8

bribable, describable, indescribable.

228.16.9

breakable, unbreakable, unshakable, mistakable, unmistakable.

228.16.10

medicable, predicable (able to be affirmed), applicable, explicable, amicable, despicable, extricable, practicable, eradicable, inapplicable, inexplicable, communicable, inextricable, impracticable, incommunicable.

228.16.11

drinkable, sinkable, thinkable, undrinkable, unsinkable, unthinkable.

228.16.12

reachable, teachable, impeachable, unteachable, unimpeachable.

228.16.13

approachable, reproachable, irreproachable, unapproachable.

228.16.14

edible, credible, beddable, inedible, incredible.

228.16.15

biddable, formidable.

228.16.16

audible, fordable, laudable, recordable, inaudible, rewardable.

228.16.17

expandable, understandable.

228.16.18

mendable, vendible, unbendable, commendable, dependable, expendable, extendible, recommendable.

228.16.19

litigable, mitigable, navigable, indefatigable, circumnavigable.

228.16.20

knowledgeable, negligible, manageable, marriageable, dirigible, corrigible, salvageable, incorrigible.

228.16.20.1

eligible, ineligible, intelligible, unintelligible.

228.16.21

frangible (breakable), tangible, refrangible (able to be refracted), infrangible, intangible, irrefrangible (inviolable).

228.16.22

bailable, scalable, saleable, sailable, resaleable, available, unassailable, unavailable.

228.16.23

syllable, willable, refillable, monosyllable.

228.16.24

controllable, uncontrollable, inconsolable.

228.16.25

calculable, regulable, inoculable, incalculable.

228.16.26

flammable, inflammable, nonflammable, programmable.

228.16.27

explainable, attainable, obtainable, unexplainable, unattainable, unobtainable.

228.16.28

discernible, returnable, indiscernible, nonreturnable.

228.16.29

terminable, imaginable, determinable, interminable, abominable, unimaginable, indeterminable.

228.16.30

finable (liable to a fine), definable, reclinable, inclinable, indefinable, indeclinable.

228.16.31

questionable, pardonable, personable, fashionable, actionable, conscionable, governable, alienable, unquestionable, impressionable, objectionable, unconscionable, ungovernable, inalienable, companionable.

228.16.31.1

pensionable, unmentionable.

228.16.31.2

reasonable, seasonable, unreasonable, unseasonable.

228.16.32

capable, incapable, inescapable.

228.16.33

bearable, tearable, wearable, unbearable, repairable, untearable, unwearable.

228.16.34

curable, durable, insurable, incurable, endurable.

228.16.35

saturable, preferable, tolerable, colourable, memorable, admirable, generable (able to be generated), venerable, honourable, vulnerable, operable, comparable, answerable, mensurable, alterable, favourable, miserable.

considerable, imponderable, insufferable, intolerable, innumerable, dishonourable, invulnerable, inoperable, insuperable, incomparable, unanswerable, commensurable, immensurable, unutterable, inalterable, unfavourable, inexorable.

inconsiderable, indecipherable, irrecoverable.

228.16.35.1

reparable, separable, irreparable, inseparable.

228.16.35.2

pleasurable, measurable, immeasurable.

228.16.36

traceable, effaceable, replaceable, ineffaceable, irreplaceable.

228.16.37
expressible, accessible, irrepressible, inexpressible, inaccessible.

228.16.38
coercible, submersible, reversible, conversable, incoercible, irreversible.

228.16.39
kissable, miscible, immiscible, omissible, permissible, admissible, noticeable, serviceable, impermissible, inadmissible.

228.16.40
sensible, tensible (able to be stretched), defensible, dispensable, insensible, ostensible, extensible, indefensible, apprehensible, reprehensible, comprehensible, indispensable, incomprehensible.

228.16.41
vincible, invincible, convincible, inconvincible.

228.16.42
depreciable, appreciable, inappreciable.

228.16.43
punishable, perishable, imperishable, distinguishable, extinguishable, indistinguishable, inextinguishable.

228.16.44
sociable, negotiable, dissociable, unsociable.

228.16.45
rateable, debatable, inflatable, untranslatable.

228.16.46
forgettable, regrettable, unforgettable.

228.16.47
convertible, inconvertible, incontrovertible.

228.16.48
eatable, beatable, unbeatable, repeatable.

228.16.49
habitable, dubitable, marketable, creditable, profitable, hospitable, equitable, charitable, heritable, veritable, irritable, indubitable, discreditable, unprofitable,

illimitable, inimitable, indomitable, inhospitable, inequitable, inevitable.

228.16.50
indictable, excitable, extraditable.

228.16.51
portable, supportable, insupportable.

228.16.52
reputable, attributable, irrefutable, disreputable.

228.16.53
suitable, mutable, inscrutable, unsuitable, immutable, commutable, imputable, disputable, incommutable, incomputable, indisputable.

228.16.54
deductible, destructible, ineluctable (inescapable), indestructible.

228.16.55
preventable, presentable, unpreventable, unpresentable.

228.16.56
accountable, surmountable, unaccountable, insurmountable.

228.16.57
merchantable, lamentable, warrantable, unwarrantable.

228.16.58
perceptible, susceptible, acceptable, imperceptible, unacceptable.

228.16.59
suggestible, comestible, digestible, arrestable, detestable, contestable, indigestible, incontestable.

228.16.60
combustible, adjustable, incombustible.

228.16.61
achievable, believable, retrievable, conceivable, unbelievable, irretrievable, inconceivable.

228.16.62
movable, provable, immovable, removable, improvable, irremovable.

228.16.63
risible, visible, divisible, invisible, indivisible.

228.16.64

sizable, devisable, advisable, realizable, recognizable, inadvisable, unrecognizable.

228.16.65

usable, fusible (able to be melted), excusable, infusible, irrecusable (unable to be rejected), inexcusable.

228.17

amble, Campbell, gamble, gambol, ramble, bramble, scramble, shamble, preamble, unscramble.

228.18

Kemble (English acting family), tremble, dissemble, assemble, resemble, disassemble.

228.19

cackle, hackle, mackle (printing term), crackle, grackle (US songbird), shackle, tackle, hamshackle (fetter a horse), ramshackle, tabernacle.

228.20

darkle (grow dark), sparkle, debacle, monarchal.

228.21

deckle, Jekyll, heckle, speckle, freckle, shekel, kenspeckle (*Scot* easily recognized).

228.22

circle, encircle, semicircle.

228.23 [also **38** + *-al*]

chicle (ingredient of chewing-gum), fickle, mickle (*Dialect* much), nickel, pickle, prickle, trickle, sickle, tickle.

vehicle, stoical, cubicle, cubical (relating to volume), radicle (embryonic plant root), radical, magical, biblical, chemical, rhythmical, funicle (botany term), tunicle (Catholic bishop's vestment), technical, apical (at the apex), typical, auricle (heart's upper chamber), curricle (two-wheeled open carriage), metrical, utricle (part of ear), ventricle, fascicle (bundle of branches), classical, farcical, vesical (relating to bladder), vesicle (small cavity), versicle, icicle, bicycle, tricycle, ossicle (small bone in ear), Popsicle (*Trademark*), dropsical, article, particle, vertical, nautical, canti-

cle, sceptical, optical, testicle, ethical, mythical, clavicle, cervical, lexical (relating to vocabulary), musical, whimsical.

veridical (truthful), juridical (relating to law), pontifical, encyclical, inimical, cupronickel, pumpernickel, atypical, cylindrical, theatrical, symmetrical, electrical, nonsensical, elliptical, unmusical.

hierarchical, philosophical, biochemical, aeronautical, dialectical, paradoxical, lackadaisical, ecclesiastical.

228.23.1

medical, pedicle (small plant stalk), premedical, paramedical.

228.23.2

methodical, periodical, immethodical.

228.23.3

graphical, geographical, biographical, typographical, autobiographical.

228.23.4

surgical, liturgical, metallurgical, neurosurgical.

228.23.5 [further rhymes may be derived from **16.108.4**]

logical, illogical, geological, biological, zoological, ecological, psychological, chronological, technological, pathological, mythological.

228.23.6

helical, pellicle (thin surface layer), angelical, evangelical.

228.23.7

silicle (type of fruit), umbilical.

228.23.8

follicle, symbolical, diabolical.

228.23.9

comical, economical, astronomical, gastronomical, anatomical.

228.23.10

panicle (type of inflorescence), sanicle (flowering plant), mechanical, tyrannical, botanical, puritanical.

228.23.11

galenical (pharmacology term), arsenical, ecumenical.

228.23.12
clinical, cynical, rabbinical, dominical (relating to the Lord).

228.23.13
conical, chronicle, canonical, ironical.

228.23.14
tropical, topical, subtropical.

228.23.15
spherical, clerical, chimerical (fanciful), numerical, hysterical, anticlerical.

228.23.16
lyrical, empirical, satirical.

228.23.17
rhetorical, historical, metaphorical, allegorical, categorical, oratorical.

228.23.18
sabbatical, grammatical, fanatical, mathematical, ungrammatical.

228.23.19
reticle (grid in optical instrument), heretical, alphabetical, catechetical (by question and answer), theoretical, antithetical, hypothetical.

228.23.20
critical, political, analytical, apolitical, diacritical, hypocritical, hypercritical.

228.23.21
cuticle, pharmaceutical.

228.23.22
practical, tactical, impractical.

228.23.23
denticle (small tooth), identical, conventicle (secret group of worshippers).

228.23.24
mystical, statistical, egotistical.

228.23.25
physical, quizzical, metaphysical.

228.24
Michael, cycle, recycle, unicycle, motorcycle.

228.25
cockle, grockle, socle (plinth), corncockle (European wayside plant), streptococcal.

228.26
focal, local, vocal, yokel, bifocal, matrilocal (living with wife's family), patrilocal (living with husband's family).

228.27
buckle, chuckle, muckle (*Scot* much), knuckle, truckle, suckle, parbuckle (rope sling), turnbuckle (device for tightening wire), unbuckle, pinochle (card game), honeysuckle.

228.28
tubercle, manacle, barnacle, cenacle (supper room), binnacle (housing for ship's compass), pinnacle, monocle, miracle, spiracle (respiratory aperture), oracle, coracle, spectacle, pentacle (star-shaped figure), tentacle, obstacle, reciprocal, receptacle, conceptacle (botany term), equivocal, unequivocal.

228.28.1
zodiacal, maniacal, ammoniacal, paradisiacal.

228.29
wrinkle, crinkle, sprinkle, tinkle, winkle, twinkle, besprinkle, periwinkle, Rip Van Winkle.

228.30
uncle, nuncle (*Dialect* uncle), carbuncle, peduncle (flower stalk), furuncle (a boil).

228.31
addle, paddle, raddle, straddle, saddle, staddle, skedaddle, unsaddle, packsaddle, fiddle-faddle.

228.32
diddle, fiddle, middle, piddle, riddle, griddle, twiddle, infidel, tarradiddle (nonsense), pyramidal.

228.33 [also **92.7** + *-al*]
idol, idle, Rydal (English village), bridal, bridle, sidle, tidal, unbridle, suicidal, spermicidal, homicidal.

228.34
coddle, doddle, model, noddle, toddle, waddle, swaddle, twaddle, remodel, mollycoddle.

228.35

Goidel (Gaelic-speaking Celt), spheroidal (approximately spherical), adenoidal, sinusoidal (maths term).

228.36

buddle (trough for washing ore), cuddle, fuddle, huddle, muddle, puddle, ruddle (red dye for sheep), befuddle, Tolpuddle.

228.37

boodle, doodle, noodle, poodle, strudel, feudal, caboodle, flapdoodle (*Slang* foolish talk), canoodle.

228.38

apodal (without feet), citadel, hebdomadal, antipodal.

228.39

candle, scandal, dandle (bounce child on knee), Handel, handle, sandal, vandal, manhandle, panhandle, mishandle.

228.40

kindle, spindle, brindle, Tyndale (English Protestant), dwindle, swindle, rekindle, enkindle.

228.41

skiffle, sniffle, piffle, riffle, whiffle (behave unpredictably), apocryphal.

228.42

scuffle, duffel, muffle, snuffle, ruffle, truffle, shuffle, kerfuffle, reshuffle.

228.43

gaggle, haggle, draggle (hang trailing), straggle, waggle, bedraggle, raggle-taggle (unkempt).

228.44

bagel (Jewish ring-shaped roll), Hegel (German philosopher), plagal (musical term), vagal (anatomy term), finagle.

228.45

eagle, beagle, legal, regal, porbeagle, illegal, viceregal, inveigle.

228.46

giggle, jiggle, niggle, squiggle, wriggle, wiggle, prodigal, madrigal.

228.47

boggle, goggle, joggle, toggle, woggle, boondoggle (*US* do futile work), hornswoggle (*Slang* to cheat).

228.48

jugal (relating to the cheekbone), frugal, bugle, fugal, centrifugal.

228.49

angle, bangle, dangle, jangle, mangle, spangle, wrangle, strangle, tangle, wangle, triangle, fandangle (elaborate ornament), galangal (Oriental plant), bespangle, quadrangle, rectangle, entangle, untangle, disentangle.

228.50

ingle, dingle (small wooded dell), jingle, mingle, cringle (nautical term), single, shingle, tingle, swingle (flax-beating instrument), commingle (to mix), Kriss Kringle (*US* Santa Claus), surcingle (horse's girth), intermingle.

228.51

camel, mammal, trammel (hindrance), stammel (coarse red woollen cloth), enamel, entrammel.

228.52

gimmal (part of rotating joint), animal, minimal, lacrimal, optimal, maximal, proximal.

228.52.1

decimal, millesimal, centesimal, duodecimal (relating to number twelve), hexadecimal (number system), Quadragesimal (relating to Lent), infinitesimal.

228.53

formal, normal, informal, abnormal, subnormal, paranormal.

228.54

dismal, abysmal, baptismal, paroxysmal.

228.55

annal, cannel (type of coal), channel, flannel, panel, empanel.

228.56

anal, decanal (relating to a dean).

228.57

kennel, fennel, crenel (indentation in battlement), unkennel.

228.58

colonel, kernel, journal, vernal, diurnal, hibernal, infernal, supernal (celestial), eternal, maternal, paternal, fraternal, nocturnal, internal, external, sempiternal (everlasting).

228.59

penal, renal, venal, adrenal, duodenal.

228.60

ginnel (*Dialect* passageway between buildings), cardinal, ordinal, marginal, virginal, germinal (embryonic), terminal, Quirinal (hill of ancient Rome), sentinel, Juvenal (Roman satirist), inguinal, vaccinal, original, intestinal, aboriginal.

228.60.1

testudinal (relating to tortoises), longitudinal, latitudinal.

228.60.2

paginal (page-for-page), imaginal (relating to an image).

228.60.3

seminal, trigeminal (anatomy term).

228.60.4

liminal (psychology term), criminal, Viminal (hill of ancient Rome), subliminal.

228.60.5

nominal, abdominal, prenominal (placed before a noun), phenomenal, binominal (biology term), pronominal (relating to a pronoun).

228.60.6

vicinal (neighbouring), medicinal.

228.61

final, spinal, rhinal (relating to the nose), vaginal, urinal, doctrinal, semifinal, quarterfinal, isoclinal (sloping in same direction), matutinal (occurring in the morning), cerebrospinal.

228.62

tonal, zonal, hormonal, coronal (anatomy term), atonal.

228.63

regional, coronal (garland for head), arsenal, personal, factional, fractional, fictional, frictional, functional, optional, seasonal, antiphonal, diagonal, octagonal, hexagonal, orthogonal (relating to right angles), impersonal, proportional, instructional, constructional, exceptional, occasional, divisional, provisional, meridional, unexceptional.

228.63.1

bacchanal (drunken celebration), diaconal (relating to a deacon).

228.63.2

national, passional, rational, irrational, multinational, international.

228.63.3

vocational, sensational, recreational, educational, irrigational, congregational, navigational, occupational, inspirational, operational, conversational, gravitational, coeducational, denominational, representational.

228.63.4

professional, confessional, congressional, recessional, processional, unprofessional, semiprofessional.

228.63.5

additional, traditional, conditional, nutritional, transitional, unconditional.

228.63.6

notional, emotional, promotional, devotional.

228.63.7

institutional, constitutional, unconstitutional.

228.63.8

sectional, directional.

228.63.9

intentional, conventional, three-dimensional, two-dimensional, unintentional, unconventional.

228.64

apple, chapel, dapple, grapple, crabapple, Whitechapel, pineapple.

228.65

peepul (Indian tree), people, steeple, unpeople, townspeople.

228.66

fipple (mouthpiece of wind instrument), nipple, ripple, cripple, triple, tipple, stipple, maniple (unit of Roman soldiers), manciple (steward who buys provisions), principle, principal, multiple, municipal, participle.

228.67

Siple (mountain in Antarctica), stipel (small leaflike structure), disciple, archetypal.

228.68

hopple (hobble), popple, topple, estoppel (legal term).

228.69

opal, copal (hard aromatic resin), nopal (red-flowered cactus), Constantinople.

228.70

sample, example.

228.71

equal, sequel, unequal.

228.72

barrel, Carol, carol, carrel (study cubicle in library), apparel.

228.73

coral, laurel, moral, quarrel, sorrel, amoral, immoral, Balmoral.

228.74

aural, oral, choral, goral (small goat antelope), chloral (oily liquid), floral, aboral (away from the mouth), binaural, monaural.

228.75

jural (relating to law), plural, pleural, rural, crural, Ural, mural, neural, epidural, intramural, extramural.

228.76

liberal, pickerel (US freshwater fish), cockerel, mackerel, natural, structural, cultural, scriptural, sculptural, federal, doggerel, humeral, numeral, admiral, general, mineral, funeral, corporal, temporal, nonpareil, visceral, mensural, lateral, literal, littoral, guttural, doctoral, pastoral, several.
illiberal, unnatural, peripheral, bicameral, puerperal, bilateral, trilateral, collateral, postdoctoral, parenteral (medical term), Canaveral, inaugural, behavioural.
supernatural, preternatural, horticultural, unicameral, unilateral, equilateral, quadrilateral, multilateral.

228.76.1

conjectural, architectural.

228.76.2

femoral, ephemeral.

228.76.3

pectoral, electoral.

228.77

tumbrel, adumbral (shadowy).

228.78

dihedral (two-sided), anhedral (aircraft wing's downward inclination), cathedral, polyhedral, rhombohedral, procathedral (church serving as cathedral).

228.79

citral (fragrant plant oil), arbitral (relating to arbitration), diametral (relating to diameter).

228.80

central, ventral, dorsoventral.

228.81

kestrel, orchestral, campestral (relating to fields), ancestral.

228.82

mistral, magistral (pharmacology term), sinistral (relating to left side).

228.83

castle, parcel, tarsal, Newcastle, metatarsal.

228.84

tercel (male falcon or hawk), succursal (subsidiary), rehearsal, demersal (living in deep water), dispersal, reversal, transversal, universal.

228.85

kissel (Russian fruit dessert), missal, bristle, gristle, thistle, whistle, abyssal, dismissal, epistle, cacomistle (cat-like mammal).

228.86

fossil, jostle, throstle, colossal, apostle, hypoglossal (beneath the tongue).

228.87

bustle, hustle, mussel, muscle, Russell, rustle, tussle, corpuscle.

228.88

pencil, stencil, commensal (biology term), utensil.

228.89

consul, tonsil, proconsul.

228.90

martial, marshal, partial, impartial.

228.91

facial, glacial, spatial, racial, abbatial, palatial, preglacial, subglacial, postglacial, multiracial.

228.92

Herschel (English astronomer), tertial (ornithology term), commercial, uncommercial, controversial.

228.93

judicial, official, seneschal (medieval household steward), initial, altricial (ornithology term), prejudicial, beneficial, sacrificial, artificial, unofficial, superficial, interstitial.

228.94

social, precocial (ornithology term), asocial, unsocial, antisocial.

228.95

financial, substantial, insubstantial, circumstantial.

228.96

sciential (knowledgeable), prudential, tangential, sequential, essential, potential, influential, pestilential, exponential, consequential, inessential, nonessential, quintessential, penitential, existential, expediential, experiential, inconsequential.

228.96.1

credential, confidential, evidential, providential, residential, presidential.

228.96.2

torrential, deferential, preferential, differential, inferential, reverential.

228.97

battle, cattle, chattel, rattle, prattle, tattle, Seattle, embattle, tittle-tattle, Quetzalcoatl (Aztec god).

228.98

startle, Nahuatl (American Indian).

228.99

fatal, natal, ratel (burrowing mammal), prenatal, postnatal, perinatal, antenatal.

228.100

kettle, fettle, metal, mettle, nettle, petal, settle, nonmetal, gunmetal, resettle, unsettle, Citlaltépetl (Mexican volcano), Popocatépetl (Mexican volcano).

228.101

betel, beetle, chital (Asian deer), fetal, decretal (papal edict), centripetal.

228.102

it'll, skittle, little, spittle, brittle, tittle, victual, whittle.

orbital, cubital (relating to the forearm), sagittal (resembling an arrow), vegetal (relating to plant life), digital, skeletal, belittle, Doolittle, remittal, committal, genital, Capitol, capital, hospital, lickspittle (servile person), acquittal, marital.

parietal (anatomy term), varietal (relating to biological variety), noncommittal, congenital, bicipital (relating to the biceps), occipital (anatomy term), premarital, extramarital.

228.103

title, vital, requital, recital, subtitle, entitle, disentitle.

228.104

bottle, dottle (tobacco remnant in pipe), glottal, mottle, throttle, wattle, bluebottle, axolotl, Aristotle.

228.105

chortle, mortal, portal, immortal.

228.106
total, teetotal, subtotal, sacerdotal (relating to priests), anecdotal.

228.107
cuttle, scuttle, subtle, shuttle, rebuttal.

228.108
Bootle, footle, rootle, brutal, tootle, Kwakiutl (American Indian).

228.109
cantle (part of saddle), mantle, mantel, Fremantle, dismantle, overmantel (shelf over mantlepiece), consonantal.

228.110
dental, gentle, mental, rental, cental (unit of weight), fragmental, segmental, parental, placental, oriental, transcendental, monumental, departmental, compartmental, continental, developmental, transcontinental, intercontinental.

228.110.1
incidental, accidental, Occidental, coincidental.

228.110.2
regimental, elemental, incremental, detrimental, sentimental, experimental.

228.110.3
fundamental, ornamental, sacramental, instrumental, temperamental.

228.110.4
governmental, environmental.

228.111
quantal (physics term), horizontal, periodontal (around a tooth).

228.112
buntal (straw from palm leaves), frontal, full-frontal, disgruntle, balibuntal (Philippine straw hat), contrapuntal.

228.113
festal (festive), vestal, agrestal (growing as a weed).

228.114
distal (anatomy term), mistal (*Scot* cowshed), pistol, Bristol, crystal, pedestal.

228.115
costal, hostel, Pentecostal, intercostal.

228.116
borstal, Saint Austell.

228.117
cavil, gavel, ravel, gravel, travel, unravel.

228.118
bevel, devil, level, revel, daredevil, bedevil, dishevel.

228.119
evil, shrieval (relating to a sheriff), weevil, coeval (belonging to same age), medieval, upheaval, primeval, retrieval.

228.120
snivel, drivel, frivol (behave frivolously), shrivel, civil, swivel, carnival, Percival, uncivil, festival.

228.121
nival (growing in snow), rival, arrival, aestival (occurring in the summer), revival, survival, adjectival.

228.122
removal, approval, disapproval.

228.123
Daniel, spaniel, Nathaniel.

228.124
basil, Basil, dazzle, frazzle, bedazzle, razzle-dazzle.

228.125
hazel, nasal, phrasal, appraisal.

228.126
kursaal (building at health resort), mangelwurzel (Eurasian beet plant).

228.127
deposal, proposal, disposal, counterproposal.

228.128
ouzel, foozle (bungle golf shot), fusel (poisonous oily liquid), bamboozle, perusal, accusal, refusal.

228.129
housel (medieval name for Eucharist), spousal (marriage ceremony), tousle, espousal, arousal, carousal.

229 -am

am, Cam, cam, damn, dam, gam (school of whales), jam, jamb, ham, lam, lamb, clam, slam, mam, Spam (*Trademark*), ram, cram, scram, dram, gram, pram, tram, sham, wham, swam, yam.

iamb, Siam, pro-am, Edam, goddamn, milldam, quondam (former), Potsdam (German city), Corfam (*Trademark*), doorjamb, mallam (West African Islamic scholar), Balaam (Old Testament character), flimflam (nonsense), Annam (part of Vietnam), dirham (Moroccan currency), Bairam (Muslim festival), programme, engram (psychology term), tangram, Assam, cheongsam (Chinese dress), wigwam, exam.

cofferdam (watertight underwater chamber), Rotterdam, Amsterdam, cryptogam (non-flowering plant), Abraham, oriflamme (scarlet medieval French flag), Surinam, Vietnam, dithyramb, diaphragm, telegram, milligram, epigram, centigram, cablegram, ad nauseam.

229.1

diagram, logogram, hologram, anagram, monogram, chronogram (phrase concealing Roman numerals), phonogram (symbol representing sound), barogram, aerogram, tetragram (four-letter word), hectogram, cryptogram (secret symbol), histogram, hexagram (star-shaped figure), roentgenogram (*US* x-ray), hierogram (sacred symbol), parallelogram, encephalogram, electro-encephalogram.

229.1.1

cardiogram, radiogram, ideogram (symbol representing concept), stereogram, electrocardiogram.

229.1.2

kilogram, oscillogram (oscilloscope record), dactylogram (*US* fingerprint).

230 -arm

arm, balm, calm, charm, farm, harm, malm (greyish limestone), ma'am, smarm, palm, qualm, psalm, Guam (Pacific island).

rearm, embalm, gendarme, Islam, imam, schoolmarm, unarm, napalm, copalm (brown resin), ihram (Muslim pilgrim's white robes), firearm, forearm, disarm.

Notre Dame, underarm, overarm, Omar Khayyam.

230.1

alarm, salaam, Dar es Salaam (capital of Tanzania).

231 -ame

aim, came, dame, fame, game, hame, lame, flame, claim, flame, maim, name, frame, same, shame, tame.

became, defame, endgame, declaim, reclaim, acclaim, proclaim, disclaim, quitclaim (legal term), exclaim, aflame, inflame, surname, rename, forename, nickname, doorframe, selfsame, overcame, counterclaim.

232 -em

em (printer's measure), feme (legal term for woman), gem, hem, phlegm, crème, Shem (Noah's eldest son), stem, them.

phloem, proem (preface), Yquem (French vineyard), modem, condemn, mayhem, ahem, xylem, golem (resurrection in Jewish legend), in rem (legal term), contemn (to scorn).

requiem, per diem, diadem, Bethlehem, meristem (plant tissue), apophthegm, chernozem (black soil).

233 -erm

firm, germ, perm, sperm, squirm, term, therm, worm.

affirm, infirm, confirm, bookworm, hookworm, silkworm, midterm, inchworm, threadworm, woodworm, blindworm, roundworm, pinworm, ringworm, tapeworm, flatworm, earthworm.

pachyderm, periderm (protective plant layer), endoderm (part of embryo), mesoderm (part of embryo), ectoderm (part of embryo), reaffirm, disaffirm, endosperm (seed's nutritive tissue), gymnosperm (cone-bearing plant), zoosperm (spermatozoon), isotherm.

234 -eem

beam, scheme, deem, haem, fleam (blood-letting lancet), gleam, ream, bream, cream, scream, dream, stream, seam, seem, team, teem, steam, theme.

abeam, hornbeam (Eurasian tree), sunbeam, moonbeam, crossbeam, whitebeam (European tree), hakim (Muslim judge), redeem, grapheme (letter), morpheme (grammatical unit), blaspheme, agleam, phoneme (distinguishable speech sound), toneme (linguistics term), harem, Tarim (Chinese river), bireme, spireme (tangled mass of chromosomes), trireme, ice cream, daydream, supreme, airstream, headstream, millstream, mainstream, downstream, slipstream, upstream, extreme, raceme, regime, centime, esteem.

Hasidim (Jewish sect), academe (place of learning), quinquereme, monotreme, self-esteem, disesteem.

235 -im

skim, dim, gym, him, hymn, limb, slim, quim, rim, brim, scrim (strong fabric), Grimm, grim, prim, trim, shim (thin washer), vim, whim, swim.

poem, Sikkim (Indian state), bedim, forelimb, Muslim, paynim, denim, Blenheim, minim, Purim (Jewish holiday), megrim, pilgrim, Leitrim, Antrim, Shittim (Old Testament place), victim, maxim.

Ephraim (Old Testament character), cherubim, seraphim, pseudonym, allonym (assumed name), homonym, synonym, eponym, toponym, acronym, metonym (linguistics term), antonym, Kuskokwim (Alaskan river), interim, Abd-el-Krim (Moroccan chief), verbatim.

seriatim (in a series), literatim (letter for letter).

236 -ime

I'm, chyme (digested food in stomach), chime, dime, lime, climb, clime, slime, mime, rime, rhyme, crime, grime, prime, cyme (type of inflorescence), time, thyme.

Trondheim (Norwegian port), Sondheim (US songwriter), Mannheim (German city), sublime, quicklime, birdlime, begrime, daytime, playtime, foretime (the past), wartime, bedtime, half-time, lifetime, ragtime, full-time, sometime, meantime, noontime,

springtime, longtime, pastime, peacetime, mistime, part-time, enzyme.

paradigm, Anaheim (Californian city), pantomime, maritime, flexitime, summertime, wintertime, overtime, lysozyme (enzyme), coenzyme (biochemical compound).

237 -om

bomb, dom (title of Catholic monks), hom (ancient Persian sacred plant), mom, pom, from, prom, Tom, tom, firebomb, non-com (*short for* noncommissioned officer), sitcom, coulomb, aplomb, pom-pom, therefrom, wherefrom, maelstrom, intercom.

238 -orm

corm, dorm, form, forme (printing equipment), haulm (thatching material), Maugham, norm, shawm (medieval type of oboe), storm, warm, swarm.

re-form, biform, landform, inform, conform, transform, platform, waveform, Cairngorm, lukewarm, snowstorm, sandstorm, windstorm, hailstorm, barnstorm, rainstorm, brainstorm, aswarm.

Cominform (Communist Information Bureau), misinform, thunderstorm.

238.1

deform, reform.

deiform (godlike in form), cubiform, pediform, fungiform, aliform (wingshaped), stelliform, filiform (threadlike), piliform (hairlike), ramiform (branchlike), vermiform, uniform, cuneiform, aeriform (gaseous), variform, cribriform (sievelike), fibriform, dendriform (branching), gasiform, cruciform, falciform (sickle-shaped), unciform (hook-shaped), multiform, dentiform (tooth-shaped), lentiform (lens-shaped), oviform, fusiform (spindle-shaped).

238.2

perform, chloroform, iodoform (crystalline substance), electroform (form by electrolysis), nitrochloroform.

239 -ome

ohm, Om (Hindu sacred syllable), comb, dome, foam, home, loam, gnome, nome (modern Greek province), pome (fruit of apple), Rome, roam, brome (type of grass), chrome, tome.

Beerbohm, backcomb, cockscomb, radome (radar antenna's protective housing), megohm (one million ohms), Stockholm, genome (group of chromosomes), Jerome, prodrome (symptom indicating disease), syndrome, rhizome.

honeycomb, currycomb, astrodome (transparent dome on aircraft), tumblehome (nautical term), metronome, gastronome, polychrome (multicoloured), haemochrome (blood pigment), monochrome, velodrome (cycle-racing arena), cosmodrome (spacecraft launching-site), hippodrome, aerodrome, palindrome, ribosome (part of living cell), chromosome, centrosome (part of living cell), leptosome (slender person), schistosome (blood parasite), microtome (biologist's cutting instrument), dermatome (surgical instrument).

240 -um

bum, come, scum, chum, dumb, gum, hum, glum, plumb, plum, slum, mum, numb, rum, crumb, scrum, drum, strum, thrum, sum, some, tum, thumb, swum.

become, succumb, income, outcome, dumdum, benumb, eardrum, humdrum.

misbecome (be unsuitable for), overcome, Tweedledum, sugarplum, kettledrum.

241 -oom

boom, cwm (valley or hollow), coomb (short valley), doom, whom, loom, bloom, flume, gloom, plume, rheum, room, broom, groom, vroom, tomb, womb, fume, Hume, spume, zoom.

foredoom, heirloom, illume (illuminate), abloom (in flower), broadloom, deplume (deprive of feathers), simoom (desert wind), barroom, playroom, tearoom, storeroom, showroom, darkroom, workroom, stockroom, cloakroom, guardroom, bedroom, headroom, boardroom, wardroom, legroom, bridegroom, saleroom, grillroom, ballroom, greenroom, strongroom, taproom, classroom, houseroom, washroom, mushroom,

stateroom, courtroom, bathroom, boxroom, Khartoum, entomb, enwomb, perfume, legume, inhume (to inter), exhume, volume, assume, subsume, consume, costume, resume, presume.

catacomb, nom de plume, anteroom, elbowroom, hecatomb, disentomb, El Faiyum (Egyptian city).

242 -'m

'em, Graham, Priam, brougham, Newham, sebum, album, plumbum, Rackham, Shechem (ancient Jordanian town), caecum, Ockham (English philosopher), Morecambe, oakum (fibre from unravelled rope), hokum, Malcolm, welcome, dinkum, bunkum, Beecham, stardom, heirdom, Edom, freedom, sedum (fleshy-leaved plant), Sodom, boredom, whoredom, serfdom, sheikdom, dukedom, seldom, earldom, Oldham, condom, kingdom, popedom, princedom, wisdom, begum, Egham, sorghum, Dodgem (*Trademark*), Belgium, Nahum (Old Testament prophet), alum, Harlem, slalom, Salem, Elam (ancient Asian kingdom), coelom (body cavity), column, solemn, problem, emblem, bedlam, hoodlum, peplum (flared ruffle on garment), Moslem, Barnum, Arnhem, Farnham, venom, sphagnum (bog moss), magnum, Clapham, wampum (American Indian shell money), carom (billiards term), marram, durum, Durham, sacrum, buckram, fulcrum, wolfram, pogrom, grogram (coarse fabric), ashram (Hindu religious retreat), antrum (anatomy term), tantrum, threesome, fearsome, tiresome, awesome, dorsum (the back), foursome, noisome, gruesome, twosome, gladsome, handsome, balsam, toilsome, wholesome, fulsome, hansom, ransom, transom, winsome, lonesome, Epsom, gypsum, eightsome, jetsam, lightsome, flotsam, toothsome, lithesome, blithesome, loathsome, Heysham, Qeshm (island in Persian Gulf), Gresham, Evesham, atom, Chatham, bottom, scutum, sputum, rectum, dictum, sanctum, bantam, phantom, quantum, symptom, system, anthem, fathom, ovum, darksome, Wrexham, irksome, buxom, trillium (three-leaved plant),

William, besom, seism (earthquake), bosom.

unwelcome, poppadom, martyrdom, corundum (very hard mineral), Christendom, heathendom, amalgam, stratagem, Brummagem, exemplum, minimum, optimum, maximum, cardamom, Pergamum (ancient Asian city), per annum, arcanum (profound secret), solanum (plant genus), envenom, jejunum, cerebrum, panjandrum, Trivandrum (Indian city), conundrum, pyrethrum, sargassum (floating brown seaweed), omasum (compartment of cow's stomach), cumbersome, venturesome, bothersome, Hilversum, unwholesome, troublesome, meddlesome, cuddlesome, quarrelsome, burdensome, nasturtium, Lewisham, petersham, omentum (anatomy term), lomentum (plant pod), momentum, tomentum (biology term), Chrysostom (Greek patriarch), frolicsome, unbosom.

rehoboam, jeroboam, Eboracum (Roman name for York), crinkumcrankum (twisted object), officialdom, duodenum, jus divinum (divine law), interregnum, hydrargyrum, candelabrum, hippeastrum (South American plant), ecosystem, microcosm, macrocosm.

242.1

geum, Te Deum, lyceum, museum, hypogeum (underground burial vault), propylaeum (portico forming temple entrance), mausoleum, perineum, athenaeum (institution promoting learning), colosseum, peritoneum.

242.2

labium, erbium (element), terbium (element), cambium, ischium, scandium, indium (element), allium (plant genus), gallium (element), pallium (vestment or mantle), thallium (element), Valium (*Trademark*), fermium (element), cadmium, holmium (element), osmium, Samnium (ancient Italian city), atrium, yttrium (element), calcium, Latium (region of Italy), Actium, strontium, lithium, axiom.

ytterbium (element), aerobium (organism requiring oxygen), rhizobium (rod-shaped bacterium), niobium (element),

exordium (beginning of a speech), compendium, sporangium (spore-producing plant organ), nobelium (element), triennium, millennium, quinquennium, quadrennium, decennium, Capernaum, selenium (element), proscenium, ruthenium (element), principium (fundamental principle), marsupium, colloquium, tellurium, anthurium (tropical plant), opprobrium, potassium, sestertium (ancient Roman currency), consortium, Byzantium, promethium (element), Erechtheum (temple on the Acropolis), quadrivium (medieval branch of learning), lixivium (alkaline solution), eluvium (mass of rock particles), alluvium, colluvium (mixture of rock fragments), effluvium, Elysium, symposium.

epicardium, pericardium, endocardium, myocardium, horologium (clock tower), Verulamium, neodymium (element), californium (element), equilibrium, endometrium, corpus luteum (tissue in ovary), periosteum (membrane covering bone), mendelevium (element).

242.2.1

radium, stadium, caladium (cultivated tropical plant), palladium, vanadium (element).

242.2.2

medium, tedium, soredium (reproductive organ of lichens), uredium (spore-producing fungal structure), cypripedium (large-flowered orchid).

242.2.3

idiom, rubidium, ctenidium (mollusc's gill), conidium (fungal spore), gonidium (botany term), iridium, nephridium (tubelike excretory organ), clostridium (rod-shaped bacterium), presidium, ascidium (pitcher-shaped plant part), osmiridium (alloy), post meridiem, hesperidium (citrus fruit), antheridium (plant's male sex organ), miracidium (larva of parasitic fluke), ante meridiem.

242.2.4

odium, podium, rhodium, sodium, allodium (former property law term), plasmodium (biology term), sympodium (botany term), pseudopodium, lycopodium (non-flowering plant).

242.2.5

helium, Sealyham, telium (spore-producing fungal structure), berkelium (element), mycelium (fungal body), epithelium, endothelium, meso-thelium.

242.2.6

Ilium (ancient Troy), ilium (part of hip-bone), ileum (part of small intestine), milium (nodule on skin), cilium, beryl-lium, penicillium.

242.2.7

scholium (marginal note), folium (geo-metrical curve), trifolium (clover-like plant), linoleum, petroleum.

242.2.8

premium, gelsemium (climbing shrub).

242.2.9

chromium, encomium, prostomium (zoology term), ferrochromium (iron–chromium alloy).

242.2.10

cranium, germanium, geranium, urani-um, titanium, Herculaneum (ancient Italian city), pericranium, endo-cranium, actinouranium (isotope of uranium).

242.2.11

minium (red lead), delphinium, tri-clinium (ancient Roman dining room), dominium (property law term), actini-um, gadolinium, aluminium, condo-minium, protactinium (element).

242.2.12

conium (hemlock), zirconium (ele-ment), meconium, euphonium, polonium (element), harmonium, ammonium, plutonium, archegonium (plant's female sex organ), sporogoni-um (spore-bearing plant part), pelargo-nium, pandemonium, positronium (physics term).

242.2.13

opium, europium (element).

242.2.14

barium, herbarium (collection of dried plants), sudarium (cloth for wiping face), caldarium (Roman hot-bath room), solarium, samarium (element), aquarium, terrarium (container for small organisms), sacrarium (church sanctuary), vivarium, rosarium, colum-barium (dovecote), oceanarium, cinerarium (place for cremation ashes), honorarium, planetarium, sanitarium, insectarium, armamentarium (doctor's equipment).

242.2.15

cerium (element), imperium (ancient Roman supreme power), deuterium, bacterium, psalterium (part of cow's stomach), mezereum (fragrant Eurasian shrub), puerperium, elaterium (greenish sediment), ministerium (body of Lutheran ministers), nototherium (extinct marsupial).

242.2.16

Miriam, delirium, collyrium (eye lotion).

242.2.17

corium (deep layer beneath skin), thori-um, ciborium (Christian communion vessel), triforium (part of a church), emporium, sensorium (area of the brain), scriptorium (writing room in monastery), in memoriam, aspersorium (basin containing holy water), auditori-um, sudatorium (Roman steam-bath room), crematorium, fumatorium (air-tight fumigation chamber), sanatorium, moratorium.

242.2.18

tritium (isotope of hydrogen), syn-cytium (zoology term), satellitium (astrology term).

242.2.19

dichasium (type of inflorescence), gym-nasium, polychasium (type of inflores-cence), monochasium (type of inflorescence).

242.2.20

caesium, magnesium, trapezium.

242.3

vacuum, residuum, continuum.

242.4

colchicum (Eurasian plant), modicum, capsicum, triticum (cereal grass), High Wycombe, hypericum (flowering plant), Illyricum (ancient Roman province), viaticum.

242.5

Adam, madam, macadam.

242.6

random, tandem, memorandum, avizandum (Scottish legal term), nil desperandum.

242.7

credendum (Christian article of faith), pudendum, addendum, corrigendum, referendum, definiendum (something to be defined).

242.8

phellem (cork), pelham (horse's bit), vellum, cribellum (spider's spinning organ), labellum (part of orchid flower), post-bellum, flagellum, clitellum (part of earthworm's body), scutellum (shield-shaped structure), cerebellum, antebellum.

242.9

phylum, filum (thread-like anatomical part), hilum (botany term), subphylum, asylum.

242.10

Fulham, speculum, vasculum (botanist's specimen container), osculum (mouth-like aperture), Tusculum (ancient city near Rome), pendulum, frenulum (bristle on insect's wing), tenaculum (surgical instrument), vibraculum (type of polyp), capitulum (biology term), tintinnabulum (small high-pitched bell), acetabulum (cavity in hipbone), infundibulum (funnel-shaped anatomical part).

242.10.1

cubiculum (Roman underground burial chamber), Janiculum (ancient Roman hill), curriculum, reticulum, diverticulum.

242.11

cimbalom (type of dulcimer), Absalom, tantalum (element), Jerusalem.

242.12

chrysanthemum, mesembryanthemum.

242.13

Burnham, sternum, viburnum, laburnum.

242.14

platinum, molybdenum.

242.15

crinum (tropical plant), glucinum (element), antirrhinum, mediastinum (anatomy term).

242.16

galbanum (bitter gum resin), Twickenham, laudanum, labdanum (resinous plant juice), Dagenham, tympanum, Cheltenham, lanthanum (element), olibanum (frankincense), polygonum (plant with jointed stems).

242.17

gingham, Buckingham, Gillingham, Immingham, Sandringham, Altrincham, Walsingham, Nottingham.

242.18

arum, Fareham, Sarum, harum-scarum.

242.19

serum, theorem, disulfiram (a drug), antiserum.

242.20

aurum (gold), forum, jorum (large drinking bowl), quorum, decorum, variorum (containing scholarly annotations), indecorum, Karakoram (mountain system in Kashmir), cockalorum (self-important person), ad valorem (according to value), pons asinorum (geometry theorem), sanctum sanctorum, schola cantorum.

242.21

labarum (Christian banner), marjoram, asarum (dried wild ginger root), Rotherham, Kanchipuram (Indian city), omnium-gatherum (miscellaneous collection).

242.22

plectrum, spectrum, electrum (gold–silver alloy).

242.23

nostrum, rostrum, colostrum.

242.24

jissom, lissom, crissum (ornithology term), alyssum, wearisome, worrisome, fideicommissum (civil law term).

242.25

blossom, possum, opossum, odonto-glossum (tropical orchid).

242.26

stratum, postpartum, erratum, substra-tum, superstratum, desideratum.

242.27

datum, relatum (logic term), ideatum (philosophy term), petrolatum (petro-leum jelly), ultimatum, ageratum (tropical plant), corpus striatum (part of brain).

242.28

pinetum (conifer plantation), acetum (vinegar), Antietam (US battle site), arboretum, equisetum (a plant).

242.29

item, ad infinitum.

242.30

autumn, postmortem.

242.31

notum (entomology term), scrotum, totem, teetotum (spinning top), facto-tum.

242.32

custom, frustum, accustom, disaccus-tom.

242.33

rhythm, logarithm, algorithm.

242.34

chasm, spasm, sarcasm, orgasm, phan-tasm, chiliasm (Christian belief), endoplasm, cytoplasm, protoplasm, ectoplasm, pleonasm (use of superflu-ous words), enthusiasm, iconoclasm.

242.35

ism, chrism (oil used for anointing), chrisom (baptismal robe), prism, schism.

Maoism, cubism, plumbism (lead poi-soning), sadism, Buddhism, nudism, sophism, Sufism (mystical doctrine), Gaullism, holism, bromism (bromine poisoning), Thomism (doctrine of Thomas Aquinas), Jainism, monism (philosophy term), bonism (semi-opti-mistic doctrine), tropism, tsarism, verism (extreme realism), porism (mathematical proposition), tourism, purism, Tantrism (Hindu or Buddhist movement), Graecism, Nazism, fascism, rightism, autism, leftism, baptism, Marxism, sexism.

Dadaism, Bahaism (religious system), fideism (trust placed in faith), Judaism, Hebraism, Mithraism (ancient Persian religion), prosaism (prosaic style), Lamaism (form of Buddhism), Lamarckism, catechism, iodism (iodine poisoning), monadism (philosophical doctrine), faradism (medical use of elec-tricity), Methodism, pacifism, imagism (poetic movement), cataclysm, alarmism, extremism, euphemism, Muslimism, animism (primitive belief), pessimism, optimism, totemism, cocainism, communism, escapism, pri-apism, sinapism, vampirism, helichry-sum (flowering plant), pentaprism (five-sided prism), erythrism (abnormal red coloration), ostracism, exorcism, solipsism (philosophy term), English-ism, Irishism, fetishism, Britishism, defeatism, elitism, occultism, gigan-tism, erethism (high degree of sensitivi-ty), atavism (recurrence of primitive characteristics), paroxysm, Spinozism.

diastrophism (movement of earth's crust), catastrophism (geological theo-ry), parallelism, alcoholism, nicotinism, opportunism, malapropism, ventrilo-quism, egocentrism, ethnocentrism (belief in race's superiority).

hypothyroidism, hyperthyroidism, Eurocommunism.

242.35.1

deism, Shiism (Islamic belief), theism, misoneism (hatred of anything new), absenteeism.

242.35.2

archaism, Trotskyism, cockneyism, atheism, ditheism (belief in two gods), tritheism (belief in the Trinity), pantheism, McCarthyism, polytheism, monotheism.

242.35.3

Taoism (Chinese philosophy), echoism (linguistics term), locoism (disease of cattle), egoism, jingoism, heroism, dichroism (crystallography term), Titoism, xanthochroism (skin condition in goldfish).

242.35.4

truism, Hinduism, altruism, euphuism (Elizabethan prose style).

242.35.5

abysm, syllabism (system of writing).

242.35.6

anarchism, monarchism, masochism, sadomasochism.

242.35.7

Orphism (ancient Greek religion), dwarfism, polymorphism (existence of different forms), isomorphism (similarity of form), allomorphism (variation in crystalline form), metamorphism, anthropomorphism.

242.35.8

syllogism, synergism (medical term), geophagism (practice of eating earth), dialogism (philosophy term), paralogism (invalid argument), neologism, psychologism (belief in psychology).

242.35.9

nihilism, pugilism, virilism (medical term), pointillism, immobilism (reactionary political policy), probabilism (philosophical doctrine), zoophilism (emotional attachment to animals), necrophilism (desire to be dead), evangelism, puerilism (immature behaviour by adult), infantilism, mercantilism (economic theory).

242.35.10

formulism (adherence to formulas), botulism, somnambulism.

242.35.11

loyalism, royalism, dualism, verbalism, tribalism, embolism, symbolism, localism, vocalism (exercise of the voice), feudalism, vandalism, legalism (strict adherence to law), mongolism, formalism, finalism (philosophical doctrine), moralism, pluralism, neutralism, centralism, racialism, specialism, socialism, fatalism, vitalism (philosophical doctrine).

diabolism (devil worship), anabolism (metabolic process), metabolism, catabolism (metabolic process), cannibalism, radicalism, syndicalism (workers' revolutionary movement), clericalism (power of the clergy), classicalism (architectural style), animalism (preoccupation with physical matters), liberalism, structuralism, literalism, naturalism, commercialism, provincialism, capitalism, medievalism, revivalism.

phenomenalism (philosophy term), universalism (universal characteristic), existentialism, sacerdotalism (principles of the priesthood).

242.35.11.1

realism, idealism, surrealism.

242.35.11.2

colonialism, colloquialism, mercurialism (mercury poisoning), industrialism, territorialism.

242.35.11.2.1

serialism, imperialism, materialism, immaterialism (philosophy term).

242.35.11.3

gradualism (seeking change gradually), sensualism, ritualism, textualism (adherence to text), spiritualism, conceptualism (philosophy term), transsexualism, intellectualism, individualism.

242.35.11.4

journalism, paternalism, externalism (philosophical doctrine).

242.35.11.5

regionalism, personalism (idiosyncrasy), functionalism, professionalism, traditionalism, emotionalism, conventionalism, institutionalism, constitutionalism.

242.35.11.5.1

nationalism, rationalism, internationalism.

242.35.11.5.2
sensationalism, Congregationalism, denominationalism, representationalism (philosophy term).

242.35.11.6
mentalism (philosophy term), Orientalism, transcendentalism, sentimentalism, fundamentalism, instrumentalism (philosophy term), departmentalism (division into departments), experimentalism, environmentalism.

242.35.12
reformism, transformism (theory of evolution), nonconformism.

242.35.13
rabbinism (teachings of rabbis), albinism, morphinism, Stalinism, Hellenism, feminism, Leninism, strychninism, alpinism, foreignism, Latinism, cretinism, chauvinism, Calvinism, Darwinism, determinism, illuminism (belief in special enlightenment), ultramontanism (Roman Catholic doctrine), hyperinsulinism.

242.35.14
eonism (psychiatry term), pianism (piano-playing skill), Zionism, mechanism, tokenism (doing the minimum necessary), hedonism, modernism, paganism, organism, melanism, shamanism (Asian religion), Brahmanism, Germanism, demonism (worship of demons), Mormonism, Romanism (Roman Catholicism), humanism, pelmanism (card game), onanism, synchronism (simultaneous occurrence), Jansenism, saturnism (lead poisoning), Platonism, Satanism, Teutonism, daltonism, westernism, galvanism, unionism.

antagonism, hooliganism, anachronism, asynchronism (occurrence at different times), immersionism (Christian doctrine), traducianism (theology term), Confucianism, abstractionism (theory of abstract art), perfectionism, protectionism, expansionism, revisionism, illusionism, charlatanism, Italianism, nonunionism.

servomechanism, Mohammedanism, microorganism, exhibitionism.

242.35.14.1
Fabianism, lesbianism, Canadianism, Pelagianism (heretical Christian doctrine), Australianism, Nestorianism (theological doctrine), presbyterianism, Zoroastrianism.

242.35.14.1.1
Arianism (heretical doctrine), Tractarianism, millenarianism (Christian belief), vegetarianism, unitarianism, utilitarianism, humanitarianism, parliamentarianism.

242.35.14.2
Gallicanism (French Catholic movement), Anglicanism, Africanism, Vaticanism, republicanism, Americanism.

242.35.14.3
creationism (theological belief), inflationism, isolationism, restorationism (theological belief), presentationism (philosophy term), associationism (psychology term).

242.35.14.4
impressionism, expressionism, post-impressionism, neoimpressionism.

242.35.15
barbarism, labourism, Quakerism, naturism, futurism, aphorism, rigorism (strictness in judgment), algorism (decimal system of counting), vulgarism, plagiarism, bowdlerism, Hitlerism, mesmerism, mannerism, spoonerism, terrorism, asterism (printing symbol), Lutherism, aneurysm.

anachorism (geographical misplacement), hypocorism (pet name), adventurism, metamerism (animal's division into segments), euhemerism (historical interpretation of myths), consumerism, militarism, behaviourism.

242.35.16
stoicism, Anglicism, cynicism, classicism, narcissism, Briticism, criticism, witticism, vorticism (English art movement), scepticism, mysticism, Gnosticism, Gothicism, Hispanicism (word borrowed from Spanish), Hibernicism (Irishism), historicism (theory of history), athleticism, asceti-

cism, aestheticism, romanticism, agnosticism, academicism (conventionalism), neoclassicism.

242.35.16.1

phallicism (worship of phallus), Gallicism (word borrowed from French), Italicism.

242.35.16.2

solecism, Catholicism.

242.35.16.3

lyricism, empiricism.

242.35.16.4

Atticism (simple clear expression), fanaticism, dichromaticism (crystallography term).

242.35.16.5

Scotticism, eroticism, neuroticism.

242.35.16.6

scholasticism, monasticism, ecclesiasticism.

242.35.17

Chartism (English reform movement), Bonapartism.

242.35.18

magnetism, syncretism (tendency to combine beliefs), Docetism (early Christian heresy), sovietism, Jesuitism, fortuitism (philosophy term), favouritism, anti-Semitism, geomagnetism, ferromagnetism, electromagnetism.

242.35.19

mutism, absolutism.

242.35.20

quietism (form of mysticism), narcotism, ergotism, egotism, helotism (sociopolitical system), prelatism (Church government by prelates), schematism (general arrangement), traumatism, rheumatism, pragmatism, stigmatism, dogmatism, hypnotism, nepotism, despotism, teratism (malformed fetus), patriotism, suprematism, animatism, systematism (practice of classifying), automatism, astigmatism, separatism, conservatism.

242.35.21

scientism, tarantism (nervous disorder), immanentism (belief in God's omnipresence), Protestantism, indifferentism (indifference to religion).

242.35.22

passivism, nativism (protection of native cultures), activism, recidivism, primitivism, positivism, negativism, relativism, objectivism, subjectivism, collectivism, constructivism (abstract art movement).

243 -elm

elm, helm, realm, Wilhelm, unhelm (remove the helmet of), Anselm, overwhelm.

244 -ilm

film, microfilm.

245 -an [some *-man* words in **261** may be pronounced to rhyme with this group]

Anne, an, ban, can, Cannes, scan, dan, Dan, fan, gan (*Dialect* to go), Han (Chinese dynasty), clan, flan, plan, man, nan, pan, Pan, span, ran, bran, tan, than, van.

cyan (greenish-blue colour), Cheyenne, yuan (Chinese currency), pecan, oilcan, cancan, Houdan (breed of domestic fowl), randan (rowing boat), began, Afghan, yulan (Chinese magnolia), unman, outman, Hainan (Chinese island), Tainan (Chinese city), honan (silk fabric), Hunan (Chinese province), tarpan (extinct wild horse), claypan (subsurface clay layer), kneepan (kneecap), Saipan (Pacific island), taipan (venomous snake), Chopin, bedpan, deadpan, skidpan, jampan (sedan chair), sampan, brainpan (skull), wingspan, dustpan, FORTRAN, outran, Pusan (South Korean port), Bashan (biblical region), Anshan (Chinese city), Nan Shan (Chinese mountain range), rattan, kaftan, suntan, divan, Lausanne, Kazan (Russian city).

Caliban, billycan, astrakhan, turbofan, Kordofan (Sudanese province), tryptophan (amino acid), Callaghan, Catalan, Ku Klux Klan, overman, spick-and-span, also-ran, constantan (copper–

nickel alloy), mercaptan (chemical compound), caravan.

245.1

redan (type of fortification), sedan, shandrydan (two-wheeled cart).

245.2

Milan, gamelan (East Indian percussion orchestra), Acrilan (*Trademark*).

245.3

trepan (surgical instrument), marzipan.

245.4

Japan, tragopan (Asian pheasant), Belmopan (capital of Belize), Matapan (promontory in southern Greece).

245.5

Oran, saran (resin), Teleran (*Trademark* navigational aid), trimaran, overran, catamaran.

245.6

soutane (Catholic priest's cassock), orang-utan.

245.7

tisane, Parmesan, artisan, partisan, courtesan, bipartisan, nonpartisan.

246 -arn

Arne (English composer), barn, khan, darn, Han (Chinese imperial dynasty), Marne (French river), San (language group), Shan (Mongoloid people), tarn, Van (Turkish city), guan (South American bird), yarn.

barchan (sand dune), lucarne (dormer window), machan (tiger-hunting platform), maidan (Indian open meeting place), Sudan, goldarn, Tzigane, Oman, Amman, Teheran, Iran, Koran, buran (Asian blizzard), Tourane (Vietnamese port), Cwmbran, Khotan (Chinese oasis), Wotan (Germanic god), Bhutan (central Asian kingdom), Sevan (Russian lake), pavane, dewan (Indian minister of state), Taiwan, Jawan (Indian soldier), Szechwan (Chinese province), San Juan, Aswan, Dayan, kalian (Oriental pipe), azan (Islamic call to prayer), Fezzan (region of Libya).

Vientiane, autobahn, Kublai Khan, Aga Khan, Genghis Khan, Abadan (Iranian port), Ramadan, Lindisfarne, Abidjan

(capital of Ivory Coast), Omdurman (Sudanese city), Suleiman (sultan of Ottoman empire), Hanuman (monkey), Alcoran (Koran), Yucatán (Mexican state), Hindustan, Bantustan, macedoine, Azerbaijan (region of Iran).

246.1

Pakistan, Turkestan (region of Asia), Kurdistan (Asian plateau), Nuristan (region of Afghanistan), Baluchistan (region of Asia), Afghanistan.

247 -ane

ain (*Scot* own), bane, Cain, cane, skein, chain, Dane, deign, feign, fain, gain, Jane, lain, lane, blain (blister or sore), plain, plane, slain, Maine, mane, main, pane, pain, Spain, rein, reign, rain, brain, crane, drain, grain, sprain, train, strain, sane, Seine, tain (tinfoil mirror-backing), stain, thane, vein, vain, vane, Wayne, wane, wain, swain, twain, Twain.

cowbane (marsh plant), urbane, flea-bane (daisy-like plant), wolfbane (poisonous plant), bugbane (insect-repelling plant), henbane (poisonous plant), ratsbane (rat poison), arcane, Cockaigne (medieval imaginary land), procaine, alkane (chemical compound), cinquain (five-line poem), enchain, unchain, ordain, mundane, disdain, Sinn Fein, regain, Elaine, poleyn (armour protecting knee), chilblain, Maclean, airplane, terreplein (top of rampart), skiplane, deplane (disembark from aircraft), seaplane, biplane, triplane, warplane, sailplane (high-performance glider), tailplane (aerofoil at aircraft's tail), emplane (board an aircraft), complain, explain, germane, pearmain, demesne, remain, romaine (*US* cos lettuce), ptomaine (chemical compound), chow mein, humane, mortmain (legal term), propane, Bahrain, terrain, Lorraine, moraine, borane (chemical compound), forebrain, crackbrain (insane person), midbrain, endbrain, hindbrain, membrane, Ukraine, refrain, migraine, Igraine (King Arthur's mother), grosgrain (heavy ribbed fabric), ingrain, vicereine (viceroy's wife), detrain (disembark from train), quatrain, entrain (board a train), distrain, restrain, eyestrain, constrain, Hussein, insane, butane, obtain, octane, Beltane (ancient Celtic festival), maintain, contain, sustain, abstain, bloodstain, ethane, methane, vervain (flowering plant), sixain (six-line poem), fusain (fine charcoal pencil).

Tubal-cain (biblical character), preordain, foreordain, transmundane (beyond this world), peneplain (flattish land surface), multiplane (multi-winged aircraft), hydroplane (motorboat), aquaplane, aeroplane, gyroplane (self-propelled aircraft), inhumane, frangipane (almond-flavoured pastry), windowpane, counterpane, scatterbrain, featherbrain, Pontchartrain (US lake), halothane (chemical compound), paravane (device on minesweeper).

demimondaine, polyurethane.

247.1
chicane, hurricane.

247.2
cocaine, lignocaine (local anaesthetic), marocain (ribbed crepe fabric), Novocaine (*Trademark*).

247.3
profane, hydrophane (variety of opal), allophane (mineral), cellophane.

247.4
delaine (wool fabric), Kwajalein (Pacific atoll), Tamerlane (Mongol conqueror), chatelaine (mistress of castle).

247.5
domain, Charlemagne, legerdemain, El Alamein.

247.6
inane, Dunsinane (Scottish hill), catenane (chemistry term).

247.7
campaign, champagne, elecampane (flowering plant).

247.8
arraign, serein (fine tropical rain), souterrain (underground chamber), suzerain (feudal overlord).

247.9
detain, retain, Aquitaine.

247.10
attain, pertain, appertain, chevrotain (Asian mammal), ascertain, entertain.

247.11
Fonteyn, montane, Bloemfontein (South African city), tramontane (across the mountains), submontane (on lower mountain slopes), ultramontane (beyond the mountains).

248 -en
en (printer's measure), Ben, ben, Ken, ken, den, fen, gen, hen, Len, glen, men, Penn, pen, wren, Bren, ten, Sten, then, when, wen (cyst on scalp), yen, Zen.

cayenne, doyenne, Chechen (Russian people), Ardennes, again, greyhen (female black grouse), moorhen, amen, semen, hymen, limen (psychology term), vimen (flexible plant shoot), nomen (ancient Roman's clan name), dolmen, playpen, Guienne (former French province), Fukien (Chinese province).

Ogaden (region of Ethiopia), tappithen, madrilène (tomato-flavoured consommé), regimen, praenomen (ancient Roman's first name), agnomen (ancient Roman's fourth name), cognomen (ancient Roman's family name), acumen, samisen (Japanese stringed instrument), Sun Yat-sen (Chinese statesman), Debrecen (Hungarian city), Longyearbyen (Norwegian island village), Sinhailien (Chinese city).

248.1
julienne (cookery term), tragedienne, comedienne, Tyrolienne (Tyrolean peasant dance), equestrienne, Valenciennes (fine lace).

248.2
flamen (Roman priest), stamen, velamen (enveloping membrane of root), foramen (hole in a bone), duramen (woody tissue), putamen (fruit stone), gravamen (legal term).

248.3
rumen, numen (ancient Roman deity), cerumen (earwax), hegumen (Eastern Church monastic leader), catechumen (convert receiving pre-baptismal

instruction), energumen (possessed person).

249 -ern

urn, earn, erne (eagle), Bern, burn, kern (printing term), churn, fern, hern (*Dialect* heron), learn, spurn, quern (stone hand mill), tern, turn, stern, Verne, yearn.

Tyburn, Blackburn, windburn, Swinburne, sunburn, Hepburn, heartburn, sojourn, adjourn, unlearn, inurn, epergne (dinner-table ornament), discern, lucerne, Lucerne, concern, Saturn, Sauternes, nocturne, intern, upturn, astern, extern, casern (soldier's billet).

Bannockburn, unconcern, overturn, Comintern (international Communist organization).

249.1

gittern (guitar-like instrument), return, cittern (medieval stringed instrument), taciturn.

250 -airn

bairn, cairn, Nairn (Scottish Highland region), Pitcairn (Pacific island), moderne (architectural style), Auvergne (region of France).

251 -een

been, bean, keen, skean (double-edged dagger), dene (narrow wooded valley), dean, gean (sweet cherry), Jean, gene, lean, clean, glean, spleen, mean, mien, peen (part of hammer), queen, screen, green, preen, treen (wooden), seen, scene, sheen, teen, wean.

shebeen (illegal drinking place), buckbean (marsh plant), Azbine (region of Sahara desert), has-been, takin (large goatlike mammal), achene (one-seeded fruit), Tolkien, nankeen, sardine, sourdine (organ stop), codeine, dudeen (clay pipe), undine (female water spirit), caffeine, trephine (surgical instrument), dauphine (French princess), morphine, beguine (South American dance), hygiene, phosgene (colourless poisonous gas), praline, phthalein (chemical compound), scalene, valine (amino acid), Hellene (a Greek), colleen, choline (biochemical compound), proline (amino acid), unclean, Crimplene (*Trademark*), Kathleen,

Amin, ammine (chemical compound), gamine (slim boyish girl), demean, bromine (dark red liquid), Benin (African republic), quinine, strychnine, terpene (chemical compound), spalpeen (*Irish* rascal), McQueen, terrine, serene, dourine (infectious disease of horses), fluorine, purine (crystalline compound), windscreen, shagreen (sharkskin), gangrene, vitrine (glass display-case), latrine, fascine (bundle of long sticks), glassine (translucent bookcovering), arsine (colourless poisonous gas), narceine (chemical compound), Essene (member of Jewish sect), foreseen, obscene, unseen, dasheen (Asian plant), ratine (loosely-woven cloth), sateen (glossy fabric resembling satin), eighteen, thirteen, poteen (*Irish* illicit whiskey), fourteen, protein, routine, fifteen, canteen, dentine, pentene (colourless liquid), nineteen, tontine (annuity scheme), umpteen, Christine, pristine, cystine (amino acid), Sistine, sixteen, Slovene, subvene, convene, between, vaccine, cuisine, benzene.

Hallowe'en, toluene (colourless liquid), jellybean, terebene (chemical compound), palanquin (Oriental covered litter), Balanchine (US choreographer), pethidine, brigandine (medieval coat of mail), Josephine, carrageen (edible red seaweed), indigene (native person or organism), epigene (formed at earth's surface), hypogene (formed beneath earth's surface), philhellene (lover of Greece), bellarmine (large earthenware jar), mavourneen (Irish term of endearment), cyanine (blue dye), mezzanine, reserpine (medicinal plant extract), Philippine, atropine, Hippocrene (poetic inspiration), multiscreen, wintergreen, evergreen, unforeseen, aubergine, subroutine, velveteen, barquentine (sailing ship), brigantine (sailing ship), Argentine, galantine, clementine, quarantine, seventeen, brilliantine, mangosteen (East Indian tree), polythene, olivine (mineral), gobetween, bombazine, magazine, limousine.

piperidine (colourless liquid), tetracycline (antibiotic), physostigmine (medicinal alkaloid), nitrobenzene (chemical compound).

251.1

gradine (step or ledge), iodine, Aberdeen, gaberdine, Engadine (Swiss tourist centre), grenadine.

251.2

Terylene (*Trademark*), Vaseline (*Trademark*), ethylene, methylene, acetylene, polypropylene, oxyacetylene, polytetrafluoroethylene.

251.3

baleen (whalebone), malines (silk net fabric), Abilene (Texan city), percaline (light cotton fabric), mescaline (hallucinogenic drug), Magdalene, tourmaline (mineral), trampoline, citrulline (amino acid), gasoline, naphthalene.

251.4

rhodamine (red dye), melamine, prolamine (plant protein), Dramamine (*Trademark*), protamine (protein), glutamine (amino acid), catecholamine (biochemical compound).

251.5

pyrene (chemical compound), styrene (colourless liquid), polystyrene.

251.6

chlorine, Maureen, taurine (chemical compound), helleborine (type of orchid).

251.7

careen (sway), marine, tureen, tambourine, saccharine, sapphirine (rare blue mineral), gregarine (microscopic parasitic animal), figurine, margarine, algerine (striped woollen cloth), tangerine, pelerine (woman's narrow cape), submarine, curarine (muscle relaxant), wolverine (large mammal), Nazarene, aquamarine, ultramarine, nitroglycerine.

251.8

colchicine (medicinal alkaloid), epicene (having bisexual characteristics), Plasticine (*Trademark*), australopithecine.

251.9

Pliocene, Miocene, Eocene, Neocene, Holocene, damascene, ferrocene (crystalline compound), kerosene, tyrosine (amino acid), nigrosine (black pigment), Pleistocene, Oligocene, Palaeocene, adenosine (biochemical compound).

251.10

machine, crepe de Chine.

251.11

lateen (having a triangular sail), creatine (compound found in muscles), libertine, nicotine, tricotine (woollen fabric), gelatine, guillotine, carotene, astatine (chemical element).

251.12

ravine, supervene, margravine, landgravine, contravene, intervene.

252 -in

in, inn, bin, kin, skin, chin, din, fin, Finn, gin, Lynn, Min (Chinese dialect), pin, spin, quin, grin, sin, shin, tin, thin, win, whin (gorse), Gwyn, twin.

ruin, bruin, cabin, sabin (physics unit), Harbin (Chinese city), bobbin, dobbin, robin, dubbin, nubbin (*US* undeveloped fruit), Reuben, dustbin, firkin, gherkin, jerkin, merkin (pubic wig), Pekin, Wrekin, bodkin, lambkin, napkin, pipkin (small cooking pot), limpkin (wading bird), bumpkin, pumpkin, bearskin, deerskin, griskin (cut of pork), siskin (Eurasian finch), foreskin, doeskin, buskin (type of boot), Ruskin, redskin, kidskin, calfskin, scarfskin (outermost skin layer), pigskin, sealskin, oilskin, moleskin, wineskin, sheepskin, goatskin, Pushkin, catkin, sharkskin, snakeskin, buckskin, urchin, kitchen, Odin (Norse god), biffin (red cooking apple), griffin, tiffin, boffin, coffin, dauphin, bowfin (US fish), redfin (small fish), threadfin (tropical fish), dolphin, bargain, begin, biggin (close-fitting cap), piggin (small wooden bucket), noggin, Elgin, margin, virgin, engine, carline (Eurasian plant), marlin (tropical fish), Stalin, Berlin, merlin (small falcon), Merlin, purlin (horizontal roof beam), mullein (Mediterranean plant), Boleyn, goblin, Dublin, Brooklyn, franklin, maudlin, Kremlin, gremlin, drumlin, dunlin, Chaplin, chaplain, Joplin, poplin, purslane (trailing weed), porcelain, javelin, ravelin (type of fortification), Evelyn, muslin, King's Lynn, Brahmin, cumin, lumen, admin, Bodmin, jasmine, plasmin (enzyme), tannin, renin (enzyme), Turpin, hairpin, pippin, tiepin, lupin, crankpin, linchpin, tenpin, unpin, kingpin, Crispin, tailspin, topspin, hatpin, backspin, Tarquin, sequin, therein, wherein, Erin, herein, stearin, Turin, urine, burin (a chisel), murrain, chagrin, doctrine, brethren, sovereign, pepsin, Latin, matin, satin, martin, Martin, marten, cretin, chitin, actin (protein), pectin, plantain, fountain, mountain, Austin, within, Swithin, spavin (growth on horse's hock), savin (juniper bush), Irvine, Calvin, Kelvin (British physicist), Darwin, Edwin, Godwin, Goodwin, Baldwin, anguine (resembling a snake), sanguine, penguin, Colwyn, Gershwin, fuchsin (red dye), seisin (legal term), rosin.

casein (protein), xanthein (plant pigment), Bedouin, genuine, Menuhin, Scriabin (Russian composer), Jacobin, cannabin (cannabis resin), grimalkin (old female cat), Potemkin (Russian statesman), Algonquin (American Indian people), onionskin, capuchin, Aladdin, Dunedin, gliadin (protein), muscadine (US grape plant), paladin (peer of Charlemagne's court), Saladin, Borodin, paraffin, Godolphin (English statesman), imagine, tarpaulin, hobgoblin, Dunfermline, discipline, Ho Chi Minh, albumen, bitumen, illumine, legumen (protein), Vietminh, melanin, underpin, terrapin, harlequin, porphyrin (pigment), aspirin, ephedrine (medicinal alkaloid), Sanhedrin, Benzedrine (*Trademark*), peregrine, Lohengrin, alpestrine, assassin, myosin (protein), niacin, eosin (red dye), moccasin, characin (freshwater fish), Wisconsin, hoatzin (South American bird), freemartin (female twin calf), biotin (vitamin), gelatin, haematin (dark pigment), keratin (protein), nystatin (antibiotic), travertine (porous rock), lecithin (biochemical compound), thick-and-thin, Angevin (inhabitant of Anjou), alevin (young salmon or trout).

haemoglobin, bilirubin (bile pigment), Rumpelstiltskin, biliverdin (bile pig-

ment), prostaglandin (hormone-like compound), digitalin (poisonous chemical compound), tatty-peelin (*Scot* pretentious), indiscipline, bacitracin (antibiotic), Taliesin (Welsh bard), vasopressin (hormone), oxytocin (hormone), acriflavine (brownish antiseptic powder), riboflavin (vitamin).

252.1
Owen, heroin, heroine, Halesowen (English town), benzoin (gum resin), hydantoin (crystalline substance).

252.2
Larkin, parkin, Suakin (Sudanese port).

252.3
chicken, spillikin, ramekin, cannikin (small can), mannequin (fashion model), manikin (dwarf), pannikin (*Dialect* small cup), henequen (plant yielding rope fibre), larrikin (*Austral* hooligan), lambrequin (ornamental hanging).

252.4
akin, baldachin (silk and gold brocade), manakin (South American bird), dunnakin (*Dialect* lavatory), catechin (chemical compound).

252.5
muffin, puffin, ragamuffin.

252.6
pidgin, origin.

252.7
Helen, Welwyn, Llewellyn, vitellin (protein), Helvellyn, gibberellin (plant hormone).

252.8
myelin, Kerguelen (archipelago in Indian Ocean), aniline (oily liquid), vanillin (crystalline substance), Enniskillen (Northern Irish town), penicillin.

252.9
bowline, francolin (partridge), pangolin (scaly anteater).

252.10
globulin, masculine, insulin, botulin, tuberculin, folliculin (hormone), immunoglobulin.

252.11

kaolin, hyaline (clear and translucent), ptyalin (enzyme), violin, Gobelin, chamberlain, madeleine, magdalen (reformed prostitute), mandolin, formalin (preservative for biological specimens), lanolin (fatty extract from wool), crinoline, capelin (marine fish), zeppelin, encephalin (chemical in the brain), adrenaline, noradrenaline (hormone).

252.12

famine, gamin (street urchin), examine, re-examine.

252.13

ermine, vermin, determine, predetermine.

252.14

women, specimen, maximin (maths term).

252.15

thiamine, Benjamin, jessamine (jasmine), vitamin, histamine, arsphenamine (drug containing arsenic), amphetamine, provitamin (precursor of vitamin), antihistamine.

252.16

Lenin, rennin, venin (poisonous part of venom), antivenin.

252.17

linen, feminine, agglutinin (antibody).

252.18

foreign, florin, Ilorin (Nigerian city).

252.19

tambourin (Provençal folk dance), purpurin (crystalline substance), aventurine (dark metal-flecked glass).

252.20

suberin (waxy plant substance), saccharin, muscarine (poisonous chemical compound), mandarin, warfarin, tamarin (small monkey), coumarin (chemical compound), heparin (biochemical substance), glycerine, nectarine, Catherine, culverin (heavy cannon), luciferin (light-emitting compound), nitroglycerin.

252.21

medicine, salicin (crystalline substance), sericin (protein), ceresin (white wax), haemolysin (biochemical compound), fibrinolysin (enzyme).

252.22

lysin (substance that destroys cells), ricin (protein), streptomycin, tyrothricin (antibiotic), actinomycin (antibiotic).

252.23

bulletin, palmitin (chemical compound), ferritin (protein), quercetin (yellow plant pigment), precipitin (antibody), phenacetin (crystalline substance).

252.24

cutin (waxy plant substance), Rasputin, highfalutin.

252.25

captain, Sahaptin (American Indian).

252.26

destine, predestine, clandestine, progestin (hormone), intestine.

252.27

Justin, Augustine.

252.28

Bevin (British statesman), Previn, replevin (legal term).

252.29

tocsin, toxin, digitoxin (poisonous chemical compound), antitoxin, zootoxin (toxin produced by animal), phytotoxin (plant poison).

252.30

resin, muezzin (Islamic mosque official).

253 -ine

bine (climbing stem), kine (cattle), chine, dyne, dine, fine, Jain (member of Hindu sect), line, cline (ecology term), spline, mine, nine, pine, spine, Rhine, brine, shrine, sine, sign, shine, Tyne, tine, stein, thine, vine, whine, wine, swine, twine.

Sabine, carbine, turbine, woodbine, combine, turdine (relating to thrushes), indign (undeserving), condign (well-deserved), define, refine, confine, saline, airline, hairline, beeline, feline, skyline, dyeline (type of blueprint), Pauline (relating to Saint Paul), shoreline, towline, neckline, touchline, deadline, headline, breadline, guideline, sideline, lifeline, tramline, hemline, streamline, pipeline, baseline, dateline, outline, waistline, coastline, clothesline, carmine, canine, Pennine, rapine (forcible seizure of property), repine (be fretful), orpine (succulent plant), opine (hold an opinion), lupine, supine, alpine, vulpine (relating to foxes), vespine (relating to wasps), equine, larine (relating to gulls), taurine, murrhine (Roman vase material), eccrine, caprine (relating to goats), enshrine, Petrine (relating to Saint Peter), ursine, hircine (lascivious), quercine (relating to the oak), piscine, porcine, cosine, phocine (relating to seals), ensign, consign, shoeshine, sunshine, moonshine, outshine, pontine (relating to bridges), Holstein, Bernstein, Einstein, Epstein, cervine (relating to deer), divine, corvine (relating to crows), ovine, bovine, grapevine, entwine, design, resign.

concubine, hirundine (relating to swallows), celandine, almandine (violet-red garnet), superfine, androgyne (bisexual), aquiline, induline (blue dye), Ursuline (Catholic teaching nun), vituline (relating to calves), monocline (geology term), microcline (feldspar mineral), isocline (geology term), undermine, calamine, leonine, falconine (relating to falcons), saturnine, pavonine (relating to peacocks), porcupine, subalpine, cisalpine, transalpine, sciurine (relating to squirrels), colubrine (relating to snakes), endocrine, holocrine (physiology term), apocrine (physiology term), merocrine (physiology term), exocrine (physiology term), auld lang syne, gegenschein (faint glow in sky), vespertine (occurring in the evening), Tridentine (orthodox Roman Catholic), Aventine (ancient Roman hill), transpontine (across a bridge), argentine (relating to silver), valentine, eglantine, serpentine, turpentine, Florentine, Constantine, levantine (silk cloth), Hammerstein, Rubinstein,

Frankenstein, Liechtenstein, Eisenstein (Russian film director), Wittgenstein, intertwine, disentwine.

Alexandrine, accipitrine (relating to hawks), internecine, terebinthine, labyrinthine, hyacinthine.

253.1

combine, columbine.

253.2

aerodyne (heavier-than-air machine), anodyne, heterodyne (electronics term).

253.3

align, malign, moline (heraldic term), zibeline (sable fur), alkaline, borderline, underline, opaline, Caroline, coralline, metalline, interline, crystalline, Capitoline (ancient Roman hill).

253.4

decline, recline, helicline (spiral-shaped ramp), pericline (white mineral), anticline (rock formation).

253.5

incline, syncline (rock formation), disincline, geosyncline (depression in earth's crust).

253.6

benign, asinine.

253.7

saccharine, vulturine, leporine (relating to hares), passerine, anserine (relating to geese), uterine, riverine, estuarine, adulterine (fake), intrauterine, extrauterine.

253.8

assign, thylacine (Tasmanian wolf), limacine (relating to slugs), psittacine (relating to parrots), countersign, haversine (maths term).

253.9

Byzantine, elephantine, diamantine, adamantine (having diamond-like lustre).

253.10

pristine, Philistine, amethystine.

254 -on

on, Bonn, con, scone, don, Don, phon (unit of loudness), gone, John, shone, wan, won (Korean currency), swan, yon.

kaon (physics particle), rayon, neon, Creon (king of Thebes), gluon (hypothetical particle in physics), Huon (Tasmanian river), muon (elementary particle in physics), Gabon, bonbon, zircon, icon, Yukon, chaconne (musical term), radon (radioactive element), chiffon, argon, Sargon (Assyrian king), bygone, trigon (triangular harp), Saigon, doggone, foregone, trogon (tropical bird), salon, nylon, Orlon (*Trademark*), Teflon (*Trademark*), mouflon (wild mountain sheep), gnomon (part of sundial), xenon, Nippon, coupon, jupon (short sleeveless garment), upon, tampon, pompon, thereon, whereon, Chiron (Greek centaur), giron (heraldic term), neuron (nerve cell), Hebron (Jordanian city), macron (phonetic symbol), Dacron (*Trademark*), micron, nephron (kidney tubule), neutron, Tucson, baton, cretonne, piton, photon, proton, pluton (geology term), mouton (processed sheepskin), crouton, canton, Canton, won ton (Chinese filled dumpling), lepton (Greek coin), krypton, axon, taxon (biology term), bouillon, meson (elementary particle in physics), boson (elementary particle in physics), Luzon (largest Philippine island), blouson.

Ratisbon (German city), Comecon, Myrmidon (Greek mythological race), Macedon, stegodon (extinct mammal), celadon (Oriental porcelain), sphenodon (tuatara lizard), mastodon, parergon (additional employment), demijohn, eidolon (apparition), etymon (original form of word), kikumon (Japanese royal emblem), thereupon, whereupon, hereupon, elytron (insect's hard outer wing), positron (physics term), phytotron (experimental plant-growing unit), cyclotron (physics apparatus), electron, cabochon (unfaceted polished gem), feuilleton (part of newspaper), magneton (unit in physics), phlogiston (hypothetical substance causing combustion), trilithon (structure comprising three stones), telethon, sabayon (light foamy dessert), Cro-Magnon, liaison.

Esdraelon (Israeli plain), sine qua non, Agamemnon, antineutron (physics term), hyperbaton (reversed order of words), automaton, demicanton (part of Swiss canton), anacoluthon (rhetoric term).

254.1

logion (authentic saying of Christ), nucleon, baryon (particle in physics), Sicyon (ancient Greek city), gnathion (point on lower jaw), triskelion (three-legged symbol), Anacreon (Greek poet), antinucleon (particle in physics).

254.2

Laocoon (Greek mythological priest), entozoon (animal living inside another), protozoon, spermatozoon.

254.3

colophon (publisher's emblem on book), Bellerophon (Greek mythological hero).

254.4

begone, woebegone, polygon.

254.5

decagon, glucagon (hormone), undergone, nonagon, Nipigon (Canadian lake), estragon (tarragon), octagon, pentagon, heptagon, hexagon, dodecagon, undecagon, trimetrogon (method of aerial photography).

254.6

Ceylon, Chillon (Swiss castle), papillon (breed of spaniel), epsilon, upsilon, haematoxylon (thorny tree).

254.7

Miquelon (French territorial island group), echelon, etalon (physics device), Avalon, encephalon (the brain).

254.8

anon, guenon (African monkey), argonon (a gas), organon (philosophy term), Parthenon, olecranon (projection behind elbow joint).

254.9

hereon, interferon.

254.10

boron, moron, thoron (radioisotope of radon), oxymoron (rhetoric term).

254.11

Oberon, Acheron (Greek mythological river), megaron (tripartite rectangular room), aileron, operon (genetics term), Percheron (breed of carthorse), enteron (animal's digestive tract), ephemeron (short-lived organism), mesenteron (animal's midgut), hexaemeron (the Creation).

254.12

chignon, filet mignon, boeuf Bourguignon.

255 -orn

awn, born, borne, bourn, corn, scorn, dawn, fawn, faun, horn, lawn, lorn (forsaken), mourn, morn, Norn (Norse goddess), pawn, spawn, brawn, drawn, prawn, thrawn (*Dialect* crooked), sawn, shorn, Sean, torn, thorn, Vaughan, warn, worn, sworn, yawn.

airborne, chairborne, reborn, freeborn, seaborne, highborn, lowborn, newborn, stillborn, inborn, unborn, baseborn, first-born, Eastbourne, Osborne, earth-born, acorn, bicorn (having two horns), tricorn (cocked hat), Runcorn, popcorn, adorn, dehorn, shoehorn, inkhorn (ink container), stinkhorn (foul-smelling fungus), leghorn, foghorn, crumhorn (medieval woodwind instrument), greenhorn, longhorn, pronghorn (small US deer), alphorn, shorthorn, althorn (brass instrument), saxhorn (brass instrument), frogspawn, withdrawn, indrawn, hawthorn, blackthorn, buckthorn, careworn, forewarn, timeworn, forsworn.

peppercorn, leprechaun, Apeldoorn (Dutch town), Matterhorn, flugelhorn, alpenhorn, overdrawn, weatherworn, waterworn, Finsteraarhorn (Swiss mountain).

255.1

suborn, waterborne, winterbourne (stream caused by rainfall).

255.2

barleycorn, unicorn, Capricorn, cavicorn (having hollow horns), clavicorn (beetle), lamellicorn (beetle).

256 -oin

Boyne, coin, quoin (external corner of wall), join, loin, groyne, groin, sainfoin (Eurasian plant), rejoin, adjoin, subjoin, enjoin, conjoin, disjoin, purloin, sirloin, Boulogne, tenderloin, frankalmoign (English legal history term), talapoin (small monkey), Assiniboine (Canadian river).

257 -oan

own, bone, Beaune, cone, scone, phone, Joan, hone, loan, lone, blown, clone, flown, Sloane, moan, mown, known, pone (maize bread), Rhône, roan, crone, drone, grown, groan, prone, throne, thrown, sewn, sown, sone (unit of loudness), shown, tone, stone, zone.

thighbone, jawbone, backbone, cheekbone, aitchbone (cut of beef), whalebone, trombone, shinbone, hipbone, wishbone, breastbone, dracone (container towed by ship), condone, earphone, sulphone (chemical compound), alone, Cologne, cologne, flyblown, windblown, full-blown, cyclone, high-flown, bemoan, hormone, unknown, depone (Scottish legal term), repone (Scottish legal term), Capone, postpone, Tyrone, pyrone (chemical compound), neurone, ingrown, oestrone (hormone), dethrone, enthrone, disown, ketone, tritone (musical term), lactone (chemical compound), halftone, intone, peptone, keystone, freestone (fine-grained stone), kerbstone, touchstone, headstone, lodestone, toadstone (igneous rock), sandstone, grindstone, flagstone, hailstone, millstone, bilestone, milestone, gallstone, gemstone, brimstone, limestone, tombstone, rhinestone, moonstone, copestone, soapstone, whetstone, birthstone, gravestone, flavone (crystalline substance), hexone (chemical compound), ozone, evzone (Greek soldier).

marrowbone, collarbone, knucklebone, anklebone, cuttlebone, herringbone, silicone, methadone (narcotic drug), telephone, polyphone (linguistics term), Francophone, chordophone (stringed instrument), megaphone, mellophone (brass-band instrument), xylophone, Anglophone, gramophone, homophone (word pronounced like another), vibraphone (percussion instrument), microphone, Dictaphone (*Trademark*), saxophone, sousaphone, heckelphone (bass oboe), overblown, pheromone, unbeknown, undergrown, overgrown, overthrown, ecdysone (hormone), holystone (sandstone for scrubbing decks), thunderstone (long tapering object), cornerstone, cobblestone, staddlestone, prednisone (steroid drug), cortisone.

radiophone, anticyclone.

257.1

coumarone (aromatic liquid), chaperon, progesterone, aldosterone, androsterone, testosterone.

257.2

barbitone, semitone, baritone, baryton (bass viol), acetone, phenobarbitone.

257.3

atone, duotone (printing process), undertone, monotone, isotone (chemistry term), overtone.

258 -oun

down, gown, clown, noun, brown, crown, drown, frown, town.

godown (Asian warehouse), hoedown, lowdown, slowdown, showdown, markdown, breakdown, shakedown, touchdown, comedown, sundown, splashdown, shutdown, Piltdown, countdown, nightgown, renown, pronoun, nutbrown, Motown, midtown, downtown, uptown.

hand-me-down, eiderdown, omadhaun (*Irish* a fool), Portadown, upside-down, tumble-down, thistledown, shantytown, Chinatown, cabbagetown (city slum).

259 -un

bun, dun, done, fun, gun, Hun, none, nun, pun, spun, run, son, sun, shun, ton, tonne, tun, stun, one, won.

undone, outdone, begun, handgun, popgun, shotgun, outgun, Falun (Swedish city), homespun, finespun, rerun, forerun, millrun, outrun, godson, grandson, stepson, someone.

underdone, overdone, overrun, kiloton, megaton, anyone, everyone.

260 -oon

boon, coon, Scone (Scottish parish), goon, June, loon, moon, noon, poon (Asian tree), spoon, rune, croon, prune, soon, shoon, swoon, dune, tune.

baboon, tycoon, cocoon, puccoon (US plant), raccoon, tuchun (Chinese military governor), cardoon (European plant), bridoon (horse's bit), typhoon, buffoon, lagoon, dragoon, Rangoon, jejune, cohune (US tropical palm), shalloon (light woollen fabric), Walloon, Kowloon, doubloon, forenoon, harpoon, lampoon, teaspoon, gombroon (Oriental pottery), quadroon, Gudrun, gadroon (decorative patterned moulding), poltroon (contemptible coward), Sassoon, gossoon (*Irish* servant boy), bassoon, monsoon, matzoon (fermented milk product), cartoon, spittoon, pontoon, spontoon (short pike), festoon, triune (three in one), tribune, immune, commune, repugn, oppugn, impugn, Neptune.

rigadoon (old Provençal dance), Dehra Dun (Indian city), demilune (crescentshaped formation), perilune (point in lunar orbit), honeymoon, tablespoon, dessertspoon, Behistun (Iranian village), picayune (*US* of little value).

Tutankhamun, autoimmune.

260.1

balloon, galloon (decorative cord), saloon, apolune (point in lunar orbit), pantaloon (pantomime character).

260.2

Dunoon, afternoon.

260.3

maroon, macaroon, picaroon (adventurer), Scandaroon (fancy pigeon), Cameroon, octoroon, Iskenderun (Turkish port), vinegarroon (large scorpion-like arachnid).

260.4

platoon, saskatoon (Canadian fruit shrub), Saskatoon (Canadian city).

260.5

fortune, misfortune, importune.

260.6

attune, opportune, inopportune.

261 -'n

ebon, leben (African curdled milk), gibbon, ribbon, auburn, corban (biblical gift), Bourbon, Oban, stubborn, Cuban, Melbourne, Gisborne (New Zealand port), Lisbon, Brisbane, blacken, slacken, bracken, beckon, Deccan, reckon, Brecon, liken, lichen, silken, Vulcan, Lincoln, Duncan, drunken, shrunken, sunken, scutcheon, scuncheon (part of door jamb), luncheon, puncheon (large cask), truncheon, Christian, Arden, Baden, Dardan (Trojan), garden, harden, lardon (strip of fat), pardon, bourdon (organ stop), hoyden (tomboy), Croydon, loden (thick wool), Snowdon, Woden (Anglo-Saxon god), louden, sudden, wooden, Camden, tendon, linden, Swindon, bounden, London, Hampden, Dresden, deafen, hyphen, siphon, often, soften, orphan, roughen, toughen, lagan (wreckage on sea bed), Skagen (cape in Denmark), Dagan (Babylonian god), jargon, Hagen (German legendary character), Keegan, vegan, tigon (tiger–lion hybrid), bogan (*Canadian* side stream), Hogan, Logan, slogan, brogan (heavy boot), roentgen, largen, Georgian, Trojan, Belgian, Injun, St John, dungeon, Allen, Alan, gallon, talon, Galen (Greek physician), pylon, fallen, sullen, woollen, raglan, barman, carman, Raman (Indian physicist), Brahman, Emmen (Dutch city), lemon, German, Herman, merman, sermon, Sherman, pieman, Simon, Cimon (Athenian military commander), fireman, wireman (*US* electrician), common, doorman, foreman, lawman, Mormon, Norman, bowman (oarsman), cowman, ploughman, summon, cabman, kirkman (*Scot* church member), workman, socman (tenant farmer), stockman, milkman, linkman, churchman, Scotchman, watchman, coachman, Dutchman, henchman,

Frenchman, adman, badman, madman, Bradman (Australian cricketer), headman, birdman, freedman, goodman, woodman, sandman, bagman (travelling salesman), flagman, ragman, swagman, Bergman, dogman (*Austral* crane-driver's assistant), frogman, dolman (long Turkish robe), coalman, oilman, Pullman, penman, gunman, hangman, strongman, apeman, Helpmann (Australian ballet dancer), gasman, baseman (fielder in baseball), spaceman, horseman, Norseman, houseman, batsman, statesman, Scotsman, yachtsman, sportsman, craftsman, draughtsman, huntsman, freshman, bushman, Welshman, batman, atman (Hindu self), Pitman, pitman, Whitman (US poet), boatman, footman, postman, dustman, caveman, marksman, spokesman, Manxman, Tasman, Osman (Turkish sultan), oarsman, tribesman, guardsman, tradesman, herdsman, sidesman (church warden's assistant), swordsman, bandsman, landsman, roundsman, groundsman, bailsman (person who stands bail), dalesman, salesman, clansman, Klansman (Ku Klux Klan member), kinsman, linesman, townsman, Canaan, Lennon, pennon, tenon, happen, sharpen, tarpon (Atlantic fish), weapon, cheapen, deepen, steepen, Ripon, Crippen, ripen, open, dampen, lampern (European lamprey), crampon, hempen, lumpen (stupid), aspen, saucepan, Aran, Arran, barren, baron, Karen, marron (chestnut), Sharon, heron, perron (flight of steps), Aaron, Charon (Greek mythological character), sporran, warren, squadron, children, cauldron, pauldron (armour plate protecting shoulder), saffron, apron, matron, natron (a mineral), patron, citron, plectron, chevron, bison, hyson (Chinese green tea), grison (predatory mammal), coarsen, Dawson, whoreson, hoarsen, Porson (English classical scholar), moisten, Preussen (German name for Prussia), boatswain, bosun, loosen, Ibsen, Gibson, Hudson, Belsen, kelson (strengthening beam on keel), Nelson, Wilson, Samson, Jansen, Nansen, Johnson, sponson (ship's outboard gun platform), Bunsen, Simpson,

Thompson, stetson, Whitsun, Watson, Martian, cushion, auction, sanction, sponsion (sponsorship), Dayton (US city), phaeton (horse-drawn carriage), straighten, straiten (embarrass financially), Satan, oaten (made of oats), croton (tropical shrub), Acton, Clacton, lectern, Stockton, plankton, chieftain, Carlton, Charlton, Chiltern, Milton, Stilton, Wilton, Dalton (English scientist), saltern (saltworks), Walton, Bolton, molten, sultan, Danton (French revolutionary leader), lantern, Scranton (Pennsylvanian city), Paignton, Denton (English town), lenten, Trenton (US city), wanton, Taunton, hapten (medical term), Clapton (English rock guitarist), Skipton, Hampton, Aston, pastern, eastern, Boston, postern, pleuston (mass of floating microorganisms), Houston, Gladstone, Maidstone, charleston, Princeton, Dunstan (English saint), tungsten, capstan, Ashton, Caxton, Paxton (English architect), sexton Folkestone, Buxton, Nathan, earthen, python, lengthen, strengthen, heathen, northern, southern, smoothen, cavern, raven, tavern, proven, sylvan (relating to woods), Malvern, Jackson, klaxon, flaxen, Saxon, waxen, Texan, Nixon, vixen, oxen, Oxon., coxswain, bullion, Julian, onion, bunion, Bunyan, Runyon (US writer), grunion (Californian fish), trunnion (pivot), Tarzan, cousin, cozen (to trick), dozen, damson, crimson.

Don Juan, Moroccan, Monacan, Faliscan (ancient Italian language), Franciscan, escutcheon, unchristian, exhaustion, combustion, Basildon, Wimbledon, abandon, Ugandan, Clarendon, Abingdon, Hillingdon, Huntingdon, toboggan, Aragon, paragon, tarragon, suffragan (assistant bishop), Monaghan (Irish county), downfallen (dilapidated), chapfallen (dejected), crestfallen, gonfalon (banner), mamelon (small rounded hillock), ortolan (small bird), biathlon, decathlon, pentathlon, uncommon, Roscommon (Irish county), husbandman, Orangeman, patrolman, stableman, nobleman, middleman, rifleman, signalman, muscleman, cattleman, gentleman, midshipman, policeman, busi-

nessman, serviceman, warehouseman, Englishman, Irishman, aircraftman, merchantman (merchant ship), harvestman (arachnid), talisman, exciseman, ombudsman, backwoodsman, Lebanon, reopen, half-open, Saharan, Anderson, Jefferson, Emerson, Saracen, Paterson, Peterson, Richardson, Nicholson, Mendelssohn, Williamson, Robinson, Dickinson, Atkinson, Stephenson, pincushion, infarction, decoction (medicinal preparation), concoction, distinction, extinction, emulsion, repulsion, propulsion, impulsion, compulsion, expulsion, revulsion, avulsion (forcible separation), convulsion, pre-emption, redemption, exemption, occasion, equation, abrasion, pervasion, evasion, invasion, persuasion, dissuasion, quieten, Pinkerton, charlatan, tarlatan (cotton fabric), Sheraton, Chatterton, Chesterton, doubleton (bridge term), subaltern, Shackleton, Middleton, singleton, Hamilton, simpleton, Edmonton, Bebington, Tarkington (US novelist), Arlington (Virginian county), Darlington, Ellington (US jazz musician), Wellington, Burlington, Islington, Leamington, Lymington, Warrington, Accrington, Washington, Whittington, Lexington (US city), Kensington, Northampton, Southampton, Augustan, Palmerston, autochthon (country's earliest-known inhabitant), Carmarthen, cordovan (fine leather), Donovan, Amazon.

Muhammadan, solenodon (shrew-like mammal), Tutankhamen, polyhedron, decahedron, tetrahedron, octahedron, hexahedron, rhododendron, philodendron (climbing plant), hobson-jobson (folk etymology), Wolverhampton, Aldermaston, Saskatchewan, Elizabethan.

261.1

crayon, Malayan, Ghanaian, Pompeiian.

261.2

Ian, aeon, Behan (Irish writer), peon (Spanish-American farm labourer), paean (song of praise), Archaean (geology term), Judaean, Andean, Pandean (relating to Pan), Aegean, Fijian, Augean (very dirty), Crimean, Tarpeian, protean (variable in form).

amoebaean, Caribbean, Hebridean, Sisyphean (endless and futile), herculean, Coeur de Lion, Ponce de León (Spanish explorer), Pyrenean, European, empyrean (relating to the heavens).

antipodean, epicurean.

261.2.1

plebeian, Jacobean, Maccabean, scarabaean (type of beetle).

261.2.2

spelaean (relating to caves), Achillean, Galilean.

261.2.3

Korean, Terpsichorean, Pythagorean.

261.2.4

Odyssean, Laodicean.

261.3

Ian, lien (legal term).

Serbian, Nubian, Albion, lesbian, guardian, Freudian, Scandian (Scandinavian), Mandaean (member of Iraqi sect), Indian, Orphean, ruffian, galleon, talion (making punishment fit crime), Bodleian, Anglian, ganglion, Wesleyan, camion (lorry), Samian (relating to Samos), Permian, thermion (high-temperature electron), amnion, Jungian, apian (relating to bees), scorpion, campion, champion, lampion (oil-burning lamp), rampion (Eurasian plant), Grampian, tampion (plug for gun's muzzle), Caspian, Thespian, Syrian, Tyrian (relating to ancient Tyre), Zyrian (language group), quarrian (Australian bird), Cambrian, Adrian, Hadrian, Cyprian, Bactrian, Austrian, hessian, Ossian (legendary Irish bard), Lucian (ancient Greek writer), halcyon, Haitian, Gratian (Roman emperor), bastion, Parthian, pantheon, Scythian, Pythian (relating to Delphi), Lothian, Latvian, Marxian.

Columbian, Lamarckian, Noachian (relating to Noah), batrachian (amphibian), Pickwickian, Gulbenkian (British industrialist), Algonquian (language group), Comanchean, accordion, Edwardian, cerulean (deep blue), Bohemian, anthemion (ancient Greek floral design), acromion (part of shoulder blade), Hibernian, quaternion (maths term), Mancunian, Neptunian, Olympian, Tocharian (member of Asian culture), Amphitryon (Greek mythological character), pedestrian, equestrian, Circassian, Gilbertian, nemertean (ribbon-like marine worm), amphictyon (ancient Greek religious councillor), Atlantean, Carpathian, Promethean (creative or original), Erechtheion (temple on Acropolis), Midlothian, Venusian, Carthusian (Roman Catholic monk), Malthusian (relating to population theory), Dickensian.

Appalachian, Amerindian, Christadelphian, theologian, Carolingian (Frankish dynasty), Merovingian (Frankish dynasty), Liverpudlian, Mississippian, Alexandrian, mitochondrion (microscopic structure in cell), demibastion (type of fortification), Yugoslavian, Czechoslovakian.

261.3.1

Fabian, gabion (stone-filled cylinder), Arabian.

261.3.2

Gibeon (ancient Palestinian town), Libyan, amphibian.

261.3.3

radian, Arcadian, circadian (relating to biological rhythm), Orcadian (relating to the Orkneys), Acadian (French settler in Canada), gammadion (swastika), Canadian, steradian (unit in geometry).

261.3.4

median, tragedian, comedian, Archimedean.

261.3.5

Gideon, Midian (biblical nation), ophidian (snake-like), viridian (green pigment), meridian, ascidian (tiny marine animal), obsidian (volcanic rock), quotidian, Dravidian (language group), postmeridian, antemeridian.

261.3.6
Rhodian (relating to Rhodes),
melodeon (small accordion), collodion
(syrupy liquid), custodian, nickelodeon.

261.3.7 [see also 261.37]
Phrygian, Stygian (relating to river
Styx), callipygian (having shapely buttocks), Cantabrigian, crossopterygian
(bony fish), malacopterygian (soft-
finned fish), acanthopterygian (spiny-
finned fish).

261.3.8
alien, Salian (relating to Frankish
group), Deucalion (Greek mythological
character), mammalian, Pygmalion,
Australian, bacchanalian, sesquipedalian (using very long words), episcopalian.

261.3.9 [see also 261.119]
Sabellian (extinct language group),
Orwellian, Cromwellian, Machia-
vellian.

261.3.10
Pelion (Greek mountain), Caelian
(ancient Roman hill), parhelion (meteorology term), aphelion (point in planet's orbit), anthelion (meteorology
term), chameleon, carnelian (gemstone), Aurelian (Roman emperor),
perihelion (point in planet's orbit),
Aristotelian.

261.3.11 [see also 261.120]
Ilion (Greek name for Troy), skillion
(*Austral* lean-to), Gillian, penillion
(Welsh sung poetry), caecilian (limbless
amphibian), Sicilian, Quintilian
(Roman teacher), reptilian, Castilian
(relating to Castile), Abbevillian
(archaeological period), Basilian
(Eastern Christian monk), Brazilian,
crocodilian, Maximilian, lacertilian
(lizard), vaudevillian.

261.3.12
Aeolian, Mongolian, Napoleon,
Anatolian.

261.3.13
scullion, mullion, Tertullian
(Carthaginian Christian theologian),
slubberdegullion (slovenly person).

261.3.14
Simeon, simian (resembling a monkey),
Endymion, prosimian (zoology term).

261.3.15
Albanian, vulcanian (volcanic),
Jordanian, Rumanian, Tasmanian,
Iranian, Uranian, Ukrainian,
Lithuanian, Panamanian,
Transylvanian, Pennsylvanian.

261.3.15.1
Pomeranian, subterranean,
Mediterranean.

261.3.16
Fenian (19th-century Irish revolution-
ary), Armenian, Tyrrhenian (part of
Mediterranean), sirenian (zoology
term), Ruthenian (language group),
Athenian.

261.3.17 [see also 261.122]
Sardinian, Arminian, Socinian (relating
to religious doctrine), Justinian
(Byzantine emperor), Darwinian,
Carthaginian, Valentinian (Roman
emperor), Augustinian.

261.3.18
chthonian (relating to the underworld),
aeonian (everlasting), Ionian, Dra-
conian, chelonian (tortoise or turtle),
Johnsonian, Smithsonian, Etonian,
Plutonian (infernal), Newtonian,
Miltonian, Estonian, Devonian, favon-
ian (relating to west wind), Oxonian,
Caledonian, Macedonian, Aberdonian,
Babylonian, Apollonian, Thessalonian,
Ciceronian (eloquent), Amazonian,
Lacedaemonian (Spartan).

261.3.19
Fallopian, Utopian, Ethiopian.

261.3.20
carrion, clarion, Marian, orpharion
(large lute).

261.3.21
Arian, Darien (part of Panama), Parian
(relating to fine marble).
barbarian, Icarian (relating to Icarus),
Bulgarian, vulgarian (vulgar person),
Hungarian, valerian (Eurasian plant),
grammarian, planarian (non-parasitic
flatworm), riparian, librarian, agrarian,

fruitarian (person eating only fruit), Rotarian, sectarian, ovarian, Bavarian, Caesarean, rosarian (person who cultivates roses).

apiarian (relating to beekeeping), Rastafarian, antiquarian, Sabbatarian (strict observer of Sabbath), libertarian (believer in free thought).

abecedarian (person learning the alphabet), infralapsarian (theology term), supralapsarian (theology term), parliamentarian.

261.3.21.1

millenarian (relating to a thousand), seminarian (student at seminary), centenarian, octogenarian, nonagenarian, quinquagenarian, quadragenarian, sexagenarian, disciplinarian, veterinarian, predestinarian (believer in predestination), valetudinarian (chronically sick person), latitudinarian (permitting religious freedom), septuagenarian.

261.3.21.2

vegetarian, proletarian, Trinitarian (believer in the Trinity), unitarian, egalitarian, totalitarian, futilitarian, humanitarian, ubiquitarian (believer in Christ's omnipresence), authoritarian.

261.3.22

Pierian (relating to the Muses), Iberian, Siberian, Nigerian, Algerian, Cimmerian (very dark), Sumerian (ancient Babylonian), Wagnerian, Hyperion, Shakespearean, Chaucerian, criterion, presbyterian, metatherian (marsupial), Hanoverian.

261.3.23

chorion (embryonic membrane), Dorian (ancient Greek), morion (16th-century helmet), saurian (resembling a lizard), Gregorian, Victorian, stentorian, historian, Hyperborean (inhabitant of extreme north), prehistorian.

261.3.24

turion (plant bud), durian (Asian tree), Ben-Gurion, tellurian (relating to the earth), Silurian, decurion (Roman councillor), pagurian (hermit crab), centurion, Arthurian, Khachaturian

(Russian composer), holothurian (sea cucumber).

261.3.25

Umbrian (extinct language group), Cumbrian, Northumbrian.

261.3.26

Lancastrian, Zoroastrian.

261.3.27

fustian, Procrustean (producing conformity ruthlessly).

261.3.28

Corinthian, labyrinthian, pericynthion (point in lunar orbit), apocynthion (point in lunar orbit).

261.3.29

avian, Shavian, subclavian, Moravian, Octavian, Scandinavian.

261.3.30

Vivian, Bolivian, oblivion.

261.3.31

Jovian, Harrovian.

261.3.32

alluvion (overflow), Peruvian, vesuvian (match for lighting cigars), postdiluvian (existing after biblical Flood), antediluvian.

261.3.33

nasion (point on skull), Caucasian, Malaysian, Vespasian, Rabelaisian.

261.3.34 [see also 261.90]

artesian, Cartesian (relating to Descartes), Polynesian, Indonesian, Melanesian.

261.3.35 [see also 261.91]

Elysian, Parisian, Dionysian.

261.4

ion, iron, lion, Mayan, Ryan, Brian, scion, Zion, sadiron (heavy iron), midiron (golf club), gridiron, andiron (logstand in fireplace), antlion (tropical insect), anion, cation, flatiron, Hawaiian, dandelion.

261.4.1

Orion, zwitterion (charged particle).

261.5

doyen, Illinoisan, Iroquoian (American Indian language).

261.6

Iowan (Australian bird), rowan, Caddoan (language group), Minoan, dipnoan (lungfish), hydrozoan (small aquatic animal), sporozoan (microscopic parasitic animal), protozoan (microscopic animal).

261.7

Papuan, gargantuan.

261.8

Schwaben (region of Germany), carbon, graben (trough of land), hydrocarbon, radiocarbon.

261.9

urban, bourbon, Durban, turban, suburban.

261.10

Aachen, darken, hearken, kraken (legendary sea monster), Interlaken.

261.11

bacon, shaken, taken, waken, Jamaican, forsaken, unshaken, mistaken, awaken, godforsaken, undertaken, overtaken.

261.12

beacon, deacon, weaken, subdeacon, archdeacon, Mohican.

261.13

quicken, stricken, sicken, thicken, Barbican, Rubicon, Helicon (Greek mountain), helicon (bass tuba), pelican, Millikan (US physicist), silicon, publican, Anglican, pemmican (American Indian food), salpicon (chopped food in sauce), hurricane, African, Corsican, Vatican, lexicon, Mexican, catholicon (remedy for all diseases), republican, Dominican, pantechnicon (large van), American, ferrosilicon (iron–silicon alloy), stereopticon (type of projector).

261.14

oaken, spoken, broken, token, woken, Hoboken (Belgian city), unspoken, outspoken, unbroken, heartbroken, betoken.

261.15

Lucan, toucan, lebkuchen (German biscuit), Chinookan (American Indian language).

261.16

Balkan, falcon, gyrfalcon (large rare falcon).

261.17

Tuscan, Etruscan.

261.18

question, digestion, suggestion, ingestion, congestion, indigestion, autosuggestion.

261.19

gladden, madden, sadden, Ibadan (Nigerian city), Abaddon (the devil).

261.20

Aden, Aidan, laden, Blaydon (English town), maiden, menhaden (US fish), unladen, handmaiden.

261.21

deaden, leaden, redden, Armageddon.

261.22

burden, guerdon (reward), lurdan (stupid), unburden, disburden.

261.23

Eden, Sweden, boustrophedon (relating to writing method), cotyledon, dicotyledon, monocotyledon.

261.24

bidden, hidden, midden (*Dialect* rubbish heap), ridden, forbidden, unbidden, oppidan (urban), harridan, Sheridan, bedridden, Mohammedan.

261.25

guidon (small military flag), Haydn, Leiden (Dutch city), Dryden, Sidon (Phoenician city), widen, Poseidon.

261.26

Flodden (Northumbrian battlefield), modern, trodden, sodden, Culloden (Scottish battlefield), downtrodden, untrodden, ultramodern.

261.27
Auden, cordon, Gordon, Jordan, broaden, warden, firewarden (*US* fire-prevention officer), churchwarden.

261.28
olden, golden, embolden, beholden.

261.29
griffon, stiffen, antiphon (response).

261.30
flagon, dragon, wagon, pendragon (leader of ancient Britons), snapdragon, bandwagon.

261.31
pagan, Reagan, Nijmegen (Dutch town), Copenhagen.

261.32
Wigan, cardigan, Milligan, Mulligan, hooligan, ptarmigan, larrigan (leather moccasin boot), perigon (angle of 360°), origan (marjoram), Oregon, Michigan, Rattigan (English dramatist), shenanigan.

261.33
organ, Gorgon, Morgan, Glamorgan, Demogorgon (mythological god).

261.34
Trajan (Roman emperor), contagion.

261.35
burgeon, gurjun (Asian tree), surgeon, sturgeon, neurosurgeon.

261.36
legion, region, collegian, subregion, Norwegian, Glaswegian.

261.37 [see also **261.3.7**]
smidgen, pigeon, wigeon (Eurasian duck), religion, florigen (hypothetical plant hormone), cultigen (cultivated plant), antigen, oxygen, irreligion.

261.38
dudgeon, gudgeon, bludgeon, trudgen (swimming stroke), curmudgeon.

261.39
biogen (hypothetical protein), cryogen (freezing mixture), habergeon (coat of mail), allergen, halogen, glycogen (biochemical compound), phellogen (cork-producing cells), collagen, pyrogen (substance causing fever), acrogen (type of flowerless plant), hydrogen, androgen, nitrogen, oestrogen, mutagen (substance causing mutation), histogen (plant tissue), pathogen, fibrinogen (blood protein), carcinogen, pepsinogen (enzyme), trypsinogen (enzyme), hallucinogen.

261.40
felon, melon, Magellan, muskmelon (type of melon), pademelon (small wallaby), watermelon.

261.41
billon (alloy used for coins), Dylan, villain, villein, Babylon, Macmillan, castellan (keeper of castle), abutilon (flowering shrub).

261.42
pollen, pollan (whitefish), Hohenzollern (German noble family).

261.43
colon, Nolan, Solon (Athenian statesman), stolen, stollen (rich sweet bread), swollen, semicolon.

261.44
Ammon (biblical character), gammon, mammon, salmon, shaman (Asian priest), backgammon.

261.45
cayman (US crocodile), layman, Bremen, highwayman, railwayman.

261.46
airman, chairman, repairman.

261.47
demon, he-man, freeman, seaman, eudemon (benevolent spirit), pentstemon (US plant), Lacedaemon (Sparta), cacodemon (evil spirit).

261.48
handyman, bogeyman, clergyman, tallyman, journeyman, dairyman, quarryman, juryman, laundryman, nurseryman, countryman, Everyman, persimmon (tropical tree), cavalryman, infantryman, committeeman, artilleryman.

261.49

omen, bowman, foeman, snowman, Roman, showman, yeoman, locoman (engine-driver), dragoman (professional interpreter).

261.50

woman, charwoman, churchwoman, horsewoman, sportswoman, batwoman, townswoman, washerwoman, needlewoman, gentlewoman.

261.51

Truman, Schumann, Yuman (language group), human, Newman, subhuman, inhuman, ichneumon (mongoose), superhuman.

261.52

Turkoman (Asian people), Inkerman (Crimean battle site), Betjeman, trencherman (hearty eater), spiderman, abdomen, ealdorman (Anglo-Saxon judicial official), alderman, landammann (Swiss council chairman), telamon (supporting pillar), Solomon, cyclamen, cinnamon, Chinaman, superman, cameraman, ataman (leader of the Cossacks), ottoman, slaughterman (slaughterhouse employee), waterman (skilled boatman) Ulsterman, weatherman, remainderman (legal term), newspaperman.

261.52.1

fisherman, militiaman.

261.53

chessman, desman (small amphibious mammal), pressman, yes-man, Congressman.

261.54

steersman, frontiersman.

261.55

cannon, canon, fanon (papal vestment), Shannon, Buchanan, colcannon (boiled cabbage and potatoes), Clackmannan.

261.56

finnan, noumenon (philosophy term), phenomenon, prolegomenon (critical introduction).

261.57

capon, unshapen, misshapen.

261.58

Byron, Myron (Greek sculptor), siren, environ, lepidosiren (South American fish).

261.59

Huron, aleurone (protein), Van Buren (US president), anuran (tailless amphibian), thysanuran (primitive wingless insect).

261.60

longeron (part of aircraft), cateran (former Scottish brigand), veteran, Lutheran, Aldebaran (star), poriferan (a sponge), erigeron (flowering plant), hemipteran (type of insect), chiropteran (relating to bats), orthopteran (type of insect).

261.61

arson, Carson, fasten, parson, sarsen (sandstone boulder), unfasten.

261.62

basin, caisson (watertight structure), chasten, Jason, hasten, mason, washbasin, freemason, stonemason.

261.63

lesson, lessen, delicatessen.

261.64

person, worsen, Macpherson, unperson.

261.65

listen, glisten, Nissen, christen, Addison, Madison, Edison, Tennyson, venison, unison, Morrison, jettison, diocesan, archdiocesan.

261.65.1

garrison, Harrison, parison (unshaped glass before moulding), warison (bugle note ordering attack), caparison (horse's decorated covering), comparison.

261.66

ashen, fashion, passion, ration, impassion, compassion, dispassion.

261.67

Asian, nation, station.

striation, Croatian, libation, vacation, truncation, laudation (praise), foundation, purgation, lallation (speech defect), dilation, collation, ablation, oblation (religious offering), deflation, reflation, stagflation (economics term), inflation, translation, formation, summation, Dalmatian, vernation (leaf arrangement in bud), venation (arrangement of veins), zonation, damnation, serration, gyration, oration, libration (oscillating), vibration, migration, titration, filtration, castration, prostration, frustration, cassation (legal term), cessation, Alsatian, pulsation, flirtation, citation, dictation, lactation, temptation, gustation (tasting), crustacean, substation, outstation, lavation (washing), starvation, nivation (geology term), privation, ovation, novation (legal term), salvation, fixation, causation.

conurbation, incubation, titubation, education, inculcation, coruscation (gleam of light), retardation, denudation, exudation, inundation, subjugation, conjugation, promulgation, elongation, prolongation, insolation (exposure to solar radiation), contemplation, legislation, deformation, malformation, conformation, exhumation, subornation, indignation, assignation, designation, resignation, condemnation, usurpation, occupation, syncopation, aspiration, inspiration, expiration, lucubration (laborious study), desecration, consecration, dehydration, conflagration, arbitration, penetration, infiltration, concentration, orchestration, sequestration, illustration, demonstration, conversation, deportation, importation, transportation, exportation, exhortation, exploitation, affectation, delectation, expectation, eructation (belching), exaltation, exultation, auscultation, consultation, implantation, transplantation, confrontation, presentation, acceptation, adaptation, forestation, devastation, salivation, elevation, derivation, deprivation, titivation, motivation, activation, cultivation, captivation, aestivation (biology term), excavation, renovation, innovation, aggravation,

depravation, conservation, reservation, preservation, observation, accusation. coeducation, preoccupation, intermigration.

261.67.1
creation, radiation, mediation, expiation, variation, recreation, re-creation, procreation, aviation.
irradiation, repudiation, retaliation, delineation, columniation (arrangement of architectural columns), inebriation, appropriation, repatriation, expatriation, dissociation, association, expatiation, ingratiation, depreciation, appreciation, negotiation, substantiation, asphyxiation.
transubstantiation, consubstantiation, differentiation.

261.67.1.1
filiation (lineage), affiliation, humiliation, conciliation, disaffiliation, reconciliation.

261.67.1.2
foliation, spoliation, defoliation, despoliation.

261.67.1.3
caseation (formation of cheese), glaciation, emaciation.

261.67.1.4
enunciation, denunciation, renunciation, annunciation, pronunciation, mispronunciation.

261.67.1.5
vitiation, officiation, initiation.

261.67.1.6
deviation, abbreviation, alleviation.

261.67.2
menstruation, arcuation (arrangement of arches), graduation, valuation, situation, fluctuation, punctuation, evacuation, evaluation, devaluation, revaluation, attenuation, insinuation, continuation, infatuation, perpetuation, accentuation, superannuation.

261.67.3
probation, approbation, reprobation, perturbation, masturbation, disapprobation, exacerbation.

261.67.4

embarkation, demarcation, disembarkation.

261.67.5

dedication, medication, claudication (lameness), abdication, indication, vindication, defecation, publication, application, replication, supplication, duplication, implication, complication, explication, formication (skin sensation), fornication, fabrication, lubrication, imprecation, metrication, mastication.

eradication, adjudication, multiplication, reduplication, communication, prevarication, domestication, sophistication, prognostication, intoxication.

excommunication, intercommunication, telecommunication.

261.67.5.1 [further rhymes may be derived from **7.3**]

modification, qualification, ramification, classification, specification, fortification, notification, justification, electrification, identification.

261.67.6

location, vocation, bifurcation, suffocation, allocation, collocation, dislocation, embrocation, altercation, evocation, revocation, provocation, advocation, invocation, convocation, equivocation.

261.67.7

predation, sedation, validation, trepidation, liquidation, fluoridation, depredation, oxidation, consolidation, intimidation, dilapidation, elucidation.

261.67.8

gradation, backwardation (stock exchange term), degradation, accommodation, biodegradation.

261.67.9

emendation, commendation, recommendation.

261.67.10

legation (diplomatic mission), negation, allegation, delegation, relegation, obligation, fumigation, denegation (denial), abnegation, irrigation, segregation, congregation, litigation,

mitigation, castigation, instigation, navigation, desegregation, investigation, circumnavigation.

261.67.11

rogation, propagation, expurgation, abrogation (official cancellation), subrogation (legal term), interrogation.

261.67.12

elation, gelation (freezing), relation.

jubilation, congelation, appellation, cupellation (metallurgical process), compilation, correlation, fibrillation, vacillation, tessellation, oscillation, cancellation, titillation, scutellation (arrangement of animal's scales), mutilation, ventilation, scintillation, distillation, constellation.

invigilation, dissimilation, assimilation, horripilation (gooseflesh), interrelation.

malassimilation, hyperventilation.

261.67.13

serrulation (notch), tribulation, maculation (spotted pattern), speculation, circulation, calculation, adulation, modulation, undulation, regulation, emulation, formulation, cumulation, annulation (formation of rings), granulation, copulation, population, insulation, postulation, ovulation.

perambulation, ejaculation, vermiculation, matriculation, articulation, denticulation (finely-toothed structure), gesticulation, inoculation, miscalculation, emasculation, demodulation (electronics term), coagulation, accumulation, capitulation, expostulation, recapitulation.

261.67.13.1

tabulation, confabulation, tintinnabulation.

261.67.13.2

angulation, strangulation, triangulation.

261.67.13.3

simulation, stimulation, dissimulation.

261.67.13.4

stipulation, manipulation.

261.67.14

halation (photography term), spallation (nuclear physics reaction), vallation (construction of fortifications), escalation, inhalation, exhalation, immolation, desolation, isolation, consolation, installation, revelation, de-escalation, extrapolation, interpolation.

261.67.14.1

violation, annihilation.

261.67.15

cremation, sublimation, animation, lacrimation (secretion of tears), decimation, intimation, estimation, approximation, underestimation, overestimation.

261.67.16

affirmation, defamation, reformation, information, confirmation, transformation, acclamation, declamation, reclamation, proclamation, exclamation, inflammation, consummation, automation, misinformation, amalgamation.

261.67.17

carnation, tarnation, incarnation, reincarnation.

261.67.18

crenation (biology term), ruination, combination, machination, pollination, declination, inclination, culmination, fulmination, chlorination, urination, destination, divination, vaccination, recombination, miscegenation (interbreeding of races), desalination, disinclination, insemination, peregrination, indoctrination, hallucination, concatenation (series of interconnected events), agglutination, procrastination, predestination, rejuvenation.

261.67.18.1

ordination, preordination, coordination, subordination, incoordination, insubordination.

261.67.18.2

pagination, imagination, invagination (infolding of tubular structure).

261.67.18.3

lamination, contamination, examination, decontamination, cross-examination.

261.67.18.4

germination, termination, vermination (infestation with vermin), determination, extermination.

261.67.18.5

elimination, recrimination, incrimination, discrimination.

261.67.18.6

domination, nomination, abomination, predomination, denomination.

261.67.18.7

rumination, illumination.

261.67.18.8

fascination, assassination.

261.67.19

conation (psychology term), donation, carbonation, hibernation, condonation, profanation, hyphenation, explanation, emanation, coronation, detonation, alternation, intonation, consternation, alienation, impersonation.

261.67.20

obstipation, constipation, emancipation.

261.67.20.1

dissipation, participation, anticipation.

261.67.21

Eurasian, duration, conjuration, carburation, procuration, suppuration, mensuration (measuring), maturation, trituration (grinding into fine powder), configuration, transfiguration, inauguration.

261.67.22

Horatian, narration.
liberation, decoration, saturation, adoration, federation, moderation, perforation, figuration, toleration, coloration, declaration, exploration, glomeration (cluster), numeration, admiration, reparation, preparation, separation, corporation, desperation, respiration, perspiration, peroration, laceration,

ulceration, alteration, restoration, botheration.

reverberation, deliberation, confederation, consideration, proliferation, exaggeration, refrigeration, deceleration, acceleration, exhilaration, discoloration, commemoration, agglomeration, conglomeration, enumeration, incineration, remuneration, evaporation, recuperation, vituperation, exasperation, expectoration, perseveration (psychology term), commiseration.

amelioration, deterioration.

261.67.22.1

aberration, collaboration.

261.67.22.2

generation, veneration, degeneration, regeneration.

261.67.22.3

operation, cooperation, noncooperation.

261.67.22.4

iteration, literation (representing sounds by letters), reiteration, alliteration, obliteration, transliteration.

261.67.23

calibration, celebration, cerebration (thinking), vertebration, equilibration.

261.67.24

emigration, immigration, integration, redintegration (act of renewal), disintegration.

261.67.25

registration, fenestration (arrangement of windows), ministration, defenestration (throwing person from window), administration, maladministration.

261.67.26

sensation, condensation, compensation, dispensation, aftersensation, overcompensation.

261.67.27

cetacean (whale), habitation, dubitation (doubt), meditation, agitation, vegetation, imitation, limitation, sanitation, capitation, palpitation, equitation, irritation, recitation, jactitation

(boasting), gravitation, levitation, invitation, excitation, visitation.

cohabitation, premeditation, regurgitation, decapitation, precipitation, interpretation, felicitation, sollicitation, resuscitation.

prestidigitation, rehabilitation, misinterpretation.

261.67.28

dotation (endowment), flotation, notation, potation (drinking), quotation, rotation, annotation, denotation, connotation, misquotation, dextrorotation (rotation to right), laevorotation (rotation to left).

261.67.29

mutation, nutation (nodding), refutation, salutation, permutation, commutation, sternutation (sneezing), deputation, reputation, amputation, imputation, computation, disputation, transmutation.

261.67.30

natation, dilatation, dissertation, constatation (process of establishing truth).

261.67.31

plantation, recantation, incantation.

261.67.32

dentation (tooth-like projections), tentation (method of adjusting machine), indentation, lamentation, fermentation, cementation, fomentation, fragmentation, segmentation, pigmentation, augmentation, frequentation, ostentation, sustentation (nourishment), orientation, documentation, argumentation, ornamentation, instrumentation, representation, misrepresentation.

261.67.32.1

sedimentation, regimentation, alimentation, implementation, experimentation.

261.67.33

gestation, infestation, molestation, attestation, detestation, protestation, manifestation.

261.67.34

laxation (defecation), taxation, relaxation.

261.67.35

vexation, annexation.

261.67.36 [also **516** + *-ation*]

sterilization, fertilization, civilization, realization, centralization, organization, dramatization, improvisation, nationalization, generalization.

261.68

freshen, session, cession.

profession, confession, discretion, regression, digression, aggression, progression, transgression, depression, repression, oppression, suppression, impression, compression, expression, recession, precession, secession, obsession, concession, accession, succession, possession.

indiscretion, reimpression, decompression, repossession, prepossession, selfpossession, dispossession.

261.68.1

procession, supersession, intercession.

261.69

Persian, tertian (recurring every other day), version, coercion, recursion (returning), incursion, excursion, immersion, dispersion, aspersion, assertion, insertion, Cistercian (member of religious order), reversion, diversion, subversion, inversion, conversion, exertion, desertion, animadversion (criticism).

261.69.1

aversion, perversion, introversion, extroversion.

261.70

Rhaetian (language group), Grecian, deletion, depletion, repletion, completion, Venetian, Capetian (relating to French dynasty), secretion, accretion, incretion (secretion into bloodstream), concretion, excretion, Helvetian, Diocletian (Roman emperor).

261.71

fission, mission, Titian.

coition, fruition, tuition, ambition, audition, rendition, condition, logician, magician, emission, demission, remission, submission, admission, transmission, monition (warning), munition, technician, ignition, cognition, suspicion, detrition (wearing away by friction), nutrition, contrition, partition, mortician, sortition (casting lots), beautician, tactician, dentition, optician, musician, transition.

intuition, prohibition, imbibition (absorption), inhibition, exhibition, erudition, recondition, precondition, ammunition, mechanician, premonition, admonition, inanition, precognition (foreknowledge), recognition, parturition, micturition, apparition, rhetorician, preterition (act of omitting), obstetrician, malnutrition, electrician, repartition, tripartition, deglutition, logistician, statistician, acoustician, superstition, Ordovician (geological period).

equipartition, mathematician, diagnostician.

261.71.1

edition, sedition, expedition.

261.71.2

addition, perdition, tradition, extradition.

261.71.3

volition, coalition, abolition, ebullition, demolition.

261.71.4

omission, commission, Domitian (Roman emperor), permission, intromission (insertion), intermission, academician.

261.71.5

Phoenician, clinician, definition.

261.71.6

attrition, patrician, paediatrician, geriatrician.

261.71.7

petition, dietitian, politician, cosmetician, phonetician, repetition, competition, aesthetician, theoretician.

261.71.8

physician, acquisition, requisition, inquisition, disquisition (formal discourse), metaphysician.

261.71.9

position, apposition, deposition, preposition, reposition, opposition, proposition, supposition, malposition, imposition, composition, disposition, transposition, exposition, presupposition, juxtaposition, decomposition, predisposition, indisposition.

261.72

caution, portion, torsion, abortion, precaution, retorsion (reprisal), intorsion (spiral twisting), contortion, distortion, extortion.

261.72.1

apportion, proportion, disproportion.

261.73

ocean, Goshen (region of ancient Egypt), lotion, motion, notion, potion, groschen (Austrian coin), emotion, demotion, devotion.

261.73.1

promotion, commotion, locomotion.

261.74

Russian, Prussian, percussion, concussion, discussion, repercussion, Byelorussian.

261.75

crucian (European fish), dilution, ablution, Confucian, Rosicrucian, attribution, retribution, contribution, distribution, persecution, prosecution, execution, diminution, Lilliputian, destitution, restitution, prostitution, substitution, institution, constitution.

261.75.1

pollution, solution, volution (spiral motion), dissolution, absolution, revolution, evolution, devolution, involution (complication), convolution, resolution, circumvolution (turning around central axis), irresolution, counter-revolution.

261.75.2

locution, allocution (formal speech), elocution, interlocution (conversation), circumlocution, electrocution.

261.76

action, faction, fraction, traction.

reaction, inaction, diffraction, refraction, detraction, retraction, attraction, protraction, subtraction, contraction, distraction, abstraction, extraction, exaction, transaction.

abreaction (psychiatry term), retroaction, tumefaction (swelling), benefaction, stupefaction, liquefaction, rarefaction, petrifaction, putrefaction, satisfaction, interaction, dissatisfaction.

261.77

lection (variation in text), flexion, section.

defection, refection, affection, perfection, infection, confection, ejection, dejection, rejection, objection, subjection, injection, bolection (architectural term), collection, deflection, reflection, inflection, complexion, connection, inspection, bisection, subsection, midsection, detection, protection, advection (heat transfer in air), convection.

imperfection, disinfection, recollection, retroflexion, genuflection, retrospection, introspection, intersection, overprotection.

261.77.1

projection, introjection (psychology term), interjection.

261.77.2

election, selection, re-election, predilection, intellection (thought).

261.77.3

erection, direction, indirection, misdirection.

261.77.4

correction, insurrection, resurrection.

261.77.5

dissection, resection (surgical removal of part), venesection (incision into vein), vivisection.

261.78

diction, fiction, friction, nonfiction, affliction, depiction, restriction, constriction, eviction, conviction, jurisdiction, crucifixion, dereliction, derestriction.

261.78.1

prediction, malediction, valediction, benediction.

261.78.2

addiction, contradiction, interdiction (prohibition).

261.79

fluxion, ruction, suction, deduction, reduction, seduction, abduction, induction, conduction, destruction, obstruction, instruction, construction, reconstruction, misconstruction.

261.79.1

adduction, production, reproduction, introduction, underproduction.

261.80

unction, function, junction, malfunction, dysfunction, injunction, conjunction, disjunction, compunction.

261.81

scansion, mansion, stanchion (support), expansion.

261.82

gentian, mention, pension, tension. declension, dimension, suspension, Lawrentian, ascension, detention, retention, pretension, intention, contention, abstention, extension, prevention, subvention, invention, convention. hypotension, contravention, intervention, circumvention.

261.82.1

prehension (act of grasping), apprehension, reprehension, comprehension, misapprehension, incomprehension.

261.82.2

dissension, recension (critical literary revision), condescension.

261.82.3

attention, inattention, hypertension.

261.83

caption, recaption (legal term), contraption.

261.84

obreption (obtaining by deceit), subreption (concealment of facts), deception, reception, inception, conception, exception, self-deception, preconception, misconception.

261.84.1

perception, apperception (psychology term), contraception, intussusception (medical term).

261.85

Egyptian, conniption (*US* fit of rage), description, prescription, proscription, ascription, subscription, transcription, inscription, conscription, circumscription.

261.86

option, adoption.

261.87

sorption (adsorption or absorption), absorption, adsorption, chemisorption (chemistry term).

261.88

eruption, corruption, abruption (breaking off), disruption, interruption.

261.89

gumption, assumption, subsumption (inclusion under general heading), consumption, resumption, presumption.

261.90 [see also 261.3.34]

lesion, Friesian, Ephesian, cohesion, adhesion, inhesion (inherence).

261.91 [see also 261.3.35]

Frisian (language of Netherlands), scission, vision, elision, collision, derision, misprision (concealment of treasonable act), abscission (shedding of plant parts), incision, concision, envision, excision, circumcision.

261.91.1

decision, recision (cancellation), precision, precisian (strict observer of rules), indecision, imprecision.

261.91.2
division, revision, prevision, subdivision, television.

261.91.3
provision, Eurovision, supervision, stereovision.

261.92
plosion (phonetics term), eclosion (emergence of insect), implosion, explosion, erosion, corrosion.

261.93
fusion, allusion, collusion, seclusion, occlusion, inclusion, conclusion, exclusion, protrusion, obtrusion, intrusion, extrusion, effusion, diffusion, profusion, infusion, confusion, transfusion, contusion, malocclusion (dentistry term).

261.93.1
illusion, delusion, disillusion.

261.94
batten, fatten, latten (thin sheet metal), flatten, platan (plane tree), platen (plate in printing press), slattern, pattern, patten (wooden clog), Patton (US general), Grattan, Mountbatten, Manhattan, harmattan.

261.95
Barton, carton, hearten, smarten, Spartan, tartan, Dumbarton, dishearten, kindergarten, Akhenaten (Egyptian king).

261.96
jetton (gambling token), Breton, threaten, Tibetan.

261.97
Burton, curtain, Merton, certain, uncertain.

261.98
Eton, eaten, beaten, Keaton, neaten, Cretan, Seaton, wheaten, sweeten, unbeaten, Nuneaton, weather-beaten.

261.99
bittern, bitten, kitten, mitten, smitten, written, Britain, Briton, Britten, witan (Anglo-Saxon advisory council), frostbitten, skeleton, Honiton, puritan, handwritten, unwritten, Mahometan,

Samaritan, endoskeleton, exoskeleton, Neapolitan, cosmopolitan, metropolitan.

261.100
chiton (ancient Greek tunic), heighten, lighten, righten (return to normal position), Brighton, brighten, Crichton, frighten, Triton (Greek sea god), triton (marine mollusc), tighten, Titan, whiten, enlighten.

261.101
cotton, gotten, rotten, guncotton, begotten, forgotten, ill-gotten, misbegotten, unforgotten.

261.102
Laughton, Morton, quartern (measure of weight), quartan (recurring every third day), shorten, tauten, foreshorten.

261.103
button, glutton, mutton, Sutton, unbutton, bellybutton.

261.104
Luton, gluten, Newton, Teuton (member of Germanic people), rambutan (Asian tree).

261.105
Minton, quintan (recurring every fourth day), badminton.

261.106
Preston, teston (former French silver coin), western, Avestan (ancient language).

261.107
piston, Tristan, cistern, Ilkeston (English town), Eddystone, Germiston (South African city), Coniston, sacristan.

261.108
Kingston, Livingstone.

261.109
Phaëthon (Greek mythological character), Jonathan, marathon, leviathan (biblical sea monster).

261.110
carven, Cuxhaven (German port), Caernarvon.

261.111

Avon, haven, raven, craven, graven, shaven, Newhaven, clean-shaven, unshaven.

261.112

Bevan (British statesman), Devon, heaven, leaven, Severn, seven, Midheaven (astrology term), eleven.

261.113

even, Leven (Scottish loch), Stephen, Genevan, uneven.

261.114

given, Niven, riven, driven, forgiven, Sullivan, unforgiven.

261.115

Ivan, liven, wyvern (heraldic beast), enliven.

261.116

cloven, woven, Eindhoven (Dutch city), Beethoven, interwoven.

261.117

oven, coven, govern, sloven, misgovern.

261.118

scallion, stallion, rapscallion, medallion, Italian, battalion.

261.119 [see also **261.3.9**]

hellion (troublesome person), rebellion, Trevelyan.

261.120 [see also **261.3.11**]

billion, million, pillion, trillion, zillion, tourbillion (whirlwind), modillion (architectural ornament), vermilion, carillon, decillion (10^{60}), cotillion, centillion (10^{600}), postilion, civilian, pavilion.

261.121

banyan, canyon, fanion (surveyor's small flag), companion.

261.122 [see also **261.3.17**]

minion, pinion, dominion, opinion.

261.123

union, reunion, communion, nonunion, intercommunion.

261.124

blazon, raisin, brazen, emblazon, diapason (organ stop).

261.125

reason, treason, season, unreason.

261.126

mizzen, risen, prison, wizen, malison (a curse), benison, denizen, orison, arisen, imprison, citizen.

261.127

greisen (light-coloured rock), horizon, spiegeleisen (type of pig iron).

261.128

foison (plentiful supply), poison, empoison.

261.129

chosen, frozen, lederhosen.

262 -iln

kiln, Milne, limekiln.

263 -ang

bang, bhang (narcotic from Indian hemp), dang, fang, gang, hang, Lang, clang, slang, pang, rang, prang, sprang, sang, Shang (Chinese dynasty), Tang (Chinese dynasty), tang, vang (nautical term), whang, twang.

kiang (Tibetan wild ass), shebang, gangbang, Nanchang (Chinese city), padang (Malaysian field), Malang (Indonesian city), boomslang (venomous snake), Penang (Malaysian island and state), trepang (Oriental sea cucumber), linsang (forest-dwelling mammal), mustang, Shenyang (Chinese city), Pyongyang (capital of North Korea).

overhang, siamang (large black gibbon), navarin, Mazarin, burrawang (Australian plant).

Heilungkiang (Chinese province), ylang-ylang (aromatic Asian tree), goreng pisang (Malaysian banana fritters), orang-outang.

263.1

probang (surgical instrument), charabanc, interrobang (punctuation mark).

263.2

harangue, meringue, Serang (Indonesian island), boomerang.

264 -eng

Kaifeng (Chinese city), ronggeng (Malay traditional dance), ginseng.

265 -ing [further rhymes may be created by adding -ing to appropriate verbs]

king, Ching (Chinese dynasty), ding, ling, cling, fling, sling, Ming, ping, wring, ring, bring, spring, string, sing, ting, sting, thing, wing, swing, zing.

gnawing, drawing, webbing, dubbing, rubbing, tubing, backing, blacking, packing, cracking, sacking, whacking, Barking, marking, parking, working, sneaking, Peking, speaking, liking, striking, Viking, smoking, soaking, Woking, ducking, fucking, trucking, sucking, booking, cooking, erlking (mythical malevolent spirit), hulking, Nanking, banking, planking, spanking, ranking, catching, etching, fetching, searching, I Ching (Chinese book of divination), teaching, breeching (harness strap), itching, stitching, witching, coaching, poaching, scorching, touching, cladding, padding, wording, bidding, sodding, wadding, budding, pudding, gelding, balding, wingding, surfing, briefing, spiffing, offing, stuffing, roofing, lagging, flagging, rigging, frigging, wigging, edging, lodging, grudging, swingeing, curling, hurling, sterling, Stirling, tiling, hireling, schooling, ruling, tooling, marbling, stabling, sibling, gambling, rambling, crackling, weakling, inkling, sprinkling, twinkling, reedling (Eurasian songbird), seedling, fiddling, middling, piddling, codling (variety of cooking apple), worldling (materialist), handling, brandling (small red earthworm), kindling, spindling (long and slender), foundling, groundling, rifling (grooves inside gun barrel), trifling, stifling, niggling, juggling, smuggling, angling, gangling, fledgling, changeling, greenling (Pacific fish), weanling, grappling, sapling, Kipling, crippling, stripling, coupling, dumpling, nestling, wrestling, nursling, brisling (Norwegian sprat), whistling, princeling, unsling, Gatling (machine-gun), rattling, footling, scantling (narrow rafter), mantling (heraldic term), earthling,

riesling, quisling (collaborator), gosling, gaming, flaming, lemming, Fleming, slimming, trimming, swimming, priming, timing, canning, planning, awning, mourning, morning, warning, browning, tuning, lightning, evening, hanging, longing, Epping, skipping, chipping, clipping, flipping, ripping, dripping, gripping, shipping, whipping, piping, typing, hopping, sopping, shopping, topping, stopping, whopping, coping, sloping, grouping, scalping, helping, camping, rasping, grasping, barring, sparring, herring, bullring, hairspring, headspring, handspring, offspring, mainspring, drawstring, bowstring, shoestring, hamstring, unstring, passing, nursing, piercing, icing, crossing, coursing, dancing, fencing, bouncing, flouncing, dashing, lashing, flashing, smashing, crashing, thrashing, Pershing, washing, Flushing (Dutch port), Cushing, pushing, ruching, batting, matting, tatting, parting, skirting, shirting, beating, heating, fleeting, meeting, greeting, seating, sheeting, boating, coating, floating, outing, Scouting, cutting, nutting, putting, footing, fluting, suiting, shooting, belting, felting, lilting, quilting, halting, malting, vaulting, fainting, painting, printing, wanting, daunting, haunting, pointing, bunting, hunting, tempting, costing, frosting, posting, roasting, plaything, nothing, something, farthing, bathing, scathing, Worthing, breathing, teething, loathing, clothing, soothing, carving, starving, diving, driving, loving, moving, shelving, forewing, redwing (European thrush), gull-wing, lapwing, lacewing (insect), batwing, waxwing (songbird), boxing, foxing, pleasing, freezing, seizing, dowsing, housing, rousing.

dairying, disturbing, absorbing, woodworking, beseeching, bird-watching, unflinching, regarding, forbidding, unyielding, scaffolding, demanding, commanding, intriguing, obliging, unchanging, towelling, gruelling, sanderling (small sandpiper), underling, panelling, ting-a-ling, snivelling, fosterling (foster child), hostelling, travelling, bloodcurdling, programming, performing, brainstorming, adjoining, belonging, galloping, walloping, unceasing, refreshing, brainwashing, first-footing, comforting, shoplifting, weightlifting, revolting, imprinting, excepting, blockbusting, disgusting, anything, everything, revolving, underwing.

pony trekking, overcrowding, corresponding, overwhelming, embarrassing, conveyancing, unrelenting, disappointing.

265.1

Maying (celebration of May Day), saying, bricklaying, soothsaying, surveying.

265.2

being, skiing, seeing, wellbeing, sightseeing.

265.3

dying, dyeing, flying, spying, crying, trying, undying, outlying, underlying.

265.4

owing, bowing, going, knowing, rowing, sewing, showing, seagoing, foregoing, churchgoing, ingoing, ongoing, outgoing, following, unknowing, harrowing, ingrowing, easy-going, thoroughgoing, overflowing.

265.5

doing, brewing, viewing, undoing, wrongdoing, canoeing.

265.6

baking, making, taking, waking, haymaking, dressmaking, lovemaking, backbreaking, housebreaking, heartbreaking, earthshaking, stocktaking, breathtaking, painstaking, merrymaking, undertaking.

265.7

licking, ticking, Mafeking, pigsticking (hunting wild boar), politicking (political canvassing).

265.8

smocking, frocking (coarse material), shocking, stocking, bluestocking.

265.9

corking, Dorking, hawking, walking, sleepwalking.

265.10

blinking, pinking, sinking, stinking, thinking, unblinking, freethinking, unthinking, unwinking.

265.11

fading, lading (cargo), braiding, trading, shading, unfading, degrading.

265.12

bedding, heading, leading (printing term), Reading, wedding, subheading, featherbedding.

265.13

beading, leading, bleeding, pleading, reading, breeding, sheading (Manx region), misleading, sight-reading, preceding, proceeding, exceeding.

265.14

guiding, hiding, sliding, gliding, riding, siding, abiding, confiding, providing, law-abiding.

265.15

boarding, hoarding, recording, according, rewarding, unrewarding.

265.16

loading, foreboding.

265.17

building, gilding, shipbuilding, outbuilding.

265.18

scolding, holding, moulding, stockholding, roadholding, smallholding.

265.19

landing, standing, crashlanding, freestanding, upstanding, outstanding, understanding, notwithstanding, misunderstanding.

265.20

ending, mending, pending, spending, unbending, unending, impending, heart-rending, moneylending, condescending.

265.21

binding, finding, blinding, winding, bookbinding.

265.22

grounding, sounding, surrounding, astounding, resounding.

265.23

jogging, logging, flogging, frogging (decoration on uniform), pettifogging.

265.24

ageing, staging, engaging.

265.25

bridging, packaging, managing.

265.26

Carling, darling, sparling (a fish), starling.

265.27

ailing, failing, paling, railing, grayling (freshwater fish), sailing, tailing, whaling, unfailing, prevailing, unveiling, unavailing.

265.28

spelling, telling, dwelling, swelling, compelling, misspelling, fortune-telling.

265.29

Ealing, feeling, peeling, ceiling, shieling (*Scot* shepherd's hut), stealing, unfeeling, Darjeeling, revealing, freewheeling.

265.30

billing, killing, filling, milling, thrilling, shilling, schilling (former Austrian currency), willing, spine-chilling, atheling (Anglo-Saxon prince), unwilling.

265.31

calling, galling, crawling, sprawling, snowballing, appalling, enthralling.

265.32

bowling, polling, rolling, potholing.

265.33

cowling (metal covering), fowling, howling, antifouling (protective paint).

265.34

buckling (bloater), duckling, swashbuckling.

265.35

charming, farming, alarming, disarming.

265.36

scheming, seeming, teeming, redeeming, daydreaming.

265.37

combing, coaming (frame around ship's hatches), homing, gloaming, Wyoming.

265.38

coming, plumbing, becoming, homecoming, incoming, oncoming, shortcoming, forthcoming, unbecoming.

265.39

blooming, grooming, assuming, unassuming.

265.40

caning, graining, training, veining, remaining, entertaining.

265.41

burning, churning, learning, turning, discerning, concerning.

265.42

leaning, cleaning, meaning, Sining (Chinese city), dry-cleaning, demeaning, overweening.

265.43

inning, spinning, winning, beginning, underpinning.

265.44

fining (process of clarifying liquid), lining, mining, refining, divining, designing, interlining.

265.45

cunning, gunning, running, stunning, gunrunning.

265.46

ironing, reckoning, sickening, thickening, questioning, maddening, gardening, happening, opening, fastening, christening, sweetening, frightening, shortening, ravening (voracious), reasoning, seasoning, conditioning.

265.47
springing, singing, swinging, mudslinging, upbringing, bell-ringing.

265.48
mapping, wrapping, strapping, overlapping.

265.49
keeping, weeping, sweeping, safekeeping, book-keeping, housekeeping.

265.50
dumping, thumping, showjumping.

265.51
furring, purring, shirring, stirring, recurring, unerring.

265.52
airing, bearing, daring, fairing, glaring, paring, sparing, raring, tearing, wearing, uncaring, seafaring, unsparing, cheeseparing, overbearing.

265.53
earring, gearing, hearing, clearing, searing, steering, endearing, god-fearing, veneering, sheepshearing, engineering, mountaineering, electioneering, orienteering.

265.54
firing, tiring, wiring, aspiring, inspiring, inquiring, retiring, untiring, uninspiring.

265.55
boring, flooring, roaring, warring, skijoring (snow sport), outpouring.

265.56
mooring, during, alluring, enduring, reassuring.

265.57
flowering, towering, overpowering.

265.58
neighbouring, timbering, lumbering, doddering, rendering, wandering, thundering, offering, suffering, staggering, fingering, conjuring, colouring, ashlaring (building material), murmuring, scattering, flattering, smattering, catering, Kettering, lettering, guttering, shuttering (wooden mould for concrete), sweltering, plastering, gathering, feathering (plumage), weathering, blithering, Havering (Greater London borough).
considering, self-catering, woolgathering (daydreaming), manufacturing, mouthwatering.

265.58.1
flavouring, unwavering.

265.59
casing, facing, lacing, placing, spacing, racing, bracing, tracing, interfacing.

265.60
blessing, dressing, pressing, hairdressing, depressing, distressing, prepossessing, unprepossessing.

265.61
kissing, missing, promising.

265.62
mincing, convincing, unconvincing.

265.63
fishing, furnishing, perishing, ravishing, astonishing.

265.64
skating, plating, slating, rating, grating, weighting, vacillating, calculating, fulgurating (piercingly painful), penetrating, excruciating, accommodating, unhesitating.

265.64.1
fascinating, discriminating.

265.65
netting, petting, setting, blood-letting, typesetting, upsetting, thermosetting (hardening after heating).

265.66
fitting, splitting, knitting, sitting, bracketing, marketing, picketing, pipefitting, hairsplitting, permitting, carpeting, unwitting, unremitting.

265.67
biting, fighting, lighting, slighting, writing, whiting, backbiting, bullfighting, infighting, moonlighting, skywriting, handwriting, typewriting, inviting, exciting, uninviting.

265.68

jotting, knotting, potting, rotting, yachting, train-spotting, globetrotting.

265.69

courting, sporting, Storting (Norwegian parliament), supporting.

265.70

acting, distracting, exacting, overacting.

265.71

affecting, respecting, expecting, self-respecting, unsuspecting.

265.72

slanting, enchanting.

265.73

mounting, accounting.

265.74

casting, lasting, blasting, contrasting, everlasting.

265.75

nesting, resting, testing, arresting.

265.76

listing, consisting, harvesting, interesting.

265.77

caving, paving, raving, craving, saving, shaving, engraving, timesaving.

265.78

Irving, serving, unnerving, unswerving, deserving, undeserving.

265.79

sleeving (wire insulation), grieving, thieving, weaving, unbelieving.

265.80

living, forgiving, misgiving, thanksgiving.

265.81

glazing, raising, phrasing, grazing, stargazing, amazing, self-raising, double-glazing.

265.82

rising, uprising, surprising, enterprising, appetizing, advertising, uncompromising.

265.83

closing, nosing (projecting edge), supposing, imposing.

265.84

losing, bruising, confusing, amusing.

266 -ong

bong, Caen, dong, gong, long, flong (printing term), pong, wrong, prong, strong, throng, song, tong, thong.

Mekong, Hong Kong, quandong (Australian fruit tree), ding-dong, bogong (Australian moth), dugong, mahjong, élan, daylong, furlong, belong, Shillong (Indian city), oolong, oblong, headlong, sidelong, endlong, lifelong, nightlong, livelong, chaise longue, kampong (Malaysian village), ping-pong (*Trademark*), headstrong, Armstrong, croissant, plainsong, singsong, souchong (black tea), penchant, diphthong, morwong (Australian fish), foo yong (Chinese omelette), bouffant.

billabong, aide-de-camp, Vietcong, wobbegong (shark), Chittagong (Bangladeshi port), Wollongong (Australian city), denouement, binturong (Asian mammal), cradlesong, evensong, contretemps, currawong (Australian songbird).

266.1

along, prolong, overlong.

266.2

sarong, restaurant.

267 -ung

bung, dung, hung, lung, clung, flung, slung, mung (Australian bean), wrung, rung, sprung, strung, sung, tongue, stung, swung, young, among, unstrung, unsung, Nantung (Chinese city), Shantung (Chinese province), shantung (heavy silk fabric), underhung (protruding from beneath), overhung, aqualung, highly-strung.

268 -ap

bap, cap, chap, dap, gap, Jap, Lapp, lap, clap, flap, slap, map, nap, snap, pap, rap, wrap, crap, scrap, trap, strap, sap, tap, yap, zap.

kneecap, recap, snowcap, toecap, mobcap, hubcap, blackcap (European bird), madcap, skullcap, uncap, icecap, nightcap, whitecap (white-crested wave), foolscap, stopgap, mishap, burlap (coarse fabric), dewlap, earflap, kidnap, unsnap, catnap, enwrap, unwrap, flytrap, firetrap, giftwrap, mantrap, entrap, suntrap, claptrap, mousetrap, watchstrap, bootstrap, rattrap, deathtrap, jockstrap, heeltap.

handicap, overlap, thunderclap, genipap (West Indian tree), rattletrap (broken-down car), wentletrap (marine mollusc), Tonle Sap (Cambodian lake).

269 -arp

carp, scarp, harp, sharp, tarp (*Austral* tarpaulin), syncarp (fleshy multiple fruit), escarp (side of fortification ditch), cardsharp, watap (American Indian sewing thread), Polycarp (Christian saint), epicarp (outer skin of fruit), ascocarp (part of a fungus), mesocarp (fleshy part of fruit), counterscarp (side of fortification ditch), vibraharp (percussion instrument).

270 -ape

ape, cape, gape, jape, nape, rape, crepe, scrape, drape, grape, shape, tape, seascape, escape, cloudscape, landscape, inscape (person's inner nature), townscape, agape, broomrape (plant parasite), reshape, shipshape, misshape, nametape, waterscape, Sellotape (*Trademark*).

271 -ep

skep (beehive), hep, schlep (*US* to drag), pep, rep, prep, cep (edible fungus), step, steppe, Dieppe, salep (dried orchid tuber), doorstep, sidestep, instep, footstep, quickstep, overstep, Amenhotep (Egyptian pharaoh), Gaziantep (Turkish city).

272 -erp

Earp, burp, chirp, slurp, twerp, Antwerp, usurp.

273 -eep

beep, keep, cheep, cheap, deep, jeep, heap, leap, bleep, sleep, neap, neep (*Dialect* turnip), peep, reap, creep, seep, sheep, steep, weep, sweep, upkeep,

scrapheap, asleep, upsweep, oversleep, cassareep (juice of cassava root), Lakshadweep (islands in Arabian Sea).

274 -ip

kip, skip, chip, dip, gyp, hip, lip, blip, clip, flip, slip, nip, snip, pip, quip, rip, scrip (written certificate), drip, grip, trip, strip, sip, ship, tip, whip, zip.
rosehip, harelip, fillip, Philip, polyp, julep (sweet drink), tulip, cowslip, sideslip, gymslip, nonslip, oxlip (woodland plant), turnip, parsnip, equip, hairgrip, handgrip, unrip, cantrip (magic spell), airstrip, outstrip, gossip, worship, airship, heirship, mayorship, warship, hardship, headship, midship, Lordship, wardship, friendship, flagship, judgeship, steamship, kinship, township, unship, kingship, longship, troopship, spaceship, transship, lightship, courtship, bullwhip (long rawhide whip), horsewhip, bunyip (*Austral* legendary monster), unzip.
paperclip, pillowslip, trusteeship, Ladyship, fellowship, comradeship, battleship, internship, studentship, fingertip, apprenticeship.

274.1

membership, leadership, lectureship, readership, scholarship, ownership, partnership, censorship, sponsorship, authorship, premiership, chancellorship, councillorship, governorship, dictatorship, directorship, receivership, ambassadorship.

274.2

seamanship, showmanship, workmanship, brinkmanship, penmanship, horsemanship, marksmanship, swordsmanship, salesmanship, gamesmanship, statesmanship, sportsmanship, guardianship, championship, oneupmanship, relationship, musicianship, companionship, citizenship, librarianship.

275 -ipe

hype, slype (covered passageway in cathedral), snipe, pipe, ripe, gripe, tripe, stripe, type, stipe (plant's reproductive stalk), wipe, swipe.
jacksnipe (Eurasian bird), blowpipe, standpipe, windpipe, bagpipe, tailpipe,

drainpipe, hornpipe, downpipe, stovepipe, hawsepipe (nautical term), rareripe (*US* ripening early), unripe, pinstripe, subtype, ectype (a copy), tintype (photographic print), sideswipe.

guttersnipe, liripipe (tip of graduate's hood), underripe, overripe, archetype, Teletype (*Trademark*), antetype (earlier form).

275.1

biotype (biology term), ecotype (ecology term), logotype, collotype (printing process), holotype (original biological type specimen), genotype (organism's genetic constitution), phenotype (biology term), Linotype (*Trademark*), monotype (single print), phototype (photographically-produced printing plate), prototype, countertype (opposite type), stereotype, cyanotype (blueprint), daguerreotype, electrotype (electroplated printing plate), somatotype (classification of physique).

276 -op

bop, cop, kop (prominent isolated African hill), scop (Anglo-Saxon minstrel), chop, fop, hop, lop, flop, plop, slop, mop, pop, crop, drop, prop, strop, sop, shop, top, stop, whop (to hit), swap.

coop, bebop, Cu-bop (jazz music), carhop (drive-in restaurant waiter), hedgehop (fly near ground level), bellhop, orlop (nautical term), Dunlop, clip-clop, flip-flop, slipslop (weak drink), rollmop, coin-op, joypop (*Slang* take drugs), sharecrop (*US* cultivate farmland), stonecrop (fleshy-leaved plant), airdrop, eardrop (pendant earring), snowdrop, dewdrop, gumdrop, raindrop, eavesdrop, Aesop, soursop (West Indian tree), sweetsop (West Indian tree), Worksop, milksop, teashop, workshop, bookshop, pawnshop, sweatshop, sweetshop, hardtop, tiptop, estop (legal term), doorstop, housetop, nonstop, unstop, flattop.

escalope, lollipop, overcrop (cultivate excessively), paradrop (delivery by parachute), turboprop, agitprop (Russian propaganda bureau), barbershop.

276.1

atop, overtop.

277 -orp

scaup (diving duck), dorp (small South African village), gawp, Thorpe, warp, Scunthorpe, mouldwarp (*Dialect* mole), Krugersdorp (South African city), Australorp (domestic fowl).

278 -ope

cope, scope, dope, hope, lope, slope, mope, nope, pope, rope, grope, trope (word used figuratively), soap, tope, taupe (brownish-grey colour), stope (mine excavation).

myope, pyrope (yellowish-red garnet), towrope, dragrope, manrope (rope railing on ship), tightrope, sandsoap (gritty soap).

radarscope, telescope, periscope, interlope, envelope, antipope, phalarope (aquatic shore bird), lycanthrope (werewolf), misanthrope, isotope, radioisotope.

278.1

stroboscope, bronchoscope, endoscope, seismoscope, chronoscope, snooperscope (US military instrument), baroscope (atmospheric-pressure measurer), gyroscope, horoscope, microscope, hydroscope (instrument for underwater observation), hygroscope (humidity indicator), gastroscope, otoscope, stethoscope, stereoscope, kaleidoscope, pharyngoscope, laryngoscope, ophthalmoscope, urethroscope, tachistoscope (instrument displaying images momentarily).

278.1.1

bioscope (early film projector), skiascope (eye-examining instrument), diascope (optical projector).

278.1.2

spectroscope (spectrum-producing instrument), electroscope (electric-charge detector).

278.2

elope, antelope.

278.3

allotrope (chemistry term), thaumatrope (optical illusion toy), heliotrope, azeotrope (chemistry term).

279 -up

up, cup, scup (Atlantic fish), pup, sup, tup, yup, backup, make-up, checkup, teacup, hiccup, eyecup, cockup, kingcup, roundup, close-up, lash-up (temporary connection of equipment), wickiup (American Indian hut), giddy-up, buttercup.

280 -oop

coop, coupe (shallow glass), scoop, whoop, hoop, loop, loupe (jeweller's magnifying glass), sloop, snoop, poop, roup (respiratory disease of birds), croup, droop, drupe (fleshy fruit), group, troupe, troop, soup, stoop, stoup (basin for holy water), swoop, dupe, stupe (hot medicated compress).

recoup, hencoop, regroup, subgroup, Woop Woop (*Austral* backward remote town), nincompoop.

280.1

saloop (infusion of aromatic herbs), Guadeloupe, cantaloupe.

281 -'p

ketchup, gallop, Gallup, jalap (Mexican plant), Salop, shallop (rowing boat), stanhope (one-seater carriage), larrup (*Dialect* to beat), chirrup, syrup, stirrup, Europe, satrap (Persian governor), caltrop (tropical plant), hyssop (aromatic herb), bishop, tittup (*US* prance), arch-bishop.

281.1

develop, envelop, redevelop, under-develop, overdevelop.

281.2

collop (*Dialect* slice of meat), scallop, dollop, gollop (to eat greedily), lollop, trollop, Trollope (British novelist), wallop, codswallop.

282 -alp

alp, scalp, palp, pedipalp (zoology term).

283 -elp

kelp, skelp (*Dialect* to slap), chelp (*Dialect* to chatter), help, whelp, yelp.

284 -ulp

gulp, pulp.

285 -amp

amp, camp, scamp, champ, damp, gamp (umbrella), lamp, clamp, ramp, cramp, tramp, tamp (pat down firmly), stamp, vamp, decamp, encamp, firedamp, blackdamp (gas in mines), whitedamp (gas in mines), blowlamp, revamp, afterdamp (gas in mines).

286 -emp

hemp, temp.

287 -imp

imp, skimp, chimp, gimp (stiffened fabric trimming), guimpe (short blouse), limp, blimp (small airship), pimp, crimp, scrimp, primp, shrimp.

288 -omp

comp, chomp, clomp, pomp, romp, trompe (apparatus in a forge), stomp, swamp.

289 -ump

bump, chump, dump, jump, hump, lump, clump, plump, slump, pump, rump, crump (to thud), scrump, frump, grump, trump, sump, tump (*Dialect* small mound), stump, thump, mug-wump (politically neutral person), gazump, undertrump, overtrump.

290 -asp

gasp, hasp, clasp, rasp, grasp, hand-clasp, enclasp, unclasp.

291 -isp

lisp, crisp, wisp, will-o'-the-wisp.

292 -osp

wasp, galliwasp (American lizard).

293 -ass

ass, bass, gas, lass, mass, wrasse (marine fish), crass, frass (insect excrement), trass (volcanic rock), strass (glass for imitation gemstones), sass, Tass.

Troas (region of Asia Minor), jackass, ACAS, degas, alas, amass, admass (people susceptible to advertising), landmass, groundmass, en masse, vinasse (residue in a still), cuirass, morass, Patras, Mithras (Persian god), Alsace, crevasse.

anabas (freshwater fish), Caiaphas, Ladislas (Hungarian saint and king), biomass (biology term), Maecenas (Roman statesman), hippocras (spiced wine), sassafras, demitasse (small coffee cup), tarantass (Russian horse-drawn carriage).

Leonidas (king of Sparta), Epaminondas (ancient Greek general).

293.1

Phidias (Greek sculptor), galleass (type of warship), palliasse, Lysias (Athenian orator), Herodias (mother of Salome), Asturias (former Spanish kingdom), materfamilias (female head of family), paterfamilias (male head of family).

294 -arse

arse, carse (*Scot* low-lying land), farce, class, glass, pass, sparse, brass, grass, kvass (Russian alcoholic drink).

volte-face, springhaas (African rodent), declass, subclass, outclass, eyeglass, spyglass, hourglass, wineglass, surpass, bypass, impasse, Madras, bluegrass (folk music), eelgrass (marine plant), goose-grass, knotgrass (weedy plant).

superclass (group in classification system), Plexiglass (*Trademark*), galloglass (Irish chieftain's military retainer), fibreglass, weatherglass (barometer), isinglass, underpass, overpass, sparrow-grass (*Dialect* asparagus).

295 -ace

ace, base, bass, case, chase, dace, face, lace, place, plaice, mace, pace, space, race, brace, grace, trace, Thrace.

debase, subbase (base of pedestal), wheelbase, staircase, bookcase, crankcase (part of car engine), watch-case, seedcase, briefcase, encase, slipcase (protective case for books), typecase, notecase, nutcase, suitcase, reface, coalface, typeface, outface, shoelace, enlace, unlace, replace, fire-place, showplace, emplace (put in position), someplace, displace, misplace, birthplace, bootlace, Lovelace (English poet), grimace, tenace (bridge term),

airspace, backspace, embrace, main-brace, headrace, landrace (breed of pig), scapegrace, disgrace, tailrace, millrace, retrace, rosace (rose window).

steeplechase, interface, interlace, orthoclase (mineral), commonplace, marketplace, hyperspace, aerospace, interspace, Samothrace (Greek island).

295.1

abase, rheobase (minimum nerve impulse), diabase (type of rock), contra-bass.

295.2

showcase, pillowcase.

295.3

efface, deface, Boniface (Anglo-Saxon saint).

295.4

apace, carapace.

296 -ess

Bess, chess, fesse (heraldic term), guess, jess (falconry term), Hesse (German state), less, bless, mess, Ness, cress, dress, press, tress, stress, cess, Tess, yes.

profess, confess, largess, noblesse, unless, Sheerness, Foulness, Caithness, liquesce, fluoresce, duress, redress, address, headdress, undress, sundress, nightdress, egress, regress, digress, progress, aggress, ingress, congress, transgress, depress, repress, impress, compress, winepress, express, prestress, distress, recess, precess, process, assess, abscess, obsess, princess, access, excess, success, possess.

acquiesce, SOS, bouillabaisse, recru-desce, incandesce, intumesce, deli-quesce, effloresce, watercress, retrogress, decompress, effervesce, repossess, prepossess, dispossess.

296.1

coalesce, nonetheless, obsolesce, conva-lesce, nevertheless.

296.2

finesse, luminesce.

296.3

Lyonnesse (place in Arthurian legend), Dungeness, pythoness, evanesce, Inverness, rejuvenesce.

296.4

caress, phosphoresce, manageress.

296.5

oppress, suppress, letterpress.

297 -erse

Erse, burse (*Scot* student allowance), curse, hearse, Merse (Scottish lowland area), nurse, purse, terse, verse, worse.

coerce, disburse, rehearse, immerse, commerce, disperse, cutpurse, sesterce (Roman coin), traverse, diverse, averse, perverse, obverse, adverse, inverse, converse, transverse, reimburse.

297.1

asperse, intersperse.

297.2

reverse, universe.

298 -eece

geese, lease, fleece, niece, Nice, peace, piece, crease, Greece, grease, cease.

obese, pelisse (fur-trimmed cloak), release, coulisse, police, sublease, hairpiece, earpiece, eyepiece, showpiece, headpiece, codpiece, tailpiece, timepiece, crosspiece, mouthpiece, decrease, increase, Dumfries, degrease, caprice, cassis, decease, Métis (person of mixed parentage).

chimneypiece, battlepiece (painting commemorating a battle), mantelpiece, frontispiece, ambergris, predecease.

298.1

chersonese (peninsula), Peloponnese.

298.2

apiece, altarpiece, centrepiece, masterpiece.

299 -eerse

fierce, pierce, tierce (fencing position), transpierce.

300 -iss [further rhymes may be created by adding *-less* to appropriate verbs or *-ness* to appropriate adjectives]

kiss, Dis (Roman god), hiss, bliss, miss, piss, kris (Malayan knife), sis, this, Swiss.

dais, Saïs (ancient Egyptian city), Thaïs (Athenian courtesan), Powys, prowess,

Jewess, Lewes, Lewis, abbess, ibis, Colchis (ancient Asian country), purchase, duchess, caddis, Sardis (ancient Asian city), jaundice, aphis (aphid), preface, surface, office, Memphis, haggis, Burgess, burgess (citizen of borough), dehisce (burst open), Alice, chalice, malice, palace, Tallis, starless, Ellis, trellis, airless, heirless, careless, hairless, treeless, cheerless, fearless, peerless, tearless, eyeless, tireless, wireless, Aulis (ancient Greek town), lawless, flawless, shoreless, joyless, jobless, tubeless, backless, trackless, feckless, necklace, reckless, smokeless, luckless, thankless, matchless, speechless, headless, wordless, heedless, needless, seedless, beardless, lidless, godless, cloudless, cordless, bloodless, childless, endless, friendless, kindless (heartless), mindless, boundless, groundless, soundless, lifeless, selfless, legless, ageless, changeless, guileless, soulless, goalless, armless, harmless, aimless, blameless, nameless, frameless, shameless, dreamless, seamless, limbless, timeless, homeless, formless, gormless, painless, brainless, stainless, skinless, chinless, sinless, spineless, boneless, toneless, stoneless, sunless, moonless, tuneless, hapless, strapless, shapeless, surplice, sleepless, topless, hopeless, helpless, classless, baseless, faceless, graceless, ceaseless, creaseless, priceless, voiceless, useless, hatless, artless, heartless, stateless, weightless, flightless, sightless, spotless, thoughtless, doubtless, gutless, bootless, rootless, fruitless, tactless, thriftless, shiftless, guiltless, faultless, dauntless, pointless, countless, tasteless, waistless, restless, listless, faithless, breathless, mirthless, worthless, ruthless, toothless, sleeveless, nerveless, loveless, sexless, noiseless, Amis, premiss, commis (agent), promise, pumice, pomace, kumiss (drink of fermented milk), dismiss, anise (Mediterranean plant), greyness, Ennis (Irish town), Denis, menace, tennis, Venice, furnace, Furness, lenis (linguistics term), penis, dearness, clearness, nearness, Highness, slyness, dryness, shyness, coyness, sourness, blueness, newness, Tunis, drabness, blackness, darkness, bleakness, sleekness, meekness, weakness, likeness, frankness, brusqueness, richness, muchness, badness, gladness, madness, sadness, hardness, staidness, deadness, redness, weirdness, oddness, loudness, goodness, lewdness, rudeness, shrewdness, mildness, wildness, baldness, oldness, boldness, coldness, fondness, roundness, soundness, Daphnis (Greek mythological character), deafness, stiffness, roughness, gruffness, toughness, Agnes, vagueness, smugness, strangeness, paleness, staleness, illness, stillness, vileness, smallness, tallness, foulness, dullness, fullness, coolness, calmness, lameness, sameness, tameness, firmness, dimness, slimness, grimness, warmness, dumbness, glumness, numbness, plainness, sternness, keenness, cleanness, meanness, greenness, thinness, fineness, proneness, oneness, sharpness, cheapness, steepness, ripeness, dampness, plumpness, crispness, sparseness, baseness, coarseness, hoarseness, closeness, looseness, rashness, harshness, freshness, fatness, flatness, smartness, lateness, greatness, straightness, wetness, hotness, shortness, stoutness, strictness, deftness, swiftness, softness, faintness, quaintness, gauntness, bluntness, aptness, promptness, smoothness, braveness, business, lapis, Apis (ancient Egyptian sacred bull), coppice, hospice, auspice, marquess, marquis, Harris, Paris, derris (Asian climbing plant), Ferris, peeress, orris (iris plant), Boris, Doris, Horace, Maurice, Morris, hubris, laundress, Negress, Tigris, tigress, ogress, empress, mattress, waitress, traitress, fortress, portress (female porter), buttress, temptress, mistress, seamstress, Francis, lattice, brattice (mining term), gratis, lettuce, Thetis (Greek goddess), poultice, countess, hostess, justice, solstice, Jarvis, parvis (church porch), Davis, Mavis, service, novice, Clovis (Frankish king), pelvis, lexis (complete vocabulary), Zeuxis (ancient Greek painter).

prejudice, Charybdis, edifice, benefice, orifice, artifice, flowerless, powerless, regardless, bottomless, fathomless, accomplice, remorseless, purposeless, effortless, comfortless, relentless, grotesqueness, forwardness, back-

wardness, awkwardness, aloofness, handsomeness, remoteness, quietness, exactness, pleasantness, abruptness, earnestness, precipice, Polaris, ex libris, dentifrice, verdigris, heritress, cockatrice (legendary monster), seductress, conductress, instructress, enchantress, schoolmistress, housemistress, catharsis, pertussis (whooping cough), clematis, apprentice, interstice, armistice, injustice, Glenrothes (Scottish town), self-service, disservice.

unpleasantness, ambassadress, Nunc Dimittis (canticle), epiglottis, amanuensis.

300.1

loess, Powys (English writer), allantois (embryology term).

300.2

pubis, Anubis.

300.3

abyss, cannabis.

300.4

bodice, goddess, demigoddess.

300.5

stewardess, cowardice, leopardess, hendiadys (rhetorical device).

300.6

aegis, Lyme Regis, Bognor Regis, Curia Regis (Norman king's court).

300.7

rayless, lumbricalis (worm-like muscle), digitalis, Corona Australis (constellation), aurora australis, Corona Borealis (constellation), aurora borealis.

300.8

cilice (haircloth), bodiless, syphilis, penniless, weariless, merciless, pitiless, amaryllis.

300.9

polis (ancient Greek city-state), solace, Wallace, Cornwallis (British general), torticollis.

300.10

cullis (gutter), Dulles (US statesman), portcullis.

300.11
bullace (damson tree), valueless.

300.12
clueless, viewless, parulis (gumboil).

300.13
numberless, featureless, riderless, odourless, Argolis (region of ancient Greece), colourless, humourless, mannerless, chrysalis, pleasureless, measureless, fatherless, motherless, flavourless, driverless, oxalis (flowering plant), corydalis (climbing plant), Persepolis, Camelopardalis (constellation).

300.13.1
Annapolis (capital of Maryland), Minneapolis, Indianapolis.

300.13.2
propolis (substance collected by bees), cosmopolis, necropolis (burial ground), Acropolis, metropolis, Heliopolis (ancient Egyptian city), megalopolis (complex of adjacent towns).

300.14
questionless, passionless, motionless, expressionless.

300.15
wingless, meaningless.

300.16
senseless, defenceless.

300.17
witless, profitless, limitless, spiritless.

300.18
kermis (Dutch carnival), dermis, vermis (part of brain), epidermis.

300.19
remiss, Artemis, epididymis (anatomy term).

300.20
amiss, Salamis (Greek island), Semiramis (legendary Assyrian queen).

300.21
harness, unharness, Kiwanis (US community service organization).

300.22
bareness, fairness, unfairness, awareness.

300.23
finis (the end), Guinness, pinnace (small boat).

shabbiness, flabbiness, grubbiness, tubbiness, stickiness, cockiness, silkiness, sulkiness, hardiness, sturdiness, neediness, greediness, giddiness, tidiness, moodiness, rowdiness, dauphiness, fluffiness, stuffiness, earliness, burliness, curliness, surliness, silliness, holiness, lowliness, godliness, worldliness, friendliness, kindliness, ugliness, cleanliness, loneliness, stateliness, ghostliness, liveliness, loveliness, reminisce, gloominess, happiness, sleepiness, sloppiness, airiness, wariness, dreariness, weariness, hungriness, iciness, spiciness, bossiness, sauciness, fussiness, dirtiness, prettiness, naughtiness, daintiness, emptiness, nastiness, thirstiness, healthiness, filthiness, heaviness, laziness, easiness, dizziness, noisiness, cosiness, drowsiness, clumsiness.

foolhardiness, untidiness, orderliness, scholarliness, ungodliness, cowardliness, unworldliness, unfriendliness, unhappiness, unhealthiness.

300.23.1
readiness, steadiness, unsteadiness.

300.24
cornice, rawness, soreness, notornis (rare flightless bird), archaeornis (extinct bird), aepyornis (extinct flightless bird), ichthyornis (extinct sea bird).

300.25
lowness, slowness, Adonis, callowness, shallowness, hollowness, narrowness, lex talionis (law of retaliation).

300.26 [see also **300.31**]
lioness, soberness, deaconess, wilderness, slenderness, tenderness, eagerness, villainess, canoness, baroness, thoroughness, patroness, marchioness, bitterness, otherness, cleverness, governess, togetherness.

300.27
lychnis (flowering plant), sickness, thickness, airsickness, seasickness, homesickness.

300.28

Widnes, nakedness, wickedness, crookedness, wretchedness, sordidness, raggedness, doggedness, ruggedness, hurriedness, sacredness, cussedness, vividness.

clear-headedness, bigheadedness, pig-headedness, light-headedness, hot-headedness, cold-bloodedness, broad-mindedness, kind-heartedness, half-heartedness, downheartedness, light-heartedness, softheartedness, belatedness, quick-wittedness, far-sightedness, near-sightedness, long-sightedness, short-sightedness, sure-footedness, flat-footedness.

level-headedness, narrow-mindedness, feeble-mindedness, single-mindedness, open-mindedness, absent-mindedness, unexpectedness.

300.28.1

candidness, left-handedness, offhandedness, underhandedness.

300.29

kindness, blindness, unkindness.

300.30

feebleness, nimbleness, fickleness, idleness, carefulness, cheerfulness, awfulness, thankfulness, dreadfulness, painfulness, scornfulness, hopefulness, helpfulness, gracefulness, peacefulness, usefulness, gratefulness, spitefulness, thoughtfulness, doubtfulness, boastfulness, faithfulness, truthfulness, suppleness, brittleness, gentleness, evilness.

forgetfulness, unfaithfulness, untruthfulness.

300.31 [see also 300.26]

stubbornness, drunkenness, suddenness, sullenness, commonness, openness, barrenness, rottenness, evenness, unevenness.

300.32

willingness, nothingness, unwillingness.

300.33

carelessness, cheerlessness, fearlessness, tirelessness, lawlessness, joblessness, recklessness, lucklessness, thanklessness, heedlessness, godlessness, childlessness, friendlessness, mindlessness, lifelessness, selflessness, changelessness, harmlessness, aimlessness, shamelessness, timelessness, homelessness, painlessness, tunelessness, shapelessness, sleeplessness, hopelessness, helplessness, classlessness, pricelessness, uselessness, artlessness, heartlessness, weightlessness, sightlessness, spotlessness, thoughtlessness, fruitlessness, tactlessness, thriftlessness, faultlessness, pointlessness, tastelessness, restlessness, listlessness, breathlessness, worthlessness, ruthlessness.

mercilessness, pitilessness, powerlessness, meaninglessness, remorselessness, purposelessness, limitlessness, spiritlessness, effortlessness, relentlessness.

300.33.1

senselessness, defencelessness.

300.34

joyousness, righteousness, callousness, zealousness, pompousness, monstrousness, spaciousness, graciousness, preciousness, cautiousness, consciousness, nervousness, biliousness, hazardousness, contagiousness, scrupulousness, dangerousness, boisterousness, facetiousness, infectiousness, subconsciousness, unconsciousness, covetousness, mischievousness, unscrupulousness, semiconsciousness.

300.34.1

dubiousness, tediousness, studiousness, seriousness, deviousness, fastidiousness, melodiousness, lasciviousness.

300.34.2

sensuousness, sumptuousness, conspicuousness, impetuousness, voluptuousness.

300.34.3

viciousness, officiousness, capriciousness, surreptitiousness.

300.34.4

pretentiousness, conscientiousness.

300.35

snobbishness, childishness, selfishness, foolishness, ticklishness, squeamishness, sheepishness, lavishness, peevishness, unselfishness, feverishness.

300.36
curtness, pertness, alertness.

300.37
neatness, sweetness, completeness, incompleteness.

300.38
fitness, witness, unfitness, eyewitness, appropriateness, inappropriateness.

300.39
lightness, rightness, brightness, triteness, tightness, whiteness, politeness, uprightness, impoliteness.

300.40
cuteness, acuteness, astuteness.

300.41
directness, correctness, indirectness, incorrectness.

300.42
fastness, vastness, steadfastness.

300.43
forgiveness, furtiveness, activeness, plaintiveness, impressiveness, possessiveness, decisiveness, explosiveness, impulsiveness, offensiveness, talkativeness, effectiveness, inventiveness, inquisitiveness.

300.44
heiress, mayoress, Seferis (Greek poet), millionairess, Apollinaris (mineral water).

300.45
iris, Iris, Osiris (Egyptian god).

300.46
loris, cantoris (musical term).

300.47
prioress, berberis (cultivated shrub), Sybaris (ancient Greek colony), liquorice, murderess, sorceress, clitoris, avarice, ephemeris (astronomical table), mons veneris, sui generis (unique), angina pectoris.

300.48
actress, benefactress.

300.49
classis (governing body of church), glacis (a slope), Onassis.

300.50
Acis (Greek mythological character), basis, stasis, oasis, haemostasis.

300.51
thesis, noesis (functioning of intellect), mimesis, ascesis (self-discipline), exegesis, epiclesis (invocation of Holy Spirit), anamnesis (recollection), diuresis, anuresis, enuresis, catachresis (incorrect use of words), erotesis (rhetorical question), leucopoiesis (white blood cell formation), psychokinesis (parapsychology term), photokinesis (movement towards light), telekinesis, erythropoiesis (red blood cell formation), amniocentesis.

300.51.1
paresis (muscular weakness), diaphoresis, cataphoresis (analytical technique), electrophoresis (analytical technique).

300.52
ecdysis (shedding of outer layer), symphysis, synthesis, prosthesis, diaphysis (shaft of long bone), epiphysis (end of long bone), hypophysis (pituitary gland), apophysis (outgrowth), dieresis, haemoptysis (coughing up of blood), diathesis (hereditary susceptibility to disease), metathesis (linguistics term), antithesis, epenthesis (linguistics term), parenthesis, photosynthesis.

300.52.1
dialysis, analysis, paralysis, catalysis, urinalysis, cryptanalysis (study of codes), haemodialysis, psychoanalysis, microanalysis.

300.52.2
biolysis (disintegration of organic matter), glycolysis (breakdown of glucose), thermolysis (loss of body heat), haemolysis (red blood cell disintegration), hydrolysis, cytolysis (disintegration of cells), autolysis (self-destruction of cells), histolysis (disintegration of tissues), electrolysis.

300.52.3
emesis, Nemesis, haematemesis (vomiting of blood).

300.52.4

genesis, agenesis (imperfect development), psychogenesis, morphogenesis (development of organism's form), thermogenesis (heat production), sporogenesis (spore formation), histogenesis (tissue and organ formation), pathogenesis (development of a disease), osteogenesis (bone formation), anthropogenesis (study of man's origin), haematogenesis (formation of blood).

300.52.5

prothesis (linguistics term), hypothesis.

300.53

Isis, lysis, crisis, epicrisis (pathology term).

300.54

proboscis, salpiglossis (flowering plant).

300.55

Phocis (district in ancient Greece), gnosis (knowledge of spiritual things), ptosis (drooping of the eyelid).

thrombosis, narcosis, mycosis (disease caused by fungus), psychosis, sycosis (inflammation of hair follicles), lordosis, kyphosis, alphosis (absence of skin pigmentation), phimosis (tightness of foreskin), zymosis (any infectious disease), osmosis, prognosis, hypnosis, pyrosis (heartburn), neurosis, fibrosis, necrosis, hidrosis (sweat), nephrosis (kidney disease), mitosis.

silicosis, varicosis, toxicosis, psittacosis, acidosis, ankylosis (abnormal immobility of joint), brucellosis (disease of cattle), ecchymosis (skin discoloration through bruising), syndesmosis (type of joint), cyanosis, melanosis (skin condition), diagnosis, siderosis (lung disease), diarthrosis (freely movable joint), enarthrosis (ball-and-socket joint), synarthrosis (immovable joint), asbestosis.

metempsychosis (migration of soul), Winnipegosis (Canadian lake), anastomosis, autohypnosis, osteoporosis.

300.55.1

symbiosis, scoliosis, ichthyosis, apotheosis, mononucleosis, pneumoconiosis, endometriosis.

300.55.2

meiosis, miosis (constriction of pupil), pyosis (pus formation), abiosis (absence of life), antibiosis, necrobiosis (normal death of cells), anabiosis (resuscitation), parabiosis (union of two individuals).

300.55.3

tuberculosis, pediculosis (infestation with lice), furunculosis (skin condition), diverticulosis.

300.55.4

kenosis (theology term), stenosis, trichinosis (parasitic disease), pollinosis (hay fever), byssinosis (industrial lung disease), hallucinosis (mental disorder), avitaminosis, hypervitaminosis.

300.55.5

sclerosis, cirrhosis, xerosis (abnormal dryness of tissues), atherosclerosis (disease of arteries), arteriosclerosis.

300.55.6

ketosis (pathology term), halitosis, amitosis (form of cell division), spirochaetosis (disease).

300.55.7

dermatosis, haematosis (oxygenation of blood), keratosis (skin condition), myxomatosis, carcinomatosis.

300.56

Eleusis (Greek town), anacrusis.

300.57

emphasis, protasis (conditional clause), entasis (architectural term), anabasis (ancient Persian military expedition), parabasis (speech of Greek chorus), catabasis (descent), apodosis (main clause), periphrasis, diastasis (separation of joined parts), metastasis (spreading of disease), bronchiectasis (dilation of bronchial tubes), atelectasis (lung collapse).

300.57.1

diocese, trichiasis (inversion of eyelashes), archdiocese, taeniasis (tapeworm infestation), phthiriasis (infestation with lice), psoriasis, mydriasis (abnormal pupil dilation), amoebiasis (parasitic infection), satyriasis, acariasis (hair infestation), filariasis (tropical disease), bilharziasis (tropical disease), elephantiasis, trypanosomiasis (sleeping sickness).

300.57.2
paedomorphosis (zoology term), anamorphosis (distorted image), metamorphosis, anthropomorphosis.

300.58
Chalcis (Greek city), peristalsis, diastalsis (medical term).

300.59
sepsis, syllepsis (linguistics term), prolepsis (rhetorical device), asepsis, antisepsis.

300.60
stypsis (medical term), ellipsis.

300.61
synopsis, caryopsis (one-seeded fruit), stereopsis (stereoscopic vision), coreopsis (tropical plant), thanatopsis (meditation on death).

300.62
mitis (malleable iron), phlebitis, orchitis, rachitis (rickets), bronchitis, carditis, mephitis (foul stench), colitis, rhinitis, iritis, neuritis, nephritis, metritis (inflammation of womb), gastritis, arthritis, bursitis, glossitis (inflammation of tongue), otitis, mastitis, cystitis, vulvitis.

tracheitis, osteitis, thyroiditis, mastoiditis (inflammation in ear), meningitis, pharyngitis, laryngitis, ophthalmitis, pneumonitis, urethritis, sinusitis, fibrositis, dermatitis, hepatitis, parotitis (mumps), keratitis (inflammation of cornea), prostatitis, synovitis (inflammation in a joint).

encephalitis, appendicitis, osteoarthritis.

300.62.1
myelitis (inflammation of spinal cord), spondylitis (inflammation of vertebrae), tonsillitis, pyelitis (inflammation of kidney), osteomyelitis (inflammation of bone marrow), poliomyelitis.

300.62.2
cellulitis (inflammation of body tissues), uvulitis, valvulitis (inflammation

of heart valve), utriculitis (inflammation of inner ear), diverticulitis.

300.62.3
splenitis, adenitis (inflammation of a gland), vaginitis, retinitis, duodenitis.

300.62.4
colonitis, tympanitis, peritonitis.

300.62.5
blepharitis (inflammation of eyelids), arteritis, enteritis, ovaritis, gastroenteritis.

300.62.6
gingivitis, conjunctivitis.

300.63
fortis (phonetics term), mortise, rigor mortis.

300.64
notice, stephanotis, myosotis.

300.65
factice (soft rubbery material), practice, practise, malpractice.

300.66
mantis, Atlantis.

300.67
pastis, hydrastis (flowering plant).

300.68
testis, Alcestis (Greek mythological queen), ovotestis (snail's reproductive organ).

300.69
clevis (coupling device), crevice, Ben Nevis.

300.70
axis, praxis (practice), taxis (movement), prophylaxis, thermotaxis (movement towards heat), phototaxis (movement towards light), epistaxis (nosebleed), anaphylaxis.

301 -ice
ice, bice (medium blue colour), dice, lice, splice, slice, mice, gneiss, nice, spice, rice, price, trice, thrice, syce (Indian servant), vice, twice.
de-ice, choc-ice, suffice, allspice, half-price, precise, concise, entice, device, advice.

paradise, merchandise, sacrifice, overnice, underprice, imprecise, edelweiss, self-sacrifice.

302 -oss

os, boss, Kos (Greek island), cos (variety of lettuce), doss, fosse (ditch), joss (Chinese deity), Jos (Nigerian city), loss, floss, gloss, moss, Ross, cross, crosse (lacrosse stick), dross, toss.

chaos, Keos (Greek island), Eos (Greek goddess), Chios (Greek island), emboss, Lesbos (Greek island), reredos, kudos, Paphos (village in Cyprus), Argos (ancient Greek city), Lagos, Carlos, Delos (Greek island), Melos (Greek island), bugloss, Amos, Samos (Greek island), demos (nation as political unit), Patmos (Greek island), cosmos, Minos, Lemnos (Greek island), tripos, saros (cycle of eclipses), Pharos (ancient Greek lighthouse), Skyros (Greek island), Eros, kaross (African garment), uncross, crisscross, outcross, Andros (Greek island), Kinross, Thásos (Greek island), bathos, pathos, ethos, pithos (ceramic oil container), mythos (beliefs of specific group), Naxos (Greek island).

Barbados, intrados (inner curve of arch), extrados (outer curve of arch), Calvados, omphalos (sacred conical object), candyfloss, rallycross, doublecross, Charing Cross, albatross, Thanatos (Greek personification of death), Hephaistos (Greek god).

302.1

Phobos (satellite of Mars), Villa-Lobos (Brazilian composer).

302.2

across, lacrosse, autocross, motocross, intercross (crossbreed).

302.3

Sestos (ancient Turkish town), asbestos.

303 -orse

coarse, course, force, gorse, horse, hoarse, Morse, morse (cloak fastening), Norse, source, sauce.

recourse, forecourse (boat's sail), concourse, dampcourse, racecourse, discourse, endorse, drayhorse, sawhorse, warhorse, packhorse, workhorse, cockhorse, studhorse, unhorse, racehorse,

carthorse, clotheshorse, remorse, introrse (turned inwards), extrorse (turned outwards), divorce, resource.

watercourse, intercourse, hobbyhorse, sinistrorse (spiralling right to left).

303.1

perforce, Wilberforce.

303.2

enforce, reinforce.

304 -oice

Boyce, choice, Joyce, voice, rejoice, Rolls Royce (*Trademark*), devoice (phonetics term), revoice (to echo), invoice, unvoice (phonetics term).

305 -oce

Bose (Indian physicist), kos (Indian unit of distance), dose, close, gross, chausses (medieval garment).

verbose, globose (spherical), thrombose, floccose (covered with woolly tufts), jocose, viscose, nodose, rugose (wrinkled), filose (threadlike), pilose (covered with fine hairs), ramose (having branches), osmose (undergo osmosis), venose, spinose, necrose, engross, setose (bristly).

bellicose, varicose, verrucose (covered with warts), overdose, cellulose, squamulose (covered with small scales), ramulose (having small branches), lachrymose (tearful), racemose (botany term), farinose (flour-like), anthracnose (fungal disease), adipose, comatose, keratose (having a horny skeleton), chaparejos (cowboy's leather overalls).

305.1

grandiose, foliose (leafy), otiose (futile), religiose (sanctimonious).

305.2

morose, suberose (relating to cork), tuberose, acerose (needle-shaped).

306 -ouse

scouse, douse, gauss (unit in physics), house, louse, mouse, nous, spouse, grouse, Strauss, souse.

lobscouse, degauss (demagnetize), playhouse, warehouse, teahouse, whorehouse, storehouse, poorhouse, Bauhaus, clubhouse, bakehouse, steakhouse, workhouse, cookhouse, madhouse, guardhouse, birdhouse, roadhouse, Wodehouse, roundhouse, doghouse, alehouse, jailhouse, tollhouse, schoolhouse, farmhouse, henhouse, greenhouse, glasshouse, dosshouse, gatehouse, Statehouse (*US* state capitol), lighthouse, hothouse, pothouse (small pub), courthouse, boathouse, outhouse, penthouse, guest-house, bathhouse, almshouse, delouse, Nicklaus, woodlouse, reremouse (*Dialect* bat), dormouse, fieldmouse, titmouse, woodgrouse, sandgrouse.

bawdyhouse, powerhouse, summer-house, Charterhouse, slaughterhouse, porterhouse, chapterhouse (building attached to cathedral), flittermouse (*Dialect* bat).

307 -uss

us, bus, cuss, fuss, Gus, jus (legal right), huss (dogfish), plus, muss (*US* rumple), pus, Russ, crus (lower leg), truss, suss, thus, wuss.

airbus, debus, embus, succuss, percuss, concuss, discuss, cuscus (Australasian marsupial), nonplus, untruss.

minibus, omnibus, blunderbuss, motor-bus, overplus.

308 -oos

puss, Grus (constellation), schuss, Tungus (member of Mongoloid people), Anschluss (political or economic union), sourpuss, Vilnius (Russian city), ceteris paribus (other things being equal).

309 -uce

goose, juice, loose, sluice, moose, mousse, noose, Bruce, spruce, truce, use, deuce, puce, Zeus.

cayuse (*US* small pony), caboose, cam-boose (lumberjack's cabin), couscous (North African spicy dish), mongoose, wayzgoose (printing works' annual out-ing), verjuice (juice of unripe grapes), recluse, unloose, footloose, vamoose, burnoose (Arab's hooded cloak), slip-noose, papoose, ceruse (white lead), Elbrus (Russian mountain), abstruse, abuse, excuse, educe (logic term), deduce, reduce, seduce, produce, induce, conduce, refuse, diffuse, pro-fuse, ill-use, almuce (monk's fur-lined cape), prepuce, disuse, misuse, obtuse.

charlotte russe, superinduce (introduce as additional factor).

309.1

adduce (cite as proof), produce, traduce (speak badly of), reproduce, introduce.

310 -'s

joyous, psoas (muscle in loin), Phoebus, rebus, bulbous, nimbus, rhombus, thrombus, Orcus (Roman god), caucus, Dorcas, glaucous (covered with waxy bloom), raucous, ruckus, incus, rhonchus (rattling breathing sound), bronchus, righteous, Judas, Indus, Pindus (Greek mountain range), Dreyfus, scyphus (ancient Greek drink-ing cup), typhus, Rufus, Argus, negus (port and lemon drink), bogus, Angus, fungus, fungous, gorgeous, balas (red gemstone), Callas, callous, callus, Dallas, phallus, parlous (dangerous or difficult), talus, Troilus, bolus (ball of chewed food), troublous, windlass, Douglas, surplus, atlas, cutlass, Lammas, spermous (relating to sperm whale), Thermos (*Trademark*), Remus, primus, timeous (*Scot* timely), thymus, Thomas, Comus (Roman god), Momus (Greek god), houmous (Middle Eastern creamy dip), grumous (consisting of granular tissue), humus, dolmas (stuffed vine leaves), isthmus, Christmas, litmus, Xmas, stannous (containing tin), magnus, carpus (wrist), purpose, lupus (skin disease), upas (Javan tree), pompous, trespass, scabrous, glabrous (smooth-skinned), fibrous, hydrous, wondrous, walrus, leprous, Cyprus, cypress, cuprous, cit-rous, nitrous, oestrus, lustrous, mon-strous, dextrous, thyrsus (Bacchus' staff), versus, rhesus, Croesus, lapsus (error), Thapsus (ancient town near Carthage), precious, luscious, factious, fractious, noxious, anxious, conscious, captious, bumptious, scrumptious, Plautus (Roman dramatist), tortoise, cactus, ictus (poetry term), rictus (gap of open mouth), Sanctus (hymn in Eucharist), linctus, Faustus, nervous, canvas, canvass, plexus, nexus, Texas, Jesus, Kansas.

Barabbas, succubus (female demon), incubus (male demon), syllabus, colobus (monkey), Barnabas, Damascus, self-righteous, unrighteous, solidus, Lepidus (ancient Roman statesman), tremendous, stupendous, horrendous, Josephus (Jewish historian), Sisyphus (Greek mythological king), pemphigus (blistering skin disease), egregious, Tibullus (Roman poet), Lucullus (Roman general), Agulhas (South African headland), Catullus (Roman lyric poet), Wenceslas, enormous, posthumous, nystagmus, Michaelmas, Candlemas, Martinmas, Erasmus, marasmus (wasting away), alumnus, Vertumnus (Roman god), Olympus, tenebrous, ludicrous, chivalrous, disastrous, Caucasus, Pegasus, Confucius, infectious, obnoxious, rambunctious, preconscious, subconscious, self-conscious, unconscious, singultus, Hephaestus (Greek god), Augustus, Oireachtas (Irish parliament), mischievous, abraxas (ancient magic charm).

Menelaus (Greek mythological king), philadelphus (fragrant shrub), creophagous (flesh-eating), zoophagous (feeding on animals), sarcophagus, carpophagous (feeding on fruit), coprophagous (feeding on dung), oesophagus, analogous, homologous, Galápagos, asparagus, cunnilingus, gladiolus, nucleolus (part of cell nucleus), alveolus (small cavity), Nostradamus, borborygmus, metacarpus (bones of the hand), multipurpose, idolatrous, ambidextrous, Dionysus (Greek god), Paracelsus (Swiss physician), semiprecious, semiconscious, microdontous (having unusually small teeth), Pocahontas (American Indian woman).

cumulonimbus, Camelopardus (constellation).

310.1

Dias (Portuguese navigator), Aeneas, Linnaeus, Piraeus, uraeus (ancient Egyptian sacred serpent), gluteus (muscle in buttock), Manichaeus (Persian prophet), coryphaeus (ancient Greek chorus leader), Ptolemaeus (crater on moon).

310.2

scabious, rubious (dark red), dubious, Roscius (ancient Roman actor), sardius (Old Testament precious stone), radius, tedious, Claudius, studious, Orpheus, Morpheus (Greek god), malleus, Peleus (father of Achilles), pileus (part of mushroom), coleus, nucleus, nauplius (larva of crustacean), Ennius (Roman poet), igneous, ligneous, clypeus (part of insect's head), copious, Gropius (US architect), impious, aqueous, nacreous, pancreas, citreous (greenish-yellow), vitreous, gaseous, caseous, Theseus, osseous, Celsius, courteous, piteous, Grotius (Dutch statesman), Proteus (Greek god), luteous (light greenish-yellow), beauteous, duteous, plenteous, bounteous, struthious (relating to the ostrich), pervious, devious, previous, obvious, envious, nauseous.

Eusebius (early Christian bishop), amphibious, Polybius (ancient Greek historian), compendious, Pelagius (British monk), rebellious, Equuleus (constellation), aculeus (prickle), abstemious, calumnious, Asclepius (Greek god), subaqueous, obsequious, opprobrious, lugubrious, salubrious, industrious, illustrious, caduceus (Hermes' staff), Lucretius (Roman poet), Helvétius (French philosopher), discourteous, rumbustious, Boethius (Roman philosopher), impervious, trapezius.

impecunious, Aesculapius (Roman god), Belisarius (Byzantine general), Stradivarius.

310.2.1

hideous, perfidious, insidious, fastidious, invidious.

310.2.2

odious, melodious, commodious, Asmodeus (Jewish prince of demons), incommodious.

310.2.3

alias, Sibelius, Vesalius (Flemish anatomist).

310.2.4

Delius, Aurelius (Roman emperor), Berzelius (Swedish chemist), contumelious (insolent).

310.2.5

ileus (obstruction of intestine), bilious, Marsilius (Italian political philosopher), Lucilius (Roman satirist), punctilious, supercilious.

310.2.6

calcaneus (heel bone), Comenius (Czech educational reformer), extraneous, cutaneous, spontaneous, miscellaneous, percutaneous, subcutaneous, simultaneous, instantaneous, contemporaneous, extemporaneous.

310.2.7

genius, splenius (neck muscle), ingenious, arsenious (relating to arsenic), homogeneous, heterogeneous.

310.2.8

Arminius (Dutch theologian), vimineous (producing long flexible shoots), Flaminius (Roman general), gramineous (relating to grasses), sanguineous (relating to blood), ignominious.

310.2.9

euphonious, felonious, harmonious, erroneous, Petronius (Roman satirist), Suetonius (Roman historian), inharmonious.

310.2.9.1

ceremonious, acrimonious, parsimonious, sanctimonious, unceremonious.

310.2.10

Arius (Greek Christian theologian), carious, Marius (Roman general), various, Briareus (Greek giant), precarious, vicarious, calcareous, gregarious, hilarious, denarius, Aquarius, retiarius (Roman gladiator), Sagittarius.

310.2.10.1

nefarious, omnifarious (of all sorts), multifarious.

310.2.11

serious, cereus (large cactus), Tiberius, cinereous (greyish), imperious, mysterious, deleterious.

310.2.12

Sirius, delirious.

310.2.13

aureus (Roman coin), Boreas (Greek god), glorious, arboreous (thickly wooded), laborious, inglorious, uproarious, censorious, sartorius, Sertorius (Roman soldier), notorious, victorious, Nestorius (Syrian churchman), uxorious, meritorious.

310.2.14

curious, furious, spurious, injurious, usurious, incurious, penurious, luxurious.

310.2.15

Nicias (Athenian statesman), piceous (relating to pitch), griseous (streaked with grey), Odysseus, Dionysius.

310.2.16

Statius (Roman poet), Ignatius (early Christian saint), fieri facias (legal term).

310.2.17

niveous (resembling snow), oblivious, lascivious.

310.2.18

pluvious, Vesuvius.

310.3

eyas (nestling hawk or falcon), bias, Gaius (Roman jurist), lias (blue limestone rock), pious, Pius, Elias, Matthias, Ananias, Zacharias, hamadryas (type of baboon), nisi prius (former legal term).

310.4

congruous, menstruous, vacuous, nocuous, arduous, sensuous, fatuous, virtuous, tortuous, fructuous, unctuous, flexuous.

superfluous, mellifluous, incongruous, innocuous, promiscuous, deciduous, assiduous, ambiguous, contiguous, exiguous (scanty), impetuous, spirituous (containing alcohol), anfractuous (convoluted), tumultuous, voluptuous, contemptuous, tempestuous, incestuous.

310.4.1

perspicuous, transpicuous (transparent), conspicuous, inconspicuous.

310.4.2

strenuous, tenuous, ingenuous, disingenuous.

310.4.3

sinuous, continuous, discontinuous.

310.4.4

sumptuous, presumptuous.

310.5

gibbous, arquebus (long-barrelled gun), Erebus (Greek god), circumbendibus (circumlocution).

310.6

plumbous (containing lead), Columbus.

310.7

Bacchus, Gracchus (Roman tribune), Caracas.

310.8

carcass, sarcous (muscular or fleshy), Hipparchus (Greek astronomer), Aristarchus (crater on moon).

310.9

circus, cercus (zoology term), cysticercus (tapeworm larva).

310.10

distichous (arranged in two rows), tristichous (arranged in three rows), Cyzicus (ancient Greek colony), umbilicus, Autolycus, Copernicus, ulotrichous (having curly hair), Leviticus.

310.11

coccus (spherical bacterium), floccus (downy covering on birds), pneumococcus, gonococcus, micrococcus, streptococcus.

310.12

focus, locus, crocus, hocus-pocus.

310.13

fucus (brown seaweed), mucous, mucus, Seleucus (Macedonian general), caducous (biology term), Ophiuchus (constellation).

310.14

abacus, Spartacus, Antiochus (Syrian king), diplodocus (herbivorous dinosaur), Telemachus (son of Odysseus), Callimachus (Greek poet), Lysimachus (king of Thrace), Caratacus (ancient British chieftain).

310.15

discus, viscous, hibiscus, meniscus, lemniscus (nerve fibres in brain).

310.16

Midas, Cnidus (ancient Greek city), nidus (insect's nest), Abydos (ancient Egyptian town), Nabonidus (Old Testament character).

310.17

exodus, hazardous, Enceladus (Greek mythological giant), ceratodus (extinct fish).

310.18

amorphous, polymorphous, rhizomorphous (resembling a root), anthropomorphous.

310.19

magus (Zoroastrian priest), tragus (projection in ear), Tagus (European river), vagus, choragus (ancient Greek chorus leader), Las Vegas.

310.20

courageous, umbrageous (shady), outrageous, contagious, advantageous, disadvantageous.

310.21

prodigious, religious, litigious, prestigious, irreligious, sacrilegious.

310.22

jealous, Hellas (ancient name for Greece), zealous, Marcellus (Roman general), ocellus (insect's simple eye), entellus (monkey).

310.23

villous (covered with long hairs), obelus (symbol in text), strobilus (plant cone), trochilus (humming-bird), Aeschylus, Angelus, perilous, scurrilous, bacillus, nautilus, Theophilus (crater on moon), zoophilous (pollinated by animals), Herophilus (Greek anatomist), xerophilous (living in dry conditions), hygrophilous (growing in wet places), coprophilous (growing on dung), aspergillus, erysipelas.

310.24

hilus (anatomy term), stylus, monostylous (botany term).

310.25

garrulous, fabulous, sabulous (gritty), nebulous, bibulous (addicted to alcohol), tubulous (tube-shaped), calculus, modulus, pendulous, scrofulous, Regulus (Roman general), famulus (sorcerer's attendant), hamulus (hooklike projection), emulous (competitive), tremulous, limulus (type of crab), stimulus, Romulus, annulus, populace, populous, scrupulous.
miraculous, tuberculous, homunculus (miniature man), ranunculus (plant genus), unscrupulous, convolvulus.

310.25.1

querulous, glomerulus (anatomy term).

310.25.2

ridiculous, ventriculus (bird's gizzard), meticulous, caniculus (small channel).

310.25.3

credulous, sedulous, incredulous.

310.25.4

stridulous, acidulous.

310.25.5

cumulus, tumulus, cirrocumulus, stratocumulus, altocumulus.

310.26

libellous, embolus, Daedalus, scandalous, carolus (former English coin), Tantalus (Greek mythological king), marvellous, frivolous, astragalus (anklebone), anomalous, asepalous (having no sepals), apetalous (having no petals), Sardanapalus (Assyrian king), Papadopoulos.

310.26.1

obolus (Greek unit of weight), discobolus (discus thrower).

310.26.2

Nicholas, limicolous (living in mud), terricolous (living in soil), saxicolous (living on rocks), arenicolous (living in sandy places), stercoricolous (living in dung).

310.26.3

bicephalous (having two heads), Bucephalus, acephalous (headless), hydrocephalus.

310.27

famous, squamous (biology term), ramus (biology term), mandamus (legal term), uniramous (undivided), ignoramus.

310.28

didymous (in pairs), blasphemous, ginglymus (hinge joint), minimus, mittimus (legal term), maximus.

310.28.1

animus, unanimous, magnanimous, pusillanimous.

310.28.2

onymous (bearing author's name), euonymus (cultivated tree), pseudonymous, synonymous, anonymous, eponymous, antonymous, Hieronymus, heteronymous (spelt alike).

310.29

infamous, venomous, Pyramus, monogamous, autonomous, anadromous (migrating up river), catadromous (migrating down river).

310.29.1

bigamous, polygamous.

310.29.2

calamus (Asian palm), thalamus, hypothalamus.

310.29.3

xylotomous (boring into wood), hippopotamus.

310.30

trismus (lockjaw), strabismus, vaginismus (painful vaginal spasm).

310.31

anus, Janus, heinous, manus (wrist and hand), pandanus (palm-like plant), Uranus, Silvanus (Roman god), Coriolanus.

310.32

genus, venous, Venus, Albinus (English scholar), subgenus, Silenus (Greek satyr), scalenus (muscle in neck),

Comnenus (Byzantine family), Campinas (Brazilian city), intravenous, arteriovenous.

310.33

ruinous, tendinous (relating to tendons), terminus, verminous, ominous, gangrenous, Circinus (constellation), mountainous, resinous.

libidinous, rubiginous (rust-coloured), indigenous, fuliginous (smoky or sooty), terrigenous (of the earth), vertiginous, vortiginous (whirling), endogenous, homogenous, erogenous, hydrogenous, androgynous, nitrogenous, misogynous, autogenous (originating within the body), ferruginous (containing iron), gelatinous.

multitudinous, oleaginous (resembling oil), cartilaginous.

310.33.1

luminous, numinous (awe-inspiring), aluminous (resembling aluminium), voluminous, albuminous (containing albumin), leguminous, bituminous.

310.33.2

glutinous, mutinous, velutinous.

310.34

Minas, minus, Ninus (Assyrian king), spinous (resembling a thorn), sinus, vinous (relating to wine), echinus (sea urchin), Longinus (Greek writer), Aquinas, Quirinus (Roman god), uncinus (small hooked structure), Plotinus (Roman philosopher), botulinus (bacterium), matriclinous (resembling female parent), patriclinous (resembling male parent), Flamininus (Roman general), Antoninus (Roman emperor).

310.35

onus, bonus, Jonas, clonus (type of convulsion), Cronus, tonus (muscle tone), Tithonus (Greek mythological character), Amazonas (Brazilian state).

310.36

Dardanus (mythological founder of Troy), villainous, membranous, synchronous, tetanus, gluttonous, cavernous, ravenous, poisonous, Eridanus (constellation), diaphanous, cacophonous, homophonous (pronounced the same), Telegonus (son of Odysseus), Antigonus (Macedonian king), monotonous, allochthonous (geology term), autochthonous (geology term).

310.37

Oedipus, polypus, Lysippus (Greek sculptor), Leucippus (Greek philosopher), platypus, eohippus, Aristippus (Greek philosopher).

310.38

corpus, porpoise, habeas corpus.

310.39

opus, Scopas (Greek sculptor), Canopus.

310.40

octopus, amphitropous (botany term), orthotropous (botany term), pithecanthropus.

310.41

campus, lampas (swelling in horse's mouth), pampas, grampus, hippocampus.

310.42

compass, rumpus, encompass, gyrocompass, astrocompass.

310.43

arras, Arras (French town), harass, embarrass, nonparous (never having given birth), disembarrass.

310.44

ferrous, terrace, nonferrous.

310.45

sclerous (hard or bony), serous, Severus (Roman emperor), Ahasuerus (Old Testament king).

310.46

Pyrrhus, cirrus, scirrhus (cancerous growth), Algeciras (Spanish port).

310.47

gyrus (fold on brain surface), Cyrus, virus, papyrus, Epirus (region of Greece), desirous, echovirus, ultravirus.

310.48

aurous (containing gold), chorus, Horus (Egyptian sun god), porous, sorus (plant's spore-producing structure),

Taurus, torus, pelorus (type of gyrocompass), pylorus (opening in stomach), thesaurus, Centaurus (constellation), Epidaurus (ancient Greek port), Matamoros (Mexican port), Cassiodorus (Roman writer), tubuliflorous (having tubular flowers).

310.48.1

brontosaurus, brachiosaurus, tyrannosaurus.

310.49

Eurus (Greek mythological wind), Honduras, anurous (tailless), coenurus (larva of tapeworm), Arcturus (star), mercurous, Epicurus.

310.50

barbarous, Cerberus (three-headed dog), tuberous, slumberous, decorous, Icarus, lecherous, treacherous, rapturous, murderous, odorous, Pandarus (Greek mythological character), slanderous, ponderous, chunderous (*Austral* nauseating), thunderous, Zephyrus (Greek god), sulphurous, phosphorus, phosphorous, rigorous, vigorous, languorous, dangerous, valorous, dolorous, amorous, clamorous, glamorous, timorous, humorous, humerus, numerous, generous, onerous, sonorous, vaporous, viperous (relating to a viper), copperas (chemical compound), Hesperus, Bosporus (Turkish strait), prosperous, ulcerous, cancerous, traitorous, Tartarus (Greek mythological place), stertorous (characterized by heavy snoring), uterus, icterus (jaundice), apterous (wingless), dipterous (having two wings), boisterous, Lazarus.

indecorous, adventurous, malodorous, inodorous, Pythagoras, obstreperous, uniparous, multiparous, viviparous, oviparous, dinoceras (extinct mammal), rhinoceros, Monoceros (constellation), adulterous, preposterous, cadaverous.

310.50.1

cankerous, rancorous, cantankerous.

310.50.2

splendiferous, stelliferous (full of stars), melliferous (producing honey), mammiferous (having breasts), auriferous, ossiferous (containing bones), vociferous, calciferous, lactiferous, fructiferous, umbelliferous, fossiliferous, metalliferous, odoriferous, sudoriferous (producing sweat).

310.50.2.1

coniferous, carboniferous.

310.50.3

herbivorous, frugivorous (fruit-eating), vermivorous (worm-eating), granivorous (grain-eating), carnivorous, omnivorous, piscivorous, baccivorous (berry-eating), graminivorous (grass-eating), insectivorous.

310.51

Lassus (Flemish composer), passus (part of medieval narrative), Crassus, Parnassus, Manassas (US town), Halicarnassus (ancient Greek city).

310.52

Tarsus, tarsus, metatarsus.

310.53

Issus (ancient Turkish battle site), byssus (zoology term), Ephesus, narcissus.

310.54

Knossos, colossus.

310.55

census, consensus.

310.56

spacious, gracious.

herbaceous, sebaceous, bulbaceous (bulb-shaped), audacious, mordacious (bitingly sarcastic), mendacious, fugacious (passing quickly away), sagacious, pugnacious, capacious, rapacious, loquacious, veracious, ceraceous (waxy), voracious, flirtatious, cretaceous (relating to chalk), crustaceous (having a shell), curvaceous, vivacious, vexatious, rosaceous.

alliaceous, liliaceous, foliaceous (resembling a leaf), coriaceous (relating to leather), contumacious (obstinate), saponaceous, carbonaceous, Athanasius (saint), arboraceous (resembling a tree), stercoraceous (relating to dung), disputatious, ostentatious, ranunculaceous (botany term).

310.56.1
efficacious, perspicacious, ericaceous, inefficacious.

310.56.2
edacious (greedy), predacious (predatory), orchidaceous, iridaceous, amaryllidaceous.

310.56.3
fallacious, salacious, corollaceous (relating to petals).

310.56.4
minacious (threatening), tenacious, gallinaceous (ornithology term), farinaceous, erinaceous (relating to hedgehogs), pertinacious.

310.57
specious, synoecious (botany term), facetious, autoecious (botany term).

310.58
vicious, ambitious, judicious, officious, flagitious (utterly wicked), delicious, malicious, pernicious, propitious, auspicious, suspicious, sericeous (covered with silky hairs), lubricious, capricious, nutritious, factitious, fictitious, injudicious, inauspicious, meretricious, repetitious, adscititious (additional), adventitious, surreptitious, superstitious, suppositious.

310.58.1
seditious, expeditious.

310.58.2
Mauritius, avaricious.

310.59
cautious, tortious (legal term), incautious.

310.60
stotious (*Irish* drunk), precocious, ferocious, atrocious.

310.61
Prudentius (Latin Christian poet), tendentious, dissentious, licentious, pretentious, sententious, contentious, conscientious.

310.62
flatus, stratus, status, meatus, hiatus, afflatus (creative power), conatus (striving of natural impulse), apparatus, nimbostratus, cirrostratus, altostratus, cumulostratus.

310.63
fetus, Cetus (constellation), quietus, boletus (brownish fungus), Admetus (Greek mythological king), Servetus (Spanish theologian), Epictetus (Greek philosopher).

310.64
coitus, habitus (physical state), vomitus (vomited matter), impetus, spiritous, acetous (resembling vinegar), Tacitus, covetous, circuitous, fortuitous, gratuitous, Hippolytus (Greek mythological character), calamitous, precipitous, ubiquitous, iniquitous, emeritus, Theocritus (Greek poet), Democritus (Greek philosopher), necessitous, felicitous, solicitous.

310.65
situs (location of body part), Titus, tinnitus (ringing in ears), pruritus, detritus, Saint Vitus, Polyclitus (Greek sculptor), Heraclitus (Greek philosopher).

310.66
lotus, Notus (Greek mythological wind), Duns Scotus (Scottish theologian), Polygnotus (Greek painter).

310.67
Brutus, arbutus.

310.68
riotous, Herodotus, eczematous, sclerodermatous (having hard scaly covering), microstomatous (having unusually small mouth).

310.69
rectus (straight muscle), prospectus, conspectus (overall view).

310.70
argentous (relating to silver), momentous, portentous, sedimentous, ligamentous.

310.71
Aegyptus (mythological Egyptian king), eucalyptus.

310.72

canthus (corner of the eye), Xanthus (ancient Asian city), acanthus, strophanthus (tropical tree), ailanthus (deciduous tree), helianthus (sunflower), polyanthus, amianthus (variety of asbestos), Erymanthus (Greek mountain), agapanthus (African lily).

310.73

naevus, grievous, longevous (long-lived).

311 -ilse

fils (Middle Eastern coin), grilse.

312 -orlse

false, waltz.

313 -ulse

dulse (red seaweed), pulse, repulse, impulse, convulse.

314 -ance

Hanse (medieval guild of merchants), manse, stance, askance, romance, finance, expanse, Penzance.

315 -arnce

chance, dance, lance, glance, France, prance, trance, seance, faïence, nuance, perchance, mumchance (dumbstruck), mischance, enhance, freelance, entrance, advance, Afrikaans, contredanse (Continental dance), fer-de-lance (venomous snake), vraisemblance.

316 -ence

dense, fence, hence, flense (strip blubber from whale), pence, cense (burn incense), sense, tense, thence, whence, condense, defence, offence, immense, commence, prepense (premeditated), dispense, suspense, expense, incense, pretence, intense, self-defence, recommence, recompense, frankincense.

317 -ince

mince, quince, rinse, prince, since, wince, evince, province, convince.

318 -once

bonce, sconce, nonce, ponce, ensconce, response.

319 -ounce

ounce, bounce, jounce (jolt), flounce, pounce, trounce, enounce, denounce, renounce, announce, pronounce, mispronounce.

320 -unce

once, dunce, punce (*Dialect* kick or hit).

321 -'nce [further rhymes may be derived from **420**]

cadence, voidance (annulment), prudence, vengeance, parlance, silence, penance, ordnance, fourpence, sixpence, sequence, Clarence, cumbrance, hindrance, fragrance, entrance, monstrance (receptacle for consecrated Host), license, licence, absence, nonsense, patience, sentience (awareness), conscience, substance, instance, Constance, grievance, brilliance, pleasance (secluded part of garden), presence.

abeyance, purveyance, conveyance, flamboyance, annoyance, clairvoyance, allowance, pursuance, disturbance, accordance, concordance, discordance, avoidance, impudence, decadence, abundance, elegance, emergence, resurgence, insurgence, divergence, convergence, allegiance, indulgence, vigilance, pestilence, condolence, virulence, turbulence, ambulance, opulence, corpulence, flatulence, petulance, performance, transhumance (seasonal migration of livestock), permanence, assonance, dissonance, consonance (agreement), sustenance, governance, resonance, repugnance, subsequence, consequence, eloquence, forbearance, recurrence, occurrence, incurrence, concurrence, remembrance, encumbrance, remonstrance, obeisance, renaissance, innocence, impatience, advertence, importance, inductance (electrical property), conductance (electrical property), reluctance, acquaintance, susceptance (magnetic property), acceptance, circumstance, observance, relevance, connivance, contrivance, ebullience, complaisance, cognizance.

significance, jurisprudence, correspondence, inadvertence, inobservance, omnipresence, recognizance.

overabundance, overindulgence.

321.1

ambience, radiance, audience, variance, prurience, miscreance, nescience, prescience, transience, irradiance, obedience, resilience, convenience, experience, omniscience, disobedience, inconvenience, inexperience.

321.1.1

dalliance, mésalliance (marriage with social inferior).

321.2

science, defiance, affiance (betroth), reliance, alliance, appliance, compliance, misalliance.

321.3

affluence, effluence, influence, confluence, congruence, issuance, continuance.

321.4

credence, impedance (physics term), antecedence.

321.5

riddance, forbiddance, diffidence, confidence, precedence, incidence, evidence, providence, accidence (linguistics term), residence, self-confidence, coincidence.

321.6

guidance, subsidence.

321.7

resplendence, dependence, attendance, intendance (French public department), independence, condescendence (Scottish legal term).

321.8

arrogance, extravagance.

321.9

diligence, negligence, intelligence, intransigence, counterintelligence.

321.10

balance, valance, imbalance, unbalance, counterbalance.

321.11

valence (chemistry term), surveillance.

321.12

violence, indolence, somnolence, insolence, excellence, nonviolence, ambivalence, equivalence.

321.12.1

prevalence, malevolence, benevolence.

321.13

semblance, resemblance.

321.14

ordinance, eminence, dominance, prominence, luminance (brightness of light), pertinence, maintenance, countenance, abstinence, provenance, preeminence, appurtenance, impertinence, discountenance, incontinence.

321.15

twopence, comeuppance.

321.16

Terence, aberrance, deterrence.

321.17

clearance, coherence, adherence, inherence, appearance, interference, incoherence, reappearance, nonappearance, disappearance, perseverance.

321.18

Lawrence, Florence, Torrance (Californian city), abhorrence.

321.19

durance (imprisonment), assurance, insurance, endurance, reassurance, coinsurance.

321.20

furtherance, deference, reference, preference, difference, sufferance, inference, conference, transference, tolerance, ignorance, temperance, utterance, protuberance, exuberance, indifference, circumference, belligerence, intolerance, deliverance.

321.20.1

reverence, severance, irreverence.

321.21

essence, quiescence, pubescence, frondescence (leaf-producing process), tumescence, senescence, florescence (flowering process), excrescence, vitrescence (glass-producing process), quintessence.

acquiescence, iridescence, incandescence, adolescence, opalescence, obsolescence, convalescence, detumescence, intumescence, luminescence, juvenescence, deliquescence, efflorescence, inflorescence, fluorescence, phosphorescence, vaporescence (production of vapour), effervescence.

321.22
reticence, beneficence, munificence, magnificence, reminiscence, reconnaissance, concupiscence.

321.23
nuisance, translucence.

321.24
pittance, quittance, remittance, admittance, transmittance, penitence, appetence, competence, acquittance, concomitance, impenitence, incompetence, inheritance, capacitance (electrical property).

321.25
impotence, omnipotence.

321.26
sentence, repentance.

321.27
distance, outdistance, assistance, persistence, subsistence, insistence, resistance, existence, coexistence.

321.28
brisance (shattering effect of explosion), defeasance (annulment), malfeasance (illegal act), nonfeasance (legal term), misfeasance (legal term).

322 -aps [also **268** + -*s*]
apse, lapse, schnapps, craps, taps, perhaps, elapse, relapse, prolapse, collapse, synapse.

323 -apes [also **270** + -*s*]
gapes (disease of domestic fowl), drapes, traipse, jackanapes.

324 -eps [also **271** + -*s*]
Steppes, biceps, triceps, anableps (tropical fish), quadriceps, editio princeps (first printed edition).

325 -erps [also **272** + -*s*]
turps, stirps (line of descendants).

326 -eeps [also **273** + -*s*]
Pepys, creeps.

327 -ips [also **274** + -*s*]
snips (small metal-cutting shears), Cripps (British Labour statesman), thrips, Mendips, ellipse, Phillips, eclipse, forceps, amidships, apocalypse.

328 -ipes [also **275** + -*s*]
cripes, swipes (*Slang* weak beer), bagpipes, panpipes, stovepipes (tight trousers).

329 -ops [also **276** + -*s*]
Ops (Roman goddess), copse, chops, drops, tops, stops, Cheops (ancient Egyptian king), Pelops (Greek mythological character), stylops (parasitic insect), Cyclops, Cecrops (Greek mythological character), eardrops, muttonchops (side-whiskers), triceratops (rhinoceros-like dinosaur).

330 -orps [also **277** + -*s*]
corpse, Cleethorpes.

331 -imps [also **287** + -*s*]
timps (*short for* timpani), glimpse.

332 -umps [also **289** + -*s*]
dumps, mumps, trumps.

333 -ats [also **365** + -*s*]
flats, rats, dingbats (*Austral* delirium tremens), ersatz.

334 -arts [also **366** + -*s*]
arts, darts, Ghats (Indian mountain range), Harz (German mountain range), clarts (*Dialect* lumps of mud).

335 -aits [also **367** + -*s*]
Bates, Fates (Greek goddesses controlling destiny), rates, Greats (course at Oxford University), othergates (otherwise).

336 -ets [also **368** + -*s*]
let's, Metz (French city), Donets (Russian river), assets, pantalets, chervonets (Russian coin), solonetz (saltrich soil), castanets.

337 -erts [also **369** + -s]
hertz, outskirts, kilohertz.

338 -eets [also **370** + -s]
eats, Keats.

339 -its [also **371** + -s]
its, it's, blitz, splits, spitz (breed of dog), quits, grits (coarsely ground grain), wits, blewits (edible fungus), kibitz (US interfere), rackets (game resembling squash), rickets, Saint Kitts (West Indian island), credits, giblets, minutes, Leibnitz, Biarritz, Auschwitz, Austerlitz (Napoleonic battle site), applesnits (Canadian apple dish), Saint Moritz, separates, Horowitz (Russian pianist), slivovitz, Massachusetts.

340 -ites [also **372** + -s]
lights, nights, tights, whites, daylights, footlights, Dolomites.

341 -ots [also **373** + -s]
bots (digestive disease of horses), Scots, lots, Notts, culottes, fleshpots.

342 -orts [also **374** + -s]
orts (*Dialect* scraps), sports, quartz, shorts.

343 -oats [also **376** + -s]
Oates, oats, groats, John o'Groats.

344 -outs [also **377** + -s]
grouts, thereabouts, whereabouts, hereabouts.

345 -oots [also **379** + -s]
foots (dregs), toots (term of endearment), kibbutz.

346 -utes [also **380** + -s]
boots, hoots, gumboots, cahoots.

347 -ants [also **407** + -s]
Hants, pants, Northants, Konstanz (German city), underpants.

348 -ints [also **412** + -s]
chintz, Linz (Austrian port), blintz (thin filled pancake).

349 -ash
ash, bash, cash, cache, dash, gash, hash, lash, clash, flash, splash, slash, mash, smash, gnash, Nash, pash (*Slang* infatuation), rash, brash, crash, trash, thrash, sash, tache (*short for* moustache), stash.

earbash (*Austral* talk incessantly), Wabash (US river), encash, slapdash, rehash, eyelash, goulash, calash (horse-drawn carriage), backlash, unlash, whiplash, Shamash (Assyrian sun god), quamash (US plant), mishmash, panache, gate-crash, midrash (Jewish biblical commentaries), potash, soutache (narrow braid).

balderdash, pebble-dash, synchroflash (camera mechanism), photoflash (flash bulb), callipash (edible part of turtle), sabretache (cavalryman's leather case), succotash (*US* cooked mixed vegetables).

349.1
abash, calabash (US tropical tree).

350 -arsh
harsh, marsh, gouache (art term), moustache, Chuvash (Russian people).

351 -esh
flesh, mesh, nesh, crèche, fresh, thresh, tête-bêche (philately term), parfleche (dried rawhide), horseflesh, enmesh, refresh, afresh, Marrakech, Bangladesh, synchromesh, Gilgamesh (legendary Sumerian king), Andhra Pradesh (Indian state), Uttar Pradesh (Indian state), Madhya Pradesh (Indian state).

352 -eesh
quiche, fiche (*short for* microfiche), leash, niche, babiche (rawhide thongs), unleash, hashish, baksheesh, schottische (19th-century German dance), pastiche, microfiche, ouananiche (Atlantic salmon), nouveau riche.

353 -ish [further rhymes may be created by adding -ish to appropriate adjectives and nouns]
bish (*Slang* mistake), kish (carbon-rich graphite), dish, fish, knish (stuffed dumpling), squish, wish, whish, swish. Laoighis (Irish county), greyish, boyish, Jewish, bluish, shrewish, newish, furbish, snobbish, rubbish, blackish, brackish, rakish, peckish, Turkish, freakish, mawkish, bookish, Frankish, pinkish, monkish, reddish, Kurdish, Swedish, modish, loudish, rudish, prud-

ish, childish, fiendish, roundish, raffish, garfish, starfish, crayfish, offish, oarfish, crawfish, sawfish, oafish, blowfish, roughish, jewfish, bluefish, rockfish, stockfish, monkfish, trunkfish, codfish, swordfish, goldfish, dogfish, hogfish, frogfish, batfish, catfish, flatfish, ratfish, whitefish, saltfish, waggish, biggish, piggish, priggish, doggish, hoggish, roguish, sluggish, largish, Salish (American Indian language), churlish, girlish, stylish, Gaulish, smallish, Polish, owlish, bullish, foolish, ghoulish, mulish, publish, ticklish, English, purplish, famish, rammish, blemish, Flemish, skirmish, squeamish, Rhemish (relating to Rheims), warmish, banish, clannish, mannish, Spanish, vanish, garnish, tarnish, varnish, Danish, greenish, burnish, furnish, swinish, Cornish, clownish, brownish, Hunnish (barbarous), punish, longish, apish, sheepish, foppish, popish, uppish, impish, lumpish (clumsy), frumpish, waspish, vanquish, parish, cherish, perish, Irish, boarish, moreish, boorish, Moorish, flattish, rattish, latish, fetish, Lettish, pettish, skittish, British, rightish, whitish, Scottish, goatish, loutish, sluttish, ruttish, Jutish (ancient dialect of Kent), brutish, coltish, Kentish, lavish, ravish, slavish, knavish, dervish, peevish, elvish, anguish, languish, unwish.

babyish, tomboyish, refurbish, Cavendish, jellyfish, killifish, standoffish, silverfish, angelfish, cuttlefish, damselfish, devilish, establish, accomplish, schoolmarmish, Carchemish (ancient Syrian city), womanish, kittenish, heathenish, relinquish, tovarisch (Russian term of address), distinguish, extinguish, disestablish.

353.1

caddish, faddish, radish, horseradish.

353.2

blandish, brandish, standish (inkstand), outlandish.

353.3

elfish, selfish, shellfish, unselfish.

353.4

hellish, relish, embellish, disrelish (dislike).

353.5

polish, abolish, demolish.

353.6

Rhenish, replenish.

353.7

finish, Finnish, diminish.

353.8

donnish, admonish, astonish.

353.9

bearish, fairish, garish, squarish, nightmarish.

353.10

flourish, nourish, undernourish.

353.11

gibberish, lickerish, feverish, liverish, amateurish, impoverish.

354 -osh

bosh, Bosch (Dutch painter), cosh, gosh, josh (US to tease), cloche, slosh, nosh, posh, quash, squash, tosh, wash, swash (splash noisily).

brioche, kibosh, cohosh (US plant), backwash, musquash, eyewash, siwash (Canadian knitted sweater), awash, hogwash, brainwash, whitewash, mouthwash.

tokoloshe (Bantu mythical malevolent creature), mackintosh.

355 -oshe

gauche, troche (lozenge).

356 -ush

Cush (biblical character), gush, hush, lush, blush, flush, plush, slush, mush, rush, brush, crush, thrush, tush, airbrush, hairbrush, sagebrush (US shrub), nailbrush, paintbrush, toothbrush, bulrush, inrush, onrush, uprush, outrush, underbrush (US undergrowth), bottlebrush (Australian shrub).

357 -oosh

bush, mush (Slang face), push, shush, whoosh, swoosh, shadbush (US shrub), ambush, spicebush (US shrub), Hindu Kush (Asian mountain range).

358 -ushe

douche, louche (shifty), ruche, tar-boosh (brimless Muslim cap), Ingush (Russian people), capuche (friar's large hood), barouche (horse-drawn carriage), cartouche, Kiddush (Jewish traditional blessing).

359 -arzh

plage (mark on sun's surface), bocage (French wooded countryside), sondage (archaeological trench), collage, ménage, barrage, garage, mirage, massage, dressage, corsage, frottage (rubbing), montage, gavage (forced feeding).

fuselage, persiflage, camouflage, badinage, decoupage (decoration with cut-outs), entourage, arbitrage (stock exchange term), repechage (contest for runners-up), curettage (surgical process), reportage, cabotage (coastal navigation), sabotage, décolletage.

espionage, photomontage, counter-espionage.

360 -azhe

beige, greige (undyed), Liège, manège (riding school), cortège.

361 -erzh

concierge, demivierge.

362 -eezh

prestige, noblesse oblige.

363 -ozhe

loge (theatre box), Limoges.

364 -uzhe

luge, rouge, Bruges, vouge (medieval weapon).

365 -at

at, bat, cat, scat, chat, fat, hat, flat, plait, Platte (US river system), splat, slat, mat, matt, gnat, pat, Pat, spat, rat, brat, drat, prat, sprat, sat, tat, that, vat, VAT, twat.

Croat, sabbat (period of rest), brickbat, combat, wombat, numbat (small Australian marsupial), dingbat, meerkat (South African mongoose), Sno-Cat (*Trademark*), mudcat (US catfish), wild-cat, hellcat, polecat, hepcat, tipcat (a game), muscat, backchat, woodchat,

whinchat, stonechat, chitchat, Sadat, SOGAT, sunhat, doormat, format, cow-pat, thereat, whereat, hereat, muskrat, comsat (*short for* communications satellite), Darmstadt (German city), Dumyat (Egyptian town).

Uniat (denoting Eastern Church group), caveat, acrobat, concordat (treaty), butterfat, marrowfat, Astolat (town in Arthurian legend), cervelat (smoked sausage), diplomat, Laundromat (*Trademark*), automat, pitapat, ziggurat, Ballarat (Australian town), Ararat, dandiprat (16th-century English coin), Intelsat (communications satellite), habitat, aegrotat, ratatat, rheostat (electrical component), chemostat (apparatus for bacteria culture), haemostat (device to stop bleeding), thermostat, aerostat (lighter-than-air craft), Photostat (*Trademark*), rubáiyát.

Magnificat, requiescat, anastigmat (type of lens), ratatat-tat.

365.1

begat, Kattegat.

365.2 [further rhymes may be derived from **16.307.5**]

democrat, Eurocrat, bureaucrat, autocrat, plutocrat, aristocrat.

365.3

cravat, savate (form of boxing), avadavat (Asian weaverbird).

366 -art

art, baht (Thai currency), cart, chart, dart, fart, ghat (steps leading to river), heart, hart, mart, smart, part, tart, start, wat (Thai Buddhist monastery).

Hobart, Rabat (capital of Morocco), Descartes, teacart, go-kart, handcart, dogcart, dustcart, Bogart, Earhart (US aviatrix), Bernhardt, sweetheart, Eilat (Israeli port), Kalat (division of Pakistan), outsmart, depart, forepart, rampart, impart, mouthpart, Mozart, diktat (imposed decree), redstart, upstart, kick-start.

à la carte, undercart (undercarriage), applecart, Bundesrat (German federal council).

366.1

apart, Bonaparte, counterpart.

367 -ait

eight, bate, bait, skate, date, fate, fête, gait, gate, hate, late, plate, slate, mate, pate, spate, rate, crate, freight, great, grate, prate, trait, straight, strait, sate, Tate, state, weight, wait.

striate, debate, rebate, tubate (tubular), whitebait, furcate (to fork), plicate (pleated), spicate (having spikes), falcate (sickle-shaped), truncate, cheapskate, predate, caudate (having a tail), cordate (heart-shaped), backdate, mandate, update, misdate, outdate, postdate, sulphate, phosphate, Margate, floodgate, tailgate, tollgate, Vulgate, sluicegate, Ramsgate, alate (having wings), chelate (having claws), dilate, ablate (spheroidal), deflate, reflate, inflate, conflate (combine), endplate, nameplate, hotplate, footplate, breastplate, translate, playmate, squamate (scale-like), primate, comate (hairy), bromate, chromate, plumate (having feathers), checkmate, stalemate, schoolmate, roommate, inmate, shipmate, helpmate, classmate, messmate, flatmate, pennate (having feathers), connate (congenital), ornate, agnate (having common male ancestor), magnate, stagnate, cognate (related), pupate, baldpate, palpate, makeweight, ferrate (chemical compound), serrate, aerate, irate, gyrate, orate, chlorate, prorate, librate (to waver), vibrate, third-rate, hydrate, quadrate (make square), migrate, ingrate, tartrate, nitrate, titrate, filtrate, castrate, first-rate, prostrate, lustrate (purify through religious rituals), frustrate, substrate, pulsate, scutate (covered with bony plates), mutate, lactate, tractate (short tract), dictate, restate, estate, downstate, upstate, misstate, ovate, flyweight, Kuwait, catchweight, lightweight, fixate, luxate (dislocate).

inchoate (just beginning), benzoate (chemical compound), incubate, intubate (medical term), demarcate, educate, confiscate, obfuscate (to obscure), coruscate (to sparkle), inundate, fecundate, caliphate, bisulphate, abrogate, subjugate, conjugate, corrugate, promulgate, elongate, Billingsgate, insufflate (blow into), numberplate, boilerplate, copperplate, contemplate, legislate, impregnate, designate, syncopate, extirpate, inculpate, exculpate, lucubrate (to study), adumbrate, dehydrate, second-rate, transmigrate, deflagrate (burn fiercely), infiltrate, concentrate, sequestrate, illustrate, demonstrate, remonstrate, commutate (reverse electric current), amputate, auscultate, understate, intrastate, interstate, devastate, overstate, reinstate, pennyweight (unit of weight), heavyweight, hundredweight, middleweight, bantamweight, Bassenthwaite. circumvallate (surround with defensive fortification), interpellate, electroplate, carbohydrate, extravasate (exude), tergiversate.

367.1

create, brachiate (swing through trees), radiate, mediate, ideate (imagine), cochleate (shaped like snail's shell), permeate, expiate, re-create, procreate, miscreate (create badly), aviate, obviate, nauseate, roseate.

irradiate, repudiate, enucleate, delineate, calumniate, excoriate, infuriate, luxuriate, inebriate, appropriate, impropriate (transfer to laity), expropriate, repatriate, expatriate, enunciate, denunciate, annunciate (announce), depreciate, appreciate, excruciate, exuviate (shed outer covering), asphyxiate.

367.1.1

maleate (chemical compound), retaliate.

367.1.2

filiate (fix legal paternity of), affiliate, humiliate, conciliate, disaffiliate.

367.1.3

oleate (chemical compound), spoliate (despoil), defoliate, bifoliate (having two leaves), exfoliate (flake off).

367.1.4

caseate (become cheese-like), glaciate, emaciate.

367.1.5

satiate, expatiate, ingratiate.

367.1.6

vitiate, officiate, initiate, propitiate.

367.1.7
negotiate, dissociate, associate, disassociate.

367.1.8
substantiate, instantiate (represent by an example), transubstantiate, circumstantiate.

367.1.9
potentiate (make potent), differentiate.

367.1.10
deviate, alleviate, abbreviate.

367.2
actuate, menstruate, graduate, fluctuate, punctuate, eventuate (to result), accentuate, evacuate, evaluate, attenuate, extenuate, insinuate, infatuate, perpetuate, effectuate (bring about), individuate (give individuality to), disambiguate, superannuate.

367.2.1
situate, habituate.

367.3
lobate, globate, probate, bilobate, trilobate, conglobate (form into ball).

367.4
abate, stylobate (architectural term), approbate (Scottish legal term), reprobate, acerbate (embitter), masturbate, exacerbate.

367.5
dedicate, medicate, predicate, abdicate, indicate, syndicate, vindicate, defecate, spiflicate (*Slang* destroy), triplicate, supplicate, implicate, complicate, explicate (make explicit), fornicate, muricate (having a roughened surface), suricate (South African mongoose), fabricate, lubricate, rubricate (mark with red), deprecate, imprecate, metricate, extricate, desiccate, vesicate (to blister), rusticate.
eradicate, adjudicate, nidificate (build a nest), certificate, pontificate, canonicate (office of canon), communicate, prevaricate, divaricate (diverge at wide angle), prefabricate, decorticate, authenticate, domesticate, sophisticate, prognosticate, hypothecate (legal term), intoxicate, excommunicate.

367.5.1
duplicate, quadruplicate, reduplicate, centuplicate, quintuplicate.

367.5.2
masticate, elasticate, scholasticate (Jesuit's probation period).

367.6
locate, placate, vacate, bifurcate, suffocate, allocate, collocate, dislocate, embrocate, altercate, advocate, reciprocate, equivocate.

367.7
sulcate (marked with parallel grooves), inculcate, bisulcate (cleft or cloven).

367.8
sedate, candidate, validate, lapidate (pelt with stones), liquidate, fluoridate, depredate, antedate, oxidate, invalidate, consolidate, intimidate, dilapidate, elucidate.

367.9
gradate, vanadate (chemical compound), accommodate.

367.10
negate, delegate, relegate, colligate (join together), obligate, fumigate, abnegate, variegate, irrigate, aggregate, segregate, congregate, litigate, mitigate, castigate, instigate, navigate, levigate (grind into powder), desegregate, investigate, circumnavigate.

367.11
objurgate (scold), propagate, expurgate, arrogate (claim without justification), Watergate, homologate (ratify).

367.11.1
derogate (disparage), interrogate.

367.12
elate, relate, sibilate (speak with hissing sound), flagellate, crenellate, depilate, correlate, vacillate, tessellate, oscillate, titillate, mutilate, cantillate (to chant), ventilate, scintillate, invigilate, dissimilate, assimilate, interrelate, salicylate (chemical compound), carboxylate (chemical compound).

367.12.1
jubilate, obnubilate (to darken).

367.13

tubulate (form into a tube), ambulate, peculate (embezzle), speculate, circulate, calculate, osculate (to kiss), adulate, modulate, undulate, regulate, pullulate, ululate, emulate, formulate, cumulate, cannulate (medical term), granulate, sporulate (produce spores), insulate, postulate, pustulate, ovulate.

somnambulate, perambulate, ejaculate, miscalculate, emasculate, acidulate (make slightly acid), coagulate, accumulate, encapsulate, congratulate, capitulate, absquatulate (decamp), expostulate.

discombobulate (throw into confusion), circumambulate, recapitulate.

367.13.1

tabulate, confabulate.

367.13.2

vermiculate (decorate with wavy markings), corniculate (having horns), matriculate, articulate, reticulate (covered with a network), gesticulate, disarticulate.

367.13.3

flocculate (form into aggregated mass), deflocculate, inoculate.

367.13.4

angulate, strangulate, triangulate.

367.13.5

simulate, stimulate, dissimulate.

367.13.6

stipulate, manipulate.

367.13.7

copulate, populate, depopulate.

367.14

collate, decollate, escalate, immolate, desolate, isolate, insolate (expose to sunlight), oxalate (chemical compound), faveolate (honeycombed), machicolate (fortifications term), deescalate, cardinalate, extrapolate, interpolate.

367.14.1

violate, annihilate.

367.14.2

percolate, intercalate.

367.15

cremate, collimate (adjust optical instrument), sublimate, animate, decimate, intimate, estimate, guesstimate, legitimate, approximate, underestimate.

367.16

carbamate (chemical compound), cyclamate, diplomate (holder of a diploma), desquamate (scale off), consummate, automate, glutamate, meprobamate (tranquillizer), amalgamate.

367.17

innate, pinnate.

cachinnate (laugh loudly), machinate, pollinate, declinate (drooping), reclinate (bent backwards), culminate, fulminate, supinate, carinate (keelshaped), marinate, chlorinate, fluorinate, urinate, lancinate, catenate (arrange in rings), Latinate, pectinate (comb-shaped), pulvinate (cushionlike), vaccinate, resinate.

subordinate, coordinate, originate, oxygenate, hydrogenate, desalinate, disseminate, inseminate, eliminate, recriminate, incriminate, discriminate, peregrinate, indoctrinate, hallucinate, agglutinate, procrastinate, rejuvenate, ratiocinate (argue logically).

367.17.1

raffinate (chemistry term), decaffeinate.

367.17.2

paginate, evaginate (turn inside out), invaginate.

367.17.3

laminate, deaminate (biochemistry term), delaminate (divide into thin layers), contaminate, interlaminate, decontaminate.

367.17.4

germinate, terminate, exterminate.

367.17.5

dominate, nominate, abominate, predominate, denominate.

367.17.6
ruminate, illuminate, aluminate (chemical compound), acuminate (make pointed).

367.17.7
fascinate, deracinate (uproot), assassinate.

367.18
donate, neonate, carbonate, hibernate, cybernate (control with mechanism), hyphenate, emanate, personate (act the part of), fractionate (separate into constituents), detonate, alternate, sultanate, intonate, consternate, alienate, resonate, decarbonate, permanganate, impersonate.

367.19
constipate, emancipate.

367.19.1
dissipate, participate, anticipate.

367.20
equate, liquate (separate by melting), antiquate.

367.21
berate, cirrate (biology term), aspirate, butyrate (chemical compound).

367.22
mercurate (treat with mercury), sulphurate, fulgurate, depurate (purify), suppurate, maturate, saturate, triturate (grind into fine powder), obturate (block up), micturate, inaugurate.

367.23
narrate, liberate, decorate, federate, moderate, underrate, perforate, camphorate, tolerate, separate, operate, perorate, sororate (marriage custom), acerate (needle-shaped), lacerate, macerate, susurrate (make whispering sound), ulcerate, overrate.
elaborate, collaborate, reverberate, deliberate, corroborate, redecorate, edulcorate (purify by washing), acculturate (assimilate another group's culture), confederate, desiderate (long for), preponderate, proliferate, vociferate, invigorate, exaggerate, refrigerate, decelerate, accelerate, exhilarate, commemorate, agglomerate, conglomerate,
enumerate, incinerate, itinerate (travel about), exonerate, remunerate, evaporate, cooperate, incorporate, recuperate, vituperate, exasperate, incarcerate, chelicerate (spider-like animal), eviscerate, expectorate, adulterate, coelenterate, exenterate (remove by surgery), asseverate (declare emphatically), commiserate.
ameliorate, deteriorate.

367.23.1
generate, venerate, degenerate, regenerate, intenerate (make tender).

367.23.2
iterate, reiterate, alliterate, obliterate, transliterate.

367.24
calibrate, celebrate, cerebrate, concelebrate (celebrate mass together), equilibrate, decerebrate (remove brain).

367.25
desecrate, consecrate, execrate, deconsecrate.

367.26
emigrate, immigrate, denigrate, integrate, redintegrate (make whole again), disintegrate.

367.27
citrate, arbitrate, penetrate, perpetrate, impetrate (obtain by prayer).

367.28
orchestrate, magistrate, administrate.

367.29
sensate, condensate (substance formed by condensation), compensate, insensate.

367.30
meditate, agitate, sagittate (arrow-shaped), vegetate, digitate, cogitate, imitate, capitate (headlike), crepitate (to crackle), palpitate, irritate, nictitate (to blink), gravitate, levitate, hesitate, premeditate, regurgitate, excogitate (devise), decapitate, precipitate, necessitate, felicitate, resuscitate.

367.30.1
militate, debilitate, habilitate (*US* equip and finance), facilitate, rehabilitate.

367.30.2
acetate, subacetate (crystalline compound), capacitate (make legally competent), incapacitate.

367.31
notate, rotate, annotate, dissertate, tête-à-tête.

367.32
dentate, edentate, commentate, potentate, orientate, disorientate.

367.33
gestate, testate, intestate.

367.34
costate (having ribs), prostate, apostate.

367.35
nervate (having veins), incurvate (curve inwards), innervate (supply nerves to).

367.36
salivate, elevate, titivate, motivate, activate, cultivate, captivate, aestivate, deactivate, reactivate, inactivate, radioactivate.

367.37
excavate, enervate, renovate, innovate, aggravate.

367.38
await, underweight, paperweight, welterweight, counterweight, featherweight, overweight.

368 -et
ate, bet, debt, get, jet, het, Lett, let, met, net, pet, ret (soak textile fibre), fret, threat, set, sett, stet, vet, whet, wet, sweat, yet.

layette, maquette (sculptor's preliminary model), snackette (snack bar), moquette, coquette, coquet (behave flirtatiously), croquette, banquette, vedette, mofette (opening in volcano), Tophet (Old Testament place), baguette, beget, forget, georgette, Colette, toilette, roulette, inlet, outlet, kismet, hairnet, dinette, nonet, lunette, brunette, dragnet, fishnet, pipette, fleurette (flower-shaped ornament), curet, burette, soubrette (pert girl), aigrette (long feather on hat), regret, asset, cassette, placet (vote of assent),

tacet (musical term), reset, fossette (small depression in bone), subset, headset, handset, offset, filmset, inset, onset, unset, sunset, typeset, upset, outset, fléchette (missile dropped from aircraft), brochette, couchette, planchette (board for spirit messages), courgette, quartet, motet, octet, quintet, septet, sestet (six-line verse), sextet, curvet (dressage term), revet (face with stones), corvette (small escort ship), cuvette (shallow dish), quickset (type of hedge), thickset, paillette (sequin), vignette, lorgnette, noisette, rosette.

oubliette (type of dungeon), winceyette, serviette, turbojet, suffragette, aiguillette (ornament on military uniform), landaulet (small horse-drawn carriage), flageolet, flannelette, epaulet, novelette, calumet (peace pipe), Antoinette, stockinet, kitchenette, midinette (Parisian salesgirl), clarinet, bassinet, satinet, martinet, alkanet (flowering plant), falconet (small falcon), wagonette (horse-drawn vehicle), burgonet (16th-century helmet), Internet, maisonette, canzonet (short lively song), salopette, imaret (Turkish hospice for pilgrims), vinaigrette, photoset, letterset, avocet, trebuchet (medieval weapon), epithet, minivet (Asian songbird), vilayet (Turkish administrative division), chemisette (underbodice), anisette.

Tafilalet (Moroccan oasis), marionette.

368.1
duet, silhouette, pirouette, minuet, statuette.

368.2
Tibet, quodlibet.

368.3
abet, alphabet.

368.4
piquet (card game), briquette (brick of compressed fuel), etiquette.

368.5
cadet, Bernadette.

368.6
barrette (hair clasp), Leatherette (*Trademark*), Launderette (*Trademark*),

cigarette, majorette, collarette, solleret (part of armour), swimmeret (zoology term), bannerette, lanneret (large male falcon), minaret, spinneret, usherette.

368.7

beset, salicet (organ stop), scilicet (that is), videlicet (namely).

368.8

musette (type of bagpipe), crêpe suzette.

368.9

gazette, marmoset.

369 -ert

curt, skirt, dirt, girt, hurt, blurt, flirt, pert, spurt, quirt (whip with leather thong), squirt, cert, shirt, Sturt (English explorer), wort.

seagirt, alert, inert, unhurt, expert, assert, insert, concert, Blackshirt, night-shirt, pervert, terre-verte (painting pigment), divert, overt, subvert, advert, invert, convert, stitchwort, woundwort, ragwort, stonewort (green alga), pipewort, soapwort, desert, dessert, exert.

miniskirt, underskirt, malapert (saucy), inexpert, disconcert, undershirt, reconvert, pennywort, moneywort, bladderwort, slipperwort, liverwort, animadvert (criticize strongly).

369.1

evert, revert, ambivert (psychology term), antevert (displace by tilting forwards).

369.2

avert, pervert, introvert, controvert, extrovert.

370 -eet

eat, beet, beat, skeet, cheat, feet, feat, heat, leet (former manorial court), leat (trench conveying water), bleat, cleat, fleet, gleet (gonorrhoeal discharge), pleat, sleet, meet, meat, mete, neat, peat, Crete, greet, treat, street, seat, sheet, teat, wheat, sweet, suite, tweet.

browbeat, deadbeat, offbeat, drumbeat, downbeat, upbeat, heartbeat, mesquite (small tropical tree), escheat (legal term), dustsheet, effete, defeat, reheat, elite, delete, deplete, replete, complete,

athlete, gamete, pigmeat, forcemeat, mincemeat, sweetmeat, repeat, compete, buckwheat, secrete, accrete, concrete, discreet, discrete, excrete, afreet (Arabian mythological monster), retreat, maltreat, entreat, mistreat, bystreet, backstreet, reseat, deceit, receipt, unseat, conceit, freesheet (free newspaper), foresheet, broadsheet, groundsheet, mainsheet (nautical term), slipsheet (printing term), petite, aesthete.

polychaete (marine worm), lorikeet (small parrot), parakeet, spirochaete (bacterium), exegete (interpreter of biblical text), superheat (heat above boiling point), overheat, obsolete, paraclete (mediator), incomplete, marguerite, Masorete (Hebrew scholar or rabbi), overeat, indiscreet, meadowsweet, bittersweet.

371 -it

it, bit, kit, skit, chit, dit (short sound in code), fit, git, hit, lit, flit, split, slit, mitt, Schmidt, nit, knit, pit, Pitt, spit, quit (*Slang* insignificant person), writ, Brit, grit, sprit (nautical term), sit, shit, tit, wit, Whit, whit, twit.

striate, poet, debit, rarebit, obit (*short for* obituary), Cobbett (English journalist), gobbet (chunk of raw meat), orbit, sorbet, cubit, ambit, gambit, titbit, Beckett, banket (gold-bearing rock), blanket, trinket, junket, gasket, basket, casket, biscuit, brisket, frisket (printing term), bosket (thicket), musket, hatchet, ratchet, rochet (bishop's white surplice), crotchet, adit, audit, plaudit, bandit, Chindit (World War II soldier), conduit, pundit, surfeit, prophet, profit, soffit (architectural term), forfeit, buffet, tuffet, nymphet, comfit, unfit, outfit, agate, garget (inflammation of cow's udder), target, legate (envoy), Reigate, nugget, drugget (floor-covering fabric), Newgate, Tlingit (American Indian), ringgit (Malaysian currency), gadget, digit, fidget, midget, Bridget, widget, budget, legit, mallet, palate, palette, sallet (15th-century helmet), valet, scarlet, starlet, varlet, playlet, raylet, islet, eyelet, stylet (wire in surgical instrument), twilit, Smollett (Scottish novelist), wallet, toilet, owlet, cullet (waste glass), gullet, mullet, tablet, driblet (small amount), boblet (two-man bobsleigh), goblet, doublet, circlet, pikelet, spikelet (small grass flower), booklet, brooklet, anklet, cloudlet, leaflet, pamphlet, eaglet, piglet, singlet, camlet (tough waterproof cloth), hamlet, armlet, gimlet, omelette, unlit, sunlit, moonlit, kinglet (small warbler), ringlet, winglet, chaplet (wreath for head), ripplet (small ripple), triplet, droplet, couplet, template, bracelet, corselet (foundation garment), flatlet, Bartlett, martlet (heraldic symbol resembling swallow), partlet (16th-century shawl), tartlet, platelet, notelet, cutlet, gauntlet, wristlet (bracelet), wavelet, valvelet, Hazlitt, haslet (meat loaf), emmet (*Dialect* ant), hermit, permit, climate, omit, plummet, summit, submit, admit, helmet, pelmet, transmit, Barnet, garnet, genet (catlike mammal), jennet (female donkey), rennet, senate, tenet, unit, magnet, unknit, close-knit, tightknit, Capet, lappet (small hanging flap), tappet, carpet, fleapit, snippet, pipit, frippet (frivolous young woman), sippet (small piece), tippet (fur cape), whippet, moppet, poppet, puppet, cockpit, chalkpit, sandpit, pulpit, armpit, limpet, crumpet, trumpet, strumpet, respite, acquit, banquet, barret (small cap), garret, pirate, lyrate (lyre-shaped), floret, curate, turret, worrit (*Dialect* tease), secret, Sanskrit, quadrate (cube), pomfret (liquorice sweet), egret, culprit, bowsprit, portrait, basset, facet, tacit, resit, cosset, posset, corset, Dorset, faucet, gusset, russet, dulcet, transit, lancet, Consett, whatsit, freshet (sudden overflowing of river), bullshit, horseshit, bluetit, tomtit, davit (crane-like device), brevet, rivet, privet, trivet, civet, private, covet, velvet, peewit, godwit (large shore bird), halfwit, dimwit, nitwit, outwit, exit, Tilsit (Russian town).

sobeit, howbeit, albeit, post-obit (legal term), advocate, Photofit (*Trademark*), counterfeit, discomfit, conjugate, Harrogate, surrogate, quadruplet, quintuplet, sextuplet, manumit (free from slavery), decrepit, adequate, priorate (office of prior), floweret, vertebrate,

hypocrite, interpret, self-portrait, Somerset, aquavit, margravate, nimble-wit (*US* clever person), thimblewit (*US* dunce).

lickety-split (*US* very quickly), predestinate (foreordained), inadequate, invertebrate, misinterpret, Narraganset (American Indian), affidavit, electromagnet.

371.1

gladiate (sword-shaped), radiate (radiating), foliate, nucleate (having a nucleus), craniate (having a skull), lineate (streaked), cuneate (wedge-shaped), opiate, cruciate.

chalybeate (containing iron salts), immediate, collegiate, vicariate (rank of vicar), inebriate, appropriate, repatriate, expatriate, initiate (novice), patriciate (rank of patrician), novitiate, associate, licentiate.

intermediate, unifoliate, multifoliate, multinucleate, inappropriate.

371.1.1

Juliet, aculeate (pointed).

371.1.2

aureate (gilded), laureate, baccalaureate, professoriate.

371.2

arcuate (arc-shaped), graduate, Inuit (Eskimo), sinuate (botany term), Jesuit, postgraduate, attenuate (weakened), undergraduate.

371.3

bluet (flowering plant), cruet, suet, intuit (know instinctively).

371.4

babbitt (line with alloy), habit, rabbit, drabbet (coarse yellowish-brown fabric), cohabit, inhabit.

371.5

gibbet, zibet (Asian catlike mammal), prohibit, inhibit, celibate, exhibit, flibbertigibbet.

371.6

jacket, placket (dressmaking term), packet, racquet, racket, bracket, blue-jacket, straitjacket, lumberjacket, leatherjacket.

371.7
market, Newmarket, matriarchate, patriarchate, Euromarket, hypermarket, supermarket.

371.8
circuit, bifurcate, trifurcate, microcircuit.

371.9
snicket (*Dialect* passageway), picket, cricket, pricket (young male deer), ticket, thicket, wicket, predicate, syndicate, delicate, silicate, triplicate, tunicate (marine animal), affricate (speech sound), intricate, corticate (having rind or bark), certificate, pontificate, indelicate, umbilicate (having a navel), divaricate (branching), Identikit (*Trademark*), sophisticate.

371.9.1
duplicate, quadruplicate, reduplicate (repeated), centuplicate.

371.10
docket, locket, pocket, rocket, brocket (small deer), Crockett, sprocket, socket, pickpocket, skyrocket, retrorocket.

371.11
bucket, tucket (flourish on trumpet), trebucket (medieval weapon), gutbucket (style of jazz-playing), Nantucket.

371.12
edit, credit, coedit, subedit, accredit, discredit, disaccredit.

371.13
befit, benefit.

371.14
frigate, delegate, profligate, aggregate, congregate (assembled).

371.15
pellet, prelate, stellate, flabellate (fan-shaped), appellate (relating to appeals), Marprelate (Puritan author), varicellate (marked with small ridges).

371.16
billet, skillet, fillet, millet, rillet, willet (US shore bird), flagellate (whip-like), distillate, penicillate (having tufts of hairs), verticillate (arranged in whorls).

371.17
bullet, pullet, culet (base of gemstone), virgulate (rod-shaped), ligulate (strap-shaped), angulate (having angles), ungulate, amulet, cumulate, annulate (having rings), consulate, spatulate, postulate, pustulate, rivulet, tuberculate (covered with nodules), avunculate (assigning rights to uncle), coagulate (product of coagulation).

371.17.1
sacculate (biology term), ejaculate (semen), immaculate.

371.17.2
vermiculate (relating to worms), auriculate (having ears), articulate, reticulate (in form of network), testiculate (having an oval shape), unguiculate (having claws), inarticulate.

371.18
chocolate, desolate, coverlet, disconsolate, apostolate.

371.18.1
violet, inviolate, ultraviolet.

371.19
emit, limit, remit, delimit, animate, ultimate, intimate, estimate, guesstimate, proximate (nearest or next), inanimate, legitimate, penultimate, approximate, illegitimate, underestimate.

371.20
comet, grommet, vomit, Mahomet.

371.21
commit, permit, recommit, consummate, intermit (suspend activity at intervals).

371.22
Banat (plain in eastern Europe), gannet, Janet, planet, granite, Thanet, pomegranate.

371.23
burnet (flowering plant), gurnet (European marine fish), ternate (consisting of three parts), alternate.

371.24
linnet, minute, spinet, cabinet, rabbinate (office of rabbi), turbinate

(scroll-shaped), definite, infinite, laminate, staminate (having stamens), nominate, basinet (medieval helmet), uncinate (hook-shaped), obstinate, indefinite, effeminate, determinate, discriminate, innominate, predeterminate, indeterminate, indiscriminate.

371.24.1
ordinate, coordinate, subordinate, inordinate, incoordinate, insubordinate.

371.24.2
vaginate (having a sheath), Plantagenet, invaginate (folded back on itself).

371.25
bonnet, sonnet, unbonnet, sunbonnet.

371.26
cornet, hornet, bicornate.

371.27
punnet, whodunit.

371.28
bayonet, dragonet (spiny-finned fish), pulmonate (having lungs), baronet, coronet, passionate, bicarbonate, diaconate (office of deacon), compassionate, dispassionate, affectionate, Italianate, companionate.

371.28.1
fortunate, unfortunate, importunate.

371.28.2
proportionate, extortionate, disproportionate.

371.29
cygnet, signet, designate.

371.30
parapet, episcopate.

371.31
ferret, merit, serrate, terret (ring on harness), wherrit (to worry), inherit, demerit, disinherit.

371.32
cerate (hard ointment), emirate, vizierate.

371.33
skirret (plant with edible roots), spirit, aspirate, dispirit, inspirit (fill with

vigour), levirate (marrying brother's widow), triumvirate.

371.34
accurate, obdurate, indurate (hardened), inaccurate, barbiturate.

371.35
federate, moderate, numerate, separate, corporate, temperate, desperate, disparate, literate, doctorate, favourite, leveret.

deliberate, confederate, considerate, immoderate, imperforate, agglomerate, conglomerate, innumerate, degenerate, regenerate (restored), subtemperate, intemperate, commensurate, illiterate, electorate, inspectorate, directorate, protectorate.

inconsiderate, unregenerate (unrepentant), incommensurate, semiliterate.

371.35.1
tabaret (upholstery fabric), taboret (low stool), elaborate.

371.35.2
preterite, inveterate.

371.36
licit, deficit, elicit, illicit, solicit, implicit, explicit, inexplicit.

371.37
vervet (South African monkey), incurvate (curved inwards), acervate (growing in clusters), enervate (weakened).

371.38
visit, marquisate, marquessate, requisite, perquisite, exquisite, prerequisite.

371.39
closet, posit (postulate), deposit, reposit (put away).

371.40
apposite, opposite, composite, inapposite.

372 -ite
bite, byte, bight (indentation of shoreline), kite, skite (*Austral* to boast), fight, height, light, blight, flight, plight, sleight, slight, might, mite, smite, knight, night, spite, quite, rite, right, write, Wright, bright, krait (venomous snake), fright, sprite, trite, sight, cite,

site, tight, Wight, white, twite (European finch).

Shiite, fleabite, backbite, snakebite, frostbite, Melchite (Eastern Church member), cordite (an explosive), Luddite, indict, graphite, cockfight, dogfight, bullfight, gunfight, prizefight, halite (rock salt), marlite (type of marl), starlight, daylight, perlite (volcanic rock), skylight, highlight, stylite (pillar-dwelling recluse), twilight, searchlight, deadlight (nautical term), headlight, sidelight, floodlight, half-light, tail-light, limelight, fanlight, sunlight, moonlight, hoplite (ancient Greek infantryman), droplight (movable electric light), stoplight, gaslight, flashlight, streetlight, spotlight, Hamite (member of African people), samite (heavy silk fabric), Marmite (*Trademark*), Boehmite (mineral), termite, Semite, finite, crinite (covered with soft hairs), dunnite (an explosive), Sunnite (orthodox Muslim), unite, stibnite (mineral), weeknight, ichnite (fossilized footprint), midnight, good-night, fortnight, despite, requite, playwright, ferrite, pyrite (mineral), eyebright (flowering plant), Arkwright, dendrite, chondrite (meteorite), affright, wheelwright, millwright, alright, wainwright, downright, shipwright, typewrite, upright, Cartwright, outright, contrite, ghostwrite, birthright, forthright, eyesight, foresight, website, hindsight, calcite (mineral), bombsight, insight, incite, quartzite (type of rock), ratite (flightless bird), partite (divided), airtight, skintight, uptight, Levite, cleveite (mineral), invite, excite, bauxite.

Trotskyite, Moabite, coenobite (member of religious order), Jacobite, Rechabite (teetotaller), trilobite, malachite (mineral), blatherskite (foolish talkative person), erudite, recondite (abstruse), Wycliffite, epiphyte (plant growing on another), neophyte (novice), bryophyte (botany term), cryophyte (plant growing on snow), Fahrenheit, apartheid, nummulite (fossil), granulite, lazulite, overflight, candlelight, eremite (Christian hermit), Adamite (member of nudist sect), sodomite, dolomite, dynamite, wolframite (mineral), catamite, stalagmite,

disunite, reunite, belemnite, copyright, azurite (gemstone), lazurite (lapis lazuli), achondrite (meteorite), second-sight, bipartite, tripartite, stalactite, transvestite, Muscovite, Hepplewhite.

osteophyte (small bony outgrowth), heteroclite (irregularly formed word), archimandrite (Greek Orthodox monastery head), multipartite.

anthropophagite (cannibal), itacolumite (type of sandstone).

372.1
lyddite (an explosive), expedite.

372.2
troglodyte, andradite (gemstone), extradite, hermaphrodite.

372.3
delight, phyllite (type of rock), rubellite (gemstone), argillite (type of rock), proselyte, apophyllite (mineral), toxophilite (archer), pyrophyllite (mineral), Mutazilite (8th-century liberal Muslim).

372.4
alight, polite.

hyalite (variety of opal), cryolite (mineral), oolite (sedimentary rock), acolyte, Bakelite (*Trademark*), Carmelite, impolite, corallite (fossil coral), microlight, coprolite, chrysolite (gemstone), socialite, quarterlight, graptolite (fossil), crystallite (minute crystal in rock).

Israelite, metabolite (substance produced in metabolism), amphibolite (type of rock), crocidolite (variety of asbestos), theodolite, Pre-Raphaelite, electrolyte.

372.4.1
satellite, stromatolite (type of rock).

372.5
melinite (an explosive), selenite (variety of gypsum), encrinite (fossil), retinite (resin), kaolinite (mineral), gadolinite (mineral).

372.6
tonight, urbanite (city dweller), aconite (poisonous plant), taconite (type of rock), vulcanite (hard rubber), melanite (black variety of garnet), ammonite,

Canaaanite, Maronite (Syrian Christian), overnight, Midianite, suburbanite, amazonite (gemstone).

372.7
ignite, lignite, gelignite.

372.8
aright, Labourite, sybarite, anchorite, underwrite, dolerite (type of rock), Minorite (Franciscan friar), overwrite, Nazarite (Old Testament ascetic), meteorite, ozocerite (wax), grossularite (gemstone).

372.9
recite, lewisite (poisonous liquid), plebiscite, magnesite (mineral), variscite (mineral).

372.10
oocyte (immature female germ cell), marcasite, leucocyte, lymphocyte (type of blood cell), kamacite (iron–nickel alloy), haemocyte (any blood cell), jarosite (mineral), parasite, anthracite, outasight, oversight, erythrocyte, spermatocyte (immature male germ cell), anorthosite (type of rock).

372.11
Hittite, mimetite (mineral), granitite (type of granite), magnetite (mineral), appetite.

372.12
steatite (variety of talc), haematite (mineral), apatite (mineral), watertight, goniatite (fossil), peridotite (type of rock).

373 -ot
bot (larva of botfly), cot, Scot, Scott, dot, phot (unit of illumination), got, jot, hot, lot, blot, clot, plot, slot, motte, knot, not, snot, pot, spot, squat, rot, grot (grotto), trot, sot, shot, tot, what, watt, swot, swat, yacht.

robot, boycott, cocotte, dovecot, begot, forgot, inkblot, subplot, motmot (tropical bird), cannot, slipknot, topknot, whatnot, repot, teapot, jackpot, crackpot, stockpot, stinkpot, tinpot, despot, tosspot, fusspot, sunspot, nightspot, cachepot (container for flowerpot), dashpot (mechanism for damping vibration), hotpot, sexpot, Pequot

(American Indian), loquat (Oriental fruit tree), kumquat, garotte, dogtrot (gentle trot), foxtrot, earshot, eyeshot, bowshot, buckshot, bloodshot, gunshot, moonshot, slingshot (US catapult), slapshot (ice hockey shot), snapshot, grapeshot, upshot, gavotte, abwatt (electrical unit), somewhat.

carrycot, apricot, massicot (mineral), Sialkot (Pakistani city), peridot (gemstone), microdot, Wyandotte (breed of domestic fowl), Camelot, ocelot, sansculotte, polyglot, underplot (subsidiary plot in story), counterplot, guillemot, bergamot, Arbuthnot, coffeepot, galipot (earthenware pot for ointments), galipot (pine resin), talipot (palm tree), chimneypot, flowerpot, aliquot (maths term), Paraquat (*Trademark*), tommyrot, Aldershot, undershot, overshot, Hottentot, kilowatt, megawatt, forgetme-not.

373.1
allot, calotte (Catholic priest's skullcap), shallot, cachalot (sperm whale), eschalot (shallot).

374 -ort
ought, aught, bought, caught, court, fought, fort, mort (call on hunting horn), nought, naught, snort, port, sport, quart, rort (*Austral* noisy party), wrought, brought, fraught, sought, sort, short, tort, taut, taught, torte (rich cake), thought, wart, thwart.

abort, forecourt, escort, hillfort, cohort, onslaught, fearnought (heavy woollen fabric), Connaught, dreadnought, carport, purport, airport, seaport, Newport, Stockport, Coalport, import, comport, passport, spaceport, disport (enjoy oneself), Gosport, spoilsport, transport, jetport, outport, Southport, export, distraught, re-sort, assort, consort, retort, self-taught, untaught, contort, bistort (Eurasian plant), distort, extort, methought, forethought, cavort, athwart, resort, exhort.

Agincourt, Argonaut, juggernaut, cosmonaut, aquanaut, aeronaut, astronaut, reimport, davenport, re-export, overwrought, ultrashort (having very short wavelength), aforethought, afterthought, worrywart (habitual worrier).

374.1

deport, report, heliport, misreport.

374.2

support, hoverport.

375 -oit

coit (*Austral* buttocks), quoit, doit (former Dutch coin), droit, dacoit (armed robber), exploit, adroit, Detroit, maladroit, Massasoit (American Indian chief).

376 -oat

oat, boat, coat, cote, dote, goat, bloat, float, gloat, mote, moat, smote, note, quote, rote, wrote, groat, troat (to bellow), throat, shoat (recently-weaned piglet), tote, stoat, vote.

rowboat, showboat, speedboat, lifeboat, whaleboat, steamboat, gunboat, swingboat, longboat, houseboat, surcoat (medieval knight's tunic), redcoat, Rajkot (Indian city), raincoat, turncoat, sheepcote, topcoat, waistcoat, housecoat, greatcoat, dovecote, zygote (fertilized egg cell), afloat, emote, demote, gemot (Anglo-Saxon legal assembly), remote, promote, keynote, denote, connote, woodnote (natural song), footnote, capote (long hooded cloak), compote, unquote, misquote, whitethroat (songbird), cutthroat, devote, outvote.

powerboat, motorboat, petticoat, undercoat, overcoat, antidote, anecdote, table d'hôte, redingote (overcoat), papillote (paper frill around cutlet), matelote (fish with wine sauce), underquote, creosote, asymptote.

377 -out

out, owt, bout, scout, doubt, gout, lout, clout, flout, nowt, snout, pout, spout, rout, drought, grout, sprout, trout, shout, tout, stout.

throughout, blackout, stakeout (*US* police surveillance), lockout, knockout, cookout (*US* barbecue), lookout, redoubt, dugout, mahout (elephant keeper), fallout, umlaut, amaut (Eskimo woman's hood), brownout (*US* power reduction), dropout, eelpout (marine fish), downspout, without, devout.

waterspout, sauerkraut.

377.1

about, layabout, walkabout, gadabout, roundabout, turnabout, runabout.

378 -ut

butt, but, cut, scut, phut, gut, jut, hut, glut, slut, mutt, smut, nut, putt, rut, strut, shut, tut.

rebut, abut, hackbut (long-barrelled gun), blackbutt (eucalyptus tree), sackbut, haircut, woodcut, uncut, crosscut, foregut, midgut, hindgut, catgut, rotgut, peanut, doughnut, cobnut, beechnut, groundnut, gallnut (plant gall), walnut, chestnut, half-shut.

scuttlebutt (ship's drinking fountain), Calicut (Indian port), linocut, uppercut, coconut, bladdernut (European shrub), butternut, butternut, candlenut, hazelnut, sinciput (part of skull), occiput.

379 -oot

foot, put, soot, barefoot, crowfoot (flowering plant), webfoot, Blackfoot (American Indian), finfoot (aquatic bird), coltsfoot (European plant), flatfoot, hotfoot, cocksfoot (Eurasian grass), kaput, throughput, Rajput (Hindu military caste member), input, output, pussyfoot, cajuput (Australian shrub).

379.1

afoot, tenderfoot, underfoot.

380 -ute

boot, coot, scoot, jute, hoot, lute, loot, flute, moot, snoot (*Slang* nose), root, route, brute, brut, bruit (*US* to report), croute (small piece of toast), fruit, suit, chute, shoot, toot, Ute (American Indian), Bute, beaut, butte (steep-sided hill), cute, mute, newt.

freeboot, jackboot, dilute, Hakluyt (English geographer), folkmoot (medieval district assembly), Beirut, cheroot, snakeroot (*US* plant), recruit, jackfruit (Asian fruit tree), breadfruit, grapefruit, enroot, en route, unroot, taproot, uproot, beetroot, playsuit, lawsuit, tracksuit, swimsuit, sunsuit, spacesuit, pantsuit, offshoot, outshoot, refute, confute, Salyut, solute, volute, commute, permute, deafmute, transmute, minute, Canute, impute, compute, dispute, Asyut (ancient Egyptian city), hirsute, pursuit, statute, astute.

overboot (protective boot), bandicoot, malamute (Eskimo dog), briarroot (wood for tobacco pipes), arrowroot, crinkleroot (flowering plant), coralroot (leafless orchid), Hatshepsut (ancient Egyptian queen), undershoot, parachute, overshoot, persecute, prosecute, execute, comminute (reduce to small fragments).

380.1

galoot (*US* clumsy person), pollute, salute, dissolute, absolute, involute (intricate), convolute, resolute, irresolute.

380.2

tribute, attribute, contribute, distribute.

380.3

acute, subacute (medical term), electrocute.

380.4

depute, repute, disrepute.

380.5

destitute, prostitute, substitute, institute, constitute, reconstitute.

381 -'t

Fiat (*Trademark*), Stuart, abbot, burbot (freshwater fish), Herbert, sherbet, turbot, nobbut (*Dialect* nothing but), Robert, Schubert, Egbert, Albert, Talbot, filbert, Gilbert, Lambert, Cuthbert, Urquhart, ducat, Alcott, Ascot, mascot, wainscot, effort, Beaufort, Frankfurt, comfort, faggot, maggot, braggart, ergot (crop disease), bigot, Piggott, spigot (cask stopper), boggart (*Dialect* poltergeist), yogurt, ingot, ballot, harlot, Charlotte, Helot (serf), zealot, pilot, Pilate, gamut, marmot, Connacht (Northern Irish province), donnert (*Scot* stunned), caput, Rupert, carat, carrot, claret, parrot, divot, pivot, covert, lovat (colour mixture in tweeds), culvert, stalwart, Quixote, desert.

halibut, Port Talbot, Ethelbert, discomfort, copilot.

Connecticut, autopilot.

381.1

idiot, galiot (small galley), Eliot, Herriot, Cypriot, patriot, Cheviot, soviet, exeat, compatriot, commissariat, proletariat, secretariat.

381.1.1

chariot, lariat, Marryat, Iscariot.

381.2

diet, fiat (official permission), quiet, ryot (Indian peasant), riot, Wyatt, unquiet, disquiet.

382 -act [also 32 + -*ed*]

act, fact, pact, bract, tract, tact.

react, hunchbacked, unbacked, humpbacked, redact (prepare for publication), enact, impact, compact, infract (violate), detract, retract, attract, protract, subtract, entr'acte, contract, distract, abstract, extract, intact, contact, exact, transact.

abreact (psychology term), retroact, artefact, re-enact, underact, tesseract (four-dimensional figure), cataract, interact, counteract, overact, precontract, subcontract, inexact.

overreact, autodidact (self-taught person).

382.1

diffract, refract, Pontefract.

383 -arct [also 33 + -*ed*]

gedact (organ pipe), infarct (dead tissue), unmarked.

384 -aked [also 34 + -*ed*]

half-baked, unslaked.

385 -ect [also 35 + -*ed*]

sect, unchecked, defect, prefect, infect, eject, deject, reject, project, abject, object, subject, inject, collect, deflect, reflect, inflect, neglect, connect, landsknecht (mercenary foot soldier), henpecked, aspect, respect, prospect, suspect, inspect, expect, erect, direct, bisect, trisect, transect, insect, protect.

disinfect, genuflect, disconnect, selfrespect, disrespect, retrospect, introspect, circumspect, indirect, misdirect, intersect.

interconnect, overprotect.

385.1
effect, defect, aftereffect.

385.2
affect, perfect, disaffect.

385.3
project, traject (to transport), retroject (throw backwards), introject (psychology term), interject.

385.4
elect, prelect (to lecture), select, intellect.

385.5
collect, dialect, recollect, idiolect (individual's language).

385.6
correct, incorrect, resurrect.

385.7
dissect, resect (remove surgically), quadrisect, vivisect.

385.8
detect, architect.

386 -eeked [also **37** + *-ed*]
beaked, peaked, streaked.

387 -ict [also **38** + *-ed*]
Pict, strict, addict, verdict, edict, predict, perfect, object, subject, relict, afflict, inflict, conflict, depict, district, restrict, constrict, evict, convict, maledict (utter a curse), Benedict, pluperfect, imperfect, derelict, derestrict.

387.1
addict, contradict, interdict.

388 -oct [also **40** + *-ed*]
decoct (extract by boiling), concoct, landlocked, unlocked, ectoproct (aquatic animal).

389 -uct [also **43** + *-ed*]
duct, deduct, product, abduct, induct, conduct, eruct (to belch), destruct, obstruct, instruct, construct, aqueduct, oviduct, viaduct, misconduct, usufruct, reconstruct.

390 -ooked [also **44** + *-ed*]
hooked, uncooked.

391 -anct [also **51** + *-ed*]
unthanked, sacrosanct.

392 -inct [also **52** + *-ed*]
tinct (tinted), precinct, distinct, instinct, extinct, succinct, indistinct.

393 -unct [also **54** + *-ed*]
defunct, adjunct, conjunct.

394 -asked [also **56** + *-ed*]
masked, unasked.

395 -atched [also **62** + *-ed*]
well-matched, detached, unscratched, unattached, semidetached.

396 -aft [also **158** + *-ed*]
aft, daft, haft (knife handle), raft, craft, kraft (strong wrapping-paper), draught, draft, graft, shaft, waft.
abaft, aircraft, witchcraft, woodcraft, handcraft, stagecraft, spacecraft, statecraft, redraft, engraft, crankshaft, camshaft.
handicraft, hovercraft, needlecraft, overdraft, homograft, autograft, understaffed, overstaffed.
anti-aircraft, heterograft.

397 -eft
eft, deft, heft (assess weight of), left, cleft, klepht (Greek brigand), theft, weft, bereft.

398 -ift [also **163** + *-ed*]
gift, lift, rift, drift, shrift, thrift, sift, shift, swift, airlift, uplift, festschrift (commemorative collection of writings), snowdrift, adrift, spindrift (sea spray), spendthrift, gearshift, makeshift.

399 -oft [also **165** + *-ed*]
oft, loft, croft, soft, toft (homestead), aloft, cockloft, Ashcroft, Lowestoft, undercroft (underground chamber).

400 -uft [also **168** + *-ed*]
chuffed, tuft, stuffed, candytuft (flowering plant).

401 -alt
alt (high in pitch), shalt, asphalt, gestalt (overall structure).

402 -elt

belt, Celt, dealt, felt, gelt (*Slang* money), melt, smelt, knelt, pelt, spelt, Scheldt (European river), veld, svelte, welt, dwelt, unbelt, backveld (remote rural area), heartfelt, Danegelt, jacksmelt (marine fish), underfelt, Tafilelt (largest oasis in Sahara), Roosevelt.

403 -ilt

built, kilt, guilt, gilt, jilt, hilt, lilt, milt, spilt, quilt, silt, tilt, stilt, wilt, rebuilt, well-built, atilt (tilted), uptilt, Vanderbilt.

404 -orlt

Balt (person from Baltic States), fault, halt, malt, smalt (dark blue glass), salt, vault, cobalt, default, basalt, exalt.

404.1

assault, somersault.

405 -oalt

bolt, Boult, colt, dolt, jolt, Holt, moult, smolt (young salmon), poult (young domestic fowl), volt, Humboldt, unbolt, kingbolt (steering bolt on carriage), ringbolt (bolt with ring attached), revolt, abvolt (electrical unit), thunderbolt, kilovolt, electron-volt.

406 -ult

cult, occult, adult, indult (Catholic dispensation), tumult, penult (penultimate syllable), insult, consult, result, exult, difficult, catapult, jurisconsult.

407 -ant

ant, Kant, cant, scant, pant, rant, Brabant (Belgian province), decant, recant, descant, gallant, Rembrandt, enceinte (enclosure), extant, confidant, commandant, sycophant, hierophant (ancient Greek high priest).

407.1

levant (patterned leather), gallivant.

408 -arnt

aunt, aren't, can't, chant, plant, slant, grant, shan't, plainchant, enchant, supplant, eggplant, implant, transplant, ashplant, waxplant (flowering plant), aslant, détente, disenchant, debutante.

409 -aint

ain't, feint, faint, plaint (legal term), paint, quaint, saint, taint, complaint, repaint, greasepaint, acquaint, distraint (legal term), restraint, constraint.

410 -ent

bent, Kent, dent, Ghent, gent, lent, leant, Lent, meant, pent, spent, rent, Brent, brent (small goose), Trent, cent, sent, scent, tent, vent, went, Gwent.

hellbent, unbent, indent, relent, fragment, comment, torment, loment (plant pod), augment, unmeant, anent (*Scot* concerning), repent, well-spent, frequent, besprent (sprinkled over), descent, dissent, docent (US lecturer), assent, ascent, per cent, absent, consent, portent, intent, content, extent, advent, invent, forwent, forewent, accent.

orient, document, overspent, malcontent, discontent, circumvent, underwent, disorient.

410.1

dement, cement, regiment, aliment, supplement, implement, complement, compliment, experiment, fibrocement.

410.2

foment, ferment, lament, ornament.

410.3

event, prevent, nonevent.

410.4

resent, present, represent, re-present, misrepresent.

411 -ernt

burnt, learnt, weren't, mowburnt (agricultural term), sunburnt, unlearnt.

412 -int

bint (*Slang* girl), skint, dint, hint, lint, flint, Flint, glint, splint, mint, squint, print, sprint, tint, stint.

suint (substance in sheep's wool), skinflint, gunflint, varmint, spearmint, horsemint (European plant), catmint, asquint (glancing furtively), reprint, blueprint, offprint (separate reprint of article), imprint, thumbprint, misprint, voiceprint, footprint, newsprint.

calamint (Eurasian plant), peppermint, microprint, fingerprint, mezzotint, monotint (painting technique), aquatint (copper-etching technique), Septuagint.

413 -ynt

pint, cuckoopint.

414 -ont

font, quant (pole used for punting), want, Vermont, Beaumont, Piedmont (region of Italy), Egmont, symbiont, Negropont (Greek island), Hellespont, halobiont (salt-water organism), Dandie Dinmont.

415 -ornt

daunt, gaunt, jaunt, haunt, flaunt, taunt, vaunt, Broederbond (South African secret society).

416 -oint

joint, point, conjoint, disjoint, anoint, repoint, pourpoint (medieval doublet), viewpoint, breakpoint, checkpoint, midpoint, standpoint, ballpoint, pinpoint, gunpoint, needlepoint.

416.1

appoint, disappoint, counterpoint, silverpoint (drawing technique).

417 -oant

don't, wont, won't.

418 -ount

count, fount, mount, re-count, recount, viscount, account, discount, miscount, surmount, demount (remove from mounting), seamount (underwater mountain), dismount.

418.1

amount, paramount, catamount (feline animal), tantamount.

419 -unt

bunt, cunt, dunt (*Dialect* a blow), hunt, blunt, punt, runt, brunt, front, grunt, shunt, stunt, manhunt, seafront, forefront, breakfront (having projecting central section), confront, exeunt.

419.1

affront, waterfront.

420 -'nt [further rhymes may be cre-

ated by adding -*ment* to appropriate verbs]

mayn't, lambent, bacchant (drunken reveller), vacant, merchant, couchant (heraldic term), trenchant, hadn't, pedant, verdant, trident, strident, rodent, infant, pageant, argent (silver), sergeant, Sargent, agent, regent, sejant (heraldic term), cogent, pungent, sealant, silent, Solent, volant (heraldic term), coolant, ament (catkin), garment, clement, moment, parchment, oddment, fragment, segment, figment, pigment, lodgment, judgment, treatment, vestment, pavement, stagnant, regnant (prevalent), pregnant, remnant, serpent, dopant (chemistry term), rampant, parent, spirant (phonetics term), tyrant, vibrant, hydrant, quadrant, flagrant, fragrant, vagrant, migrant, entrant, nascent, absent, quotient, Ushant (French island), ancient, potent, octant (eighth part of circle), instant, constant, sextant, Havant, haven't, savant, solvent, convent, Derwent, unguent, valiant, brilliant, poignant, hasn't, wisent (European bison), isn't, wasn't.

absorbent, adsorbent, recumbent, incumbent, impeccant (free from sin), decadent, elephant, triumphant, reagent, newsagent, sibilant, jubilant, flagellant, vigilant, pestilent, inclement, deferment, preferment, interment, agreement, requirement, retirement, endowment, embankment, impeachment, enrichment, debouchment (outlet), embranchment, retrenchment, entrenchment, bombardment, débridement (removal of dead tissue), commandment, amendment, intendment (legal term), secondment, enlargement, engagement, infringement, concealment, fulfilment, instalment, enrolment, annulment, enjambment (poetry term), adjournment, discernment, internment, alignment, assignment, consignment, adornment, postponement, atonement, escarpment, escapement, encampment, impressment (conscription into government service), assessment, enticement, inducement, advancement, commencement, announcement, pronouncement, refreshment, department, apartment, compartment, revetment (protective facing of stones), maltreatment, indictment, incitement, excitement, allotment, ballottement (medical term), deportment, comportment, assortment, abutment, recruitment, enactment, enchantment, contentment, resentment, presentment, investment, adjustment, achievement, bereavement, amazement, appeasement, chastisement, amusement, complainant, alternant, indignant, malignant, benignant, repugnant, discrepant, occupant, delinquent, godparent, grandparent, stepparent, aspirant, figurant, fulgurant, celebrant, emigrant, immigrant, integrant (part of a whole), re-entrant, registrant (person who registers trademark), ministrant, remonstrant, renascent, adjacent, subjacent (forming a foundation), complacent, innocent, dissentient, presentient, consentient (being in agreement), excitant, important, prepotent (greater in power), reactant, surfactant, attractant, reluctant, consultant, resultant, exultant, repentant, accountant, acceptant, inconstant, relevant, pursuivant, connivent, adjuvant (helping), insolvent, dissolvent, resolvent, emollient, ebullient, complaisant, cognizant, recusant (insubordinate).

equipollent (equal in effect), undergarment, overgarment, disagreement, disengagement, development, divertissement, advertisement, disenchantment, maladjustment, misdemeanant, inadvertent, unimportant, idempotent (maths term), executant, irrelevant, incognizant, redevelopment.

420.1

ambient, radiant, gradient, salient, suppliant, fainéant, sapient, variant, orient, miscreant, nutrient, transeunt (philosophy term), sentient, deviant, transient.

resilient, defoliant, recipient, percipient, incipient, invariant, aperient, inebriant, omniscient, insouciant, officiant, negotiant, assentient (approving), insentient, subservient, asphyxiant.

420.1.1

mediant, obedient, expedient, ingredient, disobedient, inexpedient.

420.1.2

lenient, prevenient (preceding), convenient, inconvenient.

420.1.3

prurient, esurient (greedy), parturient (relating to childbirth), luxuriant.

420.2

giant, client, pliant, defiant, reliant, compliant, supergiant, incompliant.

420.3

buoyant, flamboyant, foudroyant (sudden and severe), chatoyant (changing in lustre), clairvoyant.

420.4

affluent, effluent, confluent, congruent, diluent, issuant, fluctuant, evacuant (promoting bowel evacuation), attenuant, continuant, substituent, constituent.

420.5

fluent, truant, eluent (chemistry term), pursuant.

420.6

piquant, secant, cosecant.

420.7

predicant (relating to preaching), mendicant, indicant, applicant, supplicant, lubricant, desiccant, vesicant (blistering substance), toxicant (a poison), significant, communicant, intoxicant, insignificant.

420.8

ardent, guardant (heraldic term), regardant (heraldic term), retardant.

420.9

needn't, credent, decedent (deceased person), antecedent.

420.10

didn't, diffident, confident, precedent, dissident, incident, evident, provident, accident, oxidant, occident, self-confident, coincident, improvident, overconfident, antioxidant.

420.10.1
resident, president, nonresident.

420.11
mordant, mordent (melodic ornament), accordant, concordant, discordant.

420.12
couldn't, shouldn't, wouldn't, impudent.

420.13
prudent, student, imprudent, jurisprudent.

420.14
pendant, pendent (dangling), defendant, resplendent, dependant, dependent, descendant, ascendant, transcendent, attendant, intendant (provincial official), independent, interdependent, superintendent.

420.15
fondant, despondent, respondent (legal term), correspondent, co-respondent.

420.16
abundant, redundant, superabundant.

420.17
elegant, fumigant, congregant, litigant, inelegant.

420.18
termagant, arrogant, extravagant.

420.19
urgent, emergent, resurgent, insurgent, detergent, divergent, convergent.

420.20
indigent, diligent, negligent, exigent (urgent), intelligent, intransigent, unintelligent.

420.21
fulgent (resplendent), indulgent, effulgent (radiant), refulgent (shining), self-indulgent.

420.22
plangent (resonant or plaintive), tangent, cotangent, subtangent.

420.23
ringent (botany term), stringent, refringent (refractive), astringent, contingent.

420.24
gallant, talent, topgallant (ship's mast).

420.25
inhalant, exhalant (emitting a vapour), assailant, bivalent, divalent, trivalent, polyvalent, univalent, monovalent.

420.26
repellent, appellant (person who appeals), propellant, expellant, interpellant (interrupting with question).

420.27
virulent, purulent, turbulent, ambulant, feculent (filthy), flocculent (fleecy), truculent, succulent, esculent (edible), fraudulent, undulant, tremulant, simulant, stimulant, crapulent, opulent, corpulent, flatulent, petulant, postulant, pustulant, pulverulent (consisting of dust), coagulant, puberulent (covered with down), anticoagulant.

420.28
violent, libellant, redolent, indolent, somnolent, insolent, nonchalant, excellent, nonviolent, sanguinolent (containing blood), equivalent.

420.28.1
prevalent, malevolent, benevolent.

420.29
claimant, clamant (noisy), payment, raiment, repayment.

420.30
cerement (burial clothes), endearment.

420.31
vehement, rudiment, condiment, regiment, aliment, element, supplement, implement, compliment, complement, liniment, muniment, orpiment (mineral), worriment, decrement (diminution), recrement (waste matter), increment, excrement, detriment, nutriment, sentiment, embodiment, habiliment (dress), presentiment, accompaniment.

420.31.1
pediment, sediment, impediment.

420.31.2
merriment, experiment.

420.32

dormant, informant.

420.33

enjoyment, deployment, employment, redeployment, unemployment.

420.34

document, argument, monument, integument (outer protective layer), emolument.

420.35

adamant, fundament (buttocks), wonderment, parliament, filament, armament, firmament, tenement, ornament, tournament, sacrament, instrument, measurement, betterment, testament, lineament, medicament, predicament, bewilderment, disarmament, temperament, accoutrement.

420.35.1

ligament, disfigurement.

420.36

catchment, hatchment (heraldic term), detachment, attachment.

420.37

management, abridgment, acknowledgment, disparagement, encouragement, discouragement.

420.38

derangement, arrangement, estrangement, rearrangement.

420.39

ailment, bailment (legal term), derailment, curtailment.

420.40

battlement, settlement, devilment, puzzlement, entanglement, entitlement, embezzlement.

420.41

attainment, containment, entertainment.

420.42

government, abandonment, environment, apportionment, enlightenment, imprisonment.

420.43

shipment, equipment.

420.44

basement, casement, placement, subbasement, replacement, emplacement, displacement.

420.45

endorsement, enforcement, reinforcement.

420.46

harassment, embarrassment.

420.47

punishment, nourishment, embellishment, establishment, accomplishment, astonishment.

420.48

statement, abatement, affreightment (contract hiring cargo ship), understatement, reinstatement.

420.49

fitment, commitment.

420.50

ointment, anointment, appointment, disappointment.

420.51

movement, improvement.

420.52

pennant, tenant, cotenant, subtenant, lieutenant, sublieutenant.

420.53

eminent, imminent, culminant, fulminant (sudden and violent), pertinent, continent, revenant, pre-eminent, appurtenant, impertinent, subcontinent, incontinent.

420.53.1

germinant, determinant.

420.53.2

dominant, prominent, predominant, subdominant.

420.53.3

ruminant, illuminant.

420.54

sonant (phonetics term), deponent (linguistics term), opponent, proponent, component, exponent.

420.55
permanent, immanent (existing within), assonant, dissonant, consonant, covenant, resonant, impermanent, inconsonant.

420.56
flippant, participant, anticipant.

420.57
frequent, sequent, infrequent.

420.58
aliquant (maths term), subsequent, consequent, inconsequent.

420.59
eloquent, ineloquent, grandiloquent, magniloquent (lofty in style).

420.60
arrant, apparent, transparent.

420.61
errant, gerent (ruler or manager), aberrant, vicegerent, deterrent.

420.62
coherent, adherent, inherent, incoherent.

420.63
torrent, warrant, abhorrent.

420.64
currant, current, recurrent, blackcurrant, redcurrant, concurrent, crosscurrent, undercurrent, intercurrent (occurring between).

420.65
afferent (conducting inwards), efferent (conducting outwards), deferent, referent, different, tolerant, colorant, cormorant, ignorant, operant, reverent.

corroborant, protuberant, exuberant, deodorant, preponderant, indifferent, belligerent, refrigerant, accelerant, exhilarant, intolerant, decolorant, itinerant, expectorant, adulterant, irreverent, antiperspirant.

420.66
penetrant, recalcitrant.

420.67
crescent, quiescent, rubescent, pubescent, tabescent (wasting away), albescent (becoming white), confessant, turgescent, spumescent (producing froth), tumescent, liquescent, decrescent (decreasing in size), increscent (increasing in size), excrescent, nigrescent (blackish), depressant, vitrescent (turning into glass), putrescent, incessant, frutescent, lactescent.

acquiescent, iridescent, viridescent (becoming green), incandescent, adolescent, opalescent, obsolescent, convalescent, deliquescent, fluorescent, arborescent (treelike), phosphorescent, antidepressant.

420.67.1
senescent, juvenescent.

420.67.2
canescent (becoming hoary), evanescent.

420.67.3
flavescent (turning yellow), effervescent, ingravescent (becoming worse).

420.68
versant (mountain side), dispersant, conversant.

420.69
decent, recent, indecent.

420.70
dehiscent, reticent, Stuyvesant (Dutch colonial administrator), maleficent, beneficent, munificent, magnificent, omnificent, indehiscent, reminiscent.

420.71
lucent, translucent, abducent (anatomy term).

420.72
demulcent (soothing), convulsant, anticonvulsant.

420.73
patient, impatient, inpatient, outpatient, calefacient (causing warmth), stupefacient, liquefacient, abortifacient.

420.74
efficient, deficient, proficient, sufficient, coefficient, inefficient, self-sufficient, insufficient.

420.75
latent, blatant, natant (floating on water), patent, dilatant, supernatant (floating on the surface).

420.76
militant, volitant (moving rapidly), remittent, penitent, competent, irritant, hesitant, visitant, annuitant (person receiving annuity), inhabitant, exorbitant, concomitant, intermittent, impenitent, precipitant, incompetent, counterirritant.

420.77
mutant, nutant (botany term), pollutant, disputant.

420.78
combatant, adjutant, impotent, non-combatant, coadjutant, armipotent (strong in battle), plenipotent (having full authority), omnipotent.

420.79
humectant, expectant, disinfectant.

420.80
digestant, contestant, decongestant.

420.81
distant, assistant, persistent, insistent, consistent, Protestant, resistant, existent, equidistant, inconsistent, nonresistant, coexistent, nonexistent.

420.82
fervent, servant, maidservant, bondservant, manservant, observant.

420.83
accent, relaxant.

420.84
bezant (Byzantine gold coin), pheasant, pleasant, peasant, present, unpleasant, omnipresent.

421 -apt [also 268 + -ed]
apt, rapt, snowcapped, adapt, inapt, unapt, periapt (amulet).

422 -ept [also 271 + -ed]
kept, leapt, slept, crept, sept (clan), wept, swept, adept, inept, percept (object of perception), precept, transept, concept, unwept, windswept, backswept, except, accept, nympholept, overslept, intercept.

423 -erpt [also 272 + -ed]
excerpt, usurped.

424 -ipt [also 274 + -ed]
crypt, script, Egypt, decrypt (decode), prescript, subscript, transcript, conscript, typescript, postscript, nondescript, telescript (script for television), manuscript, superscript.

425 -opt [also 276 + -ed]
opt, Copt, coopt, adopt, unstopped.

426 -upt [also 279 + -ed]
erupt, irrupt, abrupt, bankrupt, disrupt.

426.1
corrupt, incorrupt, interrupt.

427 -ulpt
sculpt, gulped, pulped.

428 -empt
kempt (tidy), tempt, pre-empt, unkempt, attempt, contempt, exempt.

429 -ompt [also 288 + -ed]
prompt, swamped.

430 -ast [also 293 + -ed]
bast (plant tissue), hast, bombast, dicast (Athenian juror), gymnast, peltast (ancient Greek foot soldier), fantast (visionary), lymphoblast (immature white blood cell), neuroblast (embryonic nerve cell), chloroplast (chlorophyll-containing structure), pederast, erythroblast (cell in bone marrow), osteoblast (bone-forming cell), osteoclast (surgical instrument), iconoclast (opponent of established beliefs).

430.1
scholiast (medieval annotator), cineaste (film enthusiast), encomiast (writer of eulogies), gymnasiast (European secondary school student), ecdysiast (striptease artist), enthusiast.

431 -arst [also 294 + -ed]
cast, caste, karst, fast, last, blast, mast, past, vast.
precast, die-cast, forecast, broadcast, half-caste, roughcast, wormcast, downcast, typecast, miscast, sportscast,

outcast, newscast, holdfast (hook or clamp), Belfast, oblast (Russian administrative division), sandblast, outlast, durmast (oak tree), foremast, half-mast, mainmast, topmast, repast, contrast, avast.

telecast, overcast, simulcast (simultaneous radio–television broadcast), opencast, colourfast, counterblast, mizzenmast, Elastoplast (*Trademark*).

431.1

aghast, flabbergast.

432 -aste [also 295 + -*ed*]

baste, chaste, haste, paste, taste, waste, waist, lambaste (*Slang* beat severely), barefaced, two-faced, shamefaced, posthaste, unplaced, toothpaste, foretaste, distaste, aftertaste, pantywaist (*US* childish person).

433 -est [also 296 + -*ed*]

best, chest, guest, jest, lest, blest, nest, pest, quest, wrest, rest, Brest, breast, crest, dressed, test, vest, west, zest.

Trieste, gabfest (*US* gathering for conversation), infest, egest (excrete), digest, suggest, ingest, congest, behest, celeste, molest, unblessed, bequest, request, inquest, conquest, abreast, redbreast, goldcrest (small warbler), headrest, well-dressed, armrest, unrest, depressed, impressed, footrest, unstressed, incest, detest, attest, protest, contest, revest (restore power), divest, invest, northwest, southwest, possessed.

second-best, manifest, disinfest, predigest, Almagest (Ptolemy's treatise on astronomy), alkahest (universal solvent in alchemy), Budapest, rinderpest (disease of cattle), anapaest (metrical foot), overdressed, unimpressed, unexpressed, undervest, self-possessed.

433.1

arrest, Bucharest.

434 -erst [also 297 + -*ed*]

burst, durst, first, Hearst, thirst, versed, worst, wurst, cloudburst, sunburst, outburst, headfirst, Pankhurst, Sandhurst, knackwurst (type of sausage), athirst (longing), bratwurst (type of sausage), liverwurst.

435 -eest [also 298 + -*ed*]

east, beast, feast, geest (German heathland), least, piste, priest, yeast, modiste (fashionable milliner or dressmaker), beanfeast, archpriest, deceased, batiste (cotton fabric), artiste, northeast, southeast, wildebeest, hartebeest, arriviste (unscrupulously ambitious person).

436 -ist [Also 300 + -*ed*. Further rhymes may be derived from 242.35 or by adding -*ist* to appropriate adjectives.]

kist (*Dialect* large coffer), fist, gist, hist, list, Liszt, mist, wrist, grist, tryst, cyst, cist (box holding ritual objects), schist, whist, twist, xyst (long portico).

deist, Maoist, cubist, cambist (foreign-exchange dealer), stockist, Yorkist, sadist, modest, feudist (person involved in feud), nudist, eldest, damnedest, sophist, druggist, Hengist (Jute settler in Britain), legist, cellist, stylist, Gaullist, blacklist, cyclist, enlist, chemist, demist, tanist (heir of Celtic chieftain), earnest, honest, hymnist, Trappist, typist, tempest, Marist (member of Christian sect), centrist (person with moderate views), bassist (double bass player), subsist, insist, consist, fascist, latticed, artist, chartist, latest, greatest, statist (supporter of state power), rightist, flautist, leftist, Baptist, farthest, furthest, harvest, linguist, Marxist, sexist, desist, resist, exist.

lobbyist, copyist, atheist, oboist, egoist, soloist, altruist, casuist, anarchist, monarchist, masochist, immodest, pacifist, strategist, violist, extremist, conformist, hygienist, machinist, dishonest, trombonist, communist, columnist, Decembrist (former Russian revolutionary), Septembrist (former French revolutionary), exorcist, defeatist, unpractised, scientist, amethyst, reservist, archivist, Bolshevist, activist, coexist.

propagandist, gymnosophist (member of Indian sect), motorcyclist, biochemist, taxidermist, nonconformist, ventriloquist, equilibrist (person performing balancing acts), optometrist, psychiatrist, parachutist, orthodontist, Anabaptist (16th-century Protestant).

encyclopedist, audiotypist.

436.1
Judaist, épéeist, Hebraist (student of Hebrew culture), essayist, Ptolemaist, algebraist.

436.2
Buddhist, Talmudist (Jewish scholar), unprejudiced.

436.3
melodist, rhapsodist, Methodist, chiropodist.

436.4 [further rhymes may be derived from **16.108.4**]
suffragist, liturgist, biologist, zoologist, psychologist, graphologist, technologist, apologist (person defending by argument), archaeologist, radiologist, sociologist, gynaecologist, ornithologist, meteorologist.

436.4.1
allergist, dialogist (contributor to dialogue), metallurgist, genealogist.

436.5
idyllist, pugilist, Familist (member of Christian sect), evangelist.

436.6
fabulist, oculist, Populist (member of People's Party), funambulist, somnambulist.

436.7
loyalist, royalist, arbalest (medieval crossbow), herbalist, verbalist, symbolist, vocalist, medallist, journalist, finalist, moralist, racialist, specialist, socialist, fatalist, novelist.
minimalist, immoralist, generalist (person with broad knowledge), naturalist, capitalist, medievalist, revivalist, removalist (*Austral* furniture remover).
semifinalist, bibliopolist (dealer in rare books), universalist, existentialist.

436.7.1
realist, idealist, surrealist.

436.7.2
aerialist (trapeze artist), glacialist (person studying ice effects), imperialist, materialist, memorialist (writer of memoirs), industrialist.

436.7.3
sensualist, spiritualist, individualist.

436.7.4
analyst, panellist, psychoanalyst.

436.7.5
nationalist, rationalist, sensationalist, educationalist, Congregationalist, conversationalist.

436.7.6
catalyst, philatelist, anticatalyst, biocatalyst (enzyme).

436.7.7
instrumentalist, environmentalist.

436.8
palmist, psalmist, alarmist.

436.9
pessimist, optimist, legitimist (supporter of legitimate ruler).

436.10
alchemist, monogamist, economist, anatomist.

436.10.1
bigamist, polygamist.

436.11
Hellenist (devotee of Greek civilization), feminist, alpinist, Latinist, lutenist (lute player), chauvinist, violinist, determinist.

436.12
balloonist, bassoonist, cartoonist, opportunist.

436.13
hedonist, symphonist, organist, colonist, harmonist, Romanist (supporter of Catholicism), timpanist, Satanist, botanist, alienist (type of psychiatrist), unionist, tobacconist, telephonist, saxophonist, misogynist, accompanist, impressionist, excursionist, abortionist, contortionist, percussionist, destructionist, obstructionist, receptionist, illusionist, exclusionist, evolutionist, interventionist.

436.13.1
pianist, Orleanist.

436.13.2

agonist (type of muscle), protagonist, antagonist, deuteragonist (character in Greek drama).

436.13.3

humanist, phillumenist (collector of matchbox labels).

436.13.4

vacationist (*US* holidaymaker), salvationist, segregationist, revelationist (believer in divine revelation), conservationist.

436.13.5

nutritionist, prohibitionist, exhibitionist, abolitionist.

436.13.6

perfectionist, projectionist, protectionist, resurrectionist (body-snatcher), vivisectionist.

436.14

papist, rapist, escapist, landscapist.

436.15

therapist, philanthropist, misanthropist, psychotherapist, radiotherapist, physiotherapist.

436.16

tsarist, guitarist.

436.17

dearest, querist (questioner), careerist.

436.18

forest, florist, deforest, afforest, rainforest, reafforest, disafforest.

436.19

jurist, tourist, purist, manicurist, caricaturist.

436.20

theorist, diarist, arborist (specialist in tree-cultivation), labourist (supporter of workers' rights), Eucharist, naturist, plagiarist, amorist, humorist, terrorist, satirist, motorist, interest, Everest, apiarist, miniaturist, ocularist, militarist, disinterest, Redemptorist (Catholic missionary), behaviourist, lepidopterist.

436.21

Biblicist (biblical scholar), publicist, Anglicist, lyricist, classicist, physicist, geneticist.

436.22

assist, persist, pharmacist, macrocyst, statocyst (organ of balance), blastocyst, supremacist, nematocyst (animal's stinging organ).

436.23

cornetist, librettist, clarinetist.

436.24

Semitist (student of Semitic culture), phonetist, portraitist, hereditist (supporter of heredity's influence).

436.25

protist (microscopic organism), unnoticed.

436.26

egotist, dramatist, pragmatist, dogmatist, Donatist (Christian heretic), hypnotist, systematist, numismatist, separatist, anaesthetist.

436.27

dentist, apprenticed, Adventist (member of Christian sect), irredentist.

437 -iced [also **301** + -*ed*]

heist, Kleist (German dramatist), Christ, Zeist (Dutch city), unpriced, poltergeist, Antichrist.

438 -ost [also **302** + -*ed*]

cost, lost, frost, accost, volost (Russian peasant community), riposte, compost, defrost, hoarfrost, Bifrost (Norse mythological rainbow bridge), teleost (type of fish), Pentecost, permafrost.

439 -orst [also **303** + -*ed*]

horst (ridge of land), exhaust, holocaust, hypocaust (Roman heating system).

440 -oist [also **304** + -*ed*]

foist, joist, hoist, moist, unvoiced.

441 -oast [also **305** + -*ed*]

oast, boast, coast, ghost, host, most, post, roast, toast.
seacoast, rearmost, foremost, backmost, midmost (in the middle), endmost,

hindmost, almost, topmost, utmost, doorpost, bedpost, guidepost, soundpost, milepost, signpost, lamppost, gatepost, outpost, milquetoast (*US* timid person).

undermost, innermost, uppermost, outermost, farthermost, nethermost, furthermost, bottommost, northernmost, southernmost, westernmost, easternmost.

442 -oust [also **306** + *-ed*]

oust, Faust, joust, roust (rout out), frowst (stuffy atmosphere).

443 -ust [also **307** + *-ed*]

bust, dust, gust, just, lust, must, rust, crust, trust, thrust, robust, combust, stardust, sawdust, august, disgust, adjust, unjust, piecrust, encrust, entrust, distrust, mistrust, upthrust, readjust, wanderlust.

444 -oost [also **309** + *-ed*]

boost, roost, Proust, langouste (spiny lobster).

445 -'st [also **310** + *-ed*]

locust, breakfast, steadfast, August, ballast, Sallust (Roman historian), dynast, Bathurst (Australian city), provost, unbiased.

446 -idst

didst, midst.

447 -enst [also **316** + *-ed*]

unfenced, against, fornenst (*Scot* situated against).

448 -'nst [also **321** + *-ed*]

unlicensed, inexperienced.

449 -ished [also **353** + *-ed*]

unfurnished, unfinished, malnourished, unaccomplished, undernourished, undistinguished.

450 -ext [also **496** + *-ed*]

next, sext (Catholic prayer time), text, pretext, context, undersexed, oversexed.

451 -ixt [also **498** + *-ed*]

mixed, sixte (fencing position), betwixt.

452 -ath

Gath (biblical city), hath, Plath (US poet), strath (*Scot* glen), polymath, aftermath, chaetognath (wormlike marine animal), plectognath (spinyfinned fish), psychopath, allopath (orthodox medical practitioner), sociopath, osteopath, naturopath.

453 -arth

bath, Bath, garth (cloistered courtyard), hearth, lath, path, eyebath, birdbath, Hogarth, bypath (little-used track), warpath, towpath, footpath.

454 -aith

faith, wraith, saithe (food fish), Galbraith.

455 -eth

Beth, death, breath, Seth, Macbeth, Japheth (biblical character), megadeath (death of million people), shibboleth, Ashtoreth (biblical character).

456 -erth

earth, berth, birth, dearth, firth, girth, mirth, Perth, worth, rebirth, childbirth, stillbirth, unearth, afterbirth, pennyworth.

457 -eeth

heath, Leith, Meath, neath, wreath, Reith, sheath, teeth, beneath, B'nai B'rith (Jewish fraternal society), Monteith, underneath.

458 -ith

kith, myth, Smith, pith, grith (place of safety), withe (twig used for binding). Hadith (Mohammedan tradition), Judith, Griffith, tallith (Jewish prayer shawl), Lilith (biblical demon), goldsmith, gunsmith, tunesmith, blacksmith, locksmith, zenith, turpeth (plant yielding purgative), Asquith, Penrith. sixtieth, eightieth, thirtieth, fortieth, fiftieth, twentieth, ninetieth, Meredith, eolith (stone tool), neolith (stone tool), megalith, regolith (earth's mantle rock), granolith (paving material), monolith, urolith (stone in urinary tract), acrolith (type of sculpture), microlith (flint tool), gastrolith (stone in the stomach), batholith (large mass of granite), Ladysmith, Hammersmith, silversmith.

seventieth, Aberystwyth.

459 -oth

Goth, cloth, moth, wrath, broth, froth, Naboth (biblical character), haircloth, cerecloth (waxed waterproof cloth), backcloth, sackcloth, neckcloth, broadcloth (closely woven fabric), sailcloth, oilcloth, loincloth, dishcloth, cheesecloth, azoth (mercury), Visigoth, Ostrogoth, tablecloth, saddlecloth, behemoth (biblical monster).

460 -orth

Forth, forth, fourth, north, swath (strip of cut grass), henceforth.

461 -oath

oath, both, loath, sloth, quoth, wroth (angry), growth, troth, Thoth (ancient Egyptian deity), Arbroath, ingrowth, upgrowth, outgrowth, undergrowth, overgrowth.

462 -outh

Louth (Irish county), mouth, south, loudmouth, bigmouth, goalmouth, blabbermouth.

463 -ooth

couth, sleuth, Ruth, crwth (ancient stringed instrument), truth, strewth, sooth, tooth, youth, uncouth, Duluth (US port), Redruth, untruth, forsooth, eyetooth, bucktooth, dogtooth.

464 -'th

Sabbath, Lambeth, mammoth, Yarmouth, Weymouth, vermouth, Plymouth, Falmouth, Monmouth, Bournemouth, Portsmouth, Dartmouth, bismuth, ha'p'orth, Hepworth, Bosworth, Wordsworth, Wandsworth, Goliath, azimuth, Nazareth, Kenilworth, Elizabeth, altazimuth (astronomy instrument).

465 -elth

health, stealth, wealth, Commonwealth.

466 -ilth

filth, tilth (process of tilling land).

467 -anth

hydranth (type of polyp), perianth (part of flower), tragacanth (Asian plant), coelacanth (primitive bony fish), amaranth (flowering plant).

468 -enth

nth, tenth.

469 -eenth

eighteenth, thirteenth, fourteenth, fifteenth, nineteenth, umpteenth, sixteenth, seventeenth.

470 -inth

plinth, helminth (parasitic worm), Corinth, jacinth (gemstone), absinthe, terebinth (small Mediterranean tree), labyrinth, hyacinth.

471 -'nth

millionth, billionth, trillionth, thousandth, dozenth.

471.1

seventh, eleventh.

472 -ength

length, strength, wavelength.

473 -athe

bathe, scathe, lathe, spathe (botany term), rathe (blossoming early), swathe, sunbathe, enswathe.

474 -edh

edh (runic character), Gwynedd, Gorsedd (Welsh bardic institution).

475 -eethe

wreathe, breathe, seethe, sheathe, teethe, Westmeath (Irish county), bequeath, enwreath, unsheathe, Pontypridd.

476 -idh

with, therewith, wherewith, herewith, forthwith.

477 -ithe

lithe, blithe, Blyth, writhe, scythe, tithe.

478 -othe

loathe, clothe, reclothe, unclothe, betroth.

479 -oothe

booth, smooth, soothe, tollbooth.

480 -av

have, lav (*short for* lavatory), grav (unit of acceleration).

481 -arve

carve, calve, halve, Slav, Graves (type of wine), starve, varve (geology term), suave, Zouave (French infantryman), Yugoslav.

482 -ave

cave, gave, slave, nave, knave, pave, rave, brave, crave, grave, trave (cage for shoeing horses), save, shave, stave, they've, waive, wave.

concave, forgave, behave, enclave, conclave, exclave, enslave, outbrave, margrave, burgrave (medieval German governor), Redgrave, waldgrave (medieval German forest officer), landgrave, engrave, deprave, spokeshave.

biconcave, misbehave, autoclave (pressurized container), architrave (moulding), aftershave, microwave, photoengrave.

483 -erve

curve, derv, MIRV (type of missile), nerve, perv (*short for* pervert), serve, verve, swerve, recurve, innerve (stimulate), unnerve, subserve (be helpful), conserve, deserve, reserve, preserve, observe.

484 -eve

Eve, eve, heave, leave, cleave, sleeve, peeve, reeve, breve, grieve, greave (piece of armour), sheave, thieve, we've, weave.

naive, achieve, khedive (viceroy of Egypt), upheave, shirtsleeve, bereave, aggrieve, Congreve (English dramatist), reprieve, retrieve, perceive, conceive, qui vive, inweave.

interleave, semibreve, preconceive, misconceive, Genevieve, Tel Aviv, interweave.

underachieve, overachieve, recitative.

484.1

believe, relieve, disbelieve.

484.2

deceive, receive, undeceive.

485 -iv

chiv (*Slang* knife), div, give, live, spiv, sieve, Tiv (member of African people).

forgive, misgive (be apprehensive), relive, olive, unlive, outlive, octave, plaintive, costive (constipated).

gerundive, abrasive, pervasive, evasive, invasive, dissuasive, persuasive, cohesive, adhesive, purposive, repulsive, impulsive, compulsive, expulsive, convulsive, expansive, responsive, expletive, subjunctive, conjunctive, disjunctive, substantive, descriptive, prescriptive, proscriptive, inscriptive, adoptive, absorptive, eruptive, disruptive, pre-emptive, consumptive, presumptive, exhaustive, reflexive.

irresponsive, retributive, attributive, contributive, distributive, consecutive, executive, diminutive, substitutive, institutive, constitutive.

485.1

massive, passive, impassive.

485.2

regressive, digressive, depressive, repressive, oppressive, suppressive, impressive, compressive, expressive, recessive, obsessive, concessive, excessive, successive, possessive, inexpressive.

485.2.1

aggressive, progressive, retrogressive.

485.3

cursive, coercive, incursive, discursive, excursive (tending to digress), dispersive, aversive, perversive, subversive.

485.4

missive, permissive, submissive, admissive, dismissive.

485.5

derisive, decisive, incisive, divisive, indecisive.

485.6

plosive (phonetics term), explosive, erosive, corrosive.

485.7

jussive (linguistics term), percussive (relating to percussion), antitussive (alleviating coughing).

485.8

elusive, illusive, delusive, allusive, reclusive, seclusive, inclusive, conclusive, exclusive, protrusive, obtrusive, intrusive, extrusive, abusive, conducive, effusive, diffusive, inconclusive, unobtrusive.

485.9

pensive, tensive (causing tension), defensive, offensive, suspensive, expensive, intensive, ostensive, extensive, inoffensive, apprehensive, comprehensive, inexpensive, coextensive, counteroffensive.

485.10

dative, native, stative (linguistics term), creative, collative, concentrative, gravitative.

485.11

furtive, assertive.

485.12

additive, fugitive, volitive (relating to the will), primitive, genitive, lenitive (soothing pain), unitive, punitive, cognitive, secretive, nutritive, transitive, sensitive, partitive.

intuitive, prohibitive, exhibitive (illustrative), definitive, infinitive, interpretive, intransitive, insensitive, repetitive, competitive, acquisitive, inquisitive.

photosensitive, hypersensitive, radiosensitive.

485.12.1

positive, prepositive (linguistics term), appositive (linguistics term), suppositive (involving supposition), postpositive, diapositive, electropositive.

485.13

sportive, abortive, supportive.

485.14

motive, votive, emotive, promotive, locomotive, automotive, electromotive.

485.15 [further rhymes may be derived from **367**]

probative (providing evidence), combative, talkative, sedative, negative, purgative, ablative, conative (linguistics term), calmative, donative (gift), lucrative, portative (portable), optative (expressing a wish), laxative, fixative, causative.

rebarbative, reprobative, educative, superlative, contemplative, legislative, affirmative, alternative, imperative, pejorative, restorative, suppurative, illustrative, appreciative, initiative, associative, consultative, facultative, conservative, preservative, innovative, accusative.

investigative, approximative, administrative, inappreciative.

485.15.1

fricative (phonetics term), siccative (substance causing drying), judicative, indicative, applicative, explicative, affricative (phonetics term), significative, multiplicative, communicative, uncommunicative.

485.15.2

locative, vocative, evocative, provocative.

485.15.3

derogative, prerogative, interrogative.

485.15.4

relative, appellative (name or title), irrelative (unrelated), correlative (mutually related).

485.15.5

speculative, calculative, cumulative, copulative, coagulative, accumulative, manipulative.

485.15.6

formative, normative (establishing a norm), reformative, performative (linguistics term), informative.

485.15.7

combinative, carminative, nominative, ruminative, imaginative, determinative, denominative (naming), agglutinative.

485.15.8

narrative, declarative, preparative, comparative.

485.15.9

curative, durative (linguistics term), depurative (purifying).

485.15.10

decorative, figurative, generative, separative, operative, corporative, ulcerative, alterative (therapeutic drug), deliberative, corroborative, desiderative (expressing desire), alliterative, commemorative, remunerative, cooperative, inoperative, postoperative, vituperative, noncooperative.

485.15.11

demonstrative, remonstrative, undemonstrative.

485.15.12

meditative, vegetative, cogitative, qualitative, imitative, quantitative, authoritative, interpretative.

485.15.13

rotative, denotative.

485.15.14

putative (supposed), commutative (involving substitution).

485.15.15

tentative, augmentative, frequentative (linguistics term), preventative, argumentative, representative.

485.15.16

privative, derivative.

485.16

active, tractive, reactive, inactive, refractive, attractive, subtractive, extractive, retroactive, photoactive (responsive to light), hyperactive, interactive, overactive, unattractive, radioactive.

485.17

effective, defective, affective (arousing emotions), perfective, infective, projective, objective, subjective, elective, selective, collective, reflective, connective, respective, perspective, prospective, directive, corrective, detective, protective, invective, ineffective, imperfective, irrespective, retrospective, introspective, circumspective.

485.18

fictive, predictive, addictive, vindictive, adjective, conflictive, restrictive, constrictive, convictive, nonrestrictive.

485.19

deductive, seductive, productive, inductive, conductive, destructive, obstructive, instructive, constructive, reproductive, unproductive, counterproductive.

485.20

distinctive, instinctive, extinctive (serving to extinguish), indistinctive.

485.21

incentive, retentive, attentive, preventive, inventive, disincentive, irretentive, inattentive.

485.22

captive, adaptive.

485.23

deceptive, receptive, preceptive (didactic), perceptive, inceptive (beginning), exceptive (forming an exception), nociceptive (causing pain), imperceptive (lacking in perception), contraceptive.

485.24

festive, restive, digestive, suggestive, congestive, indigestive.

486 -ive

I've, skive, chive, dive, five, jive, hive, live, Clive, rive (split asunder), drive, shrive, strive, thrive, shive (flat cork), wive.

skydive, endive, ogive, beehive, alive, connive, derive, arrive, deprive, contrive, revive, survive, overdrive.

487 -ov

of, Pavlov, thereof, whereof, hereof, Rostov (Russian port), Baal Shem Tov (Jewish religious leader).

488 -ove

cove, Jove, Hove, hove, clove, mauve, rove, drove, grove, shrove, trove, strove, stove, wove, alcove, behove, mangrove, Bromsgrove.

489 -uv

dove, guv, love, glove, shove, above, ringdove, truelove, foxglove, turtledove, ladylove.

490 -oove

move, groove, prove, you've, remove, reprove, approve, improve, disprove, interfluve (land between two rivers), countermove, disapprove.

491 -alve

salve, valve, bivalve, univalve.

492 -elve

delve, helve (handle of tool), shelve, twelve.

493 -olve

solve, evolve, devolve, revolve, involve, dissolve, resolve, absolve.

494 -ax [also 32 + -*s*]

axe, Bax (English composer), fax, Sfax (Tunisian port), jacks, lax, flax, slacks, pax, sax, tax, wax.

coax, pickaxe, addax (large antelope), carfax (crossroads), Fairfax, Ajax, relax, smilax (climbing shrub), poleaxe (battle-axe), toadflax, climax, Lomax, larnax (terracotta coffin), Fornax (constellation), hyrax (herbivorous mammal), styrax (tropical tree), borax, storax (tropical plant), thorax, anthrax, surtax, syntax, earwax, paxwax (*Dialect* ligament in neck), beeswax.

Halifax, parallax, minimax, subclimax, supertax, overtax.

Adirondacks (US mountain range), anticlimax, Astyanax (Greek mythological character).

495 -arx [also 33 + -*s*]

Berks, Marx.

496 -ex [also 35 + -*s*]

ex, kex (flowering plant), hex, lex (body of laws), flex, specs, Rex, sex, vex.

ibex, caudex (woody base of stem), codex (volume of ancient manuscripts), index, telex, ilex (evergreen tree), silex (heat-resistant glass), pollex (first digit on forelimb), scolex (head of tapeworm), culex (type of mosquito), reflex, Triplex (*Trademark*), suplex (wrestling hold), duplex, perplex, simplex (electronics term), complex, cimex (bedbug), annex, annexe, Kleenex (*Trademark*), apex, Perspex (*Trademark*), auspex (Roman soothsayer), Pyrex (*Trademark*), Lurex (*Trademark*), Durex (*Trademark*), murex (spiny-shelled mol-

lusc), unsex, latex, vertex, cortex, vortex, convex.

subindex, spinifex (Australian grass), pontifex (senior Catholic cleric), retroflex, circumflex, multiplex (electronics term), quadruplex (fourfold), googolplex (large number), haruspex (ancient Roman priest), interrex (interim ruler), unisex, intersex, Middlesex, biconvex.

497 -erx [also 36 + -*s*]

fireworks, steelworks, gasworks, glassworks, waterworks, ironworks.

498 -ix [also 38 + -*s*]

fix, mix, nix, Nyx (Greek goddess), pix, pyx (container for Eucharist), six, Styx.

spadix (type of inflorescence), radix, affix, graphics, prefix, suffix, affix, infix, unfix, transfix, postfix (add to the end), calyx, helix, kylix (two-handled drinking vessel), prolix (long and boring), rhythmics, technics, tropics, varix (varicose vein), oryx (African antelope), classics, Essex, Wessex, Sussex, glyptics (engraving precious stones), optics, chopsticks, ethics, cervix, civics (study of citizens' rights), coccyx, physics.

heroics, aerobics, appendix, strategics (military strategy), hydraulics, spondulix, polemics, phonemics (branch of linguistics), eurhythmics, mechanics, sardonyx (gemstone), philippics (bitter invective), subtropics, cicatrix, Bellatrix (star), dioptrics (branch of optics), kinesics (study of body language), forensics (formal debating), politics, orthoptics, ekistics (study of human settlements), logistics, sphragistics (study of document seals), ballistics, statistics, linguistics, acoustics, fiddlesticks.

logopaedics (speech therapy), orthopaedics, bionomics (ecology), economics, ergonomics (study of work), agronomics (land economics), pyrotechnics, zootechnics (animal domestication and breeding), executrix, semiotics (study of symbols), aeronautics, astronautics, hermeneutics (science of scriptural interpretation), therapeutics, pharmaceutics, dialectics, orthodontics, prosthodontics, diagnostics, geophysics, astrophysics, biophysics, metaphysics.

498.1

crucifix, antefix (ornament on roof), hieroglyphics.

498.2

dynamics, ceramics, thermodynamics, aerodynamics, electrodynamics.

498.3

eugenics (selective breeding), dysgenics (reducing quality of race), euthenics (study of environment control), cryogenics, callisthenics.

498.4

phoenix, hygienics, irenics (branch of theology).

498.5

onyx, phonics (phonetic teaching method), bionics, cryonics (freezing corpses for preservation), harmonics, mnemonics, tectonics, thermionics (branch of electronics), histrionics, avionics, quadraphonics, eudemonics (art of happiness), geoponics (science of agriculture), hydroponics (method of plant cultivation), electronics, architectonics (science of architecture), microelectronics.

498.6

spherics, hysterics, atmospherics.

498.7

apteryx (kiwi), Vercingetorix (Gallic chieftain), archaeopteryx.

498.8

theatrics, paediatrics, geriatrics, physiatrics (*US* physiotherapy).

498.9

matrix, testatrix, aviatrix, generatrix (geometry term), separatrix (oblique stroke).

498.10

metrics (use of poetic metre), obstetrics, psychometrics (branch of psychology), isometrics, econometrics (branch of economics).

498.11

statics, chromatics (science of colour), pneumatics (branch of physics), rheumatics, dramatics, aquatics, ecstatics, aerobatics, acrobatics, kinematics (branch of physics), systematics (study of systems), diplomatics, mathematics, numismatics, hydrostatics (study of stationary fluids), thermostatics, electrostatics (branch of physics).

498.12

poetics, athletics, kinetics, genetics, magnetics, aesthetics, prosthetics, exegetics (study of textual interpretation), homiletics (art of preaching sermons), theoretics, dietetics, anaesthetics, apologetics (branch of theology).

498.12.1

phonetics, cybernetics, aerodonetics (study of gliding flight).

498.13

tactics, didactics (science of teaching), syntactics (study of symbol systems).

498.14

antics, semantics.

498.15

gymnastics, ceroplastics (wax modelling), onomastics (study of proper names).

499 -ox [also **40** + -s]

ox, box, cox, fox, lox (smoked salmon), phlox, Knox, Nox (Roman goddess), pox, stocks, vox (voice).

gearbox, firebox, jukebox, matchbox, soundbox, snuffbox, mailbox, pillbox, strongbox, soapbox, icebox, horsebox, loosebox, hatbox, paintbox, postbox, boondocks (*US* wild desolate country), outfox, cowpox, smallpox, swinepox, Xerox (*Trademark*), aurochs.

tinderbox, chatterbox, gogglebox, goldilocks, equinox, chickenpox.

499.1

paradox, orthodox, heterodox, unorthodox.

500 -orx [also **41** + -s]

Fawkes, lawks, Yorks.

501 -oax [also **42** + -*s*]

coax, hoax.

502 -ux [also **43** + -*s*]

ducks, dux (*Scot* best pupil), lux (unit of illumination), flux, crux, shucks, de luxe, efflux (flowing out), reflux, influx, conflux (merging of rivers), Benelux.

503 -'x [also **46** + -*s*]

hallux (first digit on foot), bollocks, Pollux, lummox (clumsy person), flummox, barracks, Trossachs, Appomattox (US Civil War site).

504 -anx [also **51** + -*s*]

Manx, thanks, Fairbanks, phalanx.

505 -inx [also **52** + -*s*]

sphinx, jinx, Lincs, lynx, links, minx, high jinks, pharynx, larynx, syrinx (bird's vocal organ), methinks, androsphinx (sphinx representing man's head), pilliwinks (medieval instrument of torture), tiddlywinks, hieracosphinx (hawk-headed sphinx).

506 -unx [also **54** + -*s*]

trunks, quincunx (arrangement of five objects).

507 -az

as, jazz, has, Boaz (Old Testament character), Hejaz (Saudi Arabian province), La Paz (Bolivian city), topaz, whereas, Alcatraz, razzmatazz.

508 -arz [also **1** + -*s*]

Mars, parse, vase, Abkhaz (Russian people), Shiraz (Iranian city), memoirs, handlebars, churidars (Indian long trousers).

509 -aze [also **2** + -*s*]

baize, daze, phase, faze, gaze, haze, laze, blaze, glaze, maze, maize, Naze (Essex headland), raise, raze, braise, braze (decorate with brass), craze, fraise (neck ruff), phrase, graze, praise, prase (variety of quartz), chaise (horse-drawn carriage), stays.

ukase (tsar's edict), prophase (biology term), stargaze, malaise, ablaze, amaze, manes (Roman minor deities), lipase (enzyme), erase, mores, rephrase, upraise, appraise, dispraise, lactase (enzyme), sideways, endways, edge-ways, always, longways, leastways, lengthways.

peptidase (enzyme), oxidase (enzyme), nowadays, hollandaise, polyphase (having alternating voltages), amylase (enzyme), Bordelaise (sauce with red wine), Marseillaise, lyonnaise (cooked with onions), Béarnaise (rich sauce), mayonnaise, Bolognese, polonaise, paraphrase, metaphrase (literal transla-tion), écossaise, invertase (enzyme), phosphatase (enzyme).

broderie anglaise, enterokinase (enzyme).

509.1

liaise, nuclease (enzyme), casease (enzyme), protease (enzyme), ribonu-clease (enzyme).

510 -ez

fez, Baez (US folk singer), Boulez (French composer), Cortes.

511 -erz [also **3** + -*s*]

furze, hers, Meuse, chartreuse, masseuse, mitrailleuse (machine gun), Betelgeuse (star), secateurs.

512 -airz [also **4** + -*s*]

airs, theirs, stairs, wares, affairs, upstairs, backstairs, downstairs, unawares, Armentières.

513 -eeze [also **5** + -*s*]

ease, bise (cold northerly wind), cheese, he's, lees, please, sneeze, pease (*Dialect* pea), squeeze, breeze, freeze, frieze, seize, she's, tease, Tees, these, wheeze, tweeze.

scabies, rabies, tabes (wasting of body organ), soubise (onion sauce), pubes, marquise, headcheese (*US* brawn), Hades, Andes, Ganges, tales (legal term), Thales (Greek philosopher), displease, Burmese, Hermes, Manes (Persian prophet), Menes (ancient Egyptian king), Chinese, stapes (bone in ear), herpes, appease, trapeze, Tabriz (Iranian city), refreeze, unfreeze, deepfreeze, reprise, fasces (Roman magistrate's insignia), bases, faeces, heartsease, species, bêtise, Maltese, striptease, Dives (New Testament char-acter), axes, Xerxes, disease.

Celebes (Indonesian island), Caribbees (West Indian islands), Maccabees (Jewish patriotic family), gourmandise, Portuguese, meninges, Hercules, Pericles, Sophocles, Damocles, Heracles, Androcles, talipes (club foot), antifreeze, indices, helices (*plural of* helix), Ulysses, Rameses, apices (*plural of* apex), varices (varicose veins), matrices, vertices, vortices, subspecies, penates (Roman household gods), Laertes, expertise, velites (Roman troops), equites (Roman cavalry), pyrites (mineral), barytes (mineral), Boötes (constellation), litotes (understatement), Cervantes, Orontes (Asian river).

Diogenes, cheval-de-frise (barrier of spikes), ecospecies, cacoethes (uncontrollable urge).

513.1
sanies (discharge from wound), caries, paries (wall of body organ), calvities (baldness).

513.2
Héloïse, Genoese, Faeroese, Averroës (Arab philosopher).

513.3
aedes (type of mosquito), heredes (heirs), Archimedes, Diomedes (Greek mythological king).

513.4
Hebrides, Parmenides (Greek philosopher), Eumenides (Greek Furies), Maimonides (Jewish philosopher), Simonides (Greek poet), Pheidippides (Athenian athlete), Euripides, cantharides (former medicine), Hesperides (Greek mythological characters), Pierides (Greek Muses).

513.5
Hyades (cluster of stars), Pleiades, Cyclades, Sporades, antipodes.

513.6
Achilles, Ramillies (Belgian battle site), Antilles, Los Angeles, isosceles, Praxiteles (Greek sculptor).

513.6.1
anopheles (type of mosquito), Mephistopheles.

513.7
valise, vocalise (vocal exercise), legalese, Sinhalese (language of Sri Lanka), journalese, novelese, officialese.

513.8
camise (medieval loose smock), chemise, Siamese, Assamese, Vietnamese.

513.9
Viennese, Lebanese, Pekinese, manganese, Milanese, Japanese, Pyrenees, Cantonese, Dodecanese, Demosthenes (Athenian statesman), Aristophanes (Greek comic dramatist).

513.10
Aries, Ares (Greek god), lares (Roman household gods), nares (nostrils), Antares (star).

513.11
heres (heir), series, Ceres (Roman goddess), congeries (collection).

513.12
cerise, Kanarese (Indian people).

513.13
Pisces, Cambyses (Persian king), Anchises (Trojan prince), Polynices (Greek mythological character).

513.14
menses, Waldenses (members of Catholic sect), Albigenses (medieval French heretics).

513.15
nates (buttocks), Achates (loyal friend), Euphrates, Mithridates (ancient Greek king).

513.16
DT's, Aeëtes (Greek mythological king), Sudetes (European mountain range), diabetes.

513.17
Socrates, Xenocrates (Greek philosopher), Hippocrates, Isocrates (Athenian orator).

513.18
cerastes (venomous snake), Ecclesiastes.

513.19
testes, Thyestes (Greek mythological character), Orestes (Greek mythological character).

514 -eerz [also 6 + -s]
cheers, shears, Algiers, Pamirs (Asian mountainous region), arrears, Cordeliers (French political club).

515 -iz [Also 16 + -s. Further rhymes may be created by adding -es to appropriate nouns and verbs.]
is, fizz, phiz (*Slang* face), his, Ms, quiz, frizz, 'tis, whizz, swizz (*Slang* disappointment).

Suez, darbies, showbiz, Rockies, riches, breeches, clutches, crutches, goodies, Cádiz, Indies, undies, Kirghiz (Mongoloid people), ages, wages, wellies, Scillies, willies, kermes (dried insect bodies), Orkneys, Jeffreys, glasses, braces, falsies, rushes (film-making term), treatise, panties, civvies, blazes, Moses, Menzies.

damages, obsequies, exequies, Benares (Indian city), eyeglasses (*US* spectacles), sunglasses, galoshes, equities, assizes.

heebie-jeebies, Buenos Aires, elevenses.

515.1
Stannaries, groceries, Potteries, ivories, preliminaries.

515.2
masses, molasses.

515.3
missis, Mrs, premises.

516 -ize [also 7 + -s]
guise, rise, prize, prise, size, wise.
franchise, disguise, stylize, surmise, cognize (perceive), despise, sunrise, moonrise, uprise, comprise, misprize (undervalue), abscise (to separate), excise, incise, capsize, outsize, baptize, chastise, Levis (*Trademark*), advise, crabwise, likewise, clockwise, somewise (in some way), unwise, crosswise, slantwise, widthwise.

Judaize, archaize, catechize, affranchise (release from obligation), enfranchise, disfranchise, fluidize, liquidize, hybridize, subsidize, oxidize, iodize (treat with iodine), standardize,

melodize, anodize, jeopardize, rhapsodize, bastardize, methodize, merchandise, gormandize (eat greedily), aggrandize, nebulize (atomize), capsulize, butterflies, manyplies (cow's stomach), immunize, recognize, solemnize, sulphurize, symmetrize, cicatrize (heal), exorcise, circumcise, amortize, deputize, supervise, improvise, otherwise.

propagandize, apostrophize, philosophize, anticlockwise, counterclockwise, soliloquize, ventriloquize, panegyrize (extol), anthropomorphize (ascribe human form to).

516.1
elegize, eulogize, energize, analogize (draw comparisons), geologize (study geology of), neologize (invent new words), theologize, apologize, mythologize, anthologize (compile an anthology), entomologize (study insects), demythologize.

516.2
stabilize, mobilize, tranquillize, sterilize, fossilize, fertilize, subtilize (refine), utilize, civilize, demobilize, immobilize, lyophilize (freeze-dry), evangelize, volatilize (change into vapour).

516.3
dialyse, symbolize, localize, vocalize, alkalize, idolize, feudalize, scandalize, vandalize, legalize, formalize, normalize, penalize, finalize, signalize, equalize, paralyse, moralize, pluralize, ruralize, hydrolyse, mongrelize, neutralize, centralize, specialize, socialize, catalyse, metallize, vitalize, totalize, brutalize, tantalize, crystallize, breathalyse, novelize (convert into a novel), nasalize.

parabolize (explain by a parable), metabolize, cannibalize, illegalize, animalize, decimalize, caramelize, communalize, monopolize, demoralize, electrolyse, decentralize, commercialize, initialize (computer term), digitalize (treat with digitalis), capitalize, hospitalize, devitalize, revitalize, immortalize.

universalize, Orientalize, Occidentalize, sentimentalize, departmentalize, compartmentalize.

516.3.1
realize, idealize.

516.3.2
bestialize, trivialize, mercurialize, industrialize.

516.3.2.1
serialize, materialize, etherealize, immaterialize, dematerialize.

516.3.2.2
memorialize (commemorate), editorialize, territorialize.

516.3.3
actualize, visualize, ritualize, conceptualize, contextualize (put into context), desexualize (castrate or spay), intellectualize, individualize.

516.3.4
verbalize, hyperbolize (exaggerate).

516.3.5
analyse, canalize, channelize, psychoanalyse.

516.3.6
journalize (record in a journal), vernalize (botany term), internalize, externalize.

516.3.7
personalize, nationalize, rationalize, fictionalize, depersonalize, impersonalize, denationalize, conventionalize, internationalize, institutionalize.

516.3.8
liberalize, federalize, generalize, mineralize, gutturalize, naturalize, demineralize, denaturalize.

516.4
demise, remise (legal term), premise (state as a premiss), euphemize (use euphemisms), minimize, victimize, optimize, maximize, synonymize, legitimize.

516.5
randomize, infamize (make infamous), Islamize, compromise, atomize, item-

ize, customize, macadamize, economize, epitomize, dichotomize (divide into two).

516.6
trichinize (infest with parasitic worms), Hellenize (make like ancient Greeks), feminize, scrutinize, divinize (deify), homogenize, nitrogenize, aluminize (cover with aluminium), bituminize, attitudinize (adopt opinion for effect), platitudinize.

516.6.1
Latinize, platinize (coat with platinum), gelatinize (become jelly-like), keratinize (biology term).

516.7
ionize, lionize, carbonize, ebonize (finish to resemble ebony), urbanize, mechanize, preconize (announce publicly), volcanize (subject to volcanic heat), Balkanize (divide into warring states), vulcanize, cinchonize (treat with quinine), Christianize, modernize, euphonize (make pleasant-sounding), jargonize, paganize, organize, colonize, harmonize, Germanize, sermonize, Romanize, womanize, humanize, canonize, tyrannize, synchronize, patronize, Russianize, fraternize, Platonize (use Platonic principles), botanize, Teutonize (make German), westernize, heathenize, galvanize, unionize.

decarbonize, suburbanize, reorganize, disorganize, decolonize, dehumanize, skeletonize (reduce to minimum framework), Italianize.

Europeanize, Australianize, pedestrianize, republicanize, Americanize, Mohammedanize, revolutionize.

516.7.1
agonize, antagonize.

516.8
arise, theorize, barbarize, rubberize, moisturize, slenderize, tenderize, vulgarize, plagiarize, grangerize (illustrate with borrowed pictures), valorize (fix artificial price for), polarize, solarize (treat with sun's rays), bowdlerize, burglarize (US burgle), glamorize, memorize, summarize, mesmerize, vaporize, pauperize (impoverish), temporize, ter-

rorize, mercerize, pressurize, satirize, cauterize, motorize, notarize (authenticate as notary), factorize, pasteurize, authorize, pulverize.

miniaturize, deodorize, categorize, revalorize (revalue), polymerize (chemistry term), containerize, contemporize, extemporize, depressurize, computerize, characterize, transistorize, familiarize.

516.8.1
secularize, circularize (distribute circulars to), regularize, singularize, popularize, particularize.

516.8.2
militarize, catheterize, demilitarize.

516.9
apprise, surprise, enterprise.

516.10
laicize (remove ecclesiastical status), Gallicize (make French), publicize, anglicize, plasticize, mythicize, synthesize, italicize, catholicize, Hispanicize (make Spanish), fanaticize, poeticize, romanticize, hypothesize, parenthesize, photosynthesize.

516.10.1
criticize, politicize, depoliticize.

516.11
assize, emphasize, ostracize, fantasize, oversize, exercise, metastasize (medical term), apotheosize (glorify).

516.12
digitize, sanitize, monetize (establish as legal tender), magnetize, concretize, sensitize, proselytize (convert to another faith), demonetize, remonetize, parasitize, desensitize, hyposensitize, photosensitize (make sensitive to light), hypersensitize.

516.13
narcotize, schematize, traumatize, stigmatize, dogmatize, hypnotize, advertise, alphabetize, emblematize, acclimatize, automatize, aromatize (make aromatic), achromatize (remove colour from), demagnetize, dehypnotize, democratize, bureaucratize, hypostatize (regard as real), apostatize (abandon one's faith), anaesthetize.

516.13.1
dramatize, melodramatize, epigrammatize, anagrammatize.

516.13.2
systematize, legitimatize, anathematize (to curse).

516.14
empathize, sympathize, telepathize.

516.15
devise, revise, televise, collectivize.

517 -oz
Oz, Boz (pen name of Dickens), cos, was, 'twas, because, Badajoz (Spanish city).

518 -orz [also 9 + -s]
cause, gauze, hawse (nautical term), clause, Mors (Roman god), pause, drawers, tawse, yours, yaws, indoors, outdoors, applause, jackstraws, Azores, Doukhobors (Russian Christian sect), Santa Claus, menopause.

519 -oize [also 11 + -s]
noise, poise, turquoise, equipoise (equilibrium), centipoise (unit in physics), counterpoise (counterbalancing force), corduroys.

520 -oze [also 12 + -s]
chose, doze, hose, close, nose, pose, rose, brose (*Scot* porridge), froze, prose, throes, those.

ribose (a sugar), glucose, bulldoze, bellows, parclose (church screen), foreclose, enclose, unclose, disclose, bluenose (*US* puritanical person), hooknose, depose, repose, impose, compose, dispose, transpose, expose, Faeroes, Burroughs, Ambrose, rockrose, sucrose, refroze, unfroze, primrose, Montrose, dextrose, ketose (a sugar), lactose, fructose, maltose, pentose.

Berlioz, pantihose, ankylose, amylose (component of starch), cellulose, dominoes, bladdernose (type of seal), diagnose, bottlenose (type of dolphin), shovelnose (US freshwater sturgeon), decompose, recompose, discompose, predispose, indispose, quelquechose (insignificant thing), pettitoes, galactose (a sugar).

metamorphose, anastomose, superimpose, underexpose, overexpose.

520.1
aloes, gallows, Allhallows, lignaloes (Asian tree).

520.2
appose, oppose, propose, suppose, superpose (maths term), presuppose, interpose, juxtapose.

520.3
arose, tuberose (Mexican plant), saccharose, guelder-rose.

521 -ouze [also **13** + -s]
bouse (nautical term), Cowes, dowse, house, blouse, mouse (hunt mice), rouse, browse, drowse, trouse (close-fitting Irish breeches), rehouse, espouse, arouse, carouse.

522 -uz
buzz, does, fuzz, muzz (make muzzy), abuzz, Hormuz (Iranian island).

523 -ooze [also **15** + -s]
ooze, Ouse, booze, choose, who's, whose, lose, blues, flews (bloodhound's fleshy upper lip), schmooze (US chat), snooze, ruse, bruise, cruise, cruse, Druse (religious sect in Lebanon), trews, use, fuse, Hughes, muse, mews, news.

Toulouse, peruse, abuse, accuse, excuse, defuse, effuse, diffuse, refuse, infuse, confuse, transfuse, bemuse, amuse, misuse, contuse (to bruise), enthuse.

Veracruz (Mexican state), Santa Cruz (Argentine province), St Andrews, disabuse, hypotenuse.

523.1
perfuse (permeate through), suffuse, interfuse (intermingle).

524 -'z [also **17** + -s]
pliers, chequers, sneakers, knickers, blinkers, bonkers, conkers, Yonkers (US city), withers, waders, glanders, Flanders, rounders, taggers (tin-coated iron sheet), staggers (type of vertigo), cobblers, bloomers, honours, Connors, clippers, jodhpurs, champers, rompers, vespers, horrors, Messrs, pincers, bitters, afters, hipsters, divers, tweezers, scissors, trousers.

Moluccas, dividers, malanders (horse disease), pyjamas, Bahamas, headquarters.

Himalayas, camiknickers, knickerbockers, butterfingers, binoculars, Cordilleras (American mountain range).

525 -ads [also **83** + -s]
adze, scads (US lots).

526 -eeds [also **89** + -s]
Leeds, needs, proceeds.

527 -ides [also **92** + -s]
ides, besides, burnsides (US sidewhiskers), ironsides (person with great stamina).

528 -ords [also **95** + -s]
cords, Lords, Broads, sideboards, towards.

529 -odes [also **98** + -s]
Rhodes, crossroads.

530 -uds [also **100** + -s]
buds, suds.

531 -'ds [also **103** + -s]
innards, backwards, seawards, forwards, inwards, onwards, downwards, upwards, outwards, westwards, eastwards, northwards, southwards, billiards, afterwards, heavenwards.

532 -ends [also **131** + -s]
bends, amends, calends (day in Roman calendar).

533 -ounds [also **139** + -s]
bounds, zounds (archaic interjection).

534 -'nds [also **143** + -s]
Highlands, Midlands, Netherlands, Bury St Edmunds.

535 -egs [also **181** + -s]
dregs, sheerlegs (lifting device), spindlelegs.

536 -ales [also **214** + -s]
Dales, tails, Wales, entrails.

537 -els [also **215** + -s]
Wells, Seychelles.

538 -ools [also **227** + -s]
pools, gules (heraldic term).

539 - 'ls [also **228** + -*s*]

Peebles, Gorbals, doubles, shambles, gimbals (device enabling free suspension), hackles, Eccles, oodles, singles, shingles, annals, flannels, finals, Naples, Brussels, nuptials, Beatles, skittles, victuals, bristols, measles, bifocals, spectacles, genitals, incidentals, regimentals (regiment's uniform and insignia), unmentionables.

539.1

cobbles, collywobbles.

539.2

clericals, theatricals, academicals.

539.2.1

Chronicles, canonicals.

540 -arms [also **230** + -*s*]

arms, alms, Brahms, Psalms.

541 -ems [also **232** + -*s*]

hems, Thames.

542 -imes [also **236** + -*s*]

sometimes, betweentimes.

543 - 'ms [also **242** + -*s*]

Adams, doldrums, customs, Williams.

544 -ans [also **245** + -*s*]

banns, cans (headphones), glans, Volans (constellation), Octans (constellation), Prestonpans (Scottish battle site), Lytham St Anne's.

545 -ains [also **247** + -*s*]

pains, reins, Staines, remains, afterpains.

546 -ens [also **248** + -*s*]

ens (metaphysics term), Fens, gens (Roman aristocratic family), lens, cleanse, Valens (Roman emperor), impatiens (flowering plant), locum tenens, vas deferens, Homo sapiens, delirium tremens.

547 -eens [also **251** + -*s*]

jeans, means, greens, teens, Milton Keynes, Grenadines (West Indian islands), Philippines, smithereens.

548 -ins [also **252** + -*s*]

gubbins (object of little value), Rubens, Dickens, dickens, Hawkins, Wilkins, Jenkins, Hopkins, moleskins, buckskins, Higgins, juggins (silly fellow), muggins, Collins, tenpins, ninepins, matins, Athens, avens (flowering plant), spillikins, withershins (*Scot* anticlockwise), galligaskins (17th-century men's breeches).

549 -ons [also **254** + -*s*]

bonze (Buddhist priest), pons (bridge of connecting tissue), bronze, frons (entomology term), long johns, nylons.

550 -oans [also **257** + -*s*]

Jones, nones, sawbones, crossbones, headphones, lazybones.

551 - 'ns [also **261** + -*s*]

siemens (unit of electrical conductance), summons, Evans, evens, St Albans, Gay Gordons, environs, abducens (cranial nerve), munitions, House of Commons.

551.1

relations, Galatians, combinations, congratulations, telecommunications.

552 -ings [also **265** + -*s*]

doings, makings, takings, tidings, leggings, lodgings, dealings, filings, earnings, gleanings (useful crop remnants), screenings (refuse separated by sifting), innings, trappings, droppings, heartstrings, Hastings, beestings (first milk from cow), hustings, shavings, leavings, outgoings, surroundings, chitterlings (cooked intestines of pig), belongings, furnishings.

553 -eves [also **484** + -*s* and plurals of some nouns in **162**]

eaves, heaves (disease of horses), greaves (residue of tallow), Hargreaves, Anne of Cleves.

554 -ives [also **486** + -*s* and plurals of some nouns in **164**]

fives (ball game), hives, St Ives, archives.

555 -elves [also **492** + -*s* and plurals of some nouns in **172**]

ourselves, themselves.

Index

A

aa 1
Aachen 261.10
aardvark 33
aardwolf 175
Aaron 261
abaca 17.42
aback 32.2
abacus 310.14
Abadan 246
Abaddon 261.19
abaft 396
abalone 16.233.1
abampere 4
abandon 261
abandoned 143
abandonee 5.14
abandonment 420.42
abase 295.1
abash 349.1
abate 367.4
abatement 420.48
abattoir 1.17
abaxial 228.3.18
Abba 17.9
abbacy 16.307
Abbasid 91
abbatial 228.91
abbé 2
abbess 300
Abbevillian 261.3.11
abbey 16.5
abbot 381
abbreviate 367.1.10
abbreviation 261.67.1.6
Abd-el-Krim 235

abdicate 367.5
abdication 261.67.5
abdomen 261.52
abdominal 228.60.5
abducens 551
abducent 420.71
abduct 389
abduction 261.79
abeam 234
abecedarian 261.3.21
abed 86.1
Abednego 12.29
Abel 228.11
Abelard 84
abelmosk 59
Abeokuta 17.351
Aberdare 4
Aberdeen 251.1
Aberdonian 261.3.18
abernethy 16.369
aberrance 321.16
aberrant 420.61
aberration 261.67.22.1
Aberystwyth 458
abet 368.3
abeyance 321
abhor 9
abhorrence 321.18
abhorrent 420.63
abide 92
abiding 265.14
Abidjan 246
Abigail 214
Abilene 251.3
ability 16.333.9.2
Abingdon 261
abiosis 300.55.2

abject 385
abjure 10
Abkhaz 508
ablate 367
ablation 261.67
ablative 485.15
ablaze 509
able 228.11
abloom 241
ablution 261.75
abnegate 367.10
abnegation 261.67.10
abnormal 228.53
abnormality 16.333.8.5
Abo 12
aboard 95.1
abode 98
aboideau 12
abolish 353.5
abolition 261.71.3
abolitionist 436.13.5
abominable 228.16.29
abominate 367.17.5
abomination 261.67.18.6
aboral 228.74
aboriginal 228.60
aborigine 16.229.1
abort 374
abortifacient 420.73
abortion 261.72
abortionist 436.13
abortive 485.13
Aboukir 6
abound 139
about 377.1
above 489
abracadabra 17.280

abrade 85
Abraham 229
abrasion 261
abrasive 485
abraxas 310
abreact 382
abreaction 261.76
abreast 433
abridge 197
abridgment 420.37
abroad 95
abrogate 367
abrogation 261.67.11
abrupt 426
abruption 261.88
abruptness 300
Absalom 242.11
abscess 296
abscise 516
abscissa 17.302
abscission 261.91
abscond 136
abseil 214
absence 321
absent 410
absent 420
absentee 5.24
absenteeism 242.35.1
absente reo 12.2
absent-mindedness
    300.28
absinthe 470
absolute 380.1
absolutely 16.193
absolution 261.75.1
absolutism 242.35.19
absolve 493
absorb 27
absorbent 420
absorber 17.17
absorbing 265
absorption 261.87
absorptive 485
absquatulate 367.13
abstain 247
abstainer 17.227
abstemious 310.2
abstention 261.82
abstinence 321.14
abstract 382
abstraction 261.76
abstractionism 242.35.14
abstruse 309
absurd 87
absurdity 16.333

Abu Dhabi 16.6
abulia 17.3.23
abundance 321
abundant 420.16
abuse 309
abuse 523
abusive 485.8
abut 378
abutilon 261.41
abutment 420
abutter 17.349
abuzz 522
abvolt 405
abwatt 373
Abydos 310.16
abysm 242.35.5
abysmal 228.54
abyss 300.3
abyssal 228.85
Abyssinia 17.3.34
acacia 17.322
academe 234
academia 17.3.26
academic 38.25
academicals 539.2
academician 261.71.4
academicism 242.35.16
academy 16.222
Acadia 17.3.7
Acadian 261.3.3
acajou 15
acanthoid 97
acanthopterygian
    261.3.7
acanthus 310.72
Acapulco 12
acariasis 300.57.1
acarid 91.27
acaroid 97.12
acarology 16.108.4.13
ACAS 293
accede 89
accelerant 420.65
accelerate 367.23
acceleration 261.67.22
accelerator 17.338.9
accelerometer 17.342.3.4
accent 410
accent 420.83
accentor 17.368
accentual 228.9
accentuate 367.2
accentuation 261.67.2
accept 422
acceptable 228.16.58

acceptance 321
acceptant 420
acceptation 261.67
access 296
accessible 228.16.37
accession 261.68
accessory 16.274.34
acciaccatura 17.277
accidence 321.5
accident 420.10
accidental 228.110.1
accidie 16.63
accipiter 17.342
accipitrine 253
acclaim 231
acclamation 261.67.16
acclamatory 16.274.43.5
acclimatize 516.13
acclivity 16.333.35
accolade 85
accommodate 367.9
accommodating 265.64
accommodation
    261.67.8
accompaniment 420.31
accompanist 436.13
accompany 16.237
accomplice 300
accomplish 353
accomplishment 420.47
accord 95.3
accordance 321
accordant 420.11
according 265.15
accordingly 16.175
accordion 261.3
accost 438
account 418
accountable 228.16.56
accountancy 16.312
accountant 420
accounting 265.73
accoutre 17.351
accoutrement 420.35
Accra 1
accredit 371.12
accrete 370
accretion 261.70
Accrington 261
accrue 15
acculturate 367.23
accumulate 367.13
accumulation 261.67.13
accumulative 485.15.5
accumulator 17.338.6

accuracy 16.307
accurate 371.34
accursed 91
accusal 228.128
accusation 261.67
accusative 485.15
accusatorial 228.3.12.2
accusatory 16.274.43
accuse 523
accused 156
accuser 17.444
accustom 242.32
accustomed 127
ace 295
acedia 17.3.8
acentric 38.47
acephalous 310.26.3
acerate 367.23
acerbate 367.4
acerbic 38
acerbity 16.333
acerose 305.2
acervate 371.37
acetabulum 242.10
acetaldehyde 92
acetanilide 92.2
acetate 367.30.2
acetic 38.51
acetone 257.2
acetous 310.64
acetum 242.28
acetyl 218
acetylene 251.2
acetylide 92.2
acey-deucy 16.306
Achaea 17.2
Achaemenid 91.21
Achates 513.15
ache 34
achene 251
Achernar 1
Acheron 254.11
achievable 228.16.61
achieve 484
achievement 420
Achillean 261.2.2
Achilles 513.6
achondrite 372
achondroplasia 17.3.59
achromatic 38.49.2
achromatize 516.13
acid 91.28
acidic 38
acidify 7.3.1
acidimeter 17.342.2

acidimetry 16.285.1
acidity 16.333.5.1
acidosis 300.55
acidulate 367.13
acidulous 310.25.4
Acis 300.50
ack-ack 32
ackee 5
acknowledge 197.2
acknowledgment 420.37
acme 16
acne 16.238
acolyte 372.4
aconite 372.6
acorn 255
acouchi 16.326
acoustic 38
acoustician 261.71
acoustics 498
acquaint 409
acquaintance 321
acquainted 91.45
acquiesce 296
acquiescence 321.21
acquiescent 420.67
acquire 8
acquisition 261.71.8
acquisitive 485.12
acquit 371
acquittal 228.102
acquittance 321.24
acre 17.30
acreage 197
acrid 91
acridity 16.333.5
acriflavine 252
Acrilan 245.2
acrimonious 310.2.9.1
acrimony 16.237
acrobat 365
acrobatic 38.49
acrobatics 498.11
acrogen 261.39
acrolith 458
acromegaly 16.131.2
acromion 261.3
acronym 235
acronymic 38.28
acrophobia 17.3.4
acrophobic 38.3
Acropolis 300.13.2
acrospire 8.2
across 302.2
acrostic 38.71
acrylic 38.21

acrylonitrile 219
act 382
actin 252
acting 265.70
actinia 17.3.34
actinic 38.34
actinide 92
actinium 242.2.11
actinoid 97.8
actinomere 6.3
actinometer 17.342.3
actinomycin 252.22
actinouranium 242.2.10
action 261.76
actionable 228.16.31
Actium 242.2
activate 367.36
activation 261.67
activator 17.338.11
active 485.16
actively 16.206
activeness 300.43
activism 242.35.22
activist 436
activity 16.333.35.2
Acton 261
actor 17.353
actress 300.48
actual 228.9.4
actuality 16.333.8.2
actualize 516.3.3
actually 16.131.1
actuarial 228.3.10
actuary 16.274.2
actuate 367.2
acuity 16.333.3
aculeate 371.1.1
aculeus 310.2
acumen 248
acuminate 367.17.6
acupuncture 17.68
acute 380.3
acuteness 300.40
ad 83
Ada 17.79
adage 197
adagio 12.3
Adam 242.5
adamant 420.35
adamantine 253.9
Adamite 372
Adams 543
adapt 421
adaptable 228.16
adaptation 261.67

adapter 17.374
adaptive 485.22
adaxial 228.3.18
add 83
addax 494
addend 131
addendum 242.7
adder 17.77
addict 387
addict 387.1
addiction 261.78.2
addictive 485.18
Addis Ababa 17.21
Addison 261.65
addition 261.71.2
additional 228.63.5
additive 485.12
addle 228.31
address 296
addressee 5.19
Addressograph 158.1
adduce 309.1
adduction 261.79.1
adductor 17.357
Adelaide 85
Aden 261.20
adenitis 300.62.3
adenoid 97.8
adenoidal 228.35
adenoidectomy
16.222.5.1
adenoma 17.215
adenosine 251.9
adept 422
adequacy 16.307
adequate 371
adhere 6
adherence 321.17
adherent 420.62
adhesion 261.90
adhesive 485
ad hoc 40
adieu 15.8
ad infinitum 242.29
adipocere 6.7
adipose 305
Adirondacks 494
adit 371
Adivasi 16.295
adjacent 420
adjectival 228.121
adjective 485.18
adjoin 256
adjoining 265
adjourn 249

adjournment 420
adjudge 203
adjudicate 367.5
adjudication 261.67.5
adjudicator 17.338.2
adjunct 393
adjure 10
adjust 443
adjustable 228.16.60
adjustment 420
adjutant 420.78
adjuvant 420
Adler 17.183
ad-lib 24
adman 261
admass 293
admeasure 17.333
Admetus 310.63
admin 252
administer 17.384.1
administrate 367.28
administration 261.67.25
administrative 485.15
administrator 17.338
admirable 228.16.35
admiral 228.76
admiralty 16.352
admiration 261.67.22
admire 8
admirer 17.274
admissible 228.16.39
admission 261.71
admissive 485.4
admit 371
admittance 321.24
admittedly 16.148
admixture 17.76
admonish 353.8
admonition 261.71
ad nauseam 229
ado 15.3
adobe 16.12
adolescence 321.21
adolescent 420.67
Adonis 300.25
adopt 425
adopted 91
adoption 261.86
adoptive 485
adorable 228.16
adoration 261.67.22
adore 9.4
adorn 255
adornment 420
adrenal 228.59

adrenaline 252.11
adrenergic 38.16
Adrian 261.3
Adriatic 38.49
adrift 398
adroit 375
adscititious 310.58
adsorb 27
adsorbent 420
adsorption 261.87
adulate 367.13
adulation 261.67.13
adulatory 16.274.40.2
adult 406
adulterant 420.65
adulterate 367.23
adulterer 17.279
adulterine 253.7
adulterous 310.50
adultery 16.274
adulthood 101
adumbral 228.77
adumbrate 367
Aduwa 1
ad valorem 242.20
advance 315
advancement 420
advantage 197
advantageous 310.20
advection 261.77
advent 410
Adventist 436.27
adventitia 17.3.49
adventitious 310.58
adventure 17.70
adventurer 17.279
adventurism 242.35.15
adventurous 310.50
adverb 22
adverbial 228.3
adversary 16.274
adverse 297
adversity 16.333.26
advert 369
advertence 321
advertise 516.13
advertisement 420
advertiser 17.441
advertising 265.82
advice 301
advisable 228.16.64
advise 516
advised 154
advisedly 16.148
adviser 17.441

advisory 16.274.53
advocaat 1
advocacy 16.307
advocate 367.6
advocate 371
advocation 261.67.6
adze 525
aedes 513.3
aedile 219
Aeëtes 513.16
Aegean 261.2
Aegina 17.232
Aegir 6
aegis 300.6
aegrotat 365
Aegyptus 310.71
Aeneas 310.1
Aeneid 91.1
Aeolian 261.3.12
Aeolic 38.22
aeon 261.2
aeonian 261.3.18
aepyornis 300.24
aerate 367
aerial 228.3.10
aerialist 436.7.2
aeriform 238.1
aerify 7.3
aerobatics 498.11
aerobe 28
aerobic 38.3
aerobics 498
aerobium 242.2
aerodonetics 498.12.1
aerodrome 239
aerodynamic 38.24
aerodynamics 498.2
aerodyne 253.2
aerofoil 222.1
aerogram 229.1
aeromechanic 38.31
aerometer 17.342.3
aeronaut 374
aeronautical 228.23
aeronautics 498
aerophagia 17.3.12
aerophobia 17.3.4
aeroplane 247
aerosol 220
aerospace 295
aerosphere 6.1
aerostat 365
aerugo 12.32
aery 16.264
Aeschylus 310.23

Aesculapius 310.2
Aesop 276
aesthesia 17.3.60
aesthete 370
aesthetic 38.50
aesthetician 261.71.7
aestheticism 242.35.16
aesthetics 498.12
aestival 228.121
aestivate 367.36
aestivation 261.67
aetiology 16.108.4.1
afar 1
affable 228.16
affair 4.3
affairs 512
affect 385.2
affectation 261.67
affected 91.43
affecting 265.71
affection 261.77
affectionate 371.28
affective 485.17
affenpinscher 17.331
afferent 420.65
affiance 321.2
affidavit 371
affiliate 367.1.2
affiliation 261.67.1.1
affinity 16.333.17
affirm 233
affirmation 261.67.16
affirmative 485.15
affix 498
affix 498
affixture 17.76
afflatus 310.62
afflict 387
affliction 261.78
affluence 321.3
affluent 420.4
afford 95
afforest 436.18
affranchise 516
affray 2
affreightment 420.48
affricate 371.9
affricative 485.15.1
affright 372
affront 419.1
Afghan 245
afghani 16.224
Afghanistan 246.1
aficionado 12.16
afield 115.1

afire 8.1
aflame 231
afloat 376
afoot 379.1
afore 9.6
aforementioned 143
aforesaid 86
aforethought 374
a fortiori 7.11
afoul 224
afraid 85
afreet 370
afresh 351
Africa 17.34
African 261.13
Africanism 242.35.14.2
Afrikaans 315
Afrikaner 17.226.2
Afro 12
afrormosia 17.3.62
aft 396
after 17.358
afterbirth 456
afterburner 17.229
aftercare 4
afterdamp 285
afterdeck 35
aftereffect 385.1
afterglow 12.46
afterimage 197.3
afterlife 164
aftermath 452
afternoon 260.2
afterpains 545
afters 524
aftersensation 261.67.26
aftershave 482
aftershock 40
aftertaste 432
afterthought 374
afterwards 531
afterword 87
afterworld 114
aga 17.124
Agadir 6
again 248
against 447
Aga Khan 246
agama 17.218
Agamemnon 254
agamic 38.24
agapanthus 310.72
agape 270
Agape 16.254
agar 17.125

agaric 38.44
Agartala 1.9
agate 371
agateware 4.9
agave 16.379
age 193
aged 91
agee 5.7
ageing 265.24
ageless 300
agency 16.312
agenda 17.101
agenesis 300.52.4
agent 420
ageratum 242.27
ages 515
agger 17.144
agglomerate 367.23
agglomerate 371.35
agglomeration 261.67.22
agglutinate 367.17
agglutination 261.67.18
agglutinative 485.15.7
agglutinin 252.17
aggrade 85.6
aggrandize 516
aggravate 367
aggravate 367.37
aggravation 261.67
aggregate 367.10
aggregate 371.14
aggress 296
aggression 261.68
aggressive 485.2.1
aggressor 17.300
aggrieve 484
aggro 12
aghast 431.1
agile 219
agility 16.333.9
Agincourt 374
agiotage 197
agitate 367.30
agitation 261.67.27
agitator 17.338.10
agitprop 276
Aglaia 17.4
agleam 234
agley 2
aglitter 17.342
aglow 12.46
agma 17.220
agnate 367
Agnes 300
agnomen 248

agnostic 38.71
agnosticism 242.35.16
ago 12.33
agog 185.2
à gogo 12.31
agonist 436.13.2
agonize 516.7.1
agony 16.237
agora 1.14
agora 17.279
agoraphobia 17.3.4
agoraphobic 38.3
agouti 16.343
agraffe 157
agrapha 17.120
agrarian 261.3.21
agree 5
agreeable 228.16.1
agreed 89
agreement 420
agrestal 228.113
agrestic 38.69
Agricola 17.176.2
agriculture 17.69
agrimony 16.237
Agrippa 17.253
Agrippina 17.230
agronomics 498
agronomy 16.222.3
aground 139.2
agrypnotic 38.53.2
ague 15
Agulhas 310
ah 1
aha 1.5
Ahab 18
Ahasuerus 310.45
ahead 86.5
ahem 232
Ahmed 86
ahoy 11
ai 16.1
aid 85
Aidan 261.20
aide 85
aide-de-camp 266
aider 17.79
aigrette 368
aiguille 217
aiguillette 368
aikido 12.19
ail 214
ailanthus 310.72
aileron 254.11
ailing 265.27

ailment 420.39
ailurophile 219.1
ailurophilia 17.3.21.2
ailurophobe 28
aim 231
aimless 300
aimlessness 300.33
ain 247
ain't 409
aïoli 16.126
air 4
Aïr 6
airborne 255
airbrick 38
airbrush 356
airbus 307
aircraft 396
aircraftman 261
aircrew 15
airdrop 276
Airedale 214
airfield 115
airflow 12
airfoil 222
airhead 86
airiness 300.23
airing 265.52
airless 300
airlift 398
airline 253
airliner 17.232
airlock 40
airman 261.46
airplane 247
airport 374
airs 512
airship 274
airsick 38
airsickness 300.27
airspace 295
airspeed 89
airstream 234
airstrip 274
airtight 372
airway 2
airworthy 16.375
airy 16.264
airy-fairy 16.264
Aisha 1
aisle 219
aitchbone 257
Ajaccio 12.3
ajar 1
Ajax 494
Akbar 1

Akela 17.162
Akhenaten 261.95
akimbo 12.6
akin 252.4
Akkad 83
à la 1.7
Alabama 17.205
alabaster 17.380
à la carte 366
alack 32
alackaday 2.8
alacrity 16.333
Aladdin 252
alameda 17.79
Alamo 12
à la mode 98
alamode 98.1
Alan 261
Alanbrooke 44
alannah 17.225
alar 17.162
Alaric 38.44
alarm 230.1
alarmed 123
alarming 265.35
alarmism 242.35
alarmist 436.8
alary 16.274
alas 293
Alaska 17.47
alate 367
albacore 9.2
Alba Longa 17.142
Albania 17.3.31
Albanian 261.3.15
Albany 16.237
albatross 302
albeit 371
Albert 381
Alberta 17.340
albescent 420.67
Albigenses 513.14
albinic 38.34
albinism 242.35.13
albino 12.54
Albinus 310.32
Albion 261.3
album 242
albumen 252
albuminoid 97.8
albuminous 310.33.1
albuminuria 17.3.42.1
Albuquerque 16.23
alcaide 85
alcalde 16.73

Alcatraz 507
alcazar 1.19
Alcestis 300.68
alchemic 38.25
alchemist 436.10
alchemy 16.222
alcheringa 17.141
Alcock 40
alcohol 220
alcoholic 38.22
alcoholicity 16.333.28
alcoholism 242.35
alcoholometer 17.342.3
Alcoran 246
Alcott 381
alcove 488
Alcyone 16.237.1
Aldabra 17.280
Aldebaran 261.60
aldehyde 92
alder 17.96
alderman 261.52
aldermanic 38.31
Aldermaston 261
Alderney 16.237
Aldershot 373
aldosterone 257.1
ale 214
aleatory 16.274.43.1
Alec 38.19
alee 5.9
alehouse 306
alembic 38
Aleppo 12.58
alert 369
alertness 300.36
aleurone 261.59
alevin 252
alewife 164
Alexander 17.99
Alexander Nevski 16.43
Alexandra 17.287
Alexandria 17.3
Alexandrian 261.3
Alexandrine 253
alexia 17.3.57
alfalfa 17.121
Alfred 91
alfresco 12.14
algae 5
algebra 17.283
algebraic 38.1.1
algebraist 436.1
Algeciras 310.46
Algeria 17.3.39

Algerian 261.3.22
algerine 251.7
algicide 92.7
algid 91
Algiers 514
Algol 220
ALGOL 220
Algonquian 261.3
Algonquin 252
algophobia 17.3.4
algorism 242.35.15
algorithm 242.33
Alhambra 17.284
Al Hufuf 170
alias 310.2.3
Ali Baba 17.10
alibi 7
Alicante 16.353
Alice 300
alidad 83
alidade 85
alien 261.3.8
alienable 228.16.31
alienate 367.18
alienation 261.67.19
alienee 5.14
alienist 436.13
aliform 238.1
alight 372.4
align 253.3
alignment 420
alike 39
aliment 410.1
aliment 420.31
alimentary 16.274.47
alimentation 261.67.32.1
alimony 16.237
aliped 86.6
aliphatic 38.49
aliquant 420.58
aliquot 373
alive 486
alkahest 433
alkali 7.7
alkalic 38.19
alkalify 7.3
alkalimeter 17.342.2
alkalimetry 16.285.1
alkaline 253.3
alkalinity 16.333.17.1
alkalize 516.3
alkaloid 97.6
alkane 247
alkanet 368
all 221

Allah 17.160
allantoid 97
allantois 300.1
allay 2.12
allegation 261.67.10
allege 194
alleged 109
allegedly 16.148
allegiance 321
allegoric 38.41
allegorical 228.23.17
allegory 16.274.9
allegretto 12.75
allegro 12
allele 217
alleluia 17.432
allemande 129
Allen 261
allergen 261.39
allergenic 38.32.1
allergic 38.32.1
allergic 38.16
allergist 436.4.1
allergy 16.108.2
alleviate 367.1.10
alleviation 261.67.1.6
alley 16.112
alleyway 2
Allhallows 520.1
Allhallowtide 92
allheal 217
alliaceous 310.56
alliance 321.2
allied 92
alligator 17.338.3
alliterate 367.23.2
alliteration 261.67.22.4
alliterative 485.15.10
allium 242.2
Alloa 17.6
allocate 367.6
allocation 261.67.6
allochthonous 310.36
allocution 261.75.2
allodial 228.3
allodium 242.2.4
allograph 158.1
allomorph 166.1
allomorphism 242.35.7
allonym 235
allopath 452
allopathic 38.72
allopathy 16.373.1
allophane 247.3
allopurinol 220.3

allot 373.1
allotment 420
allotrope 278.3
allotropic 38.37.2
allottee 5
allow 13
allowable 228.16.5
allowance 321
Alloway 2.28
alloy 11
alloy 11.1
allspice 301
allude 102.1
allure 10.4
alluring 265.56
allusion 261.93
allusive 485.8
alluvial 228.3.17
alluvion 261.3.32
alluvium 242.2
ally 7
ally 7.7
Almagest 433
alma mater 17.337
almanac 32
almandine 253
Alma-Tadema 17.211
almighty 16.334
Almohade 85
almond 143
almoner 17.239
Almoravide 92.13
almost 441
alms 540
almshouse 306
almucantar 17.365
almuce 309
aloe 12.38
aloes 520.1
aloft 399
aloha 17.6
alone 257
along 266.1
alongshore 9
alongside 92
aloof 170
aloofness 300
alopecia 17.325
aloud 99
alp 282
alpaca 17.28
alpenhorn 255
alpenstock 40
alpestrine 252
alpha 17.121

alphabet 368.3
alphabetic 38.50.2
alphabetical 228.23.19
alphabetize 516.13
Alpha Centauri 16.269
alphanumeric 38.39
alphorn 255
alphosis 300.55
alpine 253
alpinism 242.35.13
alpinist 436.11
already 16.60
alright 372
Alsace 293
Alsatian 261.67
also 12
also-ran 245
alt 401
Altaic 38.1
Altair 4
altar 17.363
altarpiece 298.2
altazimuth 464
alter 17.363
alterable 228.16.35
alteration 261.67.22
alterative 485.15.10
altercate 367.6
altercation 261.67.6
alter ego 12.28
alternant 420
alternate 367.18
alternate 371.23
alternately 16.189
alternation 261.67.19
alternative 485.15
alternator 17.338.8
althorn 255
although 12
altimeter 17.342.2
altimetry 16.285.1
altitude 102.2
alto 12.82
altocumulus 310.25.5
altogether 17.402
Altona 17.236
altostratus 310.62
altricial 228.93
Altrincham 242.17
altruism 242.35.4
altruist 436
altruistic 38.70
alum 242
aluminate 367.17.6
aluminium 242.2.11

ampoule 227
ampulla 17.174
amputate 367
amputation 261.67.29
amputee 5.23
Amravati 16.344
amrita 17.341
Amritsar 17.320
Amsterdam 229
amulet 371.17
Amur 10.1
amuse 523
amused 156
amusement 420
amusing 265.84
Amy 16.212
amygdala 17.176
amygdaloid 97.6
amyl 218
amylase 509
amyloid 97.5
amylose 520
an 245
ana 17.226
Anabaptist 436
anabas 293
anabasis 300.57
anabiosis 300.55.2
anableps 324
anabolic 38.22
anabolism 242.35.11
anabranch 78
anachorism 242.35.15
anachronic 38.35
anachronism 242.35.14
anachronistic 38.70.4
anacoluthia 17.3
anacoluthon 254
anaconda 17.104
anacoustic 38
Anacreon 254.1
anacrusis 300.56
anadromous 310.29
anaemia 17.3.26
anaemic 38.27
anaerobic 38.3
anaesthesia 17.3.60
anaesthetic 38.50
anaesthetics 498.12
anaesthetist 436.26
anaesthetize 516.13
anaglyph 163
anaglypta 17.376
anagoge 16.106
anagram 229.1

anagrammatic 38.49.2
anagrammatize 516.13.1
Anaheim 236
anal 228.56
analemma 17.208
analeptic 38.65
analgesia 17.3.60
analgesic 38
analgia 17.3.16
analogize 516.1
analogous 310
analogue 185
analogy 16.108.2
analphabetic 38.50.2
analysand 128
analyse 516.3.5
analysis 300.52.1
analyst 436.7.4
analytic 38.52.1
analytical 228.23.20
Anambra 17.284
anamnesis 300.51
anamorphosis 300.57.2
Ananias 310.3
anapaest 433
anaphora 17.279
anaphylactic 38.58
anaphylaxis 300.70
anaplasty 16.361.1
anarchic 38
anarchism 242.35.6
anarchist 436
anarchy 16.33
Anastasia 17.3.59
anastigmat 365
anastigmatic 38.49.3
anastomose 520
anastomosis 300.55
anathema 17.218
anathematize 516.13.2
Anatolia 17.3.22
Anatolian 261.3.12
anatomical 228.23.9
anatomist 436.10
anatomy 16.222
Anaximander 17.98
ancestor 17.382
ancestral 228.81
ancestry 16.292
Anchises 513.13
anchor 17.43
anchorage 197
anchorite 372.8
anchovy 16.385
anchusa 17.308

ancient 420
ancillary 16.274.16
and 128
Andalusia 17.3
andante 16.353
andantino 12.54
Andean 261.2
Anderson 261
Andes 513
Andhra Pradesh 351
andiron 261.4
Andorra 17.276
Andover 17.417
andradite 372.2
Andrea 17.3.45
Andrew 15
Androcles 513
androgen 261.39
androgenic 38.32.1
androgyne 253
androgynous 310.33
android 97
Andromache 16.33
Andromeda 17.83
Andros 302
androsphinx 505
androsterone 257.1
Andy 16.77
anecdotage 197.13
anecdotal 228.106
anecdote 376
anechoic 38.2
anemochore 9.2
anemography 16.90.2.3
anemology 16.108.4.9
anemometer 17.342.3
anemometry 16.285.2
anemone 16.237.6
anent 410
anergic 38.16
aneurysm 242.35.15
anew 15
anfractuous 310.4
angel 228
angelfish 353
angelic 38.20
angelica 17.34
angelical 228.23.6
angelology 16.108.4
Angelus 310.23
anger 17.140
Angevin 252
angina 17.232
angina pectoris 300.47
angle 228.49

angler 17.194
Anglesey 16.308
Anglia 17.3
Anglian 261.3
Anglican 261.13
Anglicanism 242.35.14.2
Anglice 16.300
Anglicism 242.35.16
Anglicist 436.21
anglicize 516.10
angling 265
Anglomania 17.3.31.1
Anglophile 219.1
Anglophilia 17.3.21.2
Anglophobe 28
Anglophobia 17.3.4
Anglophone 257
Angola 17.171
angora 17.276
angostura 17.277
angry 16
Anguilla 17.166
anguine 252
anguish 353
angular 17.174
angularity 16.333.20.3
angulate 367.13.4
angulate 371.17
angulation 261.67.13.2
Angus 310
anhedral 228.78
Anhwei 2
anhydride 92
ani 16.224
Aniakchak 32
aniconic 38.35
aniline 252.8
anima 17.211
animadversion 261.69
animadvert 369
animal 228.52
animalcule 227
animalism 242.35.11
animality 16.333.8
animalize 516.3
animate 367.15
animate 371.19
animation 261.67.15
animatism 242.35.20
animé 4
animism 242.35
animosity 16.333.30
animus 310.28.1
anion 261.4
anise 300

aniseed 89.2
anisette 368
anisogamy 16.222.2
anisole 223.4
Ankara 17.279
ankh 51
ankle 228
anklebone 257
anklet 371
ankylose 520
ankylosis 300.55
Anna 17.225
Annaba 17.21
annal 228.55
annals 539
Annam 229
Annapolis 300.13.1
annatto 12.72
Anne 245
anneal 217.1
annelid 91
Anne of Cleves 553
annex 496
annexation 261.67.35
annexe 496
Annie 16.223
annihilate 367.14.1
annihilation 261.67.14.1
anniversary 16.274.35
anno Domini 7.10
annotate 367.31
annotation 261.67.28
announce 319
announcement 420
announcer 17.317
annoy 11
annoyance 321
annoyed 97.9
annual 228.9.2
annuitant 420.76
annuity 16.333.3
annul 225
annular 17.174.9
annulate 371.17
annulation 261.67.13
annulment 420
annulus 310.25
annunciate 367.1
annunciation 261.67.1.4
annunciator 17.338.1
anode 98
anodize 516
anodyne 253.2
anoint 416
anointment 420.50

anomalous 310.26
anomaly 16.131
anomie 16.219
anon 254.8
anonymity 16.333.12
anonymous 310.28.2
anopheles 513.6.1
anorak 32.3
anorexia 17.3.57
anorexia nervosa 17.306
anorthosite 372.10
another 17.408
anoxaemia 17.3.26.1
anoxia 17.3
Anschluss 308
Anselm 243
anserine 253.7
Anshan 245
answer 17.313
answerable 228.16.35
ant 407
antacid 91.28
antagonism 242.35.14
antagonist 436.13.2
antagonistic 38.70.4
antagonize 516.7.1
antalkali 7.7
Antarctic 38.59
Antarctica 17.34
Antares 513.10
ante 16.353
anteater 17.341
antebellum 242.8
antecede 89.2
antecedence 321.4
antecedent 420.9
antechoir 8.3
antedate 367.8
antediluvian 261.3.32
antefix 498.1
antelope 278.2
antemeridian 261.3.5
ante meridiem 242.2.3
antenatal 228.99
antenna 17.228
anterior 17.3.39
anteroom 241
antetype 275
antevert 369.1
anthelion 261.3.10
anthelmintic 38
anthem 242
anthemion 261.3
anther 17.399
antheridium 242.2.3

anthologize 516.1
anthology 16.108.4
anthotaxy 16.386
anthracite 372.10
anthracitic 38.52.3
anthracnose 305
anthracoid 97
anthrax 494
anthropogenesis
  300.52.4
anthropoid 97
anthropology
  16.108.4.12
anthropometry 16.285.2
anthropomorphic 38.14
anthropomorphism
  242.35.7
anthropomorphize 516
anthropomorphosis
  300.57.2
anthropomorphous
  310.18
anthropophagi 7.4
anthropophagic 38.15
anthropophagite 372
anthropophagy 16.108.1
anthroposophy 16.90.4
anthurium 242.2
anti 16.353
anti-aircraft 396
antiar 1
antibiosis 300.55.2
antibiotic 38.53.1
antibody 16.65
antic 38.62
anticatalyst 436.7.6
Antichrist 437
anticipant 420.56
anticipate 367.19.1
anticipation 261.67.20.1
anticipatory 16.274.40
anticlerical 228.23.15
anticlimactic 38.58
anticlimax 494
anticline 253.4
anticlockwise 516
anticoagulant 420.27
anticonvulsant 420.72
Anticosti 16.367
antics 498.14
anticyclone 257
anticyclonic 38.35
antidepressant 420.67
antidote 376
Antietam 242.28

antifebrile 219
antifouling 265.33
antifreeze 513
antigen 261.37
Antigone 16.237
Antigonus 310.36
Antigua 17.128
antihero 12.63
antihistamine 252.15
antiknock 40
Antilles 513.6
antilog 185
antilogy 16.108.3
antimacassar 17.298
antimagnetic 38.50
antimalarial 228.3.10
antimatter 17.336
antimissile 219.2
antimony 16.237
antineutron 254
antinode 98
antinucleon 254.1
Antioch 40
Antiochus 310.14
antioxidant 420.10
Antipater 17.352
antipathetic 38.50.6
antipathy 16.373
antiperspirant 420.65
antiphon 261.29
antiphonal 228.63
antiphony 16.237.2
antipodal 228.38
antipode 98
antipodean 261.2
antipodes 513.5
antipope 278
antipsychiatry 16.286.1
antipyretic 38.50
antiquarian 261.3.21
antiquary 16.274
antiquate 367.20
antiquated 91.34
antique 37
antiquity 16.333
antirrhinum 242.15
antiscorbutic 38.56
anti-Semitic 38.52
anti-Semitism 242.35.18
antisepsis 300.59
antiseptic 38.65
antiserum 242.19
antislavery 16.274.50
antisocial 228.94
antispasmodic 38.9

antistatic 38.49
antistrophe 16.90.3
antitank 51
antithesis 300.52
antithetical 228.23.19
antitoxin 252.29
antitussive 485.7
antivenin 252.16
antiworld 114
antler 17.203
antlike 39
antlion 261.4
Antofagasta 17.379
Antoinette 368
Antoninus 310.34
Antonio 12.3.4
Antonioni 16.233
antonomasia 17.3.59
Antony 16.237
antonym 235
antonymous 310.28.2
antre 17.365
Antrim 235
antrum 242
Antwerp 272
Anubis 300.2
anuran 261.59
anuresis 300.51
anuria 17.3.42
anurous 310.49
anus 310.31
anvil 218
anxiety 16.333.2
anxious 310
any 16.226
anybody 16.65
anyhow 13
anyone 259
anything 265
anyway 2
anywhere 4.7
Anzac 32
aorta 17.345
aortic 38.54
aoudad 83
apace 295.4
Apache 16.46
apagoge 16.106
apart 366.1
apartheid 372
apartment 420
apathetic 38.50.6
apathy 16.373
apatite 372.12
ape 270

Apeldoorn 255
apelike 39
apeman 261
aperient 420.1
aperiodic 38.9
apéritif 162
aperture 17.62
apery 16.274
apetalous 310.26
apex 496
aphagia 17.3.12
aphasia 17.3.59
aphelion 261.3.10
aphid 91
aphis 300
aphonia 17.3.36
aphonic 38.35.2
aphorism 242.35.15
aphoristic 38.70.5
aphotic 38.53
aphrodisiac 32.1
Aphrodite 16.334
aphtha 17.398
apian 261.3
apiarian 261.3.21
apiarist 436.20
apiary 16.274.1
apical 228.23
apices 513
apiece 298.2
Apis 300
apish 353
aplanatic 38.49.5
aplasia 17.3.59
aplastic 38.68
aplenty 16.355
aplomb 237
Apo 12.57
apocalypse 327
apocalyptic 38.66
apocope 16.254
apocrine 253
Apocrypha 17.114
apocryphal 228.41
apocynthion 261.3.28
apodal 228.38
apodosis 300.57
apogee 5.7
apolitical 228.23.20
Apollinaris 300.44
Apollo 12.43
Apollonian 261.3.18
apologetic 38.50.3
apologetics 498.12
apologia 17.3.15

apologist 436.4
apologize 516.1
apologue 185
apology 16.108.4.12
apolune 260.1
apophthegm 232
apophyge 16.103
apophyllite 372.3
apophysis 300.52
apoplectic 38.60
apoplexy 16.387
apostasy 16.307
apostate 367.34
apostatize 516.13
a posteriori 7.11
apostle 228.86
apostolate 371.18
apostolic 38.22
apostrophe 16.90
apostrophic 38.13
apostrophize 516
apothecary 16.274.4
apotheosis 300.55.1
apotheosize 516.11
appal 221
Appalachia 17.3
Appalachian 261.3
appalling 265.31
Appaloosa 17.308
apparatus 310.62
apparel 228.72
apparent 420.60
apparition 261.71
appeal 217
appear 6.6
appearance 321.17
appease 513
appeasement 420
appellant 420.26
appellate 371.15
appellation 261.67.12
appellative 485.15.4
appellee 5
append 131
appendage 197
appendectomy 16.222.5
appendicectomy
  16.222.5
appendicitis 300.62
appendicular 17.174.6
appendix 498
apperception 261.84.1
appertain 247.10
appetence 321.24
appetite 372.11

appetizer 17.441
appetizing 265.82
applaud 95
applause 518
apple 228.64
applecart 366
applejack 32
applesnits 339
appliance 321.2
applicable 228.16.10
applicant 420.7
application 261.67.5
applicative 485.15.1
applicator 17.338.2
applicatory 16.274.40.1
applied 92
appliqué 2.6
apply 7.9
appoggiatura 17.277
appoint 416.1
appointee 5
appointment 420.50
appointor 17.371
Appomattox 503
apportion 261.72.1
apportionment 420.42
appose 520.2
apposite 371.40
apposition 261.71.9
appositive 485.12.1
appraisal 228.125
appraise 509
appreciable 228.16.42
appreciate 367.1
appreciation 261.67.1
appreciative 485.15
apprehend 131.1
apprehensible 228.16.40
apprehension 261.82.1
apprehensive 485.9
apprentice 300
apprenticed 436.27
apprenticeship 274
apprise 516.9
approach 70
approachable 228.16.13
approbate 367.4
approbation 261.67.3
appropriate 367.1
appropriate 371.1
appropriateness 300.38
appropriation 261.67.1
approval 228.122
approve 490
approved 150

approximate 367.15
approximate 371.19
approximately 16.189.1
approximation
 261.67.15
approximative 485.15
appurtenance 321.14
appurtenant 420.53
apraxia 17.3.56
après-ski 5
apricot 373
April 228
a priori 7.11
apron 261
apropos 12.59
apse 322
apt 421
apterous 310.50
apterygial 228.3.3
apteryx 498.7
aptitude 102.2
aptness 300
apyretic 38.50
Aqaba 17.21
aqualung 267
aquamarine 251.7
aquanaut 374
aquaphobia 17.3.4
aquaplane 247
aqua regia 17.3.13
aquarelle 215
aquarium 242.2.14
Aquarius 310.2.10
aquatic 38.49
aquatics 498.11
aquatint 412
aquavit 371
aqua vitae 7.13
aqueduct 389
aqueous 310.2
aquifer 17.114
Aquila 17.166
aquilegia 17.3.13
aquiline 253
Aquinas 310.34
Aquitaine 247.9
Ara 17.268
Arab 31
arabesque 57
Arabia 17.3.1
Arabian 261.3.1
Arabic 38
arable 228.16
Araby 16.15
Arachne 16.238

arachnid 91.22
arachnoid 97
Aragon 261
Araguaia 17.4
Arak 33
Aramaic 38.1
Aran 261
araneid 91.2
Arapaho 12.37
Ararat 365
araroba 17.18
Araucania 17.3.31
araucaria 17.3.38
arbalest 436.7
arbiter 17.342
arbitrage 359
arbitral 228.79
arbitrary 16.274
arbitrate 367.27
arbitration 261.67
arboraceous 310.56
arboreal 228.3.12
arboreous 310.2.13
arborescent 420.67
arboretum 242.28
arboriculture 17.69
arborist 436.20
arbor vitae 7.13
arbour 17.10
Arbroath 461
Arbuthnot 373
arbutus 310.67
arc 33
arcade 85
Arcadia 17.3.7
Arcadian 261.3.3
arcana 17.227
arcane 247
arcanum 242
arcature 17.62
arch 63
Archaean 261.2
archaeologist 436.4
archaeology 16.108.4.1
archaeopteryx 498.7
archaeornis 300.24
archaic 38.1
archaism 242.35.2
archaize 516
archangel 228
archbishop 281
archbishopric 38
archdeacon 261.12
archdeaconry 16.284
archdiocesan 261.65

archdiocese 300.57.1
archducal 228
archduchy 16.52
archduke 45
archegonium 242.2.12
archer 17.51
archery 16.274
archespore 9
archetypal 228.67
archetype 275
archfiend 133
archimage 193
archimandrite 372
Archimedean 261.3.4
Archimedes 513.3
archipelagic 38.15
archipelago 12.33
architect 385.8
architectonic 38.35
architectonics 498.5
architectural 228.76.1
architecture 17.64
architrave 482
archives 554
archivist 436
archpriest 435
archway 2
arctic 38.59
Arcturus 310.49
arcuate 371.2
arcuation 261.67.2
Arden 261
Ardennes 248
ardent 420.8
ardour 17.78
arduous 310.4
are 7.13
area 17.3.38
areca 17.34
arena 17.230.1
arenicolous 310.26.2
aren't 408
Arequipa 17.252
Ares 513.10
arethusa 17.444
Arezzo 12.71
argent 420
argentic 38.63
Argentina 17.230
argentine 253
Argentine 251
argentous 310.70
argil 218
argillite 372.3
Argo 12.26

argol 220
Argolis 300.13
argon 254
Argonaut 374
argonon 254.8
Argos 302
argosy 16.307
argot 12.26
arguable 228.16.6
argue 15
argufy 7
argument 420.34
argumentation 261.67.32
argumentative 485.15.15
Argus 310
argy-bargy 16.99
Argyll 219
aria 17.3
Arian 261.3.21
Arianism 242.35.14.1.1
arid 91.25
aridity 16.333.5
Ariel 228.3.10
Aries 513.10
arietta 17.339
aright 372.8
Arimathea 17.2
arise 516.8
arisen 261.126
Aristarchus 310.8
Aristippus 310.37
aristocracy 16.307.5
aristocrat 365.2
aristocratic 38.49.6
Aristophanes 513.9
Aristotelian 261.3.10
Aristotle 228.104
arithmetic 38.50
arithmetic 38.57
Arius 310.2.10
Arizona 17.236
ark 33
Arkansas 9
Arkwright 372
Arlington 261
arm 230
armada 17.78
armadillo 12.42
Armageddon 261.21
Armagh 1.10
Armagnac 32
armament 420.35
armamentarium
  242.2.14
armature 10.5

armband 128
armchair 4
armed 123
Armenia 17.3.33
Armenian 261.3.16
Armentières 512
armful 226
armhole 223
armiger 17.150
armillary 16.274.16
Arminian 261.3.17
Arminius 310.2.8
armistice 300
armless 310.2.7
armlet 371
armoire 1
armorial 228.3.12
armour 17.206
armoured 103
armourer 17.279
armoury 16.274.20
armpit 371
armrest 433
arms 540
Armstrong 266
army 16.211
Arne 246
Arnhem 242
arnica 17.34
Arno 12.51
Arnold 122
aroma 17.215
aromatic 38.49.2
aromatize 516.13
arose 520.3
around 139.1
arousal 228.129
arouse 521
arpeggio 12.3
arquebus 310.5
arrack 46
arraign 247.8
Arran 261
arrange 207
arrangement 420.38
arranger 17.156
arrant 420.60
arras 310.43
Arras 310.43
array 2.19
arrears 514
arrest 433.1
arrestable 228.16.59
arrester 17.382

arresting 265.75
arrhythmia 17.3
arrival 228.121
arrive 486
arriviste 435
arrogance 321.8
arrogant 420.18
arrogate 367.11
arrow 12.60
arrowhead 86.3
arrowroot 380
arse 294
arsenal 228.63
arsenic 38
arsenical 228.23.11
arsenide 92.4
arsenious 310.2.7
arsine 251
ars nova 17.417
arson 261.61
arsphenamine 252.15
arsy-versy 16.298.1
art 366
Art Deco 12.9
artefact 382
artel 215
Artemis 300.19
arterial 228.3.11
arteriole 223.1
arteriosclerosis 300.55.5
arteriovenous 310.32
arteritis 300.62.5
artery 16.274
artesian 261.3.34
artful 226
arthralgia 17.3.16
arthralgic 38
arthritic 38.52
arthritis 300.62
arthropod 94.1
Arthur 17.397
Arthurian 261.3.24
artichoke 42
article 228.23
articular 17.174.6
articulate 367.13.2
articulate 371.17.2
articulation 261.67.13
articulator 17.338.6
artifice 300
artificer 17.302
artificial 228.93
artificiality 16.333.8.1
artillery 16.274.16
artilleryman 261.48

artisan 245.7
artist 436
artiste 435
artistic 38.70
artistry 16.293
artless 300
artlessness 300.33
arts 334
artwork 36
arty 16.328
Aruba 17.20
arum 242.18
Arundel 228
Aruwimi 16.215
as 507
asafoetida 17.83
Asantehene 16.226
asarum 242.21
asbestos 302.3
asbestosis 300.55
ascarid 91.27
ascend 131
ascendancy 16.312.2
ascendant 420.14
ascension 261.82
Ascensiontide 92.12
ascent 410
ascertain 247.10
ascesis 300.51
ascetic 38.50
asceticism 242.35.16
ascidian 261.3.5
ascidium 242.2.3
Asclepius 310.2
ascocarp 269
Ascot 381
ascribe 25
ascription 261.85
asdic 38
asepalous 310.26
asepsis 300.59
aseptic 38.65
asexual 228.9
Asgard 84
ash 349
ashamed 124
ashamedly 16.148
Ashanti 16.353
Ashcroft 399
ashen 261.66
Asher 17.321
Ashkenazi 16.392
ashkey 5
ashlaring 265.58
ashore 9

ashplant 408
ashram 242
Ashton 261
Ashtoreth 455
ashtray 2
Ashurbanipal 212
ashy 16.319
Asia 17.322
Asian 261.67
Asiatic 38.49
aside 92.8
asinine 253.6
asininity 16.333.17
Asir 6
ask 56
askance 314
askew 15
aslant 408
asleep 273
ASLEF 160
Asmodeus 310.2.2
asocial 228.94
Asoka 17.38
asparagus 310
aspect 385
aspectual 228.9.5
aspen 261
asper 17.265
aspergillus 310.23
asperity 16.333.21
asperse 297.1
aspersion 261.69
aspersorium 242.2.17
asphalt 401
asphodel 215.1
asphyxia 17.3.58
asphyxiant 420.1
asphyxiate 367.1
asphyxiation 261.67.1
aspic 38
aspidistra 17.297
aspirant 420
aspirate 367.21
aspirate 371.33
aspiration 261.67
aspirator 17.338
aspire 8.2
aspirin 252
aspiring 265.54
asquint 412
Asquith 458
ass 293
assail 214
assailant 420.25
Assam 229

Assamese 513.8
assassin 252
assassinate 367.17.7
assassination 261.67.18.8
assault 404.1
assay 2
assay 2.20
assegai 7.4
assemblage 197
assemble 228.18
assembly 16.138
assent 410
assentient 420.1
assentor 17.368
assert 369
assertion 261.69
assertive 485.11
assess 296
assessment 420
assessor 17.300
asset 368
assets 336
asseverate 367.23
assiduity 16.333.3
assiduous 310.4
assign 253.2
assignation 261.67
assignee 5.13
assignment 420
assignor 9
assimilate 367.12
assimilation 261.67.12
Assiniboine 256
assist 436.22
assistance 321.27
assistant 420.81
assize 516.11
assizes 515
associate 367.1.7
associate 371.1
association 261.67.1
associationism
   242.35.14.3
associative 485.15
assonance 321
assonant 420.55
assort 374
assorted 91
assortment 420
assuage 193
assume 241
assuming 265.39
assumption 261.89
Assur 17.298
assurance 321.19

assure 10
assured 96
assuredly 16.148
Assyria 17.3.40
Astaire 4
Astarte 16.328
astatine 251.11
aster 17.379
asteriated 91.34.1
asterisk 58
asterism 242.35.15
astern 249
asteroid,meteoroid 97.12
asthenia 17.3.33
asthenic 38.32
asthenopia 17.3.37
asthma 17
asthmatic 38.49
Asti 16.361
astigmatic 38.49.3
astigmatism 242.35.20
astilbe 16.16
astir 3
Astolat 365
Aston 261
astonish 353.8
astonishing 265.63
astonishment 420.47
Astor 17.379
Astoria 17.3.41
astound 139
astounded 91.14
astounding 265.22
astragalus 310.26
astrakhan 245
astral 228
astraphobia 17.3.4
astray 2
astride 92
astringent 420.23
astrocompass 310.42
astrodome 239
astrogeology 16.108.4.1
astrolabe 20
astrologer 17.154
astrology 16.108.4
astronaut 374
astronautic 38.54
astronautics 498
astronomer 17.218.1
astronomic 38.29.1
astronomical 228.23.9
astronomy 16.222.3
astrophotography
    16.90.2.6

astrophysics 498
Asturias 293.1
astute 380
astuteness 300.40
Astyanax 494
astylar 17.167
asunder 17.108
Aswan 246
aswarm 238
asylum 242.9
asymmetric 38.46
asymmetry 16.285.1
asymptomatic 38.49.2
asymptote 376
asymptotic 38.53
asynchronism 242.35.14
asyndetic 38.50
Asyut 380
at 365
ataman 261.52
ataraxia 17.3.56
ataraxic 38
Atatürk 36
atavism 242.35
ataxia 17.3.56
ate 368
Ate 16.329
atelectasis 300.57
atelier 2
Athabaska 17.47
Athanasius 310.56
atheism 242.35.2
atheist 436
atheistic 38.70
atheling 265.30
Athena 17.230
athenaeum 242.1
Athenian 261.3.16
Athens 548
atherosclerosis 300.55.5
athirst 434
athlete 370
athletic 38.50
athleticism 242.35.16
athletics 498.12
athwart 374
atilt 403
Atkinson 261
Atlanta 17.365
Atlantean 261.3
Atlantic 38.62
Atlantis 300.66
atlas 310
Atli 16.187
atman 261

atmosphere 6.1
atmospheric 38.39
atmospherics 498.6
atoll 220
atom 242
atomic 38.29
atomicity 16.333.28
atomize 516.5
atomizer 17.441
atonal 228.62
atonality 16.333.8
atone 257.3
atonement 420
atonic 38.35
atony 16.237
atop 276.1
atrial 228.3
atrium 242.2
atrocious 310.60
atrocity 16.333.30
atrophic 38.13
atrophy 16.90
atropine 251
attaboy 11
attach 62
attaché 2.22
attachment 420.36
attack 32.4
attacker 17.28
attain 247.10
attainable 228.16.27
attainder 17.100
attainment 420.41
attar 17.336
attempt 428
attemptable 228.16
attempter 17.378
Attenborough 17.279
attend 131
attendance 321.7
attendant 420.14
attender 17.101
attention 261.82.3
attentive 485.21
attenuant 420.4
attenuate 367.2
attenuate 371.2
attenuation 261.67.2
attenuator 17.338
attest 433
attestation 261.67.33
attic 38.49
Attic 38.49
Attica 17.34.3
Atticism 242.35.16.4

Attila 17.166
attire 8
attitude 102.2.1
attitudinize 516.6
Attlee 16.186
attorney 16.227
attract 382
attractant 420
attraction 261.76
attractive 485.16
attributable 228.16.52
attribute 380.2
attribution 261.75
attributive 485
attrition 261.71.6
attune 260.6
atypical 228.23
aubergine 251
aubrietia 17.325
auburn 261
Auckland 143
auction 261
auctioneer 6.5
audacious 310.56
audacity 16.333.25
Auden 261.27
audible 228.16.16
audience 321.1
audio 12.3
audiogenic 38.32.1
audiometer 17.342.3.1
audiophile 219.1
audiotypist 436
audiovisual 228.9
audit 371
audition 261.71
auditor 17.342
auditorium 242.2.17
auditory 16.274.41
au fait 2
Augean 261.2
auger 17.132
aught 374
augment 410
augmentation 261.67.32
augmentative 485.15.15
augur 17.132
augury 16.273
august 443
August 445
Augusta 17.388
Augustan 261
Augustine 252.27
Augustinian 261.3.17
Augustus 310

auk 41
au lait 2
auld 118
auld lang syne 253
aulic 38.23
Aulis 300
aunt 408
au pair 4
aura 17.276
aural 228.74
aureate 371.1.2
Aurelian 261.3.10
Aurelius 310.2.4
aureole 223.1
aureus 310.2.13
auric 38.42
auricle 228.23
auricula 17.174.6
auriculate 371.17.2
auriferous 310.50.2
Auriga 17.130
aurochs 499
aurora 17.276
aurora australis 300.7
aurora borealis 300.7
aurous 310.48
aurum 242.20
Auschwitz 339
auscultate 367
auscultation 261.67
auspex 496
auspice 300
auspicious 310.58
austere 6
austerity 16.333.21
Austerlitz 339
Austin 252
Australasia 17.3.59
Australia 17.3.18
Australian 261.3.8
Australiana 17.226.1
Australianism
   242.35.14.1
Australianize 516.7
australopithecine 251.8
Australorp 277
Austria 17.3
Austrian 261.3
Austronesia 17.334
autacoid 97
autarchy 16.20
autarky 16.20
authentic 38.63
authenticate 367.5
authenticity 16.333.28

author 17
authoritarian 261.3.21.2
authoritative 485.15.12
authority 16.333.22
authorize 516.8
authorship 274.1
autism 242.35
autistic 38.70
auto 12.78
autobahn 246
autobiographical
   228.23.3
autobiography 16.90.2
autocade 85
autochthon 261
autochthonous 310.36
autoclave 482
autocracy 16.307.5
autocrat 365.2
autocratic 38.49.6
autocross 302.2
autocue 15
auto-da-fé 2.9
autodidact 382
autoecious 310.57
autogenous 310.33
autogiro 12.64
autograft 396
autograph 158.1
autohypnosis 300.55
autohypnotic 38.53.2
autoimmune 260
autokinetic 38.50.4
Autolycus 310.10
autolysis 300.52.2
automat 365
automata 17.352
automate 367.16
automatic 38.49.2
automation 261.67.16
automatism 242.35.20
automatize 516.13
automaton 254
automobile 217
automotive 485.14
autonomic 38.29.1
autonomous 310.29
autonomy 16.222.3
autopilot 381
autopista 17.383
autoplasty 16.361.1
autopsy 16.315
autostrada 17.78
autosuggestion 261.18
autotimer 17.212

autotrophic 38.13
autumn 242.30
autumnal 228
Auvergne 250
auxiliary 16.274.1.1
avadavat 365.3
avail 214
availability 16.333.9.2
available 228.16.22
avalanche 78
Avalon 254.7
avant-garde 84
Avar 1
avarice 300.47
avaricious 310.58.2
avast 431
avatar 1
ave 16.378
Avebury 16.274
avenge 208
avens 548
Aventine 253
aventurine 252.19
avenue 15.9
aver 3
average 197
Averroës 513.2
averse 297
aversion 261.69.1
aversive 485.3
avert 369.2
Avesta 17.382
Avestan 261.106
avian 261.3.29
aviary 16.274.1
aviate 367.1
aviation 261.67.1
aviator 17.338.1
aviatrix 498.9
Avicenna 17.228
avid 91
avidity 16.333.5
Aviemore 9
avifauna 17.234
avionic 38.35.1
avionics 498.5
avitaminosis 300.55.4
avizandum 242.6
avocado 12.16
avocet 368
Avogadro 12
avoid 97
avoidable 228.16
avoidance 321
Avon 261.111

avow 13
avowal 228.8
avowed 99
avulsion 261
avuncular 17.174
avunculate 371.17
await 367.38
awake 34
awaken 261.11
award 95.4
aware 4.8
awareness 300.22
awash 354
away 2.28
awe 9
aweigh 2.28
awesome 242
awful 226.1
awfully 16.129
awfulness 300.30
awhile 219
awkward 103
awkwardness 300
awl 221
awn 255
awning 265
awoke 42
AWOL 220
awry 7.12
axe 494
axenic 38.33
axes 513
axial 228.3.18
axil 218
axilla 17.166
axillary 16.274.16
axiom 242.2
axiomatic 38.49.2
axis 300.70
axle 228
axletree 5
Axminster 17.394
axolotl 228.104
axon 254
ay 2
ay 7
ayah 17.4
ayatollah 17.168
Aycliffe 163
aye 7
aye-aye 7
Aylesbury 16.274
Aymara 1.14
Ayr 4
Ayrshire 6

Ayurveda 17.79
azalea 17.3.18
azan 246
Azbine 251
azedarach 32.3
azeotrope 278.3
Azerbaijan 246
Azerbaijani 16.224
azide 92
azimuth 464
Azores 518
azoth 459
azotic 38.53
azotobacter 17.353
Aztec 35
azure 17
azurite 372

B

baa 1
Baal 213
Baalbek 35
Baal Shem Tov 487
baba 1
Babbage 197
babbitt 371.4
babble 228
babe 20
Babel 228.11
Babi 16.6
babiche 352
babirusa 17.308
baboon 260
babul 227
baby 16.7
babyhood 101
babyish 353
Babylon 261.41
Babylonia 17.3.36
Babylonian 261.3.18
baby-snatcher 17.50
baccalaureate 371.1.2
baccarat 1.14
Bacchae 5
bacchanal 228.63.1
bacchanalia 17.3.18.1
bacchanalian 261.3.8
bacchant 420
Bacchic 38.6
Bacchus 310.7
baccivorous 310.50.3
baccy 16.19
Bach 33
Bacharach 32.3

balletomania 17.3.31.1
ballista 17.384
ballistic 38.70.2
ballistics 498
balloon 260.1
balloonist 436.12
ballot 381
ballottement 420
ballpark 33
ballpoint 416
ballroom 241
bally 16.112
ballyhoo 15
balm 230
Balmoral 228.73
balmy 16.211
baloney 16.233.1
balsa 17.310
balsam 242
balsamic 38.24
Balt 404
Balthazar 1.19
Baltic 38
Baltimore 9
Baluchi 16.53
Baluchistan 246.1
baluster 17.390
balustrade 85
Balzac 32
Bamberg 182
bambino 12.54
bamboo 15
bamboozle 228.128
ban 245
banal 213.1
banality 16.333.8.7
banana 17.226
Banat 371.22
Banbury 16.274
band 128
bandage 197
bandanna 17.225
bandeau 12.23
banderilla 17.2.2
banderillero 12.62
banderole 223.3
bandicoot 380
bandit 371
bandmaster 17.380
bandoleer 6
bandore 9
bandsman 261
bandstand 128
bandwagon 261.30
bandy 16.77

bane 247
baneful 226.4
bang 263
Bangalore 9.8
banger 17.245
Bangkok 40
Bangladesh 351
bangle 228.49
Bangor 17.140
banish 353
banister 17.384
banjo 12
Banjul 227
bank 51
bankable 228.16
bankbook 44
banker 17.43
banket 371
banking 265
bankroll 223
bankrupt 426
bankruptcy 16
banksia 17.3
banner 17.225
bannerette 368.6
bannock 46
Bannockburn 249
banns 544
banquet 371
banquette 368
banshee 5
bantam 242
bantamweight 367
banter 17.365
Bantu 15
Bantustan 246
banyan 261.121
banzai 7
baobab 18
bap 268
baptism 242.35
baptismal 228.54
Baptist 436
baptistry 16.293
baptize 516
bar 1
Barabbas 310
barathea 17.2
barb 19
Barbados 302
barbarian 261.3.21
barbaric 38.38
barbarism 242.35.15
barbarity 16.333.20
barbarize 516.8

Barbarossa 17.304
barbarous 310.50
Barbary 16.274
barbecue 15
barbel 228
barbell 215
barber 17.10
barbershop 276
Barbican 261.13
Barbirolli 16.122
barbitone 257.2
barbiturate 371.34
Barbuda 17.91
barcarole 223.3
Barcelona 17.236
barchan 246
bard 84
bardolatry 16.286.2
bare 4
bareback 32
barefaced 432
barefoot 379
barehanded 91.12
bareheaded 91.7
barely 16.117
bareness 300.22
bargain 252
barge 192
bargepole 223
Bari 16.261
baric 38
baric 38.38
barilla 17.166.3
baritone 257.2
barium 242.2.14
bark 33
barker 17.29
Barking 265
barley 16.113
barleycorn 255.2
barmaid 85
barman 261
Barmecide 92.7
barmy 16.211
barn 246
Barnabas 310
barnacle 228.28
Barnard 84
Barnardo 12.16
Barnet 371
barney 16.224
barnstorm 238
Barnum 242
barnyard 84
Baroda 17.88

barogram 229.1
barograph 158.1
barometer 17.342.3.4
barometric 38.46
baron 261
baronage 197
baroness 300.26
baronet 371.28
baronetage 197.12
baronetcy 16.317
baronial 228.3.8
barony 16.237
baroque 40
baroscope 278.1
barouche 358
barque 33
barquentine 251
barrack 46
barracks 503
barracouta 17.351
barracuda 17.91
barrage 359
barramunda 17.108
barranca 17.43
barratry 16.286
barré 2.16
barrel 228.72
barren 261
barrenness 300.31
barret 371
barrette 368.6
barricade 85
Barrie 16.260
barrier 17.3
barring 265
barrister 17.384
barroom 241
barrow 12.60
Barry 16.260
Barrymore 9
Barsac 32
bartender 17.101
barter 17.337
Bartholomew 15
Bartlett 371
Bartók 40
Barton 261.95
barycentre 17.368.1
baryon 254.1
barysphere 6
barytes 513
baryton 257.2
basal 228
basalt 404
basaltware 4

bascule 227
base 295
baseball 221
baseborn 255
baseless 300
baseline 253
baseman 261
basement 420.44
baseness 300
bases 513
bash 349
Bashan 245
bashaw 9
bashful 226
bashibazouk 45
Bashkir 6
basic 38
basically 16.142
Basie 16.296
basify 7.3
basil 228.124
Basil 228.124
Basildon 261
Basilian 261.3.11
basilic 38.21
basilica 17.34
basilisk 58
basin 261.62
basinet 371.24
Basingstoke 42
basis 300.50
bask 56
Baskerville 218.3
basket 371
basketball 221
basketry 16.285
basketwork 36
Basle 213
Basque 55
bas-relief 162.1
bass 293
bass 295
Bassenthwaite 367
basset 371
Basse-Terre 4
bassinet 368
bassist 436
basso 12.68
bassoon 260
bassoonist 436.12
bast 430
bastard 103
bastardize 516
bastardry 16.277
bastardy 16.72

baste 432
Bastille 217
bastinado 12.17
bastion 261.3
bat 365
batch 62
bate 367
bateau 12.72
Bates 335
batfish 353
bath 453
Bath 453
bathe 473
bathetic 38.50.6
bathhouse 306
bathing 265
batholith 458
bathometer 17.342.3
bathos 302
bathrobe 28
bathroom 241
Bathsheba 17.13
bathtub 29
Bathurst 445
bathymetry 16.285.1
bathyscaph 157
bathysphere 6
batik 38.49
batiste 435
Batley 16.186
batman 261
baton 254
batrachian 261.3
batsman 261
battalion 261.118
batten 261.94
Battenburg 182
batter 17.336
battery 16.274
batting 265
battle 228.97
battledore 9
battlefield 115
battlement 420.40
battlepiece 298
battler 17.200
battleship 274
battue 15
batty 16.327
batwing 265
batwoman 261.50
bauble 228
Bauchi 16.51
baud 95
Bauhaus 306

bauxite 372
Bavaria 17.3.38
Bavarian 261.3.21
bawbee 5
bawd 95
bawdry 16.276
bawdy 16.66
bawdyhouse 306
bawl 221
Bax 494
bay 2
bayonet 371.28
bayou 15
baywood 101
bazaar 1.19
bazoo 15.10
bazooka 17.41
be 5
beach 66
beachcomber 17.215
Beach-la-Mar 1.12
beacon 261.12
Beaconsfield 115
bead 89
beading 265.13
beadle 228
beady 16.62
beagle 228.45
beak 37
beaked 386
beaker 17.33
beam 234
bean 251
beanbag 178
beanery 16.274.25
beanfeast 435
beanie 16.228
beano 12.54
beanpole 223
beanstalk 41
bear 4
bearable 228.16.33
beard 90
bearded 91
beardless 300
bearer 17.271
bearing 265.52
bearish 353.9
Béarnaise 509
bearskin 252
beast 435
beastly 16.200
beat 370
beatable 228.16.48
beaten 261.98

beater 17.341
beatific 38.12
beatify 7.3.8
beating 265
beatitude 102.2.1
Beatles 539
beatnik 38
Beatty 16.332
beau 12
Beaufort 381
beaujolais 2.12
beau monde 136
Beaumont 414
Beaune 257
beaut 380
beauteous 310.2
beautician 261.71
beautiful 226
beautify 7.3
beauty 16.343
beaux-arts 1
beaver 17.413
Beaverbrook 44.1
Bebington 261
bebop 276
becalmed 123
became 231
because 517
beccafico 12.10
béchamel 215
bêche-de-mer 4.4
Bechuanaland 143.4
beck 35
Beckett 371
beckon 261
becloud 99
become 240
becoming 265.38
bed 86
bedaub 27
bedazzle 228.124
bedbug 189
beddable 228.16.14
bedder 17.80
bedding 265.12
Bede 89
bedeck 35
bedevil 228.118
bedew 15.7
bedfellow 12.40
Bedford 103.2
Bedfordshire 6
bedim 235
Bedivere 6.11
bedlam 242

Bedouin 252
bedpan 245
bedpost 441
bedraggle 228.43
bedraggled 122
bedridden 261.24
bedrock 40
bedroll 223
bedroom 241
bedside 92
bedsitter 17.342
bedsore 9
bedspread 86
bedstead 86
bedstraw 9
bedtime 236
bedwarmer 17.214
bee 5
Beeb 23
beebread 86
beech 66
Beecham 242
beechnut 378
beef 162
beefburger 17.127
beefcake 34
beefeater 17.341
beefsteak 34
beefy 16.84
beehive 486
beekeeper 17.252
beeline 253
Beelzebub 29
been 251
beep 273
beer 6
Beerbohm 239
Beersheba 17.13
beery 16.265
beestings 552
beeswax 494
beet 370
Beethoven 261.116
beetle 228.101
beetroot 380
befall 221
befell 215
befit 371.13
befog 185.1
befool 227
before 9.5
beforehand 128
befoul 224
befriend 131
befuddle 228.36

beg 181
began 245
begat 365.1
beget 368
beggar 17.126
beggarly 16.131.2
beggary 16.274
begin 252
beginner 17.231
beginning 265.43
begird 87
begone 254.4
begonia 17.3.36
begorra 17.275
begot 373
begotten 261.101
begrime 236
begrudge 203
beguile 219
beguine 251
begum 242
begun 259
behalf 158
Behan 261.2
behave 482
behaviour 17.436
behavioural 228.76
behaviourism 242.35.15
behaviourist 436.20
behaviouristic 38.70.5
behead 86.2
beheld 113
behemoth 459
behest 433
behind 135
behindhand 128
Behistun 260
behold 120.1
beholden 261.28
beholder 17.97
behove 488
beige 360
being 265.2
Beirut 380
bejewel 228.10
bel 215
belabour 17.11
belated 91.34.5
belatedness 300.28
belay 2.11
belch 75
beleaguer 17.128
belemnite 372
Belfast 431
belfry 16

Belgae 5
Belgian 261
Belgium 242
Belgrade 85
Belgravia 17.3.53
Belial 228.3
belie 7.5
belief 162.1
believable 228.16.61
believe 484.1
believer 17.413
Belisarius 310.2
Belisha 17.325
belittle 228.102
bell 215
belladonna 17.233.1
bellarmine 251
Bellatrix 498
bellboy 11
belle 215
Belleek 37
Bellerophon 254.3
bellhop 276
bellicose 305
bellicosity 16.333.30.3
belligerence 321.20
belligerency 16.312
belligerent 420.65
Belloc 40
Bellona 17.236
bellow 12.40
bellows 520
bell-ringing 265.47
bellwether 17.402
belly 16.115
bellyband 128
bellybutton 261.103
bellyful 226
Belmopan 245.4
belong 266
belonging 265
belongings 552
beloved 91
below 12.42
Bel Paese 16.393
Belsen 261
Belshazzar 17.437
belt 402
Beltane 247
belting 265
beltway 2
beluga 17.136
belvedere 6
bema 17.210
Bemba 17.24

bemire 8
bemoan 257
bemuse 523
bemused 156
ben 248
Ben 248
Benares 515
bench 79
bencher 17.70
bend 131
bender 17.101
Bendigo 12.29
bends 532
bendy 16.78
beneath 457
benedicite 16.333.29
Benedict 387
benediction 261.78.1
benefaction 261.76
benefactor 17.353
benefactress 300.48
benefic 38
benefice 300
beneficence 321.22
beneficent 420.70
beneficial 228.93
beneficiary 16.274.1.2
benefit 371.13
Benelux 502
benevolence 321.12.1
benevolent 420.28.1
Bengal 221
Bengali 16.123
Benghazi 16.392
Ben-Gurion 261.3.24
benighted 91.39
benign 253.6
benignant 420
benignity 16.333.19
Benin 251
benison 261.126
Benjamin 252.15
Ben Nevis 300.69
benny 16.226
Benoni 16.233
bent 410
Bentinck 52
Bentley 16.197
bentwood 101
Benue 2.3
benumb 240
benzaldehyde 92
Benzedrine 252
benzene 251
benzoate 367

benzoin 252.1
Beowulf 175
bequeath 475
bequeather 17.404
bequest 433
Berar 1
berate 367.21
Berber 17.12
Berbera 17.279
berberis 300.47
bereave 484
bereavement 420
bereft 397
beret 2
berg 182
bergamot 373
Bergman 261
beriberi 16.262
berk 36
Berkeley 16.140
berkelium 242.2.5
Berks 495
Berkshire 6
Berlin 252
Berlioz 520
Bermuda 17.91
Bern 249
Bernadette 368.5
Bernhardt 366
Bernie 16.227
Bernstein 253
berry 16.262
berserk 36
berth 456
Berwick 38.39
Berwick-upon-Tweed 89
beryl 218.2
Beryl 218.2
beryllium 242.2.6
Berzelius 310.2.4
beseech 66
beseeching 265
beset 368.7
beside 92.7
besides 527
besiege 196
besmear 6
besmirch 65
besom 242
besotted 91.40
bespangle 228.49
bespatter 17.336
bespeak 37
bespectacled 122
bespoke 42

bespread 86
besprent 410
besprinkle 228.29
Bess 296
Bessarabia 17.3.1
best 433
bestial 228.3.14
bestiality 16.333.8.1
bestialize 516.3.2
bestiary 16.274.1
bestir 3
bestow 12
bestowal 228.7
bestrew 15
bestride 92
bet 368
beta 17.341
betake 34
betel 228.101
Betelgeuse 511
Beth 455
Bethany 16.237
Bethel 228
Bethlehem 232
Bethsaida 17.79
betide 92
bêtise 513
Betjeman 261.52
betoken 261.14
betony 16.237
betook 44
betray 2
betrayal 228.1
betroth 478
betrothal 228
betrothed 145
better 17.339
betterment 420.35
between 251
betweentimes 542
betwixt 451
Beulah 17.175
Bevan 261.112
bevel 228.118
beverage 197
Beverly 16.131
Bevin 252.28
bevvy 16.380
bevy 16.380
bewail 214
beware 4.7
Bewick 38
bewilder 17.95
bewilderment 420.35
bewitch 67

bey 2
beyond 136
bezant 420.84
bezel 228
bezique 37
Bhagalpur 10
Bhagavad-Gita 17.341
bhang 263
bhindi 16.79
Bhopal 213
Bhutan 246
biannual 228.9.2
Biarritz 339
bias 310.3
biathlon 261
biaxial 228.3.18
bib 24
bibber 17.14
bibelot 12
Bible 228
biblical 228.23
Biblicist 436.21
bibliography 16.90.2.1
bibliolatry 16.286.2.1
bibliomania 17.3.31.1
bibliophile 219.1
bibliopole 223
bibliopolist 436.7
bibliotheca 17.33
bibulous 310.25
bicameral 228.76
bicarb 19
bicarbonate 371.28
bice 310
bicentenary 16.274.25
bicephalous 310.26.3
biceps 324
bicipital 228.102
bicker 17.34
biconcave 482
biconvex 496
bicorn 255
bicornate 371.26
bicuspid 91
bicycle 228.23
bid 7
bidarkee 5.3
biddable 228.16.15
bidden 261.24
bidder 17.83
bidding 265
biddy 16.63
bide 92
bidet 2
Biel 217

bield 115
biennial 228.3
bier 6
bierkeller 17.163
biff 163
biffin 252
bifid 91
bifocal 228.26
bifocals 539
bifoliate 367.1.3
biform 238
Bifrost 438
bifurcate 367.6
bifurcate 371.8
bifurcation 261.67.6
big 184
bigamist 436.10.1
bigamous 310.29.1
bigamy 16.222.1
biggin 252
biggish 353
bighead 86
bigheaded 91.7
bigheadedness 300.28
bight 372
bigmouth 462
bigot 381
bigoted 91
bigotry 16.286
bigwig 184
Bihar 1.6
Bihari 16.261
bijou 15
bijouterie 16.274
bike 39
bikini 16.228
bilateral 228.76
Bilbao 12
bilberry 16.274
bile 219
bilestone 257
bilharziasis 300.57.1
biliary 16.274.1.1
bilinear 17.3.34
bilingual 228
bilious 310.2.5
biliousness 300.34
bilirubin 252
biliverdin 252
bilk 49
bill 218
billabong 266
billboard 95
billet 371.16
billet-doux 15.2

billfold 120
billhook 44
billiard 103
billiards 531
billing 265.30
Billingsgate 367
billion 261.120
billionaire 4.5
billionth 471
billon 261.41
billow 12.42
billowy 16.3
billposter 17.387
billy 16.120
billycan 245
billyo 12.3.2
bilobate 367.3
bimbo 12.6
bimestrial 228.3.13
bimetallic 38.19.1
bimonthly 16.205
bin 252
binary 16.274.27
binaural 228.74
bind 135
binder 17.103
bindi-eye 7.1
binding 265.21
bindweed 89
bine 253
binge 209
bingo 12.36
binnacle 228.28
binocular 17.174.7
binoculars 524
binomial 228.3
binominal 228.60.5
bint 412
binturong 266
bio-assay 2.20
biocatalyst 436.7.6
biochemical 228.23
biochemist 436
biochemistry 16.293
biocide 92.8
biodegradable 228.16
biodegradation 261.67.8
biofeedback 32
biogen 261.39
biogeography 16.90.2.1
biographer 17.120.1
biographical 228.23.3
biography 16.90.2
biological 228.23.5
biologist 436.4

biology 16.108.4.2
biolysis 300.52.2
biomass 293
biometry 16.285.2
bionic 38.35
bionics 498.5
bionomics 498
biophysics 498
biopsy 16.315
bioptic 38.67
bioscope 278.1.1
biosphere 6.1
biota 17.347
biotic 38.53.1
biotin 252
biotype 275.1
bipartisan 245.7
bipartite 372
biped 86
biplane 247
bipod 94
bipolar 17.171
birch 65
bird 87
birdbath 453
birdcage 193
birdhouse 306
birdie 16.61
birdlime 236
birdman 261
birdseed 89
bird-watching 265
bireme 234
biretta 17.339
biriani 16.224
Birkenhead 86
Biro 12.64
birr 3
birth 456
birthday 2
birthmark 33
birthplace 295
birthright 372
birthstone 257
Biscay 2
biscuit 371
bise 513
bisect 385
bisection 261.77
bisector 17.354
bisexual 228.9
bish 353
bishop 281
bishopric 38
Bismarck 33

bismuth 464
bison 261
bisque 58
bissextile 219.8
bistort 374
bistoury 16.274.49
bistre 17.384
bistro 12
bisulcate 367.7
bisulphate 367
bisymmetric 38.46
bit 371
bitch 67
bitchy 16.49
bite 372
Bithynia 17.3.34
biting 265.67
bitser 17.320
bitten 261.99
bitter 17.342
bittern 261.99
bitterness 300.26
bitternut 378
bitters 524
bittersweet 370
bitty 16.333
bitumen 252
bituminize 516.6
bituminous 310.33.1
bivalent 420.25
bivalve 491
bivouac 32
bivvy 16.382
biweekly 16.141
biyearly 16.119
bizarre 1
Bizerte 17.340
Bizet 2.30
blab 18
blabber 17.9
blabbermouth 462
black 32
blackball 221
Blackbeard 90
blackberry 16.274
blackbird 87
blackboard 95
Blackburn 249
blackbutt 378
blackcap 268
blackcurrant 420.64
blackdamp 285
blacken 261
blackfly 7
Blackfoot 379

blackguard 84
blackhead 86
blacking 265
blackish 353
blackjack 32
blackleg 181
blacklist 436
blackmail 214
blackmailer 17.162
Black Maria 17.4.2
blackness 300
blackout 377
Blackpool 227
Blackshirt 369
blacksmith 458
blackthorn 255
Blackwall 221
bladder 17.77
bladdernose 520
bladdernut 378
bladderwort 369
bladderwrack 32.3
blade 85
blah 1
blain 247
Blake 34
blame 231
blameful 226
blameless 300
blameworthy 16.375
blanch 78
bland 128
blandish 353.2
blank 51
blanket 371
blankly 16.144
blare 4
blarney 16.224
blasé 2
blaspheme 234
blasphemer 17.210
blasphemous 310.28
blasphemy 16.216
blast 431
blasted 91.51
blastema 17.210
blasting 265.74
blastocoel 217.2
blastocyst 436.22
blastoff 165
blastomere 6.3
blastula 17.174
blatancy 16.312.6
blatant 420.75
blather 17.400

blatherskite 372
Blaydon 261.20
blaze 509
blazer 17.439
blazes 515
blazon 261.124
blazonry 16.284
bleach 66
bleak 37
bleakness 300
bleary 16.265
bleat 370
bleb 21
bleed 89
bleeder 17.82
bleeding 265.13
bleep 273
blemish 353
blench 79
blend 131
blender 17.101
Blenheim 235
blenny 16.226
blepharitis 300.62.5
bless 296
blessed 91
blessing 265.60
blest 433
blew 15
blewits 339
Bligh 7
blight 372
blighter 17.343
Blighty 16.334
blimey 16.217
blimp 287
blind 135
blindfold 120
blinding 265.21
blindly 16.155
blindness 300.29
blindstorey 16.269
blindworm 233
blini 16.229
blink 52
blinker 17.44
blinkers 524
blinking 265.10
blintz 348
blip 274
bliss 300
blissful 226
blister 17.384
blithe 477
blithering 265.58

blithesome 242
blitz 339
blitzkrieg 183
blizzard 103
bloat 376
bloated 91.41
bloater 17.347
blob 26
bloc 40
block 40
blockade 85
blockage 197
blockboard 95
blockbuster 17.388
blockbusting 265
blocker 17.36
blockhead 86
Bloemfontein 247.11
bloke 42
blond 136
blonde 136
blood 100
bloodcurdling 265
bloodhound 139
bloodless 300
blood-letting 265.65
bloodshed 86
bloodshot 373
bloodstain 247
bloodstained 130
bloodstock 40
bloodsucker 17.39
bloodthirsty 16.365
bloody 16.69
bloody-minded 91
bloom 241
bloomer 17.217
bloomers 524
bloomery 16.274.22
blooming 265.39
Bloomsbury 16.274
blooper 17.259
blossom 242.25
blot 373
blotch 68
blotchy 16.50
blotter 17.344
blotto 12.77
blouse 521
blouson 254
blow 12
blower 17.6
blowfish 353
blowfly 7
blowhard 84

blowhole 223
blowlamp 285
blown 257
blowpipe 275
blowtorch 69
blowy 16.3
blowzy 16.400
blub 29
blubber 17.19
blubbery 16.274
bludge 203
bludgeon 261.38
blue 15
Bluebeard 90
bluebell 215
blueberry 16.274
bluebill 218
bluebird 87
blue-blooded 91.11
bluebook 44
bluebottle 228.104
bluefish 353
bluegrass 294
bluejacket 371.6
blueness 300
bluenose 520
blueprint 412
blues 523
bluestocking 265.8
bluet 371.3
bluetit 371
bluey 16.4
bluff 168
bluffer 17.118
bluish 353
blunder 17.108
blunderbuss 307
blunge 211
blunger 17.159
blunt 419
bluntness 300
blur 3
blurb 22
blurry 16.263
blurt 369
blush 356
blusher 17.329
bluster 17.388
blustery 16.274
Blyth 477
B'nai B'rith 457
boa 16.7
Boadicea 17.2
boar 9
board 95

boarder 17.86
boarding 265.15
boardroom 241
boardwalk 41
boarhound 139
boarish 353
boast 441
boastful 226
boastfulness 300.30
boat 376
boatel 215.4
boater 17.347
boathook 44
boathouse 306
boating 265
boatload 98
boatman 261
boatswain 261
Boaz 507
bob 26
bobbery 16.274.3
bobbin 252
bobble 228
bobby 16.11
bobbysoxer 17.428
boblet 371
bobolink 52
bobotie 16.342
bobowler 17.172
bobsleigh 2
bobtail 214
bocage 359
boccia 17.57
bock 40
bod 94
bode 98
bodega 17.128
bodge 199
bodger 17.152
bodgie 16.104
bodice 300.4
bodiless 300.8
bodily 16.120
bodkin 252
Bodleian 261.3
Bodmin 252
Bodoni 16.233
body 16.65
bodyguard 84.1
body-snatcher 17.50
bodywork 36
Boehmite 372
Boeotia 17.328
Boer 10
Boethius 310.2

boeuf Bourguignon
254.12
boffin 252
bog 185
bogan 261
Bogarde 84
Bogart 366
bogey 16.96
bogeyman 261.48
boggart 381
boggle 228.47
boggy 16.94
bogie 16.96
bogle 228
Bognor Regis 300.6
bogong 266
Bogotá 1
bogus 310
bogwood 101
Bohemia 17.3.26
Bohemian 261.3
boil 222
boiler 17.170
boilermaker 17.30
boilerplate 367
Boise 16.398
boisterous 310.50
boisterousness 300.34
bokmakierie 16.265
bola 17.171
bold 120
boldness 300
bole 223
bolection 261.77
bolero 12.62
boletus 310.63
Boleyn 252
bolide 92
Bolingbroke 44
bolivar 17.3
Bolivia 17.3.54
Bolivian 261.3.30
boll 223
bollard 103.3
bollocks 503
bolo 12.44
Bolognese 509
Bolshevik 38.74
Bolshevist 436
bolster 17.392
bolt 405
bolter 17.364
Bolton 261
bolus 310
bomb 237

bombard 84
bombardier 6
bombardment 420
bombast 430
bombastic 38.68
Bombay 2
bombazine 251
bombé 2
bomber 17.213
bombora 17.276
bombshell 215
bombsight 372
bombycid 91.29
bona fide 16.64
Bonaire 4
bonanza 17.445
Bonaparte 366.1
Bonapartism 242.35.17
bona vacantia 17.3.50
Bonaventura 17.277
bonbon 254
bonce 318
bond 136
bondage 197
bonded 91
bondservant 420.82
bone 257
bonehead 86
boneless 300
boner 17.236
bonesetter 17.339
boneshaker 17.30
boneyard 84
bonfire 8
bong 266
bongo 12
bonhomie 16.222.3
Boniface 295.3
bonism 242.35
bonito 12.76
bonkers 524
Bonn 254
bonnet 371.25
bonny 16.231
bonsai 7
bonsela 17.163
bonus 310.35
bony 16.233
bonze 549
boo 15
boob 30
boobook 44
booby 16.14
boodle 228.37
boogie 16.98

boogie-woogie 16.98
boohoo 15
book 44
bookbinder 17.103
bookbindery 16.274.8
bookbinding 265.21
bookcase 295
bookie 16.31
booking 265
bookish 353
book-keeper 17.252
book-keeping 265.49
booklet 371
bookmaker 17.30
bookmark 33
bookshop 276
bookstall 221
bookworm 233
Boole 227
boom 241
boomer 17.217
boomerang 263.2
boomslang 263
boon 260
boondocks 499
boondoggle 228.47
boor 10
boorish 353
boost 444
booster 17.389
boot 380
bootblack 32
booted 91.42
bootee 5
Boötes 513
booth 479
bootlace 295
Bootle 228.108
bootleg 181
bootlegger 17.126
bootless 300
bootlick 38
bootlicker 17.34
boots 346
bootstrap 268
booty 16.343
booze 523
boozer 17.444
boozy 16.402
bop 276
bora 17.276
Bora Bora 17.276
boracic 38.48
borage 197
borane 247

borax 494
borborygmus 310
Bordeaux 12
Bordelaise 509
bordello 12.40
border 17.86
bordereau 12
borderer 17.279
borderland 143.4
borderline 253.3
bordure 10
bore 9
boreal 228.3.12
Boreas 310.2.13
boredom 242
boree 5
borer 17.276
Borg 186
Borgia 17.153
boric 38.42
boride 92.5
boring 265.55
Boris 300
born 255
borne 255
Borneo 12.3
borneol 220.1
Borodin 252
Borodino 12.54
boron 254.10
borough 17.278
borrow 12.65
borrower 17.6
borstal 228.116
borzoi 11
boscage 197
Bosch 354
Bose 305
bosh 354
bosk 59
bosket 371
Bosnia 17.3
bosom 242
bosomy 16.222
boson 254
Bosporus 310.50
boss 302
bossa nova 17.417
bossiness 300.23
bossy 16.302
Boston 261
bosun 261
Boswell 228
Bosworth 464
bot 373

botanical 228.23.10
botanist 436.13
botanize 516.7
botany 16.237.7
botargo 12.26
botch 68
botcher 17.57
botchy 16.50
botfly 7
both 461
bother 17.407
botheration 261.67.22
bothersome 242
bothy 16.371
bots 341
Botswana 17.226
bottle 228.104
bottlebrush 356
bottleneck 35
bottlenose 520
bottom 242
bottomless 300
bottommost 441
botulin 252.10
botulinus 310.34
botulism 242.35.10
bouchée 2
bouclé 2
Boudicca 17.34
boudoir 1
bouffant 266
Bougainville 218
bougainvillea 17.3.21
bough 13
bought 374
bougie 5
bouillabaisse 296
bouillon 254
boulder 17.97
boule 227
boulevard 1
boulevardier 2.1
Boulez 510
Boulogne 256
Boult 405
bounce 319
bouncer 17.317
bouncing 265
bound 139
boundary 16.274
bounden 261
bounder 17.107
boundless 300
bounds 533
bounteous 310.2

bountiful 226
bounty 16.359
bouquet 2
bouquet garni 5.10
bourbon 261.9
Bourbon 261
bourdon 261
bourg 187
bourgeois 1
bourgeoisie 5
bourn 255
Bournemouth 464
bourrée 2.18
bouse 521
boustrophedon 261.23
bout 377
boutique 37
boutonniere 4.1
bouzouki 16.32
bovid 91
bovine 253
Bovril 218
bovver 17.416
bow 12
bow 13
bowdlerism 242.35.15
bowdlerize 516.8
bowel 228.8
bower 14
bowerbird 87
bowfin 252
bowhead 86.3
bowing 265.4
bowl 223
bow-legged 91
bowler 17.171
bowlful 226
bowline 252.9
bowling 265.32
bowman 261
bowman 261.49
bowser 17.443
bowshot 373
bowsprit 371
bowstring 265
bow-wow 13
bowyer 17.431
box 499
boxcar 1
boxer 17.428
boxing 265
boxroom 241
boy 11
Boyce 304
boycott 373

Boyd 97
boyfriend 131
boyhood 101
boyish 353
Boyle 222
Boyne 256
boysenberry 16.274
Boz 517
bra 1
Brabant 407
brace 295
bracelet 371
bracer 17.299
braces 515
brachial 228.3
brachiate 367.1
brachiopod 94.1
brachiosaurus 310.48.1
brachylogy 16.108.3
bracing 265.59
bracken 261
bracket 371.6
bracketing 265.66
brackish 353
Bracknell 228
bract 382
brad 83
bradawl 221
Bradford 103
Bradley 16.146
Bradman 261
Bradshaw 9
bradycardia 17.3.6
brae 2
brag 178
braggadocio 12.3
braggart 381
bragger 17.123
Brahma 17.206
Brahman 261
Brahmanic 38.31
Brahmanism 242.35.14
Brahmaputra 17.294
Brahmin 252
Brahminic 38.34
Brahms 540
braid 85
braided 91.6
braiding 265.11
Braille 214
brain 247
brainchild 117
brainless 300
brainpan 245
brainsick 38

brainstorm 238
brainstorming 265
brainwash 354
brainwashing 265
brainy 16.225
braise 509
brake 34
bramble 228.17
bran 245
branch 78
branchia 17.3
branchiopod 94.1
Brancusi 16.402
brand 128
Brandenburg 182
brandish 353.2
brandling 265
Brando 12.23
brandy 16.77
brash 349
Brasília 17.3.21
brass 294
brassard 84
brassbound 139
brasserie 16.274
brassica 17.34
brassie 16.294
brassiere 17.3.46
brassy 16.295
brat 365
Bratislava 17.409
brattice 300
bratwurst 434
bravado 12.16
brave 482
braveness 300
bravery 16.274.50
bravissimo 12.48
bravo 12
bravura 17.277
braw 9
brawl 221
brawler 17.169
brawn 255
brawny 16.232
braxy 16.386
bray 2
braze 509
brazen 261.124
brazier 17.3.59
Brazil 218
Brazilian 261.3.11
breach 66
bread 86
breadboard 95

breadfruit 380
breadline 253
breadwinner 17.231
break 34
breakable 228.16.9
breakage 197
breakaway 2.28
breakdown 258
breaker 17.30
breakfast 445
breakfront 419
breakneck 35
breakpoint 416
breakwater 17.345
bream 234
breast 433
breastbone 257
breastplate 367
breaststroke 42
breastwork 36
breath 455
breathalyse 516.3
Breathalyzer 17.441
breathe 475
breather 17.404
breathing 265
breathless 300
breathlessness 300.33
breathtaking 265.6
breathy 16.369
breccia 17.3
Brecknockshire 6
Brecon 261
Breconshire 6.8
bred 86
Breda 17.82
bree 5
breech 66
breechblock 40
breeches 515
breeching 265
breed 89
breeder 17.82
breeding 265.13
breeze 513
breezy 16.395
bregma 17.221
Bremen 261.45
Bren 248
brent 410
Brent 410
Brentwood 101
br'er 3
Brest 433
brethren 252

Breton 261.96
breve 484
brevet 371
breviary 16.274.1
brevity 16.333.34
brew 15
brewage 197
brewer 17.8
brewery 16.274
brewing 265.5
Brezhnev 160
Brian 261.4
Brian Boru 15.6
briar 17.4
Briareus 310.2.10
briarroot 380
bribable 228.16.8
bribe 25
briber 17.15
bribery 16.274
bric-a-brac 32
brick 38
brickbat 365
bricklayer 17.1
bricklaying 265.1
brickwork 36
brickyard 84
bricole 223
bridal 228.33
bride 92
bridegroom 241
bridesmaid 85
bridewell 215
bridge 197
Bridget 371
bridgework 36
bridging 265.25
Bridgwater 17.345
bridie 16.64
bridle 228.33
bridler 17.187
bridoon 260
Brie 5
brief 162
briefcase 295
briefing 265
briefly 16.158
brig 184
brigade 85.1
brigadier 6
brigalow 12.45
brigand 143
brigandine 251
brigantine 251
bright 372

brighten 261.100
brightness 300.39
Brighton 261.100
brightwork 36
Brigid 91.15
brill 218
brilliance 321
brilliant 420
brilliantine 251
brim 235
brimful 226
brimstone 257
brindle 228.40
brindled 122
brine 253
bring 265
brink 52
brinkmanship 274.2
briny 16.230
brioche 354
briquette 368.4
brisance 321.28
Brisbane 261
brisk 58
brisket 371
brisling 265
bristle 228.85
bristly 16.181
Bristol 228.114
bristols 539
Brit 371
Britain 261.99
Britannia 17.3.29
Britannic 38.31
Briticism 242.35.16
British 353
Britisher 17.326
Britishism 242.35
Briton 261.99
Brittany 16.237
Britten 261.99
brittle 228.102
brittleness 300.30
broach 70
broad 95
broadcast 431
broadcaster 17.380
broadcloth 459
broaden 261.27
broadloom 241
broadly 16.150
broad-minded 91
broad-mindedness
 300.28
Broadmoor 9

Broads 528
broadsheet 370
broadside 92
broadsword 95
broadtail 214
Broadway 2
brocade 85
brocatelle 215
broccoli 16.131
broché 2
brochette 368
brochure 10
brock 40
brocket 371.10
broderie anglaise 509
Broederbond 415
brogan 261
brogue 188
broil 222
broiler 17.170
broke 42
broken 261.14
brokenhearted 91.33
broker 17.38
brokerage 197
brolga 17.138
brolly 16.122
bromate 367
brome 239
bromeliad 83.1
bromic 38
bromide 92
bromidic 38
bromine 251
bromism 242.35
Bromsgrove 488
bronchi 7
bronchia 17.3
bronchial 228.3
bronchiectasis 300.57
bronchiole 223.1
bronchitic 38.52
bronchitis 300.62
bronchopneumonia
 17.3.36
bronchoscope 278.1
bronchus 310
bronco 12
broncobuster 17.388
Brontë 16.357
brontosaurus 310.48.1
bronze 549
brooch 70
brood 102
brooder 17.91

broody 16.71
brook 44
brooklet 371
Brooklyn 252
broom 241
broomrape 270
broomstick 38
brose 520
broth 459
brothel 228
brother 17.408
brotherhood 101
brother-in-law 9
brotherly 16.131
brougham 242
brought 374
brouhaha 1.5
brow 13
browbeat 370
brown 258
brownie 16.234
browning 265
brownish 353
brownout 377
browse 521
browser 17.443
Brubeck 35
Bruce 309
brucellosis 300.55
Bruges 364
bruin 252
bruise 523
bruised 156
bruiser 17.444
bruising 265.84
bruit 380
Brummagem 242
Brummell 228
Brummie 16.220
brunch 82
Brunei 7
Brunel 215
brunette 368
Brunhild 116
Brunswick 38
brunt 419
brush 356
brushoff 165
brushwood 101
brushwork 36
brusque 60
brusqueness 300
Brussels 539
brut 380
brutal 228.108

brutality 16.333.8
brutalize 516.3
brute 380
brutify 7.3
brutish 353
Brutus 310.67
bryology 16.108.4.2
bryony 16.237.1
bryophyte 372
Brythonic 38.35
bubal 228
bubble 228.14
bubbly 16.136
bubo 12
bubonic 38.35
buccaneer 6.5
buccinator 17.338.7
Bucephalus 310.26.3
Buchanan 261.55
Bucharest 433.1
buck 43
buckaroo 15.6
buckbean 251
buckboard 95
bucket 371.11
buckeye 7
Buckingham 242.17
Buckinghamshire 6
buckjumper 17.264
buckle 228.27
buckling 265.34
bucko 12
buckram 242
bucksaw 9
buckshee 5
buckshot 373
buckskin 252
buckskins 548
buckthorn 255
bucktooth 463
buckwheat 370
bucolic 38.22
bud 100
Budapest 433
Buddha 17
Buddhism 242.35
Buddhist 436.2
budding 265
buddle 228.36
buddleia 17.3
buddy 16.69
budge 203
budgerigar 1.4
budget 371
budgie 16.107

buds 530
Buenos Aires 515
buff 168
buffalo 12.45
buffer 17.118
buffet 2
buffet 371
bufflehead 86
buffoon 260
buffoonery 16.274.28
bug 189
bugaboo 15.1
Buganda 17.98
bugbane 247
bugbear 6
bugger 17.134
buggery 16.274.10
buggy 16.97
bugle 228.48
bugleweed 89.7
bugloss 302
build 116
builder 17.95
building 265.17
built 403
Bukhara 17.268
bulbaceous 310.56
bulbous 310
bulbul 226
Bulgaria 17.3.38
Bulgarian 261.3.21
bulge 205
bulimia 17.3.27
bulk 50
bulkhead 86
bulky 16.35
bull 226
bulla 17.174
bullace 300.11
bulldog 185
bulldoze 520
bulldozer 17.442
bullet 371.17
bulletin 252.23
bulletproof 170
bullfight 372
bullfighter 17.343
bullfighting 265.67
bullfinch 80
bullfrog 185
bullion 261
bullish 353
bullock 46
bullring 265
bullshit 371

buttery 16.274
buttock 46
button 261.103
buttonhole 223
buttress 300
butty 16.341
butyrate 367.21
buxom 242
Buxton 261
buy 7
buyer 17.4
buzz 522
buzzard 103
bwana 17.226
by 7
bye 7
Byelorussian 261.74
bygone 254
bylaw 9
bypass 294
bypath 453
Byrd 87
byre 8
byroad 98
Byron 261.58
Byronic 38.35
byssinosis 300.55.4
byssus 310.53
bystander 17.98
bystreet 370
byte 372
byway 2.26
byword 87
Byzantine 253.9
Byzantium 242.2

C

cab 18
cabal 212
caballero 12.62
cabaret 2.19
cabbage 197
cabbagetown 258
cabbala 17.161
cabby 16.5
caber 17.11
cabin 252
cabinet 371.24
cable 228.11
cablegram 229
cableway 2
cabman 261
cabochon 254
caboodle 228.37

caboose 309
cabotage 359
cabriole 223.1
cabriolet 2.12
cacao 12
cacciatore 16.269
cachalot 373.1
cache 349
cachepot 373
cachet 2.22
cachexia 17.3.57
cachinnate 367.17
cachou 15
cachucha 17.61
cacique 37
cack-handed 91.12
cackle 228.19
cacodemon 261.47
cacodyl 218
cacoepy 16.245
cacoethes 513
cacography 16.90.2
cacology 16.108.4.6
cacomistle 228.85
cacophonous 310.36
cacophony 16.237.3
cactus 310
cad 83
cadaster 17.379
cadaver 17.410
cadaverous 310.50
caddie 16.57
caddis 300
caddish 353.1
Caddoan 261.6
caddy 16.57
cade 85
cadelle 215.1
cadence 321
cadenza 17.446
cadet 368.5
cadge 191
cadger 17.144
cadi 16.58
Cadillac 32
Cádiz 515
cadmium 242.2
cadre 17.78
caduceus 310.2
caducity 16.333
caducous 310.13
caecilian 261.3.11
caecum 242
Caelian 261.3.10
Caen 266

Caernarvon 261.110
Caernarvonshire 6.8
Caerphilly 16.120
Caesar 17.440
Caesarea 17.2.2
Caesarean 261.3.21
caesium 242.2.20
caesura 17.277
café 2
cafeteria 17.3.39
caff 157
caffeine 251
cage 193
cagey 16.100
Cagliari 16.261
cagoule 227
cahoots 346
Caiaphas 293
Cain 247
caïque 37
cairn 250
Cairngorm 238
Cairo 12.64
caisson 261.62
Caithness 296
caitiff 163
cajole 223
cajolery 16.274.17
cajuput 379
cake 34
cakewalk 41
Calabar 1.2
calabash 349.1
Calabria 17.3
caladium 242.2.1
Calais 2
calamander 17.98
calamine 253
calamint 412
calamitous 310.64
calamity 16.333.11
calamus 310.29.2
calandria 17.3.45
calash 349
calcaneus 310.2.6
calcareous 310.2.10
calceolaria 17.3.38.1
calciferol 220.4
calciferous 310.50.2
calcific 38.12
calcify 7.3
calcite 372
calcium 242.2
calculable 228.16.25
calculate 367.13

calculated 91.34
calculating 265.64
calculation 261.67.13
calculative 485.15.5
calculator 17.338.6
calculus 310.25
Calcutta 17.349
caldarium 242.2.14
caldera 17.271
Caldwell 215
Caledonia 17.3.36
Caledonian 261.3.18
calefacient 420.73
calefactory 16.274.44
calendar 17.102
calender 17.102
calends 532
calendula 17.174
calenture 10
calf 158
calfskin 252
Calgary 16.274
Caliban 245
calibrate 367.24
calibration 261.67.23
calibre 17.14
calico 12.11
Calicut 378
California 17.3.35
californium 242.2
Caligula 17.174
calipee 5
caliph 163.1
caliphate 367
call 221
calla 17.160
Callaghan 245
Callas 310
callboy 11
caller 17.169
calligraphy 16.90
Callimachus 310.14
calling 265.31
calliope 16.254
callipash 349
calliper 17.253
callipygian 261.3.7
callisthenic 38.32
callisthenics 498.3
callosity 16.333.30
callous 310
callousness 300.34
callow 12.38
callowness 300.25
callus 310

calm 230
calmative 485.15
calmness 300
calomel 215
caloric 38.41
calorie 16.274.15
calorific 38.12.1
calorimeter 17.342.2.1
calotte 373.1
calpac 32
calque 47
caltrop 281
calumet 368
calumniate 367.1
calumnious 310.2
calumny 16
Calvados 302
Calvary 16.274
calve 481
Calvin 252
Calvinism 242.35.13
calvities 513.1
calypso 12
calyx 498
cam 229
Cam 229
Camagüey 2
camaraderie 16.274.6
camarilla 17.166.3
camber 17.23
Camberwell 215
cambist 436
cambium 242.2
Cambodia 17.3
cambogia 17.3.15
camboose 309
Cambria 17.3.43
Cambrian 261.3
cambric 38
Cambridge 197
Cambridgeshire 6
Cambyses 513.13
Camden 261
came 231
camel 228.51
cameleer 6
camellia 17.3.20
camelopard 84
Camelopardalis 300.13
Camelopardus 310
Camelot 373
cameo 12.3
camera 17.279
camera lucida 17.83
cameraman 261.52

camera obscura 17.277
Cameroon 260.3
camiknickers 524
camion 261.3
camise 513.8
camisole 223.4
camlet 371
camomile 219
camoodi 16.71
Camorra 17.275
camouflage 359
camp 285
campaign 247.7
campaigner 17.227
Campania 17.3.31
campanile 16.118
campanology
   16.108.4.11
campanula 17.174.9
Campbell 228.17
camper 17.261
campestral 228.81
camphire 8
camphor 17.122
camphorate 367.23
camphoric 38.41
Campinas 310.32
camping 265
campion 261.3
campus 310.41
camshaft 396
can 245
Cana 17.227
Canaan 261
Canaanite 372.6
Canada 17.92
Canadian 261.3.3
Canadianism
   242.35.14.1
canaigre 17.130
canal 212
caniculus 310.25.2
canalize 516.3.5
canapé 16.254
canard 84
canary 16.264
canasta 17.379
canaster 17.390
Canaveral 228.76
Canberra 17.279
cancan 245
cancel 228
cancellation 261.67.12
cancer 17.312
Cancer 17.312

cancerous 310.50
cancroid 97
candela 17.165
candelabrum 242
candid 91.12
candidacy 16.307
candidate 367.8
candidness 300.28.1
candied 91.12
candle 228.39
candlelight 372
Candlemas 310
candlenut 378
candlestick 38
candlewick 38
candlewood 101
candour 17.98
candy 16.77
candyfloss 302
candytuft 400
cane 247
canella 17.163
canescent 420.67.2
canine 253
caning 265.40
canister 17.384
canker 17.43
cankerous 310.50.1
cannabin 252
cannabis 300.3
Cannae 5
canned 128
cannel 228.55
cannelloni 16.233
cannelure 10.4
canner 17.225
cannery 16.274
Cannes 245
cannibal 228.12
cannibalism 242.35.11
cannibalistic 38.70.2
cannibalize 516.3
cannikin 252.3
canning 265
Cannock 46
cannon 261.55
cannonade 85.3
cannonball 221
cannoneer 6.5
cannonry 16.284
cannot 373
cannula 17.174.9
cannulate 367.13
canny 16.223
canoe 15

canoeing 265.5
canon 261.55
canoness 300.26
canonical 228.23.13
canonicals 539.2.1
canonicate 367.5
canonize 516.7
canonry 16.284
canoodle 228.37
Canopus 310.39
canopy 16.254
Canossa 17.304
cans 544
cant 407
can't 408
Cantab. 18
cantabile 16.120
Cantabrigian 261.3.7
cantaloupe 280.1
cantankerous 310.50.1
cantata 17.337
canteen 251
canter 17.365
Canterbury 16.274
cantharides 513.4
canthus 310.72
canticle 228.23
cantilena 17.227
cantilever 17.413
cantillate 367.12
cantina 17.230
cantle 228.109
canto 12.83
canton 254
Canton 254
Cantonese 513.9
cantor 9
cantoris 300.46
cantrip 274
Cantuar. 1
Canute 380
canvas 310
canvass 310
canvasser 17.309
canyon 261.121
canzone 16.233
canzonet 368
caoutchouc 45
cap 268
capability 16.333.9.2
capable 228.16.32
capacious 310.56
capacitance 321.24
capacitate 367.30.2
capacitor 17.342

capacity 16.333.25.1
cap-a-pie 5
caparison 261.65.1
cape 270
capelin 252.11
Capella 17.163
caper 17.249
Capernaum 242.2
Capet 371
Capetian 261.70
capillarity 16.333.20.2
capillary 16.274.16
capital 228.102
capitalism 242.35.11
capitalist 436.7
capitalistic 38.70.2
capitalize 516.3
capitate 367.30
capitation 261.67.27
Capitol 228.102
Capitoline 253.3
capitular 17.174.12
capitulate 367.13
capitulation 261.67.13
capitulum 242.10
capo 12
capon 261.57
Capone 257
caporal 213
capote 376
Cappadocia 17.3
cappuccino 12.54
Capri 5
capriccio 12.3
caprice 298
capricious 310.58
capriciousness 300.34.3
Capricorn 255.2
caprifig 184
caprine 253
capriole 223.1
capsicum 242.4
capsid 91.31
capsize 516
capstan 261
capsule 227
capsulize 516
captain 252.25
captaincy 16.311
caption 261.83
captious 310
captivate 367.36
captivation 261.67
captive 485
captive 485.22

captivity 16.333.35
captor 17.374
capture 17.72
Capua 17.7
capuche 358
capuchin 252
caput 381
capybara 17.268
car 1
carabao 12.1
carabid 91.4
carabineer 6.4
caracal 212
Caracalla 17.160
caracara 17.268
Caracas 310.7
caracole 223
caracul 225
carafe 157
caramba 17.23
caramel 228
caramelize 516.3
carapace 295.4
carat 228
Caratacus 310.14
caravan 245
caravanserai 7.12
caravel 215
caraway 2.28
carbamate 367.16
carbazole 223
carbide 92
carbine 253
carbohydrate 367
carbolic 38.22
carbon 261.8
carbonaceous 310.56
carbonade 85.3
carbonado 12.17
Carbonari 16.261
carbonate 367.18
carbonation 261.67.19
carbonic 38.35
carboniferous 310.50.2.1
carbonize 516.7
carboxylate 367.12
carbuncle 228.30
carbuncular 17.174
carburation 261.67.21
carburettor 17.339
carcass 310.8
Carchemish 353
carcinogen 261.39
carcinogenic 38.32.1.1
carcinoma 17.215

carcinomatosis 300.55.7
card 84
cardamom 242
cardboard 95
cardiac 32.1
cardialgia 17.3.16
Cardiff 163
cardigan 261.32
Cardiganshire 6.8
cardinal 228.60
cardinalate 367.14
cardiogram 229.1.1
cardiograph 158.1.1
cardiography 16.90.2.1
cardiomegaly 16.131.2
carditis 300.62
cardoon 260
cardsharp 269
cardsharper 17.248
care 4
careen 251.7
career 6
careerist 436.17
carefree 5
careful 226
carefulness 300.30
careless 300
carelessness 300.33
caress 296.4
caretaker 17.30
careworn 255
Carey 16.264
carfare 4.2
carfax 494
cargo 12.26
carhop 276
Caria 17.3.38
Carib 24
Caribbean 261.2
Caribbees 513
caribou 15
caricature 10.5
caricaturist 436.19
caries 513.1
CARIFTA 17.359
carillon 261.120
carillonneur 3
Carina 17.230.1
carinate 367.17
Carinthia 17.3.52
carioca 17.38
cariogenic 38.32.1
cariole 223.1
carious 310.2.10
Carl 213

carline 252
Carling 265.26
Carlisle 219
Carlos 302
Carlow 12.39
Carlton 261
Carlyle 219
carman 261
Carmarthen 261
Carmarthenshire 6.8
Carmelite 372.4
carminative 485.15.7
carmine 253
carnage 197
carnal 228
carnassial 228.3
Carnatic 38.49
carnation 261.67.17
carnelian 261.3.10
carnet 2.14
Carniola 17.171
carnival 228.120
carnivore 9.13
carnivorous 310.50.3
Carnot 12.51
carob 31
carol 228.72
Carol 228.72
Carolina 17.232
Caroline 253.3
Carolingian 261.3
carolus 310.26
carom 242
carotene 251.11
carotenoid 97.8
carotid 91.40
carousal 228.129
carouse 521
carousel 215.2
carouser 17.443
carp 269
carpal 228
Carpathian 261.3
carpel 228
Carpentaria 17.3.38
carpenter 17.369
carpentry 16.289
carpet 371
carpetbag 178.1
carpetbagger 17.123
carpeting 265.66
carpophagous 310
carport 374
carpus 310
carrack 46

carrageen 251
Carrara 17.268
carrefour 9.6
carrel 228.72
carriage 197.9
carriageway 2.29
carrier 17.3
carrion 261.3.20
carrot 381
carroty 16.344
carry 16.260
carryall 221
carrycot 373
carse 294
carsick 38
Carson 261.61
cart 366
cartage 197
carte blanche 78
cartel 215
Carter 17.337
Cartesian 261.3.34
cartful 226
Carthage 197
Carthaginian 261.3.17
carthorse 303
Carthusian 261.3
cartilage 197.1
cartilaginous 310.33
cartload 98
cartography 16.90.2
cartomancy 16.309
carton 261.95
cartoon 260
cartoonist 436.12
cartouche 358
cartridge 197
cartulary 16.274.18
cartwheel 217
Cartwright 372
carve 481
carven 261.110
carver 17.409
carvery 16.274
carving 265
caryatid 91.32
caryopsis 300.61
carzey 16.392
casaba 17.10
Casablanca 17.43
Casanova 17.417
cascade 85
cascara 17.268
cascarilla 17.166.3
case 295

casease 509.1
caseate 367.1.4
caseation 261.67.1.3
casebound 139
casefy 7.3
casein 252
casement 420.44
caseous 310.2
casern 249
casework 36
cash 349
cashew 15
cashier 6
cashmere 6
casing 265.59
casino 12.54
cask 56
casket 371
Caspar 17.265
Caspian 261.3
casque 55
cassareep 273
cassata 17.337
cassation 261.67
cassava 17.409
casserole 223.3
cassette 368
cassia 17.3.46
cassimere 6.2
Cassiodorus 310.48
Cassiopeia 17.2.1
cassis 298
cassock 46
cassoulet 2
cassowary 16.264
cast 431
castanets 336
castaway 2.28
caste 431
castellan 261.41
castellated 91.34.5
caster 17.380
castigate 367.10
castigation 261.67.10
Castile 217
Castilian 261.3.11
casting 265.74
castle 228.83
Castlereagh 2
castor 17.380
castrate 367
castration 261.67
castrato 12.73
Castro 12
casual 228.9

casualty 16.352
casuarina 17.232
casuist 436
casuistic 38.70
casuistry 16.293
cat 365
catabasis 300.57
catabolic 38.22
catabolism 242.35.11
catachresis 300.51
cataclysm 242.35
cataclysmic 38
catacomb 241
catadromous 310.29
catafalque 47
Catalan 245
catalepsy 16.313
catalogue 185
Catalonia 17.3.36.2
catalyse 516.3
catalysis 300.52.1
catalyst 436.7.6
catalytic 38.52.1
catamaran 245.5
catamenia 17.3.33
catamite 372
catamount 418.1
cataphoresis 300.51.1
catapult 406
cataract 382
catarrhal 228
catastrophe 16.90
catastrophic 38.13
catastrophism 242.35
catatonia 17.3.36
Catawba 17.17
catcall 221
catch 62
catcher 17.50
catching 265
catchment 420.36
catchpenny 16.226
catchpole 223
catchweight 367
catchword 87
catchy 16.46
catechetical 228.23.19
catechin 252.4
catechism 242.35
catechize 516
catecholamine 251.4
catechumen 248.3
categoric 38.41
categorical 228.23.17
categorize 516.8

centenarian 261.3.21.1
centenary 16.274.25
centennial 228.3
centesimal 228.52.1
centesimo 12.48
centigrade 85.5
centigram 229
centilitre 17.341
centillion 261.120
centime 234
centimetre 17.341
centipede 89.1
centipoise 519
cento 12.84
central 228.80
centralism 242.35.11
centrality 16.333.8
centralization 261.67.36
centralize 516.3
centre 17.368
centreboard 95.1
centrefold 120
centrepiece 298.2
centric 38.47
centrifugal 228.48
centrifuge 204
centripetal 228.101
centrist 436
centrobaric 38.38
centrosome 239
centrosphere 6.1
centuplicate 367.5.1
centuplicate 371.9.1
centurion 261.3.24
century 16.274
cep 271
cephalad 83
cephalalgia 17.3.16
cephalic 38.19
Cephalonia 17.3.36.2
cephalopod 94.1
ceraceous 310.56
ceramic 38.24
ceramics 498.2
cerastes 513.18
cerate 371.32
ceratodus 310.17
Cerberus 310.50
cercaria 17.3.38
cercopithecoid 97.3
cercus 310.9
cereal 228.3.11
cerebellum 242.8
cerebral 228
cerebrate 367.24

cerebration 261.67.23
cerebrospinal 228.61
cerebrum 242
cerecloth 459
cerement 420.30
ceremonial 228.3.8
ceremonious 310.2.9.1
ceremony 16.237
Ceres 513.11
ceresin 252.21
cereus 310.2.11
ceria 17.3.39
cerise 513.12
cerium 242.2.15
cerography 16.90.2
ceroplastic 38.68
ceroplastics 498.15
cert 369
certain 261.97
certainly 16.174
certainty 16.360
certifiable 228.16.3.1
certificate 367.5
certificate 371.9
certified 92.1
certify 7.3
certiorari 17
certitude 102.2
cerulean 261.3
cerumen 248.3
ceruse 309
Cervantes 513
cervelat 365
cervical 228.23
cervid 91.55
cervine 253
cervix 498
cess 296
cessation 261.67
cession 261.68
cessionary 16.274.29.2
cesspool 227
cestode 98
cestoid 97
cetacean 261.67.27
ceteris paribus 308
Cetus 310.63
Ceylon 254.6
chablis 16.132
cha-cha 1
chacma 17.219
chaconne 254
Chad 83
Chadic 38.7
chaeta 17.341

chaetognath 452
chaetopod 94.1
chafe 159
chafer 17.111
chaff 158
chaffer 17.110
chaffinch 80
chagrin 252
chain 247
chair 4
chairborne 255
chairman 261.46
chaise 509
chaise longue 266
chalaza 17.439
chalcedony 16.237
Chalcidice 16.300
Chalcis 300.58
Chaldee 5
chalet 2
chalice 300
chalicothere 6.10
chalk 41
chalkboard 95
chalkpit 371
chalky 16.28
challah 17.161
challenge 209
challenger 17.157
challis 16.112
chalybeate 371.1
chamber 17
chamberlain 252.11
chambermaid 85
chambray 2
chameleon 261.3.10
chameleonic 38.35.1
chamfer 17.122
chamois 16.210
Chamonix 16.237
champ 285
champagne 247.7
champers 524
champerty 16.344
champion 261.3
championship 274.2
Champs Élysées 2.30
chance 315
chancel 228
chancellery 16.274.19
chancellor 17.176
chancellorship 274.1
chancery 16.274
chancre 17.43
chancroid 97

chelicerate 367.23
Chelmsford 103
chelonian 261.3.18
chelp 283
Chelsea 16
Cheltenham 242.16
chemical 228.23
chemin de fer 4.3
chemise 513.8
chemisette 368
chemisorb 27
chemisorption 261.87
chemist 436
chemistry 16.293
chemostat 365
chemotherapy 16.254
chempaduk 43
Chenab 18
chenille 217.1
cheongsam 229
Cheops 329
cheque 35
chequebook 44
chequer 17.31
chequerboard 95.1
chequered 103
chequers 524
Cherbourg 187
cherish 353
chernozem 232
Cherokee 5
cheroot 380
cherry 16.262
chersonese 298.1
Chertsey 16.316
cherub 31
cherubic 38.4
cherubim 235
Cherubini 16.228
chervil 218
chervonets 336
Chesapeake 37
Cheshire 6
chess 296
chessboard 95
chessman 261.53
chest 433
Chester 17.382
chesterfield 115.1
Chesterfield 115.1
Chesterton 261
chestnut 378
chesty 16.364
Chetnik 38
cheval-de-frise 513

chevet 2
Cheviot 381.1
chevron 261
chevrotain 247.10
chevy 16.380
chew 15
chewy 16.4
Cheyenne 245
chiack 32
Chiang Kai-shek 35
chianti 16.353
chiaroscuro 12.66
chiasma 17.223
chic 37
Chicago 12.26
chicalote 2.24
chicane 247.1
chicanery 16.274
Chichester 17.384
chichi 5
chick 38
chickabiddy 16.63
chickadee 5.4
Chickasaw 9.11
chicken 252.3
chicken-hearted 91.33
chickenpox 499
chickpea 5
chickweed 89.6
chicle 228.23
chico 12.10
chicory 16.274.4
chide 92
chief 162
chiefly 16.158
chieftain 261
chiffchaff 157
chiffon 254
chiffonier 6.5
chigger 17.129
chignon 254.12
chigoe 12.29
chihuahua 1
chilblain 247
child 117
childbed 86
childbirth 456
childhood 101
childish 353
childishness 300.35
childless 300
childlessness 300.33
childlike 39
children 261
Chile 16.120

chiliad 83.1
chiliasm 242.34
chill 218
chilli 16.120
chilli con carne 16.224
Chillon 254.6
chilly 16.120
chilopod 94.1
Chiltern 261
chime 236
chimera 17.272
chimerical 228.23.15
chimney 16
chimneypiece 298
chimneypot 373
chimp 287
chimpanzee 5
chin 252
china 17.232
China 17.232
chinaberry 16.274
Chinagraph 158.1
Chinaman 261.52
Chinatown 258
chinaware 4.8
chincherinchee 5
chinchilla 17.166
Chindit 371
chine 253
chiné 2
Chinee 5.13
Chinese 513
Ching 265
chink 52
chinless 300
chino 12.54
chinoiserie 5.17
Chinook 45
Chinookan 261.15
chintz 348
chinwag 178
chionodoxa 17.428
Chios 302
chip 274
chipboard 95
chipmunk 54
chipolata 17.337.1
Chippendale 214
chipper 17.253
chipping 265
chippy 16.248
chiromancy 16.309
Chiron 254
chiropodist 436.3
chiropody 16.72

churchwoman 261.50
churchyard 84
churidars 508
churinga 17.141
churl 216
churlish 353
churn 249
churning 265.41
chute 380
chutney 16
Chuvash 350
chyle 219
chyme 236
ciao 13
ciborium 242.2.17
cicada 17.78
cicatrix 498
cicatrize 516
cicely 16.131
Cicero 12
cicerone 16.233
Ciceronian 261.3.18
cichlid 91
cider 17.84
cig 184
cigar 1.4
cigarette 368.6
cigarillo 12.42
ciggy 16.93
cilia 17.3.21
ciliary 16.274.1.1
cilice 300.8
cilium 242.2.6
cimbalom 242.11
cimex 496
Cimmerian 261.3.22
Cimon 261
cinch 80
cinchona 17.236
cinchonize 516.7
Cincinnati 16.327
cincture 17.67
cinder 17.102
Cinderella 17.163
cine 16.229
cineaste 430.1
cinema 17.211
cinematic 38.49.1
cinematograph 158.1
cinematography
 16.90.2.6
Cinerama 17.206
cineraria 17.3.38
cinerarium 242.2.14
cinereous 310.2.11

Cinna 17.231
cinnabar 1.2
cinnamon 261.52
cinquain 247
cinquefoil 222
Cinzano 12.51
cipher 17.115
circa 17.32
circadian 261.3.3
Circassia 17.3.46
Circassian 261.3
Circe 16.298
Circinus 310.33
circle 228.22
circlet 371
circuit 371.8
circuitous 310.64
circuitry 16.285
circular 17.174.5
circularize 516.8.1
circulate 367.13
circulation 261.67.13
circulatory 16.274.40.2
circumambulate 367.13
circumbendibus 310.5
circumcise 516
circumcision 261.91
circumference 321.20
circumflex 496
circumlocution 261.75.2
circumlocutory
 16.274.42
circumlunar 17.238
circumnavigable
 228.16.19
circumnavigate 367.10
circumnavigation
 261.67.10
circumscissile 219.2
circumscribe 25
circumscription 261.85
circumspect 385
circumspective 485.17
circumstance 321
circumstantial 228.95
circumstantiate 367.1.8
circumvallate 367
circumvent 410
circumvention 261.82
circumvolution 261.75.1
circus 310.9
ciré 2
Cirencester 17.382
cirque 36
cirrate 367.21

cirrhosis 300.55.5
cirrhotic 38.53
cirripede 89.1
cirrocumulus 310.25.5
cirrostratus 310.62
cirrus 310.46
cisalpine 253
cisco 12.15
cislunar 17.238
cist 436
Cistercian 261.69
cistern 261.107
cisterna 17.229
citadel 228.38
citation 261.67
cite 372
cithara 17.279
citified 92.1
citify 7.3
citizen 261.126
citizenry 16.284
citizenship 274.2
Citlaltépetl 228.100
citral 228.79
citrate 367.27
citreous 310.2
citric 38
citron 261
citronella 17.163
citronellal 212
citrulline 251.3
citrus 310
cittern 249.1
city 16.333
civet 371
civic 38.74
civics 498
civil 228.120
civilian 261.120
civility 16.333.9
civilization 261.67.36
civilize 516.2
civilized 154
civvies 515
civvy 16.382
clack 32
Clackmannan 261.55
Clacton 261
clad 83
cladding 265
claim 231
claimant 420.29
clair-obscure 10
clairvoyance 321
clairvoyant 420.3

clam 229
clamant 420.29
clambake 34
clamber 17.23
clammy 16.210
clamorous 310.50
clamour 17.205
clamp 285
clan 245
clandestine 252.26
clang 263
clanger 17.245
clangour 17.140
clank 51
clannish 353
clansman 261
clap 268
Clapham 242
clapper 17.247
clapperboard 95.1
Clapton 261
claptrap 268
claque 32
clarabella 17.163.1
Clare 4
Clarence 321
Clarendon 261
claret 381
clarify 7.3.4
clarinet 368
clarinetist 436.23
clarion 261.3.20
clarity 16.333.20
Clark 33
clarkia 17.3
claro 12.61
clarts 334
clash 349
clasp 290
class 294
classic 38.48
classical 228.23
classicalism 242.35.11
classicism 242.35.16
classicist 436.21
classics 498
classifiable 228.16.3.1
classification 261.67.5.1
classified 92.1
classify 7.3.6
classis 300.49
classless 300
classlessness 300.33
classmate 367
classroom 241

classy 16.295
clastic 38.68
clatter 17.336
claudication 261.67.5
Claudius 310.2
clause 518
claustrophobia 17.3.4
claustrophobic 38.3
claver 17.410
clavichord 95.2
clavicle 228.23
clavicorn 255.2
clavier 17.3
claw 9
clay 2
claymore 9
claypan 245
claytonia 17.3.36
clean 251
cleaner 17.230
cleaning 265.42
cleanliness 300.23
cleanly 16.171
cleanly 16.172
cleanness 300
cleanse 546
cleanser 17.446
clean-shaven 261.111
clear 6
clearance 321.17
clearcole 223
clear-headedness 300.28
clearing 265.53
clearness 300
clear-sighted 91.39
clearway 2
cleat 370
cleavage 197
cleave 484
cleaver 17.413
cleck 35
Cleethorpes 330
clef 160
cleft 397
cleg 181
clematis 300
clemency 16.312
clement 420
clementine 251
clench 79
Cleo 12.2
cleome Dahomey 16.219
Cleopatra 17.291
clerestory 16.269
clergy 16.102

clergyman 261.48
cleric 38.39
clerical 228.23.15
clericalism 242.35.11
clericals 539.2
clerihew 15
clerk 33
clerkly 16.140
cleveite 372
Cleveland 143
clever 17.411
cleverness 300.26
clevis 300.69
clew 15
cliché 2
cliché'd 85
Clichy 5
click 38
clicker 17.34
client 420.2
clientele 215
cliff 163
cliffhanger 17.245
climacteric 38.44
climactic 38.58
climate 371
climatic 38.49
climatology
  16.108.4.15.1
climax 494
climb 236
climber 17.212
clime 236
clinch 80
clincher 17.71
cline 253
cling 265
clinger 17.246
clinic 38.34
clinical 228.23.12
clinician 261.71.5
clink 52
clinker 17.44
clinometer 17.342.3
clip 274
clipboard 95
clip-clop 276
clipper 17.253
clippers 524
clippie 16.248
clipping 265
clique 37
cliquey 16.24
clishmaclaver 17.410
clitellum 242.8

clitic 38.52
clitoris 300.47
Clive 486
cloaca 17.30
cloak 42
cloakroom 241
clobber 17.16
cloche 354
clock 40
clockmaker 17.30
clockwise 516
clockwork 36
clod 94
clodhopper 17.255
clog 185
cloisonné 2
cloister 17.386
cloistered 103
cloistral 228
clomp 288
clone 257
clonic 38.35
clonk 53
clonus 310.35
close 305
close 520
closed 155
close-grained 130
close-hauled 118
close-knit 371
closely 16.182
closeness 300
closer 17.442
close-stool 227
closet 371.39
close-up 279
closing 265.83
clostridium 242.2.3
closure 17.335
clot 373
cloth 459
clothbound 139
clothe 478
clotheshorse 303
clothesline 253
clothier 17.3
clothing 265
cloture 17.59
cloud 99
cloudberry 16.274
cloudburst 434
cloudless 300
cloudlet 371
cloudscape 270
cloudy 16.68

Clough 168
clout 377
clove 488
cloven 261.116
clover 17.417
cloverleaf 162
Clovis 300
clown 258
clownery 16.274
clownish 353
cloy 11
club 29
clubby 16.13
club-footed 91
clubhouse 306
clubland 143
cluck 43
clucky 16.30
clue 15
clueless 300.12
clumber 17.27
clump 289
clumsiness 300.23
clumsy 16
clung 267
clunk 54
Cluny 16.236
clupeid 91.2
cluster 17.388
clutch 72
clutches 515
clutter 17.349
Clwyd 91.3
Clyde 92
Clydebank 51
Clydesdale 214
clypeus 310.2
clyster 17.384
Cnidus 310.16
coach 70
coaching 265
coachman 261
coachwork 36
coadjutant 420.78
coadjutor 17.350
coagulant 420.27
coagulate 367.13
coagulate 371.17
coagulation 261.67.13
coagulative 485.15.5
coal 223
coaler 17.171
coalesce 296.1
coalface 295
coalfield 115

coalition 261.71.3
coalman 261
Coalport 374
coaming 265.37
coarse 303
coarsen 261
coarseness 300
coast 441
coastal 228
coaster 17.387
coastguard 84
coastline 253
coat 376
coated 91.41
coatee 5
coati 16.328
coating 265
coax 494
coax 501
coaxer 17.429
coaxial 228.3.18
cob 26
cobalt 404
cobber 17.16
Cobbett 371
cobble 228
cobbler 17.178
cobblers 524
cobbles 539.1
cobblestone 257
cobia 17.3.4
cobnut 378
COBOL 220
cobra 17
Coburg 182
cobweb 21
cobwebbed 104
coca 17.38
Coca-Cola 17.171
cocaine 247.2
cocainism 242.35
cocci 7
coccus 310.11
coccyx 498
cochineal 217
cochlea 17.3
cochleate 367.1
cock 40
cockade 85
cock-a-doodle-doo 15
Cockaigne 247
cock-a-leekie 16.24
cockalorum 242.20
cockatiel 217
cockatoo 15

cockatrice 300
cockchafer 17.111
cocker 17.36
cockerel 228.76
cockeye 7
cockeyed 92
cockfight 372
cockhorse 303
cockiness 300.23
cockle 228.25
cocklebur 3
cockleshell 215
cockloft 399
cockney 16.239
cockneyfy 7.3
cockneyism 242.35.2
cockpit 371
cockroach 70
cockscomb 239
cocksfoot 379
cockshy 7
cockspur 3
cocksure 10
cocktail 214
cockup 279
cocky 16.27
cocoa 12.12
coco de mer 4.4
coconut 378
cocoon 260
cocotte 373
cod 94
coda 17.88
coddle 228.34
coddler 17.188
code 98
codeine 251
coder 17.88
codex 496
codfish 353
codger 17.152
codicil 218
codicology 16.108.4.4
codify 7.3
codling 265
codpiece 298
co-driver 17.415
codswallop 281.2
Cody 16.67
co-ed 86
coedit 371.12
coeducation 261.67
coeducational 228.63.3
coefficient 420.74
coelacanth 467

coelenterate 367.23
coeliac 32.1
coelom 242
coenobite 372
coenurus 310.49
coenzyme 236
coerce 297
coercible 228.16.38
coercion 261.69
coercive 485.3
coeternity 16.333.16.1
Coeur de Lion 261.2
coeval 228.119
coexist 436
coexistence 321.27
coexistent 420.81
coextend 131
coextensive 485.9
coffee 16.86
coffeepot 373
coffer 17.116
cofferdam 229
coffin 252
coffle 228
cog 185
cogent 420
cogitate 367.30
cogitative 485.15.12
Cognac 32
cognate 367
cognition 261.71
cognitive 485.12
cognizance 321
cognizant 420
cognize 516
cognomen 248
cognoscenti 16.355
cogwheel 217
cohabit 371.4
cohabitation 261.67.27
cohere 6
coherence 321.17
coherent 420.62
cohesion 261.90
cohesive 485
coho 12
cohort 374
cohosh 354
cohune 260
coiffeur 3
coil 222
coin 256
coincide 92.9
coincidence 321.5
coincident 420.10

coincidental 228.110.1
coin-op 276
coinsurance 321.19
coinsure 10.2
Cointreau 12
coir 17.5
coit 375
coition 261.71
coitus 310.64
coke 42
col 220
cola 17.171
colander 17.109
colcannon 261.55
Colchester 17.384
colchicine 251.8
colchicum 242.4
Colchis 300
colcothar 1
cold 120
cold-blooded 91.11
cold-bloodedness 300.28
cold-hearted 91.33
coldness 300
Cole 223
coleorhiza 17.441.1
Coleridge 197
coleslaw 9
Colette 368
coleus 310.2
coley 16.126
colic 38.22
colicweed 89.6
colitis 300.62
collaborate 367.23
collaboration 261.67.22.1
collaborator 17.338.9
collage 359
collagen 261.39
collapsar 1
collapse 322
collapsible 228.16
collar 17.168
collarbone 257
collarette 368.6
collate 367.14
collateral 228.76
collation 261.67
collative 485.10
collator 17.338
colleague 183
collect 385
collect 385.5
collectanea 17.3.31

commensurate 371.35
comment 410
commentary 16.274.48
commentate 367.32
commentator 17.338
commerce 297
commercial 228.92
commercialism 242.35.11
commercialistic 38.70.2
commerciality 16.333.8.1
commercialize 516.3
commère 4
commingle 228.50
comminute 380
commis 300
commiserate 367.23
commiseration 261.67.22
commissar 1
commissariat 381.1
commissary 16.274.36
commission 261.71.4
commissionaire 4.5
commissioner 17.239.2
commissure 10
commit 371.21
commitment 420.49
committal 228.102
committee 16.333
committeeman 261.48
commode 98.1
commodious 310.2.2
commodity 16.333.6
commodore 9.4
common 261
commonality 16.333.8.7
commonalty 16.352
commoner 17.239
commonly 16.174
commonness 300.31
commonplace 295
commonweal 217
Commonwealth 465
commotion 261.73.1
communal 228
communalize 516.3
communard 84
commune 260
communicable 228.16.10
communicant 420.7
communicate 367.5
communication 261.67.5
communicative 485.15.1

communion 261.123
communiqué 2.7
communism 242.35
communist 436
communistic 38.70
community 16.333.18
commutable 228.16.53
commutate 367
commutation 261.67.29
commutative 485.15.14
commutator 17.338
commute 380
commuter 17.351
Comnenus 310.32
Como 12.49
comp 288
compact 382
compactly 16.194
companion 261.121
companionable 228.16.31
companionate 371.28
companionship 274.2
companionway 2
company 16.237
comparable 228.16.35
comparative 485.15.8
comparatively 16.206
comparator 17.352
compare 4
comparison 261.65.1
compartment 420
compartmental 228.110
compartmentalize 516.3
compass 310.42
compassion 261.66
compassionate 371.28
compatibility 16.333.9.2
compatible 228.16
compatriot 381.1
compeer 6
compel 215
compelling 265.28
compendious 310.2
compendium 242.2
compensate 367.29
compensation 261.67.26
compensatory 16.274.40
compere 4
compete 370
competence 321.24
competent 420.76
competition 261.71.7
competitive 485.12
competitor 17.342

compilation 261.67.12
compile 219
compiler 17.167
complacency 16.312
complacent 420
complain 247
complainant 420
complaint 409
complaisance 321
complaisant 420
complement 410.1
complement 420.31
complementary 16.274.47
complete 370
completeness 300.37
completion 261.70
complex 496
complexion 261.77
complexity 16.333
compliance 321.2
compliant 420.2
complicate 367.5
complicated 91.34.3
complication 261.67.5
complicity 16.333.28
compliment 410.1
compliment 420.31
complimentary 16.274.47
comply 7
component 420.54
comport 374
comportment 420
compose 520
composed 155
composer 17.442
composite 371.40
composition 261.71.9
compositor 17.342.5
compost 438
composure 17.335
compote 376
compound 139
comprador 9.4
comprehend 131.1
comprehensible 228.16.40
comprehension 261.82.1
comprehensive 485.9
compress 296
compression 261.68
compressive 485.2
compressor 17.300
comprise 516

compromise 516.5
Comptometer 17.342.3
compulsion 261
compulsive 485
compulsory 16.274
compunction 261.80
computation 261.67.29
compute 380
computer 17.351
computerize 516.8
comrade 85
comradeship 274
comsat 365
comstockery 16.274.5
Comus 310
con 254
con amore 16.269
conation 261.67.19
conative 485.15
conatus 310.62
con brio 12.2
concatenation 261.67.18
concave 482
concavity 16.333.33
conceal 217
concealment 420
concede 89.5
conceit 370
conceited 91.37
conceivable 228.16.61
conceive 484
concelebrate 367.24
concentrate 367
concentration 261.67
concentrative 485.10
concentre 17.368
concentric 38.47
concentricity 16.333.28
concept 422
conceptacle 228.28
conception 261.84
conceptual 228.9
conceptualism
 242.35.11.3
conceptualize 516.3.3
concern 249
concerned 132
concernedly 16.148
concerning 265.41
concert 369
concertante 16.353
concerted 91.36
concertgoer 17.6
concertina 17.230
concerto 12

concession 261.68
concessionaire 4.5
concessionary
 16.274.29.2
concessive 485.2
conch 53
conchology 16.108.4
concierge 361
conciliar 17.3.21
conciliate 367.1.2
conciliation 261.67.1.1
conciliatory 16.274.43.1
concise 301
concision 261.91
conclave 482
conclude 102
conclusion 261.93
conclusive 485.8
concoct 388
concoction 261
concomitance 321.24
concomitant 420.76
concord 95
concordance 321
concordant 420.11
concordat 365
Concorde 95
concourse 303
concrete 370
concretion 261.70
concretize 516.12
concubinage 197.7
concubine 253
concupiscence 321.22
concur 3
concurrence 321
concurrent 420.64
concuss 307
concussion 261.74
condemn 232
condemnation 261.67
condemnatory 16.274.40
condensate 367.29
condensation 261.67.26
condense 316
condenser 17.314
condescend 131
condescendence 321.7
condescending 265.20
condescension 261.82.2
condign 253
condiment 420.31
condition 261.71
conditional 228.63.5
conditioned 143.5

conditioner 17.239.2
conditioning 265.46
condole 223.2
condolence 321
condom 242
condominium 242.2.11
condonation 261.67.19
condone 257
condor 9
condottiere 16.264
conduce 309
conducive 485.8
conduct 389
conductance 321
conduction 261.79
conductive 485.19
conductivity 16.333.35.3
conductor 17.357
conductress 300
conduit 371
condyle 218
cone 257
confab 18
confabulate 367.13.1
confabulation
 261.67.13.1
confection 261.77
confectioner 17.239
confectionery
 16.274.29.4
confederacy 16.307.4
confederate 367.23
confederate 371.35
confederation 261.67.22
confer 3
conferee 5
conference 321.20
conferrer 17.270
conferva 17.412
confess 296
confessant 420.67
confessedly 16.148
confession 261.68
confessional 228.63.4
confessor 17.300
confetti 16.330
confidant 407
confide 92
confidence 321.5
confident 420.10
confidential 228.96.1
confidentiality
 16.333.8.1.1
confiding 265.14
configuration 261.67.21

confine 253
confinement 420
confirm 233
confirmand 128
confirmation 261.67.16
confiscate 367
Confiteor 9.1
confiture 10
conflagration 261.67
conflate 367
conflict 387
conflictive 485.18
confluence 321.3
confluent 420.4
conflux 502
conform 238
conformable 228.16
conformation 261.67
conformist 436
conformity 16.333.13
confound 139
confounded 91.14
confraternity 16.333.16
confrère 4
confront 419
confrontation 261.67
Confucian 261.75
Confucianism 242.35.14
Confucius 310
con fuoco 12.12
confuse 523
confusedly 16.148
confusing 265.84
confusion 261.93
confute 380
conga 17.142
congé 2
congeal 217
congelation 261.67.12
congener 17.230
congenial 228.3.6
congeniality 16.333.8.1
congenital 228.102
conger 17.142
congeries 513.11
congest 433
congestion 261.18
congestive 485.24
conglobate 367.3
conglomerate 367.23
conglomerate 371.35
conglomeration 261.67.22
Congo 12
congrats 333

congratulate 367.13
congratulations 551.1
congratulatory 16.274.40.2
congregant 420.17
congregate 367.10
congregate 371.14
congregation 261.67.10
congregational 228.63.3
Congregationalism 242.35.11.5.2
Congregationalist 436.7.5
congress 296
congressional 228.63.4
Congressman 261.53
Congreve 484
congruence 321.3
congruent 420.4
congruity 16.333.3
congruous 310.4
conic 38.35
conical 228.23.13
conidium 242.2.3
conifer 17.114
coniferous 310.50.2.1
Coniston 261.107
conium 242.2.12
conjectural 228.76.1
conjecture 17.64
conjoin 256
conjoint 416
conjugal 228
conjugate 367
conjugate 371
conjugation 261.67
conjunct 393
conjunction 261.80
conjunctiva 17.415
conjunctive 485
conjunctivitis 300.62.6
conjuncture 17.68
conjuration 261.67.21
conjure 10
conjure 17.159
conjurer 17.279
conjuring 265.58
conk 53
conker 17.45
conkers 524
con moto 12.79
Connacht 381
connate 367
Connaught 374
connect 385

Connecticut 381
connection 261.77
connective 485.17
connector 17.354
Connemara 17.268
conniption 261.85
connivance 321
connive 486
connivent 420
connoisseur 3
Connors 524
connotation 261.67.28
connote 376
connubial 228.3
conquer 17.45
conqueror 17.279
conquest 433
conquistador 9.4
Conrad 83
consanguinity 16.333.17
conscience 321
conscientious 310.61
conscientiousness 300.34.4
conscionable 228.16.31
conscious 310
consciousness 300.34
conscript 424
conscription 261.85
consecrate 367.25
consecration 261.67
consecutive 485
consensual 228.9
consensus 310.55
consent 410
consentient 420
consequence 321
consequent 420.58
consequential 228.96
consequently 16.198
conservancy 16.312
conservation 261.67
conservationist 436.13.4
conservatism 242.35.20
conservative 485.15
conservatoire 1.17
conservator 17.338
conservatory 16.274.43
conserve 483
Consett 371
consider 17.83
considerable 228.16.35
considerate 371.35
consideration 261.67.22
considering 265.58

copyright 372
copywriter 17.343
coquelicot 12.11
coquet 368
coquetry 16.285
coquette 368
coquito 12.76
Cora 17.276
coracle 228.28
coral 228.73
coralline 253.3
corallite 372.4
coralloid 97.6
coralroot 380
cor anglais 2
corban 261
corbel 228
corbicula 17.174.6
cor blimey 16.217
cord 95
cordate 367
corded 91.9
Cordeliers 514
cordial 228.3.2
cordiality 16.333.8.1
cordillera 17.271
Cordilleras 524
cordite 372
cordless 300
cordoba 17.21
cordon 261.27
cordovan 261
cords 528
corduroy 11
corduroys 519
core 9
coreopsis 300.61
corer 17.276
co-respondent 420.15
corf 166
Corfam 229
Corfu 15
corgi 16.95
coriaceous 310.56
coriander 17.98.1
Corinth 470
Corinthian 261.3.28
Coriolanus 310.31
corium 242.2.17
cork 41
Cork 41
corkage 197
corkboard 95
corker 17.37
corking 265.9

corkscrew 15
corm 238
cormorant 420.65
corn 255
corncob 26
corncockle 228.25
corncrake 34
cornea 17.3.35
corneal 228.2
corned 137
corner 17.234
cornerstone 257
cornet 371.26
cornetist 436.23
cornfield 115
cornflour 14
cornflower 14
cornhusk 60
cornice 300.24
corniculate 367.13.2
Cornish 353
cornstarch 63
cornucopia 17.3.37
Cornwall 221
Cornwallis 300.9
corny 16.232
corolla 17.168
corollaceous 310.56.3
corollary 16.274
corona 17.236
Corona Australis 300.7
Corona Borealis 300.7
coronach 46
coronagraph 158.1.2
coronal 228.62
coronal 228.63
coronary 16.274.29
coronation 261.67.19
coroner 17.239
coronet 371.28
coroneted 91.35
corpora 17.279
corporal 228.76
corporate 371.35
corporation 261.67.22
corporative 485.15.10
corporeal 228.3.12
corporeity 16.333.1
corps 9
corpse 330
corpulence 321
corpulent 420.27
corpus 310.38
Corpus Christi 16.366
corpuscle 228.87

corpuscular 17.174.8
corpus delicti 7
corpus luteum 242.2
corpus striatum 242.27
corpus vile 16.121
corral 213
correct 385.6
correction 261.77.4
correctitude 102.2
corrective 485.17
correctly 16.195
correctness 300.41
Corregidor 9.3
correlate 367.12
correlation 261.67.12
correlative 485.15.4
correspond 136
correspondence 321
correspondent 420.15
corresponding 265
corridor 9.3
corrie 16.268
corrigendum 242.7
corrigible 228.16.20
corroborant 420.65
corroborate 367.23
corroborative 485.15.10
corroboree 16.274.3
corrode 98
corrosion 261.92
corrosive 485.6
corrugate 367
corrugator 17.338.4
corrupt 426.1
corruptible 228.16
corruption 261.88
corsac 32
corsage 359
corsair 4
corselet 371
corset 371
corsetier 6
corsetry 16.285
Corsica 17.34
Corsican 261.13
cortège 360
Cortes 510
cortex 496
corticate 371.9
corticosteroid 97.10
cortisol 220
cortisone 257
corundum 242
Corunna 17.237
coruscate 367

coruscation 261.67
corvée 2
corvette 368
corvine 253
corydalis 300.13
coryphaeus 310.1
coryphée 2
coryza 17.441.1
cos 302
cos 517
cosecant 420.6
cosh 354
cosher 17.327
cosignatory 16.274.43
cosine 253
cosiness 300.23
cosmetic 38.50
cosmetician 261.71.7
cosmic 38
cosmodrome 239
cosmogony 16.237.4
cosmography 16.90.2
cosmology 16.108.4
cosmonaut 374
cosmopolis 300.13.2
cosmopolitan 261.99
cosmos 302
COSPAR 1
Cossack 32
cosset 371
cost 438
costa 17.385
Costa Brava 17.409
costal 228.115
Costa Rica 17.33
costate 367.34
costermonger 17.143
costing 265
costive 485
costly 16
costume 241
costumier 17.3
cosy 16.399
cot 373
cotangent 420.22
cote 376
cotenant 420.52
coterie 16.274
cotillion 261.120
cotinga 17.141
cotoneaster 17.379
Cotswold 120
cottage 197
cottager 17.150
cotter 17.344

cottier 17.3
cotton 261.101
cottonade 85.3
cottonseed 89.5
cottontail 214
cottonweed 89
cottony 16.237.7
cotyledon 261.23
cotyloid 97.5
couch 71
couchant 420
couchette 368
cougar 17.136
cough 165
could 101
couldn't 420.12
coulee 2
coulisse 298
couloir 1
coulomb 237
coulometer 17.342.3
coulter 17.364
coumarin 252.20
coumarone 257.1
council 228
councillor 17.176
councillorship 274.1
counsel 228
counsellor 17.176
count 418
countdown 258
countenance 321.14
counter 17.372
counteract 382
counterattack 32.4
counterbalance 321.10
counterblast 431
counterchange 207
countercharge 192
counterclaim 231
counterclockwise 516
counterculture 17.69
counterespionage 359
counterfeit 371
counterfeiter 17.342
counterfoil 222.1
counterglow 12.46
counterinsurgency
   16.312.3
counterintelligence
   321.9
counterirritant 420.76
countermand 129
countermarch 63
countermeasure 17.333

countermove 490
counteroffensive 485.9
counterpane 247
counterpart 366.1
counterplot 373
counterpoint 416.1
counterpoise 519
counterproductive
   485.19
counterproposal 228.127
counter-revolution
   261.75.1
counterscarp 269
countersign 253.8
countersink 52
counterspy 7
countertenor 17.228
countertype 275.1
countervail 214
counterweigh 2.28
counterweight 367.38
counterwork 36
countess 300
countless 300
countrified 92.1
countrify 7.3
country 16.290
countryman 261.48
countryside 92.7
county 16.359
coup 15
coup d'état 1
coupe 280
coupé 2
couple 228
couplet 371
coupling 265
coupon 254
courage 197.10
courageous 310.20
courgette 368
courier 17.3.42
course 303
courser 17.305
coursing 265
court 374
Courtelle 215.3
courteous 310.2
courtesan 245.7
courtesy 16.300
courthouse 306
courtier 17.3
courting 265.69
courtly 16.192
courtroom 241

courtship 274
courtyard 84
couscous 309
cousin 261
couteau 12.80
couth 463
couthie 16.372
couture 10
couturier 2.1
cove 488
coven 261.117
covenant 420.55
covenantee 5.24
Coventry 16.291
cover 17.418
coverage 197
coverlet 371.18
covert 381
covet 371
covetous 310.64
covetousness 300.34
covey 16.383
cow 13
coward 103
cowardice 300.5
cowardliness 300.23
cowardly 16.152
cowbane 247
cowbell 215
cowbind 135
cowboy 11
cower 14
Cowes 521
cowgirl 216
cowherb 22
cowherd 87
cowhide 92
cowitch 67
cowl 224
cowlick 38
cowling 265.33
cowman 261
cowpat 365
cowpea 5
cowpox 499
cowry 16.271
cowslip 274
cox 499
coxa 17.428
coxalgia 17.3.16
coxswain 261
coy 11
coyness 300
coyote 16.339
coypu 15

cozen 261
crab 18
crab-apple 228.64
crabbed 91
crabber 17.9
crabby 16.5
crabstick 38
crabwise 516
crack 32
crackbrain 247
crackbrained 130
cracker 17.28
crackerjack 32
cracking 265
crackle 228.19
crackling 265
cracknel 228
crackpot 373
Cracow 13
cradle 228
cradle-snatcher 17.50
cradlesong 266
craft 396
craftsman 261
crafty 16.345
crag 178
cragged 91
craggy 16.91
Craig 180
crake 34
cram 229
crambo 12
crammer 17.205
cramoisy 16.398
cramp 285
crampon 261
cranage 197
cranberry 16.274
crane 247
cranesbill 218
cranial 228.3.5
craniate 371.1
craniology 16.108.4.1
craniometer 17.342.3.1
craniometry 16.285.2.1
craniotomy 16.222.4.1
cranium 242.2.10
crank 51
crankcase 295
crankpin 252
crankshaft 396
cranky 16.36
cranny 16.223
crap 268
crappy 16.243

craps 322
crapulent 420.27
craquelure 10.4
crash 349
crashing 265
crashlanding 265.19
crass 293
Crassus 310.51
crate 367
crater 17.338
cravat 365.3
crave 482
craven 261.111
craving 265.77
craw 9
crawfish 353
crawl 221
crawler 17.169
Crawley 16.123
crawling 265.31
cray 2
crayfish 353
crayon 261.1
craze 509
crazed 152
crazy 16.393
creak 37
creaky 16.24
cream 234
creamer 17.210
creamery 16.274
creamy 16.215
crease 298
creaseless 300
create 367.1
creatine 251.11
creation 261.67.1
creationism 242.35.14.3
creative 485.10
creativity 16.333.35
creator 17.338.1
creature 17.55
crèche 351
Crécy 16.297
credence 321.4
credendum 242.7
credent 420.9
credential 228.96.1
credenza 17.446
credibility 16.333.9.2
credible 228.16.14
credit 371.12
creditable 228.16.49
creditor 17.342.1
credits 339

crossopterygian 261.3.7
crossover 17.417
crosspatch 62
crosspiece 298
crossroads 529
crosstalk 41
crosstree 5
crosswalk 41
crosswind 134
crosswise 516
crossword 87
crotch 68
crotchet 371
crotchety 16.333
croton 261
crouch 71
croup 280
croupier 17.3
croute 380
crouton 254
crow 12
crowbar 1
crowberry 16.274
crowd 99
crowded 91
crowfoot 379
crown 258
Croydon 261
cru 15
crucial 228
crucian 261.75
cruciate 371.1
crucible 228.12
crucifer 17.114
crucifix 498.1
crucifixion 261.78
cruciform 238.1
crucify 7.3
cruck 43
crud 100
crude 102
crudity 16.333
cruel 228.10
cruelty 16.352
cruet 371.3
Cruickshank 51
cruise 523
cruiser 17.444
crumb 240
crumble 228
crumbly 16.139
crumby 16.220
crumhorn 255
crummy 16.220
crump 289

crumpet 371
crumple 228
crunch 82
crunchy 16.56
crupper 17.258
crura 17.277
crural 228.75
crus 307
crusade 85
crusader 17.79
cruse 523
crush 356
crusher 17.329
crust 443
crustacean 261.67
crustaceous 310.56
crusted 91.54
crusty 16.368
crutch 72
crutches 515
crux 502
crux ansata 17.338
cruzeiro 12.62
crwth 463
cry 7
crybaby 16.7
crying 265.3
cryobiology 16.108.4.2
cryogen 261.39
cryogenics 498.3
cryolite 372.4
cryometer 17.342.3
cryonics 498.5
cryophilic 38.21
cryophyte 372
cryosurgery 16.274.13
cryotherapy 16.254
crypt 424
cryptaesthesia 17.3.60
cryptanalysis 300.52.1
cryptic 38.66
cryptogam 229
cryptogenic 38.32.1
cryptogram 229.1
cryptograph 158.1
cryptography 16.90.2
cryptology 16.108.4.17
cryptozoic 38.2
crystal 228.114
crystalline 253.3
crystallite 372.4
crystallize 516.3
crystallography 16.90.2.2
crystalloid 97.6
ctenidium 242.2.3

ctenoid 97.7
ctenophore 9.6
cub 29
Cuba 17.20
Cuban 261
cubature 17.62
cubbyhole 223
cube 2
cube 30
cubeb 21
cubic 38.4
cubical 228.23
cubicle 228.23
cubiculum 242.10.1
cubiform 238.1
cubism 242.35
cubist 436
cubit 371
cubital 228.102
cuboid 97
Cu-bop 276
cuckold 122
cuckoldry 16.278
cuckoo 15
cuckoopint 413
cucumber 17.27
cud 100
cuddle 228.36
cuddlesome 242
cuddly 16.151
cudgel 228
cudgerie 16.274
cue 15
cuff 168
cuirass 293
cuirassier 6.7
cuisine 251
culch 77
cul-de-sac 32
culet 371.17
culex 496
culicid 91.29
culinary 16.274.26
cull 225
cullet 371
cullis 300.10
Culloden 261.26
cully 16.128
culminant 420.53
culminate 367.17
culmination 261.67.18
culottes 341
culpa 1
culpable 228.16
culprit 371

cult 406
cultigen 261.37
cultivar 1
cultivate 367.36
cultivated 91.34
cultivation 261.67
cultivator 17.338.11
cultural 228.76
culture 17.69
cultured 103
culver 17.424
culverin 252.20
culvert 381
cumber 17.27
Cumberland 143.4.1
Cumbernauld 118
cumbersome 242
cumbrance 321
Cumbria 17.3.44
Cumbrian 261.3.25
cumin 252
cummerbund 140
cumulate 367.13
cumulate 371.17
cumulation 261.67.13
cumulative 485.15.5
cumulonimbus 310
cumulostratus 310.62
cumulus 310.25.5
cuneal 228.3
cuneate 371.1
cuneiform 238.1
cunnilingus 310
cunning 265.45
cunt 419
cup 279
cupbearer 17.271
cupboard 103
cupcake 34
cupel 228
cupellation 261.67.12
Cupid 91
cupidity 16.333.5
cupola 17.176
cuppa 17.258
cupric 38
cupronickel 228.23
cuprous 310
cur 3
curable 228.16.34
Curaçao 12
curacy 16.307
curare 16.261
curarine 251.7
curate 371

curative 485.15.9
curator 17.338
curb 22
curd 87
curdle 228
curdler 17.185
cure 10
curet 368
curettage 359
curfew 15
curia 17.3.42
Curia Regis 300.6
Curie 16.270
curio 12.3
curiosity 16.333.30.1
curious 310.2.14
curl 216
curler 17.164
curlew 15
curlicue 15
curliness 300.23
curling 265
curly 16.116
curmudgeon 261.38
currant 420.64
currawong 266
currency 16.312
current 420.64
curricle 228.23
curriculum 242.10.1
curriculum vitae 7.13
currier 17.3
curriery 16.274.1
curry 16.272
currycomb 239
curse 297
cursed 91
cursive 485.3
cursor 17.301
cursorial 228.3.12
cursory 16.274.35
curt 369
curtail 214
curtailment 420.39
curtain 261.97
curtness 300.36
curtsy 16.316
curvaceous 310.56
curvature 17.62
curve 483
curvet 368
curvilinear 17.3.34
curvy 16.381
cuscus 307
Cush 356

Cushing 265
cushion 261
Cushitic 38.52
cushy 16.325
CUSO 12
cuspid 91
cuspidor 9.3
cuss 307
cussed 91
cussedness 300.28
custard 103
Custer 17.388
custodial 228.3
custodian 261.3.6
custody 16.72
custom 242.32
customary 16.274
customer 17.218
customize 516.5
customs 543
cut 378
cutaneous 310.2.6
cutaway 2.28
cutback 32
cutch 72
cute 380
cuteness 300.40
Cuthbert 381
cuticle 228.23.21
cutie 16.343
cutin 252.24
cutlass 310
cutler 17.202
cutlery 16.274
cutlet 371
cutpurse 297
Cuttack 32
cutter 17.349
cutthroat 376
cutting 265
cuttle 228.107
cuttlebone 257
cuttlefish 353
cutty 16.341
cuvette 368
Cuxhaven 261.110
cwm 241
Cwmbran 246
cyan 245
cyanide 92.4
cyanine 251
cyanosis 300.55
cyanotype 275.1
Cybele 16.120
cybernate 367.18

cybernetic 38.50.5
cybernetics 498.12.1
cycad 83
Cyclades 513.5
cyclamate 367.16
cyclamen 261.52
cycle 228.24
cyclic 38
cyclist 436
cycloid 97
cyclometer 17.342.3
cyclone 257
cyclonic 38.35
cyclopedia 17.3.8
Cyclops 329
cyclorama 17.206
cyclostyle 219.7
cyclotron 254
cygnet 371.29
cylinder 17.102
cylindrical 228.23
cylindroid 97
cymar 1.11
cymbal 228
cymbalo 12.45
cyme 236
Cymric 38
Cynewulf 175
cynic 38.34
cynical 228.23.12
cynicism 242.35.16
cynosure 10
Cynthia 17.3.52
cy pres 2
cypress 310
Cyprian 261.3
cyprinid 91
Cypriot 381.1
cypripedium 242.2.2
Cyprus 310
Cyrenaica 17.33
Cyril 228
Cyrillic 38.21
Cyrus 310.47
cyst 436
cystectomy 16.222.5
cystic 38.70
cysticercoid 97.2
cysticercus 310.9
cystine 251
cystitis 300.62
cystocele 217.2
cystoid 97
cystotomy 16.222.4
Cythera 17.272

cytology 16.108.4.14
cytolysis 300.52.2
cytoplasm 242.34
Cyzicus 310.10
Czech 35
Czechoslovak 32
Czechoslovakia 17.3
Czechoslovakian 261.3

D

dab 18
dabber 17.9
dabble 228
dabbler 17.177
dabchick 38
da capo 12.57
Dacca 17.28
dace 295
dacha 17.50
dachshund 141
dacoit 375
dacoity 16.338
Dacron 254
dactyl 218
dactylic 38.21
dactylogram 229.1.2
dactylography 16.90.2.2
dactylology 16.108.4.8
dad 83
Dada 1
Dadaism 242.35
daddy 16.57
dado 12.17
Daedalus 310.26
daff 157
daffodil 218
daffy 16.82
daft 396
Dagan 261
Dagenham 242.16
dagger 17.123
daglock 40
dagoba 17.21
daguerreotype 275.1
dah 1
dahlia 17.3.18
daily 16.114
daintiness 300.23
dainty 16.354
daiquiri 16.266
dairy 16.264
dairying 265
dairyman 261.48
dais 300

daisy 16.393
daisycutter 17.349
Dakar 17.28
Dakota 17.347
dal 213
Dalai Lama 17.206
dalasi 16.295
dale 214
Dales 536
dalesman 261
Dalhousie 16.400
Dali 16.113
Dallas 310
dalliance 321.1.1
dally 16.112
Dalmatia 17.322
Dalmatian 261.67
dalmatic 38.49
Dalton 261
daltonism 242.35.14
dam 229
damage 197
damages 515
Damara 17.268
damascene 251.9
Damascus 310
damask 61
dame 231
dammar 17.205
damn 229
damnable 228.16
damnation 261.67
damnatory 16.274.43
damnedest 436
damnify 7.3
Damocles 513
damp 285
dampcourse 303
dampen 261
damper 17.261
damply 16.178
dampness 300
damsel 228
damselfish 353
damselfly 7
damson 261
dan 245
Dan 245
Danaë 5.1
dance 315
dancer 17.313
dancing 265
dandelion 261.4
dander 17.98
Dandie Dinmont 414

debag 178
debar 1.1
debark 33
debase 295
debatable 228.16.45
debate 367
debater 17.338
debauch 69
debauchee 5
debauchery 16.274
debenture 17.70
debilitate 367.30.1
debility 16.333.9.2
debit 371
debonair 4.5
Deborah 17.279
debouch 71
debouchment 420
Debrecen 248
débridement 420
debrief 162
debris 16
debt 368
debtor 17.339
debug 189
debunk 54
debus 307
Debussy 16.306
debut 15
debutante 408
decade 85
decadence 321
decadent 420
decaffeinate 367.17.1
decagon 254.5
decahedron 261
decal 212
decalcomania 17.3.31.1
Decalogue 185
decamp 285
decanal 228.56
decant 407
decanter 17.365
decapitate 367.30
decapitation 261.67.27
decapod 94.1
decarbonate 367.18
decarbonize 516.7
decathlon 261
decay 2.7
Deccan 261
decease 298
deceased 435
decedent 420.9
deceit 370

deceitful 226
deceive 484.2
deceiver 17.413
decelerate 367.23
deceleration 261.67.22
decelerometer 17.342.3.4
December 17.24
Decembrist 436
decency 16.312
decennary 16.274.23
decennium 242.2
decent 420.69
decentralize 516.3
deception 261.84
deceptive 485.23
decerebrate 367.24
decibel 215
decide 92.7
decided 91.8
decidedly 16.148
decider 17.84
decidua 17.7
deciduous 310.4
decillion 261.120
decimal 228.52.1
decimalize 516.3
decimate 367.15
decimation 261.67.15
decipher 17.115
decision 261.91.1
decisive 485.5
decisiveness 300.43
deck 35
deckle 228.21
declaim 231
declamation 261.67.16
declamatory 16.274.43.5
declaration 261.67.22
declarative 485.15.8
declaratory 16.274.43
declare 4
declarer 17.271
declass 294
declassify 7.3.6
declension 261.82
declinate 367.17
declination 261.67.18
decline 253.4
declivity 16.333.35
declutch 72
decoct 388
decoction 261
decode 98
decoder 17.88
decoke 42

decollate 367.14
décolletage 359
décolleté 2
decolonize 516.7
decolorant 420.65
decompose 520
decomposer 17.442
decomposition 261.71.9
decompress 296
decompression 261.68
decongestant 420.80
deconsecrate 367.25
decontaminate 367.17.3
decontamination 261.67.18.3
decontrol 223
décor 9
decorate 367.23
decoration 261.67.22
decorative 485.15.10
decorator 17.338.9
decorous 310.50
decorticate 367.5
decorum 242.20
decoupage 359
decoy 11
decrease 298
decreasingly 16.175
decree 5
decree nisi 5
decrement 420.31
decrepit 371
decrepitude 102.2
decrescent 420.67
decretal 228.101
decry 7
decrypt 424
decurion 261.3.24
dedicate 367.5
dedicated 91.34.3
dedication 261.67.5
deduce 309
deduct 389
deductible 228.16.54
deduction 261.79
deductive 485.19
Dee 5
deed 89
deejay 2
deem 234
deemster 17.393
deep 273
deepen 261
deepfreeze 513
deer 6

deontic 38.64
deontology 16.108.4.16
deoxyribonucleic 38.1
depart 366
departed 91.33
department 420
departmental 228.110
departmentalism 242.35.11.6
departmentalize 516.3
departure 17.51
depend 131.3
dependable 228.16.18
dependant 420.14
dependence 321.7
dependency 16.312.2
dependent 420.14
depersonalize 516.3.7
depict 387
depiction 261.78
depilate 367.12
depilatory 16.274.43.4
deplane 247
deplete 370
depletion 261.70
deplorable 228.16
deplore 9
deploy 11
deployment 420.33
deplume 241
depoliticize 516.10.1
depone 257
deponent 420.54
depopulate 367.13.7
deport 374.1
deportation 261.67
deportee 5
deportment 420
deposal 228.127
depose 520
deposit 371.39
deposition 261.71.9
depositor 17.342.5
depository 16.274.41
depot 12.58
depravation 261.67
deprave 482
depraved 146
depravity 16.333.33
deprecate 367.5
deprecatory 16.274.40.1
depreciable 228.16.42
depreciate 367.1
depreciation 261.67.1
depredate 367.8

depredation 261.67.7
depress 296
depressant 420.67
depressed 433
depressing 265.60
depression 261.68
depressive 485.2
depressor 17.300
depressurize 516.8
deprivation 261.67
deprive 486
deprived 149
depurate 367.22
depurative 485.15.9
deputation 261.67.29
depute 380.4
deputize 516
deputy 16.342
De Quincey 16.311
deracinate 367.17.7
derail 214
derailleur 17.433
derailment 420.39
derange 207.1
derangement 420.38
Derby 16.6
Derbyshire 6
deregister 17.384
Derek 38.39
derelict 387
dereliction 261.78
derestrict 387
derestriction 261.78
deride 92
derision 261.91
derisive 485.5
derisory 16.274.37
derivation 261.67
derivative 485.15.16
derive 486
derma 17.209
dermal 228
dermatitis 300.62
dermatology 16.108.4.15
dermatome 239
dermatoplasty 16.361.1
dermatosis 300.55.7
dermis 300.18
derogate 367.11.1
derogative 485.15.3
derogatory 16.274.43.3
derrick 38.39
derrière 4.1
derring-do 15
derringer 17.157

derris 300
Derry 16.262
derv 483
dervish 353
Derwent 420
Derwentwater 17.345
desalinate 367.17
desalination 261.67.18
descant 407
Descartes 366
descend 131
descendant 420.14
descent 410
deschool 227
describable 228.16.8
describe 25
description 261.85
descriptive 485
descry 7
desecrate 367.25
desecration 261.67
desegregate 367.10
desegregation 261.67.10
desensitize 516.12
desert 369
desert 381
deserted 91.36
deserter 17.340
desertion 261.69
deserve 483
deservedly 16.148.1
deserving 265.78
desexualize 516.3.3
desiccant 420.7
desiccate 367.5
desiccated 91.34.3
desiccator 17.338.2
desiderata 17.337.2
desiderate 367.23
desiderative 485.15.10
desideratum 242.26
design 253
designate 367
designate 371.29
designation 261.67
designer 17.232
designing 265.44
desirability 16.333.9.2
desirable 228.16
desire 8
desirous 310.47
desist 436
desk 57
desman 261.53
desmid 91

desmoid 97
desolate 367.14
desolate 371.18
desolation 261.67.14
despair 4
desperado 12.16
desperate 371.35
desperation 261.67.22
despicable 228.16.10
despise 516
despite 372
despoil 222
despoliation 261.67.1.2
despondent 420.15
despot 373
despotic 38.53
despotism 242.35.20
desquamate 367.16
dessert 369
dessertspoon 260
destination 261.67.18
destine 252.26
destined 134
destiny 16.229
destitute 380.5
destitution 261.75
destroy 11
destroyer 17.5
destruct 389
destructible 228.16.54
destruction 261.79
destructionist 436.13
destructive 485.19
destructor 17.357
desuetude 102.2
desultory 16.274
detach 62
detachable 228.16
detached 395
detachment 420.36
detail 214
detailed 112
detain 247.9
detainee 5.11
detainer 17.227
detect 385.8
detectable 228.16
detection 261.77
detective 485.17
detector 17.354
détente 408
detention 261.82
deter 3
deterge 195
detergency 16.312.3

detergent 420.19
deteriorate 367.23
deterioration 261.67.22
determinable 228.16.29
determinant 420.53.1
determinate 371.24
determination
   261.67.18.4
determinative 485.15.7
determine 252.13
determined 134
determiner 17.231
determinism 242.35.13
determinist 436.11
deterrence 321.16
deterrent 420.61
detest 433
detestable 228.16.59
detestation 261.67.33
dethrone 257
detinue 15.9
Detmold 120
detonate 367.18
detonation 261.67.19
detonator 17.338.8
detour 10
detoxify 7.3
detract 382
detraction 261.76
detrain 247
detriment 420.31
detrimental 228.110.2
detrition 261.71
detritus 310.65
Detroit 375
de trop 12
detumescence 321.21
Deucalion 261.3.8
deuce 309
deuced 91.30
deuteragonist 436.13.2
deuteranopia 17.3.37.2
deuterium 242.2.15
Deuteronomy 16.222.3
deva 17.410
devaluation 261.67.2
devalue 15
Devanagari 16.274
devastate 367
devastation 261.67
develop 281.1
developer 17.260
development 420
developmental 228.110
deviant 420.1

deviate 367.1.10
deviation 261.67.1.6
device 301
devil 228.118
devilish 353
devilment 420.40
devilry 16.283
devious 310.2
deviousness 300.34.1
devisable 228.16.64
devisal 228
devise 516.15
devisee 5
devisor 17.441
devitalize 516.3
devoice 304
devoid 97
devoirs 1.18
devolution 261.75.1
devolve 493
Devon 261.112
Devonian 261.3.18
devote 376
devoted 91.41
devotee 5
devotion 261.73
devotional 228.63.6
devour 14
devout 377
dew 15
dewan 246
Dewar 17.8
dewberry 16.274
dewclaw 9
dewdrop 276
Dewey 16.4
dewlap 268
Dewsbury 16.274
dewy 16.4
dexterity 16.333.21
dextrorotation 261.67.28
dextrose 520
dextrous 310
dey 2
dhak 33
dharma 17.206
dhobi 16.12
dhoti 16.339
dhow 13
diabase 295.1
diabetes 513.16
diabetic 38.50.2
diabolic 38.22
diabolical 228.23.8
diabolism 242.35.11

digression 261.68
digressive 485.2
dihedral 228.78
dik-dik 38
diktat 366
dilapidate 367.8
dilapidated 91.34
dilapidation 261.67.7
dilatancy 16.312.6
dilatant 420.75
dilatation 261.67.30
dilate 367
dilation 261.67
dilator 17.338
dilatory 16.274.43.4
dildo 12
dilemma 17.208
dilemmatic 38.49.1
dilettante 16.353
diligence 321.9
diligent 420.20
dill 218
dilly-dally 16.112
diluent 420.4
dilute 380
dilution 261.75
diluvial 228.3.17
dim 235
dime 236
dimension 261.82
dimer 17.212
dimetric 38.46
diminish 353.7
diminuendo 12.24
diminution 261.75
diminutive 485
dimity 16.333.12
dimmer 17.211
dimness 300
dimple 228
dimwit 371
dim-witted 91.38
din 252
Dinah 17.232
dinar 1
dine 253
diner 17.232
dinette 368
ding 265
dingbat 365
dingbats 333
ding-dong 266
dinge 209
dinghy 16.242
dingle 228.50

dingo 12.36
dingy 16.110
Dinka 17.44
dinkum 242
dinky 16.37
dinner 17.231
dinoceras 310.50
dinosaur 9.11
dinothere 6.10
dint 412
diocesan 261.65
diocese 300.57.1
Diocletian 261.70
diode 98
Diogenes 513
Diomedes 513.3
Dionysia 17.3.61
Dionysiac 32.1
Dionysian 261.3.35
Dionysius 310.2.15
Dionysus 310
diopside 92.10
dioptre 17.377
dioptric 38
dioptrics 498
Dior 9.1
diorama 17.206
dioxide 92.14
dip 274
dipeptide 92
diphtheria 17.3.39
diphtherial 228.3.11
diphthong 266
diplegia 17.3.13
diplodocus 310.14
diploë 5
diploid 97
diploma 17.215
diplomacy 16.307
diplomat 365
diplomate 367.16
diplomatic 38.49.2
diplomatics 498.11
diplopia 17.3.37
dipnoan 261.6
dipole 223
dipper 17.253
dippy 16.248
dipsomania 17.3.31.1
dipsomaniac 32.1
dipstick 38
dipterous 310.50
diptych 38.66
Dirac 32
dire 8

direct 385
direction 261.77.3
directional 228.63.8
directive 485.17
directly 16.195
directness 300.41
director 17.354
directorate 371.35
directorial 228.3.12
directorship 274.1
directory 16.274.45
dirge 195
dirham 229
dirigible 228.16.20
dirk 36
dirndl 228
dirt 369
dirtiness 300.23
dirty 16.331
Dis 300
disability 16.333.9.2
disable 228.11
disabuse 523
disaccord 95.3
disaccredit 371.12
disaccustom 242.32
disadvantage 197
disadvantaged 110
disadvantageous 310.20
disaffect 385.2
disaffiliate 367.1.2
disaffiliation 261.67.1.1
disaffirm 233
disafforest 436.18
disagree 5
disagreeable 228.16.1
disagreement 420
disallow 13
disambiguate 367.2
disannul 225
disappear 6.6
disappearance 321.17
disappoint 416.1
disappointed 91.48
disappointing 265
disappointment 420.50
disapprobation 261.67.3
disapproval 228.122
disapprove 490
disarm 230
disarmament 420.35
disarming 265.35
disarrange 207
disarray 2.19
disarticulate 367.13.2

dislodge 199
disloyal 228.6
disloyalty 16.352.1
dismal 228.54
dismantle 228.109
dismantler 17.203
dismay 2
dismember 17.24
dismiss 300
dismissal 228.85
dismissive 485.4
dismount 418
Disneyland 143.2
disobedience 321.1
disobedient 420.1.1
disobey 2.4
disoblige 198
disorder 17.86
disorderly 16.131
disorganize 516.7
disorganized 154
disorient 410
disorientate 367.32
disown 257
disparage 197.9
disparagement 420.37
disparate 371.35
disparity 16.333.20
dispassion 261.66
dispassionate 371.28
dispatch 62
dispel 215
dispensable 228.16.40
dispensary 16.274.38
dispensation 261.67.26
dispensatory 16.274.43
dispense 316
dispenser 17.314
dispersal 228.84
dispersant 420.68
disperse 297
dispersion 261.69
dispersive 485.3
dispirit 371.33
dispirited 91.38
displace 295
displacement 420.44
display 2
displease 513
displeasure 17.333
disport 374
disposable 228.16
disposal 228.127
dispose 520
disposed 155

disposition 261.71.9
dispossess 296
dispossession 261.68
dispraise 509
disproof 170
disproportion 261.72.1
disproportionate
 371.28.2
disprove 490
disputable 228.16.53
disputant 420.77
disputation 261.67.29
disputatious 310.56
dispute 380
disqualifier 17.4.1
disqualify 7.3.2
disquiet 381.2
disquietude 102.2
disquisition 261.71.8
Disraeli 16.114
disregard 84.1
disrelish 353.4
disrepair 4.6
disreputable 228.16.52
disrepute 380.4
disrespect 385
disrespectful 226.10
disrobe 28
disrupt 426
disruption 261.88
disruptive 485
dissatisfaction 261.76
dissatisfied 92
dissatisfy 7
dissect 385.7
dissection 261.77.5
dissemble 228.18
disseminate 367.17
dissension 261.82.2
dissent 410
dissenter 17.368.1
dissentient 420
dissentious 310.61
dissertate 367.31
dissertation 261.67.30
disservice 300
dissident 420.10
dissimilar 17.166
dissimilarity 16.333.20.2
dissimilate 367.12
dissimilation 261.67.12
dissimilitude 102.2
dissimulate 367.13.5
dissimulation
 261.67.13.3

dissipate 367.19.1
dissipated 91.34
dissipation 261.67.20.1
dissociable 228.16.44
dissociate 367.1.7
dissociation 261.67.1
dissolute 380.1
dissolution 261.75.1
dissolve 493
dissolvent 420
dissonance 321
dissonant 420.55
dissuade 85
dissuasion 261
dissuasive 485
dissymmetry 16.285.1
distaff 158
distal 228.114
distance 321.27
distant 420.81
distaste 432
distasteful 226.12
distemper 17.262
distend 131
distich 38.70
distichous 310.10
distil 218
distillate 371.16
distillation 261.67.12
distiller 17.166
distillery 16.274.16
distinct 392
distinction 261
distinctive 485.20
distinguish 353
distinguishable
 228.16.43
distort 374
distortion 261.72
distract 382
distracting 265.70
distraction 261.76
distrain 247
distrainee 5.11
distraint 409
distrait 2
distraught 374
distress 296
distressing 265.60
distribute 380.2
distributee 5.23
distribution 261.75
distributive 485
distributor 17.350
district 387

distrust 443
distrustful 226.13
disturb 22
disturbance 321
disturbing 265
disulfiram 242.19
disulphide 92
disunite 372
disunity 16.333.18
disuse 309
disused 156
dit 371
ditch 67
ditheism 242.35.2
dither 17.405
dithyramb 229
dithyrambic 38.5
dittander 17.98
dittany 16.237
ditto 12
dittography 16.90.2.5
ditty 16.333
diuresis 300.51
diuretic 38.50
diurnal 228.58
div 485
diva 17.413
divalent 420.25
divan 245
divaricate 367.5
divaricate 371.9
dive 486
diver 17.415
diverge 195
divergence 321
divergent 420.19
divers 524
diverse 297
diversify 7.3
diversion 261.69
diversity 16.333.26
divert 369
diverticulitis 300.62.2
diverticulosis 300.55.3
diverticulum 242.10.1
divertimento 12.84
divertissement 420
Dives 513
divest 433
divide 92
dividend 131
divider 17.84
dividers 524
divi-divi 16.382
divination 261.67.18

divine 253
diviner 17.232
diving 265
divining 265.44
divinity 16.333.17
divinize 516.6
divisibility 16.333.9.2.2
divisible 228.16.63
division 261.91.2
divisional 228.63
divisive 485.5
divisor 17.441
divorce 303
divorcé 2
divorcee 5.21
divot 381
divulge 205
divvy 16.382
dixie 16.388
Dixie 16.388
Dixieland 143.2
Diyarbakir 6
dizziness 300.23
dizzy 16.396
Djaja 17.145
Djakarta 17.337
Djambi 16.17
Djerba 17.12
Djibouti 16.343
Dnieper 17.252
Dniester 17.383
do 15
doable 228.16.7
dobbin 252
dobby 16.11
Doberman pinscher
  17.331
dobla 1
doc 40
docent 410
Docetism 242.35.18
docile 219
docility 16.333.9
dock 40
dockage 197
docker 17.36
docket 371.10
dockland 143
dockyard 84
doctor 17.356
doctoral 228.76
doctorate 371.35
doctrinaire 4
doctrinal 228.61
doctrine 252

document 410
document 420.34
documentary 16.274.47
documentation
  261.67.32
dodder 17.85
doddering 265.58
doddery 16.274
doddle 228.34
dodecagon 254.5
Dodecanese 513.9
dodge 199
Dodgem 242
dodger 17.152
dodgy 16.104
dodo 12.21
doe 12
doer 17.8
does 522
doeskin 252
doff 165
dog 185
dogberry 16.274
dogcart 366
doge 201
dogfight 372
dogfish 353
dogged 91
doggedness 300.28
Dogger 17.131
doggerel 228.76
doggery 16.274.12
doggish 353
doggo 12
doggone 254
doggy 16.94
doghouse 306
dogie 16.96
dogleg 181
dogma 17
dogman 261
dogmatic 38.49
dogmatism 242.35.20
dogmatist 436.26
dogmatize 516.13
dogsbody 16.65
dogtooth 463
dogtrot 373
dogwatch 68
dogwood 101
doh 12
Doha 1
doily 16.125
doing 265.5
doings 552

doit 375
dol 220
doldrums 543
dole 223
doleful 226
dolerite 372.8
doll 220
dollar 17.168
dollop 281.2
dolly 16.122
dolman 261
dolmas 310
dolmen 248
Dolmetsch 64
dolomite 372
Dolomites 340
dolorimetry 16.285.1
doloroso 12.70
dolorous 310.50
dolour 17.168
dolphin 252
dolt 405
dom 237
domain 247.5
dome 239
domestic 38.69
domesticate 367.5
domestication 261.67.5
domesticity 16.333.28
domicile 219.2
domiciliary 16.274.1.1
dominance 321.14
dominant 420.53.2
dominate 367.17.5
domination 261.67.18.6
domineer 6.4
Dominic 38.34
Dominica 17.33
dominical 228.23.12
Dominican 261.13
dominie 16.229
dominion 261.122
dominium 242.2.11
domino 12.55
dominoes 520
Domitian 261.71.4
don 254
Don 254
Donar 1
donate 367.18
donation 261.67.19
Donatist 436.26
donative 485.15
Doncaster 17.390
done 259

donee 5
Donegal 221
Donets 336
dong 266
Donizetti 16.330
Don Juan 261
donkey 16.38
Donna 17.233
donned 136
donnert 381
donnish 353.8
donnybrook 44
donor 17.236
Donovan 261
Don Quixote 16.339
don't 417
doodah 1.3
doodle 228.37
doodlebug 189
Doolittle 228.102
doom 241
doomsday 2
door 9
doorbell 215
doorframe 231
doorjamb 229
doorkeeper 17.252
doorman 261
doormat 365
doornail 214
doorpost 441
doorsill 218
doorstep 271
doorstop 276
doorway 2
dooryard 84
dopant 420
dope 278
dopey 16.251
Doppelgänger 17.245
Doppler 17.195
Dora 17.276
Dorcas 310
Dorchester 17.384
Dorian 261.3.23
Doric 38.41
Doris 300
Dorking 265.9
dorm 238
dormant 420.32
dormer 17.214
dormie 16.218
dormitory 16.274.41
Dormobile 217
dormouse 306

dorp 277
dorsad 83
dorsal 228
Dorset 371
dorsoventral 228.80
dorsum 242
Dortmund 143
dorty 16.336
dory 16.269
dosage 197
dose 305
do-si-do 12.19
dosimeter 17.342.2
doss 302
dosser 17.304
dosshouse 306
dossier 2.1
Dostoevsky 16.43
dot 373
dotage 197.13
dotard 103
dotation 261.67.28
dote 376
dotted 91.40
dottle 228.104
dotty 16.335
Douai 2.2
double 228.14
double-breasted 91.52
double-cross 302
double-decker 17.31
double entendre 17.287
double-glazing 265.81
double-jointed 91.48
doubles 539
doublet 371
doublethink 52
doubleton 261
doubloon 260
doubly 16.136
doubt 377
doubter 17.348
doubtful 226
doubtfulness 300.30
doubtless 300
douceur 3
douche 358
dough 12
doughboy 11
doughnut 378
doughty 16.340
doughy 16.3
Douglas 310
Doukhobors 518
dour 10

drinkable 228.16.11
drinker 17.44
drip 274
dripping 265
drippy 16.248
drive 486
drivel 228.120
driven 261.114
driver 17.415
driverless 300.13
driveway 2
driving 265
drizzle 228
drizzly 16.209
drogue 188
droit 375
droll 223
drollery 16.274.17
dromedary 16.274.7
drone 257
drongo 12
drool 227
droop 280
droopy 16.253
drop 276
droplet 371
droplight 372
dropout 377
dropper 17.255
droppings 552
drops 329
dropsical 228.23
dropsy 16.315
drosophila 17.166
dross 302
drought 377
drove 488
drover 17.417
drown 258
drowse 521
drowsiness 300.23
drowsy 16.400
drub 29
drudge 203
drudgery 16.274
drug 189
drugget 371
druggist 436
drugstore 9
druid 91.3
druidic 38
drum 240
drumbeat 370
drumhead 86
drumlin 252

drummer 17.216
drumstick 38
drunk 54
drunkard 103
drunken 261
drunkenness 300.31
drupe 280
Drury 16.270
Druse 523
dry 7
dryad 83.2
dryadic 38.7
dry-cleaning 265.42
Dryden 261.25
dryer 17.4
dryness 300
Drysdale 214
DTs 513.16
dual 228.10
dualism 242.35.11
duality 16.333.8.2
dub 29
Dubai 7
dubbin 252
dubbing 265
dubiety 16.333.2
dubious 310.2
dubiousness 300.34.1
dubitable 228.16.49
dubitation 261.67.27
Dublin 252
Dubonnet 2
Dubrovnik 38
ducal 228
ducat 381
duce 16.53
duchess 300
duchy 16.52
duck 43
duckboard 95
ducking 265
duckling 265.34
ducks 502
duckweed 89
ducky 16.30
duct 389
ductile 219
dud 100
dude 102
dudeen 251
dudgeon 261.38
Dudley 16.151
due 15
duel 228.10
dueller 17.176

duenna 17.228
duet 368.1
duff 168
duffel 228.42
duffer 17.118
dug 189
dugong 266
dugout 377
duiker 17.35
duke 45
dukedom 242
dulcet 371
dulciana 17.226.1
dulcify 7.3.7
dulcimer 17.211
dulia 17.3.23
dull 225
dullard 103.4
Dulles 300.10
dullness 300
dullsville 218
dulse 313
Duluth 463
duly 16.130
Du Maurier 2.1
dumb 240
Dumbarton 261.95
dumbbell 215
dumbfound 139
dumbness 300
dumbstruck 43
dumbwaiter 17.338
dumdum 240
Dumfries 298
dummy 16.220
dump 289
dumper 17.264
dumping 265.50
dumpling 265
dumps 332
dumpy 16.257
Dumyat 365
dun 259
Dunbar 1
Duncan 261
dunce 320
Dundalk 41
Dundee 5
dunderhead 86.5
dune 260
Dunedin 252
Dunfermline 252
dung 267
dungaree 5.17
Dungeness 296.3

earplug 189
earring 265.53
earshot 373
earth 456
earthborn 255
earthbound 139
earthen 261
earthenware 4
earthling 265
earthly 16.204
earthquake 34
earthshaking 265.6
earthstar 1
earthwork 36
earthworm 233
earthy 16
earwax 494
earwig 184
ease 513
easeful 226
easel 228
easiness 300.23
east 435
East Anglia 17.3
eastbound 139
Eastbourne 255
Easter 17.383
easterly 16.131
eastern 261
Easterner 17.239
easternmost 441
Eastertide 92.11
East Kilbride 92
Eastleigh 5
eastward 103
eastwards 531
easy 16.395
easy-going 265.4
eat 370
eatable 228.16.48
eaten 261.98
eater 17.341
eats 338
eau de Javelle 215
eau de nil 217.1
eau de vie 5
eaves 553
eavesdrop 276
eavesdropper 17.255
ebb 21
ebbed 104
Ebbw Vale 214
Ebenezer 17.440
ebon 261
ebonize 516.7

ebony 16.237
Eboracum 242
ebullience 321
ebullient 420
ebullition 261.71.3
écarté 2.23
Ecbatana 17.239
ecbolic 38.22
eccentric 38.47
eccentricity 16.333.28
ecchymosis 300.55
Eccles 539
ecclesia 17.3.60
Ecclesiastes 513.18
ecclesiastic 38.68.1
ecclesiastical 228.23
ecclesiasticism
  242.35.16.6
ecclesiology 16.108.4.1
eccrine 253
ecdysiast 430.1
ecdysis 300.52
ecdysone 257
echelon 254.7
echeveria 17.3.39
echidna 17.241
echinoid 97
echinus 310.34
echo 12.9
echoic 38.2
echoism 242.35.3
echolalia 17.3.18
echopraxia 17.3.56
echovirus 310.47
éclair 4
eclampsia 17.3
éclat 1
eclectic 38.60
eclipse 327
ecliptic 38.66
eclogue 185
eclosion 261.92
ecocide 92.8
ecological 228.23.5
ecology 16.108.4
econometrics 498.10
economic 38.29.1
economical 228.23.9
economics 498
economist 436.10
economize 516.5
economy 16.222.3
écorché 2
ecospecies 513
ecosphere 6.1

écossaise 509
ecosystem 242
ecotype 275.1
écraseur 3
ecru 15
ecstasy 16.307
ecstatic 38.49
ecstatics 498.11
ectoderm 233
ectomorph 166.1
ectomorphic 38.14
ectopic 38.37
ectoplasm 242.34
ectoproct 388
ectosarc 33
ectype 275
Ecuador 9.4
ecumenical 228.23.11
eczema 17.211
eczematous 310.68
edacious 310.56.2
Edam 229
edaphic 38.11
Edda 17.80
eddo 12
eddy 16.60
Eddystone 261.107
edelweiss 301
Eden 261.23
edentate 367.32
Edgar 17
edge 194
Edgehill 218
edgeways 509
edging 265
edgy 16.101
edh 474
edible 228.16.14
edict 387
edifice 300
edify 7.3
Edinburgh 17.279
Edison 261.65
edit 371.12
edition 261.71.1
editio princeps 324
editor 17.342.1
editorial 228.3.12.1
editorialize 516.3.2.2
Edmonton 261
Edmund 143
Edom 242
educable 228.16
educate 367
educated 91.34

embracery 16.274.33
embranchment 420
embrasure 17.332
embrocate 367.6
embrocation 261.67.6
embroider 17.87
embroidery 16.274
embroil 222
embryo 12.3
embryology 16.108.4.1
embryonic 38.35.1
embus 307
emcee 5
emend 131
emendation 261.67.9
emerald 122
emerge 195
emergence 321
emergency 16.312.3
emergent 420.19
emeritus 310.64
Emerson 261
emery 16.274
emesis 300.52.3
emetic 38.50
emigrant 420
emigrate 367.26
emigration 261.67.24
émigré 2
eminence 321.14
eminent 420.53
emir 6
emirate 371.32
emissary 16.274.36
emission 261.71
emit 371.19
emitter 17.342.2
Emmanuel 228.9.2
Emmen 261
Emmenthal 213
emmer 17.208
emmet 371
Emmy 16.213
emollient 420
emolument 420.34
emote 376
emotion 261.73
emotional 228.63.6
emotionalism 242.35.11.5
emotive 485.14
empanel 228.55
empathetic 38.50.6
empathic 38.72
empathize 516.14

empathy 16.373
empennage 197.6
emperor 17.279
empery 16.274.31
emphasis 300.57
emphasize 516.11
emphatic 38.49
emphatically 16.142
emphysema 17.210
empire 8
empiric 38.40
empirical 228.23.16
empiricism 242.35.16.3
emplace 295
emplacement 420.44
emplane 247
employ 11
employable 228.16.4
employee 5
employer 17.5
employment 420.33
empoison 261.128
empower 14
empress 300
emptiness 300.23
empty 16
empty-handed 91.12
empyema 17.210
empyrean 261.2
empyreuma 17.217
emu 15
emulate 367.13
emulation 261.67.13
emulous 310.25
emulsify 7.3.7
emulsion 261
emulsoid 97
emunctory 16.274
en 248
enable 228.11
enact 382
enactment 420
enamel 228.51
enamour 17.205
enamoured 103
enarthrosis 300.55
encage 193
encamp 285
encampment 420
encapsulate 367.13
encase 295
encash 349
enceinte 407
Enceladus 310.17

encephalic 38.19
encephalin 252.11
encephalitis 300.62
encephalogram 229.1
encephalography 16.90.2.2
encephalon 254.7
enchain 247
enchant 408
enchanted 91
enchanting 265.72
enchantment 420
enchantress 300
enchilada 17.78
encipher 17.115
encircle 228.22
enclasp 290
enclave 482
enclitic 38.52
enclose 520
enclosure 17.335
encode 98
encoder 17.88
encomiast 430.1
encomium 242.2.9
encompass 310.42
encore 9
encounter 17.372
encourage 197.10
encouragement 420.37
encrinite 372.5
encroach 70
encrust 443
encumber 17.27
encumbrance 321
encumbrancer 17.318
encyclical 228.23
encyclopedia 17.3.8
encyclopedic 38.8
encyclopedist 436
end 131
endamage 197
endanger 17.156
endbrain 247
endear 6
endearing 265.53
endearment 420.30
endeavour 17.411
endemic 38.25
endermic 38.26
endgame 231
ending 265.20
endive 486
endless 300
endlong 266

entitlement 420.40
entity 16.333.32
entomb 241
entomic 38.29
entomologize 516.1
entomology 16.108.4
entopic 38.37
entourage 359
entozoic 38.2
entozoon 254.2
entr'acte 382
entrails 536
entrain 247
entrammel 228.51
entrance 315
entrance 321
entrant 420
entrap 268
entreat 370
entreaty 16.332
entrée 2
entrench 79
entrenchment 420
entrepreneur 3
entrepreneurial 228.3
entresol 220
entropy 16.254
entrust 443
entry 16.288
entwine 253
enucleate 367.1
enumerate 367.23
enumeration 261.67.22
enumerator 17.338.9
enunciate 367.1
enunciation 261.67.1.4
enuresis 300.51
envelop 281.1
envelope 278
envenom 242
envenomed 127
enviable 228.16.2
envious 310.2
environ 261.58
environment 420.42
environmental 228.110.4
environmentalism
    242.35.11.6
environmentalist 436.7.7
environs 551
envisage 197
envision 261.91
envoy 11
envy 16
enwind 135

enwomb 241
enwrap 268
enwreath 475
Enzed 86
enzyme 236
enzymology 16.108.4
Eocene 251.9
eohippus 310.37
eolith 458
Eolithic 38.73
eonism 242.35.14
Eos 302
eosin 252
eosinophil 218.1
Eozoic 38.2
Epaminondas 293
eparch 33
eparchy 16.20
epaulet 368
épée 2
épéeist 436.1
epeiric 38
epeirogeny 16.229.2
epenthesis 300.52
epergne 249
ephah 17.113
ephebe 23
ephedrine 252
ephemera 17.279.1
ephemeral 228.76.2
ephemerality 16.333.8.9
ephemerid 91.27
ephemeris 300.47
ephemeron 254.11
Ephesian 261.90
Ephesus 310.53
ephod 94
ephor 9
Ephraim 235
epic 38
epicardium 242.2
epicarp 269
epicene 251.8
epicentre 17.368.1
epiclesis 300.51
epicrisis 300.53
Epictetus 310.63
epicure 10.3
epicurean 261.2
Epicurus 310.49
Epidaurus 310.48
epidemic 38.25
epidemiology 16.108.4.1
epidermis 300.18
epididymis 300.19

epidural 228.75
epigeal 228.2
epigene 251
epiglottis 300
epigram 229
epigrammatic 38.49.2
epigrammatize 516.13.1
epigraph 158
epigraphic 38.11
epigraphy 16.90
epilepsy 16.313
epileptic 38.65
epileptoid 97
epilogue 185
epimere 6.2
epiphany 16.237.2
epiphysis 300.52
epiphyte 372
Epirus 310.47
episcopacy 16.307
episcopal 228
episcopalian 261.3.8
episcopate 371.30
episode 98
episodic 38.9
epistaxis 300.70
epistemic 38.27
epistemology 16.108.4.9
epistle 228.85
epistolary 16.274.19
epistoler 17.176
epistrophe 16.90.3
epitaph 158
epitaphic 38.11
epitaxy 16.386
epithelium 242.2.5
epithet 368
epitome 16.222
epitomize 516.5
epizootic 38.53
epoch 40
epode 98
eponym 235
eponymous 310.28.2
eponymy 16.216
épopée 5.16
epoxy 16.389
Epping 265
epsilon 254.6
Epsom 242
Epstein 253
equable 228.16
equal 228.71
equality 16.333.10
equalize 516.3

equalizer 17.441
equally 16.131
equanimity 16.333.12
equate 367.20
equation 261
equator 17.338
equatorial 228.3.12.2
equerry 16.262
equestrian 261.3
equestrienne 248.1
equiangular 17.174
equidistant 420.81
equilateral 228.76
equilibrate 367.24
equilibration 261.67.23
equilibrist 436
equilibrium 242.2
equine 253
equinoctial 228
equinox 499
equip 274
equipage 197.8
equipartition 261.71
equipment 420.43
equipoise 519
equipollent 420
equisetum 242.28
equitable 228.16.49
equitation 261.67.27
equites 513
equities 515
equity 16.333
equivalence 321.12
equivalent 420.28
equivocal 228.28
equivocate 367.6
equivocation 261.67.6
Equuleus 310.2
era 17.272
eradicable 228.16.10
eradicate 367.5
eradication 261.67.5
erasable 228.16
erase 509
eraser 17.439
Erasmus 310
erasure 17.332
Erbil 218
erbium 242.2
ere 4
Erebus 310.5
Erechtheion 261.3
Erechtheum 242.2
erect 385
erectile 219.5

erection 261.77.3
erector 17.354
eremite 372
erethism 242.35
erg 182
ergo 12
ergonomics 498
ergosterol 220.4
ergot 381
ergotism 242.35.20
Eric 38.39
Erica 17.34.2
ericaceous 310.56.1
Eridanus 310.36
Erie 16.265
erigeron 261.60
Erin 252
erinaceous 310.56.4
eristic 38.70
Eritrea 17.1
erk 36
erlking 265
ermine 252.13
erne 249
Ernie 16.227
erode 98
erogeneity 16.333.1
erogenous 310.33
Eros 302
erosion 261.92
erosive 485.6
erotesis 300.51
erotic 38.53
erotica 17.34
eroticism 242.35.16.5
erotogenic 38.32.1
erotology 16.108.4.15
erotomania 17.3.31.1
err 3
errand 143
errant 420.61
errantry 16.291
errata 17.337
erratic 38.49
erratum 242.26
erroneous 310.2.9
error 17.269
ersatz 333
Erse 297
erstwhile 219
eruct 389
eructation 261.67
erudite 372
erudition 261.71
erupt 426

eruption 261.88
eruptive 485
Erymanthus 310.72
erysipelas 310.23
erysipeloid 97.5
erythema 17.210
erythrism 242.35
erythroblast 430
erythrocyte 372.10
erythrocytic 38.52.3
erythropoiesis 300.51
Esau 9
escadrille 218
escalade 85
escalate 367.14
escalation 261.67.14
escalator 17.338
escallonia 17.3.36.2
escalope 276
escapade 85
escape 270
escapee 5.15
escapement 420
escapism 242.35
escapist 436.14
escapology 16.108.4.12
escarp 269
escarpment 420
eschalot 373.1
eschatology 16.108.4.15
escheat 370
eschew 15
escolar 1.9
Escorial 213
escort 374
escritoire 1
escrow 12
escudo 12.22
esculent 420.27
escutcheon 261
Esdraelon 254
Esher 17.325
Eskimo 12.48
esoteric 38.39
espadrille 218
esparto 12.73
especial 228
especially 16.131
Esperanto 12.83
espial 228.4
espionage 359
Espíritu Santo 12.83
esplanade 85.3
espousal 228.129
espouse 521

esprit 5
esprit de corps 9.2
espy 7
esquire 8
essay 2
essayist 436.1
essence 321.21
Essene 251
essential 228.96
Essequibo 12.5
Essex 498
establish 353
establishment 420.47
estancia 17.3.48
estate 367
esteem 234
ester 17.382
esterify 7.3.5
Esther 17.382
estimable 228.16
estimate 367.15
estimate 371.19
estimation 261.67.15
Estonian 261.3.18
estop 276
estoppel 228.68
estrade 84
estragon 254.5
estrange 207
estranged 111
estrangement 420.38
estuarial 228.3.10
estuarine 253.7
estuary 16.274.2
esurient 420.1.3
eta 17.338
etaerio 12.3
etalon 254.7
et cetera 17.293
etch 64
etching 265
eternal 228.58
eternity 16.333.16.1
ethane 247
ethanol 220
Ethelbert 381
Ethelred 86
ether 17
ethereal 228.3.11
etherealize 516.3.2.1
ethic 38
ethical 228.23
ethics 498
Ethiopia 17.3.37
Ethiopian 261.3.19

Ethiopic 38.37
ethmoid 97
ethnarch 33
ethnic 38
ethnocentrism 242.35
ethnology 16.108.4
ethos 302
ethyl 218
ethylene 251.2
ethylic 38.21
etiquette 368.4
Etna 17.244
Eton 261.98
Etonian 261.3.18
Etruria 17.3.42
Etruscan 261.17
étude 102
étui 5
etymology 16.108.4.9
etymon 254
Etzel 228
Euboea 17.2
eucalyptus 310.71
Eucharist 436.20
euchre 17.41
Euclid 91
eudemon 261.47
eudemonia 17.3.36
eudemonics 498.5
eugenic 38.32
eugenics 498.3
eugenol 220.3
euglena 17.230
euhemerism 242.35.15
eulogistic 38.70.1
eulogize 516.1
eulogy 16.108
Eumenides 513.4
eunuch 46
euonymus 310.28.2
eupatrid 91
eupepsia 17.3
euphemism 242.35
euphemistic 38.70.3
euphemize 516.4
euphonic 38.35
euphonious 310.2.9
euphonium 242.2.12
euphonize 516.7
euphony 16.237
euphorbia 17.3
euphoria 17.3.41
euphoric 38.41
euphotic 38.55
Euphrates 513.15

Euphrosyne 5.12
euphuism 242.35.4
Eurasia 17.322
Eurasian 261.67.21
eureka 17.33
eurhythmic 38.30
eurhythmics 498
Euripides 513.4
Eurocommunism 242.35
Eurocrat 365.2
Eurodollar 17.168
Euromarket 371.7
Europa 17.257
Europe 281
European 261.2
Europeanize 516.7
europium 242.2.13
Eurovision 261.91.3
Eurus 310.49
Eurydice 16.300
Eusebius 310.2
Euterpe 16.246
euthanasia 17.3.59
euthenics 498.3
eutrophic 38.13
evacuant 420.4
evacuate 367.2
evacuation 261.67.2
evacuee 5
evade 85
evaginate 367.17.2
evaluate 367.2
evaluation 261.67.2
evanesce 296.3
evanescent 420.67.2
evangelical 228.23.6
evangelism 242.35.9
evangelist 436.5
evangelistic 38.70
evangelize 516.2
Evans 551
evaporate 367.23
evaporation 261.67.22
evasion 261
evasive 485
eve 484
Eve 484
Evelyn 252
even 261.113
evening 265
evenness 300.31
evens 551
evensong 266
event 410.3
eventful 226.11

eventide 92.12
eventual 228.9
eventuality 16.333.8.2
eventually 16.131.1
eventuate 367.2
ever 17.411
Everest 436.20
evergreen 251
everlasting 265.74
evermore 9.9
evert 369.1
every 16.274
everybody 16.65
everyday 2
Everyman 261.48
everyone 259
everything 265
everywhere 4.7
Evesham 242
evict 387
eviction 261.78
evidence 321.5
evident 420.10
evidential 228.96.1
evidently 16.198
evil 228.119
evildoer 17.8
evilness 300.30
evince 317
eviscerate 367.23
evocation 261.67.6
evocative 485.15.2
evoke 42
evolution 261.75.1
evolutionary 16.274.29
evolutionist 436.13
evolve 493
evzone 257
ewe 15
ewer 17.8
ex 496
exacerbate 367.4
exacerbation 261.67.3
exact 382
exacting 265.70
exaction 261.76
exactitude 102.2
exactly 16.194
exactness 300
exaggerate 367.23
exaggerated 91.34.7
exaggeration 261.67.22
exalt 404
exaltation 261.67
exalted 91.44

exam 229
examination 261.67.18.3
examine 252.12
examinee 5.12
examiner 17.231.1
example 228.70
exanthema 17.210
exarch 33
exasperate 367.23
exasperation 261.67.22
Excalibur 17.14
ex cathedra 17.286
excavate 367
excavate 367.37
excavation 261.67
excavator 17.338
exceed 89
exceeding 265.13
exceedingly 16.175
excel 215
excellence 321.12
Excellency 16.312
excellent 420.28
excelsior 9.1
except 422
excepting 265
exception 261.84
exceptional 228.63
exceptive 485.23
excerpt 423
excess 296
excessive 485.2
exchange 207
exchequer 17.31
excise 516
exciseman 261
excision 261.91
excitable 228.16.50
excitant 420
excitation 261.67.27
excite 372
excited 91.39
excitement 420
exciting 265.67
exclaim 231
exclamation 261.67.16
exclamatory 16.274.43.5
exclave 482
exclude 102
exclusion 261.93
exclusionist 436.13
exclusive 485.8
excogitate 367.30
excommunicate 367.5

excommunication
  261.67.5
excoriate 367.1
excrement 420.31
excrescence 321.21
excrescent 420.67
excreta 17.341
excrete 370
excretion 261.70
excruciate 367.1
excruciating 265.64
exculpate 367
excursion 261.69
excursionist 436.13
excursive 485.3
excusable 228.16.65
excusatory 16.274.43
excuse 309
excuse 523
exeat 381.1
execrable 228.16
execrate 367.25
executant 420
execute 380
execution 261.75
executioner 17.239
executive 485
executor 17.350
executory 16.274.42
executrix 498
exegesis 300.51
exegete 370
exegetic 38.50
exegetics 498.12
exemplar 17.196
exemplary 16.274
exemplify 7.3
exemplum 242
exempt 428
exemption 261
exenterate 367.23
exequies 515
exercise 516.11
exerciser 17.441
exergue 182
exert 369
exertion 261.69
Exeter 17.342
exeunt 419
exfoliate 367.1.3
ex gratia 17.322
exhalant 420.25
exhalation 261.67.14
exhale 214
exhaust 439

exhaustible 228.16
exhaustion 261
exhaustive 485
exhibit 371.5
exhibition 261.71
exhibitioner 17.239.2
exhibitionism 242.35.14
exhibitionist 436.13.5
exhibitive 485.12
exhibitor 17.342
exhilarant 420.65
exhilarate 367.23
exhilaration 261.67.22
exhort 374
exhortation 261.67
exhumation 261.67
exhume 241
exigency 16.312
exigent 420.20
exiguous 310.4
exile 219
exist 436
existence 321.27
existent 420.81
existential 228.96
existentialism 242.35.11
existentialist 436.7
exit 371
ex libris 300
Exmoor 10
exocrine 253
exodus 310.17
exoergic 38.16
ex officio 12.3
exogamy 16.222.2
exonerate 367.23
exorbitant 420.76
exorcise 516
exorcise 516
exorcism 242.35
exorcist 436
exordium 242.2
exoskeleton 261.99
exosphere 6.1
exoteric 38.39
exothermic 38.26
exotic 38.53
exotica 17.34
expand 128
expandable 228.16.17
expander 17.98
expanse 314
expansible 228.16
expansile 219
expansion 261.81

expansionism 242.35.14
expansive 485
ex parte 16.328
expatiate 367.1.5
expatiation 261.67.1
expatriate 367.1
expatriate 371.1
expatriation 261.67.1
expect 385
expectable 228.16
expectancy 16.312
expectant 420.79
expectation 261.67
expecting 265.71
expectorant 420.65
expectorate 367.23
expectoration 261.67.22
expediency 16.312.1
expedient 420.1.1
expediential 228.96
expedite 372.1
expedition 261.71.1
expeditionary
  16.274.29.3
expeditious 310.58.1
expel 215
expellant 420.26
expend 131
expendable 228.16.18
expenditure 17.56
expense 316
expensive 485.9
experience 321.1
experiential 228.96
experiment 410.1
experiment 420.31.2
experimental 228.110.2
experimentalism
  242.35.11.6
experimentation
  261.67.32.1
expert 369
expertise 513
expiable 228.16.2
expiate 367.1
expiation 261.67.1
expiration 261.67
expire 8
expiry 16.267
explain 247
explainable 228.16.27
explanation 261.67.19
explanatory 16.274.43
expletive 485
explicable 228.16.10

explicate 367.5
explication 261.67.5
explicative 485.15.1
explicit 371.36
explode 98
exploit 375
exploitation 261.67
exploration 261.67.22
exploratory 16.274.43.7
explore 9
explorer 17.276
explosion 261.92
explosive 485.6
explosiveness 300.43
exponent 420.54
exponential 228.96
export 374
exportation 261.67
exporter 17.345
expose 520
exposé 2.31
exposed 155
exposition 261.71.9
expositor 17.342.5
expository 16.274.41
expostulate 367.13
expostulation 261.67.13
exposure 17.335
expound 139
express 296
expressage 197.11
expressible 228.16.37
expression 261.68
expressionism
  242.35.14.4
expressionless 300.14
expressive 485.2
expressivity 16.333.35
expresso 12.69
expressway 2
expropriate 367.1
expulsion 261
expulsive 485
expunge 211
expurgate 367.11
expurgation 261.67.11
exquisite 371.38
extant 407
extemporaneous 310.2.6
extempore 16.274.31
extemporize 516.8
extend 131
extender 17.101
extendible 228.16.18
extensible 228.16.40

faggot 381
Fahrenheit 372
faïence 315
fail 214
failing 265.27
faille 214
failure 17.433
fain 247
fainéant 420.1
faint 409
fainter 17.367
fainting 265
faintly 16.196
faintness 300
fair 4
Fairbanks 504
Fairfax 494
fairground 139
fairing 265.52
fairish 353.9
fairlead 89
fairly 16.117
fairness 300.22
fairway 2
fairy 16.264
fairyland 143.2
Faisal 228
faith 454
faithful 226
faithfulness 300.30
faithless 300
fake 34
faker 17.30
fakir 6
fa-la 1.7
Falange 206
falbala 17.176
falcate 367
falciform 238.1
falcon 261.16
falconer 17.239
falconet 368
falconine 253
falconry 16.284
falderal 212
faldstool 227
Faliscan 261
Falkirk 36
Falkland 143
fall 221
fallacious 310.56.3
fallacy 16.307
fallal 212
fallen 261
faller 17.169

fallibility 16.333.9.2
fallible 228.16
Fallopian 261.3.19
fallout 377
fallow 12.38
Falmouth 464
false 312
falsehood 101
falsetto 12.75
falsies 515
falsify 7.3
falsity 16.333
falter 17.363
Falun 259
Famagusta 17.388
fame 231
familial 228.3.4
familiar 17.3.21
familiarity 16.333.20.1
familiarize 516.8
Familist 436.5
family 16.120
famine 252.12
famish 353
famous 310.27
famulus 310.25
fan 245
fanatic 38.49.5
fanatical 228.23.18
fanaticism 242.35.16.4
fanaticize 516.10
fancied 91
fancier 17.3.48
fanciful 226
fancy 16.309
fancywork 36
fandangle 228.49
fandango 12.35
fanfare 4
fang 263
fanion 261.121
fankle 228
fanlight 372
fanny 16.223
fanon 261.55
fantail 214
fan-tailed 112
fantasia 17.3.59
fantasize 516.11
fantast 430
fantastic 38.68
fantasy 16.307
Fanti 16.353
fantoccini 16.228
far 1

farad 103
Faraday 2.8
faradic 38.7
faradism 242.35
farandole 223.2
faraway 2.28
farce 294
farci 5
farcical 228.23
farcy 16.295
fardel 228
fare 4
Fareham 242.18
farewell 215
farina 17.230.1
farinaceous 310.56.4
farinose 305
farl 213
farm 230
farmer 17.206
farmhouse 306
farming 265.35
farmland 143
farmstead 86
farmyard 84
Farnborough 17.279
Farnham 242
faro 12.62
Farouk 45
farrago 12.26
farrier 17.3
farriery 16.274.1
farrow 12.60
far-sighted 91.39
far-sightedness 300.28
fart 366
farther 17.401
farthermost 441
farthest 436
farthing 265
farthingale 214
fartlek 35
fasces 513
fascia 17.322
fascicle 228.23
fascicule 227.1
fascinate 367.17.7
fascinating 265.64.1
fascination 261.67.18.8
fascine 251
fascism 242.35
fascist 436
fashion 261.66
fashionable 228.16.31
Fashoda 17.88

fast 431
fasten 261.61
fastener 17.239
fastening 265.46
fastidious 310.2.1
fastidiousness 300.34.1
fastness 300.42
fat 365
fatal 228.99
fatalism 242.35.11
fatalist 436.7
fatalistic 38.70.2
fatality 16.333.8
fate 367
fated 91.34
fateful 226.7
Fates 335
fathead 86
father 17.401
fatherhood 101
father-in-law 9
fatherland 143.4
fatherless 300.13
fatherly 16.131
fathom 242
fathomable 228.16
fathomless 300
fatidic 38
fatigue 183
Fatima 17.211
fatness 300
fatso 12
fatted 91.32
fatten 261.94
fatty 16.327
fatuity 16.333.3
fatuous 310.4
faubourg 187
faucal 228
faucet 371
fault 404
faultless 300
faultlessness 300.33
faulty 16.351
faun 255
fauna 17.234
Fauré 2
Faust 442
Faustus 310
faux pas 1
faveolate 367.14
favonian 261.3.18
favour 17.410
favourable 228.16.35
favourite 371.35

favouritism 242.35.18
Fawkes 500
fawn 255
fax 494
fay 2
faze 509
fealty 16.352
fear 6
fearful 226
fearfully 16.129
fearless 300
fearlessness 300.33
fearnought 374
fearsome 242
feasible 228.16
feast 435
feat 370
feather 17.402
featherbedding 265.12
featherbrain 247
featherbrained 130
featheredge 194
feathering 265.58
featherstitch 67
featherweight 367.38
feathery 16.274
feature 17.55
featureless 300.13
febrific 38.12
febrifuge 204
febrile 219
febrility 16.333.9
February 16.274.2
feckless 300
fecula 17.174.4
feculent 420.27
fecund 143
fecundate 367
fecundity 16.333.7
fed 86
fedayee 5
federal 228.76
federalize 516.3.8
federate 367.23
federate 371.35
federation 261.67.22
fedora 17.276
fee 5
feeble 228
feeble-minded 91
feeble-mindedness
   300.28
feebleness 300.30
feed 89
feedback 32

feedbag 178
feeder 17.82
feel 217
feeler 17.165
feeling 265.29
feet 370
feign 247
feint 409
feldspar 1
felicitate 367.30
felicitation 261.67.27
felicitous 310.64
felicity 16.333.28
feline 253
fell 215
fellah 17.163
fellatio 12.3.6
feller 17.163
Fellini 16.228.1
fellow 12.40
fellowship 274
felo de se 5.20
felon 261.40
felonious 310.2.9
felony 16.237.5
felt 402
felting 265
felucca 17.39
female 214
feme 232
feminine 252.17
femininity 16.333.17
feminism 242.35.13
feminist 436.11
feminize 516.6
femoral 228.76.2
femur 17.210
fen 248
fence 316
fencer 17.314
fencing 265
fend 131
fender 17.101
fenestrated 91.34
fenestration 261.67.25
Fenian 261.3.16
fennec 35
fennel 228.57
fenny 16.226
Fenrir 6
Fenriswolf 175
Fens 546
fenugreek 37
feral 228
fer-de-lance 315

Ferdinand 128
feretory 16.274.41
Fergana 17.226
feria 17.3.39
ferial 228.3.11
ferity 16.333.21
Fermanagh 17.225
ferment 410.2
fermentation 261.67.32
Fermi 16.214
fermium 242.2
fern 249
fernery 16.274.24
ferocious 16.274.60
ferocity 16.333.30.5
Ferrara 17.268
Ferrari 16.261
ferrate 367
ferret 371.31
ferric 38.39
Ferris 300
ferrite 372
ferritin 252.23
ferrocene 251.9
ferrochromium 242.2.9
ferromagnetism
  242.35.18
ferrosilicon 261.13
ferrous 310.44
ferruginous 310.33
ferrule 227
ferry 16.262
fertile 219
fertility 16.333.9
fertilization 261.67.36
fertilize 516.2
fertilizer 17.441
ferula 17.174
ferule 227
fervent 420.82
fervid 91.55
fervour 17.412
fescue 15
fesse 296
festal 228.113
fester 17.382
festival 228.120
festive 485.24
festivity 16.333.35
festoon 260
festoonery 16.274.28
festschrift 398
feta 17.339
fetal 228.101
fetch 64

fetching 265
fête 367
feticide 92.7
fetid 91.35
fetish 353
fetishism 242.35
fetlock 40
fetor 17.341
fetter 17.339
fettle 228.100
fettucine 16.228
fetus 310.63
feud 102
feudal 228.37
feudalism 242.35.11
feudality 16.333.8
feudalize 516.3
feudist 436
feuilleton 254
fever 17.413
fevered 103
feverfew 15
feverish 353.11
feverishness 300.35
few 15
fey 2
fez 510
Fezzan 246
fiancé 2
Fianna fail 222.1
fiasco 12
fiat 381.2
Fiat 381
fib 24
fibber 17.14
fibre 17.15
fibreglass 294
fibriform 238.1
fibril 218
fibrillation 261.67.12
fibrinogen 261.39
fibrinolysin 252.21
fibrocement 410.1
fibroid 97
fibroma 17.215
fibrosis 300.55
fibrositis 300.62
fibrous 310
fibula 17.174.2
fiche 352
fichu 15
fickle 228.23
fickleness 300.30
fictile 219
fiction 261.78

fictional 228.63
fictionalize 516.3.7
fictitious 310.58
fictive 485.18
fid 91
fiddle 228.32
fiddle-de-dee 5
fiddle-faddle 228.31
fiddler 17.186
fiddlestick 38
fiddlesticks 498
fiddling 265
fiddly 16.148
fideicommissum 242.24
fideism 242.35
fidelity 16.333
fidget 371
fidgety 16.333
fiduciary 16.274.1
fie 7
fief 162
field 115
fielder 17.94
fieldfare 4
fieldmouse 306
fieldwork 36
fiend 133
fiendish 353
fierce 299
fieri facias 310.2.16
fiery 16.267
fiesta 17.382.1
FIFA 17.113
fife 164
Fife 164
fifteen 251
fifteenth 469
fiftieth 458
fifty 16.347
fig 184
fight 372
fighter 17.343
fighting 265.67
figment 420
figurant 420
figuration 261.67.22
figurative 485.15.10
figure 17.129
figurehead 86.5
figurine 251.7
Fijian 261.2
filament 420.35
filar 17.167
filaria 17.3.38
filariasis 300.57.1

filature 17.62
filbert 381
filch 76
file 219
filecard 84
filet mignon 254.12
filial 228.3.4
filiate 367.1.2
filiation 261.67.1.1
filibeg 181
filibuster 17.388
filicide 92.7
filiform 238.1
filigree 5.18
filings 552
Filipino 12.54
fill 218
filler 17.166
fillet 371.16
filling 265.30
fillip 274
filly 16.120
film 244
filmography 16.90.2
filmset 368
filose 305
fils 311
filter 17.362
filth 466
filthiness 300.23
filthy 16
filtrate 367
filtration 261.67
filum 242.9
fimble 228
fin 252
finable 228.16.30
finagle 228.44
final 228.61
finale 16.113
finalism 242.35.11
finalist 436.7
finality 16.333.8
finalize 516.3
finally 16.131
finals 539
finance 314
financial 228.95
financier 17.3.48
finch 80
find 135
finder 17.103
finding 265.21
fine 2
fine 253

Fine Gael 214
fineness 300
finery 16.274.27
finespun 259
finesse 296.2
finfoot 379
finger 17.141
fingerboard 95.1
fingering 265.58
fingermark 33
fingernail 214
fingerprint 412
fingerstall 221
fingertip 274
finicky 16.25
fining 265.44
finis 300.23
finish 353.7
finisher 17.326
Finisterre 4
finite 372
fink 52
Finland 143
Finn 252
finnan 261.56
finnan haddie 16.57
finned 134
finner 17.231
Finnic 38.34
Finnish 353.7
Finnmark 33
finny 16.229
fino 12.54
Finsteraarhorn 255
fipple 228.66
fir 3
Firdausi 16.304
fire 8
firearm 230
fireball 221
firebird 87
firebomb 237
firebox 499
firebrand 128
firebreak 34
firebrick 38
firebug 189
firecracker 17.28
firedamp 285
firedog 185
firedrake 34
firefly 7
fireguard 84
fireman 261
fireplace 295

fireproof 170
fireside 92
firetrap 268
firewarden 261.27
firewater 17.345
fireweed 89
firewood 101
firework 36
fireworks 497
firing 265.54
firkin 252
firm 233
firmament 420.35
firmness 300
firmware 4
firry 16.263
first 434
first-born 255
first-footer 17.350
first-footing 265
first-rate 367
firth 456
fiscal 228
fish 353
fishbowl 223
fisher 17.326
fisherman 261.52.1
fishery 16.274
fishfinger 17.141
fishgig 184
fishing 265.63
fishmonger 17.143
fishnet 368
fishwife 164
fishy 16.322
fissile 219.2
fission 261.71
fissiped 86.6
fissure 17.326
fist 436
fistic 38.70
fistula 17.174
fit 371
fitch 67
fitful 226
fitly 16.189
fitment 420.49
fitness 300.38
fitted 91.38
fitter 17.342
fitting 265.66
Fittipaldi 16.73
Fitzgerald 122.1
five 486
fivefold 120

fivepenny 16.237
fiver 17.415
fives 554
fix 498
fixate 367
fixation 261.67
fixative 485.15
fixedly 16.148
fixer 17.427
fixity 16.333
fixture 17.76
fizz 515
fizzle 228
fizzy 16.396
fjord 95
flab 18
flabbergast 431.1
flabbergasted 91.51
flabbiness 300.23
flabby 16.5
flabellate 371.15
flaccid 91.28
flag 178
flagellant 420
flagellate 367.12
flagellate 371.16
flagellum 242.8
flageolet 368
flagging 265
flaggy 16.91
flagitious 310.58
flagman 261
flagon 261.30
flagpole 223
flagrancy 16.312
flagrant 420
flagship 274
flagstaff 158
flagstone 257
flail 214
flair 4
flak 32
flake 34
flaky 16.21
flambé 2.5
flambeau 12
Flamborough 17.279
flamboyance 321
flamboyant 420.3
flame 231
flamen 248.2
flamenco 12.13
flameproof 170
flaming 265
flamingo 12.36

Flamininus 310.34
Flaminius 310.2.8
flammable 228.16.26
Flamsteed 89
flan 245
Flanders 524
flange 206
flank 51
flanker 17.43
flannel 228.55
flannelette 368
flannels 539
flap 268
flapdoodle 228.37
flapjack 32
flapper 17.247
flare 4
flash 349
flashback 32
flashboard 95
flashcube 30
flasher 17.321
flashing 265
flashlight 372
flashover 17.417
flashy 16.319
flask 56
flat 365
flatfish 353
flatfoot 379
flat-footed 91
flat-footedness 300.28
flathead 86
flatiron 261.4
flatlet 371
flatly 16.186
flatmate 367
flatness 300
flats 333
flatten 261.94
flatter 17.336
flatterer 17.279
flattering 265.58
flattery 16.274
flattish 353
flattop 276
flatulence 321
flatulent 420.27
flatus 310.62
flatworm 233
Flaubert 4
flaunch 81
flaunt 415
flaunty 16.358
flautist 436

flavescent 420.67.3
flavone 257
flavour 17.410
flavourful 226
flavouring 265.58.1
flavourless 300.13
flaw 9
flawless 300
flax 494
flaxen 261
flaxseed 89
flay 2
flea 5
fleabag 178
fleabane 247
fleabite 372
fleam 234
fleapit 371
fléchette 368
fleck 35
fled 86
fledge 194
fledgling 265
fledgy 16.101
flee 5
fleece 298
fleecy 16.299
fleet 370
fleeting 265
Fleetwood 101
Fleming 265
Flemish 353
flense 316
flesh 351
flesher 17.323
fleshly 16.185
fleshpots 341
fleshy 16.321
fletch 64
Fletcher 17.53
fleur-de-lis 5.9
fleurette 368
flew 15
flews 523
flex 496
flexibility 16.333.9.2
flexible 228.16
flexion 261.77
flexitime 236
flexor 17.426
flexuous 310.4
flibbertigibbet 371.5
flick 38
flicker 17.34
flight 372

flightless 300
flighty 16.334
flimflam 229
flimsy 16.403
flinch 80
flincher 17.71
fling 265
flint 412
Flint 412
Flintshire 6
flinty 16.356
flip 274
flip-flop 276
flippant 420.56
flipper 17.253
flipping 265
flirt 369
flirtation 261.67
flirtatious 310.56
flit 371
flitch 67
flitter 17.342
flittermouse 306
flivver 17.414
float 376
floater 17.347
floating 265
floaty 16.339
floccose 305
flocculate 367.13.3
floccule 227
flocculent 420.27
floccus 310.11
flock 40
Flodden 261.26
floe 12
flog 185
flogging 265.23
flong 266
flood 100
floodgate 367
floodlight 372
floor 9
floorage 197
floorboard 95
flooring 265.55
floozy 16.402
flop 276
floppy 16.250
flora 17.276
Flora 17.276
floral 228.74
Florence 321.18
Florentine 253
florescence 321.21

floret 371
floriated 91.34.1
floribunda 17.108
florid 91.26
Florida 17.83
florigen 261.37
florin 252.18
florist 436.18
floristic 38.70
floss 302
flossy 16.302
flotage 197.13
flotation 261.67.28
flotilla 17.166
flotsam 242
flounce 319
flouncing 265
flounder 17.107
flour 14
flourish 353.10
floury 16.274
flout 377
flow 12
flowage 197
flower 14
flowerbed 86.1
floweret 371
flowering 265.57
flowerless 300
flowerpot 373
flowery 16.274
flown 257
flu 15
fluctuant 420.4
fluctuate 367.2
fluctuation 261.67.2
flue 15
fluency 16.312
fluent 420.5
fluff 168
fluffiness 300.23
fluffy 16.88
flugelhorn 255
fluid 91.3
fluidity 16.333.5
fluidize 516
fluke 45
fluky 16.32
flume 241
flummery 16.274
flummox 503
flung 267
flunk 54
flunky 16.39
fluoresce 296

fluorescence 321.21
fluorescent 420.67
fluoridate 367.8
fluoridation 261.67.7
fluoride 92
fluorinate 367.17
fluorine 251
fluorspar 1
flurry 16.272
flush 356
Flushing 265
fluster 17.388
flute 380
fluted 91.42
fluter 17.351
fluting 265
flutter 17.349
fluvial 228.3.17
flux 502
fluxion 261.79
fly 7
flyaway 2.28
flyblown 257
flyby 7
flyer 17.4
flying 265.3
flyleaf 162
flyover 17.417
flypaper 17.249
flyspeck 35
flytrap 268
flyweight 367
flywheel 217
foal 223
foam 239
foamy 16.219
fob 26
focal 228.26
focus 310.12
fodder 17.85
foe 12
foeman 261.49
fog 185
fogbound 139
fogged 106
foggy 16.94
foghorn 255
fogy 16.96
foible 228
foil 222
foison 261.128
foist 440
Fokker 17.36
fold 120
foldaway 2.28

folder 17.97
foliaceous 310.56
foliage 197
foliar 17.3.22
foliate 371.1
foliated 91.34.1
foliation 261.67.1.2
folio 12.3.3
foliose 305.1
folium 242.2.7
folk 42
folklore 9
folkloric 38.41
folkmoot 380
follicle 228.23.8
follicular 17.174.6
folliculin 252.10
follow 12.43
follower 17.6
following 265.4
folly 16.122
foment 410.2
fomentation 261.67.32
fond 136
Fonda 17.104
fondant 420.15
fondle 228
fondness 300
fondue 15
font 414
Fontainebleau 12
fontanelle 215
Fonteyn 247.11
Foochow 13
food 102
foodstuff 168
fool 227
foolery 16.274
foolhardiness 300.23
foolhardy 16.58
foolish 353
foolishness 300.35
foolproof 170
foolscap 268
foot 379
footage 197
football 221
footballer 17.169
footboy 11
footbridge 197
footfall 221
footgear 6
foothill 218
foothold 120
footing 265

footle 228.108
footlights 340
footling 265
footloose 309
footman 261
footmark 33
footnote 376
footpad 83
footpath 453
footplate 367
footprint 412
footrest 433
foots 345
footsie 16.318
footslog 185
footsore 9
footstall 221
footstep 271
footstool 227
footway 2
footwear 4
footwork 36
footy 16.342
foo yong 266
foozle 228.128
fop 276
foppery 16.274
foppish 353
for 9
forage 197
foramen 248.2
forasmuch 72
foray 2
forbade 83
forbear 4
forbearance 321
forbid 91.4
forbiddance 321.5
forbidden 261.24
forbidding 265
forbore 9
force 303
forceful 226.6
force majeure 3
forcemeat 370
forceps 327
forcible 228.16
ford 95
fordable 228.16.16
fore 9
forearm 230
forebear 4
forebode 98
foreboding 265.16
forebrain 247

forecast 431
forecaster 17.380
foreclose 520
foreclosure 17.335
forecourse 303
forecourt 374
foredeck 35
foredoom 241
forefather 17.401
forefinger 17.141
forefront 419
forego 12
foregoing 265.4
foregone 254
foreground 139
foregut 378
forehand 128
forehanded 91.12
forehead 91.26
forehock 40
foreign 252.18
foreigner 17.231
foreignism 242.35.13
forejudge 203
foreknew 15
foreknow 12
foreknowledge 197.2
foreland 143
foreleg 181
forelimb 235
forelock 40
foreman 261
foremast 431
foremost 441
forename 231
forenamed 124
forenoon 260
forensic 38
forensics 498
foreordain 247
forepart 366
forepaw 9
forepeak 37
foreplay 2
forequarter 17.345
forerun 259
forerunner 17.237
foresail 214
foresaw 9
foresee 5.21
foreseeable 228.16.1
foreseen 251
foreshadow 12
foresheet 370
foreshore 9

Fra 1
fracas 1
fraction 261.76
fractional 228.63
fractionate 367.18
fractious 310
fracture 17.63
frae 2
fragile 219
fragility 16.333.9
fragment 410
fragment 420
fragmental 228.110
fragmentary 16.274.48
fragmentation 261.67.32
fragrance 321
fragrant 420
frail 214
fraise 509
framboesia 17.3.60
frame 231
frameless 300
framer 17.207
framework 36
franc 51
France 315
franchise 516
Francis 300
Franciscan 261
francolin 252.9
Francophile 219.1
Francophobe 28
Francophobia 17.3.4
Francophone 257
frangible 228.16.21
frangipane 247
frangipani 16.224
frank 51
Frank 51
frankalmoign 256
Frankenstein 253
Frankfurt 381
frankfurter 17.340
frankincense 316
Frankish 353
franklin 252
frankly 16.144
frankness 300
frankpledge 194
frantic 38.62
frappé 2
Fraser 17.439
frass 293
frater 17.338
fraternal 228.58

fraternity 16.333.16
fraternize 516.7
fratricide 92.7
Frau 13
fraud 95
fraudulent 420.27
fraught 374
fray 2
frazzle 228.124
freak 37
freakish 353
freaky 16.24
freckle 228.21
freckled 122
Frederick 38
free 5
freebie 16.10
freeboard 95
freeboot 380
freebooter 17.351
freeborn 255
freedman 261
freedom 242
freehold 120
freeholder 17.97
freelance 315
freeload 98
freely 16.118
freeman 261.47
freemartin 252
freemason 261.62
freemasonic 38.35.4
freemasonry 16.284
freesheet 370
freesia 17.334
freestanding 265.19
freestone 257
freestyle 219
freethinker 17.44
freethinking 265.10
freeway 2
freewheel 217
freewheeling 265.29
freeze 513
freezer 17.440
freezing 265
freight 367
freighter 17.338
freightliner 17.232
Fremantle 228.109
French 79
Frenchify 7.3
Frenchman 261
frenetic 38.50.4
frenulum 242.10

frenzied 91
frenzy 16.405
frequency 16.312
frequent 410
frequent 420.57
frequentation 261.67.32
frequentative 485.15.15
fresco 12.14
fresh 351
freshen 261.68
freshener 17.239
fresher 17.323
freshet 371
freshly 16.185
freshman 261
freshness 300
freshwater 17.345
fresnel 215
fret 368
fretful 226.8
fretted 91.35
fretwork 36
Freud 97
Freudian 261.3
Frey 2
Freya 17.1
friable 228.16.3
friar 17.4
friarbird 87
friary 16.274
fribble 228.12
fricassee 5
fricative 485.15.1
friction 261.78
frictional 228.63
Friday 2
fridge 197
friend 131
friendless 300
friendlessness 300.33
friendliness 300.23
friendly 16.154
friendship 274
Friesian 261.90
Friesland 143
frieze 513
frig 184
frigate 371.14
frigging 265
fright 372
frighten 261.100
frightening 265.46
frightful 226.9
frightfully 16.129
frigid 91.15

frigidity 16.333.5
frill 218
frilly 16.120
fringe 209
frippery 16.274.30
frippet 371
Frisbee 5
Frisco 12.15
frisé 2.30
Frisian 261.91
frisk 58
frisker 17.48
frisket 371
frisky 16.41
fritillary 16.274.16
fritter 17.342
frivol 228.120
frivolity 16.333.10
frivolous 310.26
frizz 515
frizzle 228
frizzy 16.396
fro 12
Frobisher 17.326
frock 40
frocking 265.8
frog 185
frogfish 353
frogging 265.23
froggy 16.94
froghopper 17.255
frogman 261
frogmarch 63
frogspawn 255
frolic 38.22
frolicsome 242
from 237
frond 136
Fronde 136
fronded 91
frondescence 321.21
frons 549
front 419
frontage 197
frontal 228.112
frontier 6
frontiersman 261.54
frontispiece 298
frontrunner 17.237
frost 438
frostbite 372
frostbitten 261.99
frosted 91
frosting 265
frosty 16.367

froth 459
frothy 16.371
frottage 359
froward 103
frown 258
frowst 442
frowzy 16.400
froze 520
frozen 261.129
fructiferous 310.50.2
fructose 520
fructuous 310.4
frugal 228.48
frugality 16.333.8
frugivorous 310.50.3
fruit 380
fruitarian 261.3.21
fruitcake 34
fruiter 17.351
fruiterer 17.279
fruitful 226
fruition 261.71
fruitless 300
fruitlessness 300.33
fruity 16.343
frumenty 16.360
frump 289
frumpish 353
frustrate 367
frustration 261.67
frustule 227
frustum 242.32
frutescent 420.67
fry 7
fryer 17.4
fuchsia 17
fuchsin 252
fuck 43
fucker 17.39
fucking 265
fucoid 97
fucus 310.13
fuddle 228.36
fuddy-duddy 16.69
fudge 203
fuel 228.10
fug 189
fugacious 310.56
fugal 228.48
fugitive 485.12
fugue 190
Fuji 5
Fukien 248
Fula 17.175
fulcrum 242

fulfil 218
fulfilment 420
fulgent 420.21
fulgurant 420
fulgurate 367.22
fulgurating 265.64
Fulham 242.10
fuliginous 310.33
full 226
fullback 32
full-blooded 91.11
full-blown 257
fuller 17.174
full-frontal 228.112
fullness 300
full-time 236
full-timer 17.212
fully 16.129
fully-fledged 109
fulminant 420.53
fulminate 367.17
fulmination 261.67.18
fulsome 242
fumarole 223.3
fumatorium 242.2.17
fumatory 16.274.43
fumble 228
fumbler 17.180
fume 241
fumigant 420.17
fumigate 367.10
fumigation 261.67.10
fumitory 16.274.41
fun 259
funambulist 436.6
function 261.80
functional 228.63
functionalism
    242.35.11.5
functionary 16.274.29
fund 140
fundament 420.35
fundamental 228.110.3
fundamentalism
    242.35.11.6
fundi 5
Fundy 16.80
funeral 228.76
funerary 16.274.32
funereal 228.3.11
funfair 4
fungal 228
fungi 7
fungicide 92.7
fungiform 238.1

fungoid 97
fungous 310
fungus 310
funicle 228.23
funicular 17.174.6
funk 54
funky 16.39
funnel 228
funny 16.235
fur 3
furbelow 12.42
furbish 353
furcate 367
furcula 17.174.5
furious 310.2.14
furl 216
furlong 266
furlough 12
furnace 300
Furness 300
furnish 353
furnisher 17.326
furnishing 265.63
furnishings 552
furniture 17.56
furor 9
furore 16.269
furphy 16.83
furred 87
furrier 17.3
furriery 16.274.1
furring 265.51
furrow 12
furry 16.263
further 17.403
furtherance 321.20
furthermore 9.9
furthermost 441
furthest 436
furtive 485.11
furtiveness 300.43
furuncle 228.30
furunculosis 300.55.3
fury 16.270
furze 511
fusain 247
fuse 523
fusel 228.128
fuselage 359
fusible 228.16.65
fusiform 238.1
fusilier 6
fusillade 85
fusion 261.93
fuss 307

fussiness 300.23
fusspot 373
fussy 16.305
fustanella 17.163
fustian 261.3.27
fustic 38
fusty 16.368
futhark 33
futile 219
futilitarian 261.3.21.2
futility 16.333.9
futtock 46
future 17.61
futurism 242.35.15
futuristic 38.70.5
futurity 16.333.23
futurology 16.108.4.13
fuzz 522
fuzzy 16.401
Fylde 117
fyrd 90

G

gab 18
gabble 228
gabbler 17.177
gabby 16.5
gaberdine 251.1
gabfest 433
gabion 261.3.1
gabionade 85.3
gable 228.11
gabled 122
Gabon 254
Gabor 9
Gaborone 16.233
Gabriel 228.3
gaby 16.7
gad 83
gadabout 377.1
gadfly 7
gadget 371
gadgeteer 6
gadgetry 16.285
Gadhelic 38.20
gadid 91.6
gadoid 97
gadolinite 372.5
gadolinium 242.2.11
gadroon 260
Gael 214
Gaelic 38
gaff 157
gaffe 157

gaffer 17.110
gag 178
gaga 1
Gagauzi 16.397
gage 193
gagger 17.123
gaggle 228.43
gaiety 16.344
gaillardia 17.3.6
gaily 16.114
gain 247
gainer 17.227
gainful 226.4
gainly 16.170
gainsay 2
Gainsborough 17.279
gait 367
gaiter 17.338
Gaitskell 218
Gaius 310.3
gal 212
gala 17.161
galactagogue 185.2
galactic 38.58
galactopoietic 38.50
galactose 520
galah 1.9
Galahad 83
galangal 228.49
galantine 251
Galápagos 310
galatea 17.2
Galatia 17.322
Galatians 551.1
galaxy 16.390
galbanum 242.16
Galbraith 454
gale 214
galea 17.3.18
Galen 261
galenical 228.23.11
Galibi 16.10
Galilean 261.2.2
galilee 5.8
Galilee 5.8
Galileo 12.1
galingale 214
galiot 381.1
galipot 373
gall 221
gallant 407
gallant 420.24
gallantry 16.291
galleass 293.1
galleon 261.3

gallery 16.274.15
galley 16.112
gallfly 7
galliambic 38.5
galliard 103
Gallic 38.19
Gallicanism 242.35.14.2
Gallice 16.300
Gallicism 242.35.16.1
Gallicize 516.10
galligaskins 548
gallimaufry 16.280
gallinaceous 310.56.4
galling 265.31
gallinule 227
Gallipoli 16.131.5
gallipot 373
gallium 242.2
gallivant 407.1
galliwasp 292
gallnut 378
galloglass 294
gallon 261
galloon 260.1
gallop 281
galloping 265
Galloway 2.28
gallows 520.1
gallstone 257
Gallup 281
galoot 380.1
galore 9.8
galoshes 515
Galsworthy 16.375
galumph 177
galvanic 38.31
galvanism 242.35.14
galvanize 516.7
galvanometer 17.342.3.3
galvo 12
Galway 2
galyak 32
gam 229
Gambetta 17.339
Gambia 17.3.5
gambit 371
gamble 228.17
gambler 17.179
gambling 265
gamboge 201
gambol 228.17
game 231
gamecock 40
gamekeeper 17.252
gamelan 245.2

gamely 16.165
gamesmanship 274.2
gamete 370
gametophore 9.6
gamic 38.24
gamin 252.12
gamine 251
gaming 265
gamma 17.205
gammadion 261.3.3
gammon 261.44
gammy 16.210
gamp 285
gamut 381
gamy 16.212
gan 245
gander 17.98
Gandhi 16.77
ganef 171
gang 263
gangbang 263
ganger 17.245
Ganges 513
gangland 143
gangling 265
ganglion 261.3
gangplank 51
gangrene 251
gangrenous 310.33
gangster 17
gangway 2
ganister 17.384
gannet 371.22
gansey 16.404
gantry 16.287
Ganymede 89
gap 268
gape 270
gapes 323
gar 1
garage 359
Garamond 136
garb 19
garbage 197
garble 228
Garbo 12
Garda 17.78
garden 261
gardener 17.240
gardenia 17.3.33
gardening 265.46
Gardiner 17.240
garfish 353
Gargantua 17.7.2
gargantuan 261.7

garget 371
gargle 228
gargoyle 222
garibaldi 16.75
Garibaldi 16.75
garish 353.9
garland 143
garlic 38
garlicky 16.25
garment 420
garner 17.226
garnet 371
garnish 353
garnishee 5
garniture 17.56
garotte 373
garpike 39
garret 371
Garrick 38.38
garrison 261.65.1
garrulous 310.25
garrya 17.3
garter 17.337
garth 453
Gary 16.260
gas 293
gasbag 178
gasconade 85.3
Gascony 16.237
gaseous 310.2
gash 349
gasholder 17.97
gasiform 238.1
gasify 7.3.6
Gaskell 228
gasket 371
gaslight 372
gasman 261
gasolier 6
gasoline 251.3
gasometer 17.342.3
gasp 290
Gaspé 2
gasser 17.298
gassy 16.294
gastralgia 17.3.16
gastralgic 38
gastrectomy 16.222.5
gastric 38
gastritis 300.62
gastroenteric 38.39
gastroenteritis 300.62.5
gastroenterology
    16.108.4.13
gastrolith 458

gastrology 16.108.4
gastronome 239
gastronomer 17.218.1
gastronomic 38.29.1
gastronomical 228.23.9
gastronomy 16.222.3
gastropod 94.1
gastroscope 278.1
gastrostomy 16.222.6
gastrotrich 38
gastrula 17.174
gasworks 497
gate 367
gateau 12.72
gate-crash 349
gate-crasher 17.321
gatefold 120
gatehouse 306
gatekeeper 17.252
gatepost 441
Gateshead 86
gateway 2
Gath 452
gather 17.400
gathering 265.58
Gatling 265
gauche 355
gaucherie 5.17
gaucho 12
gaudy 16.66
gauge 193
gauger 17.146
Gaul 221
Gauleiter 17.343
Gaulish 353
Gaullism 242.35
Gaullist 436
gaunt 415
gauntlet 371
gauntness 300
gauss 306
Gautama 17.218
gauze 518
gauzy 16.397
gavage 359
gave 482
gavel 228.117
gavelkind 135
gavial 228.3
gavotte 373
gawk 41
gawky 16.28
gawp 277
gay 2
Gay Gordons 551

Gay-Lussac 32
Gaynor 17.227
Gaza 17.438
gaze 509
gazebo 12.5
gazelle 215
gazette 368.9
gazetteer 6
Gaziantep 271
gazpacho 12
gazump 289
gean 251
gear 6
gearbox 499
gearing 265.53
gearshift 398
gearwheel 217
gecko 12.9
gedact 383
gee 5
gee-gee 5
geek 37
geese 298
geest 435
geezer 17.440
gegenschein 253
Gehenna 17.228
Geiger 17.130
geisha 17.322
gel 215
gelada 17.92
gelatin 252
gelatine 251.11
gelatinize 516.6.1
gelatinoid 97.8.1
gelatinous 310.33
gelation 261.67.12
geld 113
Gelderland 143.4
gelding 265
gelid 91.17
gelignite 372.7
gelsemium 242.2.8
gelt 402
gem 232
Gemini 7.10
gemma 17.208
gemot 376
gemsbok 40
gemstone 257
gen 248
gendarme 230
gendarmerie 16.274.20
gender 17.101
gene 251

genealogist 436.4.1
genealogy 16.108.2
genera 17.279
generable 228.16.35
general 228.76
generalissimo 12.48
generalist 436.7
generality 16.333.8.9
generalization 261.67.36
generalize 516.3.8
generally 16.131
generate 367.23.1
generation 261.67.22.2
generative 485.15.10
generator 17.338.9
generatrix 498.9
generic 38.39
generosity 16.333.30.5
generous 310.50
genesis 300.52.4
genet 371
genetic 38.50.4
geneticist 436.21
genetics 498.12
Geneva 17.413
Genevan 261.113
Genevieve 484
Genghis Khan 246
genial 228.3.6
geniality 16.333.8.1
genic 38.32
genie 16.228
genii 7.1
genipap 268
genital 228.102
genitalia 17.3.18
genitalic 38.19.1
genitals 539
genitive 485.12
genitor 17.342
genitourinary 16.274.26
genius 310.2.7
genoa 17.6
Genoa 17.6
genocide 92.8
Genoese 513.2
genome 239
genotype 275.1
gens 546
gent 410
genteel 217
gentian 261.82
Gentile 219.6
gentility 16.333.9
gentle 228.110

gentlefolk 42
gentleman 261
gentlemanly 16.174
gentleness 300.30
gentlewoman 261.50
gently 16.197
gentry 16.288
genuflect 385
genuflection 261.77
genuine 252
genus 310.32
geocentric 38.47
geode 98
geodesic 38
geodesy 16.300.1
geognosy 16.307.3
geographical 228.23.3
geography 16.90.2.1
geoid 97.1
geological 228.23.5
geologize 516.1
geology 16.108.4.1
geomagnetism 242.35.18
geometer 17.342.3.1
geometric 38.46
geometrid 91
geometry 16.285.2.1
geomorphic 38.14
geomorphology 16.108.4
geophagism 242.35.8
geophagy 16.108.1
geophysics 498
geoponic 38.35
geoponics 498.5
Geordie 16.66
George 200
georgette 368
Georgia 17.153
Georgian 261
georgic 38
Georgie 16.105
geostatic 38.49.7
geosyncline 253.5
geotectonic 38.35
Gerald 122.1
geranial 228.3.5
geranium 242.2.10
geratology 16.108.4.15
gerbil 218
gerent 420.61
geriatric 38.45
geriatrician 261.71.6
geriatrics 498.8
germ 233
German 261

germander 17.98
germane 247
Germanic 38.31
Germanism 242.35.14
germanium 242.2.10
Germanize 516.7
Germanophile 219.1
Germanophilia 17.3.21.2
Germanophobe 28
Germanophobia 17.3.4
Germany 16.237
germicide 92.7
germinal 228.60
germinant 420.53.1
germinate 367.17.4
germination 261.67.18.4
Germiston 261.107
Geronimo 12.48
gerontocracy 16.307.5
gerontology 16.108.4.16
gerrymander 17.98
Gershwin 252
gerund 143
gerundive 485
gesso 12.69
gestalt 401
Gestapo 12.57
gestate 367.33
gestation 261.67.33
gesticulate 367.13.2
gesticulation 261.67.13
gesture 17.73
get 368
Gethsemane 16.237.6
getter 17.339
Getty 16.330
Gettysburg 182
geum 242.1
gewgaw 9
geyser 17.440
Gezira 17.272
Ghana 17.226
Ghanaian 261.1
ghastly 16.199
ghat 366
Ghats 334
ghazi 16.392
ghee 5
Ghent 410
gherkin 252
ghetto 12.75
ghibli 16.134
ghost 441
ghostlike 39
ghostliness 300.23

ghostly 16.202
ghostwrite 372
ghostwriter 17.343
ghoul 227
ghoulish 353
giant 420.2
gibber 17.14
gibberellin 252.7
gibberish 353.11
gibbet 371.5
gibbon 261
gibbous 310.5
gibe 25
Gibeon 261.3.2
giblets 339
Gibraltar 17.363
Gibson 261
gid 91
giddiness 300.23
giddy 16.63
giddy-up 279
Gideon 261.3.5
gidgee 5.6
gie 5
Gielgud 101
gift 398
gifted 91
giftwrap 268
gig 184
gigantic 38.62
gigantism 242.35
gigantomachy 16.33
giggle 228.46
giggly 16.160
gigolo 12.45
gigot 12.28
gigue 183
Gilbert 381
Gilbertian 261.3
gild 116
gilding 265.17
Gilead 83.1
gilet 2.11
gilgai 7
Gilgamesh 351
gill 218
Gillian 261.3.11
gillie 16.120
Gillingham 242.17
gillyflower 14
gilt 403
gimbals 539
gimcrack 32
gimlet 371
gimmal 228.52

gimme 5
gimmick 38.28
gimmickry 16.275
gimmicky 16.25
gimp 287
gin 252
ginger 17.157
gingerbread 86
gingerly 16.131
gingery 16.274.14
gingham 242.17
gingiva 17.414
gingivitis 300.62.6
ginglymus 310.28
gink 52
ginnel 228.60
ginseng 264
Giotto 12.77
gippy 16.248
giraffe 158
girandole 223.2
girasol 220
gird 87
girder 17.81
girdle 228
girl 216
girlfriend 131
girlhood 101
girlie 16.116
girlish 353
giro 12.64
giron 254
girt 369
girth 456
Gisborne 261
gist 436
git 371
gittern 249.1
give 485
given 261.114
giver 17.414
gizzard 103
glabella 17.163.1
glabrous 310
glacé 16.294
glacial 228.91
glacialist 436.7.2
glaciate 367.1.4
glaciation 261.67.1.3
glacier 17.3.46
glaciology 16.108.4.1
glacis 300.49
glad 83
gladden 261.19
glade 85

gladiate 371.1
gladiator 17.338.1
gladiatorial 228.3.12
gladiolus 310
gladly 16.146
gladness 300
gladsome 242
Gladstone 261
glair 4
Glamorgan 261.33
glamorize 516.8
glamorous 310.50
glamour 17.205
glance 315
gland 128
glanders 524
glandular 17.174
glans 544
glare 4
glaring 265.52
glary 16.264
Glasgow 12
glass 294
glass-blower 17.6
glasses 515
glasshouse 306
glassine 251
glasslike 39
glassware 4
glasswork 36
glassworks 497
glassy 16.295
Glastonbury 16.274
Glaswegian 261.36
Glauce 16.303
glaucoma 17.215
glaucous 310
glaze 509
glazier 17.3.59
glazing 265.81
gleam 234
glean 251
gleanings 552
glebe 23
glee 5
gleeful 226
gleet 370
glen 248
Glencoe 12
Glendower 14
glengarry 16.260
glenoid 97.7
Glenrothes 300
gley 2
gliadin 252

glib 24
glibly 16.134
glide 92
glider 17.84
gliding 265.14
glimmer 17.211
glimpse 331
glint 412
glioma 17.215
glissade 84
glissando 12.23
glisten 261.65
glister 17.384
glitter 17.342
glittery 16.274.41
gloaming 265.37
gloat 376
glob 26
global 228.13
globate 367.3
globe 28
globetrotter 17.344
globetrotting 265.68
globigerina 17.232
globoid 97
globose 305
globular 17.174
globule 227
globulin 252.10
glockenspiel 217
glogg 185
glomeration 261.67.22
glomerulus 310.25.1
gloom 241
gloominess 300.23
gloomy 16.221
gloria 17.3.41
Gloria 17.3.41
glorify 7.3
glorious 310.2.13
glory 16.269
gloss 302
glossa 17.304
glossary 16.274
glossitis 300.62
glossolalia 17.3.18
glossy 16.302
glottal 228.104
glottic 38.53
Gloucester 17.385
Gloucestershire 6
glove 489
glover 17.418
glow 12
glower 14

gloxinia 17.3.34
glucagon 254.5
glucinum 242.15
glucose 520
glue 15
gluey 16.4
glum 240
glumly 16.168
glumness 300
gluon 254
glut 378
glutamate 367.16
glutamine 251.4
gluten 261.104
gluteus 310.1
glutinous 310.33.2
glutton 261.103
gluttonous 310.36
gluttony 16.237
glyceric 38.39
glyceride 92.6
glycerine 252.20
glycerol 220.4
glycogen 261.39
glycol 220
glycolysis 300.52.2
glycoside 92.8
glycosuria 17.3.42.2
glyph 163
glyptic 38.66
glyptics 498
glyptography 16.90.2
gnarl 213
gnash 349
gnat 365
gnathic 38.72
gnathion 254.1
gnaw 9
gnawing 265
gneiss 301
gnocchi 16.27
gnome 239
gnomic 38
gnomon 254
gnosis 300.55
gnostic 38.71
Gnosticism 242.35.16
gnu 15
go 12
goa 17.6
Goa 17.6
goad 98
go-ahead 86.5
goal 223
goalie 16.126

goalkeeper 17.252
goalless 300
goalmouth 462
goanna 17.225
goat 376
goatee 5
goatherd 87
goatish 353
goatsbeard 90
goatskin 252
goatsucker 17.39
gob 26
gobbet 371
gobble 228
gobbledegook 45
gobbler 17.178
Gobelin 252.11
go-between 251
Gobi 16.12
goblet 371
goblin 252
gobstopper 17.255
goby 16.12
god 94
godchild 117
goddamn 229
Goddard 84
goddaughter 17.345
goddess 300.4
godetia 17.325
godfather 17.401
god-fearing 265.53
godforsaken 261.11
Godhead 86
godhood 101
Godiva 17.415
godless 300
godlessness 300.33
godlike 39
godliness 300.23
godly 16.149
godmother 17.408
Godolphin 252
godown 258
godparent 420
godsend 131
godson 259
Godspeed 89
Godunov 165
Godwin 252
godwit 371
goer 17.6
goffer 17.117
Gog 185
go-getter 17.339

goggle 228.47
gogglebox 499
Gogol 220
Goiânia 17.3.30
Goidel 228.35
Goidelic 38.20
going 265.4
goitre 17.346
go-kart 366
Golconda 17.104
gold 120
goldarn 246
goldcrest 433
golden 261.28
goldeneye 7
goldenrod 94
goldfinch 80
goldfish 353
goldilocks 499
goldsmith 458
golem 232
golf 173
goliardery 16.274.6
Goliath 464
golliwog 185
gollop 281.2
golly 16.122
Gomberg 182
gombroon 260
Gomorrah 17.275
gonad 83.3
Gondar 1
gondola 17.176
gondolier 6
Gondwanaland 143.4
gone 254
goner 17.233
gonfalon 261
gong 266
Gongola 17.171
goniatite 372.12
gonidium 242.2.3
goniometer 17.342.3.1
gonk 53
gonna 17.233
gonococcus 310.11
gonorrhoea 17.2.2
goo 15
goober 17.20
good 101
goodbye 7
good-humoured 103.5
goodies 515
goodman 261
good-natured 103

goodness 300
good-night 372
goodwife 164
goodwill 218
Goodwin 252
goody 16.70
Goodyear 6
goody-goody 16.70
gooey 16.4
goof 170
goofy 16.89
googly 16.162
googol 220
googolplex 496
Goole 227
goon 260
goosander 17.98
goose 309
gooseberry 16.274
goosegog 185
goosegrass 294
gooseneck 35
goosy 16.306
gopak 32
gopher 17.117
goral 228.74
Gorbals 539
gorcock 40
Gordon 261.27
gore 9
goreng pisang 263
gorge 200
gorgeous 310
gorger 17.153
Gorgon 261.33
Gorgonzola 17.171
gorilla 17.166.3
Gorky 16.28
gormandize 516
gormless 300
gorse 303
Gorsedd 474
gory 16.269
gosh 354
goshawk 41
Goshen 261.73
gosling 265
gospel 228
gospeller 17.176
Gosport 374
gossamer 17.218
gossip 274
gossipy 16.248
gossoon 260
got 373

Goth 459
Gothenburg 182
Gothic 38
Gothicism 242.35.16
Gotland 143
gotta 17.344
gotten 261.101
gouache 350
Gouda 17.89
gouge 202
goulash 349
gourd 96
gourami 16.222
gourmand 143
gourmandise 513
gourmet 2
gout 377
goutweed 89
govern 261.117
governable 228.16.31
governance 321
governess 300.26
government 420.42
governmental 228.110.4
governor 17.239
governorship 274.1
Gower 14
gown 258
Goya 17.5
grab 18
grabble 228
graben 261.8
Gracchus 310.7
grace 295
graceful 226
gracefulness 300.30
graceless 300
gracile 219
gracility 16.333.9
gracious 310.56
graciousness 300.34
grackle 228.19
grad 83
gradate 367.9
gradation 261.67.8
grade 85
grader 17.79
gradient 420.1
gradine 251.1
gradual 228.9
gradualism 242.35.11.3
graduand 128
graduate 367.2

graduate 371.2
graduation 261.67.2
Graecism 242.35
graffiti 16.332
graffito 12.76
graft 396
grafter 17.358
Graham 242
Grail 214
grain 247
graining 265.40
grainy 16.225
gram 229
gramarye 16.274
gramercy 16.298
gramineous 310.2.8
graminivorous 310.50.3
grammar 17.205
grammarian 261.3.21
grammatical 228.23.18
gramophone 257
Grampian 261.3
grampus 310.41
Granada 17.78.1
granadilla 17.166
granary 16.274
grand 128
grandchild 117
Grand Coulee 16.130
granddad 83
granddaughter 17.345
grandee 5
grandeur 17.155
grandfather 17.401
grandiloquent 420.59
grandiose 305.1
grandiosity 16.333.30.1
grandioso 12.70
grandma 1
grand mal 212
grandmama 1.12
grandmaster 17.380
grandmother 17.408
grandpa 1
grandpapa 1
grandparent 420
grandson 259
grandstand 128
grange 207
grangerize 516.8
granite 371.22
graniteware 4.9
granitic 38.52
granitite 372.11
granivorous 310.50.3

granny 16.223
granolith 458
granophyre 8.1
grant 408
Granta 17.365
grantee 5
grantor 9
gran turismo 12.50
granular 17.174.9
granulate 367.13
granulation 261.67.13
granule 227
granulite 372
grape 270
grapefruit 380
grapeshot 373
grapevine 253
graph 158
grapheme 234
graphic 38.11
graphical 228.23.3
graphics 498
graphite 372
graphitic 38.52
graphologist 436.4
graphology 16.108.4
grapnel 228
grappa 17.247
Grappelli 16.115
grapple 228.64
grappling 265
graptolite 372.4
Grasmere 6
grasp 290
grasping 265
grass 294
grasshopper 17.255
grassland 143
grassy 16.295
grate 367
grateful 226.7
gratefulness 300.30
grater 17.338
Gratian 261.3
graticule 227.1
gratify 7.3.8
grating 265.64
gratis 300
gratitude 102.2.1
Grattan 261.94
gratuitous 310.64
gratuity 16.333.3
grav 480
gravamen 248.2
grave 16.378

grave 482
gravel 228.117
gravelly 16.131
graven 261.111
Graves 481
Gravesend 131
gravestone 257
graveyard 84
gravid 91
gravitate 367.30
gravitation 261.67.27
gravitational 228.63.3
gravitative 485.10
gravity 16.333.33
gravure 10
gravy 16.379
Gray 2
grayling 265.27
graze 509
grazier 17.3.59
grazing 265.81
grease 298
greasepaint 409
greasy 16.299
great 367
greatcoat 376
greatest 436
greatness 300
Greats 335
greave 484
greaves 553
grebe 23
Grecian 261.70
Greece 298
greed 89
greediness 300.23
greedy 16.62
Greek 37
Greeley 16.118
green 251
greenback 32
greenbrier 17.4
greenery 16.274.25
greenfinch 80
greenfly 7
greengage 193
greengrocer 17.306
greengrocery 16.274
greenhorn 255
greenhouse 306
greenish 353
Greenland 143
Greenlander 17.109
greenling 265
greenness 300

Greenock 46
greenroom 241
greens 547
Greensboro 17.279
greenshank 51
greenstick 38
greenstuff 168
greensward 95
Greenwich 197.7
greenwood 101
greet 370
greeting 265
gregarine 251.7
gregarious 310.2.10
Gregorian 261.3.23
Gregory 16.274
greige 360
greisen 261.127
gremlin 252
Grenada 17.79
grenade 85.2
grenadier 6
grenadine 251.1
Grenadines 547
Grendel 228
Grenoble 228.13
Gresham 242
gressorial 228.3.12
Gretna 17.244
grew 15
grey 2
greyback 32
greybeard 90
greyhen 248
greyhound 139
greyish 353
greylag 178
greyness 300
greywacke 17.28
gribble 228.12
grid 91
griddle 228.32
griddlecake 34
gridiron 261.4
grief 162
Grieg 183
grievance 321
grieve 484
grieving 265.79
grievous 310.73
griffin 252
Griffith 458
griffon 261.29
grig 184
grigri 5

grill 218
grillage 197.1
grille 218
grillroom 241
grilse 311
grim 235
grimace 295
Grimaldi 16.75
grimalkin 252
grime 236
Grimm 235
grimness 300
Grimsby 16
grimy 16.217
grin 252
grind 135
grinder 17.103
grindery 16.274.8
grindstone 257
gringo 12.36
grip 274
gripe 275
gripping 265
griseous 310.2.15
griskin 252
grisly 16.209
grison 261
grist 436
gristle 228.85
gristly 16.181
grit 371
grith 458
grits 339
gritty 16.333
grizzle 228
grizzled 122
grizzly 16.209
groan 257
groat 376
groats 343
grocer 17.306
groceries 515.1
grocery 16.274
grockle 228.25
grog 185
groggy 16.94
grogram 242
groin 256
Grolier 17.3.22
grommet 371.20
gromwell 228
groom 241
grooming 265.39
groove 490
groovy 16.384

grope 278
groper 17.257
Gropius 310.2
grosbeak 37
groschen 261.73
grosgrain 247
gross 305
grossularite 372.8
grot 373
grotesque 57
grotesqueness 300
grotesquery 16.274
Grotius 310.2
grotto 12.77
grouch 71
grouchy 16.51
ground 139
groundage 197
grounding 265.22
groundless 300
groundling 265
groundmass 293
groundnut 378
groundsel 228
groundsheet 370
groundsman 261
groundspeed 89
groundwork 36
group 280
grouper 17.259
groupie 16.253
grouping 265
grouse 306
grout 377
grouts 344
grouty 16.340
grove 488
grovel 228
grow 12
grower 17.6
growl 224
growler 17.172
grown 257
growth 461
groyne 256
grub 29
grubber 17.19
grubbiness 300.23
grubby 16.13
grudge 203
grudging 265
gruel 228.10
gruelling 265
gruesome 242
gruff 168

gruffness 300
grumble 228
grumbler 17.180
grumbly 16.139
grumous 310
grump 289
grumpy 16.257
Grundy 16.80
grunion 261
grunt 419
grunter 17.373
Grus 308
Gruyère 4
guacamole 16.126
Guadalcanal 212
Guadalquivir 6.11
Guadeloupe 280.1
Guam 230
guan 246
guano 12.51
Guarani 5.14
guarantee 5.24
guarantor 9
guaranty 16.360
guard 84
guardant 420.8
guarded 91.5
guardhouse 306
guardian 261.3
guardianship 274.2
guardrail 214
guardroom 241
guardsman 261
Guarneri 16.265
Guatemala 17.161.1
guava 17.409
gubbins 548
gubernatorial 228.3.12.2
guck 43
gudgeon 261.38
Gudrun 260
guelder-rose 520.3
Guelph 172
guenon 254.8
guerdon 261.22
Guernica 17.33
guerrilla 17.166.3
guess 296
guesstimate 367.15
guesstimate 371.19
guesswork 36
guest 433
guesthouse 306
Guevara 17.268
guff 168

haberdasher

guffaw 9
guidance 321.6
guide 92
guideline 253
guidepost 441
guider 17.84
guiding 265.14
guidon 261.25
Guienne 248
guild 116
guilder 17.95
Guildford 103
guildhall 221
guile 219
guileful 226
guileless 300
guillemot 373
guillotine 251.11
guilt 403
guiltless 300
guilty 16.350
guimpe 287
guinea 16.229
Guinea 16.229
guinea pig 184
Guinevere 6.11
Guinness 300.23
guipure 10
guise 516
guitar 1
guitarist 436.16
Gujarati 16.328.1
Gujranwala 17.173
Gulag 178
gular 17.175
Gulbenkian 261.3
gulch 77
gules 538
gulf 174
gull 225
gullet 371
gullibility 16.333.9.2
gullible 228.16
gull-wing 265
gully 16.128
gulp 284
gulped 427
gum 240
gumbo 12.7
gumboil 222
gumboots 346
gumdrop 276
gumma 17.216
gummy 16.220
gumption 261.89

gumshield 115
gumshoe 15
gumtree 5
gun 259
gunboat 376
guncotton 261.101
gunfight 372
gunfighter 17.343
gunfire 8
gunflint 412
gunge 211
gungy 16.111
gunk 54
gunlock 40
gunman 261
gunmetal 228.100
gunnel 228
gunner 17.237
gunnery 16.274
gunning 265.45
gunplay 2
gunpoint 416
gunpowder 17.89
gunrunner 17.237
gunrunning 265.45
gunshot 373
gunslinger 17.246
gunsmith 458
gunstock 40
gunwale 228
guppy 16.252
gurdwara 17.268
gurgle 228
gurjun 261.35
Gurkha 17.32
Gurmukhi 16.31
gurnard 103
gurnet 371.23
guru 15
Gus 307
gush 356
gusher 17.329
gushy 16.324
gusset 371
gust 443
gustation 261.67
gusto 12
gusty 16.368
gut 378
gutbucket 371.11
Gutenberg 182
gutless 300
gutta-percha 17.54
gutter 17.349
guttering 265.58

guttersnipe 275
guttural 228.76
gutturalize 516.3.8
guv 489
guy 7
Guyana 17.225
guzzle 228
guzzler 17.204
Gwalior 9.1
Gwelo 12
Gwent 410
Gwyn 252
Gwynedd 474
gwyniad 83.1
gym 235
gymkhana 17.226
gymnasiarch 33.1
gymnasiast 430.1
gymnasium 242.2.19
gymnast 430
gymnastic 38.68
gymnastics 498.15
gymnosophist 436
gymnosperm 233
gymslip 274
gynaecocracy 16.307.5
gynaecoid 97.3
gynaecologist 436.4
gynaecology 16.108.4.4
gynaecomastia 17.3
gynarchy 16.20
gyp 274
gypsophila 17.166
gypsum 242
gypsy 16.314
gyral 228
gyrate 367
gyration 261.67
gyratory 16.274.40
gyre 8
gyrfalcon 261.16
gyrocompass 310.42
gyroplane 247
gyroscope 278.1
gyrostatic 38.49.7
gyrus 310.47

H

ha 1
haar 1
Habakkuk 46
habanera 17.271
habeas corpus 310.38
haberdasher 17.321

haberdashery 16.274
habergeon 261.39
habiliment 420.31
habilitate 367.30.1
habit 371.4
habitable 228.16.49
habitat 365
habitation 261.67.27
habitual 228.9.3
habituate 367.2.1
habitué 2.3
habitus 310.64
háček 35
hachure 10
hacienda 17.101
hack 32
hackamore 9.9
hackberry 16.274
hackbut 378
hackle 228.19
hackles 539
hackney 16.238
Hackney 16.238
hackneyed 91.22
hacksaw 9
had 83
hadal 228
haddock 46
Hades 513
Hadith 458
hadn't 420
Hadrian 261.3
hae 2
haecceity 16.333.1
haem 234
haemagogue 185.2
haematemesis 300.52.3
haematic 38.49
haematin 252
haematite 372.12
haematocele 217.2
haematogenesis 300.52.4
haematoid 97
haematology 16.108.4.15
haematoma 17.215
haematosis 300.55.7
haematoxylon 254.6
haematuria 17.3.42
haemic 38.27
haemochrome 239
haemocoel 217.2
haemocyte 372.10
haemodialysis 300.52.1
haemoglobin 252

haemoglobinuria
17.3.42.1
haemolysin 252.21
haemolysis 300.52.2
haemophilia 17.3.21.2
haemophiliac 32.1.1
haemophilic 38.21
haemoptysis 300.52
haemorrhage 197
haemorrhagic 38.15
haemorrhoid 97.12
haemorrhoidectomy
16.222.5.1
haemostasis 300.50
haemostat 365
haemostatic 38.49.7
haeremai 7
haft 396
hag 178
Hagar 1
Hagen 261
Haggadah 17.78
Haggai 7
haggard 103
haggis 300
haggle 228.43
haggler 17.192
hagiocracy 16.307.5.1
Hagiographa 17.120.1
hagiography 16.90.2.1
hagiolatry 16.286.2.1
hagiology 16.108.4.1
Hague 180
ha-ha 1.5
Haifa 17.115
Haig 180
hail 214
Haile Selassie 16.294
hailstone 257
hailstorm 238
Hainan 245
hair 4
hairball 221
hairbrush 356
haircloth 459
haircut 378
hairdo 15
hairdresser 17.300
hairdressing 265.60
hairgrip 274
hairless 300
hairlike 39
hairline 253
hairnet 368
hairpiece 298

hairpin 252
hairsplitting 265.66
hairspring 265
hairstyle 219
hairy 16.264
Haiti 16.329
Haitian 261.3
Haitink 52
hajj 191
hake 34
hakim 234
Hakluyt 380
Hakodate 2.23
Halakah 1
halal 213
halation 261.67.14
halberd 103
halcyon 261.3
hale 214
Haleakala 1.7
haler 17.161
Halesowen 252.1
half 158
halfback 32
half-baked 384
half-caste 431
half-day 2
half-hearted 91.33
half-heartedness 300.28
half-life 164
half-light 372
half-mast 431
half-naked 91
half-open 261
half-price 301
half-shut 378
half-time 236
halftone 257
halfway 2
halfwit 371
halfwitted 91.38
halibut 381
Halicarnassus 310.51
halide 92
Halifax 494
halite 372
halitosis 300.55.6
hall 221
Halley 16.112
hallmark 33
hallo 12.45
halloo 15.5
hallow 12.38
hallowed 98
Hallowe'en 251

hallucinate 367.17
hallucination 261.67.18
hallucinatory 16.274.43.6
hallucinogen 261.39
hallucinogenic 38.32.1.1
hallucinosis 300.55.4
hallux 503
hallway 2
halo 12
halobiont 414
halogen 261.39
halothane 247
halt 404
halter 17.363
halting 265
halvah 1
halve 481
halyard 103
ham 229
Hama 1.10
hamadryad 83.2
hamadryas 310.3
Hamburg 182
hamburger 17.127
hame 231
Hamilcar Barca 17.29
Hamilton 261
Hamite 372
Hamitic 38.52
hamlet 371
Hammarskjöld 120
hammer 17.205
hammerhead 86.5
Hammersmith 458
Hammerstein 253
hammertoe 12
hammock 46
Hammond 143
Hammurabi 16.6
hammy 16.210
Hampden 261
hamper 17.261
Hampshire 6
Hampstead 91
Hampton 261
hamshackle 228.19
hamster 17
hamstring 265
hamulus 310.25
Han 245
Han 246
hanaper 17.260
Hancock 40
hand 128

handbag 178
handball 221
handbarrow 12.60
handbell 215
handbill 218
handbook 44
handbrake 34
handcart 366
handclasp 290
handcraft 396
handcuff 168
Handel 228.39
handfeed 89
handful 226
handgrip 274
handgun 259
handhold 120
handicap 268
handicraft 396
handiwork 36
handkerchief 163
handle 228.39
handlebar 1
handlebars 508
handled 122
handler 17
handling 265
handmade 85
handmaiden 261.20
hand-me-down 258
handrail 214
handsaw 9
handsel 228
handset 368
handshake 34
handsome 242
handsomeness 300
handspring 265
handstand 128
handwriting 265.67
handwritten 261.99
handy 16.77
handyman 261.48
hang 263
hangar 17.245
Hangchow 13
hangdog 185
hanger 17.245
hanging 265
hangman 261
hangnail 214
hangover 17.417
hank 51
hanker 17.43
hanky 16.36

hanky-panky 16.36
Hannah 17.225
Hannibal 228.12
Hanoi 11
Hanover 17.417
Hanoverian 261.3.22
Hanratty 16.327
Hansard 84
Hanse 314
Hanseatic 38.49
hansom 242
Hants 347
Hanukkah 17.42
Hanuman 246
haphazard 103
hapless 300
haploid 97
ha'p'orth 464
happen 261
happening 265.46
happiness 300.23
happy 16.243
Hapsburg 182
hapten 261
haptic 38
harakiri 16.266
harambee 2.5
harangue 263.2
Harappa 17.247
Harar 17.268
harass 310.43
harassment 420.46
Harbin 252
harbinger 17.157
harbour 17.10
harbourage 197
hard 84
hardback 32
hardbake 34
hardboard 95
harden 261
hardened 143
hardener 17.240
hardhearted 91.33
hardihood 101
hardiness 300.23
hardly 16
hardness 300
hardship 274
hardtack 32
hardtop 276
hardware 4
hardwood 101
hardy 16.58
hare 4

harebell 215
harebrained 130
harelip 274
harem 234
Hargeisa 17.299
Hargreaves 553
haricot 12.11
Haringey 2.10
hark 33
Harlem 242
harlequin 252
harlequinade 85.2
harlot 381
Harlow 12.39
harm 230
harmattan 261.94
harmful 226
harmless 300
harmlessness 300.33
harmonic 38.35
harmonica 17.34.1
harmonics 498.5
harmonious 310.2.9
harmonist 436.13
harmonium 242.2.12
harmonize 516.7
harmony 16.237
harness 300.21
Harold 122
harp 269
Harper 17.248
harpoon 260
harpsichord 95.2
harpy 16.244
harridan 261.24
harrier 17.3
Harris 300
Harrisburg 182.1
Harrison 261.65.1
Harrogate 371
Harrovian 261.3.31
harrow 12.60
Harrow 12.60
harrowing 265.4
harry 16.260
Harry 16.260
harsh 350
harshness 300
hart 366
hartebeest 435
Hartford 103
Hartlepool 227
Hartley 16.187
harum-scarum 242.18
Harun al-Rashid 89

haruspex 496
Harvard 103
harvest 436
harvester 17.384
harvesting 265.76
harvestman 261
Harvey 16.378
Harwich 197.9
Harz 334
has 507
has-been 251
Hasdrubal 228.15
hash 349
hashish 352
Hasidim 234
hask 55
haslet 371
hasn't 420
hasp 290
hassle 228
hassock 46
hast 430
haste 432
hasten 261.62
Hastings 552
hasty 16.363
hat 365
hatband 128
hatbox 499
hatch 62
hatchback 32
hatchel 228
hatchery 16.274
hatchet 371
hatchment 420.36
hatchway 2
hate 367
hateful 226.7
hater 17.338
Hatfield 115
hath 452
Hathaway 2.28
hatless 300
hatpin 252
hatred 91
Hatshepsut 380
hatter 17.336
hauberk 36
haughty 16.336
haul 221
haulage 197
haulm 238
haunch 81
haunt 415
haunted 91.47

haunting 265
Hausa 17.307
hausfrau 13
hautboy 11
hauteur 3
Havana 17.225
Havant 420
have 480
haven 261.111
haven't 420
haver 17.410
Havering 265.58
haversack 32
haversine 253.8
havildar 1
havoc 46
haw 9
Hawaii 16.2
Hawaiian 261.4
hawfinch 80
Hawhaw 9
hawk 41
hawker 17.37
hawking 265.9
Hawkins 548
hawksbill 218
hawse 518
hawsepipe 275
hawthorn 255
hay 2
haycock 40
Haydn 261.25
hayfork 41
haymaker 17.30
haymaking 265.6
hayrack 32
hayrick 38
haystack 32
haywire 8
hazard 103
hazardous 310.17
hazardousness 300.34
haze 509
hazel 228.125
hazelnut 378
Hazlitt 371
hazy 16.393
he 5
head 86
headache 34
headachy 16.21
headband 128
headboard 95
headcheese 513
headdress 296

heliograph 158.1.1
heliolatry 16.286.2.1
Heliopolis 300.13.2
heliotherapy 16.254
heliotrope 278.3
heliport 374.1
helium 242.2.5
helix 498
hell 215
he'll 217
Hellas 310.22
hellbent 410
hellcat 365
hellebore 9
helleborine 251.6
Hellene 251
Hellenic 38.32
Hellenism 242.35.13
Hellenist 436.11
Hellenistic 38.70
Hellenize 516.6
Heller 17.163
hellery 16.274
Hellespont 414
hellfire 8
hellhole 223
hellhound 139
hellion 261.119
hellish 353.4
hello 12.40
helm 243
helmet 371
helmeted 91.38
helminth 470
helminthic 38
Héloïse 513.2
Helot 381
helotism 242.35.20
helotry 16.286
help 283
helpful 226
helpfulness 300.30
helping 265
helpless 300
helplessness 300.33
Helpmann 261
helpmate 367
Helsinki 16.37
helter-skelter 17.361
helve 492
Helvellyn 252.7
Helvetia 17.325
Helvetian 261.70
Helvetic 38.50
Helvetii 7.1

Helvétius 310.2
hem 232
he-man 261.47
Hemel Hempstead 91
hemeralopia 17.3.37.1
Hemingway 2
hemiplegia 17.3.13
hemiplegic 38.17
hemipode 98
hemipteran 261.60
hemisphere 6
hemispheric 38.39
hemispheroid 97.10
hemistich 38.70
hemline 253
hemlock 40
hemmer 17.208
hemp 286
hempen 261
hems 541
hemstitch 67
hen 248
henbane 247
hence 316
henceforth 460
henceforward 103.8
henchman 261
hencoop 280
hendiadys 300.5
henequen 252.3
henge 208
Hengist 436
henhouse 306
Henley 16.171
henna 17.228
hennery 16.274.23
henpeck 35
henpecked 385
hep 271
heparin 252.20
hepatic 38.49
hepatica 17.34.3
hepatitis 300.62
Hepburn 249
hepcat 365
Hephaestus 310
Hephaistos 302
Hepplewhite 372
heptad 83
heptagon 254.5
Heptateuch 45
Hepworth 464
her 3
Hera 17.272
Heracles 513

Heraclitus 310.65
herald 122.1
heraldic 38
heraldry 16.278
herb 22
herbaceous 310.56
herbage 197
herbal 228
herbalist 436.7
herbarium 242.2.14
Herbert 381
herbicide 92.7
herbivore 9.13
herbivorous 310.50.3
herby 16.9
Herculaneum 242.2.10
herculean 261.2
Hercules 513
herd 87
herder 17.81
herdsman 261
here 6
hereabouts 344
hereafter 17.358
hereat 365
hereby 7
heredes 513.3
hereditary 16.274.41
hereditist 436.24
heredity 16.333
Hereford 103
herein 252
hereinbefore 9.5
hereinto 15
hereof 487
hereon 254.9
Herero 12.62
heres 513.11
heresiarch 33.1
heresy 16.307
heretic 38.57
heretical 228.23.19
hereto 15
heretofore 9
hereunder 17.108
hereupon 254
Hereward 103
herewith 476
heritable 228.16.49
heritage 197.12
heritor 17.342
heritress 300
Herman 261
hermaphrodite 372.2
hermaphroditic 38.52

hermeneutic 38.56
hermeneutics 498
Hermes 513
hermetic 38.50
hermit 371
hermitage 197.12
hern 249
hernia 17.3.32
herniorrhaphy 16.90.1
hero 12.63
Herod 103
Herodias 293.1
Herodotus 310.68
heroic 38.2
heroics 498
heroin 252.1
heroine 252.1
heroism 242.35.3
heron 261
heronry 16.284
Herophilus 310.23
herpes 513
herpetology 16.108.4
herring 265
herringbone 257
Herriot 381.1
hers 511
Herschel 228.92
herself 172
Hertford 103
Hertfordshire 6
hertz 337
Hertzog 185
Herzegovina 17.230
he's 513
Hesiod 94
Hesione 16.237.1
hesitancy 16.312
hesitant 420.76
hesitate 367.30
Hesperides 513.4
hesperidium 242.2.3
Hesperus 310.50
Hesse 296
hessian 261.3
het 368
hetaera 17.272
heteroclite 372
heterodox 499.1
heterodoxy 16.389
heterodyne 253.2
heterogeneous 310.2.7
heterograft 396
heteromorphic 38.14
heteronymous 310.28.2

heteroplasty 16.361.1
heteroscedasticity
  16.333.28.2
heterosexual 228.9
heterosexuality
  16.333.8.2
heterostyly 16.121
heterotopia 17.3.37.3
heuristic 38.70
hew 15
hex 496
hexad 83
hexadecimal 228.52.1
hexaemeron 254.11
hexagon 254.5
hexagonal 228.63
hexagram 229.1
hexahedron 261
hexameter 17.342
hexapod 94.1
hexastich 38
Hexateuch 45
hexone 257
hey 2
heyday 2
Heysham 242
Heywood 101
Hezekiah 17.4
hi 7
hiatus 310.62
hibachi 16.47
hibernal 228.58
hibernate 367.18
hibernation 261.67.19
Hibernia 17.3.32
Hibernian 261.3
Hibernicism 242.35.16
hibiscus 310.15
hic 38
hiccup 279
hick 38
hickey 16.25
hickory 16.274.4
hid 91
hidalgo 12.34
hidden 261.24
hide 92
hide-and-seek 37
hideaway 2.28
hidebound 139
hideous 310.2.1
hiding 265.14
hidrosis 300.55
hie 7
hieland 143.1

hieracosphinx 505
hierarch 33
hierarchical 228.23
hierarchy 16.20
hieratic 38.49
hierocracy 16.307.5
hierodule 227
hieroglyph 163
hieroglyphic 38.12
hieroglyphics 498.1
hierogram 229.1
hierology 16.108.4
Hieronymus 310.28.2
hierophant 407
hi-fi 7
Higgins 548
high 7
highball 221
highborn 255
highbrow 13
highchair 4
highfalutin 252.24
high-flown 257
high-handed 91.12
high jinks 505
highland 143
Highlander 17.109
Highlands 534
highlife 164
highlight 372
highly 16.121
highly-strung 267
high-minded 91
Highness 300
highroad 98
high-spirited 91.38
hightail 214
highway 2.26
highwayman 261.45
High Wycombe 242.4
hijack 32
hijacker 17.28
hike 39
hiker 17.35
hilarious 310.2.10
hilarity 16.333.20.2
Hilary 16.274.16
Hilda 17.95
hill 218
Hillary 16.274.16
hillbilly 16.120
hillfort 374
Hillingdon 261
hillock 46
hillside 92

hilly 16.120
hilt 403
hilum 242.9
hilus 310.24
Hilversum 242
him 235
Himalayas 524
Himeji 5.5
himself 172
Himyaritic 38.52.2
Hinayana 17.226
Hinckley 16.145
hind 135
hindbrain 247
Hindenburg 182
hinder 17.102
hinder 17.103
hindgut 378
Hindi 16.79
hindmost 441
hindquarter 17.345
hindrance 321
hindsight 372
Hindu 15
Hinduism 242.35.4
Hindu Kush 357
Hindustan 246
Hindustani 16.224
hinge 209
hinny 16.229
hint 412
hinterland 143.4
hip 274
hipbone 257
Hipparchus 310.8
hippeastrum 242
hippie 16.248
hippo 12
hippocampus 310.41
hippocras 293
Hippocrates 513.17
Hippocratic 38.49.6
Hippocrene 251
hippodrome 239
hippogriff 163
Hippolyta 17.342
Hippolyte 5.22
Hippolytus 310.64
hippopotamus 310.29.3
hipster 17.396
hipsters 524
hiragana 17.226
hircine 253
hire 8
hireling 265

hirer 17.274
Hirohito 12.76
Hiroshige 2
Hiroshima 17.210
hirsute 380
hirundine 253
his 515
Hispania 17.3.29
Hispanic 38.31
Hispanicism 242.35.16
Hispanicize 516.10
Hispaniola 17.171
hiss 300
hist 436
histamine 252.15
histaminic 38.34
histogen 261.39
histogenesis 300.52.4
histogram 229.1
histoid 97
histology 16.108.4
histolysis 300.52.2
historian 261.3.23
historic 38.41
historical 228.23.17
historicism 242.35.16
historicity 16.333.28
historiographer 17.120.1
historiography 16.90.2.1
history 16.274.49
histrionic 38.35.1
histrionics 498.5
hit 371
hitch 67
Hitchcock 40
hitchhike 39
hitchhiker 17.35
hither 17.405
hitherto 15
Hitler 17.201
Hitlerism 242.35.15
hitter 17.342
Hittite 372.11
hive 486
hives 554
ho 12
hoar 9
hoard 95
hoarder 17.86
hoarding 265.15
hoarfrost 438
hoarse 303
hoarsen 261
hoarseness 300
hoary 16.269

hoatzin 252
hoax 501
hoaxer 17.429
hob 26
Hobart 366
hobble 228
hobbledehoy 11
hobby 16.11
hobbyhorse 303
hobgoblin 252
hobnail 214
hobnailed 112
hobnob 26
hobo 12
Hoboken 261.14
hobson-jobson 261
Ho Chi Minh 252
hock 40
hockey 16.27
Hockney 16.239
Hocktide 92
hocus-pocus 310.12
hod 94
hodgepodge 199
hoe 12
hoedown 258
Hofei 2
hog 185
Hogan 261
Hogarth 453
hogback 32
hogfish 353
Hogg 185
hogged 106
hoggish 353
Hogmanay 2
hogshead 86
hogtie 7
hogwash 354
hogweed 89
Hohenzollern 261.42
hoi polloi 11.1
hoist 440
hoity-toity 16.338
hokey cokey 16.29
Hokkaido 12.20
hokum 242
Hokusai 7
Holarctic 38.59
hold 120
holdall 221
holder 17.97
holdfast 431
holding 265.18
hole 223

holey 16.126
holiday 2
holiness 300.23
Holinshed 86
holism 242.35
Holland 143
hollandaise 509
Hollandia 17.3
holler 17.168
hollow 12.43
hollowness 300.25
holly 16.122
hollyhock 40
Hollywood 101
holmium 242.2
holocaust 439
Holocene 251.9
holocrine 253
hologram 229.1
holograph 158.1
holography 16.90.2
holophytic 38.52
holothurian 261.3.24
holotype 275.1
Holstein 253
holster 17.392
Holt 405
holy 16.126
Holyhead 86.2
holystone 257
hom 237
homa 17.213
homage 197.4
hombre 2
homburg 182
home 239
homebred 86
homecoming 265.38
homeland 143
homeless 300
homelessness 300.33
homely 16
homeopathic 38.72
homeopathy 16.373.1.1
homer 17.215
Homer 17.215
Homeric 38.39
homesick 38
homesickness 300.27
homespun 259
homestead 86
homesteader 17.80
homeward 103
homework 36
homicidal 228.33

homicide 92.7
homiletic 38.50
homiletics 498.12
homily 16.120
homing 265.37
hominid 91
hominoid 97.8
hominy 16.229
homo 12.49
homocentric 38.47
homogamy 16.222.2
homogeneity 16.333.1
homogeneous 310.2.7
homogenize 516.6
homogenous 310.33
homogeny 16.229.2
homograft 396
homograph 158.1
homologate 367.11
homologous 310
homologue 185
homology 16.108.4
homonym 235
homophone 257
homophonic 38.35.2
homophonous 310.36
homophony 16.237.3
Homo sapiens 546
homoscedasticity
  16.333.28.2
homosexual 228.9
homosexuality
  16.333.8.2
homunculus 310.25
homy 16.219
honan 245
Honda 17.104
Honduras 310.49
hone 257
Honegger 17.129
honest 436
honestly 16.201
honesty 16.366
honey 16.235
honeybee 5
honeybunch 82
honeycomb 239
honeydew 15.7
honey-eater 17.341
honeyed 91
honeymoon 260
honeymooner 17.238
honeysucker 17.39
honeysuckle 228.27
Hong Kong 266

Honiara 17.268.1
Honiton 261.99
honk 53
honky-tonk 53
Honolulu 15.4
honorarium 242.2.14
honorary 16.274.32
honorific 38.12.1
honour 17.233
honourable 228.16.35
honours 524
Honshu 15
hooch 74
hood 101
hooded 91
hoodlum 242
hoodoo 15
hoodwink 52
hooey 16.4
hoof 170
Hooghly 16.162
hoo-ha 1
hook 44
hookah 17.40
hooked 390
hooker 17.40
hooknose 520
hookworm 233
hooky 16.31
hooligan 261.32
hooliganism 242.35.14
hoop 280
hoopla 1
hoopoe 15
hoorah 1.13
hooray 2
hoot 380
hootenanny 16.223
hooter 17.351
hoots 346
Hoover 17.419
hop 276
hope 278
hopeful 226
hopefully 16.129
hopefulness 300.30
Hopeh 2
hopeless 300
hopelessness 300.33
Hopi 16.251
Hopkins 548
hoplite 372
hoplology 16.108.4
hopper 17.255
hopping 265

hopple 228.68
hopsack 32
hopscotch 68
Horace 300
Horae 5
Horatian 261.67.22
horde 95
horehound 139
horizon 261.127
horizontal 228.111
horme 16.218
hormonal 228.62
hormone 257
Hormuz 522
horn 255
hornbeam 234
hornbill 218
hornblende 131
horned 137
hornet 371.26
hornpipe 275
hornswoggle 228.47
horny 16.232
horologe 199
horologium 242.2
horology 16.108.4
horoscope 278.1
horoscopy 16.254.2
Horowitz 339
horrendous 310
horrible 228.16
horribly 16.137
horrid 91.26
horrific 38.12
horrify 7.3
horripilation 261.67.12
horror 17.275
horrors 524
Horsa 17.305
horse 303
horseback 32
horsebox 499
horseflesh 351
horsefly 7
horsehair 4
horsehide 92
horseleech 66
horseman 261
horsemanship 274.2
horsemint 412
horseplay 2
horsepower 14
horseradish 353.1
horseshit 371
horseshoe 15

horsewhip 274
horsewoman 261.50
horst 439
horsy 16.303
hortatory 16.274.43
horticultural 228.76
horticulture 17.69
Horus 310.48
hosanna 17.225
hose 520
Hosea 17.2
hosier 17.3.62
hosiery 16.274.1
hospice 300
hospitable 228.16.49
hospital 228.102
hospitality 16.333.8
hospitalize 516.3
hospitaller 17.176.3
host 441
hosta 17.385
hostage 197
hostel 228.115
hosteller 17.176
hostelling 265
hostelry 16.283
hostess 300
hostile 219
hostility 16.333.9
hot 373
hotbed 86
hot-blooded 91.11
hotchpotch 68
hot dog 185
hotel 215.4
hotelier 17.3.19
hotfoot 379
hothead 86
hot-headedness 300.28
hothouse 306
hotly 16.191
hotness 300
hotplate 367
hotpot 373
Hotspur 3
Hottentot 373
hottie 16.335
Houdan 245
Houdini 16.228
houmous 310
hound 139
Hounslow 12
hour 14
hourglass 294
houri 16.270

hourly 16.127
house 306
house 521
houseboat 376
housebound 139
houseboy 11
housebreaker 17.30
housebreaking 265.6
housecarl 213
housecoat 376
housefly 7
household 120
householder 17.97
housekeeper 17.252
housekeeping 265.49
housel 228.129
houseleek 37
housemaid 85
houseman 261
housemaster 17.380
housemistress 300
House of Commons 551
houseroom 241
housetop 276
housewife 164
housewifery 16.274
housework 36
housey-housey 16.304
housing 265
Houston 261
hove 488
Hove 488
hovel 228
hover 17.416
hovercraft 396
hoverport 374.2
how 13
Howard 103
howbeit 371
howdah 17.89
howdy 16.68
howe'er 4
however 17.411
howitzer 17.320
howl 224
howler 17.172
howling 265.33
howsoever 17.411
howtowdie 16.68
hoy 11
hoya 17.5
hoyden 261
Hoylake 34
Hsi 5
hub 29

Hubbard 103
hubbub 29
hubby 16.13
hubcap 268
hubris 300
huckaback 32.2
huckleberry 16.274
Huddersfield 115
huddle 228.36
hudibrastic 38.68
Hudson 261
hue 15
hued 102
huff 168
huffy 16.88
hug 189
huge 204
huggermugger 17.134
Hughes 523
Hugo 12.32
Huguenot 12
hula 17.175
hulk 50
hulking 265
hull 225
Hull 225
hullabaloo 15.5
hum 240
human 261.51
humane 247
humanism 242.35.14
humanist 436.13.3
humanitarian 261.3.21.2
humanitarianism
  242.35.14.1.1
humanity 16.333.14
humanize 516.7
humankind 135
humanly 16.174
humanoid 97.9
Humber 17.27
Humberside 92.8
humble 228
humbly 16.139
Humboldt 405
humbug 189
humdinger 17.246
humdrum 240
Hume 241
humectant 420.79
humeral 228.76
humerus 310.50
humid 91
humidifier 17.4.1
humidify 7.3.1

humidity 16.333.5
humidor 9.3
humiliate 367.1.2
humiliation 261.67.1.1
humility 16.333.9
hummingbird 87
hummock 46
humoresque 57
humorist 436.20
humoristic 38.70.5
humorous 310.50
humour 17.217
humourless 300.13
hump 289
humpback 32
humpbacked 382
humph 177
Humphrey 16.281
humpy 16.257
humus 310
Hun 259
Hunan 245
hunch 82
hunchback 32
hunchbacked 382
hundred 103
hundredweight 367
hung 267
Hungarian 261.3.21
Hungary 16.274.11
hunger 17.143
hungriness 300.23
hungry 16
hunk 54
hunky-dory 16.269
Hunnish 353
hunt 419
hunted 91
hunter 17.373
hunting 265
Huntingdon 261
Huntingdonshire 6.8
huntsman 261
Huon 254
Hupeh 2
hurdle 228
hurdler 17.185
hurdy-gurdy 16.61
hurl 216
hurley 16.116
hurling 265
hurly-burly 16.116
Huron 261.59
hurrah 1
hurricane 247.1

hurricane 261.13
hurried 91
hurriedness 300.28
hurry 16.272
hurt 369
hurter 17.340
hurtful 226
hurtle 228
husband 143
husbandman 261
husbandry 16.279
hush 356
husk 60
husky 16.42
huss 307
hussar 1
Hussein 247
hussy 16.305
hustings 552
hustle 228.87
hustler 17.199
hut 378
hutch 72
Hutu 15
hyacinth 470
hyacinthine 253
Hyades 513.5
hyaline 252.11
hyalite 372.4
hyaloid 97.6
hybrid 91
hybridize 516
hydantoin 252.1
hydathode 98
hydatid 91
Hyde 92
hydrangea 17.156
hydrant 420
hydranth 467
hydrargyrum 242
hydrastis 300.67
hydrate 367
hydrated 91.34
hydraulic 38.23
hydraulics 498
hydride 92
hydro 12
hydrocarbon 261.8
hydrocele 217.2
hydrocephalus 310.26.3
hydrocephaly 16.131
hydrochloric 38.42
hydrochloride 92.5
hydroelectric 38

imbalance 321.10
imbecile 217
imbecility 16.333.9
imbibe 25
imbibition 261.71
imbroglio 12.3.3
imbue 15
imitate 367.30
imitation 261.67.27
imitative 485.15.12
imitator 17.338.10
immaculate 371.17.1
immanent 420.55
immanentism 242.35.21
immaterial 228.3.11
immaterialism
  242.35.11.2.1
immaterialize 516.3.2.1
immature 10.5
immaturity 16.333.23
immeasurable
  228.16.35.2
immediate 371.1
immediately 16.189
immemorial 228.3.12
immense 316
immensity 16.333.31
immensurable 228.16.35
immerse 297
immersion 261.69
immersionism 242.35.14
immethodical 228.23.2
immigrant 420
immigrate 367.26
immigration 261.67.24
imminent 420.53
Immingham 242.17
immiscible 228.16.39
immobile 219
immobilism 242.35.9
immobility 16.333.9.1
immobilize 516.2
immoderate 371.35
immodest 436
immodesty 16.366
immolate 367.14
immolation 261.67.14
immoral 228.73
immoralist 436.7
immorality 16.333.8.9
immortal 228.105
immortality 16.333.8
immortalize 516.3
immortelle 215.3
immovable 228.16.62

immune 260
immunity 16.333.18
immunize 516
immunoassay 2.20
immunogenic 38.32.1
immunoglobulin 252.10
immunology 16.108.4
immunotherapy 16.254
immure 10
immutable 228.16.53
Imo 12.47
imp 287
impact 382
impacted 91
impair 4
impala 17.161
impale 214
impalpable 228.16
impart 366
impartial 228.90
impartiality 16.333.8.1
impassable 228.16
impasse 294
impassion 261.66
impassioned 143
impassive 485.1
impatience 321
impatiens 546
impatient 420.73
impeach 66
impeachable 228.16.12
impeachment 420
impearl 216
impeccable 228.16
impeccant 420
impecunious 310.2
impedance 321.4
impede 89
impediment 420.31.1
impedimenta 17.368
impel 215
impend 131
impending 265.20
impenetrable 228.16
impenitence 321.24
impenitent 420.76
imperative 485.15
imperator 9
imperceptible 228.16.58
imperceptive 485.23
imperfect 387
imperfection 261.77
imperfective 485.17
imperforate 371.35
imperial 228.3.11

imperialism
  242.35.11.2.1
imperialist 436.7.2
imperil 218.2
imperious 310.2.11
imperishable 228.16.43
imperium 242.2.15
impermanent 420.55
impermeable 228.16.2
impermissible 228.16.39
impersonal 228.63
impersonality 16.333.8.7
impersonalize 516.3.7
impersonate 367.18
impersonation 261.67.19
impersonator 17.338.8
impertinence 321.14
impertinent 420.53
imperturbable 228.16
impervious 310.2
impetigo 12.30
impetrate 367.27
impetuosity 16.333.30.2
impetuous 310.4
impetuousness 300.34.2
impetus 310.64
impi 16.255
impiety 16.333.2
impinge 209
impious 310.2
impish 353
implacable 228.16
implant 408
implantation 261.67
implausible 228.16
implement 410.1
implement 420.31
implementation
  261.67.32.1
implicate 367.5
implication 261.67.5
implicit 371.36
implode 98
implore 9
implosion 261.92
imply 7
impolicy 16.300
impolite 372.4
impoliteness 300.39
impolitic 38.52
imponderabilia 17.3.21.1
imponderable 228.16.35
import 374
importance 321
important 420

indiscernible 228.16.28
indiscipline 252
indiscreet 370
indiscretion 261.68
indiscriminate 371.24
indispensable 228.16.40
indispose 520
indisposed 155
indisposition 261.71.9
indisputable 228.16.53
indissoluble 228.15
indistinct 392
indistinctive 485.20
indistinguishable
    228.16.43
indium 242.2
individual 228.9.1
individualism
    242.35.11.3
individualist 436.7.3
individualistic 38.70.2
individuality 16.333.8.2
individualize 516.3.3
individuate 367.2
indivisible 228.16.63
Indochina 17.232
indocile 219
indoctrinate 367.17
indoctrination 261.67.18
indole 223
indolence 321.12
indolent 420.28
indomitable 228.16.49
Indonesia 17.3.60
Indonesian 261.3.34
indoor 9
indoors 518
indrawn 255
indubitable 228.16.49
induce 309
inducement 420
induct 389
inductance 321
inductee 5
inductile 219
induction 261.79
inductive 485.19
inductor 17.357
indulge 205
indulgence 321
indulgent 420.21
induline 253
indult 406
indurate 371.34
Indus 310

industrial 228.3
industrialism
    242.35.11.2
industrialist 436.7.2
industrialize 516.3.2
industrious 310.2
industry 16
indwell 215
inebriant 420.1
inebriate 367.1
inebriate 371.1
inebriation 261.67.1
inebriety 16.333.2
inedible 228.16.14
ineducable 228.16
ineffable 228.16
ineffaceable 228.16.36
ineffective 485.17
ineffectual 228.9.5
inefficacious 310.56.1
inefficacy 16.307.1
inefficiency 16.312.5
inefficient 38.70
inelastic 38.68
inelasticity 16.333.28.2
inelegant 420.17
ineligible 228.16.20.1
ineloquent 420.59
ineluctable 228.16.54
inept 422
ineptitude 102.2
inequality 16.333.10
inequitable 228.16.49
inequity 16.333
inert 369
inertia 17.324
inescapable 228.16.32
in esse 16.297
inessential 228.96
inestimable 228.16
inevitable 228.16.49
inexact 382
inexactitude 102.2
inexcusable 228.16.65
inexhaustible 228.16
inexorable 228.16.35
inexpedient 420.1.1
inexpensive 485.9
inexperience 321.1
inexperienced 448
inexpert 369
inexplicable 228.16.10
inexplicit 371.36
inexpressible 228.16.37
inexpressive 485.2

inextinguishable
    228.16.43
inextricable 228.16.10
infallible 228.16
infamize 516.5
infamous 310.29
infamy 16.222
infancy 16.312
infant 420
infanta 17.365
infante 16.353
infanticide 92.7
infantile 219
infantilism 242.35.9
infantility 16.333.9
infantry 16.291
infantryman 261.48
infarct 383
infarction 261
infatuate 367.2
infatuated 91.34.2
infatuation 261.67.2
infect 385
infection 261.77
infectious 310
infectiousness 300.34
infective 485.17
infecund 143
infecundity 16.333.7
infelicity 16.333.28
infer 3
inference 321.20
inferential 228.96.2
inferior 17.3.39
inferiority 16.333.22
infernal 228.58
inferno 12.53
infertile 219
infertility 16.333.9
infest 433
infestation 261.67.33
infidel 228.32
infidelity 16.333
infield 115
infighting 265.67
infiltrate 367
infiltration 261.67
infinite 371.24
infinitesimal 228.52.1
infinitive 485.12
infinity 16.333.17
infirm 233
infirmary 16.274.21
infirmity 16.333
infix 498

inflame 231
inflammable 228.16.26
inflammation 261.67.16
inflammatory
 16.274.43.5
inflatable 228.16.45
inflate 367
inflation 261.67
inflationary 16.274.29.1
inflationism 242.35.14.3
inflect 385
inflection 261.77
inflexible 228.16
inflict 387
inflorescence 321.21
inflow 12
influence 321.3
influential 228.96
influenza 17.446
influx 502
info 12
inform 238
informal 228.53
informality 16.333.8.5
informant 420.32
information 261.67.16
informative 485.15.6
informer 17.214
infract 382
infra dig 184
infralapsarian 261.3.21
infrangible 228.16.21
infrared 86
infrasonic 38.35.4
infrastructure 17.66
infrequency 16.312
infrequent 420.57
infringe 209
infringement 420
infundibulum 242.10
infuriate 367.1
infuse 523
infuser 17.444
infusible 228.16.65
infusion 261.93
ingather 17.400
ingenious 310.2.7
ingénue 15
ingenuity 16.333.3.1
ingenuous 310.4.2
ingest 433
ingesta 17.382
ingestion 261.18
ingle 228.50
inglenook 44

inglorious 310.2.13
ingoing 265.4
ingot 381
ingrain 247
ingrained 130
ingrate 367
ingratiate 367.1.5
ingratiation 261.67.1
ingratitude 102.2.1
ingravescent 420.67.3
ingredient 420.1.1
ingress 296
ingrowing 265.4
ingrown 257
ingrowth 461
inguinal 228.60
Ingush 358
inhabit 371.4
inhabitant 420.76
inhalant 420.25
inhalation 261.67.14
inhale 214
inhaler 17.162
inharmonious 310.2.9
inhere 6
inherence 321.17
inherent 420.62
inherit 371.31
inheritance 321.24
inherited 91.38
inheritor 17.342
inhesion 261.90
inhibit 371.5
inhibition 261.71
inhibitor 17.342
inhospitable 228.16.49
inhospitality 16.333.8
inhuman 261.51
inhumane 247
inhumanity 16.333.14
inhume 241
inimical 228.23
inimitable 228.16.49
iniquitous 310.64
iniquity 16.333
initial 228.93
initialize 516.3
initially 16.131
initiate 367.1.6
initiate 371.1
initiation 261.67.1.5
initiative 485.15
inject 385
injection 261.77
injector 17.354

injudicious 310.58
Injun 261
injunction 261.80
injure 17.157
injurious 310.2.14
injury 16.274.14
injustice 300
ink 52
inkblot 373
Inkerman 261.52
inkhorn 255
inkling 265
inkstand 128
inkwell 215
inky 16.37
inlaid 85
inland 143
inlay 2
inlet 368
inlier 17.4
inmate 367
in memoriam 242.2.17
inn 252
innards 531
innate 367.17
inner 17.231
innermost 441
innervate 367.35
innerve 483
inning 265.43
innings 552
innkeeper 17.252
innocence 321
innocent 420
innocuous 310.4
innominate 371.24
in nomine 2.15
innovate 367
innovate 367.37
innovation 261.67
innovative 485.15
Innsbruck 44
innuendo 12.24
Innuit 371.2
innumerable 228.16.35
innumerate 371.35
inobservance 321
inoculable 228.16.25
inoculate 367.13.3
inoculation 261.67.13
inodorous 310.50
inoffensive 485.9
inoperable 228.16.35
inoperative 485.15.10
inopportune 260.6

intellection 261.77.2
intellectual 228.9.5
intellectualism
  242.35.11.3
intellectualize 516.3.3
intelligence 321.9
intelligent 420.20
intelligentsia 17.3
intelligible 228.16.20.1
Intelsat 365
intemperate 371.35
intend 131
intendance 321.7
intendant 420.14
intended 91.13
intendment 420
intenerate 367.23.1
intense 316
intensifier 17.4.1
intensify 7.3
intensity 16.333.31
intensive 485.9
intent 410
intention 261.82
intentional 228.63.9
intently 16.197
inter 3
interact 382
interaction 261.76
interactive 485.16
interatomic 38.29
interbreed 89
intercalary 16.274.19
intercalate 367.14.2
intercede 89.3
intercept 422
interceptor 17.375
intercession 261.68.1
interchange 207
interchangeable 228.16
intercity 16.333
intercom 237
intercommunication
  261.67.5
intercommunion
  261.123
interconnect 385
intercontinental 228.110
intercostal 228.115
intercourse 303
intercross 302.2
intercurrent 420.64
interdependent 420.14
interdict 387.1
interdiction 261.78.2

interdisciplinary
  16.274.26
interest 436.20
interested 91.53
interesting 265.76
interface 295
interfacing 265.59
interfere 6
interference 321.17
interferometer
  17.342.3.4
interferon 254.9
interfluve 490
interfuse 523.1
intergrade 85.6
interim 235
interior 17.3.39
interject 385.3
interjection 261.77.1
interlace 295
Interlaken 261.10
interlaminate 367.17.3
interlard 84
interlay 2.12
interleaf 162
interleave 484
interline 253.3
interlinear 17.3.34
interlining 265.44
interlink 52
interlock 40
interlocution 261.75.2
interlocutor 17.350
interlocutory 16.274.42
interlope 278
interloper 17.257
interlude 102.1
intermarriage 197.9
intermarry 16.260
intermediary 16.274.1
intermediate 371.1
interment 420
intermezzo 12.71
intermigration 261.67
interminable 228.16.29
intermingle 228.50
intermission 261.71.4
intermit 371.21
intermittent 420.76
intermixture 17.76
intern 249
internal 228.58
internalize 516.3.6
international 228.63.2

internationalism
  242.35.11.5.1
internationalize 516.3.7
internecine 253
internee 5
Internet 368
internment 420
internship 274
interpage 193
interpellant 420.26
interpellate 367
interplay 2
interplead 89
interpleader 17.82
Interpol 220
interpolate 367.14
interpolation 261.67.14
interpose 520.2
interpret 371
interpretation 261.67.27
interpretative 485.15.12
interpreter 17.342
interpretive 485.12
interregnum 242
interrelate 367.12
interrelation 261.67.12
interrex 496
interrobang 263.1
interrogate 367.11.1
interrogation 261.67.11
interrogative 485.15.3
interrogator 17.338.4
interrogatory
  16.274.43.3
interrupt 426.1
interruption 261.88
interscholastic 38.68
intersect 385
intersection 261.77
intersex 496
interspace 295
intersperse 297.1
interstate 367
interstice 300
interstitial 228.93
intertrigo 12.30
intertwine 253
interval 228
intervene 251.12
intervention 261.82
interventionist 436.13
interview 15
interviewee 5
interviewer 17.8
intervocalic 38.19

interweave 484
interwoven 261.116
intestate 367.33
intestinal 228.60
intestine 252.26
intimacy 16.307.2
intimate 367.15
intimate 371.19
intimation 261.67.15
intimidate 367.8
intimidation 261.67.7
into 15
intolerable 228.16.35
intolerance 321.20
intolerant 420.65
intonate 367.18
intonation 261.67.19
intone 257
intorsion 261.72
in toto 12.79
intoxicant 420.7
intoxicate 367.5
intoxication 261.67.5
intra-atomic 38.29
intracranial 228.3.5
intractable 228.16
intrados 302
intramural 228.75
intramuscular 17.174.8
intransigence 321.9
intransigent 420.20
intransitive 485.12
intrastate 367
intrauterine 253.7
intravenous 310.32
intrepid 91.23
intricacy 16.307.1
intricate 371.9
intrigue 183
intriguing 265
intrinsic 38
intro 12
introduce 309.1
introduction 261.79.1
introductory 16.274
introject 385.3
introjection 261.77.1
intromission 261.71.4
introrse 303
introspect 385
introspection 261.77
introspective 485.17
introversion 261.69.1
introvert 369.2
intrude 102

intruder 17.91
intrusion 261.93
intrusive 485.8
intubate 367
intuit 371.3
intuition 261.71
intuitive 485.12
intumesce 296
intumescence 321.21
intussusception 261.84.1
inundate 367
inundation 261.67
inure 10
inurn 249
invade 85
invader 17.79
invaginate 367.17.2
invaginate 371.24.2
invagination 261.67.18.2
invalid 89
invalid 91.16
invalidate 367.8
invalidity 16.333.5
invaluable 228.16.6
invariable 228.16.2
invariant 420.1
invasion 261
invasive 485
invective 485.17
inveigh 2
inveigle 228.45
invent 410
invention 261.82
inventive 485.21
inventiveness 300.43
inventor 17.368
inventory 16.274.48
inveracity 16.333.25
Invercargill 218
Inverness 296.3
inverse 297
inversion 261.69
invert 369
invertase 509
invertebrate 371
inverter 17.340
invest 433
investigate 367.10
investigation 261.67.10
investigative 485.15
investigator 17.338.3
investiture 17.56
investment 420
investor 17.382
inveterate 371.35.2

invidious 310.2.1
invigilate 367.12
invigilation 261.67.12
invigilator 17.338.5
invigorate 367.23
invincible 228.16.41
inviolable 228.16
inviolate 371.18.1
invisibility 16.333.9.2.2
invisible 228.16.63
invitation 261.67.27
invitatory 16.274.43
invite 372
inviting 265.67
in vitro 12
invocation 261.67.6
invoice 304
invoke 42
involucre 17.41
involuntary 16.274.48
involute 380.1
involution 261.75.1
involve 493
involved 151
invulnerable 228.16.35
inward 103
inwardly 16.152
inwards 531
inweave 484
Io 12.4
iodic 38.9
iodide 92
iodine 251.1
iodism 242.35
iodize 516
iodoform 238.2
ion 261.4
Iona 17.236
Ionesco 12.14
Ionia 17.3.36
Ionian 261.3.18
ionic 38.35
Ionic 38.35
ionize 516.7
ionosphere 6.1
iota 17.347
IOU 15
Iowa 17.6
ipecac 32
ipecacuanha 17.225
Ipswich 67
iracund 140
Iran 246
Iranian 261.3.15
Iraq 33

Iraqi 16.20
irascible 228.16
irate 367
ire 8
Ireland 143
Irene 16.228
irenic 38.33
irenics 498.4
iridaceous 310.56.2
iridescence 321.21
iridescent 420.67
iridium 242.2.3
iris 300.45
Iris 300.45
Irish 353
Irishism 242.35
Irishman 261
iritis 300.62
irk 36
irksome 242
iron 261.4
ironbound 139
ironclad 83
ironic 38.35
ironical 228.23.13
ironing 265.46
ironmonger 17.143
ironmongery 16.274.11
Ironside 92
ironsides 527
ironware 4
ironwork 36
ironworks 497
irony 16.237
irony 16.237.1
Iroquoian 261.5
Iroquois 11
irradiance 321.1
irradiate 367.1
irradiation 261.67.1
irrational 228.63.2
irrationality 16.333.8.7.1
Irrawaddy 16.65
irreconcilable 228.16
irrecoverable 228.16.35
irrecusable 228.16.65
irredeemable 228.16
irredentist 436.27
irreducible 228.16
irrefrangible 228.16.21
irrefutable 228.16.52
irregular 17.174
irregularity 16.333.20.3
irrelative 485.15.4
irrelevant 420

irreligion 261.37
irreligious 310.21
irremediable 228.16.2
irremovable 228.16.62
irreparable 228.16.35.1
irreplaceable 228.16.36
irrepressible 228.16.37
irreproachable 228.16.13
irresistible 228.16
irresoluble 228.15
irresolute 380.1
irresolution 261.75.1
irresolvable 228.16
irrespective 485.17
irresponsible 228.16
irresponsive 485
irretentive 485.21
irretrievable 228.16.61
irreverence 321.20.1
irreverent 420.65
irreversible 228.16.38
irrevocable 228.16
irrigate 367.10
irrigation 261.67.10
irrigational 228.63.3
irritable 228.16.49
irritant 420.76
irritate 367.30
irritation 261.67.27
irrupt 426
Irvine 252
Irving 265.78
is 515
Isaac 46
Isabel 215
Isabella 17.163.1
isagoge 16.106
Isaiah 17.4
Isar 1
Iscariot 381.1.1
ischaemia 17.3.26
ischium 242.2
Isherwood 101
Ishmael 228.1
isinglass 294
Isis 300.53
Iskander Bey 2.4
Iskenderun 260.3
Islam 230
Islamic 38.24
Islamize 516.5
island 143
islander 17.109
Islay 2
isle 219

islet 371
Islington 261
ism 242.35
Ismaili 16.118
isn't 420
isobar 1.2
isobaric 38.38
isoclinal 228.61
isocline 253
isocracy 16.307.5
Isocrates 513.17
isodiaphere 6
isogamy 16.222.2
isolate 367.14
isolation 261.67.14
isolationism 242.35.14.3
isomagnetic 38.50
isomer 17.218
isometric 38.46
isometrics 498.10
isomorph 166.1
isomorphism 242.35.7
isoniazid 91
isonomy 16.222.3
isosceles 513.6
isothere 6.10
isotherm 233
isotone 257.3
isotonic 38.35.5
isotope 278
isotopic 38.37
Israel 228.1
Israeli 16.114
Israelite 372.4
Israfil 217
issuable 228.16.6
issuance 321.3
issuant 420.4
issue 15
Issus 310.53
Istanbul 226
isthmus 310
Istria 17.3
it 371
itacolumite 372
Italian 261.118
Italianate 371.28
Italianism 242.35.14
Italianize 516.7
italic 38.19.1
Italicism 242.35.16.1
italicize 516.10
Italy 16.131
itch 67
itching 265

itchy 16.49
item 242.29
itemize 516.5
iterate 367.23.2
iteration 261.67.22.4
Ithaca 17.42
itinerancy 16.312
itinerant 420.65
itinerary 16.274.32
itinerate 367.23
it'll 228.102
its 339
it's 339
itself 172
Ivan 261.115
I've 486
ivied 91
ivories 515.1
ivory 16.274.52
ivy 16
Iwo Jima 17.210
ixia 17.3.58
Izmir 6

J

jab 18
Jabalpur 10
jabber 17.9
jabberwocky 16.27
jaborandi 16.77
jabot 12
jacamar 1.12
jaçana 1
jacaranda 17.98.2
jacinth 470
jack 32
Jack 32
jackal 221
jackanapes 323
jackass 293
jackboot 380
jackdaw 9
jackeroo 15.6
jacket 371.6
jackfruit 380
jackknife 164
jackpot 373
jacks 494
jacksmelt 402
jacksnipe 275
Jackson 261
Jacksonville 218
jackstay 2
jackstraws 518

Jacob 31
Jacobean 261.2.1
Jacobin 252
Jacobite 372
Jacquard 84
jactitation 261.67.27
jade 85
jaded 91.6
jaeger 17.125
Jael 228.1
Jaffa 17.110
jag 178
jagged 91
Jagger 17.123
jaggy 16.91
jaguar 17.7.1
jaguarundi 16.80
jai alai 7
jail 214
jailbird 87
jailbreak 34
jailer 17.162
jailhouse 306
Jain 253
Jainism 242.35
jalap 281
jalopy 16.250
jalousie 5
jam 229
Jamaica 17.30
Jamaican 261.11
jamb 229
jambalaya 17.4
jamboree 5.17
jammy 16.210
jampan 245
Jamshedpur 10
Jamshid 89
Janata 1
Jane 247
Janet 371.22
jangle 228.49
Janiculum 242.10.1
janissary 16.274.36
janitor 17.342
Jansen 261
Jansenism 242.35.14
January 16.274.2
Janus 310.31
Jap 268
Japan 245.4
Japanese 513.9
jape 270
Japheth 455
japonica 17.34.1

jar 1
jardinière 4.1
jargon 261
jargonize 516.7
jarl 213
jarosite 372.10
Jarrow 12.60
jarvey 16.378
Jarvis 300
jasmine 252
Jason 261.62
jaspé 2
jasper 17.265
jato 12.74
jaundice 300
jaunt 415
jaunty 16.358
Java 17.409
javelin 252
jaw 9
Jawan 246
jawbone 257
jawbreaker 17.30
jay 2
jaywalk 41
jaywalker 17.37
jazz 507
jazzy 16.391
jealous 310.22
jealousy 16.307
Jean 251
jeans 547
jebel 228
jeep 273
jeer 6
Jefferson 261
Jeffreys 515
Jehol 220
Jehovah 17.417
jejune 260
jejunum 242
Jekyll 228.21
jell 215
jellaba 17.21
jellied 91.17
jellify 7.3
jello 12.40
jelly 16.115
jellybean 251
jellyfish 353
jemmy 16.213
Jenkins 548
Jenner 17.228
jennet 371
jenny 16.226

Jenny 16.226
jeopardize 516
jeopardy 16.72
jequirity 16.333
jerboa 17.6
jeremiad 83.2
Jeremiah 17.4
Jericho 12.11
jerk 36
jerkin 252
jerky 16.23
jeroboam 242
Jerome 239
jerry 16.262
Jerry 16.262
jersey 16.394
Jersey 16.394
Jerusalem 242.11
jess 296
jessamine 252.15
Jesse 16.297
Jessica 17.34
jest 433
jester 17.382
Jesu 15
Jesuit 371.2
Jesuitic 38.52
Jesuitism 242.35.18
Jesus 310
jet 368
jeté 2
Jethro 12
jetliner 17.232
jetport 374
jetsam 242
jetsetter 17.339
jettison 261.65
jetton 261.96
jetty 16.330
Jew 15
jewel 228.10
jeweller 17.176
jewellery 16.283
Jewess 300
jewfish 353
Jewish 353
Jewry 16.270
Jezebel 215
Jhansi 16.310
jib 24
Jidda 17.83
jiffy 16.85
jig 184
jigger 17.129
jiggered 103

jiggery-pokery 16.274
jiggle 228.46
jigsaw 9
jihad 83
jilt 403
Jimmy 16.216
jingle 228.50
jingo 12.36
jingoism 242.35.3
jingoistic 38.70
Jinja 17.157
jink 52
jinni 5.12
jinx 505
jissom 242.24
jitter 17.342
jitterbug 189
jittery 16.274.41
jive 486
Joab 18
Joan 257
job 26
Job 28
jobber 17.16
jobbery 16.274.3
Jobcentre 17.368
jobless 300
joblessness 300.33
Jocasta 17.379
Jock 40
jockey 16.27
jockstrap 268
jocose 305
jocosely 16.182
jocular 17.174.7
jocularity 16.333.20.3
jocund 143
jocundity 16.333.7
jocundly 16.157
jodhpurs 524
Jodo 12.21
Joe 12
joey 16.3
jog 185
jogger 17.131
jogging 265.23
joggle 228.47
Johannesburg 182.1
John 254
John Dory 16.269
Johnny 16.231
John o'Groats 343
Johnson 261
Johnsonian 261.3.18
Johore 9

join 256
joinder 17.106
joiner 17.235
joinery 16.274
joint 416
jointed 91.48
jointer 17.371
joist 440
joke 42
joker 17.38
jokingly 16.175
jollify 7.3.2
jollity 16.333.10
jolly 16.122
Jolo 12.44
jolt 405
Jonah 17.236
Jonas 310.35
Jonathan 261.109
Jones 550
jonnock 46
jonquil 218
Joplin 252
Joppa 17.255
Jordan 261.27
Jordanian 261.3.15
jorum 242.20
Jos 302
Joseph 163
Josephine 251
Josephus 310
josh 354
Joshua 17.7
Josiah 17.4
joss 302
jostle 228.86
jostler 17.198
jot 373
jotter 17.344
jotting 265.68
joual 213
joule 227
jounce 319
journal 228.58
journalese 513.7
journalism 242.35.11.4
journalist 436.7
journalistic 38.70.2
journalize 516.3.6
journey 16.227
journeyman 261.48
journo 12.53
joust 442
Jove 488
jovial 228.3.16

joviality 16.333.8.1
Jovian 261.3.31
jowl 224
joy 11
Joyce 304
joyful 226
joyless 300
joyous 310
joyousness 300.34
joypop 276
joyrider 17.84
Juan de Fuca 17.41
Jubal 228
jube 16.14
jubilant 420
jubilate 367.12.1
jubilation 261.67.12
jubilee 5.8
Judaea 17.2
Judaean 261.2
Judah 17.91
Judaic 38.1
Judaica 17.33
Judaism 242.35
Judaist 436.1
Judaize 516
Judas 310
judder 17.90
Jude 102
judge 203
judgeship 274
judgment 420
judicative 485.15.1
judicatory 16.274.40.1
judicature 17.62
judicial 228.93
judiciary 16.274.1.2
judicious 310.58
Judith 458
judo 12.22
judogi 16.96
judoka 1
Judy 16.71
jug 189
jugal 228.48
juggernaut 374
juggins 548
juggle 228
juggler 17.193
jugglery 16.274
juggling 265
jugular 17.174
juice 309
juicy 16.306
jujitsu 15

juju 15
jujube 30
jukebox 499
julep 274
Julia 17.3.23
Julian 261
Juliana 17.226.1
Julie 16.130
julienne 248.1
Juliet 371.1.1
Jullundur 17.109
July 7.6
jumble 228
jumbo 12.7
jumbuck 43
Jumna 17.242
jump 289
jumper 17.264
jumpy 16.257
junction 261.80
juncture 17.68
June 260
Jungian 261.3
jungle 228
junior 17
juniper 17.253
junk 54
Junker 17.46
junket 371
junkie 16.39
junkyard 84
Juno 12
Junoesque 57
junta 17.373
Jupiter 17.342
jupon 254
Jura 17.277
jural 228.75
Jurassic 38.48
juridical 228.23
jurisconsult 406
jurisdiction 261.78
jurisprudence 321
jurisprudent 420.13
jurist 436.19
juristic 38.70
juror 17.277
jury 16.270
juryman 261.48
jus 307
jus civile 16.118
jus divinum 242
jus naturale 16.114
jussive 485.7
just 443

justice 300
justiciar 1
justiciary 16.274.1.2
justifiable 228.16.3.1
justification 261.67.5.1
justificatory 16.274.40.1
justify 7.3
Justin 252.27
Justinian 261.3.17
jut 378
jute 380
Jutish 353
Jutland 143
Juvenal 228.60
juvenescence 321.21
juvenescent 420.67.1
juvenile 219
juvenilia 17.3.21
juvenility 16.333.9.3
juxtapose 520.2
juxtaposition 261.71.9

K

kabaragoya 17.431
kabuki 16.32
Kabul 226
kachang puteh 2.25
kachina 17.230
Kaduna 17.238
kaftan 245
Kagera 17.269
Kaifeng 264
Kaiser 17.441
kaka 17.29
kakapo 12.59
kakemono 12.56
kaki 16.20
kala-azar 1.19
Kalahari 16.261.1
Kalamazoo 15.10
Kalat 366
kale 214
kaleidoscope 278.1
kaleidoscopic 38.37.1
kaleyard 84
Kalgoorlie 16.124
Kali 16.113
kalian 246
kalmia 17.3.28
Kalmuck 43
kamacite 372.10
kamala 17.161.1
Kamasutra 17.294
kami 16.211

kick 38
kickback 32
kicker 17.34
kickshaw 9
kicksorter 17.345
kickstand 128
kick-start 366
kid 91
Kidd 91
Kidderminster 17.394
Kiddush 358
kiddy 16.63
kidnap 268
kidnapper 17.247
kidney 16.240
kidskin 252
Kiel 217
Kierkegaard 84
Kiev 160.1
kif 163
kikumon 254
Kildare 4
Kilimanjaro 12.61
Kilkenny 16.226
kill 218
Killarney 16.224
killer 17.166
killick 38.21
Killiecrankie 16.36
killifish 353
killing 265.30
Kilmarnock 46
kiln 262
kilo 12.41
kilocalorie 16.274.15
kilogram 229.1.2
kilohertz 337
kilometre 17.341
kilometric 38.46
kiloton 259
kilovolt 405
kilowatt 373
kilt 403
kilted 91
Kimberley 16.131
kimono 12.56
kin 252
Kinabalu 15.5
kinaesthesia 17.3.60
kincob 26
kind 135
kindergarten 261.95
kind-hearted 91.33
kind-heartedness 300.28
kindle 228.40

kindler 17.189
kindless 300
kindliness 300.23
kindling 265
kindly 16.155
kindness 300.29
kindred 91
kine 253
kinematics 498.11
kinesics 498
kinetic 38.50.4
kinetics 498.12
king 265
kingbolt 405
kingcup 279
kingdom 242
kingfisher 17.326
kinglet 371
kingly 16.175
kingpin 252
kingship 274
King's Lynn 252
Kingston 261.108
kink 52
kinkajou 15
kinky 16.37
kinnikinnick 38.34
Kinross 302
Kinsey 16.406
kinsfolk 42
Kinshasa 17.438
kinship 274
kinsman 261
kiosk 59
kip 274
Kipling 265
kipper 17.253
Kirghiz 515
kirigami 16.211
kirk 36
Kirkby 16.9
kirkman 261
Kirkpatrick 38.45
Kirkuk 44
kish 353
kismet 368
kiss 300
kissable 228.16.39
kissel 228.85
kisser 17.302
kissing 265.61
Kissinger 17.157
kist 436
kit 371
kitbag 178.1

kitchen 252
Kitchener 17.231
kitchenette 368
kitchenware 4
kite 372
kith 458
kitsch 67
kitten 261.99
kittenish 353
kittiwake 34
kitty 16.333
Kiwanis 300.21
Klansman 261
klaxon 261
Kleenex 496
Kleist 437
Klemperer 17.279
klepht 397
kleptomania 17.3.31.1
kleptomaniac 32.1
klipspringer 17.246
Klondike 39
kloof 170
knack 32
knacker 17.28
knackwurst 434
knapsack 32
knapweed 89
knar 1
knave 482
knavery 16.274.50
knavish 353
knawel 228.5
knead 89
knee 5
kneecap 268
kneehole 223
kneel 217
kneeler 17.165
kneepad 83
kneepan 245
knell 215
knelt 402
knew 15
Knickerbocker 17.36
knickerbockers 524
knickers 524
knickknack 32
knife 164
knight 372
knighthood 101
knightly 16.190
knish 353
knit 371
knitted 91.38

knitter 17.342
knitting 265.66
knitwear 4.9
knob 26
knobbly 16.135
knobkerrie 16.262
knock 40
knocker 17.36
knock-kneed 89
knockout 377
knoll 223
Knossos 310.54
knot 373
knotgrass 294
knothole 223
knotted 91.40
knotting 265.68
knotty 16.335
knotweed 89
know 12
know-how 13
knowing 265.4
knowledge 197.2
knowledgeable 228.16.20
known 257
Knox 499
knuckle 228.27
knucklebone 257
knuckle-duster 17.388
knucklehead 86
knur 3
knurl 216
KO 12.1
koa 17.6
koala 17.161
Kobe 16.12
kobold 120
Kochi 5
Kodiak 32.1
kofta 17.360
Kohima 1.11
Kohinoor 10
kohl 223
kohlrabi 16.6
kokanee 16.223
kolinsky 16.45
Kol Nidre 2
kolo 12.44
komatik 38.49
Komi 16.219
Komodo 12.21
Komsomol 220.2
Konstanz 347
kook 45
kookaburra 17.278

kooky 16.32
Kootenay 5.14
kop 276
kopeck 35
kopje 16.250
Koran 246
Kordofan 245
Korea 17.2.2
Korean 261.2.3
korma 17.214
koruna 17.238
kos 305
Kos 302
kosher 17.328
Kota 17.347
koto 12.79
koulibiaca 17.29
kowhai 7
Kowloon 260
kowtow 13
Kra 1
kraal 213
kraft 396
krait 372
Krakatoa 17.6
kraken 261.10
Krefeld 113
Kremlin 252
kriegspiel 217
krill 218
krimmer 17.211
kris 300
Krishna 17.243
Kriss Kringle 228.50
Kristiansand 128
kromesky 16.40
krone 17.236
Kruger 17.136
Krugersdorp 277
krypton 254
Kuala Lumpur 10
Kublai Khan 246
Kubrick 38
kudos 302
kudu 15
Kufic 38
Ku Klux Klan 245
kulak 32
Kumasi 16.294
kumbaloi 11.1
kumiss 300
kumquat 373
kung fu 15
Kura 1
Kurd 87

Kurdish 353
Kurdistan 246.1
Kure 2
kursaal 228.126
Kuskokwim 235
Kutch 72
Kuwait 367
kvass 294
Kwa 1
kwacha 1
Kwajalein 247.4
Kwakiutl 228.108
kwanza 17.445
kwashiorkor 17.37
Kweisui 2
kwela 17.162
kyle 219
kylix 498
Kyoto 12.79
kyphosis 300.55
kyu 15

L

laager 17.124
lab 18
labarum 242.21
labdanum 242.16
label 228.11
labeller 17.176
labellum 242.8
labia 17.3.1
labial 228.3
labile 219
labium 242.2
lablab 18
laboratory 16.274.43.7
laborious 310.2.13
labour 17.11
labourer 17.279
labourism 242.35.15
labourist 436.20
Labourite 372.8
Labrador 9.4
laburnum 242.13
labyrinth 470
labyrinthian 261.3.28
labyrinthine 253
lac 32
lace 295
Lacedaemon 261.47
Lacedaemonian 261.3.18
lacerate 367.23
laceration 261.67.22
Lacerta 17.340

lacertilian 261.3.11
lacewing 265
lachrymose 305
lacing 265.59
lack 32
lackadaisical 228.23
lackey 16.19
lacklustre 17.388
laconic 38.35
lacquer 17.28
lacrimal 228.52
lacrimation 261.67.15
lacrimator 17.338
lacrimatory 16.274.43
lacrosse 302.2
lactary 16.274.44
lactase 509
lactate 367
lactation 261.67
lacteal 228.3
lactescent 420.67
lactic 38.58
lactiferous 310.50.2
lactogenic 38.32.1
lactone 257
lactose 520
lacuna 17.238
lacy 16.296
lad 83
ladder 17.77
laddie 16.57
lade 85
laden 261.20
la-di-da 1
lading 265.11
Ladislas 293
ladle 228
lady 16.59
ladybird 87
ladyfy 7.3
ladylike 39
ladylove 489
Ladyship 274
Ladysmith 458
Laertes 513
laevorotation 261.67.28
lag 178
lagan 261
lager 17.124
laggard 103
lagging 265
lagomorph 166.1
lagoon 260
Lagos 302
La Guardia 17.3.6

lah 1
Lahnda 17.99
Lahore 9
laic 38.1
laicize 516.10
laid 85
lain 247
lair 4
laird 88
lairy 16.264
laity 16.333
lake 34
Lakeland 143
Lakshadweep 273
laky 16.21
Lala 1.7
lallation 261.67
lallygag 178
lam 229
lama 17.206
Lamaism 242.35
Lamarckian 261.3
Lamarckism 242.35
lamb 229
lambaste 432
lambent 420
Lambert 381
Lambeth 464
lambkin 252
lambrequin 252.3
lame 231
lamé 2
lamella 17.163
lamellicorn 255.2
lamely 16.165
lameness 300
lament 410.2
lamentable 228.16.57
lamentation 261.67.32
lamented 91.46
lamia 17.3.24
lamina 17.231.1
laminate 367.17.3
laminate 371.24
lamination 261.67.18.3
Lammas 310
lammergeier 17.4
lamp 285
lampas 310.41
lampblack 32
Lampedusa 17.444
lampern 261
lampion 261.3
lamplighter 17.343
lampoon 260

lamppost 441
lamprophyre 8.1
Lanai 16.1
Lanark 46
Lancashire 6
Lancaster 17.390
Lancastrian 261.3.26
lance 315
lancer 17.313
lancet 371
lancinate 367.17
land 128
landammann 261.52
landau 9
landaulet 368
landed 91.12
landfall 221
landform 238
landgrave 482
landgravine 251.12
landing 265.19
landlady 16.59
landlocked 388
landloper 17.257
landlord 95
landlubber 17.19
landmark 33
landmass 293
landowner 17.236
landrace 295
landscape 270
landscapist 436.14
Landseer 6
landshark 33
landsknecht 385
landslide 92
landsman 261
Landtag 33
landward 103
lane 247
Lang 263
Langland 143
langouste 444
language 197
langue de chat 1
languid 91
languish 353
languor 17.140
languorous 310.50
langur 10
lank 51
lanky 16.36
lanner 17.225
lanneret 368.6
lanolin 252.11

lantana 17.227
lantern 261
lanthanide 92.4
lanthanum 242.16
lanugo 12.32
lanyard 103
Lao 13
Laocoon 254.2
Laodicea 17.2
Laodicean 261.2.4
Laoighis 353
Laotze 2
lap 268
laparotomy 16.222.4
La Paz 507
lapel 215
lapidary 16.274
lapidate 367.8
lapidify 7.3.1
lapis 300
lapis lazuli 7.6
Lapland 143
Laplander 17.109
Lapp 268
lappet 371
lapse 322
lapsus 310
lapwing 265
larboard 103
larceny 16.229.4
larch 63
lard 84
larder 17.78
lardon 261
lares 513.10
large 192
largen 261
largess 296
largish 353
largo 12.26
lariat 381.1.1
larine 253
Larisa 17.302
lark 33
Larkin 252.2
larkspur 3
larnax 494
La Rochefoucauld 12
larrigan 261.32
larrikin 252.3
larrup 281
Larry 16.260
larva 17.409
larval 228
larvicide 92.7

Larwood 101
laryngeal 228.2
laryngitic 38.52
laryngitis 300.62
laryngology 16.108.4.7
laryngoscope 278.1
laryngotomy 16.222.4
larynx 505
lasagne 17.434
La Salle 212
lascar 17.47
lascivious 310.2.17
lasciviousness 300.34.1
laser 17.439
lash 349
lashing 265
lash-up 279
lass 293
lassie 16.294
lassitude 102.2
lasso 15
Lassus 310.51
last 431
lasting 265.74
lastly 16.199
Las Vegas 310.19
latch 62
latchkey 5
late 367
latecomer 17.216
lateen 251.11
lately 16.188
latent 420.75
later 17.338
lateral 228.76
Lateran 261.60
latest 436
latex 496
lath 453
lathe 473
lather 17.401
lathery 16.274
lathi 16.328
Latimer 17.218
Latin 252
Latinate 367.17
Latinism 242.35.13
Latinist 436.11
Latinity 16.333.17
Latinize 516.6.1
Latino 12.54
latish 353
latitude 102.2.1
latitudinal 228.60.1

latitudinarian 261.3.21.1
Latium 242.2
latrine 251
latten 261.94
latter 17.336
latterly 16.131.7
lattice 300
latticed 436
Latvian 261.3
laud 95
laudable 228.16.16
laudanum 242.16
laudation 261.67
laudatory 16.274.43
Lauder 17.86
laugh 158
laughable 228.16
laughter 17.358
Laughton 261.102
launch 81
launder 17.105
Launderette 368.6
laundress 300
Laundromat 365
laundry 16
laundryman 261.48
Laura 17.276
Laurasia 17.322
laureate 371.1.2
laurel 228.73
Lausanne 245
lav 480
lava 17.409
lavage 197
Laval 212
lavation 261.67
lavatory 16.274.43
lavender 17.109
laver 17.409
laver 17.410
laverock 46
lavish 353
lavishness 300.35
law 9
law-abiding 265.14
lawbreaker 17.30
lawful 226.1
lawgiver 17.414
lawks 500
lawless 300
lawlessness 300.33
lawman 261
lawn 255
Lawrence 321.18
Lawrentian 261.82

lawsuit 380
lawyer 17.430
lax 494
laxation 261.67.34
laxative 485.15
laxity 16.333
lay 2
layabout 377.1
layer 17.1
layette 368
layman 261.45
lazar 17.437
lazaretto 12.75
Lazarus 310.50
laze 509
laziness 300.23
lazulite 372
lazurite 372
lazy 16.393
lazybones 550
L-dopa 17.257
lea 5
leach 66
Leacock 40
lead 86
lead 89
Leadbelly 16.115
leaded 91.7
leaden 261.21
leader 17.82
leadership 274.1
leading 265.12
leading 265.13
leaf 162
leafcutter 17.349
leaflet 371
leafstalk 41
leafy 16.84
league 183
Leah 6
leak 37
leakage 197
leaky 16.24
leal 217
Leamington 261
lean 251
Leander 17.98.1
leaning 265.42
leant 410
leap 273
leapfrog 185
leapt 422
Lear 6
learn 249
learned 91

learner 17.229
learning 265.41
learnt 411
lease 298
leaseback 32
leasehold 120
leaseholder 17.97
leash 352
least 435
leastways 509
leat 370
leather 17.402
leatherback 32.2
Leatherette 368.6
Leatherhead 86.5
leatherjacket 371.6
leathery 16.274
leave 484
leaved 148
leaven 261.112
leavings 552
Lebanese 513.9
Lebanon 261
leben 261
lebkuchen 261.15
Le Carré 2.16
lech 64
Lech 35
lecher 17.53
lecherous 310.50
lechery 16.274
lecithin 252
lectern 261
lection 261.77
lectionary 16.274.29.4
lector 9
lecture 17.64
lecturer 17.279
lectureship 274.1
led 86
Leda 17.82
lederhosen 261.129
ledge 194
ledger 17.147
lee 5
leeboard 95
leech 66
Leeds 526
leek 37
leer 6
leery 16.265
lees 513
leet 370
leeward 103
leeway 2

left 397
left-handed 91.12
left-handedness 300.28.1
left-hander 17.98
leftism 242.35
leftist 436
leftover 17.417
lefty 16.346
leg 181
legacy 16.307
legal 228.45
legalese 513.7
legalism 242.35.11
legality 16.333.8.4
legalize 516.3
legate 371
legatee 5
legation 261.67.10
legato 12.73
legator 9
legend 143
legendary 16.274
legendry 16.279
legerdemain 247.5
leggings 552
leggy 16.92
leghorn 255
legible 228.16
legion 261.36
legionary 16.274.29
legionnaire 4.5
legislate 367
legislation 261.67
legislative 485.15
legislator 17.338
legislatorial 228.3.12.2
legislature 17.52
legist 436
legit 371
legitimacy 16.307.2
legitimate 367.15
legitimate 371.19
legitimatize 516.13.2
legitimist 436.9
legitimize 516.4
legless 300
legroom 241
legume 241
legumen 252
leguminous 310.33.1
legwork 36
Lehár 1
lei 5.1
Leibnitz 339
Leicester 17.382

Leicestershire 6
Leiden 261.25
Leigh 5
Leipzig 184
leishmania 17.3.31
leister 17.383
leisure 17.333
leisured 103.6
leisurely 16.131
Leith 457
leitmotiv 162
Leitrim 235
lek 35
Lely 16.118
lemma 17.208
lemming 265
lemniscus 310.15
Lemnos 302
lemon 261
lemonade 85.3
lemony 16.237.6
lempira 17.272
lemur 17.210
lemuroid 97
Len 248
Lena 17.230
lend 131
lender 17.101
length 472
lengthen 261
lengthways 509
lengthy 16
leniency 16.312.1
lenient 420.1.2
Lenin 252.16
Leningrad 83
Leninism 242.35.13
lenis 300
lenitive 485.12
lenity 16.333.15
Lennon 261
leno 12.54
lens 546
lent 410
Lent 410
lentamente 16.355
lenten 261
lentic 38.63
lenticular 17.174.6
lentiform 238.1
lentigo 12.30
lentil 218
lento 12.84
Leo 12.2
Leonidas 293

leonine 253
leopard 103
leopardess 300.5
Leopold 120
leotard 84
leper 17.250
lepidopterist 436.20
lepidosiren 261.58
Lepidus 310
leporid 91.27
leporine 253.7
leprechaun 255
leprosy 16.307
leprous 310
lepton 254
leptosome 239
Lerwick 38
lesbian 261.3
lesbianism 242.35.14.1
Lesbos 302
Les Cayes 2
lese-majesty 16.366
lesion 261.90
Lesley 16.208
less 296
lessee 5.19
lessen 261.63
lesser 17.300
lesson 261.63
lessor 9
lest 433
let 368
lethal 228
lethargic 38
lethargy 16.108
Lethbridge 197
Leto 12.76
let's 336
Lett 368
letter 17.339
letterhead 86.5
lettering 265.58
letterpress 296.5
letterset 368
Lettish 353
lettuce 300
Leucippus 310.37
leucocyte 372.10
leucoderma 17.209
leucopenia 17.3.33
leucopoiesis 300.51
leucorrhoea 17.2.2
leucotomy 16.222.4
leukaemia 17.3.26
lev 160

levant 407.1
levanter 17.365
levantine 253
levator 17.338.11
levee 16.380
level 228.118
level-headed 91.7
level-headedness 300.28
leveller 17.176
Leven 261.113
lever 17.413
leverage 197
leveret 371.35
Levi 7
leviathan 261.109
levigate 367.10
levirate 371.33
Levis 516
levitate 367.30
levitation 261.67.27
Levite 372
Leviticus 310.10
levity 16.333.34
levy 16.380
lewd 102
lewdness 300
Lewes 300
Lewis 300
Lewisham 242
lewisite 372.9
lex 496
lexical 228.23
lexicography 16.90.2
lexicology 16.108.4.4
lexicon 261.13
Lexington 261
lexis 300
lex loci 7
lex non scripta 17.376
lex talionis 300.25
ley 5
liability 16.333.9.2.1
liable 228.16.3
liaise 509.1
liaison 254
liana 17.226.1
liar 17.4
liard 84
Liard 84
lias 310.3
Liassic 38.48
lib 24
libation 261.67
libel 228
libellant 420.28

libellee 5.9
libellous 310.26
liberal 228.76
liberalism 242.35.11
liberality 16.333.8.9
liberalize 516.3.8
liberate 367.23
liberation 261.67.22
liberator 17.338.9
Liberia 17.3.39
libertarian 261.3.21
libertine 251.11
liberty 16.344
libidinous 310.33
libido 12.18
Libra 17.283
librarian 261.3.21
librarianship 274.2
library 16.274
librate 367
libration 261.67
librettist 436.23
libretto 12.75
Libya 17.3.3
Libyan 261.3.2
lice 301
licence 321
license 321
licensee 5
licentiate 371.1
licentious 310.61
lichen 261
Lichfield 115
licit 371.36
lick 38
lickerish 353.11
lickety-split 371
licking 265.7
lickspittle 228.102
lictor 17.355
lid 91
lidless 300
lido 12.18
lie 7
Liebfraumilch 49
Liechtenstein 253
lied 89
lief 162
liege 196
Liège 360
lien 261.3
Lietuva 17.419
lieu 15
lieutenant 420.52
life 164

lifeblood 100
lifeboat 376
lifeguard 84
lifeless 300
lifelessness 300.33
lifelike 39
lifeline 253
lifelong 266
lifer 17.115
lifetime 236
Liffey 16.85
lift 398
liftboy 11
liftoff 165
ligament 420.35.1
ligamentous 310.70
ligand 143
ligature 17.62
liger 17.130
light 372
lighten 261.100
lightener 17.239
lighter 17.343
light-headed 91.7
light-headedness 300.28
light-hearted 91.33
light-heartedness 300.28
lighthouse 306
lighting 265.67
lightness 300.39
lightning 265
lights 340
lightship 274
lightsome 242
lightweight 367
lignaloes 520.1
ligneous 310.2
lignify 7.3.3
lignite 372.7
lignocaine 247.2
ligulate 371.17
Liguria 17.3.42
likable 228.16
like 39
likelihood 101
likely 16.143
like-minded 91
liken 261
likeness 300
likewise 516
liking 265
lilac 46
liliaceous 310.56
Lilith 458
Liliuokalani 5.10

Lilliputian 261.75
lilly-pilly 16.120
Lilo 12
lilt 403
lilting 265
lily 16.120
lima 17.212
Lima 17.210
limacine 253.8
Limassol 220
limb 235
limber 17.25
limbless 300
limbo 12.6
Limburg 182
Limburger 17.127
lime 236
limeade 85
limekiln 262
limelight 372
limen 248
limerick 38.44
Limerick 38.44
limestone 257
limey 16.217
limicolous 310.26.2
liminal 228.60.4
limit 371.19
limitary 16.274.41
limitation 261.67.27
limited 91.38
limitless 300.17
limitlessness 300.33
limitrophe 167
Limoges 363
limousine 251
limp 287
limpet 371
limpid 91
limpkin 252
Limpopo 12
limulus 310.25
limy 16.217
linchpin 252
Lincoln 261
Lincolnshire 6.8
lincrusta 17.388
Lincs. 505
linctus 310
Lindbergh 182
linden 261
Lindisfarne 246
line 253
lineage 197
lineal 228.3.7

lineament 420.35
linear 17.3.34
lineate 371.1
linen 252.17
liner 17.232
linesman 261
ling 265
lingcod 94
linger 17.141
lingerie 16.274
lingo 12.36
lingua franca 17.43
lingual 228
linguini 16.228
linguist 436
linguistic 38.70
linguistics 498
liniment 420.31
lining 265.44
link 52
linkage 197
linkboy 11
linkman 261
links 505
Linnaeus 310.1
linnet 371.24
Linnhe 16.229
lino 12
linocut 378
linoleum 242.2.7
Linotype 275.1
linsang 263
linseed 89.4
linstock 40
lint 412
lintel 228
linter 17.369
Linz 348
lion 261.4
lioness 300.26
lion-hearted 91.33
lionize 516.7
lip 274
lipase 509
lipid 91.24
lipoid 97
Lippizaner 17.226
lippy 16.248
lip-read 89
lip-reader 17.82
lipstick 38
liquate 367.20
liquefacient 420.73
liquefaction 261.76
liquefy 7.3

liquesce 296
liquescent 420.67
liqueur 10.3
liquid 91
liquidambar 17.23
liquidate 367.8
liquidation 261.67.7
liquidator 17.338
liquidity 16.333.5
liquidize 516
liquidizer 17.441
liquor 17.34
liquorice 300.47
lira 17.272
liripipe 275
Lisbon 261
lisle 219
lisp 291
Lissajous 15
lissom 242.24
list 436
listed 91.53
listen 261.65
Lister 17.384
listing 265.76
listless 300
listlessness 300.33
Liszt 436
lit 371
litany 16.237
literacy 16.307.4
literal 228.76
literalism 242.35.11
literally 16.131
literary 16.274.32
literate 371.35
literati 16.328.1
literatim 235
literation 261.67.22.4
literature 17.56
lithe 477
lithesome 242
lithia 17.3.51
lithic 38.73
lithium 242.2
lithograph 158.1
lithography 16.90.2
lithoid 97
lithology 16.108.4.18
lithosol 220
lithosphere 6.1
lithotomy 16.222.4
Lithuania 17.3.31
Lithuanian 261.3.15
litigable 228.16.19

litigant 420.17
litigate 367.10
litigation 261.67.10
litigious 310.21
litmus 310
litotes 513
litre 17.341
litter 17.342
littérateur 3.1
litterbug 189
little 228.102
littoral 228.76
liturgical 228.23.4
liturgist 436.4
liturgy 16.108
live 485
live 486
livelihood 101
liveliness 300.23
livelong 266
lively 16
liven 261.115
liver 17.414
liveried 91.27
liverish 353.11
Liverpool 227
Liverpudlian 261.3
liverwort 369
liverwurst 434
livery 16.274.51
livestock 40
liveware 4
livid 91
living 265.80
Livingstone 261.108
Livonia 17.3.36
Livy 16.382
lixivium 242.2
lizard 103
Ljubljana 17.226
llama 17.206
Llandaff 157
Llandudno 12
Llanelli 16.203
llano 12.51
Llewellyn 252.7
Lloyd 97
lo 12
loach 70
load 98
loaded 91.10
loader 17.88
loading 265.16
loaf 167
loafer 17.117

loam 239
loamy 16.219
loan 257
loath 461
loathe 478
loathing 265
loathsome 242
lob 26
lobar 17.18
lobate 367.3
lobby 16.11
lobbyist 436
lobe 28
lobelia 17.3.20
Lobengula 17.175
loblolly 16.122
lobotomy 16.222.4
lobscouse 306
lobster 17.391
lobster thermidor 9.3
lobule 227
local 228.26
locale 213
localism 242.35.11
locality 16.333.8
localize 516.3
locate 367.6
location 261.67.6
locative 485.15.2
loch 40
loci 7
lock 40
lockable 228.16
locker 17.36
locket 371.10
lockjaw 9
lockout 377
locksmith 458
loco 12.12
locoism 242.35.3
locoman 261.49
locomotion 261.73.1
locomotive 485.14
locomotor 17.347
locular 17.174.7
locule 227
locum tenens 546
locus 310.12
locus sigilli 7.5
locus standi 7
locust 445
locution 261.75.2
Lod 94
lode 98
loden 261

lodestar 1
lodestone 257
lodge 199
lodger 17.152
lodging 265
lodgings 552
lodgment 420
loess 300.1
loft 399
lofter 17.360
lofty 16.348
log 185
Logan 261
loganberry 16.274
logaoedic 38.8
logarithm 242.33
logarithmic 38.30
logbook 44
loge 363
logger 17.131
loggerhead 86.5
loggia 17.152
logging 265.23
logic 38.18
logical 228.23.5
logician 261.71
logion 254.1
logistic 38.70.1
logistician 261.71
logistics 498
logo 12.31
logogram 229.1
logograph 163
logomachy 16.33
logopaedics 498
logorrhoea 17.2.2
logotype 275.1
logwood 101
Lohengrin 252
loin 256
loincloth 459
loiter 17.346
Loki 16.29
Lola 17.171
loll 220
Lollard 103.3
lollipop 276
lollop 281.2
lolly 16.122
Lomax 494
Lombard 103
Lombardy 16.72
Lombok 40
loment 410
lomentum 242

Lomond 143
London 261
Londonderry 16.262
Londoner 17.239
lone 257
loneliness 300.23
lonely 16.173
loner 17.236
lonesome 242
long 266
longboat 376
longbow 12
longeron 261.60
longevity 16.333.34
longevous 310.73
Longfellow 12.40
Longford 103
long-haired 88
longhand 128
longhorn 255
longing 265
Longinus 310.34
longish 353
longitude 102.2
longitudinal 228.60.1
long johns 549
longship 274
longshore 9
long-sighted 91.39
long-sightedness 300.28
longtime 236
longways 509
long-winded 91
Longyearbyen 248
lonicera 17.279.2
loo 15
looby 16.14
loofah 17.119
look 44
looker 17.40
lookout 377
loom 241
loon 260
loony 16.236
loop 280
looper 17.259
loophole 223
loopy 16.253
loose 309
loosebox 499
loosely 16.183
loosen 261
looseness 300
loosestrife 164
loot 380

looter 17.351
lop 276
lope 278
lop-eared 90
lopsided 91.8
loquacious 310.56
loquacity 16.333.25
loquat 373
lor 9
lord 95
lordly 16.150
lordosis 300.55
Lords 528
Lordship 274
lordy 16.66
lore 9
Lorelei 7.7
lorgnette 368
lorica 17.35
lorikeet 370
lorimer 17.211
loris 300.46
lorn 255
Lorraine 247
lorry 16.268
lory 16.269
Los Angeles 513.6
lose 523
loser 17.444
losing 265.84
loss 302
lossy 16.302
lost 438
lot 373
Lothair 4
Lothario 12.3.5
Lothian 261.3
lotic 38.55
lotion 261.73
lots 341
lottery 16.274
lotto 12.77
lotus 310.66
louche 358
loud 99
louden 261
loud-hailer 17.162
loudish 353
loudmouth 462
loudness 300
loudspeaker 17.33
lough 40
Loughborough 17.279
louis 16.4
Louis 16.4

Louisburg 182.1
louis d'or 9.3
Louisiana 17.225.1
lounge 210
lounger 17.158
loupe 280
lour 14
louse 306
lousy 16.400
lout 377
Louth 462
loutish 353
louvre 17.419
louvred 103
lovable 228.16
lovage 197
lovat 381
love 489
lovebird 87
Lovelace 295
loveless 300
loveliness 300.23
Lovell 228
lovelock 40
lovelorn 255
lovely 16.207
lovemaking 265.6
lover 17.418
lovesick 38
lovey 16.383
lovey-dovey 16.383
loving 265
low 12
lowan 261.6
lowborn 255
lowboy 11
lowbred 86
lowbrow 13
lowdown 258
lower 17.6
Lowestoft 399
lowland 143
lowliness 300.23
lowly 16.126
lowness 300.25
Lowry 16.271
lox 499
loyal 228.6
loyalism 242.35.11
loyalist 436.7
loyalty 16.352.1
lozenge 209
lozengy 16.110
Lozi 16.399
Luanda 17.98

Luba 17.20
lubber 17.19
Lubbock 46
lubricant 420.7
lubricate 367.5
lubrication 261.67.5
lubricator 17.338.2
lubricious 310.58
lubricity 16.333.28
Lubumbashi 16.319
Lucan 261.15
lucarne 246
lucent 420.71
lucerne 249
Lucerne 249
Lucian 261.3
lucid 91.30
lucidity 16.333.5
Lucifer 17.114
luciferin 252.20
Lucilius 310.2.5
luck 43
luckless 300
lucklessness 300.33
lucky 16.30
lucrative 485.15
lucre 17.41
Lucretius 310.2
lucubrate 367
lucubration 261.67
Lucullus 310
Lucy 16.306
Luddite 372
Ludhiana 17.226.1
ludicrous 310
ludo 12.22
luff 168
luffa 17.118
lug 189
luge 364
Luger 17.136
luggage 197
lugger 17.134
lugubrious 310.2
Luke 45
lukewarm 238
lull 225
lullaby 7
Lulu 15.4
lumbago 12.27
lumbar 17.27
lumber 17.27
lumbering 265.58
lumberjack 32
lumberjacket 371.6

mackle 228.19
Maclean 247
Macleod 99.1
Macmillan 261.41
Macpherson 261.64
McQueen 251
macramé 16.211
macrobiotic 38.53.1
macrocephaly 16.131
macrocosm 242
macrocyst 436.22
macrograph 158.1
macron 254
macrophage 193.1
macroscopic 38.37.1
macula 17.174.3
macula lutea 17.3
maculation 261.67.13
macule 227
mad 83
Madagascar 17.47
madam 242.5
madcap 268
madden 261.19
maddening 265.46
madder 17.77
made 85
Madeira 17.272
madeleine 252.11
mademoiselle 215
madhouse 306
Madhya Pradesh 351
Madison 261.65
madly 16.146
madman 261
madness 300
Madonna 17.233.1
Madras 294
madrepore 9
Madrid 91
madrigal 228.46
madrilène 248
Madura 17.277
Madurai 7
maduro 12.66
Maecenas 293
maelstrom 237
maenad 83
maestoso 12.70
maestro 12
Maeterlinck 52
Mafeking 265.7
Mafia 17.3.10
mafioso 12.70
mag 178

magazine 251
magdalen 252.11
Magdalena 17.227
Magdalene 251.3
Magdeburg 182
Magellan 261.40
magenta 17.368
maggot 381
maggoty 16.344
Maghreb 31
magi 7
magic 38.15
magical 228.23
magician 261.71
Maginot 12.55
magisterial 228.3.11
magistery 16.274.49
magistracy 16.307
magistral 228.82
magistrate 367.28
magistrature 10.5
magma 17.220
magmatic 38.49
Magna Carta 17.337
magnanimity 16.333.12
magnanimous 310.28.1
magnate 367
magnesia 17.325
magnesite 372.9
magnesium 242.2.20
magnet 371
magnetic 38.50
magnetics 498.12
magnetism 242.35.18
magnetite 372.11
magnetize 516.12
magneto 12.76
magnetometer 17.342.3
magneton 254
magnetosphere 6.1
magnifiable 228.16.3.1
Magnificat 365
magnificence 321.22
magnificent 420.70
magnifico 12.11
magnifier 17.4.1
magnify 7.3
magniloquent 420.59
magnitude 102.2
magnolia 17.3.22
magnum 242
magnus 310
Magog 185
magpie 7
magus 310.19

Magyar 1
Mahabharata 17.352
maharajah 17.145
maharani 5.10
maharishi 16.322
Mahayana 17.226
Mahdi 16.58
mahjong 266
Mahler 17.161
mahogany 16.237.4
Mahomet 371.20
Mahometan 261.99
mahonia 17.3.36
mahout 377
mahseer 17.3.47
Maia 17.4
maid 85
maidan 246
maiden 261.20
maidenhair 4
maidenhead 86
Maidenhead 86
maidenhood 101
maidenly 16.174
maidservant 420.82
Maidstone 261
maieutic 38.56
mail 214
mailbag 178
mailbox 499
mailcoach 70
mailer 17.162
mailsack 32
maim 231
Maimonides 513.4
main 247
mainbrace 295
Maine 247
mainland 143
mainly 16.170
mainmast 431
mainsail 214
mainsheet 370
mainspring 265
mainstay 2
mainstream 234
maintain 247
maintenance 321.14
maisonette 368
maître d'hôtel 215.4
maize 509
majestic 38.69
majesty 16.366
major 17.146
Majorca 17.37

major-domo 12.49
majorette 368.6
majority 16.333.22
majuscule 227
Makasar 17.298
make 34
maker 17.30
makeshift 398
make-up 279
makeweight 367
making 265.6
makings 552
Makurdi 16.61
Malabar 1.2
Malacca 17.28
Malachi 7.2
malachite 372
malacology 16.108.4.6
malacopterygian 261.3.7
maladjusted 91.54
maladjustment 420
maladminister 17.384.1
maladministration 261.67.25
maladroit 375
malady 16.72
mala fide 16.64
Malagasy 16.294
malaise 509
malamute 380
malanders 524
Malang 263
malapert 369
malapropism 242.35
malapropos 12.59
malaria 17.3.38.1
malarial 228.3.10
malarkey 16.20
malassimilation 261.67.12
Malay 2.12
Malaya 17.1
Malayan 261.1
Malaysian 261.3.33
Malcolm 242
malcontent 410
male 214
Male 2
maleate 367.1.1
maledict 387
malediction 261.78.1
malefactor 17.353
malefic 38
maleficent 420.70
malevolence 321.12.1

malevolent 420.28.1
malfeasance 321.28
malformation 261.67
malformed 125
Mali 16.113
malice 300
malicious 310.58
malign 253.3
malignancy 16.312
malignant 420
malignity 16.333.19
malimprinted 91
malines 251.3
malinger 17.141
malingerer 17.279
Malinke 16.37
Malinowski 16.44
malison 261.126
mall 221
mallam 229
mallard 84
malleable 228.16.2
mallee 5
mallemuck 43
mallet 371
malleus 310.2
mallow 12.38
malm 230
Malmö 12
malnourished 449
malnutrition 261.71
malocclusion 261.93
malodorous 310.50
Malory 16.274.15
malposition 261.71.9
malpractice 300.65
malt 404
Malta 17.363
malted 91.44
Maltese 513
Malthusian 261.3
malting 265
maltose 520
maltreat 370
maltreatment 420
malty 16.351
Malvern 261
mam 229
mama 1.12
mamba 17.23
mambo 12
mamelon 261
Mameluke 45
mamilla 17.166

mamma 17.205
mammal 228.51
mammalian 261.3.8
mammalogy 16.108.2
mammary 16.274
mammiferous 310.50.2
mammon 261.44
mammoth 464
mammy 16.210
man 245
manacle 228.28
manage 197.5
manageable 228.16.20
management 420.37
manager 17.150
manageress 296.4
managerial 228.3.11
managing 265.25
manakin 252.4
Manama 17.206
Manassas 310.51
Manasseh 16.294
manatee 5
Manchester 17.384
Manchu 15
Manchuria 17.3.42
manciple 228.66
Mancunian 261.3
Mandaean 261.3
Mandalay 2.12
mandamus 310.27
mandarin 252.20
mandate 367
mandatory 16.274.43
Mande 2
mandible 228.12
mandibular 17.174.2
mandir 6
mandolin 252.11
mandorla 17.169
mandragora 17.279
mandrake 34
mandrel 228
mandrill 218
mane 247
manège 360
manes 509
Manes 513
manful 226
mangabey 2.4
Mangalore 9.8
manganese 513.9
mange 207
mangelwurzel 228.126
manger 17.156

mangle 228.49
mango 12.35
mangonel 215
mangosteen 251
mangrove 488
mangy 16.109
manhandle 228.39
Manhattan 261.94
manhole 223
manhood 101
manhunt 419
Mani 16.224
mania 17.3.31
maniac 32.1
maniacal 228.28.1
manic 38.31
Manichaeus 310.1
manicotti 16.335
manicure 10.3
manicurist 436.19
manifest 433
manifestation 261.67.33
manifesto 12.86
manifold 120
manikin 252.3
Manila 17.166.1
manilla 17.166.1
manioc 40
maniple 228.66
manipulability
  16.333.9.2
manipular 17.174
manipulate 367.13.6
manipulation
  261.67.13.4
manipulative 485.15.5
Manisa 1
Manitoba 17.18
mankind 135
manky 16.36
manlike 39
manly 16.169
manna 17.225
manned 128
mannequin 252.3
manner 17.225
mannered 103
mannerism 242.35.15
mannerless 300.13
mannerly 16.131
Mannheim 236
mannish 353
manoeuvrable 228.16
manoeuvre 17.419
man-of-war 9

manometer 17.342.3.3
manor 17.225
manorial 228.3.12
manpower 14
manrope 278
mansard 84
manse 314
manservant 420.82
Mansfield 115
mansion 261.81
manslaughter 17.345
mansuetude 102.2
manta 17.365
manteau 12.83
mantel 228.109
mantelpiece 298
mantic 38.62
mantilla 17.166
mantis 300.66
mantissa 17.302
mantle 228.109
mantling 265
Mantoux 15
mantra 17.296
mantrap 268
mantua 17.7.2
Mantua 17.7.2
manual 228.9.2
manufacture 17.63
manufacturing 265.58
manumit 371
manure 10
manus 310.31
manuscript 424
Manx 504
Manxman 261
many 16.226
manyplies 516
manzanilla 17.166.1
Maoism 242.35
Maoist 436
Maori 16.271
map 268
maple 228
mapping 265
mapping 265.48
Maputo 12.80
maquette 368
maquis 5.3
mar 1
mara 1.14
marabou 15.1
marabout 15.1
marabunta 17.373
maraca 17.28

marasca 17.47
maraschino 12.54
marasmus 310
Maratha 17.337.2
Marathi 16.328.1
marathon 261.109
maraud 95
marauder 17.86
maravedi 16.59
marble 228
marbled 122
marbling 265
Marburg 182
marc 33
marcasite 372.10
Marcel 215
Marcellus 310.22
march 63
March 63
marcher 17.51
marchioness 300.26
Marconi 16.233
Marco Polo 12.44
mardy 16.58
mare 2.17
mare 4
maremma 17.208
marg 192
margaric 38.38
margarine 251.7
margarita 17.341
Margate 367
margay 2
marge 192
margin 252
marginal 228.60
marginalia 17.3.18
marginally 16.131.3
margrave 371
margrave 482
margravine 251.12
marguerite 370
Maria 17.2.2
mariachi 16.47
Marian 261.3.20
Maribor 9
Marie 5.17
marigold 120
marijuana 17.226
marimba 17.25
marina 17.230.1
marinade 85.2
marinate 367.17
Marinduque 2
marine 251.7

mariner 17.231
Mariolatry 16.286.2.1
Mariology 16.108.4.1
marionette 368
mariposa 17.442
Marist 436
maritage 197.12
marital 228.102
maritime 236
Maritimer 17.212
Marius 310.2.10
marjoram 242.21
mark 33
Mark 33
markdown 258
markedly 16.148
marker 17.29
market 371.7
marketable 228.16.49
marketing 265.66
marketplace 295
markhor 9
marking 265
markka 1
Markova 17.417
marksman 261
marksmanship 274.2
marl 213
Marlborough 17.279
marlin 252
marlite 372
Marlowe 12.39
marmalade 85
Marmara 17.279
Marmite 372
marmoreal 228.3.12
marmoset 368.9
marmot 381
Marne 246
marocain 247.2
Maronite 372.6
maroon 260.3
marooned 142
Marprelate 371.15
marque 33
marquee 5.3
marquess 300
marquessate 371.38
marquetry 16.285
marquis 300
marquisate 371.38
marquise 513
Marrakech 351
marram 242
marriage 197.9

marriageable 228.16.20
married 91.25
marron 261
marrow 12.60
marrowbone 257
marrowfat 365
marry 16.260
Marryat 381.1.1
Mars 508
Marsala 17.161
Marseillaise 509
marsh 350
marshal 228.90
Marshalsea 5
marshland 143
marshmallow 12.38
marshy 16.320
Marsilius 310.2.5
marsupial 228.3.9
marsupium 242.2
mart 366
Martello 12.40
marten 252
Martha 17.397
martial 228.90
Martian 261
martin 252
Martin 252
martinet 368
martingale 214
martini 16.228
Martinique 37
Martinmas 310
martlet 371
martyr 17.337
martyrdom 242
martyrology 16.108.4.13
marvel 228
marvellous 310.26
Marx 495
Marxian 261.3
Marxism 242.35
Marxist 436
Mary 16.264
Maryland 143.2
marzipan 245.3
Masai 7
Masbate 16.328
mascara 17.268
mascle 228
mascot 381
masculine 252.10
masculinity 16.333.17
Masefield 115
maser 17.439

mash 349
masher 17.321
mashie 16.319
masjid 91
mask 56
masked 394
masochism 242.35.6
masochist 436
masochistic 38.70
mason 261.62
masonic 38.35.4
masonry 16.284
Masora 17.276
masque 56
Masorete 370
masque 56
masquerade 85.4
mass 293
Massachusetts 339
massacre 17.42
massage 359
massasauga 17.132
Massasoit 375
Massenet 2
masses 515.2
masseter 17.341
masseur 3
masseuse 511
Massey 16.294
massicot 373
massif 162
Massinger 17.157
massive 485.1
massy 16.294
mast 431
mastaba 17.21
mastectomy 16.222.5
master 17.380
masterful 226
masterly 16.131
mastermind 135
masterpiece 298.2
masterstroke 42
mastery 16.274
masthead 86
mastic 38.68
masticate 367.5.2
mastication 261.67.5
mastiff 163
mastitis 300.62
mastodon 254
mastoid 97
mastoiditis 300.62
masturbate 367.4
masturbation 261.67.3
Masuria 17.3.42.2

mat 365
Matabele 16.118
Matabeleland 143.2
matador 9.4
Mata Hari 16.261.1
Matamoros 310.48
Matapan 245.4
match 62
matchboard 95
matchbox 499
matchless 300
matchmaker 17.30
matchstick 38
matchwood 101
mate 367
maté 2.23
matelote 376
mater 17.338
materfamilias 293.1
material 228.3.11
materialism
 242.35.11.2.1
materialist 436.7.2
materialistic 38.70.2.1
materiality 16.333.8.1
materialize 516.3.2.1
materially 16.131
materia medica 17.34
materiel 215
maternal 228.58
maternity 16.333.16
matey 16.329
mathematical 228.23.18
mathematician 261.71
mathematics 498.11
Matilda 17.95
matin 252
matinée 2.15
matins 548
Matlock 40
matriarch 33.1
matriarchate 371.7
matriarchy 16.20
matrices 513
matricide 92.7
matriclinous 310.34
matriculate 367.13.2
matriculation 261.67.13
matrilineal 228.3.7
matrilocal 228.26
matrimonial 228.3.8
matrimony 16.237
matrix 498.9
matron 261
matronage 197

matronly 16.174
matt 365
mattamore 9.9
matted 91.32
matter 17.336
Matterhorn 255
Matthew 15
Matthias 310.3
matting 265
mattock 46
mattress 300
maturate 367.22
maturation 261.67.21
mature 10.5
maturity 16.333.23
matutinal 228.61
matza 17.319
matzoon 260
Maud 95
maudlin 252
Maugham 238
maul 221
mauler 17.169
maulstick 38
Mau Mau 13
Mauna Kea 1
Mauna Loa 1
maund 137
maunder 17.105
Maureen 251.6
Maurice 300
Mauritania 17.3.31.2
Mauritius 310.58.2
Mauser 17.443
mausoleum 242.1
mauve 488
maverick 38.44
Mavis 300
mavourneen 251
maw 9
mawkish 353
mawsie 16.397
maxi 16.386
maxilla 17.166
maxillary 16.274.16
maxim 235
maxima 17.211
maximal 228.52
Maximilian 261.3.11
maximin 252.14
maximize 516.4
maximum 242
maximus 310.28
Maxwell 228
may 2

May 2
maya 17.4
Mayan 261.4
maybe 16.7
Mayday 2
Mayfair 4
Mayflower 14
mayfly 7
mayhem 232
Maying 265.1
mayn't 420
Mayo 12.1
mayonnaise 509
mayor 4
mayoral 228
mayoralty 16.352
mayoress 300.44
mayorship 274
maypole 223
mayweed 89
Mazarin 263
maze 509
mazuma 17.217
mazurka 17.32
mazy 16.393
Mbabane 16.224
me 5
mead 89
meadow 12
meadowlark 33
meadowsweet 370
meagre 17.128
meal 217
mealy 16.118
mean 251
meander 17.98.1
meaning 265.42
meaningful 226
meaningless 300.15
meaninglessness 300.33
meanness 300
means 547
meant 410
meantime 236
meanwhile 219
meany 16.228
measles 539
measurable 228.16.35.2
measure 17.333
measured 103.6
measureless 300.13
measurement 420.35
meat 370
meatball 221
Meath 457

meatus 310.62
meaty 16.332
Mecca 17.31
Meccano 12.51
mechanic 38.31
mechanical 228.23.10
mechanician 261.71
mechanics 498
mechanism 242.35.14
mechanistic 38.70.4
mechanize 516.7
Mecklenburg 182
meconium 242.2.12
Med 86
medal 228
medallic 38.19
medallion 261.118
medallist 436.7
meddle 228
meddler 17.184
meddlesome 242
Mede 89
Medea 17.2
media 17.3.8
medial 228.3.1
median 261.3.4
mediant 420.1.1
mediastinum 242.15
mediate 367.1
mediation 261.67.1
mediator 17.338.1
medic 38
medicable 228.16.10
Medicaid 85
medical 228.23.1
medicament 420.35
Medicare 4
medicate 367.5
medication 261.67.5
medicinal 228.60.6
medicine 252.21
medick 38
medico 12.11
medieval 228.119
medievalism 242.35.11
medievalist 436.7
Medina 17.230
mediocre 17.38
mediocrity 16.333
meditate 367.30
meditation 261.67.27
meditative 485.15.12
Mediterranean
    261.3.15.1
medium 242.2.2

medlar 17.184
medley 16.147
Médoc 40
medulla 17.173
medusa 17.444
Medway 2
meek 37
meekly 16.141
meekness 300
meerkat 365
meet 370
meeting 265
megadeath 455
megalith 458
megalithic 38.73
megalocardia 17.3.6
megalomania 17.3.31.1
megalomaniac 32.1
megalopolis 300.13.2
megalosaur 9.11
megaphone 257
megaphonic 38.35.2
megapode 98
megaron 254.11
megaspore 9.10
megathere 6.10
megaton 259
megawatt 373
megillah 17.166
megohm 239
megrim 235
meiosis 300.55.2
meiotic 38.53.1
Meir 6
Meistersinger 17.246
Mekong 266
mel 215
melamine 251.4
melancholia 17.3.22
melancholic 38.22
melancholy 16.131
Melanesia 17.334
Melanesian 261.3.34
melanin 252
melanism 242.35.14
melanite 372.6
melanoid 97.9
melanosis 300.55
melaphyre 8.1
Melba 17.22
Melbourne 261
Melchior 9.1
Melchite 372
meld 113
melee 2

melinite 372.5
melisma 17.224
melliferous 310.50.2
mellifluous 310.4
mellophone 257
mellow 12.40
melodeon 261.3.6
melodic 38.9
melodious 310.2.2
melodiousness 300.34.1
melodist 436.3
melodize 516
melodrama 17.206
melodramatic 38.49.2
melodramatize 516.13.1
melody 16.72
meloid 97.4
melon 261.40
Melos 302
melt 402
Melville 218
member 17.24
membership 274.1
membrane 247
membranous 310.36
memento 12.84
memento mori 7.11
memo 12
memoir 1
memoirs 508
memorabilia 17.3.21.1
memorable 228.16.35
memoranda 17.98.2
memorandum 242.6
memorial 228.3.12
memorialist 436.7.2
memorialize 516.3.2.2
memorize 516.8
memory 16.274
Memphis 300
memsahib 24
men 248
menace 300
ménage 359
menagerie 16.274
Menai 7
Menander 17.98
menarche 16.20
mend 131
mendable 228.16.18
mendacious 310.56
mendacity 16.333.25
Mendel 228
mendelevium 242.2
Mendelssohn 261

mender 17.101
mendicant 420.7
mending 265.20
Mendips 327
Mendoza 17.442
Menelaus 310
Menelik 38.21
Menes 513
menfolk 42
menhaden 261.20
menhir 6
menial 228.3.6
meninges 513
meningitic 38.52
meningitis 300.62
meniscus 310.15
meno 12.52
menology 16.108.4
menopause 518
menorah 17.276
menorrhagia 17.3.12
Menotti 16.335
Mensa 17.314
menses 513.14
Menshevik 38.74
menstrual 228.9
menstruate 367.2
menstruation 261.67.2
menstruous 310.4
mensurable 228.16.35
mensural 228.76
mensuration 261.67.21
menswear 4
mental 228.110
mentalism 242.35.11.6
mentality 16.333.8.10
menthol 220
mentholated 91.34
mention 261.82
mentor 9.12
menu 15
Menuhin 252
Menzies 515
meow 13
Mephistopheles 513.6.1
mephitic 38.52
mephitis 300.62
meprobamate 367.16
mercantile 219
mercantilism 242.35.9
mercaptan 245
mercaptide 92
Mercator 17.338
mercenary 16.274.26
mercer 17.301

mercerize 516.8
merchandise 301
merchandise 516
merchant 420
merchantable 228.16.57
merchantman 261
Mercia 17.3
merciful 226
merciless 300.8
mercilessness 300.33
mercurate 367.22
mercurial 228.3
mercurialism 242.35.11.2
mercurialize 516.3.2
mercuric 38.43
mercurous 310.49
mercury 16.273
Mercury 16.274
mercy 16.298
mere 6
Meredith 458
merely 16.119
merengue 2
meretricious 310.58
merganser 17.312
merge 195
merger 17.148
meridian 261.3.5
meridional 228.63
meringue 263.2
merino 12.54
Merionethshire 6
meristem 232
meristic 38.70.5
merit 371.31
meritocracy 16.307.5
meritorious 310.2.13
merkin 252
merle 216
merlin 252
Merlin 252
mermaid 85
merman 261
merocrine 253
Meroë 5
Merovingian 261.3
merrily 16.120
merriment 420.31.2
merry 16.262
merry-go-round 139
merrymaker 17.30
merrymaking 265.6
Merse 297
Mersey 16.394
Merseyside 92.7

Merthyr Tydfil 218
Merton 261.97
mesa 17.299
mésalliance 321.1.1
Mesa Verde 87
mescaline 251.3
mesembryanthemum
  242.12
mesenteron 254.11
mesh 351
Meshach 32
meshy 16.321
mesmeric 38.39
mesmerism 242.35.15
mesmerize 516.8
mesocarp 269
mesoderm 233
Mesolithic 38.73
mesomorph 166.1
mesomorphic 38.14
meson 254
mesophyll 218.1
Mesopotamia 17.3.24
mesosphere 6.1
mesothelium 242.2.5
Mesozoic 38.2
mesquite 370
mess 296
message 197.11
Messalina 17.230
messenger 17.157
Messiah 17.4
messianic 38.31.1
Messina 17.230
messmate 367
Messrs 524
messy 16.297
met 368
metabolic 38.22
metabolism 242.35.11
metabolite 372.4
metabolize 516.3
metacarpal 228
metacarpus 310
metagalaxy 16.390
metal 228.100
metalanguage 197
metallic 38.19.1
metalliferous 310.50.2
metalline 253.3
metallize 516.3
metallography 16.90.2.2
metalloid 97.6
metallurgic 38.16
metallurgical 228.23.4

metallurgist 436.4.1
metallurgy 16.108.2
metalwork 36
metamerism 242.35.15
metamorphic 38.14
metamorphism 242.35.7
metamorphose 520
metamorphosis 300.57.2
metaphor 17.120
metaphoric 38.41
metaphorical 228.23.17
metaphrase 509
metaphysic 38
metaphysical 228.23.25
metaphysician 261.71.8
metaphysics 498
metapsychology
16.108.4.5
metastasis 300.57
metastasize 516.11
metatarsal 228.83
metatarsus 310.52
metatheory 16.265
metatherian 261.3.22
metathesis 300.52
mete 370
metempsychosis 300.55
meteor 17.3
meteoric 38.41
meteorite 372.8
meteoritic 38.52.2
meteorologist 436.4
meteorology 16.108.4.13
meter 17.341
methadone 257
methane 247
methanol 220
methinks 505
method 103
methodical 228.23.2
Methodism 242.35
Methodist 436.3
methodize 516
methodology 16.108.4
methought 374
Methuselah 17.176
methyl 218
methyldopa 17.257
methylene 251.2
methylic 38.21
metic 38.50
meticulous 310.25.2
métier 2.1
Métis 298
metonym 235

metonymy 16.216
metre 17.341
metric 38.46
metrical 228.23
metricate 367.5
metrication 261.67.5
metrics 498.10
metrify 7.3
metritis 300.62
metro 12
metrology 16.108.4
metronome 239
metronomic 38.29.1
metronymic 38.28
metropolis 300.13.2
metropolitan 261.99
mettle 228.100
mettled 122.2
Metz 336
meunière 4
Meuse 511
mew 15
mewl 227
mews 523
Mexicali 16.113
Mexican 261.13
Mexico 12.11
mezereum 242.2.15
mezzanine 251
mezzo 12.71
mezzotint 412
mi 5
Miami 16.210
miasma 17.223
mica 17.35
Micah 17.35
Micawber 17.17
mice 301
Michael 228.24
Michaelmas 310
Michelangelo 12.42
Michigan 261.32
Mick 38
mickle 228.23
Micmac 32
microanalysis 300.52.1
microbe 28
microbiology 16.108.4.2
microcephaly 16.131
microcircuit 371.8
microclimatology
16.108.4.15.1
microcline 253
micrococcus 310.11
microcopy 16.250

microcosm 242
microcosmic 38
microdontous 310
microdot 373
microelectronic 38.35
microelectronics 498.5
microfiche 352
microfilm 244
micrograph 158.1
micrography 16.90.2
microlight 372.4
microlith 458
micrometer 17.342.3
micron 254
Micronesia 17.334
microorganism
242.35.14
microphone 257
microphonic 38.35.2
microphotograph 158.1
microprint 412
microprocessor 17.300
microscope 278.1
microscopic 38.37.1
microscopy 16.254.2
microsecond 143
microspore 9.10
microstomatous 310.68
microtome 239
microtomy 16.222.4
microwave 482
micrurgy 16.102
micturate 367.22
micturition 261.71
mid 91
midair 4
Midas 310.16
midbrain 247
midday 2
Middelburg 182
midden 261.24
middle 228.32
middlebrow 13
middleman 261
Middlesex 496
Middleton 261
middleweight 367
middling 265
midfield 115
Midgard 84
midge 197
midget 371
midgut 378
Midheaven 261.112
midi 16.63

minimal 228.52
minimalist 436.7
minimax 494
minimize 516.4
minimum 242
minimus 310.28
mining 265.44
minion 261.122
minipill 218
miniskirt 369
minister 17.384.1
ministerial 228.3.11
ministerium 242.2.15
ministrant 420
ministration 261.67.25
ministry 16.293
minium 242.2.11
miniver 17.414
minivet 368
mink 52
Minna 17.231
Minneapolis 300.13.1
minnesinger 17.246
Minnesota 17.347
minnow 12.55
Minoan 261.6
minor 17.232
Minorca 17.37
Minorite 372.8
minority 16.333.22
Minos 302
Minotaur 9
minster 17.394
minstrel 228
minstrelsy 16.308
mint 412
mintage 197
Minton 261.105
minty 16.356
minuend 131
minuet 368.1
minus 310.34
minuscule 227
minute 371.24
minute 380
minutely 16.189
minutely 16.193
minutes 339
minutiae 5.2
minx 505
Miocene 251.9
miosis 300.55.2
Miquelon 254.7
Mira Ceti 7.13
miracidium 242.2.3

miracle 228.28
miraculous 310.25
mirage 359
Miranda 17.98
mire 8
mirepoix 1
Miriam 242.2.16
mirror 17.273
mirth 456
mirthful 226
mirthless 300
MIRV 483
miry 16.267
misadventure 17.70
misalliance 321.2
misanthrope 278
misanthropic 38.37.3
misanthropist 436.15
misanthropy 16.254
misapply 7.9
misapprehend 131.1
misapprehension
  261.82.1
misbecome 240
misbegotten 261.101
misbehave 482
misbehaviour 17.436
misbelief 162.1
miscalculate 367.13
miscalculation 261.67.13
miscarriage 197.9
miscarry 16.260
miscast 431
miscegenation 261.67.18
miscellanea 17.3.31
miscellaneous 310.2.6
miscellany 16.237.5
mischance 315
mischief 163
mischievous 310
mischievousness 300.34
miscible 228.16.39
misconceive 484
misconception 261.84
misconduct 389
misconstruction 261.79
misconstrue 15
miscount 418
miscreance 321.1
miscreant 420.1
miscreate 367.1
miscue 15
misdate 367
misdeal 217
misdeed 89

misdemeanant 420
misdemeanour 17.230
misdirect 385
misdirection 261.77.3
miser 17.441
miserable 228.16.35
misère 4
misericord 95.2
miserly 16.131
misery 16.274
misfeasance 321.28
misfile 219
misfire 8
misfortune 260.5
misgive 485
misgiving 265.80
misgovern 261.117
misguide 92
misguided 91.8
mishandle 228.39
mishap 268
mishear 6
mishmash 349
Mishnah 17.243
misinform 238
misinformation
  261.67.16
misinterpret 371
misinterpretation
  261.67.27
misjoinder 17.106
misjudge 203
mislay 2
mislead 89
misleading 265.13
misled 86
mismanage 197.5
mismatch 62
misnomer 17.215
misogamy 16.222.2
misogynist 436.13
misogynous 310.33
misogyny 16.229.2
misology 16.108.4
misoneism 242.35.1
misplace 295
misplay 2
misplead 89
misprint 412
misprision 261.91
misprize 516
mispronounce 319
mispronunciation
  261.67.1.4
misquotation 261.67.28

misquote 376
misread 89
misreport 374.1
misrepresent 410.4
misrepresentation
261.67.32
misrule 227
miss 300
missal 228.85
misshape 270
misshapen 261.57
missile 219.2
missing 265.61
mission 261.71
missionary 16.274.29.3
missis 515.3
Mississauga 17.132
Mississippi 16.248
Mississippian 261.3
missive 485.4
Missouri 16.270
misspell 215
misspelling 265.28
misspend 131
misstate 367
missy 16.300
mist 436
mistakable 228.16.9
mistake 34
mistaken 261.11
mistal 228.114
Mistassini 16.228
mister 17.384
mistigris 5.18
mistime 236
mistletoe 12
mistook 44
mistral 228.82
mistreat 370
mistress 300
mistrial 228.4
mistrust 443
misty 16.366
misunderstand 128
misunderstanding
265.19
misunderstood 101
misuse 309
misuse 523
misuser 17.444
Mitchell 228
mite 372
Mithraism 242.35
Mithras 293
Mithridates 513.15

miticide 92.7.1
mitigable 228.16.19
mitigate 367.10
mitigation 261.67.10
mitis 300.62
mitochondrion 261.3
mitosis 300.55
mitrailleuse 511
mitre 17.343
mitt 371
mitten 261.99
mittimus 310.28
mix 498
mixed 451
mixer 17.427
Mixtec 35
mixture 17.76
Mizar 1
Mizoguchi 16.53
mizzen 261.126
mizzenmast 431
mizzle 228
m'lud 100
mnemonic 38.35
mnemonics 498.5
Mnemosyne 5.12
mo 12
moa 17.6
Moab 18
Moabite 372
moan 257
moaner 17.236
moat 376
mob 26
mobcap 268
mobile 219
mobility 16.333.9.1
mobilize 516.2
mobocracy 16.307.5
mobster 17.391
moccasin 252
mocha 17.36
mock 40
mockery 16.274.5
mockingbird 87
mod 94
modal 228
modality 16.333.8
mode 98
model 228.34
modeller 17.176
modem 232
moderate 367.23
moderate 371.35
moderation 261.67.22

moderato 12.73
moderator 17.338.9
modern 261.26
moderne 250
modernism 242.35.14
modernistic 38.70.4
modernity 16.333.16
modernize 516.7
modest 436
modestly 16.201
modesty 16.366
modge 199
modicum 242.4
modifiable 228.16.3.1
modification 261.67.5.1
modifier 17.4.1
modify 7.3
modillion 261.120
modish 353
modiste 435
modular 17.174
modulate 367.13
modulation 261.67.13
modulator 17.338.6
module 227
modulus 310.25
mofette 368
mog 185
Mogadishu 15
mogul 228
mohair 4
Mohammed 91
Mohammedan 261.24
Mohammedanism
242.35.14
Mohammedanize 516.7
Mohave 16.378
Mohawk 41
Mohican 261.12
Mohorovičil 67
moider 17.87
moidore 9
moiety 16.333
moire 1
moiré 2.17
moist 440
moisten 261
moisture 17
moisturize 516.8
moisturizer 17.441
moke 42
molality 16.333.8
molar 17.171
molarity 16.333.20
molasses 515.2

Moldau 13
Moldavia 17.3.53
mole 223
molecular 17.174.4
molecule 227.1
molehill 218
moleskin 252
moleskins 548
molest 433
molestation 261.67.33
molester 17.382
moline 253.3
moll 220
mollify 7.3.2
mollusc 61
Molly 16.122
mollycoddle 228.34
mollycoddler 17.188
Molly Maguire 8
Moloch 40
Molokai 16.1
Molotov 165
molten 261
Moluccas 524
molybdenum 242.14
mom 237
Mombasa 17.298
moment 420
momentarily 16.120.1
momentary 16.274.48
momentous 310.70
momentum 242
Momus 310
Mona 17.236
Monacan 261
Monaco 12
monad 83.3
monadism 242.35
monadnock 40
Monaghan 261
Mona Lisa 17.440
monarch 46
monarchal 228.20
monarchism 242.35.6
monarchist 436
monarchy 16.33
monasterial 228.3.11
monastery 16.274
monastic 38.68
monasticism 242.35.16.6
monaural 228.74
Monday 2
mondial 228.3
Monegasque 55
monetary 16.274.41

monetize 516.12
money 16.235
moneychanger 17.156
moneyed 91
moneylender 17.101
moneylending 265.20
moneymaker 17.30
moneywort 369
Mongol 220
Mongol 228
Mongolia 17.3.22
Mongolian 261.3.12
Mongolic 38.22
mongolism 242.35.11
mongoloid 97.6
mongoose 309
mongrel 228
mongrelize 516.3
Monica 17.34.1
moniker 17.34.1
monism 242.35
monition 261.71
monitor 17.342
monitory 16.274.41
monk 54
monkey 16.39
monkfish 353
monkhood 101
monkish 353
monkshood 101
Monmouth 464
Monmouthshire 6
mono 12
Monoceros 310.50
monochasium 242.2.19
monochord 95.3
monochromatic 38.49.2
monochrome 239
monocle 228.28
monocline 253
monocoque 40
monocotyledon 261.23
monocracy 16.307.5
monocular 17.174.7
monoculture 17.69
monogamist 436.10
monogamous 310.29
monogamy 16.222.2
monogram 229.1
monogrammatic 38.49.2
monograph 158.1
monogyny 16.229.2
monolatry 16.286.2
monolingual 228
monolith 458

monolithic 38.73
monologue 185
monomania 17.3.31.1
monomark 33
monomer 17.218.1
monometer 17.342.3
monomial 228.3
monomorphic 38.14
mononuclear 17.3
mononucleosis 300.55.1
monophonic 38.35.2
monophony 16.237.3
monopolize 516.3
monopoly 16.131.6
monorail 214
monosaccharide 92.6
monosemy 16.215
monostich 38
monostrophe 16.90
monostylous 310.24
monosyllabic 38
monosyllable 228.16.23
monotheism 242.35.2
monotint 412
monotone 257.3
monotonous 310.36
monotony 16.237.7
monotreme 234
monotype 275.1
monotypic 38.36
monovalent 420.25
monoxide 92.14
Monroe 12
Monrovia 17.3.55
Monsignor 17.435
monsoon 260
monster 17
monstrance 321
monstrosity 16.333.30
monstrous 310
monstrousness 300.34
mons veneris 300.47
montage 359
Montagnard 84
Montague 15
Montana 17.225
montane 247.11
montbretia 17.325
monte 16.357
Monte Carlo 12.39
Montego 12.28
Monteith 457
Montenegro 12.67
Monterey 2.19
Monterrey 2.19

Montessori 16.269
Montezuma 17.217
Montgomery 16.274
monthly 16.205
monticule 227.1
Montreal 221
Montrose 520
Monty 16.357
monument 420.34
monumental 228.110
moo 15
mooch 74
mood 102
moodiness 300.23
moody 16.71
Moog 190
moolah 1
moon 260
moonbeam 234
mooncalf 158
mooneye 7
moonflower 14
moonless 300
moonlight 372
moonlighter 17.343
moonlighting 265.67
moonlit 371
moonquake 34
moonraker 17.30
moonrise 516
moonshine 253
moonshiner 17.232
moonshot 373
moonstone 257
moonstruck 43
moony 16.236
moor 10
Moor 10
moorage 197
moorcock 40
Moore 10
moorfowl 224
moorhen 248
mooring 265.56
Moorish 353
moorland 143
moose 309
moot 380
mop 276
mope 278
moped 86
mopoke 42
moppet 371
moquette 368
moraine 247

moral 228.73
morale 213
moralism 242.35.11
moralist 436.7
morality 16.333.8.9
moralize 516.3
Morar 17.276
morass 293
moratorium 242.2.17
Morava 17.409
Moravia 17.3.53
Moravian 261.3.29
moray 2
morbid 91
morbidity 16.333.5
morbific 38.12
morbilli 7.5
mordacious 310.56
mordacity 16.333.25
mordant 420.11
Mordecai 16.2
mordent 420.11
more 9
Morecambe 242
moreish 353
morel 215
morello 12.40
moreover 17.417
mores 509
Moresque 57
Morgan 261.33
morganatic 38.49.5
Morgan le Fay 2.9
morgue 186
moribund 140
morion 261.3.23
Morisco 12.15
Morley 16.123
Mormon 261
Mormonism 242.35.14
morn 255
mornay 2
morning 265
Moroccan 261
Morocco 12
moron 254.10
moronic 38.35
morose 305.2
morosely 16.182
morph 166
morpheme 234
Morpheus 310.2
morphia 17.3
morphine 251
morphinism 242.35.13

morphogenesis 300.52.4
morphology 16.108.4
Morris 300
Morrison 261.65
morrow 12.65
Mors 518
morse 303
Morse 303
morsel 228
mort 374
mortal 228.105
mortality 16.333.8
mortar 17.345
mortarboard 95.1
mortgage 197
mortgagee 5.6
mortgagor 17.150
mortician 261.71
mortify 7.3
Mortimer 17.211
mortise 300.63
mortmain 247
Morton 261.102
mortuary 16.274.2
morwong 266
mosaic 38.1
moschatel 215
Moscow 12
Moselle 215
Moses 515
mosey 16.399
Moslem 242
Moslemic 38.25
mosque 59
mosquito 12.76
moss 302
mossbunker 17.46
mosstrooper 17.259
mossy 16.302
most 441
mostly 16.202
mot 12
mote 376
motel 215.4
motet 368
moth 459
mothball 221
mother 17.408
motherfucker 17.39
motherhood 101
mother-in-law 9
motherland 143.4
motherless 300.13
motherly 16.131
mother-of-pearl 216

mothproof 170
mothy 16.371
motif 162
motile 219
motility 16.333.9
motion 261.73
motionless 300.14
motivate 367.36
motivation 261.67
motive 485.14
motley 16.191
motmot 373
motocross 302.2
motor 17.347
motorbike 39
motorboat 376
motorbus 307
motorcade 85
motorcar 1
motorcoach 70
motorcycle 228.24
motorcyclist 436
motorist 436.20
motorize 516.8
motorway 2.28
Motown 258
motte 373
mottle 228.104
motto 12.77
mouflon 254
mouillé 2
mould 120
moulder 17.97
moulding 265.18
mouldwarp 277
mouldy 16.76
moult 405
mound 139
mount 418
mountain 252
mountaineer 6.4
mountaineering 265.53
mountainous 310.33
Mountbatten 261.94
mountebank 51
mounted 91.49
Mountie 16.359
mounting 265.73
Mount Rushmore 9
mourn 255
mourner 17.234
mournful 226
mourning 265
mouse 306
mouse 521

mouser 17.443
mousetrap 268
moussaka 17.29
mousse 309
moustache 350
mousy 16.304
mouth 462
mouthbrooder 17.91
mouthful 226
mouthpart 366
mouthpiece 298
mouthwash 354
mouthwatering 265.58
mouton 254
movable 228.16.62
move 490
moved 150
movement 420.51
mover 17.419
movie 16.384
moving 265
Moviola 17.171
mow 12
mow 13
mowburnt 411
mower 17.6
mown 257
moxa 17.428
moxie 16.389
Mozambique 37
Mozart 366
mozzarella 17.163
mozzetta 17.339
Mr 17.384
Mrs 515.3
Ms 515
much 72
muchness 300
mucid 91.30
mucilage 197.1
muck 43
mucker 17.39
muckle 228.27
muckrake 34
mucky 16.30
mucoid 97
mucosa 17.306
mucous 310.13
mucus 310.13
mud 100
mudcat 365
muddle 228.36
muddleheaded 91.7
muddy 16.69
mudguard 84

mudlark 33
mudpack 32
mudskipper 17.253
mudslinging 265.47
muezzin 252.30
muff 168
muffin 252.5
muffle 228.42
muffler 17.191
mufti 16.349
Mufti 16.349
mug 189
Mugabe 16.6
mugger 17.134
muggins 548
muggy 16.97
mugwump 289
Muhammad 103
Muhammadan 261
Muir 10
mukluk 43
mulatto 12.72
mulberry 16.274
mulch 77
mule 227
muleta 17.339
muleteer 6
mulga 17.139
muliebrity 16.333.24
mulish 353
mull 225
Mull 225
mullah 17.173
mullein 252
mullet 371
mulley 16.128
Mulligan 261.32
mulligatawny 16.232
mullion 261.3.13
mulloway 2.28
multeity 16.333.1
multicollinearity 16.333.20.1
multicoloured 103.4
multidisciplinary 16.274.26
multifaceted 91.38
multifarious 310.2.10.1
multifoil 222
multifoliate 371.1
multiform 238.1
multigravida 17.83
multihull 225
multilateral 228.76
multilingual 228

multimedia 17.3.8
multimillionaire 4.5
multinational 228.63.2
multinuclear 17.3
multinucleate 371.1
multipara 17.279
multiparous 310.50
multipartite 372
multiplane 247
multiple 228.66
multiplex 496
multiplicand 128.1
multiplication 261.67.5
multiplicative 485.15.1
multiplicity 16.333.28.1
multiplier 17.4
multiply 7.8
multipurpose 310
multiracial 228.91
multirole 223
multiscreen 251
multistage 193
multistorey 16.269
multitude 102.2
multitudinous 310.33
multure 17.69
mum 240
mumble 228
mumbler 17.180
mumbo jumbo 12.7
mumchance 315
mummer 17.216
mummery 16.274
mummify 7.3
mummy 16.220
mumps 332
munch 82
mundane 247
mung 267
munga 17.143
Munich 38
municipal 228.66
municipality 16.333.8.8
munificence 321.22
munificent 420.70
muniment 420.31
munition 261.71
munitions 551
Munster 17.395
muntjac 32
muon 254
mural 228.75
murder 17.81
murderer 17.279
murderess 300.47

murderous 310.50
Murdoch 40
murex 496
muricate 367.5
Murillo 12.42
murk 36
murky 16.23
murmur 17.209
murmuring 265.58
Murphy 16.83
murrain 252
Murray 16.272
murrhine 253
Murrumbidgee 16.103
murther 17.403
Musca 17.49
muscadine 252
muscarine 252.20
muscat 365
muscatel 215
muscid 91
muscle 228.87
muscleman 261
muscovado 12.16
Muscovite 372
Muscovy 16.385
muscular 17.174.8
muscularity 16.333.20.3
musculature 17.62
muse 523
musette 368.8
museum 242.1
mush 356
mush 357
mushroom 241
mushy 16.324
music 38
musical 228.23
musician 261.71
musicianship 274.2
musicology 16.108.4.4
musk 60
muskellunge 211
musket 371
musketeer 6
musketry 16.285
muskmelon 261.40
muskrat 365
musky 16.42
Muslim 235
Muslimism 242.35
muslin 252
muso 12
musquash 354
muss 307

mussel 228.87
Mussolini 16.228.1
must 443
mustachio 12.3
mustang 263
mustard 103
mustee 5
muster 17.388
musty 16.368
mutable 228.16.53
mutagen 261.39
mutant 420.77
mutate 367
mutation 261.67.29
Mutazilite 372.3
mute 380
mutilate 367.12
mutilation 261.67.12
mutineer 6.4
mutinous 310.33.2
mutiny 16.229
mutism 242.35.19
mutt 378
mutter 17.349
mutton 261.103
muttonchops 329
mutual 228.9
mutuality 16.333.8.2
Muzak 32
muzz 522
muzzle 228
muzzler 17.204
muzzy 16.401
my 7
myalgia 17.3.16
myall 228.4
myasthenia 17.3.33
mycelium 242.2.5
Mycenae 5
mycology 16.108.4.5
mycorrhiza 17.441.1
mycosis 300.55
mycotic 38.53
mydriasis 300.57.1
mydriatic 38.49
myelin 252.8
myelitis 300.62.1
myeloid 97.5
myeloma 17.215
mynah 17.232
myocardial 228.3
myocardium 242.2
myogenic 38.32.1
myology 16.108.4.2
myoma 17.215

myope 278
myopia 17.3.37
myopic 38.37
myosin 252
myosotis 300.64
myotonia 17.3.36
myriad 103.1
myriapod 94.1
myrica 17.35
myrmecology 16.108.4.4
myrmecophile 219.1
Myrmidon 254
Myron 261.58
myrrh 3
myrtle 228
myself 172
Mysore 9
mystagogue 185.2
mysterious 310.2.11
mystery 16.274.49
mystic 38.70
mystical 228.23.24
mysticism 242.35.16
mystify 7.3
mystique 37
myth 458
mythical 228.23
mythicize 516.10
mythological 228.23.5
mythologize 516.1
mythology 16.108.4.18
mythos 302
myxoedema 17.210
myxomatosis 300.55.7

N

NAAFI 16.82
nab 18
nabob 26
Nabokov 165
Nabonidus 310.16
Naboth 459
nacelle 215.2
nacre 17.30
nacreous 310.2
Na-Dene 16.225
nadir 6
nae 2
naevus 310.73
nag 178
Nagari 16.274
Nagasaki 16.20
nagger 17.123
Nagoya 17.431

Nagpur 10
Nahuatl 228.98
Nahum 242
naiad 83.2
naïf 162
nail 214
nailbrush 356
nailfile 219
nailhead 86
nainsook 44
naira 17.269
Nairn 250
Nairobi 16.12
naive 484
naiveté 2
naked 91
nakedness 300.28
NALGO 12.34
namby-pamby 16.17
name 231
nameless 300
namely 16.165
nameplate 367
namesake 34
nametape 270
Namibia 17.3.3
Namur 10
nan 245
Nanchang 263
Nancy 16.309
nankeen 251
Nanking 265
nanny 16.223
nanometre 17.341
Nanook 45
nanosecond 143
Nansen 261
Nan Shan 245
Nantucket 371.11
Nantung 267
Naoise 16.299
Naomi 16.222
nap 268
napalm 230
nape 270
naphtha 17.398
naphthalene 251.3
naphthol 220
Napier 17.3
napkin 252
Naples 539
Napoleon 261.3.12
Napoleonic 38.35.1
napper 17.247
nappy 16.243

Nara 17.268
narceine 251
narcissism 242.35.16
narcissistic 38.70
narcissus 310.53
narcolepsy 16.313
narcosis 300.55
narcotic 38.53
narcotism 242.35.20
narcotize 516.13
nard 84
nares 513.10
narial 228.3.10
nark 33
Narraganset 371
narrate 367.23
narration 261.67.22
narrative 485.15.8
narrator 17.338.9
narrow 12.60
narrow-minded 91
narrow-mindedness
  300.28
narrowness 300.25
Narvik 38
narwhal 228
nary 16.264
NASA 17.298
nasal 228.125
nasalize 516.3
nascent 420
Nash 349
Nashville 218
nasion 261.3.33
Nastase 16.392
nastiness 300.23
nasturtium 242
nasty 16.362
natal 228.99
natality 16.333.8
natant 420.75
natation 261.67.30
natatory 16.274.40
natch 62
nates 513.15
Nathan 261
Nathaniel 228.123
nation 261.67
national 228.63.2
nationalism
  242.35.11.5.1
nationalist 436.7.5
nationalistic 38.70.2
nationality 16.333.8.7.1

neighbouring 265.58
neighbourly 16.131
Neil 217
Neisse 17.303
neither 17.406
nelly 16.115
Nelson 261
nematocyst 436.22
nematode 98
Nembutal 213
nemertean 261.3
nemesia 17.334
Nemesis 300.52.3
nene 2
neoanthropic 38.37.3
Neocene 251.9
neoclassicism 242.35.16
neodymium 242.2
neoimpressionism
  242.35.14.4
neolith 458
Neolithic 38.73
neologism 242.35.8
neologize 516.1
neon 254
neonate 367.18
neophyte 372
neoplasty 16.361.1
neoteny 16.237.7
Neozoic 38.2
Nepal 221
Nepali 16.123
neper 17.249
nephew 15
nephology 16.108.4
nephralgia 17.3.16
nephralgic 38
nephrectomy 16.222.5
nephridium 242.2.3
nephritic 38.52
nephritis 300.62
nephron 254
nephrosis 300.55
nepotic 38.53
nepotism 242.35.20
Neptune 260
Neptunian 261.3
nerd 87
Nereid 91.2
Nero 12.63
Nerva 17.412
nervate 367.35
nerve 483
nerveless 300
nervous 310

nervousness 300.34
nervy 16.381
nescience 321.1
nesh 351
Ness 296
nesselrode 98
nest 433
nesting 265.75
nestle 17.402
nestler 17.197
nestling 265
Nestor 9
Nestorianism
  242.35.14.1
Nestorius 310.2.13
net 368
netball 221
nether 17.402
Netherlands 534
nethermost 441
netting 265.65
nettle 228.100
network 36
neural 228.75
neuralgia 17.3.16
neuralgic 38
neurasthenia 17.3.33
neuritis 300.62
neuroblast 430
neurogenic 38.32.1
neurolemma 17.208
neurology 16.108.4
neuromuscular 17.174.8
neuron 254
neurone 257
neuropathology 16.108.4
neuropathy 16.373.1
neuropsychiatry
  16.286.1
neurosis 300.55
neurosurgeon 261.35
neurosurgery 16.274.13
neurosurgical 228.23.4
neurotic 38.53
neuroticism 242.35.16.5
neurotomy 16.222.4
neuter 17.351
neutral 228
neutralism 242.35.11
neutrality 16.333.8
neutralize 516.3
neutralizer 17.441
neutrino 12.54
neutron 254
neutrophil 218.1

Neva 17.413
Nevada 17.78
névé 2
never 17.411
nevermore 9.9
nevertheless 296.1
new 15
Newark 46
newborn 255
Newburg 182
Newbury 16.274
Newcastle 228.83
newcomer 17.216
newel 228.10
newfangled 122
Newfie 16.89
Newfoundland 143
Newgate 371
Newham 242
Newhaven 261.111
newish 353
newly 16.130
newlywed 86
Newman 261.51
Newmarket 371.7
newness 300
Newport 374
news 523
newsagent 420
newscast 431
newscaster 17.380
newshawk 41
newsletter 17.339
newspaper 17.249
newspaperman 261.52
newspeak 37
newsprint 412
newsreel 217
newsstand 128
newsworthy 16.375
newsy 16.402
newt 380
Newton 261.104
Newtonabbey 16.5
Newtonian 261.3.18
New Zealand 143.1
New Zealander 17.109
next 450
nexus 310
ngaio 12.4
ngwee 2
niacin 252
Niagara 17.289
Niamey 2
nib 24

nibble 228.12
niblick 38
Nicaragua 17.7.1
nice 301
Nice 298
nicety 16.333.29
niche 352
niche 67
Nicholas 310.26.2
Nicholson 261
Nicias 310.2.15
nick 38
nickel 228.23
nickelodeon 261.3.6
nicker 17.34
Nicklaus 306
nickname 231
Nicosia 17.2
nicotinamide 92.3
nicotine 251.11
nicotinic 38.34
nicotinism 242.35
nictitate 367.30
nide 92
nidificate 367.5
nidus 310.16
Niebuhr 10
niece 298
Nietzsche 17.55
niff 163
nifty 16.347
Niger 17.151
Nigeria 17.3.39
Nigerian 261.3.22
niggard 103
niggardly 16.152
niggle 228.46
niggling 265
niggly 16.160
nigh 7
night 372
nightcap 268
nightclub 29
nightdress 296
nightfall 221
nightgown 258
nighthawk 41
nightie 16.334
nightingale 214
nightjar 1
nightlife 164
nightlong 266
nightly 16.190
nightmare 4
nightmarish 353.9

nightrider 17.84
nights 340
nightshade 85
nightshirt 369
nightspot 373
nightwear 4
nigrescent 420.67
nigrosine 251.9
nihilism 242.35.9
Nijinsky 16.45
Nijmegen 261.31
Nikko 12.10
nil 218
nil desperandum 242.6
Nile 219
nilgai 7
nimble 228
nimbleness 300.30
nimblewit 371
nimbostratus 310.62
nimbus 310
niminy-piminy 16.229.3
Nimrod 94
Nina 17.230
nincompoop 280
nine 253
ninefold 120
ninepins 548
nineteen 251
nineteenth 469
ninetieth 458
ninety 16
Nineveh 17.414
ninny 16.229
Ninus 310.34
niobium 242.2
nip 274
nipa 17.252
Nipigon 254.5
nipper 17.253
nipple 228.66
Nippon 254
Nippur 10
nippy 16.248
nirvana 17.226
Nishapur 10
nisi 7
nisi prius 310.3
Nissen 261.65
nit 371
nitid 91.38
nitrate 367
nitre 17.343
nitric 38
nitride 92

nitrify 7.3
nitrobenzene 251
nitrochloroform 238.2
nitrogen 261.39
nitrogenize 516.6
nitrogenous 310.33
nitroglycerin 252.20
nitroglycerine 251.7
nitrometer 17.342.3
nitrous 310
nitty 16.333
nitty-gritty 16.333
nitwit 371
Niue 2.2
nival 228.121
nivation 261.67
Niven 261.114
niveous 310.2.17
nix 498
nixer 17.427
nixie 16.388
Nixon 261
Njord 95
Nkomo 12.49
Nkrumah 17.217
no 12
Noachian 261.3
Noachic 38.6
Noah 17.6
nob 26
nobble 228
nobbut 381
Nobel 215
nobelium 242.2
nobiliary 16.274.1.1
nobility 16.333.9.1
noble 228.13
nobleman 261
noblesse 296
noblesse oblige 362
nobody 16.72
nociceptive 485.23
noctule 227
nocturnal 228.58
nocturne 249
nocuous 310.4
nod 94
nodal 228
noddle 228.34
Noddy 16.65
node 98
nodose 305
nodular 17.174
nodule 227
Noel 228.7

noesis 300.51
noetic 38.50.1
nog 185
noggin 252
noil 222
noise 519
noiseless 300
noisette 368
noisiness 300.23
noisome 242
noisy 16.398
Nolan 261.43
noli-me-tangere 16.274
nomad 83
nomadic 38.7
nomarch 33
nom de guerre 4
nom de plume 241
nome 239
nomen 248
nomenclature 17.62
nominal 228.60.5
nominate 367.17.5
nominate 371.24
nomination 261.67.18.6
nominative 485.15.7
nominee 5.12
nomocracy 16.307.5
nomology 16.108.4
nomothetic 38.50.6
nonagenarian 261.3.21.1
nonagon 254.5
nonaligned 135
nonappearance 321.17
nonce 318
nonchalant 420.28
non-com 237
noncombatant 420.78
noncommissioned 143.5
noncommittal 228.102
nonconductor 17.357
nonconformism
    242.35.12
nonconformist 436
nonconformity
    16.333.13
noncontributory
    16.274.42
noncooperation
    261.67.22.3
noncooperative
    485.15.10
nondescript 424
none 259
nonentity 16.333.32

nones 550
nonessential 228.96
nonesuch 72
nonet 368
nonetheless 296.1
nonevent 410.3
nonexistent 420.81
nonfeasance 321.28
nonferrous 310.44
nonfiction 261.78
nonflammable 228.16.26
nonharmonic 38.35
nonjoinder 17.106
nonjuror 17.277
nonmember 17.24
nonmetal 228.100
nonmetallic 38.19.1
nonpareil 228.76
nonparous 310.43
nonpartisan 245.7
nonparty 16.328
nonplus 307
nonresident 420.10.1
nonresistant 420.81
nonrestrictive 485.18
nonreturnable 228.16.28
nonrigid 91.15
nonsense 321
nonsensical 228.23
non sequitur 17.342
nonslip 274
nonsmoker 17.38
nonstandard 103
nonstarter 17.337
nonstick 38
nonstop 276
nonswimmer 17.211
non-U 15
nonunion 261.123
nonunionism 242.35.14
nonviolence 321.12
nonviolent 420.28
nonvoter 17.347
noodle 228.37
nook 44
noon 260
noonday 2
noontime 236
noose 309
nopal 228.69
nope 278
nor 9
Nora 17.276
noradrenaline 252.11
Nordic 38

Norfolk 46
nork 41
norm 238
Norma 17.214
normal 228.53
normality 16.333.8.5
normalize 516.3
normally 16.131
Norman 261
Normandy 16.81
normative 485.15.6
Norn 255
Norse 303
Norseman 261
north 460
Northampton 261
Northamptonshire 6.8
Northants 347
northbound 139
northeast 435
northeasterly 16.131
northeastward 103
northerly 16.131
northern 261
Northerner 17.239
northernmost 441
Northumberland 143.4.1
Northumbria 17.3.44
Northumbrian 261.3.25
northward 103
northwards 531
northwest 433
northwesterly 16.131
northwestward 103
Northwich 67
Norway 2
Norwegian 261.36
Norwich 197
nose 520
nosebag 178
noseband 128
nosebleed 89
nosegay 2
nosh 354
nosing 265.83
nosology 16.108.4
nostalgia 17.3.16
nostalgic 38
nostoc 40
Nostradamus 310
nostril 218
nostrum 242.23
nosy 16.399
nosy-parker 17.29
not 373

notability 16.333.9.2
notable 228.16
notarize 516.8
notary 16.274
notate 367.31
notation 261.67.28
notch 68
note 376
notebook 44
notecase 295
noted 91.41
notelet 371
notepaper 17.249
noteworthy 16.375
nothing 265
nothingness 300.32
notice 300.64
noticeable 228.16.39
notifiable 228.16.3.1
notification 261.67.5.1
notify 7.3
notion 261.73
notional 228.63.6
notitia 17.3.49
notochord 95.3
notoriety 16.333.2.1
notorious 310.2.13
notornis 300.24
nototherium 242.2.15
Notre Dame 230
Nottingham 242.17
Nottinghamshire 6
Notts 341
notum 242.31
Notus 310.66
notwithstanding 265.19
nougat 1
nought 374
noumenon 261.56
noun 258
nourish 353.10
nourishment 420.47
nous 306
nouveau riche 352
nova 17.417
Nova Scotia 17.328
novation 261.67
novel 228
novelese 513.7
novelette 368
novelist 436.7
novelistic 38.70.2
novelize 516.3
novella 17.163
Novello 12.40

novelty 16.352
November 17.24
novena 17.230
novice 300
novitiate 371.1
Novocaine 247.2
now 13
nowadays 509
noway 2.27
Nowell 215
nowhere 4
nowt 377
Nox 499
noxious 310
noyade 84
noyau 12.4
nozzle 228
nth 468
nuance 315
nub 29
Nuba 17.20
nubbin 252
nubble 228.14
nubecula 17.174.4
Nubia 17.3
Nubian 261.3
nubile 219
nuclear 17.3
nuclease 509.1
nucleate 371.1
nuclei 7.1
nucleolus 310
nucleon 254.1
nucleoside 92.8
nucleotide 92.11
nucleus 310.2
nuclide 92
nuddy 16.69
nude 102
nudge 203
nudism 242.35
nudist 436
nudity 16.333
Nuffield 115
nugatory 16.274.43
nuggar 17.134
nugget 371
nuisance 321.23
nuke 45
null 225
nullah 1
nulla-nulla 17.173
nullify 7.3
nullipara 17.279
nullipore 9

nullity 16.333
Numantia 17.3.50
numb 240
numbat 365
number 17.27
numberless 300.13
numberplate 367
numbness 300
numbskull 225
numen 248.3
numeracy 16.307.4
numeral 228.76
numerary 16.274.32
numerate 371.35
numeration 261.67.22
numerator 17.338.9
numeric 38.39
numerical 228.23.15
numerology 16.108.4.13
numerous 310.50
Numidia 17.3.9
numinous 310.33.1
numismatic 38.49.4
numismatics 498.11
numismatist 436.26
nummary 16.274
nummular 17.174
nummulite 372
nun 259
nunatak 32.4
Nunc Dimittis 300
nuncio 12.3
nuncle 228.30
Nuneaton 261.98
nunhood 101
nunnery 16.274
Nupe 2
NUPE 16.253
nuptial 228
nuptials 539
Nuremberg 182
Nuristan 246.1
nurse 297
nursemaid 85
nursery 16.274.35
nurseryman 261.48
nursing 265
nursling 265
nurture 17.54
nut 378
nutant 420.77
nutation 261.67.29
nutbrown 258
nutcase 295
nutcracker 17.28

nuthatch 62
nutmeg 181
nutrient 420.1
nutriment 420.31
nutrition 261.71
nutritional 228.63.5
nutritionist 436.13.5
nutritious 310.58
nutritive 485.12
nutshell 215
nutter 17.349
nutting 265
nutty 16.341
nux vomica 17.34
nuzzle 228
nyala 17.161
Nyanja 17.434
Nyasaland 143.4
nyctalopia 17.3.37.1
nyctophobia 17.3.4
nylghau 9
nylon 254
nylons 549
nymph 176
nymphet 371
nympho 12
nympholepsy 16.313
nympholept 422
nymphomania 17.3.31.1
nymphomaniac 32.1
nystagmus 310
nystatin 252
Nyx 498

O

oaf 167
oafish 353
oak 42
oaken 261.14
oakum 242
oar 9
oared 95
oarfish 353
oarlock 40
oarsman 261
oasis 300.50
oast 441
oat 376
oatcake 34
oaten 261
Oates 343
oath 461
oatmeal 217
oats 343

Obadiah 17.4
Oban 261
obbligato 12.73
obdurate 371.34
obeah 17.3.4
obedience 321.1
obedient 420.1.1
obedientiary 16.274.39
obeisance 321
obelisk 58
obelus 310.23
Oberland 143.4
Oberon 254.11
obese 298
obesity 16.333.27
obey 2.4
obfuscate 367
obi 16.12
obit 371
obituary 16.274.2
object 385
object 387
objectify 7.3.9
objection 261.77
objectionable 228.16.31
objective 485.17
objectivism 242.35.22
objectivity 16.333.35
objurgate 367.11
oblast 431
oblate 367
oblation 261.67
obligate 367.10
obligation 261.67.10
obligatory 16.274.43
oblige 198
obligee 5.6
obliging 265
oblique 37
obliquity 16.333
obliterate 367.23.2
obliteration 261.67.22.4
oblivion 261.3.30
oblivious 310.2.17
oblong 266
obloquy 16.259
obnoxious 310
obnubilate 367.12.1
oboe 12
oboist 436
obol 220
obolus 310.26.1
Obote 2.24
obreption 261.84
obscene 251

obscenity 16.333.15
obscure 10
obscurity 16.333.23
obsequies 515
obsequious 310.2
observable 228.16
observance 321
observant 420.82
observation 261.67
observatory 16.274.43
observe 483
observer 17.412
obsess 296
obsession 261.68
obsessive 485.2
obsidian 261.3.5
obsolesce 296.1
obsolescence 321.21
obsolescent 420.67
obsolete 370
obstacle 228.28
obstetric 38.46
obstetrician 261.71
obstetrics 498.10
obstinacy 16.307
obstinate 371.24
obstipation 261.67.20
obstreperous 310.50
obstruct 389
obstruction 261.79
obstructionist 436.13
obstructive 485.19
obtain 247
obtainable 228.16.27
obtrude 102
obtrusion 261.93
obtrusive 485.8
obtund 140
obturate 367.22
obtuse 309
obverse 297
obviate 367.1
obvious 310.2
obviously 16.184
ocarina 17.230.1
O'Casey 16.296
occasion 261
occasional 228.63
occasionally 16.131.4
occident 420.10
Occidental 228.110.1
Occidentalize 516.3
occipital 228.102
occiput 378
occlude 102

occlusion 261.93
occult 406
occultism 242.35
occupancy 16.312
occupant 420
occupation 261.67
occupational 228.63.3
occupier 17.4
occupy 7
occur 3
occurrence 321
ocean 261.73
oceanarium 242.2.14
Oceania 17.3.30
oceanic 38.31.1
oceanid 91.21
oceanography 16.90.2.4
oceanology 16.108.4.11
ocellus 310.22
ocelot 373
och 40
ochlocracy 16.307.5
ochlophobia 17.3.4
ochre 17.38
ocker 17.36
Ockham 242
o'clock 40
O'Connor 17.233
octachord 95.3
octad 83
octagon 254.5
octagonal 228.63
octahedron 261
octane 247
Octans 544
octant 420
octave 485
Octavia 17.3.53
Octavian 261.3.29
octavo 12
octet 368
October 17.18
octogenarian 261.3.21.1
octopod 94.1
octopus 310.40
octoroon 260.3
octroi 1
octuple 228
ocular 17.174.7
ocularist 436.20
oculist 436.6
odalisque 58
odd 94
oddball 221
oddity 16.333.6

oddly 16.149
oddment 420
oddness 300
ode 98
Oder 17.88
Odessa 17.300
Odin 252
odious 310.2.2
odium 242.2.4
odometer 17.342.3
odontalgia 17.3.16
odontoglossum 242.25
odoriferous 310.50.2
odorous 310.50
odour 17.88
odourless 300.13
Odyssean 261.2.4
Odysseus 310.2.15
Odyssey 16.300.1
oedema 17.210
Oedipus 310.37
oeillade 84
oenology 16.108.4
Oenone 16.233
o'er 9
oersted 86
oesophageal 228.2
oesophagus 310
oestriol 220.1
oestrogen 261.39
oestrogenic 38.32.1
oestrone 257
oestrus 310
of 487
off 165
Offa 17.116
offal 228
offbeat 370
Offenbach 33
offence 316
offend 131
offender 17.101
offensive 485.9
offensiveness 300.43
offer 17.116
offering 265.58
offertory 16.274.43
offhand 128
offhandedness 300.28.1
office 300
officer 17.302
official 228.93
officialdom 242
officialese 513.7
officially 16.131

officiant 420.1
officiary 16.274.1.2
officiate 367.1.6
officiation 261.67.1.5
officious 310.58
officiousness 300.34.3
offing 265
offish 353
offprint 412
offset 368
offshoot 380
offshore 9
offside 92
offspring 265
offstage 193
oft 399
often 261
Ogaden 248
ogee 5
ogive 486
ogle 228
Ogooué 2.27
ogre 17.133
ogress 300
oh 12
Ohio 12.4
ohm 239
oil 222
oilcan 245
oilcloth 459
oiler 17.170
oilfield 115
oilfired 93
oilman 261
oilskin 252
oily 16.125
ointment 420.50
Oireachtas 310
Oita 17.346
okapi 16.244
okay 2
Okeechobee 16.12
okey-doke 42
okey-dokey 16.29
Oklahoma 17.215
okta 17.356
old 120
Old Bailey 16.114
olden 261.28
Oldenburg 182
older 17.97
oldfangled 122
old-fashioned 143
Oldham 242
oldie 16.76

oldness 300
old-timer 17.212
olé 2
oleaginous 310.33
oleander 17.98.1
oleaster 17.379
oleate 367.1.3
olecranon 254.8
olfactory 16.274.44
Olga 17.138
olibanum 242.16
olid 91.18
oligarch 33
oligarchy 16.20
Oligocene 251.9
oligopoly 16.131.6
olio 12.3.3
olivary 16.274.51
olive 485
Oliver 17.414
Olivia 17.3.54
Olivier 2.1
olivine 251
olla 17.168
olla podrida 17.82
ology 16.108.4
oloroso 12.70
Olympia 17.3
Olympiad 83.1
Olympian 261.3
Olympic 38
Olympus 310
Om 239
omadhaun 258
Omagh 1
Omaha 1
Oman 246
Omar Khayyam 230
omasum 242
Omayyad 83.2
ombre 17.26
ombudsman 261
Omdurman 246
omega 17.129
omelette 371
omen 261.49
omentum 242
omer 17.215
ominous 310.33
omissible 228.16.39
omission 261.71.4
omit 371
ommatophore 9.6
omnibus 307
omnifarious 310.2.10.1

omnific 38.12
omnificent 420.70
omnipotence 321.25
omnipotent 420.78
omnipresence 321
omnipresent 420.84
omnirange 207.1
omniscience 321.1
omniscient 420.1
omnium-gatherum 242.21
omnivore 9.13
omnivorous 310.50.3
omophagy 16.108.1
Omphale 5.9
omphalos 302
on 254
onager 17.154
onanism 242.35.14
Onassis 300.49
once 320
oncogenic 38.32.1
oncology 16.108.4
oncoming 265.38
one 259
Oneida 17.84
oneiric 38
oneness 300
oner 17.237
onerous 310.50
oneself 172
one-sided 91.8
one-upmanship 274.2
ongoing 265.4
onion 261
onionskin 252
onlooker 17.40
only 16.173
onomastic 38.68
onomastics 498.15
onomatopoeia 17.2.1
onomatopoeic 38
onrush 356
onset 368
onshore 9
onslaught 374
Ontario 12.3
onto 15
ontogeny 16.229.2
ontology 16.108.4.16
onus 310.35
onus probandi 16.77
onward 103
onwards 531
onymous 310.28.2

onyx 498.5
oocyte 372.10
oodles 539
oogamy 16.222.2
ooh 15
oolite 372.4
oolitic 38.52.1
oology 16.108.4.3
oolong 266
oompah 1
oophorectomy 16.222.5.2
ooze 523
opacity 16.333.25
opal 228.69
opalescence 321.21
opalescent 420.67
opaline 253.3
opaque 34
OPEC 35
open 261
opencast 431
opener 17.239
opening 265.46
open-minded 91
open-mindedness 300.28
openness 300.31
openwork 36
opera 17.290
operable 228.16.35
operant 420.65
operate 367.23
operatic 38.49
operation 261.67.22.3
operational 228.63.3
operative 485.15.10
operator 17.338.9
operetta 17.339
operon 254.11
ophicleide 92
ophidian 261.3.5
ophiology 16.108.4.1
Ophir 17.117
Ophiuchus 310.13
ophthalmia 17.3.28
ophthalmic 38
ophthalmitis 300.62
ophthalmology 16.108.4
ophthalmoscope 278.1
ophthalmoscopy 16.254.2
opiate 371.1
opine 253
opinion 261.122
opium 242.2.13

Oporto 12.78
opossum 242.25
Oppenheimer 17.212
oppidan 261.24
opponent 420.54
opportune 260.6
opportunism 242.35
opportunist 436.12
opportunity 16.333.18
opposable 228.16
oppose 520.2
opposite 371.40
opposition 261.71.9
oppress 296.5
oppression 261.68
oppressive 485.2
oppressor 17.300
opprobrious 310.2
opprobrium 242.2
oppugn 260
Ops 329
opt 425
optative 485.15
optic 38.67
optical 228.23
optician 261.71
optics 498
optimal 228.52
optimism 242.35
optimist 436.9
optimistic 38.70.3
optimize 516.4
optimum 242
option 261.86
optional 228.63
optometer 17.342.3
optometrist 436
optometry 16.285.2
opulence 321
opulent 420.27
opuntia 17.3
opus 310.39
or 9
orache 67
oracle 228.28
oracular 17.174.3
oracy 16.307
oral 228.74
Oran 245.5
orange 209
orangeade 85
Orangeman 261
orangery 16.274.14
orang-outang 263
orang-utan 245.6

orate 367
oration 261.67
orator 17.352
oratorical 228.23.17
oratorio 12.3
oratory 16.274.43.7
orb 27
orbicular 17.174.6
orbit 371
orbital 228.102
orc 41
Orcadian 261.3.3
orchard 103
orchestra 17.297
orchestral 228.81
orchestrate 367.28
orchestration 261.67
orchestrina 17.230
orchid 91
orchidaceous 310.56.2
orchitis 300.62
orcinol 220.3
Orcus 310
ordain 247
ordeal 217
order 17.86
orderliness 300.23
orderly 16.131
ordinal 228.60
ordinance 321.14
ordinand 128
ordinarily 16.120.1
ordinary 16.274.26
ordinate 371.24.1
ordination 261.67.18.1
ordnance 321
Ordovician 261.71
ordure 10
ore 9
oread 83.1
orectic 38.60
oregano 12.51
Oregon 261.32
Orestes 513.19
orfe 166
Orff 166
organ 261.33
organdie 16.81
organelle 215
organic 38.31
organism 242.35.14
organist 436.13
organization 261.67.36
organize 516.7
organizer 17.441

organon 254.8
organza 17.445
orgasm 242.34
orgasmic 38
orgeat 1
orgiastic 38.68.1
orgy 16.105
oriel 228.3.12
orient 410
orient 420.1
oriental 228.110
Orientalism 242.35.11.6
Orientalize 516.3
orientate 367.32
orientation 261.67.32
orienteering 265.53
orifice 300
oriflamme 229
origami 16.211
origan 261.32
origin 252.6
original 228.60
originality 16.333.8.6
originally 16.131.3
originate 367.17
Orinoco 12.12
oriole 223.1
Orion 261.4.1
orison 261.126
Orissa 17.302
Orizaba 17.10
Orkneys 515
Orlando 12.23
Orleanist 436.13.1
Orlon 254
orlop 276
Orly 5
Ormandy 16.81
ormer 17.214
ormolu 15.5
ornament 410.2
ornament 420.35
ornamental 228.110.3
ornamentation
    261.67.32
ornate 367
ornithic 38.73
ornithologist 436.4
ornithology 16.108.4.18
ornithomancy 16.309
ornithopod 94.1
ornithopter 17.377
ornithoscopy 16.254.2
orogeny 16.229.2
orology 16.108.4

Orontes 513
orotund 140
orphan 261
orphanage 197
orpharion 261.3.20
Orphean 261.3
Orpheus 310.2
Orphic 38.14
Orphism 242.35.7
orphrey 16.280
orpiment 420.31
orpine 253
orrery 16.274
orris 300
ortanique 37
orthoclase 295
orthodontic 38.64
orthodontics 498
orthodontist 436
orthodox 499.1
orthodoxy 16.389
orthoepy 16.245
orthogonal 228.63
orthography 16.90.2
orthopaedic 38.8
orthopaedics 498
orthopteran 261.60
orthoptic 38.67
orthoptics 498
orthorhombic 38
orthoscopic 38.37.1
orthotropous 310.40
ortolan 261
orts 342
Orwell 228
Orwellian 261.3.9
oryx 498
os 302
Osage 193
Osaka 17.29
Osborne 255
Oscar 17
oscillate 367.12
oscillation 261.67.12
oscillator 17.338.5
oscillogram 229.1.2
oscillograph 158.1
oscular 17.174
osculate 367.13
osculum 242.10
Oshawa 17.425
osier 17.3.62
Osiris 300.45
Oslo 12
Osman 261

Osmanli 16.169
osmiridium 242.2.3
osmium 242.2
osmose 305
osmosis 300.55
osmotic 38.53
Ossa 17.304
osseous 310.2
Ossetia 17.325
Ossian 261.3
ossicle 228.23
ossiferous 310.50.2
ossify 7.3
ossuary 16.274.2
osteal 228.3
osteitis 300.62
Ostend 131
ostensible 228.16.40
ostensive 485.9
ostentation 261.67.32
ostentatious 310.56
osteoarthritic 38.52
osteoarthritis 300.62
osteoblast 430
osteoclast 430
osteogenesis 300.52.4
osteoid 97
osteoma 17.215
osteomalacia 17.322
osteomyelitis 300.62.1
osteopath 452
osteopathic 38.72
osteopathy 16.373.1.1
osteophyte 372
osteoplasty 16.361.1
osteoporosis 300.55
osteotomy 16.222.4.1
Ostia 17.3
ostiole 223.1
ostler 17.198
ostracism 242.35
ostracize 516.11
ostracod 94
ostrich 67
Ostrogoth 459
otalgia 17.3.16
Othello 12.40
other 17.408
othergates 335
otherness 300.26
otherwhere 4.8
otherwise 516
otherworldly 16.153
otic 38.55
otiose 305.1

otitis 300.62
otolaryngology
  16.108.4.7
otology 16.108.4
otoscope 278.1
ottava 17.409
Ottawa 17.425
otter 17.344
Otto 12.77
ottoman 261.52
Ouachita 9
ouananiche 352
oubliette 368
ouch 71
Oudh 99
ought 374
Ouija 17.149
ounce 319
our 14
ourselves 555
Ouse 523
oust 442
out 377
outasight 372.10
outback 32
outbid 91
outboard 95
outbound 139
outbrave 482
outbreak 34
outbreed 89
outbuilding 265.17
outburst 434
outcast 431
outclass 294
outcome 240
outcross 302
outdate 367
outdated 91.34
outdid 91
outdistance 321.27
outdo 15
outdone 259
outdoor 9
outdoors 518
outer 17.348
outermost 441
outface 295
outfield 115
outfit 371
outfitter 17.342
outflank 51
outflow 12
outfox 499
outgo 12

overnice 301
overnight 372.6
overpaid 85
overpass 294
overpay 2
overpitch 67
overplay 2
overplus 307
overpower 14
overpowering 265.57
overprotect 385
overprotection 261.77
overran 245.5
overrate 367.23
overreach 66
overreact 382
override 92.6
overripe 275
overrule 227
overrun 259
oversee 5
overseer 17.2
oversell 215.2
oversew 12
oversexed 450
overshadow 12
overshoe 15
overshoot 380
overshot 373
oversight 372.10
oversimplify 7.3
oversize 516.11
oversized 154
oversleep 273
overslept 422
overspend 131.4
overspent 410
overspill 218
overstaffed 396
overstate 367
overstay 2
oversteer 6
overstep 271
overstuff 168
overt 369
overtake 34
overtaken 261.11
overtask 56
overtax 494
overthrew 15
overthrow 12
overthrown 257
overtime 236
overtired 93
overtone 257.3

overtook 44
overtop 276.1
overtrade 85
overtrick 38
overtrump 289
overture 10.5
overturn 249
overview 15
overwatch 68
overweening 265.42
overweigh 2.28
overweight 367.38
overwhelm 243
overwhelming 265
overwind 135
overwinter 17.369
overword 87
overwork 36
overwrite 372.8
overwrought 374
Ovid 91
oviduct 389
oviform 238.1
ovine 253
oviparity 16.333.20
oviparous 310.50
ovipositor 17.342.5
ovisac 32
ovotestis 300.68
ovoid 97
ovulate 367.13
ovulation 261.67.13
ovule 227
ovum 242
ow 13
owe 12
Owen 252.1
owing 265.4
owl 224
owlet 371
owlish 353
own 257
owner 17.236
ownership 274.1
owt 377
ox 499
oxalate 367.14
oxalis 300.13
oxblood 100
oxbow 12
Oxbridge 197
oxen 261
oxeye 7
Oxford 103
Oxfordshire 6

oxhide 92
oxidant 420.10
oxidase 509
oxidate 367.8
oxidation 261.67.7
oxide 92.14
oxidize 516
oxlip 274
Oxon 261
Oxonian 261.3.18
oxpecker 17.31
oxtail 214
oxyacetylene 251.2
oxyacid 91.28
oxygen 261.37
oxygenate 367.17
oxygenic 38.32
oxymoron 254.10
oxytocin 252
oyer 17.5
Oyo 12
oyster 17.386
oystercatcher 17.50
Oz 517
Ozalid 91
ozocerite 372.8
ozone 257
ozonic 38.35
ozonosphere 6.1

P

pa 1
pace 295
pacemaker 17.30
pacer 17.299
pacesetter 17.339
paceway 2
pachisi 16.395
pachyderm 233
pacific 38.12
Pacific 38.12
pacifier 17.4.1
pacifism 242.35
pacifist 436
pacify 7.3.6
pack 32
package 197
packager 17.150
packaging 265.25
packer 17.28
packet 371.6
packhorse 303
packing 265
packsaddle 228.31

packthread 86
pact 382
pad 83
padang 263
padding 265
paddle 228.31
paddler 17.183
paddock 46
paddy 16.57
Paddy 16.57
paddywhack 32
pademelon 261.40
padlock 40
padrone 16.233
Padua 17.7
paduasoy 11
paean 261.2
paediatric 38.45
paediatrician 261.71.6
paediatrics 498.8
paedomorphosis
  300.57.2
paedophile 219.1
paedophilia 17.3.21.2
paella 17.163
pagan 261.31
paganism 242.35.14
paganize 516.7
page 193
pageant 420
pageantry 16.291
pageboy 11
paginal 228.60.2
paginate 367.17.2
pagination 261.67.18.2
pagoda 17.88
pagurian 261.3.24
Pahari 16.261.1
Pahlavi 16.385
paid 85
Paignton 261
pail 214
paillette 368
pain 247
pained 130
painful 226.4
painfulness 300.30
painkiller 17.166
painless 300
painlessness 300.33
pains 545
painstaking 265.6
paint 409
paintbox 499
paintbrush 356

painter 17.367
painting 265
painty 16.354
pair 4
paisa 1
paisley 16
pakeha 1.6
Pakistan 246.1
Pakistani 16.224
pal 212
palace 300
paladin 252
palaeanthropic 38.37.3
palaeethnology 16.108.4
palaeobotany 16.237.7
Palaeocene 251.9
palaeoclimatology
  16.108.4.15.1
palaeography 16.90.2.1
Palaeolithic 38.73
palaeontography 16.90.2
palaeontology
  16.108.4.16
Palaeozoic 38.2
palaeozoology 16.108.4.3
palais 2
palanquin 251
palatable 228.16
palatal 228
palate 371
palatial 228.91
palaver 17.409
pale 214
paleness 300
palette 371
palindrome 239
paling 265.27
pall 221
palladium 242.2.1
palliasse 293.1
pallid 91.16
pallium 242.2
pallor 17.160
pally 16.112
palm 230
Palmerston 261
palmetto 12.75
palmist 436.8
palmistry 16.293
palmitin 252.23
palmy 16.211
palmyra 17.274
palolo 12.44
Palomar 1.12
palomino 12.54

palooka 17.41
palp 282
palpable 228.16
palpate 367
palpebral 228
palpitate 367.30
palpitation 261.67.27
palsied 91
palter 17.363
paltry 16
palynology 16.108.4.10
Pamirs 514
pampas 310.41
pamper 17.261
pamphlet 371
pamphleteer 6
Pamphylia 17.3.21
Pamplona 17.236
pan 245
Pan 245
panacea 17.2
panache 349
panada 17.78.1
Panama 1.12
Panamanian 261.3.15
panatella 17.163.2
Panay 7
pancake 34
pancreas 310.2
pancreatic 38.49
panda 17.98
pandanus 310.31
Pandarus 310.50
Pandean 261.2
pandemic 38.25
pandemonium 242.2.12
pander 17.98
Pandora 17.276
pandour 10
pandowdy 16.68
pane 247
panegyric 38.40
panegyrize 516
panel 228.55
panelling 265
panellist 436.7.4
panettone 16.233
pang 263
panga 17.140
pangolin 252.9
panhandle 228.39
panic 38.31
panicky 16.25
panicle 228.23.10
panjandrum 242

Pankhurst 434
pannage 197.5
pannier 17.3.29
pannikin 252.3
panocha 17.59
panoply 16
panoptic 38.67
panorama 17.206
panoramic 38.24
panpipes 328
pansophy 16.90
pansy 16.404
pant 407
pantalets 336
pantaloon 260.1
pantechnicon 261.13
pantheism 242.35.2
pantheon 261.3
panther 17.399
panties 515
pantihose 520
pantile 219
pantisocracy 16.307.5
panto 12.83
pantograph 158.1
pantomime 236
pantry 16.287
pants 347
pantsuit 380
pantywaist 432
panzer 17.445
Paotow 13
pap 268
papa 1
papacy 16.307
Papadopoulos 310.26
papal 228
papaya 17.4
Papeete 16.332
paper 17.249
paperback 32.2
paperbark 33
paperboard 95.1
paperboy 11
paperclip 274
papergirl 216
paperhanger 17.245
paperknife 164
paperweight 367.38
paperwork 36
papery 16.274
papeterie 16.286
Paphlagonia 17.3.36.1
Paphos 302
papier-mâché 2.22

papilla 17.166.2
papilloma 17.215
papillon 254.6
papillote 376
papist 436.14
papoose 309
paprika 17.34
Papua 17.7
Papuan 261.7
papule 227
papyrus 310.47
par 1
Pará 1.14
parabasis 300.57
parabiosis 300.55.2
parable 228.16
parabola 17.176
parabolic 38.22
parabolize 516.3
paraboloid 97.6
parabrake 34
Paracelsus 310
paracetamol 220.2
parachute 380
parachutist 436
paraclete 370
parade 85.4
paradigm 236
paradigmatic 38.49.3
paradise 301
paradisiacal 228.28.1
paradox 499.1
paradoxical 228.23
paradrop 276
paraffin 252
paragoge 16.106
paragon 261
paragraph 158.1
paragraphia 17.3.10
Paraguay 7
parakeet 370
paralipomena 17.239
parallactic 38.58
parallax 494
parallel 215
parallelism 242.35
parallelogram 229.1
paralogism 242.35.8
paralyse 516.3
paralysis 300.52.1
paralytic 38.52.1
paramedical 228.23.1
parameter 17.342
paramilitary 16.274.41
paramount 418.1

paramour 10.1
paranoia 17.5
paranoiac 46
paranoid 97.9
paranormal 228.53
parapet 371.30
paraph 171
paraphernalia 17.3.18.1
paraphrase 509
paraplegia 17.3.13
paraplegic 38.17
parapsychology
  16.108.4.5
Paraquat 373
Parashah 1
parasite 372.10
parasitic 38.52.3
parasiticide 92.7.1
parasitize 516.12
parasitology 16.108.4.14
parasol 220
parasympathetic 38.50.6
parathyroid 97.11
paratyphoid 97
paravane 247
parboil 222
parbuckle 228.27
parcel 228.83
parcenary 16.274.26
parcener 17.231
parch 63
parchment 420
parclose 520
pard 84
pardner 17.240
pardon 261
pardonable 228.16.31
pare 4
parenchyma 17.211
parent 420
parentage 197
parental 228.110
parenteral 228.76
parenthesis 300.52
parenthesize 516.10
parenthetic 38.50
parenthood 101
parergon 254
paresis 300.51.1
parfait 2
parfleche 351
parhelion 261.3.10
pariah 17.4.2
Parian 261.3.21
paries 513.1

patella 17.163.2
patency 16.312.6
patent 420.75
patentee 5.24
patently 16.198
patentor 9
pater 17.338
paterfamilias 293.1
paternal 228.58
paternalism 242.35.11.4
paternity 16.333.16
paternoster 17.385
Paterson 261
path 453
pathetic 38.50.6
pathfinder 17.103
pathogen 261.39
pathogenesis 300.52.4
pathogenetic 38.50.4
pathogenic 38.32.1
pathognomonic 38.35.3
pathological 228.23.5
pathology 16.108.4
pathos 302
pathway 2
patience 321
patient 420.73
patiently 16.198
patina 17.231
patio 12.3
patisserie 16.274
Patmos 302
patois 1
Patras 293
patrial 228.3
patriarch 33.1
patriarchate 371.7
patriarchy 16.20
patrician 261.71.6
patriciate 371.1
patricide 92.7
Patrick 38.45
patriclinous 310.34
patrilineal 228.3.7
patrilocal 228.26
patrimonial 228.3.8
patrimony 16.237
patriot 381.1
patriotic 38.53
patriotism 242.35.20
patristic 38.70
patrol 223
patrolman 261
patron 261
patronage 197

patroness 300.26
patronize 516.7
patronymic 38.28
patten 261.94
patter 17.336
pattern 261.94
Patton 261.94
patty 16.327
paucal 228
paucity 16.333
Paul 221
pauldron 261
Pauline 253
paunch 81
paunchy 16.55
pauper 17.256
pauperize 516.8
pause 518
pavane 246
pave 482
pavé 2
pavement 420
pavilion 261.120
paving 265.77
paviour 17.436
Pavlov 487
Pavlova 17.417
pavonine 253
paw 9
pawky 16.28
pawl 221
pawn 255
pawnbroker 17.38
Pawnee 5
pawnshop 276
pawpaw 9
pax 494
Paxton 261
paxwax 494
pay 2
payable 228.16
payday 2
payee 5.1
payer 17.1
payload 98
paymaster 17.380
payment 420.29
paynim 235
payola 17.171
payroll 223
pea 5
peace 298
peaceable 228.16
peaceful 226
peacefulness 300.30

peacemaker 17.30
peacetime 236
peach 66
peacock 40
peafowl 224
peak 37
peaked 386
peaky 16.24
peal 217
peanut 378
pear 4
pearl 216
pearler 17.164
pearlized 154
pearly 16.116
pearmain 247
Peary 16.265
peasant 420.84
peasantry 16.291
pease 513
peashooter 17.351
peasouper 17.259
peat 370
peaty 16.332
peau de soie 1
pebble 228
pebble-dash 349
pebbly 16.133
pecan 245
peccable 228.16
peccadillo 12.42
peccary 16.274
peccavi 5
peck 35
pecker 17.31
Peckinpah 1
peckish 353
pectin 252
pectinate 367.17
pectoral 228.76.3
peculate 367.13
peculiar 17.3.23
peculiarity 16.333.20.1
pecuniary 16.274.1
pedagogic 38.18
pedagogue 185.2
pedagogy 16.104
pedal 228
pedalfer 17.121
pedalo 12.45
pedant 420
pedantic 38.62
pedantry 16.291
peddle 228
pederast 430

pederasty 16.361
pedestal 228.114
pedestrian 261.3
pedestrianize 516.7
pedicab 18
pedicel 215
pedicle 228.23.1
pedicular 17.174.6
pediculosis 300.55.3
pedicure 10.3
pediform 238.1
pedigree 5.18
pediment 420.31.1
pedipalp 282
pedlar 17.184
pedometer 17.342.3
peduncle 228.30
pee 5
Peebles 539
peek 37
peekaboo 15.1
peel 217
peeler 17.165
peelie-wally 16.112
peeling 265.29
peen 251
peep 273
peeper 17.252
peephole 223
peepshow 12
peepul 228.65
peer 6
peerage 197
peeress 300
peerless 300
peeve 484
peevish 353
peevishness 300.35
peewee 5
peewit 371
peg 181
Pegasus 310
pegboard 95
peignoir 1.16
pejorative 485.15
peke 37
Pekin 252
Pekinese 513.9
Peking 265
pekoe 12.10
Pelagianism 242.35.14.1
pelagic 38.15
Pelagius 310.2
pelargonium 242.2.12
Pelé 2

Pelée 2.12
pelerine 251.7
Peleus 310.2
pelf 172
pelham 242.8
pelican 261.13
Pelion 261.3.10
pelisse 298
Pella 17.163
pellagra 17.289
pellet 371.15
pellicle 228.23.6
pellitory 16.274.41
pell-mell 215
pellucid 91.30
pelmanism 242.35.14
pelmet 371
Peloponnese 298.1
Pelops 329
peloria 17.3.41
pelorus 310.48
pelota 17.344
pelt 402
peltast 430
pelvic 38
pelvis 300
Pemba 17.24
Pembroke 44
Pembrokeshire 6
pemmican 261.13
pemphigus 310
pen 248
penal 228.59
penalize 516.3
penalty 16.352
penance 321
Penang 263
penates 513
pence 316
penchant 266
pencil 228.88
pendant 420.14
pendent 420.14
pendente lite 16.334
pending 265.20
pendragon 261.30
pendulous 310.25
pendulum 242.10
Penelope 16.254
peneplain 247
penetralia 17.3.18
penetrant 420.66
penetrate 367.27
penetrating 265.64
penetration 261.67

penguin 252
penicillate 371.16
penicillin 252.8
penicillium 242.2.6
penile 219
penillion 261.3.11
peninsula 17.174.11
peninsular 17.174.11
penis 300
penitence 321.24
penitent 420.76
penitential 228.96
penitentiary 16.274.39
penknife 164
penman 261
penmanship 274.2
Penn 248
penna 17.228
pennant 420.52
pennate 367
penned 131
penniless 300.8
Pennine 253
pennon 261
Pennsylvania 17.3.31
Pennsylvanian 261.3.15
penny 16.226
pennyroyal 228.6
pennyweight 367
pennywort 369
pennyworth 456
penology 16.108.4
Penrith 458
pensile 219.3
pension 261.82
pensionable 228.16.31.1
pensioner 17.239
pensive 485.9
pent 410
pentacle 228.28
pentad 83
pentagon 254.5
pentameter 17.342
pentaprism 242.35
pentastich 38
Pentateuch 45
pentathlon 261
pentatonic 38.35.5
Pentecost 438
Pentecostal 228.115
pentene 251
penthouse 306
pentimento 12.84
pentomic 38.29
pentose 520

pentstemon 261.47
penuche 16.53
penult 406
penultimate 371.19
penumbra 17.285
penurious 310.2.14
penury 16.273
Penzance 314
peon 261.2
peony 16.237
people 228.65
pep 271
peplum 242
pepper 17.250
peppercorn 255
peppermint 412
peppery 16.274
peppy 16.245
pepsin 252
pepsinogen 261.39
peptic 38.65
peptidase 509
peptide 92
peptone 257
Pepys 326
Pequot 373
per 3
peracid 91.28
peradventure 17.70
perambulate 367.17
perambulation 261.67.13
perambulator 17.338.6
per annum 242
percale 214
percaline 251.3
per capita 17.342
perceive 484
per cent 410
percentage 197.14
percentile 219.6
percept 422
perceptible 228.16.58
perception 261.84.1
perceptive 485.23
perceptual 228.9
perch 65
perchance 315
Percheron 254.11
percipient 420.1
Percival 228.120
percoid 97.2
percolate 367.14.2
percolator 17.338
percuss 307
percussion 261.74

percussionist 436.13
percussive 485.7
percutaneous 310.2.6
Percy 16.298
per diem 232
perdition 261.71.2
peregrinate 367.17
peregrination 261.67.18
peregrine 252
peremptory 16.274
perennial 228.3
perfect 385.2
perfect 387
perfectible 228.16
perfection 261.77
perfectionism 242.35.14
perfectionist 436.13.6
perfective 485.17
perfecto 12.81
perfervid 91.55
perfidious 310.2.1
perfidy 16.63
perforate 367.23
perforated 91.34.7
perforation 261.67.22
perforce 303.1
perform 238.2
performance 321
performative 485.15.6
performer 17.214
performing 265
perfume 241
perfumer 17.217
perfumery 16.274.22
perfunctory 16.274
perfuse 523.1
Pergamum 242
pergola 17.176
perhaps 322
peri 16.265
perianth 467
periapt 421
pericardium 242.2
Pericles 513
pericline 253.4
pericope 16.254.1
pericranium 242.2.10
pericynthion 261.3.28
periderm 233
peridot 373
peridotite 372.12
perigee 5.6
perigon 261.32
perihelion 261.3.10
peril 218.2

perilous 310.23
perilune 260
perilymph 176
perimeter 17.342.2.1
perimorph 166
perinatal 228.99
perineal 228.2
perineum 242.1
period 103.1
periodic 38.9
periodical 228.23.2
periodontal 228.111
periosteum 242.2
periotic 38.55
peripatetic 38.50
peripeteia 17.4
peripheral 228.76
periphery 16.274
periphrasis 300.57
periphrastic 38.68
periscope 278
periscopic 38.37
perish 353
perishable 228.16.43
perishing 265.63
peristalsis 300.58
peristaltic 38.61
peristyle 219
peritoneal 228.2
peritoneum 242.1
peritonitis 300.62.4
periwig 184
periwinkle 228.29
perjure 17.148
perjurer 17.279
perjury 16.274.13
perk 36
perky 16.23
perlite 372
perm 233
permafrost 438
permalloy 11
permanence 321
permanency 16.312
permanent 420.55
permanganate 367.18
permeability 16.333.9.2
permeable 228.16.2
permeate 367.1
Permian 261.3
permissible 228.16.39
permission 261.71.4
permissive 485.4
permit 371
permit 371.21

permitting 265.66
permittivity 16.333.35
permutation 261.67.29
permute 380
pernicious 310.58
pernickety 16.333.4
Pernod 12.53
perorate 367.23
peroration 261.67.22
peroxide 92.14
perpend 131
perpendicular 17.174.6
perpendicularity 16.333.20.3.1
perpetrate 367.27
perpetrator 17.338
perpetual 228.9
perpetuate 367.2
perpetuation 261.67.2
perpetuity 16.333.3
perplex 496
perplexity 16.333
perquisite 371.38
perron 261
perry 16.262
per se 2
persecute 380
persecution 261.75
persecutor 17.351
Persephone 16.237
Persepolis 300.13
perseverance 321.17
perseveration 261.67.22
persevere 6.11
Pershing 265
Persia 17.324
Persian 261.69
persicaria 17.3.38
persiflage 359
persimmon 261.48
persist 436.22
persistence 321.27
persistent 420.81
person 261.64
persona 17.236
personable 228.16.31
personage 197
personal 228.63
personalism 242.35.11.5
personality 16.333.8.7
personalize 516.3.7
personally 16.131.4
personalty 16.352
personate 367.18
personify 7.3

personnel 215
perspective 485.17
Perspex 496
perspicacious 310.56.1
perspicuity 16.333.3
perspicuous 310.4.1
perspiration 261.67.22
perspiratory 16.274.43
perspire 8.2
persuade 85
persuasion 261
persuasive 485
pert 369
pertain 247.10
Perth 456
pertinacious 310.56.4
pertinacity 16.333.25
pertinence 321.14
pertinent 420.53
pertness 300.36
perturb 22
perturbation 261.67.3
pertussis 300
Peru 15.6
peruke 45
perusal 228.128
peruse 523
Peruvian 261.3.32
perv 483
pervade 85
pervasion 261
pervasive 485
perverse 297
perversion 261.69.1
perversity 16.333.26
perversive 485.3
pervert 369
pervert 369.2
perverted 91.36
pervious 310.2
Pesach 33
peseta 17.338
pesewa 1
pesky 16.40
peso 12
pessary 16.274.34
pessimism 242.35
pessimist 436.9
pessimistic 38.70.3
pest 433
pester 17.382
pesticide 92.7
pestilence 321
pestilent 420
pestilential 228.96

pestle 228
pet 368
petal 228.100
petalody 16.67
petaloid 97.6
petard 84
peter 17.341
Peter 17.341
Peterborough 17.279
Peterlee 5.9
Peterloo 15.5
petersham 242
Peterson 261
pethidine 251
petiole 223.1
petit bourgeois 1
petite 370
petit four 9.5
petition 261.71.7
petitioner 17.239.2
petit mal 212
Petra 17.293
Petrarch 33
petrel 228
petrifaction 261.76
petrify 7.3
Petrine 253
petrodollar 17.168
petroglyph 163
Petrograd 83
petrography 16.90.2
petrol 228
petrolatum 242.27
petroleum 242.2.7
petrology 16.108.4
Petronius 310.2.9
petticoat 376
pettifog 185.1
pettifogger 17.131
pettifoggery 16.274.12
pettifogging 265.23
petting 265.65
pettish 353
pettitoes 520
petty 16.330
petulance 321
petulant 420.27
petunia 17.3
pew 15
pewter 17.351
peyote 16.339
pfennig 184
Phaedra 17.286
Phaëthon 261.109
phaeton 261

phage 193
phagomania 17.3.31.1
phalange 206
phalangeal 228.3
phalanger 17.155
phalanx 504
phalarope 278
phallic 38.19
phallicism 242.35.16.1
phallus 310
phantasm 242.34
phantasmagoria 17.3.41
phantasmagoric 38.41
phantom 242
Pharaoh 12.62
Pharaonic 38.35
Pharisaic 38.1
Pharisee 5.20
pharmaceutical
   228.23.21
pharmaceutics 498
pharmacist 436.22
pharmacognosy 16.307.3
pharmacology
   16.108.4.6
pharmacopoeia 17.2.1
pharmacy 16.307
Pharos 302
pharyngeal 228.2
pharyngitis 300.62
pharyngology 16.108.4.7
pharyngoscope 278.1
pharyngotomy 16.222.4
pharynx 505
phase 509
phasmid 91
phatic 38.49
pheasant 420.84
Pheidippides 513.4
phellem 242.8
phellogen 261.39
phenacetin 252.23
phenobarbitone 257.2
phenol 220
phenology 16.108.4.10
phenomena 17.231
phenomenal 228.60.5
phenomenalism
   242.35.11
phenomenology
   16.108.4.10
phenomenon 261.56
phenotype 275.1
phenylketonuria 17.3.42
pheromone 257

phew 15
phial 228.4
Phi Beta Kappa 17.247
Phidias 293.1
Philadelphia 17.3
philadelphus 310
philander 17.98
philanderer 17.279
philanthropic 38.37.3
philanthropist 436.15
philanthropy 16.254
philatelic 38.20
philatelist 436.7.6
philately 16.131.7
Philby 16.16
philharmonic 38.35
philhellene 251
Philip 274
Philippi 7
philippic 38.36
philippics 498
Philippine 251
Philippines 547
Philistine 253.10
Phillips 327
phillumenist 436.13.3
philodendron 261
philogyny 16.229.2
philology 16.108.4.8
philomel 215
Philomela 17.165
philosopher 17.120
philosophic 38.13
philosophical 228.23
philosophize 516
philosophy 16.90.4
philtre 17.362
phimosis 300.55
phiz 515
phlebitic 38.52
phlebitis 300.62
phlebotomy 16.222.4
phlegm 232
phlegmatic 38.49
phloem 232
phlogistic 38.70.1
phlogiston 254
phlox 499
phobia 17.3.4
phobic 38.3
Phobos 302.1
phocine 253
Phocis 300.55
phocomelia 17.3.20
Phoebe 16.10

Phoebus 310
Phoenicia 17.3.49
Phoenician 261.71.5
phoenix 498.4
phon 254
phone 257
phoneme 234
phonemic 38.27
phonemics 498
phonetic 38.50.5
phonetician 261.71.7
phonetics 498.12.1
phonetist 436.24
phoney 16.233
phonic 38.35
phonics 498.5
phonogram 229.1
phonograph 158.1.2
phonology 16.108.4.11
phonometer 17.342.3.3
phonotypy 16.249
phooey 16.4
phosgene 251
phosphatase 509
phosphate 367
phosphatide 92.11
phospholipid 91.24
phosphoresce 296.4
phosphorescence 321.21
phosphorescent 420.67
phosphoric 38.41
phosphorous 310.50
phosphorus 310.50
phot 373
photic 38.55
photo 12.79
photoactive 485.16
photocell 215
photocopier 17.3
photocopy 16.250
photoelectric 38
photoelectricity
   16.333.28
photoengrave 482
Photofit 371
photoflash 349
photogenic 38.32.1
photogrammetry 16.285
photograph 158.1
photographer 17.120.1
photographic 38.11
photography 16.90.2.6
photogravure 10
photokinesis 300.51
photometry 16.285.2

photomicrograph 158.1
photomontage 359
photomultiplier 17.4
photon 254
photonasty 16.361
photoperiod 103.1
photophobia 17.3.4
photophore 9.6
photopia 17.3.37
photosensitive 485.12
photosensitize 516.12
photoset 368
Photostat 365
photosynthesis 300.52
photosynthesize 516.10
photosynthetic 38.50
phototaxis 300.70
phototherapy 16.254
photothermic 38.26
phototropic 38.37.2
phototype 275.1
phrasal 228.125
phrase 509
phraseology 16.108.4.1
phrasing 265.81
phrenic 38.32
phrenology 16.108.4.10
Phrygia 17.3.14
Phrygian 261.3.7
phthalein 251
phthiriasis 300.57.1
phut 378
phycology 16.108.4.5
phylactery 16.274.44
phyle 16.121
phyllite 372.3
phylloid 97.5
phylloxera 17.272
phylogeny 16.229.2
phylum 242.9
physiatrics 498.8
physic 38
physical 228.23.25
physically 16.142
physician 261.71.8
physicist 436.21
physics 498
physiognomic 38.29
physiognomy 16.222.3.1
physiology 16.108.4.1
physiotherapist 436.15
physiotherapy 16.254
physique 37
physostigmine 251
phytogenic 38.32.1

phytology 16.108.4.14
phytosociology
   16.108.4.1
phytotoxin 252.29
phytotron 254
pi 7
piaffe 157
pianism 242.35.14
pianissimo 12.48
pianist 436.13.1
piano 12
pianoforte 16.336
Pianola 17.171
piassava 17.409
piastre 17.379
piazza 17.319
pibroch 40
pica 17.35
picador 9.4
Picardy 16.72
picaresque 57
picaroon 260.3
Picasso 12.68
picayune 260
Piccadilly 16.120
piccalilli 16.120
piccaninny 16.229
piccolo 12.45
piceous 310.2.15
pick 38
pickaback 32.2
pickaxe 494
picker 17.34
pickerel 228.76
pickerelweed 89.7
picket 371.9
picketing 265.66
pickle 228.23
pickled 122
picklock 40
pickpocket 371.10
Pickwickian 261.3
picnic 38
picnicker 17.34
picot 12.10
Pict 387
pictograph 158.1
pictorial 228.3.12
picture 17.65
picturesque 57
piddle 228.32
piddling 265
piddock 46
pidgin 252.6
pie 7

piebald 118
piece 298
piecemeal 217
piecework 36
piecrust 443
pied 92
Piedmont 414
pieman 261
pier 6
pierce 299
piercing 265
Pierian 261.3.22
Pierides 513.4
Pierrot 12.63
pietà 1
Pietermaritzburg 182.2
piety 16.333.2
piezometer 17.342.3
piffle 228.41
pig 184
pigeon 261.37
pigeonhole 223
piggery 16.274.9
piggin 252
piggish 353
Piggott 381
piggy 16.93
piggyback 32
pig-headedness 300.28
piglet 371
pigmeat 370
pigment 420
pigmentation 261.67.32
pigskin 252
pigsticking 265.7
pigsty 7
pigswill 218
pigtail 214
pigtailed 112
pigweed 89
pika 17.35
pike 39
pikelet 371
pikeperch 65
pikestaff 158
pilaster 17.379
Pilate 381
pilau 13
pilch 76
pilchard 103
pile 219
pileus 310.2
pilfer 17
pilferage 197
pilgrim 235

pilgrimage 197.3
pili 5.8
piliform 238.1
pill 218
pillage 197.1
pillar 17.166
pillbox 499
pillion 261.120
pilliwinks 505
pillory 16.274.16
pillow 12.42
pillowcase 295.2
pillowslip 274
pilose 305
pilot 381
pilotage 197
Piltdown 258
pilule 227
pimento 12.84
pimp 287
pimpernel 215
pimple 228
pimpled 122
pimply 16.179
pin 252
pinafore 9.6
pinball 221
pince-nez 2
pincer 17.315
pincers 524
pinch 80
pinchbeck 35
pinchpenny 16.226
pincushion 261
Pindar 17.102
Pindaric 38.38
Pindus 310
pine 253
pineal 228.3.7
pineapple 228.64
Pinero 12.63
pinery 16.274.27
pinetum 242.28
ping 265
pinger 17.246
ping-pong 266
pinguid 91
pinhead 86.4
pinhole 223
pinion 261.122
pink 52
Pinkerton 261
pinkeye 7
pinkie 16.37
pinking 265.10

pinkish 353
pinna 17.231
pinnace 300.23
pinnacle 228.28
pinnate 367.17
pinniped 86.6
pinny 16.229
Pinocchio 12.3
pinochle 228.27
pinpoint 416
pinprick 38
pinstripe 275
pint 413
pinta 17.369
pintadera 17.271
pintail 214
Pinter 17.369
pintle 228
pinwheel 217
pinworm 233
piny 16.230
piolet 2
pioneer 6.5
pious 310.3
pip 274
pipe 275
pipeclay 2
pipefitting 265.66
pipeline 253
piper 17.254
piperidine 251
pipette 368
pipewort 369
piping 265
pipistrelle 215
pipit 371
pipkin 252
pippin 252
pipsissewa 17.425
pipsqueak 37
piquancy 16.312
piquant 420.6
pique 37
piqué 2.6
piquet 368.4
piracy 16.307
Piraeus 310.1
piranha 17.226
pirate 371
piratic 38.49
pirogue 188
pirouette 368.1
Pisa 17.440
piscatorial 228.3.12.2
Pisces 513.13

piscina 17.230
piscine 253
piscivorous 310.50.3
pishogue 188
pismire 8
piss 300
Pissarro 12.61
pistachio 12.3
piste 435
pistil 218
pistol 228.114
pistole 223
pistoleer 6
piston 261.107
pit 371
pitapat 365
Pitcairn 250
pitch 67
pitchblende 131
pitcher 17.56
pitchfork 41
pitchy 16.49
piteous 310.2
pitfall 221
pith 458
pithead 86
pithecanthropus 310.40
pithos 302
pithy 16.370
pitiable 228.16.2
pitiful 226
pitiless 300.8
pitilessness 300.33
pitman 261
Pitman 261
piton 254
Pitot 12.76
Pitt 371
pitta 17.342
pittance 321.24
pitter-patter 17.336
Pittsburgh 182.2
pituitary 16.274.41
pituri 16.274.41
pity 16.333
Pius 310.3
pivot 381
pivotal 228
pix 498
pixie 16.388
pixilated 91.34.5
Pizarro 12.61
pizza 17
pizzeria 17.2.2
pizzicato 12.73

pleura 17.277
pleural 228.75
pleurisy 16.300
pleuston 261
Plexiglass 294
plexor 17.426
plexus 310
pliable 228.16.3
pliant 420.2
plica 17.35
plicate 367
plié 2
pliers 524
plight 372
plimsoll 228
plinth 470
Pliny 16.229
Pliocene 251.9
plissé 2
plod 94
plodder 17.85
plonk 53
plonko 12
plop 276
plosion 261.92
plosive 485.6
plot 373
Plotinus 310.34
plotter 17.344
plough 13
ploughboy 11
ploughman 261
ploughshare 4
ploughstaff 158
plover 17.418
ploy 11
pluck 43
plucky 16.30
plug 189
plum 240
plumage 197
plumate 367
plumb 240
plumbago 12.27
plumber 17.216
plumbing 265.38
plumbism 242.35
plumbous 310.6
plumbum 242
plume 241
plummet 371
plummy 16.220
plump 289
plumper 17.264
plumpness 300

plumy 16.221
plunder 17.108
plunderer 17.279
plunge 211
plunger 17.159
pluperfect 387
plural 228.75
pluralism 242.35.11
plurality 16.333.8
pluralize 516.3
plus 307
plush 356
Plutarch 33
Pluto 12.80
plutocracy 16.307.5
plutocrat 365.2
plutocratic 38.49.6
pluton 254
Plutonian 261.3.18
plutonic 38.35
plutonium 242.2.12
pluvial 228.3.17
pluvious 310.2.18
ply 7
Plymouth 464
plywood 101
pneumatic 38.49
pneumatics 498.11
pneumatology
  16.108.4.15
pneumococcus 310.11
pneumoconiosis
  300.55.1
pneumonectomy
  16.222.5
pneumonia 17.3.36
pneumonic 38.35
pneumonitis 300.62
po 12
Po 12
poach 70
poacher 17.59
poaching 265
Pocahontas 310
pochard 103
pock 40
pocket 371.10
pocketbook 44
pocketful 226
pocketknife 164
pockmark 33
poco 12.12
pococurante 16.353
pod 94
podagra 17.289

podesta 17.382
podgy 16.104
podiatry 16.286.1
podium 242.2.4
podzol 220
Poe 12
poem 235
poesy 16.396
poet 371
poetaster 17.379
poetic 38.50.1
poeticize 516.10
poetics 498.12
poetry 16.285
pogonia 17.3.36.1
pogrom 242
poi 11
poignancy 16.312
poignant 420
poinciana 17.226.1
poinsettia 17.3
point 416
pointed 91.48
pointer 17.371
pointillism 242.35.9
pointing 265
pointless 300
pointlessness 300.33
poise 519
poison 261.128
poisoner 17.239
poisonous 310.36
poke 42
poker 17.38
pokeweed 89
poky 16.29
Poland 143
polar 17.171
polarimeter 17.342.2.1
Polaris 300
polarity 16.333.20
polarize 516.8
Polaroid 97.12
polder 17.97
pole 223
Pole 223
poleaxe 494
polecat 365
polemarch 33.2
polemic 38.25
polemics 498
polenta 17.368
poleyn 247
police 298
policeman 261

precocial 228.94
precocious 310.60
precocity 16.333.30.3
precognition 261.71
preconceive 484
preconception 261.84
precondition 261.71
preconize 516.7
preconscious 310
precontract 382
precursor 17.301
precursory 16.274.35
predacious 310.56.2
predate 367
predation 261.67.7
predator 17.352
predatory 16.274.43
predecease 298
predecessor 17.300
predestinarian
   261.3.21.1
predestinate 371
predestination 261.67.18
predestine 252.26
predeterminate 371.24
predetermine 252.13
predial 228.3.1
predicable 228.16.10
predicament 420.35
predicant 420.7
predicate 367.5
predicate 371.9
predict 387
predictable 228.16
prediction 261.78.1
predictive 485.18
predictor 17.355
predigest 433
predilection 261.77.2
predispose 520
predisposition 261.71.9
prednisone 257
predominant 420.53.2
predominate 367.17.5
predomination
   261.67.18.6
pre-eclampsia 17.3
preemie 16.215
pre-eminence 321.14
pre-eminent 420.53
pre-empt 428
pre-emption 261
pre-emptive 485
pre-emptor 17.378
preen 251

prefab 18
prefabricate 367.5
preface 300
prefatory 16.274.43
prefect 385
prefectorial 228.3.12
prefecture 10
prefer 3
preferable 228.16.35
preference 321.20
preferential 228.96.2
preferment 420
preferrer 17.270
prefigure 17.129
prefix 498
preglacial 228.91
pregnable 228.16
pregnancy 16.312
pregnant 420
prehensile 219.3
prehension 261.82.1
prehistorian 261.3.23
prehistoric 38.41
prehistory 16.274.49
prehominid 91
prejudge 203
prejudice 300
prejudicial 228.93
prelacy 16.307
prelate 371.15
prelatism 242.35.20
prelect 385.4
preliminaries 515.1
preliminary 16.274.26
prelude 102
premarital 228.102
premedical 228.23.1
premeditate 367.30
premeditation 261.67.27
premenstrual 228.9
premier 17
premiere 4.1
premiership 274.1
premise 516.4
premises 515.3
premiss 300
premium 242.2.8
premolar 17.171
premonition 261.71
premonitory 16.274.41
prenatal 228.99
prenominal 228.60.5
preoccupation 261.67

preoccupied 92
preoccupy 7
preordain 247
preordination
   261.67.18.1
prep 271
prepaid 85
preparation 261.67.22
preparative 485.15.8
preparatory 16.274.43
prepare 4.6
prepay 2
prepense 316
preponderant 420.65
preponderate 367.23
preposition 261.71.9
prepositive 485.12.1
prepositor 17.342.5
prepossess 296
prepossessing 265.60
prepossession 261.68
preposterous 310.50
prepotent 420
prepuce 309
Pre-Raphaelite 372.4
prerecorded 91.9
prerequisite 371.38
prerogative 485.15.3
presage 197.11
presbyopia 17.3.37
presbyter 17.342
presbyterian 261.3.22
presbyterianism
   242.35.14.1
presbytery 16.274.41
preschool 227
prescience 321.1
prescribe 25
prescript 424
prescription 261.85
prescriptive 485
presence 321
present 410.4
present 420.84
presentable 228.16.55
presentation 261.67
presentationism
   242.35.14.3
presenter 17.368
presentient 420
presentiment 420.31
presently 16.198
presentment 420
preservation 261.67
preservative 485.15

preserve 483
preshrunk 54
preside 92
presidency 16.312
president 420.10.1
presidential 228.96.1
presidio 12.3.1
presidium 242.2.3
presignify 7.3.3
Presley 16.208
press 296
pressing 265.60
pressman 261.53
pressmark 33
pressure 17.323
pressurize 516.8
presswork 36
prestidigitation 261.67.27
prestige 362
prestigious 310.21
presto 12.86
Preston 261.106
Prestonpans 544
prestress 296
Prestwich 67
presumable 228.16
presumably 16.137
presume 241
presumption 261.89
presumptive 485
presumptuous 310.4.4
presuppose 520.2
presupposition 261.71.9
pretence 316
pretend 131.5
pretender 17.101
pretension 261.82
pretentious 310.61
pretentiousness 300.34.4
preterite 371.35.2
preterition 261.71
preternatural 228.76
pretext 450
Pretoria 17.3.41
prettify 7.3
prettiness 300.23
pretty 16.333
pretzel 228
Preussen 261
prevail 214
prevailing 265.27
prevalence 321.12.1
prevalent 420.28.1
prevaricate 367.5

prevarication 261.67.5
prevenient 420.1.2
prevent 410.3
preventable 228.16.55
preventative 485.15.15
preventer 17.368
prevention 261.82
preventive 485.21
preview 15
Previn 252.28
previous 310.2
previously 16.184
prevision 261.91.2
prewar 9
Priam 242
priapism 242.35
price 301
priceless 300
pricelessness 300.33
pricey 16.301
prick 38
pricket 371.9
prickle 228.23
prickly 16.142
pride 92
prie-dieu 3
priest 435
priesthood 101
Priestley 16.200
priestly 16.200
prig 184
priggish 353
prim 235
prima 17.210
primacy 16.307
prima donna 17.233.1
primal 228
primarily 16.120.1
primary 16.274
primate 367
primatology 16.108.4.15.1
prime 236
primer 17.212
primeval 228.119
primigravida 17.83
priming 265
primitive 485.12
primitivism 242.35.22
primo 12.47
primogenitor 17.342
primogeniture 17.56
primordial 228.3.2
primp 287
primrose 520

primula 17.174
primus 310
prince 317
princedom 242
princeling 265
princess 296
Princeton 261
principal 228.66
principality 16.333.8.8
Principe 5
principium 242.2
principle 228.66
principled 122
prink 52
print 412
printable 228.16
printer 17.369
printing 265
prior 17.4
priorate 371
prioress 300.47
priority 16.333.22
priory 16.274
Priscilla 17.166
prise 516
prism 242.35
prismatic 38.49.4
prison 261.126
prisoner 17.239
prissy 16.300
pristine 251
pristine 253.10
prithee 16.376
privacy 16.307
private 371
privateer 6.9
privation 261.67
privative 485.15.16
privet 371
privilege 197.1
privileged 110
privity 16.333.35
privy 16.382
prize 516
prizefight 372
prizefighter 17.343
pro 12
pro-am 229
probabilism 242.35.9
probability 16.333.9.2
probable 228.16
probably 16.137
proband 128
probang 263.1
probate 367.3

probation 261.67.3
probationer 17.239.1
probative 485.15
probe 28
probity 16.333
problem 242
problematic 38.49.2
proboscis 300.54
procaine 247
procathedral 228.78
procedure 17.149
proceed 89.3
proceeding 265.13
proceeds 526
process 296
procession 261.68.1
processional 228.63.4
processor 17.300
proclaim 231
proclamation 261.67.16
proclamatory 16.274.43.5
proclivity 16.333.35
Procne 16.239
proconsul 228.89
procrastinate 367.17
procrastination 261.67.18
procreate 367.1
procreation 261.67.1
Procrustean 261.3.27
proctology 16.108.4
proctor 17.356
procuration 261.67.21
procurator 17.338
procure 10
procurer 17.277
prod 94
prodigal 228.46
prodigality 16.333.8.4
prodigious 310.21
prodigy 16.103
prodrome 239
produce 309
produce 309.1
producer 17.308
product 389
production 261.79.1
productive 485.19
productivity 16.333.35.3
proem 232
prof 165
profanation 261.67.19
profane 247.3
profanity 16.333.14

profess 296
profession 261.68
professional 228.63.4
professionalism 242.35.11.5
professor 17.300
professorial 228.3.12
professoriate 371.1.2
proffer 17.116
proficiency 16.312.5
proficient 420.74
profile 219
profit 371
profitable 228.16.49
profiteer 6
profiterole 223.3
profitless 300.17
profligacy 16.307
profligate 371.14
profound 139
profoundly 16.156
profundity 16.333.7
profuse 309
profusely 16.183
profusion 261.93
prog 185
progenitor 17.342
progeny 16.229.2
progesterone 257.1
progestin 252.26
prognosis 300.55
prognostic 38.71
prognosticate 367.5
prognostication 261.67.5
programmable 228.16.26
programmatic 38.49.2
programme 229
programmer 17.205
programming 265
progress 296
progression 261.68
progressive 485.2.1
prohibit 371.5
prohibition 261.71
prohibitionist 436.13.5
prohibitive 485.12
project 385
project 385.3
projectile 219.5
projection 261.77.1
projectionist 436.13.6
projective 485.17
projector 17.354
projet 2
Prokofiev 160.1

prolamine 251.4
prolapse 322
prole 223
prolegomenon 261.56
prolepsis 300.59
proletarian 261.3.21.2
proletariat 381.1
proliferate 367.23
proliferation 261.67.22
prolific 38.12
proline 251
prolix 498
prolocutor 17.350
prologue 185
prolong 266.1
prolongation 261.67
prom 237
promenade 84
promenader 17.78.1
Promethean 261.3
promethium 242.2
prominence 321.14
prominent 420.53.2
promiscuity 16.333.3
promiscuous 310.4
promise 300
promisee 5.20
promising 265.61
promisor 9
promissory 16.274.36
promontory 16.274.48
promote 376
promoter 17.347
promotion 261.73.1
promotional 228.63.6
promotive 485.14
prompt 429
promptitude 102.2
promptness 300
promulgate 367
promulgation 261.67
prone 257
proneness 300
prong 266
pronghorn 255
pronominal 228.60.5
pronoun 258
pronounce 319
pronounceable 228.16
pronouncement 420
pronto 12.85
pronunciation 261.67.1.4
proof 170
proofread 89

proof-reader 17.82
prop 276
propaedeutic 38.56
propaganda 17.98
propagandist 436
propagandize 516
propagate 367.11
propagation 261.67.11
propagator 17.338.4
propane 247
propel 215
propellant 420.26
propeller 17.163
propensity 16.333.31
proper 17.255
properly 16.131.6
propertied 91
property 16.344
prophase 509
prophecy 16.300
prophesy 7
prophet 371
prophetic 38.50
prophylactic 38.58
prophylaxis 300.70
propinquity 16.333
propitiate 367.1.6
propitious 310.58
propolis 300.13.2
proponent 420.54
proportion 261.72.1
proportional 228.63
proportionate 371.28.2
proposal 228.127
propose 520.2
proposer 17.442
proposition 261.71.9
propound 139
proprietary 16.274.41
proprietor 17.352.1
propriety 16.333.2
proprioceptor 17.375
propulsion 261
propylaeum 242.1
pro rata 17.337
prorate 367
prorogue 188
prosaic 38.1
prosaism 242.35
proscenium 242.2
prosciutto 12.80
proscribe 25
proscription 261.85
proscriptive 485
prose 520

prosecute 380
prosecution 261.75
prosecutor 17.351
proselyte 372.3
proselytize 516.12
Proserpina 17.231
prosimian 261.3.14
prosody 16.72
prosopopoeia 17.2.1
prospect 385
prospective 485.17
prospector 17.354
prospectus 310.69
prosper 17.267
prosperity 16.333.21
prosperous 310.50
prostaglandin 252
prostate 367.34
prostatectomy 16.222.5
prostatitis 300.62
prosthesis 300.52
prosthetic 38.50
prosthetics 498.12
prosthodontics 498
prostitute 380.5
prostitution 261.75
prostomium 242.2.9
prostrate 367
prostration 261.67
prosy 16.399
protactinium 242.2.11
protagonist 436.13.2
protamine 251.4
protanopia 17.3.37.2
protasis 300.57
protean 261.2
protease 509.1
protect 385
protection 261.77
protectionism 242.35.14
protectionist 436.13.6
protective 485.17
protector 17.354
protectorate 371.35
protégé 2
protein 251
protest 433
Protestant 420.81
Protestantism 242.35.21
protestation 261.67.33
protester 17.382
Proteus 310.2
prothesis 300.52.5
protist 436.25
protocol 220

protohistory 16.274.49
protolanguage 197
protomorphic 38.14
proton 254
protoplasm 242.34
Protosemitic 38.52
prototype 275.1
protozoan 261.6
protozoology 16.108.4.3
protozoon 254.2
protract 382
protractile 219.4
protraction 261.76
protractor 17.353
protrude 102
protrusion 261.93
protrusive 485.8
protuberance 321.20
protuberant 420.65
protyle 219
proud 99
Proust 444
provable 228.16.62
prove 490
proven 261
provenance 321.14
Provençal 213
provender 17.102
proverb 22
proverbial 228.3
provide 92.13
providence 321.5
provident 420.10
providential 228.96.1
providing 265.14
province 317
provincial 228
provincialism 242.35.11
provinciality 16.333.8.1
provision 261.91.3
provisional 228.63
proviso 12
provitamin 252.15
Provo 12
provocation 261.67.6
provocative 485.15.2
provoke 42
provolone 16.233.1
provost 445
prow 13
prowess 300
prowl 224
prowler 17.172
Proxima 17.211
proximal 228.52

proximate 371.19
proximity 16.333.12
proximo 12.48
proxy 16.389
prude 102
prudence 321
prudent 420.13
prudential 228.96
Prudentius 310.61
prudish 353
prune 260
prunelle 215
pruner 17.238
prurience 321.1
prurient 420.1.3
prurigo 12.30
pruritus 310.65
Prussia 17.329
Prussian 261.74
pry 7
psalm 230
psalmist 436.8
psalmodic 38.9
psalmody 16.72
Psalms 540
psalter 17.363
psalterium 242.2.15
psaltery 16.274
psephology 16.108.4
pseud 102
Pseudepigrapha 17.120
pseudo 12.22
pseudonym 235
pseudonymous 310.28.2
pseudopodium 242.2.4
pshaw 9
psittacine 253.8
psittacosis 300.55
psoas 310
psoriasis 300.57.1
psych 39
psyche 16.26
psychedelia 17.3.19
psychedelic 38.20
psychiatric 38.45
psychiatrist 436
psychiatry 16.286.1
psychic 38
psycho 12
psychoanalyse 516.3.5
psychoanalysis 300.52.1
psychoanalyst 436.7.4
psychoanalytic 38.52.1
psychobiology
  16.108.4.2

psychodrama 17.206
psychogenesis 300.52.4
psychogenic 38.32.1
psychokinesis 300.51
psychological 228.23.5
psychologism 242.35.8
psychologist 436.4
psychology 16.108.4.5
psychometrics 498.10
psychometry 16.285.2
psychoneurotic 38.53
psychopath 452
psychopathic 38.72
psychopathology
  16.108.4
psychopathy 16.373.1
psychosis 300.55
psychosomatic 38.49.2
psychosurgery 16.274.13
psychotherapist 436.15
psychotherapy 16.254
psychotic 38.53
psystolic 38.22
ptarmigan 261.32
pterodactyl 218
pteropod 94.1
pterosaur 9.11
Ptolemaeus 310.1
Ptolemaic 38.1
Ptolemaist 436.1
Ptolemy 16.216
ptomaine 247
ptosis 300.55
ptyalin 252.11
pub 29
puberty 16.344
puberulent 420.27
pubes 513
pubescence 321.21
pubescent 420.67
pubic 38.4
pubis 300.2
public 38
publican 261.13
publication 261.67.5
publicist 436.21
publicity 16.333.28
publicize 516.10
publicly 16.142
publish 353
publisher 17.326
Puccini 16.228
puccoon 260
puce 309
puck 43

pucker 17.39
pudding 265
puddle 228.36
pudency 16.312
pudendum 242.7
pudgy 16.107
pueblo 12
puerile 219
puerilism 242.35.9
puerility 16.333.9
puerperal 228.76
puerperium 242.2.15
Puerto Rico 12.10
puff 168
puffer 17.118
puffin 252.5
puffy 16.88
pug 189
pugilism 242.35.9
pugilist 436.5
pugnacious 310.56
pugnacity 16.333.25
puke 45
pukka 17.39
pulchritude 102.2
pule 227
Pulitzer 17.320
pull 226
pullet 371.17
pulley 16.129
Pullman 261
pullover 17.417
pullulate 367.13
pulmonary 16.274.29
pulmonate 371.28
pulmonic 38.35
pulp 284
pulped 427
pulpit 371
pulsar 1
pulsate 367
pulsatile 219
pulsation 261.67
pulsator 17.338
pulsatory 16.274.43
pulse 313
pulsimeter 17.342.2
pulverize 516.8
pulverulent 420.27
pulvinate 367.17
puma 17.217
pumice 300
pummel 228
pump 289
pumpernickel 228.23

pumpkin 252
pumpkinseed 89.4
pun 259
punce 320
punch 82
punchball 221
punchbowl 223
puncheon 261
Punchinello 12.40
punchy 16.56
punctilio 12.3.2
punctilious 310.2.5
punctual 228.9
punctuality 16.333.8.2
punctuate 367.2
punctuation 261.67.2
puncture 17.68
pundit 371
pungent 420
Punic 38
punish 353
punishable 228.16.43
punishment 420.47
punitive 485.12
Punjab 19
Punjabi 16.6
punk 54
punka 17.46
punnet 371.27
punster 17.395
punt 419
punter 17.373
puny 16.236
pup 279
pupa 17.259
pupate 367
pupil 228
pupillage 197.1
pupillary 16.274.16
puppet 371
puppeteer 6
puppetry 16.285
puppy 16.252
Purbeck 35
purblind 135
Purcell 215
purchasable 228.16
purchase 300
purchaser 17.302
purdah 17.81
pure 10
purebred 86
purée 2.18
purely 16.124
purgation 261.67

purgative 485.15
purgatorial 228.3.12.2
purgatory 16.274.43
purge 195
Puri 5
purificator , 17.338.2
purifier 17.4.1
purify 7.3
Purim 235
purine 251
purism 242.35
purist 436.19
puritan 261.99
puritanical 228.23.10
purity 16.333.23
purl 216
purler 17.164
purlieu 15
purlin 252
purloin 256
purple 228
purplish 353
purport 374
purpose 310
purposeful 226
purposeless 300
purposelessness 300.33
purposely 16.184
purposive 485
purpure 10
purpurin 252.19
purr 3
purring 265.51
purse 297
purser 17.301
purslane 252
pursuance 321
pursuant 420.5
pursue 15
pursuer 17.8
pursuit 380
pursuivant 420
pursy 16.298
purulent 420.27
purvey 2
purveyance 321
purveyor 17.1
purview 15
pus 307
Pusan 245
Pusey 16.402
push 357
pushchair 4
pushing 265
Pushkin 252

pushover 17.417
pushrod 94
pushy 16.325
pusillanimity 16.333.12
pusillanimous 310.28.1
puss 308
pussy 16.305
pussyfoot 379
pustulant 420.27
pustular 17.174
pustulate 367.13
pustulate 371.17
pustule 227
put 379
putamen 248.2
putative 485.15.14
putrefaction 261.76
putrefy 7.3
putrescent 420.67
putrid 91
putt 378
puttee 16.341
putter 17.349
putting 265
putty 16.341
puzzle 228
puzzlement 420.40
puzzler 17.204
pyaemia 17.3.26
Pydna 17.241
pyelitis 300.62.1
pyelography 16.90.2.2
Pygmalion 261.3.8
pygmy 16
pyjama 17.206
pyjamas 524
pylon 261
pylorus 310.48
pyoid 97
Pyongyang 263
pyorrhoea 17.2.2
pyosis 300.55.2
pyracantha 17.399
pyramid 91.19
pyramidal 228.32
Pyramus 310.29
pyre 8
pyrene 251.5
Pyrenean 261.2
Pyrenees 513.9
pyrethrum 242
pyretic 38.50
Pyrex 496
pyrite 372
pyrites 513

pyrogen 261.39
pyrogenic 38.32.1
pyromancy 16.309
pyromania 17.3.31.1
pyromaniac 32.1
pyrometer 17.342.3
pyrone 257
pyrope 278
pyrophoric 38.41
pyrophyllite 372.3
pyrosis 300.55
pyrotechnic 38
pyrotechnics 498
Pyrrha 17.273
pyrrhic 38.40
Pyrrhus 310.46
pyrrole 223
Pythagoras 310.50
Pythagorean 261.2.3
Pythia 17.3.51
Pythian 261.3
python 261
pythoness 296.3
pythonic 38.35
pyx 498

Q

Qaboos bin Said 92.9
Qatar 1
Qeshm 242
qintar 1
quack 32
quackery 16.274
quacksalver 17.420
quad 94
quadragenarian
  261.3.21.1
Quadragesima 17.211
Quadragesimal 228.52.1
quadrangle 228.49
quadrant 420
quadraphonic 38.35.2
quadraphonics 498.5
quadrate 367
quadrate 371
quadratic 38.49
quadrature 17.62
quadrennium 242.2
quadric 38
quadriceps 324
quadriga 17.128
quadrilateral 228.76
quadrille 218
quadriplegia 17.3.13

quadriplegic 38.17
quadrisect 385.7
quadrivial 228.3.15
quadrivium 242.2
quadroon 260
quadruped 86
quadruple 228
quadruplet 371
quadruplex 496
quadruplicate 367.5.1
quadruplicate 371.9.1
quaestor 17.383
quaff 165
quagga 17.123
quaggy 16.91
quagmire 8
quahog 185
quail 214
quaint 409
quaintness 300
quake 34
Quaker 17.30
Quakerism 242.35.15
quaky 16.21
quale 16.113
qualification 261.67.5.1
qualified 92.1
qualifier 17.4.1
qualify 7.3.2
qualitative 485.15.12
quality 16.333.10
qualm 230
quamash 349
quandary 16.274
quandong 266
quango 12.35
quant 414
quantal 228.111
quantic 38.64
quantifiable 228.16.3.1
quantifier 17.4.1
quantify 7.3
quantitative 485.15.12
quantity 16.333
quantum 242
quarantine 251
quare 4
quark 33
quarrel 228.73
quarreller 17.176
quarrelsome 242
quarrian 261.3
quarrier 17.3
quarry 16.268
quarryman 261.48

quart 374
quartan 261.102
quarter 17.345
quarterage 197
quarterback 32.2
quarterdeck 35
quarterfinal 228.61
quarterlight 372.4
quarterly 16.131
quartermaster 17.380
quartern 261.102
quarterstaff 158
quartet 368
quartile 219
quarto 12.78
quartz 342
quartzite 372
quasar 1
quash 354
Quasimodo 12.21
quassia 17.327
quatercentenary
  16.274.25
quaternary 16.274.24
quaternion 261.3
quaternity 16.333.16
quatrain 247
quatre 17.291
quatrefoil 222.1
quaver 17.410
quay 5
quayside 92
queasy 16.395
Quebec 35
quebracho 12
queen 251
queencake 34
queenly 16.172
Queensberry 16.274
Queensland 143
queer 6
quell 215
quelquechose 520
quench 79
quenchable 228.16
quenelle 215
quercetin 252.23
quercine 253
querist 436.17
quern 249
querulous 310.25.1
query 16.265
quest 433
question 261.18
questionable 228.16.31

questioner 17.239
questioning 265.46
questionless 300.14
questionnaire 4.5
Quetta 17.339
quetzal 228
Quetzalcoatl 228.97
queue 15
Quezon y Molina 17.230
quibble 228.12
quiche 352
quick 38
quicken 261.13
quickie 16.25
quicklime 236
quickly 16.142
quicksand 128
quickset 368
quicksilver 17.422
quickstep 271
quick-witted 91.38
quick-wittedness 300.28
quid 91
quiddity 16.333.5
quidnunc 54
quid pro quo 12
quiescence 321.21
quiescent 420.67
quiet 381.2
quieten 261
quietism 242.35.20
quietness 300
quietude 102.2
quietus 310.63
quiff 163
quill 218
quillai 7.5
quilt 403
quilting 265
quim 235
quin 252
quinary 16.274.27
quince 317
quincentenary 16.274.25
quincunx 506
quinine 251
quinol 220.3
quinquagenarian
261.3.21.1
Quinquagesima 17.211
quinquennium 242.2
quinquereme 234
quinsy 16.406
quintal 228
quintan 261.105

quintessence 321.21
quintessential 228.96
quintet 368
Quintilian 261.3.11
quintuple 228
quintuplet 371
quintuplicate 367.5.1
quip 274
quipster 17.396
quire 8
Quirinal 228.60
Quirinus 310.34
quirk 36
quirky 16.23
quirt 369
quisling 265
quit 371
quitch 67
quitclaim 231
quite 372
Quito 12.76
quits 339
quittance 321.24
quitter 17.342
quiver 17.414
quiverful 226
quivery 16.274.51
qui vive 484
Quixote 381
quixotic 38.53
quiz 515
quizmaster 17.380
quizzical 228.23.25
quod 94
quodlibet 368.2
quoin 256
quoit 375
quokka 17.36
quondam 229
quorum 242.20
quota 17.347
quotable 228.16
quotation 261.67.28
quote 376
quoth 461
quotidian 261.3.5
quotient 420

R

Ra 1
Rabat 366
rabbi 7
rabbinate 371.24
rabbinic 38.34

rabbinical 228.23.12
rabbinism 242.35.13
rabbit 371.4
rabbiter 17.342
rabble 228
Rabelais 2.12
Rabelaisian 261.3.33
rabid 91
rabies 513
raccoon 260
race 295
racecard 84
racecourse 303
racegoer 17.6
racehorse 303
raceme 234
racemic 38.27
racemose 305
racer 17.299
racetrack 32
Rachel 228
rachitic 38.52
rachitis 300.62
Rachmaninoff 165.1
racial 228.91
racialism 242.35.11
racialist 436.7
racing 265.59
rack 32
racket 371.6
racketeer 6
rackets 339
rackety 16.333
Rackham 242
raconteur 3
racquet 371.6
racy 16.296
rad 83
RADA 17.78
radar 1
radarscope 278
Radcliffe 163
raddle 228.31
raddled 122
radial 228.3
radian 261.3.3
radiance 321.1
radiant 420.1
radiate 367.1
radiate 371.1
radiation 261.67.1
radiator 17.338.1
radical 228.23
radicalism 242.35.11
radically 16.142

radicand 128.1
radicle 228.23
radii 7.1
radio 12.3
radioactivate 367.36
radioactive 485.16
radioactivity 16.333.35.2
radiobiology 16.108.4.2
radiocarbon 261.8
radiogram 229.1.1
radiograph 158.1.1
radiographer 17.120.1
radiography 16.90.2.1
radioisotope 278
radioisotopic 38.37
radiologist 436.4
radiology 16.108.4.1
radiometer 17.342.3.1
radiopaque 34
radiophone 257
radiophonic 38.35.2
radiophony 16.237.3.1
radiosensitive 485.12
radiotelegraphy 16.90
radiotherapeutic 38.56
radiotherapist 436.15
radiotherapy 16.254
radiothermy 16.214
radiotoxic 38.75
radish 353.1
radium 242.2.1
radius 310.2
radix 498
Radnorshire 6
radome 239
radon 254
raffia 17.3.10
raffinate 367.17.1
raffish 353
raffle 228
raft 396
rafter 17.358
rag 178
raga 17.124
ragamuffin 252.5
ragbag 178
rage 193
ragged 91
raggedness 300.28
raggedy 16.63
raggle-taggle 228.43
ragi 16.91
raglan 261
ragman 261
ragout 15

ragtag 178
ragtime 236
ragweed 89
ragwort 369
raid 85
raider 17.79
rail 214
railcar 1
railhead 86
railing 265.27
raillery 16.274
railroad 98
railway 2
railwayman 261.45
raiment 420.29
rain 247
rainbird 87
rainbow 12
raincheck 35
raincoat 376
raindrop 276
rainfall 221
rainforest 436.18
Rainier 17.3.31
Rainier 2.1
rainproof 170
rainstorm 238
rainy 16.225
raise 509
raisin 261.124
raising 265.81
raj 192
rajah 17.145
Rajkot 376
Rajput 379
rake 34
raki 5.3
rakish 353
rale 213
rallentando 12.23
rally 16.112
rallycross 302
ram 229
Rama 17.206
Ramachandra 17.288
Ramadan 246
Ramakrishna 17.243
Raman 261
Rambert 4
ramble 228.17
rambler 17.179
rambling 265
rambunctious 310
rambutan 261.104
ramekin 252.3

Rameses 513
ramie 16.210
ramification 261.67.5.1
ramiform 238.1
ramify 7.3
Ramillies 513.6
rammish 353
ramose 305
ramp 285
rampage 193
rampant 420
rampart 366
rampion 261.3
ramrod 94
Ramsgate 367
ramshackle 228.19
ramulose 305
ramus 310.27
ran 245
ranch 78
ranchero 12.62
Ranchi 16.54
rancid 91
rancorous 310.50.1
rancour 17.43
rand 128
randan 245
Randolph 173
random 242.6
randomize 516.5
randy 16.77
rang 263
range 207
rangefinder 17.103
ranger 17.156
Rangoon 260
rangy 16.109
rani 16.224
rank 51
ranker 17.43
ranking 265
rankle 228
ransack 32
ransom 242
rant 407
ranunculaceous 310.56
ranunculus 310.25
rap 268
rapacious 310.56
rapacity 16.333.25.1
Rapa Nui 16.4
rape 270
rapeseed 89
Raphael 228.1
rapid 91

rapidity 16.333.5
rapier 17.3
rapine 253
rapist 436.14
rappee 5
rappel 215
rapper 17.247
rapport 9
rapporteur 3
rapscallion 261.118
rapt 421
raptor 17.374
raptorial 228.3.12
rapture 17.72
rapturous 310.50
rare 4
rarebit 371
rarefaction 261.76
rarefied 92.1
rarefy 7.3
rarely 16.117
rareripe 275
raring 265.52
rarity 16.333
Rarotonga 17.142
rascal 228
rascality 16.333.8
rascally 16.131
rash 349
rasher 17.321
rashness 300
rasp 290
raspberry 16.274
rasping 265
Rasputin 252.24
Rasta 17.379
Rastafarian 261.3.21
raster 17.379
rat 365
ratafia 17.2
ratatat 365
ratatat-tat 365
ratatouille 5
ratbag 178
ratchet 371
rate 367
rateable 228.16.45
ratel 228.99
ratepayer 17.1
rates 335
ratfink 52
ratfish 353
rathe 473
rather 17.401
ratify 7.3.8

ratine 251
ratiné 2.15
rating 265.64
ratio 12.3.6
ratiocinate 367.17
ration 261.66
rational 228.63.2
rationale 213.1
rationalism 242.35.11.5.1
rationalist 436.7.5
rationalistic 38.70.2
rationality 16.333.8.7.1
rationalize 516.3.7
Ratisbon 254
ratite 372
rats 333
ratsbane 247
rattan 245
ratter 17.336
Rattigan 261.32
rattish 353
rattle 228.97
rattler 17.200
rattlesnake 34
rattletrap 268
rattling 265
rattly 16.186
rattrap 268
ratty 16.327
raucous 310
raunchy 16.55
ravage 197
rave 482
ravel 228.117
Ravel 215
ravelin 252
raven 261
raven 261.111
ravening 265.46
Ravenna 17.228
ravenous 310.36
raver 17.410
ravine 251.12
raving 265.77
ravioli 16.126
ravish 353
ravishing 265.63
raw 9
Rawalpindi 16.79
rawboned 138
rawhide 92
rawness 300.24
ray 2
rayless 300.7

raylet 371
rayon 254
raze 509
razoo 15.10
razor 17.439
razorback 32.2
razorbill 218
razzle-dazzle 228.124
razzmatazz 507
re 2
re 5
reach 66
reachable 228.16.12
react 382
reactant 420
reaction 261.76
reactionary 16.274.29
reactivate 367.36
reactive 485.16
reactivity 16.333.35.2
reactor 17.353
read 86
read 89
readable 228.16
reader 17.82
readership 274.1
readily 16.120
readiness 300.23.1
reading 265.13
Reading 265.12
readjust 443
ready 16.60
reaffirm 233
reafforest 436.18
Reagan 261.31
reagent 420
real 213
real 228.2
realgar 17.137
realism 242.35.11.1
realist 436.7.1
realistic 38.70.2.1
reality 16.333.8.1
realizable 228.16.64
realization 261.67.36
realize 516.3.1
really 16.119
realm 243
realty 16.352
ream 234
reamer 17.210
reap 273
reaper 17.252
reappear 6.6
reappearance 321.17

rear 6
rearguard 84
rearm 230
rearmost 441
rearrange 207
rearrangement 420.38
reason 261.125
reasonable 228.16.31.2
reasoned 143.6
reasoning 265.46
reassurance 321.19
reassure 10
reassuring 265.56
Réaumur 10
reb 21
rebarbative 485.15
rebate 367
rebec 35
Rebecca 17.31
rebel 215
rebel 228
rebellion 261.119
rebellious 310.2
rebirth 456
reborn 255
rebound 139
rebuff 168
rebuild 116
rebuilt 403
rebuke 45
rebus 310
rebut 378
rebuttal 228.107
rebutter 17.349
rec 35
recalcitrant 420.66
recall 221
recant 407
recantation 261.67.31
recap 367
recapitulate 367.13
recapitulation 261.67.13
recaption 261.83
recapture 17.72
recce 16.22
recede 89.2
receipt 370
receive 484.2
receiver 17.413
receivership 274.1
recension 261.82.2
recent 420.69
receptacle 228.28
reception 261.84
receptionist 436.13

receptive 485.23
receptivity 16.333.35
receptor 17.375
recess 296
recession 261.68
recessional 228.63.4
recessive 485.2
Rechabite 372
recharge 192
recherché 2
recidivism 242.35.22
Recife 17.113
recipe 16.248
recipient 420.1
reciprocal 228.28
reciprocate 367.6
reciprocity 16.333.30
recision 261.91.1
recital 228.103
recitation 261.67.27
recitative 484
recite 372.9
reckless 300
recklessness 300.33
reckon 261
reckoner 17.239
reckoning 265.46
reclaim 231
reclamation 261.67.16
reclinable 228.16.30
reclinate 367.17
recline 253.4
recliner 17.232
reclothe 478
recluse 309
reclusive 485.8
recognition 261.71
recognizable 228.16.64
recognizance 321
recognize 516
recognizee 5
recoil 222
recollect 385.5
recollection 261.77
recombination 261.67.18
recommence 316
recommend 131.2
recommendable
228.16.18
recommendation
261.67.9
recommendatory
16.274.43.2
recommit 371.21
recompense 316

recompose 520
reconcilable 228.16
reconcile 219
reconciliation 261.67.1.1
reconciliatory
16.274.43.1
recondite 372
recondition 261.71
reconnaissance 321.22
reconnoitre 17.346
reconsider 17.83
reconstitute 380.5
reconstruct 389
reconstruction 261.79
reconvert 369
record 95
record 95.2
recordable 228.16.16
recorder 17.86
recording 265.15
recount 418
re-count 418
recoup 280
recourse 303
recover 17.418
recovery 16.274
re-create 367.1
recreation 261.67.1
re-creation 261.67.1
recreational 228.63.3
recrement 420.31
recriminate 367.17
recrimination
261.67.18.5
recrudesce 296
recruit 380
recruitment 420
recta 17.354
rectal 228
rectangle 228.49
rectangular 17.174
recti 7
rectifiable 228.16.3.1
rectifier 17.4.1
rectify 7.3.9
rectilinear 17.3.34
rectitude 102.2
recto 12.81
rectocele 217.2
rector 17.354
rectory 16.274.45
rectum 242
rectus 310.69
recumbent 420
recuperate 367.23

recuperation 261.67.22
recur 3
recurrence 321
recurrent 420.64
recurring 265.51
recursion 261.69
recurve 483
recusant 420
recycle 228.24
red 86
redact 382
redan 245.1
redbreast 433
redbrick 38
redbug 189
redcoat 376
redcurrant 420.64
redden 261.21
reddish 353
Redditch 67
redecorate 367.23
redeem 234
redeemable 228.16
redeemer 17.210
redeeming 265.36
redemption 261
redemptioner 17.239
Redemptorist 436.20
redeploy 11
redeployment 420.33
redevelop 281.1
redevelopment 420
redeye 7
redfin 252
Redford 103.2
Redgrave 482
red-handed 91.12
redhead 86
redia 17.3.8
redingote 376
redintegrate 367.26
redintegration 261.67.24
rediscover 17.418
Redmond 143
redneck 35
redness 300
redo 15
redolent 420.28
redouble 228.14
redoubt 377
redoubtable 228.16
redound 139
redpoll 220
redraft 396
redress 296

Redruth 463
redshank 51
redskin 252
redstart 366
reduce 309
reducer 17.308
reducible 228.16
reduction 261.79
redundancy 16.312
redundant 420.16
reduplicate 367.5.1
reduplicate 371.9.1
reduplication 261.67.5
reduviid 91.2
redwing 265
redwood 101
re-echo 12.9
reed 89
reedbuck 43
reedling 265
reedy 16.62
reef 162
reefer 17.113
reek 37
reel 217
re-election 261.77.2
re-enact 382
re-entrant 420
re-entry 16.288
reeve 484
re-examine 252.12
re-export 374
ref 160
reface 295
refection 261.77
refectory 16.274.45
refer 3
referee 5.17
reference 321.20
referendum 242.7
referent 420.65
referral 228
refill 218
refillable 228.16.23
refine 253
refined 135
refinement 420
refiner 17.232
refinery 16.274.27
refining 265.44
reflate 367
reflation 261.67
reflect 385
reflection 261.77
reflective 485.17

reflectivity 16.333.35
reflector 17.354
reflet 502
reflex 496
reflexive 485
reflux 502
reform 238.1
re-form 238
reformation 261.67.16
reformative 485.15.6
reformatory 16.274.43
reformed 125
reformer 17.214
reformism 242.35.12
refract 382.1
refraction 261.76
refractive 485.16
refractometer 17.342.3
refractor 17.353
refractory 16.274.44
refrain 247
refrangible 228.16.21
refreeze 513
refresh 351
refresher 17.323
refreshing 265
refreshment 420
refrigerant 420.65
refrigerate 367.23
refrigeration 261.67.22
refrigerator 17.338.9
refringent 420.23
refroze 520
refuel 228.10
refuge 204
refugee 5
refulgent 420.21
refund 140
re-fund 140
refundable 228.16
refurbish 353
refusal 228.128
refuse 309
refuse 523
refutation 261.67.29
refute 380
regain 247
regal 228.45
regale 214
regalia 17.3.18
regality 16.333.8.4
regard 84.1
regardant 420.8
regardful 226
regarding 265

regardless 300
regatta 17.336
regency 16.312
regenerate 367.23.1
regenerate 371.35
regeneration 261.67.22.2
regent 420
reggae 2
regicide 92.7
regime 234
regimen 248
regiment 410.1
regiment 420.31
regimental 228.110.2
regimentals 539
regimentation
 261.67.32.1
Regina 17.232
region 261.36
regional 228.63
regionalism 242.35.11.5
register 17.384
registrant 420
registrar 1
registration 261.67.25
registry 16.293
regnant 420
regolith 458
regorge 200
regosol 220
regress 296
regression 261.68
regressive 485.2
regret 368
regretful 226.8
regrettable 228.16.46
regroup 280
regulable 228.16.25
regular 17.174
regularity 16.333.20.3
regularize 516.8.1
regulate 367.13
regulation 261.67.13
regulator 17.338.6
Regulus 310.25
regurgitate 367.30
regurgitation 261.67.27
rehabilitate 367.30.1
rehabilitation 261.67.27
rehash 349
rehearsal 228.84
rehearse 297
reheat 370
rehoboam 242
rehouse 521

Reich 39
Reichstag 179
Reid 89
reify 7.3
Reigate 371
reign 247
reimburse 297
reimport 374
reimpression 261.68
rein 247
reincarnation 261.67.17
reindeer 6
reinforce 303.2
reinforcement 420.45
reins 545
reinstate 367
reinstatement 420.48
reinsure 10.2
reiterate 367.23.2
reiteration 261.67.22.4
Reith 457
reject 385
rejection 261.77
rejig 184
rejoice 304
rejoin 256
rejoinder 17.106
rejuvenate 367.17
rejuvenation 261.67.18
rejuvenesce 296.3
rekindle 228.40
relapse 322
relate 367.12
related 91.34.5
relation 261.67.12
relations 551.1
relationship 274.2
relative 485.15.4
relativism 242.35.22
relativistic 38.70
relativity 16.333.35.1
relator 17.338.5
relatum 242.27
relax 494
relaxant 420.83
relaxation 261.67.34
relay 2
relay 2.11
release 298
relegate 367.10
relegation 261.67.10
relent 410
relentless 300
relentlessness 300.33
relevance 321

relevant 420
reliability 16.333.9.2.1
reliable 228.16.3
reliance 321.2
reliant 420.2
relic 38.20
relict 387
relief 162.1
relieve 484.1
relieved 148
religion 261.37
religiose 305.1
religiosity 16.333.30.1
religious 310.21
relinquish 353
reliquary 16.274
reliquiae 5.2
relish 353.4
relive 485
reload 98
reluctance 321
reluctant 420
reluctivity 16.333.35.3
rely 7.5
remade 85
remain 247
remainder 17.100
remainderman 261.52
remaining 265.40
remains 545
remake 34
remand 129
remark 33.2
remarkable 228.16
remarque 33.2
remarriage 197.9
remarry 16.260
rematch 62
Rembrandt 407
remedial 228.3.1
remedy 16.63
remember 17.24
remembrance 321
remind 135
reminder 17.103
remindful 226
reminisce 300.23
reminiscence 321.22
reminiscent 420.70
remise 516.4
remiss 300.19
remission 261.71
remit 371.19
remittal 228.102
remittance 321.24

remittee 5.22
remittent 420.76
remitter 17.342.2
remnant 420
remodel 228.34
remonetize 516.12
remonstrance 321
remonstrant 420
remonstrate 367
remonstrative 485.15.11
remora 17.279.1
remorse 303
remorseful 226.6
remorseless 300
remorselessness 300.33
remote 376
remoteness 300
remould 120
removable 228.16.62
removal 228.122
removalist 436.7
remove 490
removed 150
remover 17.419
remunerate 367.23
remuneration 261.67.22
remunerative 485.15.10
Remus 310
renaissance 321
renal 228.59
rename 231
renascent 420
Renault 12.52
rend 131
render 17.101
rendering 265.58
rendezvous 15
rendition 261.71
renegade 85.1
renege 183
renew 15.9
renewable 228.16.7
renewal 228.10
Renfrew 15
renin 252
rennet 371
rennin 252.16
Reno 12.54
Renoir 1
renounce 319
renovate 367
renovate 367.37
renovation 261.67
renown 258
renowned 139

rent 410
rental 228.110
rented 91.46
renter 17.368
renunciation 261.67.1.4
renvoi 11
reopen 261
reorganize 516.7
rep 271
repaint 409
repair 4.6
repairable 228.16.33
repairer 17.271
repairman 261.46
reparable 228.16.35.1
reparation 261.67.22
repartee 5
repartition 261.71
repast 431
repatriate 367.1
repatriate 371.1
repatriation 261.67.1
repay 2
repayment 420.29
repeal 217
repeat 370
repeatable 228.16.48
repeated 91.37
repeatedly 16.148
repeater 17.341
repechage 359
repel 215
repellent 420.26
repent 410
repentance 321.26
repentant 420
repercussion 261.74
repertoire 1.17
repertory 16.274.43
repetend 131.5
repetition 261.71.7
repetitious 310.58
repetitive 485.12
rephrase 509
repine 253
replace 295
replaceable 228.16.36
replacement 420.44
replay 2
replenish 353.6
replete 370
repletion 261.70
replevin 252.28
replevy 16.380
replica 17.34

replication 261.67.5
reply 7.8
repoint 416
repone 257
report 374.1
reportage 359
reportedly 16.148
reporter 17.345
repose 520
reposit 371.39
reposition 261.71.9
repository 16.274.41
repossess 296
repossession 261.68
repot 373
repoussé 2.21
reprehend 131.1
reprehensible 228.16.40
reprehension 261.82.1
represent 410.4
re-present 410.4
representation 261.67.32
representational
  228.63.3
representationalism
  242.35.11.5.2
representative 485.15.15
repress 296
repression 261.68
repressive 485.2
reprieve 484
reprimand 129
reprint 412
reprisal 228
reprise 513
repro 12
reproach 70
reproachable 228.16.13
reproachful 226
reprobate 367.4
reprobation 261.67.3
reprobative 485.15
reproduce 309.1
reproduction 261.79.1
reproductive 485.19
reprography 16.90.2
reproof 170
reprove 490
reptile 219
reptilian 261.3.11
republic 38
republican 261.13
republicanism
  242.35.14.2
republicanize 516.7

retch 64
retention 261.82
retentive 485.21
rethink 52
retiarius 310.2.10
reticence 321.22
reticent 420.70
reticle 228.23.19
reticulate 367.13.2
reticulate 371.17.2
reticule 227.1
reticulum 242.10.1
retina 17.231
retinite 372.5
retinitis 300.62.3
retinol 220.3
retinue 15.9
retire 8
retirement 420
retiring 265.54
retorsion 261.72
retort 374
retouch 72
retrace 295
retract 382
retractable 228.16
retractile 219.4
retraction 261.76
retractor 17.353
re-tread 86
retreat 370
retrench 79
retrenchment 420
retrial 228.4
retribution 261.75
retributive 485
retrievable 228.16.61
retrieval 228.119
retrieve 484
retriever 17.413
retro 12
retroact 382
retroaction 261.76
retroactive 485.16
retrocede 89.3
retrochoir 8
retrofire 8
retroflex 496
retroflexion 261.77
retrograde 85.6
retrogress 296
retrogressive 485.2.1
retroject 385.3
retrorocket 371.10
retrospect 385

retrospection 261.77
retrospective 485.17
retroussé 2.21
retry 7
retsina 17.230
return 249.1
returnable 228.16.28
Reuben 252
reunify 7.3
reunion 261.123
reunite 372
Reuter 17.346
revalorize 516.8
revaluation 261.67.2
revalue 15
revamp 285
reveal 217
revealing 265.29
reveille 16.112
revel 228.118
revelation 261.67.14
revelationist 436.13.4
reveller 17.176
revelry 16.283
revenant 420.53
revenge 208
revengeful 226
revenue 15.9
reverberate 367.23
reverberation 261.67.22
reverberatory 16.274.43
revere 6.11
reverence 321.20.1
reverend 143
reverent 420.65
reverential 228.96.2
reverie 16.274
revers 6.11
reversal 228.84
reverse 297.2
reversi 16.298.1
reversible 228.16.38
reversion 261.69
revert 369.1
revest 433
revet 368
revetment 420
review 15
reviewer 17.8
revile 219
revise 516.15
revision 261.91.2
revisionism 242.35.14
revisory 16.274.53
revitalize 516.3

revival 228.121
revivalism 242.35.11
revivalist 436.7
revive 486
revivify 7.3
revocable 228.16
revocation 261.67.6
revoice 304
revoke 42
revolt 405
revolting 265
revolution 261.75.1
revolutionary 16.274.29
revolutionize 516.7
revolve 493
revolver 17.423
revolving 265
revue 15
revulsion 261
reward 95
rewardable 228.16.16
rewarding 265.15
rewind 135
rewinder 17.103
rewire 8
reword 87
rework 36
Rex 496
Reykjavik 38
Reynard 103
rhabdomancy 16.309
Rhaetian 261.70
Rhaetic 38.51
rhapsodic 38.9
rhapsodist 436.3
rhapsodize 516
rhapsody 16.72
rhatany 16.237
rhea 17.2
Rhea 17.2
Rhemish 353
Rhenish 353.6
rheobase 295.1
rheology 16.108.4.1
rheometer 17.342.3.1
rheostat 365
rhesus 310
rhetor 17.341
rhetoric 38.44
rhetorical 228.23.17
rhetorician 261.71
rheum 241
rheumatic 38.49
rheumatics 498.11
rheumatism 242.35.20

rheumatoid 97
rheumatology 16.108.4.15
rheumy 16.221
rhinal 228.61
Rhine 253
Rhineland 143
rhinestone 257
rhinitis 300.62
rhino 12
rhinoceros 310.50
rhinology 16.108.4
rhinoplasty 16.361.1
rhizobium 242.2
rhizome 239
rhizomorph 166.1
rhizomorphous 310.18
rhizopod 94.1
rhodamine 251.4
Rhodes 529
Rhodesia 17.325
Rhodian 261.3.6
rhodium 242.2.4
rhododendron 261
rhombic 38
rhombohedral 228.78
rhomboid 97
rhombus 310
rhonchus 310
Rhondda 17.104
Rhône 257
rhotic 38.55
rhubarb 19
rhyme 236
rhythm 242.33
rhythmic 38.30
rhythmical 228.23
rhythmics 498
ria 17.2
rial 228.4
Rialto 12.82
rib 24
ribald 122
ribaldry 16.278
riband 143
Ribble 228.12
ribbon 261
riboflavin 252
ribonuclease 509.1
ribose 520
ribosome 239
rice 301
ricer 17.303
rich 67
Richard 103

Richardson 261
Richelieu 3
riches 515
Richmond 143
richness 300
ricin 252.22
rick 38
rickets 339
rickettsia 17.3
rickety 16.333.4
rickrack 32
rickshaw 9
ricochet 2
ricotta 17.344
rictus 310
rid 91
riddance 321.5
ridden 261.24
riddle 228.32
ride 92
rider 17.84
riderless 300.13
ridge 197
ridgepole 223
ridgeway 2.29
ridicule 227.1
ridiculous 310.25.2
riding 265.14
Ridley 16.148
riesling 265
Rif 163
rife 164
riff 163
riffle 228.41
riffler 17.190
riffraff 157
rifle 228
rifleman 261
rifling 265
rift 398
rig 184
Riga 17.128
rigadoon 260
rigatoni 16.233
rigger 17.129
rigging 265
right 372
righten 261.100
righteous 310
righteousness 300.34
rightful 226.9
right-handed 91.12
right-hander 17.98
rightish 353
rightism 242.35

rightist 436
rightly 16.190
rightness 300.39
rigid 91.15
rigidify 7.3.1
rigidity 16.333.5
rigmarole 223.3
rigor 9
rigorism 242.35.15
rigor mortis 300.63
rigorous 310.50
rigour 17.129
Rig-Veda 17.79
Rijeka 17.31
rile 219
Riley 16.121
rill 218
rillet 371.16
rim 235
rime 236
Rimini 16.229.3
Rimsky-Korsakov 165
rimy 16.217
rind 135
rinderpest 433
ring 265
ringbolt 405
ringdove 489
ringent 420.23
ringer 17.246
ringgit 371
ringleader 17.82
ringlet 371
ringmaster 17.380
ringside 92
ringworm 233
rink 52
rinse 317
rinser 17.315
Rio 12.2
Rio de Janeiro 12.63
riot 381.2
rioter 17.352.1
riotous 310.68
rip 274
riparian 261.3.21
ripcord 95
ripe 275
ripen 261
ripeness 300
ripieno 12.52
Ripon 261
riposte 438
ripper 17.253
ripping 265

ripple 228.66
ripplet 371
ripply 16.177
ripsnorter 17.345
riptide 92
Rip Van Winkle 228.29
rise 516
risen 261.126
riser 17.441
risibility 16.333.9.2.2
risible 228.16.63
rising 265.82
risk 58
risker 17.48
risky 16.41
Risorgimento 12.84
risotto 12.77
risqué 2
rissole 223.4
ritardando 12.23
rite 372
ritual 228.9.3
ritualism 242.35.11.3
ritualize 516.3.3
ritzy 16.317
rival 228.121
rivalry 16.283
rive 486
riven 261.114
river 17.414
riverbed 86.1
riverine 253.7
riverside 92.8
rivet 371
Riviera 17.271
rivière 4.1
rivulet 371.17
Riyadh 84
riyal 213
roach 70
road 98
roadbed 86
roadblock 40
roadholding 265.18
roadhouse 306
roadroller 17.171
roadrunner 17.237
roadstead 86
roadway 2
roadwork 36
roadworthy 16.375
roam 239
roamer 17.215
roan 257
Roanoke 42

roar 9
roaring 265.55
roast 441
roasting 265
rob 26
robber 17.16
robbery 16.274.3
robe 28
Robert 381
Robespierre 4
robin 252
robinia 17.3.34
Robinson 261
roble 2.13
robot 373
Rob Roy 11
robust 443
roc 40
rocaille 7
rocambole 223
Rochdale 214
Rochester 17.384
rochet 371
rock 40
rockabilly 16.120
rock-and-roll 223
Rockefeller 17.163
rocker 17.36
rockery 16.274.5
rocket 371.10
rocketeer 6
rocketry 16.285
rockfish 353
Rockford 103
Rockies 515
rockrose 520
rocky 16.27
rococo 12.12
rod 94
rode 98
rodent 420
rodenticide 92.7
rodeo 12.3
rodomontade 85
roe 12
roebuck 43
roentgen 261
roentgenogram 229.1
roentgenotherapy 16.254
rogation 261.67.11
rogatory 16.274.43.3
Roger 17.152
Roget 2
rogue 188
roguery 16.274

roguish 353
roil 222
roily 16.125
roister 17.386
Roland 143
role 223
Rolf 173
roll 223
rollbar 1
roller 17.171
rollick 38.22
rolling 265.32
rollmop 276
rollneck 35
Rolls Royce 304
roly-poly 16.126
romaine 247
romaji 16.99
Roman 261.49
romance 314
Romanesque 57
Romanism 242.35.14
Romanist 436.13
Romanize 516.7
Romanov 165
romantic 38.62
romanticism 242.35.16
romanticize 516.10
Romany 16.237
Romberg 182
Rome 239
Romeo 12.3
romp 288
rompers 524
Romulus 310.25
rondeau 12
rondel 228
rondo 12
Roneo 12.3.4
ronggeng 264
roo 15
rood 102
roof 170
roofing 265
rook 44
rookery 16.274
rookie 16.31
room 241
roomful 226
roommate 367
roomy 16.221
Roosevelt 402
roost 444
rooster 17.389
root 380

rootle 228.108
rootless 300
rootstock 40
rope 278
ropewalk 41
ropy 16.251
Roquefort 9
rorqual 228
Rorschach 33
rort 374
Rosa 17.442
rosace 295
rosaceous 310.56
rosarian 261.3.21
Rosario 12.3.5
rosarium 242.2.14
rosary 16.274
Roscius 310.2
Roscommon 261
rose 520
rosé 2.31
roseate 367.1
rosebay 2
rosebud 100
rosehip 274
rosella 17.163
rosemary 16.274
roseola 17.176
Rosetta 17.339
rosette 368
rosewood 101
Rosh Hashanah 17.226
Rosicrucian 261.75
Rosie Lee 5.8
rosin 252
Rosinante 16.353
ROSPA 17.267
Ross 302
Ross and Cromarty
   16.344
Rossetti 16.330
Rossini 16.228
roster 17.385
Rostock 40
Rostov 487
Rostropovich 67
rostrum 242.23
rosy 16.399
rot 373
rota 17.347
Rotarian 261.3.21
rotary 16.274
rotate 367.31
rotation 261.67.28
rotative 485.15.13

rotator 17.338
rote 376
rotgut 378
Rotherham 242.21
Rothermere 6.3
Rothschild 117
roti 16.339
rotifer 17.114
rotisserie 16.274.36
rotogravure 10
rotor 17.347
Rotorua 17.8
rotten 261.101
rottenness 300.31
rotter 17.344
Rotterdam 229
rotting 265.68
Rottweiler 17.167
rotund 140
rotunda 17.108
Rouault 12
rouble 228
roué 2.2
rouge 364
rouge et noir 1.16
rough 168
roughage 197
roughcast 431
roughen 261
roughish 353
roughly 16.159
roughneck 35
roughness 300
roughshod 94
roulade 84
rouleau 12
roulette 368
round 139
roundabout 377.1
rounded 91.14
roundel 228
roundelay 2.11
rounder 17.107
rounders 524
Roundhead 86
roundhouse 306
roundish 353
roundly 16.156
roundness 300
roundsman 261
roundup 279
roundworm 233
roup 280
rouse 521
rousing 265

Rousseau 12
roust 442
rout 377
route 380
routemarch 63
router 17.348
routine 251
roux 15
rove 488
rover 17.417
row 12
row 13
rowan 261.6
rowboat 376
rowdiness 300.23
rowdy 16.68
rowel 228.8
rower 17.6
rowing 265.4
rowlock 46
Roy 11
royal 228.6
royalism 242.35.11
royalist 436.7
royalty 16.352.1
rub 29
rubáiyát 365
rubato 12.73
rubber 17.19
rubberize 516.8
rubberneck 35
rubbery 16.274
rubbing 265
rubbish 353
rubbishy 16.322
rubble 228.14
rube 30
rubella 17.163
rubellite 372.3
Rubens 548
rubeola 17.176
rubescent 420.67
Rubicon 261.13
rubicund 143
rubidium 242.2.3
rubiginous 310.33
Rubinstein 253
rubious 310.2
rubric 38
rubricate 367.5
ruby 16.14
ruche 358
ruching 265
ruck 43
rucksack 32

ruckus 310
ruction 261.79
rudd 100
rudder 17.90
ruddle 228.36
ruddy 16.69
rude 102
rudeness 300
rudiment 420.31
rudimentary 16.274.47
rudish 353
Rudolf 173
rue 15
rueful 226
ruff 168
ruffian 261.3
ruffle 228.42
ruffler 17.191
Rufus 310
rug 189
rugby 16
rugged 91
ruggedness 300.28
rugger 17.134
rugose 305
Ruhr 10
ruin 252
ruination 261.67.18
ruinous 310.33
Ruisdael 213
rule 227
ruler 17.175
ruling 265
rum 240
Rumania 17.3.31
Rumanian 261.3.15
rumba 17.27
rumble 228
rumbustious 310.2
Rumelia 17.3.20
rumen 248.3
ruminant 420.53.3
ruminate 367.17.6
rumination 261.67.18.7
ruminative 485.15.7
rummage 197
rummer 17.216
rummy 16.220
rumour 17.217
rumoured 103.5
rump 289
Rumpelstiltskin 252
rumple 228
rumpus 310.42
run 259

runabout 377.1
Runcorn 255
rundle 228
rune 260
rung 267
runic 38
runnel 228
runner 17.237
running 265.45
runny 16.235
Runnymede 89
runt 419
runway 2
Runyon 261
rupee 5
Rupert 381
rupture 17
rural 228.75
ruralize 516.3
Rurik 38.43
Ruritania 17.3.31.2
ruse 523
Ruse 2.21
rush 356
rushes 515
rushy 16.324
rusk 60
Ruskin 252
Russ 307
Russell 228.87
russet 371
Russia 17.329
Russian 261.74
Russianize 516.7
Russky 16.42
Russophile 219.1
Russophobe 28
rust 443
rustic 38
rusticate 367.5
rustle 228.87
rustler 17.199
rustproof 170
rusty 16.368
rut 378
rutabaga 17.125
Ruth 463
Ruthenia 17.3.33
Ruthenian 261.3.16
ruthenium 242.2
Rutherford 103
ruthful 226.14
ruthless 300
ruthlessness 300.33
rutile 219

Rutland 143
ruttish 353
rutty 16.341
Rwanda 17.98
Ryan 261.4
Rydal 228.33
rye 7
ryot 381.2

S

Saab 19
Saar 1
Saba 17.10
Sabah 1
sabayon 254
sabbat 365
Sabbatarian 261.3.21
Sabbath 464
sabbatical 228.23.18
Sabellian 261.3.9
sabin 252
Sabine 253
sable 228.11
sabotage 359
saboteur 3.1
sabra 17.281
sabre 17.11
sabretache 349
sabulous 310.25
sac 32
saccharide 92.6
saccharify 7.3.4
saccharimeter 17.342.2.1
saccharin 252.20
saccharine 251.7
saccharine 253.7
saccharoid 97.12
saccharose 520.3
sacculate 371.17.1
saccule 227
sacerdotal 228.106
sacerdotalism 242.35.11
sachet 2.22
sack 32
sackbut 378
sackcloth 459
sacking 265
sacral 228
sacrament 420.35
sacramental 228.110.3
Sacramento 12.84
sacrarium 242.2.14
sacred 91
sacredness 300.28

sacrifice 301
sacrificial 228.93
sacrilege 197.1
sacrilegious 310.21
sacristan 261.107
sacristy 16.366
sacroiliac 32.1.1
sacrosanct 391
sacrum 242
sad 83
Sadat 365
sadden 261.19
saddle 228.31
saddlebag 178
saddlecloth 459
saddler 17.183
saddlery 16.274
saddletree 5
Sadducee 5
Sade 84
sadiron 261.4
sadism 242.35
sadist 436
sadistic 38.70
sadly 16.146
sadness 300
sadomasochism 242.35.6
sadomasochistic 38.70
safari 16.261
safe 159
safeguard 84
safekeeping 265.49
safety 16
safflower 14
saffron 261
Safid Rud 102
sag 178
saga 17.124
sagacious 310.56
sagacity 16.333.25
sagamore 9.9
sage 193
sagebrush 356
saggar 17.123
Sagitta 17.342
sagittal 228.102
Sagittarius 310.2.10
sagittate 367.30
sago 12.27
Sahaptin 252.25
Sahara 17.268
Saharan 261
sahib 24
said 86
Saida 17.83

saiga 17.130
Saigon 254
sail 214
sailable 228.16.22
sailcloth 459
sailing 265.27
sailor 17.162
sailplane 247
sainfoin 256
saint 409
St Albans 551
St Andrews 523
Saint Austell 228.116
sainted 91.45
Saint Helena 17.230
Saint Helier 17.3.19
sainthood 101
St Ives 554
St John 261
Saint Kilda 17.95
Saint Kitts 339
Saint Leger 17.147
saintly 16.196
Saint Moritz 339
saintpaulia 17.3
Saint Petersburg 182
Saint Vitus 310.65
Saipan 245
Saïs 300
saithe 454
Saiva 17.415
Sakai 7
sake 16.20
sake 34
saker 17.30
saki 16.20
Saki 16.20
Sakyamuni 16.236
sal 212
salaam 230.1
salacious 310.56.3
salad 103
Saladin 252
salamander 17.98
Salambria 17.3.43
salami 16.211
Salamis 300.20
salaried 91.27
salary 16.274.15
salchow 12
sale 214
saleable 228.16.22
Salem 242
salep 271
saleroom 241

salesclerk 33
salesman 261
salesmanship 274.2
Salford 103
Salian 261.3.8
salic 38.19
salicet 368.7
salicin 252.21
salicornia 17.3.35
salicylate 367.12
salient 420.1
salina 17.232
saline 253
Salinger 17.157
salinity 16.333.17.1
salinometer 17.342.3
Salisbury 16.274
Salish 353
saliva 17.415
salivary 16.274.52
salivate 367.36
salivation 261.67
sallet 371
sallow 12.38
Sallust 445
sally 16.112
Sally 16.112
salmagundi 16.80
Salmanazar 17.437
salmon 261.44
salmonella 17.163
salmonoid 97.9
Salome 16.219
salon 254
Salonika 17.34.1
saloon 260.1
saloop 280.1
Salop 281
salopette 368
salpicon 261.13
salpiglossis 300.54
salsify 16.85
salt 404
saltarello 12.40
saltatorial 228.3.12.2
saltcellar 17.163
salted 91.44
salter 17.363
saltern 261
saltfish 353
saltigrade 85.5
saltire 8
saltpetre 17.341
saltwater 17.345
salty 16.351

salubrious 310.2
Saluki 16.32
salutary 16.274.42
salutation 261.67.29
salutatory 16.274.43
salute 380.1
Salvador 9.4
salvage 197
salvageable 228.16.20
salvation 261.67
salvationist 436.13.4
salve 491
salver 17.420
salvia 17.3
salvo 12
sal volatile 16.120
salvor 17.420
Salyut 380
Samaria 17.3.38
Samaritan 261.99
samarium 242.2.14
Samarkand 128
samba 17.23
same 231
sameness 300
Samian 261.3
samisen 248
samite 372
Samnium 242.2
Samoa 17.6
Samos 302
Samothrace 295
samovar 1.15
Samoyed 86
sampan 245
samphire 8
sample 228.70
sampler 17
Samson 261
Samuel 228.9
samurai 7
San 246
sanatorium 242.2.17
sanbenito 12.76
San Bernardino 12.54
sanctify 7.3
sanctimonious 310.2.9.1
sanctimony 16.237
sanction 261
sanctitude 102.2
sanctity 16.333
sanctuary 16.274.2
sanctum 242
sanctum sanctorum
 242.20

Sanctus 310
sand 128
sandal 228.39
sandalwood 101
sandarac 32.3
sandbag 178
sandbank 51
sandblast 431
sander 17.98
sanderling 265
sandfly 7
sandgrouse 306
Sandhurst 434
San Diego 12.27
sandman 261
sandpaper 17.249
sandpiper 17.254
sandpit 371
Sandringham 242.17
sandsoap 278
sandstone 257
sandstorm 238
sandwich 197
sandy 16.77
sane 247
San Fernando 12.23
San Francisco 12.15
sang 263
Sangraal 214
sangria 17.2
sanguinary 16.274.26
sanguine 252
sanguineous 310.2.8
sanguinolent 420.28
Sanhedrin 252
sanicle 228.23.10
sanies 513.1
sanitarium 242.2.14
sanitary 16.274.41
sanitation 261.67.27
sanitize 516.12
sanity 16.333.14
San Jose 2.31
San Juan 246
sank 51
San Marino 12.54
sannyasi 16.295
San Salvador 9.4
sans-culotte 373
sanserif 163.2
sansevieria 17.3.39
Sanskrit 371
Sanskritic 38.52
San Stefano 12.51
Santa 17.365

Santa Claus 518
Santa Cruz 523
Santa Fe 2.9
Santee 5
Santiago 12.26
Santo Domingo 12.36
santonica 17.34.1
sap 268
sapele 16.118
saphena 17.230
sapid 91
sapient 420.1
sapling 265
sapodilla 17.166
saponaceous 310.56
saponify 7.3
sapota 17.347
sapper 17.247
Sapphic 38.11
sapphire 8
sapphirine 251.7
Sappho 12
sappy 16.243
sapraemia 17.3.26
sapsago 12.33
sapsucker 17.39
saraband 128
Saracen 261
Saracenic 38.32
Saragossa 17.304
Sarah 17.271
saran 245.5
Saratoga 17.133
Sarawak 46
sarcasm 242.34
sarcastic 38.68
sarcoid 97
sarcoma 17.215
sarcophagus 310
sarcous 310.8
sard 84
Sardanapalus 310.26
sardine 251
Sardinia 17.3.34
Sardinian 261.3.17
Sardis 300
sardius 310.2
sardonic 38.35
sardonyx 498
sargasso 12.68
sargassum 242
sarge 192
Sargent 420
Sargon 254
sari 16.261

Sark 33
Sarnia 17.3.30
sarong 266.2
saros 302
sarracenia 17.3.33
sarsaparilla 17.166.3
sarsen 261.61
sartor 17.337
sartorial 228.3.12
sartorius 310.2.13
Sarum 242.18
sash 349
Saskatchewan 261
saskatoon 260.4
Saskatoon 260.4
sass 293
sassaby 16.15
sassafras 293
Sassanid 91.21
Sassenach 32
Sassoon 260
sassy 16.294
sastruga 17.136
sat 365
satai 2
Satan 261
satanic 38.31
Satanism 242.35.14
Satanist 436.13
satchel 228
sate 367
sateen 251
satellite 372.4.1
satellitium 242.2.18
satiable 228.16
satiate 367.1.5
satiety 16.333.2
satin 252
satinet 368
satinwood 101
satiny 16.229
satire 8
satiric 38.40
satirical 228.23.16
satirist 436.20
satirize 516.8
satisfaction 261.76
satisfactory 16.274.44
satisfy 7
satrap 281
satsuma 17.217
saturable 228.16.35
saturate 367.22
saturated 91.34.7
saturation 261.67.22

Saturday 2.8
Saturn 249
Saturnalia 17.3.18.1
saturniid 91.2
saturnine 253
saturnism 242.35.14
satyagrahi 5
satyr 17.336
satyriasis 300.57.1
satyric 38.40
satyrid 91
sauce 303
saucepan 261
saucer 17.305
sauciness 300.23
saucy 16.303
Saud 99
Saudi 16.68
sauerkraut 377
sauger 17.132
Saul 221
sauna 17.234
saunter 17.370
saurian 261.3.23
sauropod 94.1
saury 16.269
sausage 197
sauté 2.24
Sauternes 249
savage 197
savagery 16.282
savanna 17.225
Savannah 17.225
savant 420
savate 365.3
save 482
saveloy 11.1
saver 17.410
savin 252
saving 265.77
saviour 17.436
savoir-faire 4.2
savour 17.410
savoury 16.274.50
savoy 11
Savoy 11
Savoyard 84
savvy 16.377
saw 9
sawbones 550
sawdust 443
sawfish 353
sawhorse 303
sawmill 218
sawn 255

sawyer 17.430
sax 494
saxhorn 255
saxicolous 310.26.2
saxifrage 193
Saxon 261
saxony oniony 16.237
saxophone 257
saxophonic 38.35.2
saxophonist 436.13
say 2
saying 265.1
sayyid 91
sazerac 32.3
scab 18
scabbard 103
scabby 16.5
scabies 513
scabious 310.2
scabrous 310
scad 83
scads 525
Scafell 215
scaffold 122
scaffolding 265
scagliola 17.171
scalable 228.16.22
scalar 17.162
scald 118
scale 214
scaleboard 95
scalene 251
scalenus 310.32
scaler 17.162
scallion 261.118
scallop 281.2
scallywag 178
scaloppine 16.228
scalp 282
scalpel 228
scalping 265
scaly 16.114
scammony 16.237
scamp 285
scamper 17.261
scampi 16
scan 245
scandal 228.39
scandalize 516.3
scandalmonger 17.143
scandalous 310.26
Scandaroon 260.3
Scanderbeg 181
Scandian 261.3

scombroid 97
sconce 318
scone 254
scone 257
Scone 260
scoop 280
scoot 380
scooter 17.351
scop 276
Scopas 310.39
scope 278
scopula 17.174.10
scorbutic 38.56
scorch 69
scorcher 17.58
scorching 265
score 9
scoreboard 95
scorecard 84
scorer 17.276
scoria 17.3.41
scorify 7.3
scorn 255
scornful 226
scornfulness 300.30
scorpaenid 91.20
scorpaenoid 97.7
scorper 17.256
Scorpio 12.3
scorpioid 97
scorpion 261.3
Scot 373
scotch 68
Scotch 68
Scotchman 261
scoter 17.347
scotia 17.328
Scotland 143
scotoma 17.215
scotopia 17.3.37.3
Scots 341
Scotsman 261
Scott 373
Scotticism 242.35.16.5
Scottie 16.335
Scottish 353
scoundrel 228
scour 14
scourge 195
scouse 306
scout 377
scouter 17.348
Scouting 265
scoutmaster 17.380
scow 13

scowl 224
scrabble 228
scrag 178
scraggy 16.91
scram 229
scramble 228.17
scrambler 17.179
Scranton 261
scrap 268
scrapbook 44
scrape 270
scraper 17.249
scraperboard 95.1
scrapheap 273
scrappy 16.243
scratch 62
scratchy 16.46
scrawl 221
scrawny 16.232
scream 234
screamer 17.210
scree 5
screech 66
screed 89
screen 251
screenings 552
screenplay 2
screw 15
screwball 221
screwdriver 17.415
screwy 16.4
Scriabin 252
scribble 228.12
scribbly 16.134
scribe 25
scriber 17.15
scrim 235
scrimmage 197.3
scrimp 287
scrimshank 51
scrimshaw 9
scrip 274
script 424
scriptorium 242.2.17
scriptural 228.76
scripture 17
scriptwriter 17.343
scrofula 17.174
scrofulous 310.25
scroll 223
Scrooge 204
scrotum 242.31
scrouge 202
scrounge 210
scrounger 17.158

scrub 29
scrubber 17.19
scrubby 16.13
scrubland 143
scruff 168
scruffy 16.88
scrum 240
scrummage 197
scrump 289
scrumptious 310
scrumpy 16.257
scrunch 82
scruple 228
scrupulous 310.25
scrupulousness 300.34
scrutator 17.338
scrutineer 6.4
scrutinize 516.6
scrutiny 16.229
scry 7
scuba 17.20
scud 100
scuff 168
scuffle 228.42
scull 225
scullery 16.274
scullion 261.3.13
sculpt 427
sculptor 17
sculptural 228.76
sculpture 17
sculpturesque 57
scum 240
scumble 228
scuncheon 261
scunge 211
scungy 16.111
scunner 17.237
Scunthorpe 277
scup 279
scupper 17.258
scurf 161
scurrilous 310.23
scurry 16.272
scurvy 16.381
scut 378
scutate 367
scutcheon 261
scutellation 261.67.12
scutellum 242.8
scutter 17.349
scuttle 228.107
scuttlebutt 378
scutum 242
Scylla 17.166

scyphus 310
scythe 477
Scythia 17.3
Scythian 261.3
sea 5
seaboard 95
seaborne 255
seacoast 441
seacock 40
seadog 185
seafarer 17.271
seafaring 265.52
seafood 102
seafront 419
seagirt 369
seagoing 265.4
seal 217
sealant 420
sealer 17.165
sealery 16.274
sealskin 252
Sealyham 242.2.5
seam 234
seaman 261.47
seamanly 16.174
seamanship 274.2
seamark 33
seamless 300
seamount 418
seamstress 300
seamy 16.215
Sean 255
seance 315
seaplane 247
seaport 374
seaquake 34
sear 6
search 65
searcher 17.54
searching 265
searchlight 372
searing 265.53
seascape 270
seashell 215
seashore 9
seasick 38
seasickness 300.27
seaside 92
season 261.125
seasonable 228.16.31.2
seasonal 228.63
seasoning 265.46
seat 370
seated 91.37
seating 265

Seaton 261.98
Seattle 228.97
seaward 103
seawards 531
seaware 4
seaway 2
seaweed 89
seaworthy 16.375
sebaceous 310.56
Sebastopol 228
sebum 242
sec 35
secant 420.6
secateurs 511
secede 89.2
secession 261.68
seclude 102
secluded 91
seclusion 261.93
seclusive 485.8
second 136
second 143
secondary 16.274
second-best 433
seconder 17.109
second-hand 128
secondly 16.157
secondment 420
second-rate 367
second-sight 372
secrecy 16.300
secret 371
secretarial 228.3.10
secretariat 381.1
secretary 16.274.43
secrete 370
secretion 261.70
secretive 485.12
secretory 16.274
sect 385
sectarian 261.3.21
sectary 16.274.45
sectile 219.5
section 261.77
sectional 228.63.8
sector 17.354
secular 17.174.4
secularity 16.333.20.3
secularize 516.8.1
secure 10.3
security 16.333.23
sedan 245.1
sedate 367.8
sedation 261.67.7
sedative 485.15

sedentary 16.274.48
Seder 17.79
sedge 194
Sedgemoor 10
sediment 420.31.1
sedimentary 16.274.47
sedimentation
  261.67.32.1
sedimentous 310.70
sedition 261.71.1
seditionary 16.274.29.3
seditious 310.58.1
seduce 309
seducer 17.308
seduction 261.79
seductive 485.19
seductress 300
sedulous 310.25.3
sedum 242
see 5
Seebeck 35
seed 89
seedbed 86
seedcake 34
seedcase 295
seeder 17.82
seedless 300
seedling 265
seedy 16.62
seeing 265.2
seek 37
seeker 17.33
seem 234
seeming 265.36
seemingly 16.175
seemly 16.166
seen 251
seep 273
seepage 197
seer 17.2
seersucker 17.39
seesaw 9
seethe 475
Seferis 300.44
segment 420
segmental 228.110
segmentation 261.67.32
Segovia 17.3.55
segregate 367.10
segregation 261.67.10
segregationist 436.13.4
seigneur 3
Seine 247
seisin 252
seism 242

seismic 38
seismograph 158.1
seismography 16.90.2
seismology 16.108.4
seismoscope 278.1
seize 513
seizing 265
seizure 17.334
sejant 420
Sekondi 5
Selangor 17.245
seldom 242
select 385.4
selection 261.77.2
selective 485.17
selectivity 16.333.35
selector 17.354
selenite 372.5
selenium 242.2
selenography 16.90.2
selenology 16.108.4.10
Seleucid 91.30
Seleucus 310.13
self 172
self-assured 96
self-catering 265.58
self-centred 103
self-confidence 321.5
self-confident 420.10
self-conscious 310
self-contained 130
self-control 223
self-deception 261.84
self-defence 316
self-denial 228.4
self-esteem 234
selfheal 217
selfhood 101
self-indulgent 420.21
self-inflicted 91
selfish 353.3
selfishness 300.35
selfless 300
selflessness 300.33
self-made 85
self-opinionated 91.34
self-pity 16.333
self-portrait 371
self-possessed 433
self-possession 261.68
self-propelled 113
self-raising 265.81
self-respect 385
self-respecting 265.71
self-righteous 310

self-sacrifice 301
selfsame 231
self-service 300
self-sufficient 420.74
self-taught 374
self-willed 116
Seljuk 45
Selkirk 36
sell 215
seller 17.163
Sellotape 270
selva 17.421
selvage 197
semantic 38.62
semantics 498.14
semaphore 9.6
semaphoric 38.41
semblance 321.13
semen 248
semester 17.382
semi 16.213
semiaquatic 38.49
semiarid 91.25
semiautomatic 38.49.2
semibold 120
semibreve 484
semicircle 228.22
semicircular 17.174.5
semicolon 261.43
semiconductor 17.357
semiconscious 310
semiconsciousness
  300.34
semidetached 395
semifinal 228.61
semifinalist 436.7
semifluid 91.3
semiliterate 371.35
semilunar 17.238
seminal 228.60.3
seminar 1
seminarian 261.3.21.1
seminary 16.274.26
Seminole 223
semiotic 38.53
semiotics 498
semiparasitic 38.52.3
semiprecious 310
semipro 12
semiprofessional
  228.63.4
semiquaver 17.410
Semiramis 300.20
semirigid 91.15
semiskilled 116

semisolid 91.18
Semite 372
Semitic 38.52
Semitist 436.24
semitone 257.2
semivowel 228.8
semolina 17.230
sempiternal 228.58
senate 371
senator 17.352
senatorial 228.3.12.2
send 131
Sendai 7
sendel 228
sender 17.101
sendoff 165
Seneca 17.34
Senegal 221
Senegambia 17.3.5
senescence 321.21
senescent 420.67.1
seneschal 228.93
senile 219
senility 16.333.9.3
senior 17.435
seniority 16.333.22
Senlac 32
senna 17.228
Sennacherib 24
señor 9
señorita 17.341
sensate 367.29
sensation 261.67.26
sensational 228.63.3
sensationalism
  242.35.11.5.2
sensationalist 436.7.5
sensationalistic 38.70.2
sense 316
senseless 300.16
senselessness 300.33.1
sensibilia 17.3.21
sensibility 16.333.9.2
sensible 228.16.40
sensitive 485.12
sensitivity 16.333.35
sensitize 516.12
sensitometer 17.342.3
sensor 17.314
sensorium 242.2.17
sensory 16.274.38
sensual 228.9
sensualism 242.35.11.3
sensualist 436.7.3
sensuality 16.333.8.2

sensuous 310.4
sensuousness 300.34.2
sent 410
sentence 321.26
sententious 310.61
sentience 321
sentient 420.1
sentiment 420.31
sentimental 228.110.2
sentimentalism
    242.35.11.6
sentimentality
    16.333.8.10
sentimentalize 516.3
sentinel 228.60
sentry 16.288
Senussi 16.306
Seoul 223
sepal 228
separable 228.16.35.1
separate 367.23
separate 371.35
separates 339
separation 261.67.22
separatism 242.35.20
separatist 436.26
separative 485.15.10
separator 17.338.9
separatrix 498.9
sepia 17.3
sepoy 11
sepsis 300.59
sept 422
septa 17.375
September 17.24
Septembrist 436
septet 368
septic 38.65
septicaemia 17.3.26
septuagenarian
    261.3.21.1
Septuagesima 17.211
Septuagint 412
septuple 228
sepulchral 228
sepulchre 17
sepulture 17.69
sequel 228.71
sequence 321
sequencer 17.318
sequent 420.57
sequential 228.96
sequester 17.382
sequestrate 367
sequestration 261.67

sequin 252
sequined 134
sequoia 17.5
sera 17.272
seraglio 12.3
serail 7.12
Serang 263.2
seraph 171
seraphic 38.11
seraphim 235
Serb 22
Serbia 17.3.2
Serbian 261.3
sere 6
serein 247.8
serenade 85.2
serendipity 16.333
serene 251
serenity 16.333.15
serf 161
serfdom 242
serge 195
sergeant 420
serial 228.3.11
serialism 242.35.11.2.1
serialize 516.3.2.1
seriatim 235
sericeous 310.58
sericin 252.21
sericulture 17.69
seriema 17.210
series 513.11
series-wound 139
serif 163.2
serigraph 158
serious 310.2.11
seriously 16.184
seriousness 300.34.1
sermon 261
sermonic 38.35
sermonize 516.7
serous 310.45
serpent 420
serpentine 253
serpigo 12.30
serrate 367
serrate 371.31
serrated 91.34.7
serration 261.67
serried 91
serrulation 261.67.13
Sertorius 310.2.13
serum 242.19
serval 228
servant 420.82

serve 483
server 17.412
Servetus 310.63
service 300
serviceable 228.16.39
serviceberry 16.274
serviceman 261
serviette 368
servile 219
servility 16.333.9
serving 265.78
servitor 17.342
servitude 102.2
servo 12
servomechanism
    242.35.14
sesame 16.222
sesquipedalian 261.3.8
sessile 219
session 261.68
sesterce 297
sestertium 242.2
sestet 368
sestina 17.230
Sestos 302.3
set 368
seta 17.341
Seth 455
setose 305
sett 368
settee 5
setter 17.339
setting 265.65
settle 228.100
settlement 420.40
Sevan 246
seven 261.112
sevenfold 120
seventeen 251
seventeenth 469
seventh 471.1
seventieth 458
seventy 16.360
sever 17.411
several 228.76
severally 16.131
severalty 16.352
severance 321.20.1
severe 6.11
severity 16.333.21
Severn 261.112
Severus 310.45
Seville 218.3
sew 12
sewage 197

sheik 34
sheikdom 242
Sheila 17.165
shekel 228.21
sheldrake 34
shelduck 43
shelf 172
shell 215
she'll 217
shellac 32
shellback 32
Shelley 16.115
shellfire 8
shellfish 353.3
shell-like 39
shellproof 170
Shelta 17.361
shelter 17.361
shelve 492
shelving 265
Shem 232
Shema 1.12
Shenandoah 17.6
shenanigan 261.32
Shenyang 263
Sheol 223
shepherd 103
Sheraton 261
sherbet 381
Sheridan 261.24
sheriff 163.2
Sherman 261
Sherpa 17.251
sherry 16.262
Sherwood 101
she's 513
Shetland 143
shewbread 86
shiai 7
shibboleth 455
shield 115
shielder 17.94
shieling 265.29
shift 398
shiftless 300
shifty 16.347
shih-tzu 15
Shiism 242.35.1
Shiite 372
shillelagh 17.162
shilling 265.30
Shillong 266
shillyshally 16.112
Shiloh 12
shim 235

shimmer 17.211
shimmy 16.216
Shimonoseki 16.22
shin 252
shinbone 257
shindig 184
shindy 16.79
shine 253
shiner 17.232
shingle 228.50
shingles 539
shingly 16.163
Shinto 12
shinty 16.356
shiny 16.230
ship 274
shipboard 95
shipbuilder 17.95
shipbuilding 265.17
shipload 98
shipmate 367
shipment 420.43
shipowner 17.236
shipper 17.253
shipping 265
shipshape 270
shipway 2
shipwreck 35
shipwright 372
shipyard 84
shiralee 5.9
Shiraz 508
shire 8
Shiré 2
shirk 36
shirker 17.32
shirr 3
shirring 265.51
shirt 369
shirting 265
shirtsleeve 484
shirtwaister 17.381
shirty 16.331
shit 371
Shittim 235
shitty 16.333
shive 486
shiver 17.414
shivery 16.274.51
shoal 223
shoat 376
shock 40
shocker 17.36
shocking 265.8
shockproof 170

shod 94
shoddy 16.65
shoe 15
shoebill 218
shoeblack 32
shoehorn 255
shoelace 295
shoemaker 17.30
shoeshine 253
shoestring 265
shoetree 5
shofar 1
shoji 5
shone 254
shoo 15
shoofly 7
shook 44
shoon 260
shoot 380
shooting 265
shop 276
shopkeeper 17.252
shoplifter 17.359
shoplifting 265
shopper 17.255
shopping 265
shopsoiled 119
shoptalk 41
shopwalker 17.37
shore 9
shoreless 300
shoreline 253
shoreward 103.8
shorn 255
short 374
shortage 197
shortbread 86
shortcake 34
shortcoming 265.38
shorten 261.102
shortening 265.46
shortfall 221
short-haired 88
shorthand 128
shorthorn 255
shortie 16.336
shortly 16.192
shortness 300
shorts 342
short-sighted 91.39
short-sightedness 300.28
Shoshone 16.233
Shostakovich 67
shot 373
shotgun 259

sigmoid 97
Sigmund 143
sign 253
signal 228
signalize 516.3
signaller 17.176
signally 16.131
signalman 261
signatory 16.274.43
signature 17.56
signboard 95
signet 371.29
significance 321
significant 420.7
significative 485.15.1
signify 7.3.3
signor 9
signora 17.276
signori 16.269
signorina 17.230
signpost 441
Sigurd 96
sika 17.33
Sikh 37
Sikkim 235
silage 197
sild 116
silence 321
silencer 17.318
silent 420
Silenus 310.32
Silesia 17.3.60
silex 496
silhouette 368.1
silica 17.34
silicate 371.9
silicic 38
silicide 92.7
silicle 228.23.7
silicon 261.13
silicone 257
silicosis 300.55
silk 49
silken 261
silkiness 300.23
silkworm 233
silky 16.34
sill 218
silliness 300.23
silly 16.120
silo 12
silt 403
silty 16.350
Silurian 261.3.24
Silvanus 310.31

silver 17.422
silverfish 353
silverpoint 416.1
silverside 92.8
silversmith 458
silverware 4.8
silverweed 89
silvery 16.274
Simeon 261.3.14
simian 261.3.14
similar 17.166
similarity 16.333.20.2
simile 16.120
similitude 102.2
simmer 17.211
simnel 228
Simon 261
simoniac 32.1
Simonides 513.4
simony 16.237
simoom 241
simpatico 12.11
simper 17.263
simple 228
simpleton 261
simplex 496
simplicity 16.333.28
simplify 7.3
simplistic 38.70
simply 16.179
Simpson 261
simulant 420.27
simulate 367.13.5
simulated 91.34
simulation 261.67.13.3
simulator 17.338.6
simulcast 431
simultaneous 310.2.6
sin 252
Sinai 7
sinapism 242.35
Sinatra 17.292
since 317
sincere 6
sincerely 16.119
sincerity 16.333.21
sinciput 378
Sinclair 4
Sind 134
Sindhi 16.79
sine 16.230
sine 253
sinecure 10.3
sine qua non 254

sinew 15.9
sinfonietta 17.339
sinful 226
sing 265
Singapore 9
singe 209
singer 17.246
singing 265.47
single 228.50
single-handed 91.12
single-minded 91
single-mindedness
  300.28
singles 539
singlet 371
singleton 261
singly 16.163
singsong 266
singular 17.174
singularity 16.333.20.3
singularize 516.8.1
singultus 310
Sinhailien 248
Sinhalese 513.7
Sining 265.42
sinister 17.384.1
sinistral 228.82
sinistrorse 303
Sinitic 38.52
sink 52
sinkable 228.16.11
sinker 17.44
sinking 265.10
sinless 300
sinner 17.231
Sinn Fein 247
Sinology 16.108.4
sinter 17.369
sinuate 371.2
sinuosity 16.333.30.2
sinuous 310.4.3
sinus 310.34
sinusitis 300.62
sinusoid 97
sinusoidal 228.35
Sioux 15
sip 274
siphon 261
siphonophore 9.6
Siple 228.67
sippet 371
sir 3
sirdar 1
sire 8
siren 261.58

slanderous

sirenian 261.3.16
Sirius 310.2.12
sirloin 256
sirocco 12
sirrah 17.273
sirree 5.17
sis 300
sisal 228
Sisera 17.279.2
siskin 252
Sisley 16.181
sissy 16.300
sister 17.384
sisterhood 101
sister-in-law 9
sisterly 16.131
Sistine 251
Sisyphean 261.2
Sisyphus 310
sit 371
sitar 1
sitcom 237
site 372
sitology 16.108.4.14
sitosterol 220.4
sitter 17.342
sitting 265.66
situate 367.2.1
situation 261.67.2
situla 17.174.12
situs 310.65
Sitwell 228
sitzkrieg 183
sitzmark 33
Siva 17.413
siwash 354
six 498
sixain 247
sixfold 120
six-footer 17.350
sixpence 321
sixpenny 16.237
sixte 451
sixteen 251
sixteenth 469
sixtieth 458
sixty 16
sizable 228.16.64
size 516
sized 154
sizzle 228
sjambok 40
Skagen 261
Skagerrak 32.3
skate 367

skateboard 95
skater 17.338
skating 265.64
skean 251
skedaddle 228.31
skeet 370
skeg 181
skein 247
skeletal 228.102
skeleton 261.99
skeletonize 516.7
skelf 172
Skelmersdale 214
skelp 283
skep 271
skerry 16.262
sketch 64
sketchbook 44
sketchy 16.48
skew 15
skewbald 118
skewer 17.8
skewwhiff 163
ski 5
skiascope 278.1.1
skibob 26
skid 91
skidlid 91
skidpan 245
skidproof 170
skidway 2
skier 17.2
skiff 163
skiffle 228.41
skiing 265.2
skijoring 265.55
skilful 226.3
skill 218
skilled 116
skillet 371.16
skillion 261.3.11
skim 235
skimmer 17.211
skimmia 17.3.27
skimp 287
skimpy 16.255
skin 252
skinflint 412
skinful 226
skinhead 86.4
skink 52
skinless 300
skinner 17.231
skinny 16.229
skint 412

skintight 372
skip 274
skipjack 32
skiplane 247
skipper 17.253
skipping 265
Skipton 261
skirl 216
skirmish 353
skirret 371.33
skirt 369
skirter 17.340
skirting 265
skit 371
skite 372
skitter 17.342
skittish 353
skittle 228.102
skittles 539
skive 486
skiver 17.415
skivvy 16.382
skoal 223
skua 17.8
skulduggery 16.274.10
skulk 50
skull 225
skullcap 268
skunk 54
sky 7
skydive 486
Skye 7
skyjack 32
Skylab 18
skylark 33
skylight 372
skyline 253
skyrocket 371.10
Skyros 302
skysail 214
skyscraper 17.249
skywriting 265.67
slab 18
slack 32
slacken 261
slacker 17.28
slacks 494
slag 178
slain 247
slaister 17.381
slake 34
slalom 242
slam 229
slander 17.99
slanderous 310.50

sluttish 353
sly 7
slyness 300
slype 275
smack 32
smacker 17.28
small 221
smallboy 11
smallholder 17.97
smallholding 265.18
smallish 353
smallness 300
smallpox 499
smalt 404
smarm 230
smarmy 16.211
smart 366
smart aleck 38.19
smarten 261.95
smartie 16.328
smartness 300
smash 349
smasher 17.321
smashing 265
smatter 17.336
smattering 265.58
smear 6
smectic 38.60
smegma 17.221
smell 215
smelly 16.115
smelt 402
smelter 17.361
smew 15
smidgen 261.37
smilax 494
smile 219
smirch 65
smirk 36
smite 372
Smith 458
smithereens 547
Smithsonian 261.3.18
smithy 16.376
smitten 261.99
smock 40
smocking 265.8
smog 185
smoke 42
smokejack 32
smokeless 300
smoker 17.38
smokestack 32
smoking 265
smoko 12.12

smoky 16.29
Smollett 371
smolt 405
smooch 74
smoodge 204
smooth 479
smoothbore 9
smoothen 261
smoothness 300
smorgasbord 95
smote 376
smother 17.408
smoulder 17.97
smriti 16.333
smudge 203
smudgy 16.107
smug 189
smuggle 228
smuggler 17.193
smuggling 265
smugly 16.161
smugness 300
smut 378
smutty 16.341
Smyrna 17.229
snack 32
snackette 368
snaffle 228
snafu 15
snag 178
snail 214
snake 34
snakebite 372
snakelike 39
snakeroot 380
snakeskin 252
snaky 16.21
snap 268
snapdragon 261.30
snapper 17.247
snappy 16.243
snapshot 373
snare 4
snarl 213
snatch 62
snatchy 16.46
snazzy 16.391
sneak 37
sneakers 524
sneaking 265
sneaky 16.24
sneck 35
sneer 6
sneeze 513
snib 24

snick 38
snicker 17.34
snicket 371.9
snide 92
sniff 163
sniffle 228.41
sniffy 16.85
snifter 17.359
snigger 17.129
snip 274
snipe 275
sniper 17.254
snippet 371
snips 327
snitch 67
snivel 228.120
snivelling 265
snob 26
snobbery 16.274.3
snobbish 353
snobbishness 300.35
Sno-Cat 365
snog 185
snood 102
snook 45
snooker 17.41
snoop 280
snooper 17.259
snooperscope 278.1
snoot 380
snooty 16.343
snooze 523
snore 9
snorer 17.276
snorkel 228
snort 374
snorter 17.345
snot 373
snotty 16.335
snout 377
snow 12
snowball 221
snowballing 265.31
snowberry 16.274
snowbird 87
snowblink 52
snowbound 139
snowcap 268
snowcapped 421
Snowdon 261
Snowdonia 17.3.36
snowdrift 398
snowdrop 276
snowfall 221
snowfield 115

snowflake 34
snowman 261.49
snowmobile 217
snowplough 13
snowshoe 15
snowstorm 238
snowy 16.3
snub 29
snuff 168
snuffbox 499
snuffer 17.118
snuffle 228.42
snuffly 16.159
snuffy 16.88
snug 189
snuggery 16.274.10
snuggle 228
so 12
soak 42
soaking 265
so-and-so 12
soap 278
soapbark 33
soapbox 499
soapstone 257
soapwort 369
soapy 16.251
soar 9
sob 26
sobeit 371
sober 17.18
soberness 300.26
sobriety 16.333.2
sobriquet 2.7
soccer 17.36
sociable 228.16.44
social 228.94
socialism 242.35.11
socialist 436.7
socialistic 38.70.2
socialite 372.4
sociality 16.333.8.1
socialize 516.3
society 16.333.2
Socinian 261.3.17
sociobiology 16.108.4.2
socioeconomic 38.29.1
sociologist 436.4
sociology 16.108.4.1
sociometry 16.285.2.1
sociopath 452
sock 40
sockdologer 17.154
socket 371.10
sockeye 7

socle 228.25
socman 261
Socrates 513.17
Socratic 38.49
sod 94
soda 17.88
sodality 16.333.8
sodamide 92.3
sodden 261.26
sodding 265
sodium 242.2.4
Sodom 242
sodomite 372
sodomy 16.222
sofa 17.117
sofar 1
soffit 371
Sofia 17.3.11
soft 399
softa 17.360
soften 261
softener 17.239
softhearted 91.33
softheartedness 300.28
softness 300
software 4
softwood 101
softy 16.348
SOGAT 365
soggy 16.94
soh 12
Soho 12
soignée 2
soil 222
soilage 197
soiree 2.17
sojourn 249
solace 300.9
solander 17.98
solanum 242
solar 17.171
solarimeter 17.342.2.1
solarium 242.2.14
solarize 516.8
sold 120
solder 17.97
solderer 17.279
soldier 17
soldierly 16.131
soldiery 16.274
sole 223
solecism 242.35.16.2
solely 16.164
solemn 242
solemnify 7.3

solemnity 16.333
solemnize 516
solenodon 261
solenoid 97.8
Solent 420
sol-fa 1
solfeggio 12.3
solicit 371.36
solicitor 17.342
solicitous 310.64
solicitude 102.2
solid 91.18
solidago 12.27
solidarity 16.333.20
solidify 7.3.1
solidity 16.333.5
solidus 310
Solihull 225
soliloquize 516
soliloquy 16.259
solipsism 242.35
solitaire 4
solitary 16.274.41
solitude 102.2
solleret 368.6
sollicitation 261.67.27
solo 12.44
soloist 436
Solomon 261.52
Solomonic 38.35.3
Solon 261.43
solonetz 336
solstice 300
solubility 16.333.9
soluble 228.15
solute 380
solution 261.75.1
solve 493
solvency 16.312
solvent 420
Solway 2
soma 17.215
Somali 16.113
Somalia 17.3.17
Somaliland 143.2
somatic 38.49
somatotype 275.1
sombre 17.26
sombrero 12.62
some 240
somebody 16.72
someday 2
somehow 13
someone 259
someplace 295

somersault 404.1
Somerset 371
something 265
sometime 236
sometimes 542
someway 2
somewhat 373
somewhere 4
somewise 516
sommelier 2
somnambulate 367.13
somnambulism
   242.35.10
somnambulist 436.6
somniloquy 16.259
somnolence 321.12
somnolent 420.28
son 259
sonant 420.54
sonar 1
sonata 17.337
sonatina 17.230
sondage 359
sonde 136
Sondheim 236
sone 257
son et lumière 4.1
song 266
songbird 87
songful 226
songwriter 17.343
sonic 38.35
son-in-law 9
sonnet 371.25
sonneteer 6
sonny 16.235
sonority 16.333.22
sonorous 310.50
Soochow 13
soon 260
sooner 17.238
soot 379
sooth 463
soothe 479
soothing 265
soothsay 2
soothsayer 17.1
soothsaying 265.1
sooty 16.342
sop 276
Sophie 16.87
sophism 242.35
sophist 436
sophistic 38.70
sophisticate 367.5

sophisticate 371.9
sophisticated 91.34.3
sophistication 261.67.5
sophistry 16.293
Sophocles 513
sophomore 9.9
Sophy 16.87
sopor 17.257
soporific 38.12.1
sopping 265
soppy 16.250
soprano 12.51
sorb 27
sorbet 371
sorcerer 17.279
sorceress 300.47
sorcery 16.274
sordid 91.9
sordidness 300.28
sore 9
soredium 242.2.2
sorehead 86
sorely 16.123
soreness 300.24
sorghum 242
sorgo 12
sori 7.11
sororate 367.23
sororicide 92.7
sorority 16.333.22
sorption 261.87
sorrel 228.73
Sorrento 12.84
sorrow 12.65
sorrowful 226.2
sorry 16.268
sort 374
sorter 17.345
sortie 16.336
sortilege 197.1
sortition 261.71
sorus 310.48
SOS 296
so-so 12.70
sostenuto 12.80
sot 373
soteriology 16.108.4.1
Sothic 38
sotto voce 16.50
sou 15
soubise 513
soubrette 368
souchong 266
soufflé 2
sough 13

sought 374
soul 223
soulful 226
soulless 300
sound 139
soundbox 499
sounder 17.107
sounding 265.22
soundless 300
soundly 16.156
soundness 300
soundpost 441
soundproof 170
soundtrack 32
soup 280
soupy 16.253
sour 14
source 303
sourdine 251
sourly 16.127
sourness 300
sourpuss 308
soursop 276
Sousa 17.444
sousaphone 257
souse 306
soutache 349
soutane 245.6
souterrain 247.8
south 462
Southampton 261
southbound 139
southeast 435
southeasterly 16.131
southeastward 103
Southend 131
southerly 16.131
southern 261
Southerner 17.239
southernmost 441
southpaw 9
Southport 374
southward 103
southwards 531
Southwark 46
southwest 433
southwesterly 16.131
southwestward 103
souvenir 6.5
sou'wester 17.382
sovereign 252
sovereignty 16.360
soviet 381.1
sovietism 242.35.18
sow 12

sphagnum 242
sphenic 38.32
sphenodon 254
sphenoid 97.7
spheral 228
sphere 6
spherical 228.23.15
sphericity 16.333.28
spherics 498.6
spheroid 97.10
spheroidal 228.35
spherule 227
sphinx 505
sphragistics 498
sphygmograph 158.1
sphygmoid 97
spicate 367
spiccato 12.73
spice 301
spiceberry 16.274
spicebush 357
spicery 16.274.37
spiciness 300.23
spick-and-span 245
spicule 227.1
spicy 16.301
spider 17.84
spiderman 261.52
spidery 16.274
spiegeleisen 261.127
spiel 217
spieler 17.165
spiffing 265
spifflicate 367.5
spignel 228
spigot 381
spike 39
spikelet 371
spikenard 84
spiky 16.26
spill 218
spillage 197.1
spillikin 252.3
spillikins 548
spilt 403
spin 252
spina bifida 17.83
spinach 197.7
spinal 228.61
spindle 228.40
spindlelegs 535
spindling 265
spindrift 398
spine 253
spine-chiller 17.166

spine-chilling 265.30
spinel 215
spineless 300
spinet 371.24
spinifex 496
spinnaker 17.42
spinner 17.231
spinneret 368.6
spinney 16.229
spinning 265.43
spinose 305
spinous 310.34
Spinoza 17.442
Spinozism 242.35
spinster 17.394
spiny 16.230
spiracle 228.28
spiraea 17.2
spiral 228
spirant 420
spire 8
spireme 234
spirit 371.33
spirited 91.38
spiritless 300.17
spiritlessness 300.33
spiritous 310.64
spiritual 228.9.3
spiritualism 242.35.11.3
spiritualist 436.7.3
spirituality 16.333.8.2
spirituel 215
spirituous 310.4
spirochaete 370
spirochaetosis 300.55.6
spirograph 158.1
spirogyra 17.274
spiroid 97.11
spirometer 17.342.3
spirula 17.174
spiry 16.267
spit 371
spitchcock 40
spite 372
spiteful 226.9
spitefulness 300.30
spitfire 8
Spithead 86
spittle 228.102
spittlebug 189
spittoon 260
spitz 339
spiv 485
splash 349
splashback 32

splashboard 95
splashdown 258
splashy 16.319
splat 365
splatter 17.336
splay 2
spleen 251
splendid 91.13
splendiferous 310.50.2
splendour 17.101
splenectomy 16.222.5
splenetic 38.50.4
splenic 38.32
splenitis 300.62.3
splenius 310.2.7
splenomegaly 16.131.2
splice 301
spline 253
splint 412
splinter 17.369
split 371
splits 339
splitting 265.66
splodge 199
splodgy 16.104
splotch 68
splurge 195
splutter 17.349
Spock 40
Spode 98
spoil 222
spoilage 197
spoiler 17.170
spoilsport 374
spoke 42
spoken 261.14
spokeshave 482
spokesman 261
spoliate 367.1.3
spoliation 261.67.1.2
spondee 5
spondulix 498
spondylitis 300.62.1
sponge 211
sponger 17.159
spongy 16.111
sponsion 261
sponson 261
sponsor 17.316
sponsorship 274.1
spontaneity 16.333.1
spontaneous 310.2.6
spontoon 260
spoof 170
spook 45

staff 158
Staffa 17.110
Stafford 103
Staffordshire 6
stag 178
stage 193
stagecoach .70
stagecraft 396
stagehand 128
stager 17.146
stagflation 261.67
stagger 17.123
staggered 103
staggering 265.58
staggers 524
staghound 139
staging 265.24
Stagira 17.274
stagnant 420
stagnate 367
stagy 16.100
staid 85
staidness 300
stain 247
Staines 545
stainless 300
stair 4
staircase 295
stairhead 86
stairs 512
stairway 2
stairwell 215
stake 34
stakeout 377
stalactite 372
stalactitic 38.52
stalag 178
stalagmite 372
stalagmitic 38.52
stale 214
stalemate 367
staleness 300
Stalin 252
Stalingrad 83
Stalinism 242.35.13
stalk 41
stalker 17.37
stalky 16.28
stall 221
stallion 261.118
stalwart 381
Stambul 227
stamen 248.2
stamina 17.231.1
staminate 371.24

stammel 228.51
stammer 17.205
stammerer 17.279
stamp 285
stampede 89
stance 314
stanch 78
stanchion 261.81
stand 128
standard 103
standardize 516
standee 5
standing 265.19
standish 353.2
standoffish 353
standpipe 275
standpoint 416
standstill 218
stanhope 281
stank 51
Stanley 16.169
Stannaries 515.1
stannary 16.274
stannic 38.31
stannous 310
stanza 17.445
stapelia 17.3.20
stapes 513
staphylorrhaphy 16.90.1
staple 228
stapler 17
star 1
starboard 103
starch 63
starchy 16.47
stardom 242
stardust 443
stare 4
starfish 353
stargaze 509
stargazer 17.439
stargazing 265.81
stark 33
starless 300
starlet 371
starlight 372
starling 265.26
starry 16.261
start 366
starter 17.337
startle 228.98
starvation 261.67
starve 481
starving 265
stash 349

stasis 300.50
state 367
statecraft 396
Statehouse 306
stateless 300
stateliness 300.23
stately 16.188
statement 420.48
stateroom 241
stateside 92
statesman 261
statesmanship 274.2
static 38.49
statics 498.11
station 261.67
stationary 16.274.29.1
stationer 17.239.1
stationery 16.274.29.1
stationmaster 17.380
statist 436
statistic 38.70.6
statistical 228.23.24
statistician 261.71
statistics 498
Statius 310.2.16
stative 485.10
statocyst 436.22
stator 17.338
statuary 16.274.2
statue 15
statuesque 57
statuette 368.1
stature 17.50
status 310.62
status quo 12
statute 380
statutory 16.274.42
staunch 81
stave 482
stavesacre 17.30
stay 2
stayer 17.1
stays 509
staysail 214
stead 86
steadfast 445
steadfastness 300.42
steadily 16.120
steadiness 300.23.1
steady 16.60
steak 34
steakhouse 306
steal 217
stealing 265.29
stealth 465

stealthful 226
stealthy 16.374
steam 234
steamboat 376
steamer 17.210
steamroller 17.171
steamship 274
steamy 16.215
stearic 38.38
stearin 252
steatite 372.12
steatopygia 17.3.14
steed 89
steel 217
steelworks 497
steely 16.118
steelyard 84
steep 273
steepen 261
steeple 228.65
steeplechase 295
steeplechaser 17.299
steeplejack 32
steepness 300
steer 6
steerage 197
steerageway 2.29
steering 265.53
steersman 261.54
stegodon 254
stegosaur 9.11
stein 253
Steinbeck 35
steinbok 40
stele 16.118
stellar 17.163
stellate 371.15
stelliferous 310.50.2
stelliform 238.1
stellify 7.3
stellular 17.174
stem 232
stemma 17.208
stemware 4
Sten 248
stench 79
stencil 228.88
steno 12.52
stenograph 158.1
stenographer 17.120.1
stenography 16.90.2.4
stenosis 300.55.4
stenotypy 16.249
stentor 9.12
stentorian 261.3.23

step 271
stepbrother 17.408
stepchild 117
stepdaughter 17.345
stepfather 17.401
stephanotis 300.64
Stephen 261.113
Stephenson 261
stepladder 17.77
stepmother 17.408
step-parent 420
steppe 271
stepper 17.250
Steppes 324
stepsister 17.384
stepson 259
steradian 261.3.3
stercoraceous 310.56
stercoricolous 310.26.2
stereo 12.3
stereogram 229.1.1
stereograph 158.1.1
stereometry 16.285.2.1
stereophonic 38.35.2
stereophony 16.237.3.1
stereopsis 300.61
stereopticon 261.13
stereoscope 278.1
stereoscopic 38.37.1
stereoscopy 16.254.2
stereotomy 16.222.4.1
stereotype 275.1
stereotypic 38.36
stereotypy 16.249
stereovision 261.91.3
steric 38.39
sterigma 17.222
sterile 219
sterility 16.333.9
sterilization 261.67.36
sterilize 516.2
sterilizer 17.441
sterling 265
stern 249
sternness 300
sternum 242.13
sternutation 261.67.29
sternutator 17.338
sternutatory 16.274.43
steroid 97.10
stertor 17.340
stertorous 310.50
stet 368
stethoscope 278.1
stethoscopy 16.254.2

stetson 261
stevedore 9.3
Stevenage 197
stew 15
steward 103
stewardess 300.5
sthenic 38.32
stibnite 372
stichomythia 17.3.51
stichomythy 16.370
stick 38
sticker 17.34
stickiness 300.23
stickleback 32
stickler 17.181
stickseed 89
stickweed 89.6
sticky 16.25
stickybeak 37
stiff 163
stiffen 261.29
stiffener 17.239
stiffness 300
stifle 228
stifling 265
stigma 17.222
stigmata 17.352
stigmatic 38.49.3
stigmatism 242.35.20
stigmatize 516.13
stile 219
stiletto 12.75
still 218
stillbirth 456
stillborn 255
stillicide 92.7
stillness 300
stilt 403
stilted 91
Stilton 261
stimulant 420.27
stimulate 367.13.5
stimulation 261.67.13.3
stimulator 17.338.6
stimulus 310.25
sting 265
stinger 17.246
stingray 2
stingy 16.110
stink 52
stinker 17.44
stinkhorn 255
stinking 265.10
stinkpot 373
stinkweed 89

straphanger 17.245
strapless 300
strappado 12.17
strapping 265
strapping 265.48
Strasbourg 182
strass 293
strata 17.337
stratagem 242
strategic 38.17
strategically 16.142
strategics 498
strategist 436
strategy 16.103
Stratford 103
strath 452
Strathclyde 92
strathspey 2
stratify 7.3.8
stratigraphy 16.90
stratocracy 16.307.5
stratocumulus 310.25.5
stratosphere 6.1
stratospheric 38.39
stratum 242.26
stratus 310.62
Strauss 306
stravaig 180
straw 9
strawberry 16.274
strawboard 95
stray 2
streak 37
streaked 386
streaker 17.33
streaky 16.24
stream 234
streamer 17.210
streamline 253
streamlined 135
street 370
streetcar 1
streetlight 372
streetwalker 17.37
Streisand 128
strelitzia 17.3
strength 472
strengthen 261
strengthener 17.239
strenuosity 16.333.30.2
strenuous 310.4.2
streptococcal 228.25
streptococcus 310.11
streptomycin 252.22
stress 296

stressful 226.5
stretch 64
stretchable 228.16
stretcher 17.53
stretchy 16.48
strew 15
strewth 463
stria 17.4
striate 367
striate 371
striation 261.67
stricken 261.13
strict 387
strictness 300
stricture 17.65
stride 92
strident 420
stridor 9
stridulous 310.25.4
strife 164
strigil 218
strike 39
strikebound 139
strikebreaker 17.30
striker 17.35
striking 265
Strindberg 182
string 265
stringboard 95
stringed 107
stringency 16.312.4
stringent 420.23
stringer 17.246
stringy 16.242
strip 274
stripe 275
stripling 265
stripper 17.253
striptease 513
stripy 16.249
strive 486
strobe 28
strobic 38.3
strobila 17.167
strobilus 310.23
stroboscope 278.1
stroboscopic 38.37.1
strode 98
stroganoff 165
stroke 42
stroll 223
stroller 17.171
stromatolite 372.4.1
Stromboli 16.131
strong 266

strongbox 499
stronghold 120
strongly 16.176
strongman 261
strongroom 241
strontium 242.2
strop 276
strophanthus 310.72
strophe 16.87
strophic 38.13
stroppy 16.250
Stroud 99
strove 488
struck 43
structural 228.76
structuralism 242.35.11
structure 17.66
strudel 228.37
struggle 228
struggler 17.193
strum 240
strumpet 371
strung 267
strut 378
struthious 310.2
strychnic 38
strychnine 251
strychninism 242.35.13
Stuart 381
stub 29
stubble 228.14
stubbly 16.136
stubborn 261
stubbornness 300.31
stubby 16.13
stucco 12
stuck 43
stud 100
studbook 44
student 420.13
studentship 274
studhorse 303
studied 91.11
studio 12.3
studious 310.2
studiousness 300.34.1
study 16.69
stuff 168
stuffed 400
stuffiness 300.23
stuffing 265
stuffy 16.88
stultify 7.3
stumble 228
stump 289

substance 321
substandard 103
substantial 228.95
substantiate 367.1.8
substantive 485
substation 261.67
substituent 420.4
substitute 380.5
substitution 261.75
substitutive 485
substrate 367
substratum 242.26
substructure 17.66
subsume 241
subsumption 261.89
subtangent 420.22
subtemperate 371.35
subtenancy 16.312
subtenant 420.52
subtend 131
subterfuge 204
subterranean 261.3.15.1
subtilize 516.2
subtitle 228.103
subtle 228.107
subtlety 16.352
subtonic 38.35
subtotal 228.106
subtract 382
subtraction 261.76
subtractive 485.16
subtrahend 131
subtropical 228.23.14
subtropics 498
subtype 275
suburb 22
suburban 261.9
suburbanite 372.6
suburbanize 516.7
suburbia 17.3.2
subvene 251
subvention 261.82
subversion 261.69
subversive 485.3
subvert 369
subway 2
subzero 12.63
succeed 89
succentor 17.368
success 296
successful 226.5
succession 261.68
successive 485.2
successor 17.300

succinct 392
succinic 38.34
succory 16.274
succotash 349
succour 17.39
succubus 310
succulent 420.27
succumb 240
succursal 228.84
succuss 307
such 72
suchlike 39
suck 43
sucker 17.39
sucking 265
suckle 228.27
sucrose 520
suction 261.79
Sudan 246
sudarium 242.2.14
sudatorium 242.2.17
Sudbury 16.274
sudden 261
suddenness 300.31
Sudetenland 143
Sudetes 513.16
sudor 9
sudoriferous 310.50.2
sudorific 38.12.1
suds 530
sue 15
suede 85
suet 17.3
Suetonius 310.2.9
Suez 515
suffer 17.118
sufferance 321.20
sufferer 17.279
suffering 265.58
suffice 301
sufficiency 16.312.5
sufficient 420.74
suffix 498
suffocate 367.6
suffocation 261.67.6
Suffolk 46
suffragan 261
suffrage 197
suffragette 368
suffragist 436.4
suffuse 523.1
Sufi 16.89
Sufism 242.35
sugar 17.135
sugar daddy 16.57

sugarplum 240
sugary 16.274
suggest 433
suggestibility 16.333.9.2
suggestible 228.16.59
suggestion 261.18
suggestive 485.24
suicidal 228.33
suicide 92.7
sui generis 300.47
suint 412
suit 380
suitability 16.333.9.2
suitable 228.16.53
suitcase 295
suite 370
suiting 265
suitor 17.351
sukiyaki 16.20
Sulawesi 16.296
sulcate 367.7
Suleiman 246
sulk 50
sulkiness 300.23
sulky 16.35
Sulla 17.173
sullage 197
sullen 261
sullenness 300.31
Sullivan 261.114
sully 16.128
sulphanilamide 92.3
sulphate 367
sulphide 92
sulphonamide 92.3
sulphone 257
sulphur 17
sulphurate 367.22
sulphuric 38.43
sulphurize 516
sulphurous 310.50
sultan 261
sultana 17.226
sultanate 367.18
sultanic 38.31
sultry 16
Sulu 15.4
sum 240
sumach 32
Sumatra 17.292
Sumer 17.217
Sumerian 261.3.22
summarize 516.8
summary 16.274
summation 261.67

summer 17.216
summerhouse 306
summertime 236
summery 16.274
summit 371
summon 261
summons 551
Sumo 12
sump 289
sumptuous 310.4.4
sumptuousness 300.34.2
sun 259
sunbathe 473
sunbeam 234
sunbird 87
sunbonnet 371.25
sunburn 249
sunburnt 411
sunburst 434
sundae 2
Sunday 2
sunder 17.108
Sunderland 143.4
sundew 15
sundial 228.4
sundog 185
sundown 258
sundress 296
sundry 16
sunflower 14
sung 267
sunglasses 515
sungrebe 23
sunhat 365
sunk 54
sunken 261
sunless 300
sunlight 372
sunlit 371
Sunna 17.237
Sunni 16.235
Sunnite 372
sunny 16.235
sunray 2
sunrise 516
sunroof 170
sunset 368
sunshade 85
sunshine 253
sunshiny 16.230
sunspot 373
sunstar 1
sunstroke 42
sunsuit 380
suntan 245

suntanned 128
suntrap 268
Sun Yat-sen 248
sup 279
super 17.259
superabound 139
superabundant 420.16
superadd 83
superannuate 367.2
superannuated 91.34.2
superannuation 261.67.2
superb 22
supercharge 192
supercharger 17.145
superciliary 16.274.1.1
supercilious 310.2.5
superclass 294
superconductivity
  16.333.35.3
supercool 227
super-duper 17.259
superego 12.28
supererogatory
  16.274.43.3
superfamily 16.120
superficial 228.93
superficiality 16.333.8.1
superfine 253
superfluid 91.3
superfluity 16.333.3
superfluous 310.4
supergiant 420.2
superheat 370
superhero 12.63
superhighway 2.26
superhuman 261.51
superimpose 520
superinduce 309
superintend 131
superintendency
  16.312.2
superintendent 420.14
superior 17.3.39
superiority 16.333.22
superlative 485.15
superman 261.52
supermarket 371.7
supernal 228.58
supernatant 420.75
supernatural 228.76
supernova 17.417
supernumerary
  16.274.32
superpose 520.2
superpower 14

supersaturated 91.34.7
superscript 424
supersede 89.3
supersedure 17.149
supersession 261.68.1
supersonic 38.35.4
superstar 1
superstition 261.71
superstitious 310.58
superstratum 242.26
superstructure 17.66
supertax 494
supervene 251.12
supervise 516
supervision 261.91.3
supervisor 17.441
supervisory 16.274.53
supinate 367.17
supinator 17.338.7
supine 253
suplex 496
supper 17.258
supplant 408
supple 228
supplement 410.1
supplement 420.31
supplementary
  16.274.47
suppleness 300.30
suppliant 420.1
supplicant 420.7
supplicate 367.5
supplication 261.67.5
supplier 17.4
supply 7.9
support 374.2
supportable 228.16.51
supporter 17.345
supporting 265.69
supportive 485.13
suppose 520.2
supposed 155.1
supposedly 16.148
supposing 265.83
supposition 261.71.9
suppositious 310.58
suppositive 485.12.1
suppository 16.274.41
suppress 296.5
suppression 261.68
suppressive 485.2
suppurate 367.22
suppuration 261.67.21
suppurative 485.15
supralapsarian 261.3.21

sweetening 265.46
sweetheart 366
sweetie 16.332
sweetmeal 217
sweetmeat 370
sweetness 300.37
sweetshop 276
sweetsop 276
swell 215
swelling 265.28
swelter 17.361
sweltering 265.58
swept 422
swerve 483
swift 398
swiftie 16.347
swiftness 300
swig 184
swill 218
swim 235
swimmer 17.211
swimmeret 368.6
swimming 265
swimmingly 16.175
swimsuit 380
Swinburne 249
swindle 228.40
swindler 17.189
Swindon 261
swine 253
swineherd 87
swinepox 499
swing 265
swingboat 376
swinge 209
swingeing 265
swinger 17.246
swinging 265.47
swingle 228.50
swingometer 17.342.3
swinish 353
swipe 275
swipes 328
swirl 216
swish 353
Swiss 300
switch 67
switchback 32
switchboard 95
swither 17.405
Swithin 252
Switzer 17.320
Switzerland 143.4
swivel 228.120
swizz 515

swizzle 228
swollen 261.43
swoon 260
swoop 280
swoosh 357
sword 95
swordfish 353
swordlike 39
swordplay 2
swordsman 261
swordsmanship 274.2
swordstick 38
swordtail 214
swore 9
sworn 255
swot 373
swound 139
swum 240
swung 267
Sybaris 300.47
sybarite 372.8
sybaritic 38.52.2
Sybil 228.12
sycamore 9.9
syce 301
sycophant 407
sycophantic 38.62
sycosis 300.55
Sydney 16.240
syllabary 16.274
syllabi 7
syllabic 38
syllabify 7.3
syllabism 242.35.5
syllable 228.16.23
syllabub 29
syllabus 310
syllepsis 300.59
syllogism 242.35.8
syllogistic 38.70.1
sylva 17.422
sylvan 261
sylvatic 38.49
symbiont 414
symbiosis 300.55.1
symbiotic 38.53
symbol 228
symbolic 38.22
symbolical 228.23.8
symbolism 242.35.11
symbolist 436.7
symbolistic 38.70.2
symbolize 516.3
symbology 16.108.4
symmetrical 228.23

symmetrize 516
symmetry 16.285.1
sympathetic 38.50.6
sympathize 516.14
sympathizer 17.441
sympatholytic 38.52.1
sympathy 16.373
symphonic 38.35
symphonist 436.13
symphony 16.237
symphysis 300.52
sympodium 242.2.4
symposium 242.2
symptom 242
symptomatic 38.49.2
symptomatology
  16.108.4.15
synagogue 185.2
synalepha 17.113
synapse 322
synarthrosis 300.55
sync 52
syncarp 269
syncarpy 16.244
synchroflash 349
synchromesh 351
synchronism 242.35.14
synchronize 516.7
synchronous 310.36
syncline 253.5
syncopate 367
syncopation 261.67
syncope 16.254
syncretism 242.35.18
syncytium 242.2.18
syndesmosis 300.55
syndetic 38.50
syndic 38
syndicalism 242.35.11
syndicate 367.5
syndicate 371.9
syndrome 239
syndromic 38.29
synecdoche 16.33
synergetic 38.50.3
synergism 242.35.8
synergistic 38.70.1
synergy 16.108
synod 103
synodic 38.9
synoecious 310.57
synonym 235
synonymity 16.333.12
synonymize 516.4
synonymous 310.28.2

talisman 261
talismanic 38.31
talk 41
talkative 485.15
talkativeness 300.43
talker 17.37
talkie 16.28
tall 221
Tallahassee 16.294
tallboy 11
Tallis 300
tallith 458
tallness 300
tallow 12.38
tally 16.112
tally-ho 12
tallyman 261.48
Talmud 101
Talmudist 436.2
talon 261
taloned 143
talus 310
tamale 16.113
tamandua 17.8
tamarack 32.3
tamarin 252.20
tamarind 134
tamarindo 12.25
tamarisk 58
tamasha 17.321
Tambora 1.14
tambour 10
tamboura 17.277
tambourin 252.19
tambourine 251.7
tame 231
tameness 300
tamer 17.207
Tamerlane 247.4
Tamil 218
Tammany 16.237
tammy 16.210
tam-o'-shanter 17.365
tamp 285
Tampa 17.261
tamper 17.261
tampion 261.3
tampon 254
tan 245
tana 17.226
tanager 17.154
tanbark 33
tandem 242.6
Tandoori 16.270
tang 263

Tang 263
Tanga 17.140
Tanganyika 17.33
tangelo 12.45
tangent 420.22
tangential 228.96
tangerine 251.7
tangible 228.16.21
Tangier 6
tangle 228.49
tango 12.35
tangram 229
tangy 16.241
tanist 436
tank 51
tanka 17.43
tankard 103
tanker 17.43
tankful 226
tannage 197.5
tanner 17.225
tannery 16.274
tannic 38.31
tannin 252
tansy 16.404
Tanta 17.365
tantalize 516.3
tantalum 242.11
Tantalus 310.26
tantamount 418.1
tantivy 16.382
Tantra 17.296
Tantrism 242.35
tantrum 242
Tanzania 17.2
Taoism 242.35.3
tap 268
tapa 17.248
tape 270
taper 17.249
tapestry 16.293
tapeworm 233
tapioca 17.38
tapir 17.249
tapis 5
tappet 371
tappit-hen 248
taproom 241
taproot 380
taps 322
tar 1
taramasalata 17.337.1
tarantass 293
tarantella 17.163
tarantism 242.35.21

Taranto 12.83
tarantula 17.174
tarboosh 358
tardigrade 85.5
tardy 16.58
tare 4
target 371
tariff 163
Tarim 234
Tarkington 261
tarlatan 261
Tarmac 32
tarn 246
tarnation 261.67.17
tarnish 353
taro 12.61
tarot 12.60
tarp 269
tarpan 245
tarpaulin 252
Tarpeian 261.2
tarpon 261
Tarquin 252
tarradiddle 228.32
tarragon 261
tarry 16.260
tarry 16.261
tarsal 228.83
tarsier 17.3.47
tarsus 310.52
Tarsus 310.52
tart 366
tartan 261.95
tartar 17.337
Tartar 17.337
tartaric 38.38
Tartarus 310.50
Tartary 16.274
tartlet 371
tartrate 367
Tarzan 261
task 56
taskmaster 17.380
Tasman 261
Tasmania 17.3.31
Tasmanian 261.3.15
Tass 293
tassel 228
taste 432
tasteful 226.12
tasteless 300
tastelessness 300.33
taster 17.381
tasty 16.363
tat 365

Teleran 245.5
telescope 278
telescopic 38.37
telescopy 16.254
telescript 424
telestich 38.69
telethon 254
teletube 30
Teletype 275
televise 516.15
television 261.91.2
telewriter 17.343
telex 496
Telford 103
telic 38.20
telium 242.2.5
tell 215
Tell el Amarna 17.226
teller 17.163
telling 265.28
telltale 214
tellurian 261.3.24
telluric 38.43
telluride 92
tellurium 242.2
tellurometer 17.342.3
telly 16.115
Telstar 1
temerity 16.333.21
temp 286
temper 17.262
tempera 17.279
temperament 420.35
temperamental
  228.110.3
temperance 321.20
temperate 371.35
temperature 17.56
tempest 436
tempestuous 310.4
Templar 17.196
template 371
temple 228
tempo 12
temporal 228.76
temporality 16.333.8.9
temporary 16.274.32
temporize 516.8
tempt 428
temptation 261.67
tempter 17.378
tempting 265
temptress 300
tempura 1.13
ten 248

tenable 228.16
tenace 295
tenacious 310.56.4
tenacity 16.333.25
tenaculum 242.10
tenancy 16.312
tenant 420.52
tenantry 16.291
tench 79
tend 131
tendency 16.312.2
tendentious 310.61
tender 17.101
tenderfoot 379.1
tenderhearted 91.33
tenderize 516.8
tenderizer 17.441.1
tenderloin 256
tenderness 300.26
tendinous 310.33
tendon 261
tendril 218
tenebrosity 16.333.30
tenebrous 310
tenement 420.35
Tenerife 162.2
tenet 371
tenfold 120
Tengri Nor 9
tenner 17.228
Tennessee 5.20
tennis 300
tenno 12.52
Tennyson 261.65
tenon 261
tenor 17.228
tenorrhaphy 16.90.1
tenpenny 16.237
tenpin 252
tenpins 548
tenrec 35
tense 316
tensible 228.16.40
tensile 219.3
tensiometer 17.342.3.1
tension 261.82
tensive 485.9
tensor 17.314
tent 410
tentacle 228.28
tentacular 17.174.3
tentage 197.14
tentation 261.67.32
tentative 485.15.15
tenter 17.368

tenterhook 44
tenth 468
tenuity 16.333.3
tenuous 310.4.2
tenure 10
Tenzing Norgay 2
teocalli 16.112
teosinte 16.356
tepee 5
tepid 91.23
tequila 17.165
Terai 7.12
teraph 171
teratism 242.35.20
teratogenic 38.32.1
teratoid 97
teratology 16.108.4.15
terbium 242.2
tercel 228.84
terebene 251
terebinth 470
terebinthine 253
Terence 321.16
tergiversate 367
teriyaki 16.20
term 233
termagant 420.18
terminable 228.16.29
terminal 228.60
terminate 367.17.4
termination 261.67.18.4
terminator 17.338.7
terminology 16.108.4.10
terminus 310.33
termite 372
tern 249
ternary 16.274.24
ternate 371.23
terpene 251
terpineol 220.1
Terpsichore 16.274.4
Terpsichorean 261.2.3
terrace 310.44
terra cotta 17.344
terra firma 17.209
terrain 247
terrapin 252
terrarium 242.2.14
terreplein 247
terrestrial 228.3.13
terret 371.31
terre-verte 369
terrible 228.16
terribly 16.137
terricolous 310.26.2

terrier 17.3
terrific 38.12.1
terrify 7.3.5
terrigenous 310.33
terrine 251
territorial 228.3.12.1
territorialism 242.35.11.2
territoriality 16.333.8.1
territorialize 516.3.2.2
territory 16.274.41
terror 17.269
terrorism 242.35.15
terrorist 436.20
terrorize 516.8
Terry 16.262
terse 297
tertial 228.92
tertian 261.69
tertiary 16.274
tertium quid 91
Tertullian 261.3.13
Terylene 251.2
Tess 296
tessellate 367.12
tessellation 261.67.12
tessera 17.279
tesseract 382
tessitura 17.277
test 433
testament 420.35
testamentary 16.274.47
testate 367.33
testator 17.338
testatrix 498.9
tester 17.382
testes 513.19
testicle 228.23
testiculate 371.17.2
testify 7.3
testimonial 228.3.8
testimony 16.237
testing 265.75
testis 300.68
teston 261.106
testosterone 257.1
testudinal 228.60.1
testudo 12.22
testy 16.364
tetanic 38.31
tetanus 310.36
tetany 16.237
tetchy 16.48
tête-à-tête 367.31
tête-bêche 351
tether 17.402

tetra 17.293
tetrachloride 92.5
tetracycline 251
tetrad 83
tetragram 229.1
tetrahedron 261
tetralogy 16.108.2
tetrapod 94.1
tetrarch 33
tetrastich 38
tetter 17.339
Teucer 17.308
Teuton 261.104
Teutonic 38.35
Teutonism 242.35.14
Teutonize 516.7
Tewkesbury 16.274
Texan 261
Texas 310
text 450
textbook 44
textile 219.8
textual 228.9
textualism 242.35.11.3
textuary 16.274.2
texture 17.75
Thackeray 16.274
Thai 7
Thailand 143
Thaïs 300
thalamus 310.29.2
thalassic 38.48
thaler 17.161
Thales 513
thalidomide 92.3
thallium 242.2
thalweg 181
Thames 541
than 245
thanatopsis 300.61
Thanatos 302
thane 247
Thanet 371.22
thank 51
thankful 226
thankfulness 300.30
thankless 300
thanklessness 300.33
thanks 504
thanksgiving 265.80
Thapsus 310
Thásos 302
that 365
thatch 62
thatcher 17.50

Thatcher 17.50
thaumatology 16.108.4.15
thaumatrope 278.3
thaumaturge 195
thaw 9
thearchy 16.20
theatre 17.352
theatrical 228.23
theatricals 539.2
theatrics 498.8
theca 17.33
thee 5
theft 397
their 4
theirs 512
theism 242.35.1
them 232
thematic 38.49.1
theme 234
themselves 555
then 248
thenar 1
thence 316
theocentric 38.47
theocracy 16.307.5.1
theocrasy 16.307.5.1
Theocritus 310.64
theodicy 16.300.1
theodolite 372.4
Theodoric 38.44
theogony 16.237.4
theologian 261.3
theologize 516.1
theology 16.108.4.1
theomachy 16.33
theomancy 16.309
theomania 17.3.31.1
theonomy 16.222.3.1
theopathy 16.373.1.1
theophagy 16.108.1
theophany 16.237.3.1
Theophilus 310.23
theorem 242.19
theoretical 228.23.19
theoretician 261.71.7
theoretics 498.12
theorist 436.20
theorize 516.8
theory 16.265
theosophy 16.90.4
therapeutic 38.56
therapeutics 498
therapist 436.15
therapsid 91.31

therapy 16.254
there 4
thereabouts 344
thereafter 17.358
thereat 365
thereby 7
therefore 9
therefrom 237
therein 252
thereinto 15
thereof 487
thereon 254
Theresa 17.440
thereto 15
theretofore 9
thereunder 17.108
thereupon 254
therewith 476
therianthropic 38.37.3
theriomorphic 38.14
therm 233
thermae 5
thermaesthesia 17.3.60
thermal 228
thermion 261.3
thermionic 38.35.1
thermionics 498.5
thermocouple 228
thermodynamic 38.24
thermodynamics 498.2
thermoelectric 38
thermoelectricity
  16.333.28
thermogenesis 300.52.4
thermograph 158.1
thermolysis 300.52.2
thermolytic 38.52.1
thermometer 17.342.3.2
thermometry 16.285.2
thermonuclear 17.3
thermophile 219.1
thermophilic 38.21
thermopile 219
thermoplastic 38.68
Thermopylae 5.9
Thermos 310
thermosetting 265.65
thermostat 365
thermostatic 38.49.7
thermostatics 498.11
thermotaxis 300.70
thermotensile 219.3
theroid 97.10
theropod 94.1
thesaurus 310.48

these 513
Theseus 310.2
thesis 300.51
Thespian 261.3
Thessalonian 261.3.18
Thessaly 16.131
theta 17.341
thetic 38.50
Thetis 300
theurgy 16.102
thew 15
they 2
they'd 85
they'll 214
they're 4
they've 482
thiamine 252.15
thiazole 223
thick 38
thick-and-thin 252
thicken 261.13
thickener 17.239
thickening 265.46
thicket 371.9
thickly 16.142
thickness 300.27
thickset 368
thick-skinned 134
thief 162
thieve 484
thieving 265.79
thigh 7
thighbone 257
thimble 228
thimbleful 226
thimblerig 184
thimbleweed 89.7
thimblewit 371
thin 252
thine 253
thing 265
thingumabob 26
thingumajig 184
think 52
thinkable 228.16.11
thinker 17.44
thinking 265.10
thinner 17.231
thinness 300
thin-skinned 134
thionic 38.35
third 87
third-rate 367
Thirlmere 6
thirst 434

thirstiness 300.23
thirsty 16.365
thirteen 251
thirteenth 469
thirtieth 458
thirty 16.331
this 300
thistle 228.85
thistledown 258
thistly 16.181
thither 17.405
thitherto 15
thixotropic 38.37.2
thole 223
Thomas 310
Thomism 242.35
Thompson 261
thong 266
Thor 9
thoracic 38.48
thorax 494
thoria 17.3.41
thorium 242.2.17
thorn 255
thornbill 218
Thorndike 39
thorny 16.232
thoron 254.10
thorough 17.278
thoroughbred 86
thoroughfare 4.3
thoroughgoing 265.4
thoroughly 16.131
thoroughness 300.26
Thorpe 277
those 520
Thoth 461
thou 13
though 12
thought 374
thoughtful 226
thoughtfulness 300.30
thoughtless 300
thoughtlessness 300.33
thousand 143
thousandth 471
Thrace 295
thrall 221
thrash 349
thrasher 17.321
thrashing 265
thrawn 255
thread 86
threadbare 4
threadfin 252

torsion 261.72
torso 12
tort 374
torte 374
tortellini 16.228.1
torticollis 300.9
tortilla 17.2
tortious 310.59
tortoise 310
tortoiseshell 215
tortricid 91.29
tortuosity 16.333.30.2
tortuous 310.4
torture 17.58
torturer 17.279
torus 310.48
Tory 16.269
Toscanini 16.228
tosh 354
toss 302
tosspot 373
tot 373
total 228.106
totalitarian 261.3.21.2
totality 16.333.8
totalizator 17.338
totalize 516.3
totalizer 17.441
tote 376
totem 242.31
totemic 38.25
totemism 242.35
totter 17.344
toucan 261.15
touch 72
touchable 228.16
touchdown 258
touché 2
touching 265
touchline 253
touchstone 257
touchwood 101
touchy 16.52
tough 168
toughen 261
toughie 16.88
toughness 300
Toulouse 523
toupee 2
tour 10
touraco 12
Tourane 246
tourbillion 261.120
tourer 17.277
tourism 242.35

tourist 436.19
touristic 38.70
touristy 16.366
tourmaline 251.3
tournament 420.35
tournedos 12
tourniquet 2.7
tousle 228.129
tout 377
tovarisch 353
tow 12
towage 197
toward 95.4
towards 528
towbar 1
towel 228.8
towelling 265
tower 14
towering 265.57
tow-haired 88
towhead 86.3
towline 253
town 258
townee 5
townhall 221
townie 16.234
townscape 270
township 274
townsman 261
townspeople 228.65
townswoman 261.50
towpath 453
towrope 278
toxaemia 17.3.26.1
toxic 38.75
toxicant 420.7
toxicity 16.333.28
toxicogenic 38.32.1
toxicology 16.108.4.4
toxicosis 300.55
toxin 252.29
toxophilite 372.3
toy 11
Toyama 1.10
trace 295
traceable 228.16.36
tracer 17.299
tracery 16.274.33
trachea 17.2
tracheitis 300.62
tracheostomy 16.222.6
tracheotomy 16.222.4.1
trachoma 17.215
tracing 265.59
track 32

tracker 17.28
trackless 300
tracksuit 380
tract 382
tractable 228.16
Tractarianism
    242.35.14.1.1
tractate 367
tractile 219.4
traction 261.76
tractive 485.16
tractor 17.353
Tracy 16.296
trad 83
trade 85
trademark 33
trader 17.79
tradescantia 17.3.50
tradesfolk 42
tradesman 261
trading 265.11
tradition 261.71.2
traditional 228.63.5
traditionalism
    242.35.11.5
traditor 17.342
traduce 309.1
traducianism 242.35.14
Trafalgar 17.137
traffic 38.11
trafficator 17.338.2
trafficker 17.34
tragacanth 467
tragedian 261.3.4
tragedienne 248.1
tragedy 16.63
tragic 38.15
tragically 16.142
tragicomedy 16.63
tragicomic 38.29
tragopan 245.4
tragus 310.19
trail 214
trailblazer 17.439
trailer 17.162
train 247
trainbearer 17.271
trainee 5.11
trainer 17.227
training 265.40
train-spotting 265.68
traipse 323
trait 367
traitor 17.338
traitorous 310.50

treehopper 17.255
treeless 300
treen 251
treenail 214
treenware 4
trefoil 222
trek 35
trekker 17.31
trellis 300
trelliswork 36
trematode 98
tremble 228.18
trembly 16.138
tremendous 310
tremolo 12.45
tremor 17.208
tremulant 420.27
tremulous 310.25
trench 79
trenchant 420
trencher 17.70
trencherman 261.52
trend 131
trendy 16.78
Trent 410
Trenton 261
trepan 245.3
trepang 263
trephine 251
trepidation 261.67.7
treponema 17.210
trespass 310
trespasser 17.309
tress 296
tressure 17.323
trestle 228
trestletree 5
Trevelyan 261.119
Trevino 12.54
trews 523
trey 2
triable 228.16.3
triad 83.2
triage 197
trial 228.4
triangle 228.49
triangular 17.174
triangulate 367.13.4
triangulation
  261.67.13.2
Triassic 38.48
triatomic 38.29
triaxial 228.3.18
tribal 228
tribalism 242.35.11

tribe 25
tribesman 261
tribulation 261.67.13
tribunal 228
tribune 260
tributary 16.274.42
tribute 380.2
trice 301
tricentenary 16.274.25
triceps 324
triceratops 329
trichiasis 300.57.1
trichina 17.232
trichinize 516.6
Trichinopoly 16.131.6
trichinosis 300.55.4
trichloride 92.5
trichoid 97.3
trichology 16.108.4.4
trichomonad 83.3
trichotomy 16.222.4
trichromatic 38.49.2
trick 38
trickery 16.274.4
trickle 228.23
tricksy 16.388
tricky 16.25
triclinium 242.2.11
tricolour 17.176.2
tricorn 255
tricot 12.11
tricotine 251.11
tricuspid 91
tricycle 228.23
trident 420
Tridentine 253
triennial 228.3
triennium 242 2
Trieste 433
trifid 91
trifle 228
trifling 265
trifolium 242.2.7
triforium 242.2.17
trifurcate 371.8
trig 184
trigeminal 228.60.3
trigger 17.129
trigon 254
trigonometry 16.285.2.2
trigraph 158
trike 39
trilateral 228.76
trilby 16.16
trilinear 17.3.34

trilingual 228
trilithon 254
trill 218
trillion 261.120
trillionth 471
trillium 242
trilobate 367.3
trilobite 372
trilogy 16.108.3
trim 235
trimaran 245.5
trimer 17.212
trimester 17.382
trimetric 38.46
trimetrogon 254.5
trimmer 17.211
trimming 265
trimonthly 16.205
Trimurti 16.337
trinary 16.274.27
Trincomalee 5.9
Trinidad 83
Trinitarian 261.3.21.2
trinity 16.333.17
trinket 371
trinomial 228.3
trio 12.2
triode 98
trioxide 92.14
trip 274
tripartite 372
tripartition 261.71
tripe 275
triplane 247
triple 228.66
triplet 371
Triplex 496
triplicate 367.5
triplicate 371.9
triplicity 16.333.28.1
triploid 97
triply 16.177
tripod 94
Tripoli 16.131.5
Tripolitania 17.3.31.2
tripos 302
tripper 17.253
triptych 38.66
triptyque 37
tripwire 8
trireme 234
trisect 385
triskaidekaphobia 17.3.4
triskelion 254.1
trismus 310.30

Tubal-cain 247
tubate 367
tubbiness 300.23
tubby 16.13
tube 30
tubeless 300
tuber 17.20
tubercle 228.28
tubercular 17.174.5
tuberculate 371.17
tuberculin 252.10
tuberculosis 300.55.3
tuberculous 310.25
tuberose 305.2
tuberose 520.3
tuberosity 16.333.30.5
tuberous 310.50
tubing 265
tubular 17.174
tubulate 367.13
tubule 227
tubuliflorous 310.48
tubulous 310.25
Tucana 17.226
tuchun 260
tuck 43
tucker 17.39
tucket 371.11
Tucson 254
Tudor 17.91
Tuesday 2
tufa 17.119
tuff 168
tuffet 371
tuft 400
tufted 91
tufty 16.349
tug 189
tugrik 37
Tuileries 16.274
tuition 261.71
tulip 274
Tull 225
tulle 227
Tulsa 17.311
tum 240
tumble 228
tumble-down 258
tumblehome 239
tumbler 17.180
tumbleweed 89.7
tumbrel 228.77
tumefaction 261.76
tumefy 7.3
tumescence 321.21

tumescent 420.67
tumid 91
tummy 16.220
tumour 17.217
tump 289
tumult 406
tumultuous 310.4
tumulus 310.25.5
tun 259
tuna 17.238
tunable 228.16
tundra 17.288
tune 260
tuneful 226
tuneless 300
tunelessness 300.33
tuner 17.238
tunesmith 458
tungsten 261
Tungus 308
Tungusic 38
tunic 38
tunicate 371.9
tunicle 228.23
tuning 265
Tunis 300
Tunisia 17.3.61
tunnel 228
tunny 16.235
tup 279
tupelo 12.42
Tupi 5
tuque 45
turban 261.9
turbary 16.274
turbid 91
turbinate 371.24
turbine 253
turbocar 1
turbocharger 17.145
turbo-electric 38
turbofan 245
turbojet 368
turboprop 276
turbot 381
turbulence 321
turbulent 420.27
turd 87
turdine 253
tureen 251.7
turf 161
turfy 16.83
turgescent 420.67
turgid 91
turgor 17.127

Turin 252
turion 261.3.24
Turk 36
Turkestan 246.1
turkey 16.23
Turkey 16.23
Turkic 38
Turkish 353
Turkoman 261.52
turmeric 38.44
turmoil 222
turn 249
turnabout 377.1
turnaround 139.1
turnbuckle 228.27
turncoat 376
turncock 40
turner 17.229
turnery 16.274.24
turning 265.41
turnip 274
turnkey 5
turnpike 39
turnsole 223
turnstile 219
turntable 228.11
turpentine 253
turpeth 458
Turpin 252
turpitude 102.2
turps 325
turquoise 519
turret 371
turreted 91.38
turtle 228
turtledove 489
turtleneck 35
Tuscan 261.17
Tuscany 16.237
Tuscarora 17.276
Tusculum 242.10
tush 356
tusk 60
tusker 17.49
Tussaud 12
tussle 228.87
tussock 46
tussore 9
tut 378
Tutankhamen 261
Tutankhamun 260
tutee 5
tutelage 197.1
tutelary 16.274.16
tutor 17.351

tutorial 228.3.12
tutti 16.342
tutti-frutti 16.343
tutu 15
Tuvalu 15.5
tu-whit tu-whoo 15
tuxedo 12.18
tuyère 4
twaddle 228.34
twain 247
Twain 247
twang 263
'twas 517
twat 365
tweak 37
twee 5
tweed 89
Tweed 89
Tweedledee 5
Tweedledum 240
tweedy 16.62
tweet 370
tweeter 17.341
tweeze 513
tweezers 524
Twelfthtide 92
twelve 492
twentieth 458
twenty 16.355
'twere 3
twerp 272
Twi 5
twibill 218
twice 301
Twickenham 242.16
twiddle 228.32
twig 184
twiggy 16.93
twilight 372
twilit 371
twill 218
twin 252
twine 253
twinge 209
twink 52
twinkle 228.29
twinkler 17.182
twinkling 265
twirl 216
twist 436
twister 17.384
twisty 16.366
twit 371
twitch 67
twitcher 17.56

twite 372
twitter 17.342
two 15
two-dimensional
    228.63.9
two-faced 432
twofold 120
twopence 321.15
twopenny 16.237
two-seater 17.341
twosome 242
Tyburn 249
Tyche 16.26
Tycho 12
tycoon 260
tyke 39
Tyler 17.167
tylopod 94.1
tympanic 38.31
tympanitis 300.62.4
tympanum 242.16
Tyndale 228.40
Tyne 253
Tyneside 92
Tynwald 122
type 275
typecase 295
typecast 431
typeface 295
typescript 424
typeset 368
typesetter 17.339
typesetting 265.65
typewrite 372
typewriter 17.343
typewriting 265.67
typhoid 97
typhoon 260
typhus 310
typical 228.23
typically 16.142
typify 7.3
typing 265
typist 436
typo 12
typographical 228.23.3
typography 16.90.2
tyrannical 228.23.10
tyrannicide 92.7
tyrannize 516.7
tyrannosaur 9.11
tyrannosaurus 310.48.1
tyranny 16.237
tyrant 420
tyre 8

Tyre 8
Tyrian 261.3
tyro 12.64
Tyrol 223
Tyrolienne 248.1
Tyrone 257
tyrosine 251.9
tyrothricin 252.22
Tyrrhenian 261.3.16
Tzigane 246

U

ubiety 16.333.2
ubiquitarian 261.3.21.2
ubiquitous 310.64
udder 17.90
UFO 12
ufology 16.108.4
Uganda 17.98
Ugandan 261
Ugaritic 38.52.2
ugli 16.161
uglify 7.3
ugliness 300.23
ugly 16.161
Ugric 38
Uigur 10
uintathere 6.10
ukase 509
ukiyoe 2
Ukraine 247
Ukrainian 261.3.15
ukulele 16.114
ulcer 17.311
ulcerate 367.23
ulceration 261.67.22
ulcerative 485.15.10
ulcerous 310.50
ullage 197
Ullswater 17.345
ulotrichous 310.10
Ulster 17
Ulsterman 261.52
ulterior 17.3.39
ultima 17.211
ultimate 371.19
ultimately 16.189.1
ultimatum 242.27
ultimo 12.48
ultrahigh 7
ultramarine 251.7
ultramodern 261.26
ultramontane 247.11

ultramontanism
242.35.13
ultrashort 374
ultrasonic 38.35.4
ultrasound 139
ultraviolet 371.18.1
ultravirus 310.47
ululate 367.13
Ulysses 513
umbel 228
umbelliferous 310.50.2
umber 17.27
umbilical 228.23.7
umbilicate 371.9
umbilicus 310.10
umbo 12.7
umbra 17.285
umbrage 197
umbrageous 310.20
umbrella 17.163
Umbria 17.3.44
Umbrian 261.3.25
Umbriel 228.3
umiak 32.1
umlaut 377
umpire 8
umpteen 251
umpteenth 469
Umtali 16.113
unabated 91.34
unable 228.11
unabridged 110
unacceptable 228.16.58
unacclaimed 124
unaccompanied 91.21
unaccomplished 449
unaccountable 228.16.56
unaccustomed 127
unacquainted 91.45
unadopted 91
unadorned 137
unadulterated 91.34.7
unadvised 154
unadvisedly 16.148
unaffected 91.43
unafraid 85
unaided 91.6
unaimed 124
unaired 88
unalloyed 97.6
unanimity 16.333.12
unanimous 310.28.1
unanswerable 228.16.35
unanswered 103

unapproachable
228.16.13
unappropriated 91.34.1
unapt 421
unarm 230
unarmed 123
unary 16.274.28
unashamed 124
unashamedly 16.148
unasked 394
unassailable 228.16.22
unassisted 91.53
unassuming 265.39
unatoned 138
unattached 395
unattainable 228.16.27
unattended 91.13
unattested 91.52
unattractive 485.16
unauthorized 154
unavailable 228.16.22
unavailing 265.27
unavoidable 228.16
unaware 4.8
unawares 512
unbacked 382
unbalance 321.10
unbar 1
unbearable 228.16.33
unbeatable 228.16.48
unbeaten 261.98
unbecoming 265.38
unbeknown 257
unbelief 162.1
unbelievable 228.16.61
unbeliever 17.413
unbelieving 265.79
unbelt 402
unbend 131
unbendable 228.16.18
unbending 265.20
unbent 410
unbiased 445
unbidden 261.24
unbind 135
unbirthday 2
unblessed 433
unblinking 265.10
unbolt 405
unbolted 91
unboned 138
unbonnet 371.25
unborn 255
unbosom 242
unbound 139

unbounded 91.14
unbowed 99
unbreakable 228.16.9
unbred 86
unbridle 228.33
unbridled 122
unbroken 261.14
unbuckle 228.27
unburden 261.22
unbutton 261.103
uncaged 108
uncanny 16.223
uncap 268
uncaring 265.52
unceasing 265
unceremonious 310.2.9.1
uncertain 261.97
uncertainty 16.360
unchain 247
unchanging 265
unchaperoned 138
uncharted 91.33
unchecked 385
unchristian 261
unchurch 65
uncial 228.3
unciform 238.1
uncinate 371.24
uncinus 310.34
uncircumcised 154
uncivil 228.120
uncivilized 154
unclad 83
unclasp 290
unclassified 92.1
uncle 228.30
unclean 251
uncleaned 133
uncleanly 16.171
unclear 6
unclog 185
unclose 520
unclothe 478
unclothed 145
uncoil 222
uncomfortable 228.16
uncommercial 228.92
uncommon 261
uncommonly 16.174
uncommunicative
485.15.1
uncompromising 265.82
unconcern 249
unconcerned 132
unconcernedly 16.148

unconditional 228.63.5
unconditioned 143.5
unconformity 16.333.13
unconnected 91.43
unconscionable
  228.16.31
unconscious 310
unconsciousness 300.34
unconstitutional
  228.63.7
uncontrollable 228.16.24
unconventional 228.63.9
unconventionality
  16.333.8.7
unconvincing 265.62
uncooked 390
uncoordinated 91.34.6
uncork 41
uncounted 91.49
uncouple 228
uncouth 463
uncover 17.418
uncovered 103.7
uncross 302
uncrowned 139
unction 261.80
unctuous 310.4
uncurbed 105
uncurl 216
uncut 378
undaunted 91.47
undecagon 254.5
undeceive 484.2
undecided 91.8
undefended 91.13
undefiled 117
undemonstrative
  485.15.11
undeniable 228.16.3
under 17.108
underachieve 484
underachiever 17.413
underact 382
underage 193
underarm 230
underbelly 16.115
underbid 91.4
underbody 16.65
underbred 86
underbrush 356
undercarriage 197.9
undercart 366
undercharge 192
underclay 2
undercoat 376

undercover 17.418
undercroft 399
undercurrent 420.64
underdevelop 281.1
underdog 185
underdone 259
underemployed 97
underestimate 367.15
underestimate 371.19
underestimation
  261.67.15
underexpose 520
underexposure 17.335
underfed 86
underfeed 89
underfelt 402
underfloor 9
underfoot 379.1
underfur 3
undergarment 420
undergird 87
undergo 12.33
undergone 254.5
undergraduate 371.2
underground 139.2
undergrown 257
undergrowth 461
underhand 128
underhanded 91.12
underhandedness
  300.28.1
underhung 267
underlaid 85
underlay 2.12
underlie 7.7
underline 253.3
underling 265
underlying 265.3
undermentioned 143
undermine 253
undermost 441
underneath 457
undernourish 353.10
undernourished 449
underpaid 85
underpants 347
underpass 294
underpay 2
underpin 252
underpinning 265.43
underplay 2
underplot 373
underprice 301
underprivileged 110

underproduction
  261.79.1
underquote 376
underrate 367.23
underripe 275
underscore 9
undersea 5
underseal 217.2
undersecretary 16.274.43
undersell 215.2
undersexed 450
undersheriff 163.2
undershirt 369
undershoot 380
undershot 373
underside 92.8
undersigned 135
undersized 154
underskirt 369
undersoil 222
understaffed 396
understand 128
understandable
  228.16.17
understanding 265.19
understate 367
understatement 420.48
understood 101
understudy 16.69
undertake 34
undertaken 261.11
undertaker 17.30
undertaking 265.6
undertone 257.3
undertook 44
undertow 12
undertrick 38
undertrump 289
undervalue 15
undervest 433
underwater 17.345
underwear 4.8
underweight 367.38
underwent 410
underwing 265
underworld 114
underwrite 372.8
underwriter 17.343
undescended 91.13
undeserved 147
undeserving 265.78
undesirable 228.16
undetected 91.43
undetermined 134
undeterred 87

undiagnosed 155
undid 91
undies 515
undigested 91.52
undignified 92.1
undiluted 91.42
undine 251
undirected 91.43
undisclosed 155
undiscovered 103.7
undisguised 154
undisputed 91.42
undissolved 151
undistinguished 449
undisturbed 105
undivided 91.8
undo 15
undoing 265.5
undone 259
undoubted 91
undress 296
undrinkable 228.16.11
undue 15
undulant 420.27
undulate 367.13
undulation 261.67.13
unduly 16.130
undying 265.3
unearned 132
unearth 456
unearthly 16.204
uneasy 16.395
uneconomic 38.29.1
unedited 91.38
unemployable 228.16.4
unemployed 97
unemployment 420.33
unending 265.20
unengaged 108
unenviable 228.16.2
unequal 228.71
unequalled 122
unequivocal 228.28
unerring 265.51
UNESCO 12.14
uneven 261.113
unevenness 300.31
uneventful 226.11
unexceptional 228.63
unexpected 91.43
unexpectedness 300.28
unexpired 93
unexplainable 228.16.27
unexploded 91.10
unexposed 155

unexpressed 433
unfading 265.11
unfailing 265.27
unfair 4
unfairness 300.22
unfaithful 226
unfaithfulness 300.30
unfamiliar 17.3.21
unfamiliarity
    16.333.20.1
unfasten 261.61
unfathomable 228.16
unfathomed 127
unfavourable 228.16.35
unfeeling 265.29
unfenced 447
unfetter 17.339
unfinished 449
unfit 371
unfitness 300.38
unfix 498
unflappable 228.16
unfledged 109
unflinching 265
unfold 120
unforeseeable 228.16.1
unforeseen 251
unforgettable 228.16.46
unforgivable 228.16
unforgiven 261.114
unforgotten 261.101
unformed 125
unfortunate 371.28.1
unfounded 91.14
unframed 124
unfreeze 513
unfriendliness 300.23
unfriendly 16.154
unfrock 40
unfroze 520
unfurl 216
unfurled 114
unfurnished 449
ungainly 16.170
unglazed 152
ungodliness 300.23
ungodly 16.149
ungovernable 228.16.31
ungrammatical
    228.23.18
ungrateful 226.7
unguarded 91.5
unguent 420
unguiculate 371.17.2
ungulate 371.17

unguligrade 85.5
unhallowed 98
unhand 128
unhappiness 300.23
unhappy 16.243
unharmed 123
unharness 300.21
unhealthiness 300.23
unhealthy 16.374
unheard 87
unheeded 91
unhelm 243
unhesitating 265.64
unhinge 209
unholy 16.126
unhook 44
unhorse 303
unhurried 91
unhurt 369
uni 16.236
Uniat 365
uniaxial 228.3.18
unicameral 228.76
UNICEF 160
unicorn 255.2
unicycle 228.24
unifoliate 371.1
uniform 238.1
uniformity 16.333.13
unify 7.3
unilateral 228.76
unimaginable 228.16.29
unimpaired 88
unimpeachable
    228.16.12
unimportant 420
unimpressed 433
unimproved 150
uninformed 125
uninspired 93
uninspiring 265.54
uninsured 96
unintelligent 420.20
unintelligible
    228.16.20.1
unintentional 228.63.9
uninterested 91.53
uninvited 91.39
uninviting 265.67
union 261.123
unionism 242.35.14
unionist 436.13
unionize 516.7
uniparous 310.50
unipod 94

usury 16.274
Utah 9
Ute 380
utensil 228.88
uterine 253.7
uterus 310.50
Utgard 84
Utica 17.34
utilitarian 261.3.21.2
utilitarianism 242.35.14.1.1
utility 16.333.9
utilize 516.2
utmost 441
Utopia 17.3.37
Utopian 261.3.19
utricle 228.23
utriculitis 300.62.2
Uttar Pradesh 351
utter 17.349
utterance 321.20
utterly 16.131
uvula 17.174
uvulitis 300.62.2
Uxbridge 197
uxorial 228.3.12
uxoricide 92.7
uxorious 310.2.13

V

Vaal 213
vac 32
vacancy 16.312
vacant 420
vacate 367.6
vacation 261.67
vacationer 17.239.1
vacationist 436.13.4
vaccinal 228.60
vaccinate 367.17
vaccination 261.67.18
vaccine 251
vaccinia 17.3.34
vacillate 367.12
vacillating 265.64
vacillation 261.67.12
vacua 17.7
vacuity 16.333.3
vacuole 223
vacuous 310.4
vacuum 242.3
vagabond 136
vagabondage 197
vagal 228.44

vagary 16.274
vagina 17.232
vaginal 228.61
vaginate 371.24.2
vaginismus 310.30
vaginitis 300.62.3
vagrancy 16.312
vagrant 420
vague 180
vagueness 300
vagus 310.19
vain 247
vainglory 16.269
vainly 16.170
vair 4
valance 321.10
vale 2
vale 214
valediction 261.78.1
valedictory 16.274.46
valence 321.11
Valenciennes 248.1
valency 16.312
Valens 546
valentine 253
Valentinian 261.3.17
Valentino 12.54
valerian 261.3.21
valeric 38.39
Valerie 16.274.15
valet 371
valetudinarian 261.3.21.1
Valhalla 17.160
valiant 420
valid 91.16
validate 367.8
validation 261.67.7
validity 16.333.5
valine 251
valise 513.7
Valium 242.2
Valkyrie 16.266
vallation 261.67.14
Valletta 17.339
valley 16.112
valonia 17.3.36.2
valorize 516.8
valorous 310.50
valour 17.160
valuable 228.16.6
valuation 261.67.2
value 15
valueless 300.11
valuer 17.7

valve 491
valvelet 371
valvular 17.174
valvule 227
valvulitis 300.62.2
vamoose 309
vamp 285
vampire 8
vampiric 38.40
vampirism 242.35
van 245
Van 246
vanadate 367.9
vanadium 242.2.1
Van Buren 261.59
Vancouver 17.419
vandal 228.39
vandalism 242.35.11
vandalize 516.3
Van de Graaff 158.1
Vanderbilt 403
Van der Waal 213
Vandyke 39
vane 247
van Eyck 39
vang 263
Van Gogh 40
vanguard 84
vanilla 17.166.1
vanillic 38.21
vanillin 252.8
vanish 353
vanity 16.333.14
vanquish 353
vantage 197
vapid 91
vaporescence 321.21
vaporetto 12.75
vaporific 38.12.1
vaporize 516.8
vaporizer 17.441.1
vaporous 310.50
vapour 17.249
var 1
varactor 17.353
Varanasi 16.307
varec 35
varia 17.3.38
variable 228.16.2
variance 321.1
variant 420.1
variation 261.67.1
varicella 17.163
varicellate 371.15
varicelloid 97.4

varices 513
varicoloured 103.4
varicose 305
varicosis 300.55
varicosity 16.333.30.3
varicotomy 16.222.4
varied 91
variegate 367.10
variegated 91.34.4
varietal 228.102
variety 16.333.2.1
variform 238.1
variola 17.176.1
variometer 17.342.3.1
variorum 242.20
various 310.2.10
variscite 372.9
varistor 17.384
varix 498
varlet 371
varmint 412
varna 17.226
varnish 353
varnisher 17.326
varsity 16.333
varve 481
vary 16.264
Vasari 16.261
Vasco da Gama 17.206
vascular 17.174
vasculum 242.10
vas deferens 546
vase 508
vasectomy 16.222.5
Vaseline 251.2
vasoconstrictor 17.355
vasodilator 17.338
vasopressin 252
vassal 228
vassalage 197
vast 431
vastness 300.42
vasty 16.362
vat 365
VAT 365
vatic 38.49
Vatican 261.13
Vaticanism 242.35.14.2
Vaud 12
vaudeville 218.3
vaudevillian 261.3.11
Vaughan 255
vault 404
vaulted 91.44
vaulting 265

vaunt 415
vavasor 9.11
veal 217
vealer 17.165
vector 17.354
Veda 17.79
vedalia 17.3.18
Vedanta 17.365
Vedda 17.80
vedette 368
Vedic 38
veer 6
veg 194
Vega 17.128
vegan 261
vegetable 228.16
vegetal 228.102
vegetarian 261.3.21.2
vegetarianism
    242.35.14.1.1
vegetate 367.30
vegetation 261.67.27
vegetative 485.15.12
vehement 420.31
vehicle 228.23
vehicular 17.174.6
veil 214
veiled 112
vein 247
veining 265.40
veiny 16.225
velamen 248.2
velar 17.165
Velcro 12
veld 402
veleta 17.341
veliger 17.150
velites 513
velleity 16.333.1
Vellore 9.8
vellum 242.8
veloce 16.50
velocipede 89.1
velocity 16.333.30
velodrome 239
velours 10
velouté 2.25
velure 10.4
velutinous 310.33.2
velvet 371
velveteen 251
velvety 16.333
vena 17.230
vena cava 17.410
venal 228.59

venality 16.333.8
venatic 38.49
venation 261.67
vend 131
vendee 5
vendetta 17.339
vendible 228.16.18
vendor 17.101
vendor 9
veneer 6.4
veneering 265.53
venerable 228.16.35
venerate 367.23.1
veneration 261.67.22.2
venereal 228.3.11
venereology 16.108.4.1
venery 16.274.23
venesection 261.77.5
Venetia 17.325
Venetian 261.70
Venetic 38.50.4
Venezuela 17.162
vengeance 321
vengeful 226
venial 228.3.6
Venice 300
venin 252.16
venipuncture 17.68
venison 261.65
Venite 16.334
venom 242
venomous 310.29
venose 305
venous 310.32
vent 410
ventage 197.14
venter 17.368
ventilate 367.12
ventilation 261.67.12
ventilator 17.338.5
ventral 228.80
ventricle 228.23
ventricular 17.174.6
ventriculus 310.25.2
ventriloquism 242.35
ventriloquist 436
ventriloquize 516
ventriloquy 16.259
venture 17.70
venturesome 242
Venturi 16.270
venue 15
venule 227
Venus 310.32
Venusian 261.3

victimize 516.4
victor 17.355
Victoria 17.3.41
Victorian 261.3.23
Victoriana 17.226.1
victorious 310.2.13
victory 16.274.46
victual 228.102
victualler 17.176.3
victuals 539
vicuna 17.238
vide 16.64
videlicet 368.7
video 12.3.1
vie 7
Vienna 17.228
Viennese 513.9
Vientiane 246
Vietcong 266
Vietminh 252
Vietnam 229
Vietnamese 513.8
view 15
viewable 228.16.7
viewer 17.8
viewfinder 17.103
viewing 265.5
viewless 300.12
viewpoint 416
vigil 218
vigilance 321
vigilant 420
vigilante 16.353
vignette 368
Vigo 12.28
vigorous 310.50
vigour 17.129
Viking 265
vilayet 368
vile 219
vileness 300
vilify 7.3
vilipend 131.3
villa 17.166
village 197.1
villager 17.150
villain 261.41
villainess 300.26
villainous 310.36
villainy 16.237
Villa-Lobos 302.1
villanella 17.163
villanelle 215
villein 261.41
villi 7.5

villous 310.23
Vilnius 308
vim 235
vimen 248
Viminal 228.60.4
vimineous 310.2.8
vinaigrette 368
vinasse 293
vincible 228.16.41
vindicate 367.5
vindication 261.67.5
vindictive 485.18
vine 253
vinegar 17.129
vinegarroon 260.3
vinegary 16.274.9
vinery 16.274.27
vineyard 84
viniculture 17.69
vinificator 17.338.2
Vinland 143
vino 12.54
vinosity 16.333.30.4
vinous 310.34
vintage 197
vintager 17.150
vinyl 218
viol 228.4
viola 17.171
viola 17.176.1
viola da gamba 17.23
viola d'amore 16.269
violate 367.14.1
violation 261.67.14.1
violence 321.12
violent 420.28
violet 371.18.1
violin 252.11
violinist 436.11
violist 436
violoncello 12.40
viper 17.254
viperous 310.50
virago 12.26
viral 228
virelay 2.11
virga 17.127
Virgil 218
virgin 252
virginal 228.60
Virginia 17.3.34
virginity 16.333.17
Virgo 12
virgulate 371.17
virgule 227

viridescent 420.67
viridian 261.3.5
viridity 16.333.5
virile 219
virilism 242.35.9
virility 16.333.9
virology 16.108.4
virtual 228.9
virtually 16.131.1
virtue 15
virtuosity 16.333.30.2
virtuoso 12.70
virtuous 310.4
virulence 321
virulent 420.27
virus 310.47
visa 17.440
visage 197
vis-à-vis 5
viscacha 17.50
viscera 17.279.2
visceral 228.76
viscid 91.29
viscoid 97
viscometer 17.342.3
viscose 305
viscosity 16.333.30
viscount 418
viscous 310.50
Vishnu 15
visibility 16.333.9.2.2
visible 228.16.63
Visigoth 459
vision 261.91
visionary 16.274.29
visit 371.38
visitant 420.76
visitation 261.67.27
visitatorial 228.3.12.2
visitor 17.342.4
visor 17.441
vista 17.384
Vistula 17.174
visual 228.9
visualize 516.3.3
vital 228.103
vitalism 242.35.11
vitality 16.333.8
vitalize 516.3
vitamin 252.15
vitellin 252.7
vitiate 367.1.6
vitiation 261.67.1.5
viticulture 17.69
Vitória 17.3.41

vitreous 310.2
vitrescence 321.21
vitrescent 420.67
vitric 38
vitrify 7.3
vitrine 251
vitriol 220.1
vitriolic 38.22
vituline 253
vituperate 367.23
vituperation 261.67.22
vituperative 485.15.10
viva 17.413
viva 17.415
vivace 16.47
vivacious 310.56
vivacity 16.333.25
Vivaldi 16.73
vivarium 242.2.14
viva voce 16.50
Vivian 261.3.30
vivid 91
vividness 300.28
vivify 7.3
viviparity 16.333.20
viviparous 310.50
vivisect 385.7
vivisection 261.77.5
vivisectionist 436.13.6
vixen 261
Viyella 17.163
vizier 6
vizierate 371.32
Vlach 33
Vladimir 6.2
vocab 18
vocable 228.16
vocabulary 16.274.18
vocal 228.26
vocalic 38.19
vocalise 513.7
vocalism 242.35.11
vocalist 436.7
vocalize 516.3
vocation 261.67.6
vocational 228.63.3
vocative 485.15.2
vociferate 367.23
vociferous 310.50.2
vodka 17
vogue 188
Vogul 228
voice 304
voiceless 300
voiceprint 412

void 97
voidance 321
voile 222
voir dire 6
Volans 544
volant 420
Volapuk 44
volatile 219
volatilize 516.2
volcanic 38.31
volcanize 516.7
volcano 12
volcanology 16.108.4.11
vole 223
Volga 17.138
volitant 420.76
volition 261.71.3
volitive 485.12
volley 16.122
volleyball 221
volost 438
Volsci 5
volt 405
Volta 17.364
voltage 197
voltaic 38.1
Voltaire 4
voltameter 17.342
volte-face 294
voluble 228.15
volume 241
voluminosity
  16.333.30.4
voluminous 310.33.1
voluntary 16.274.48
volunteer 6
voluptuary 16.274.2
voluptuous 310.4
voluptuousness 300.34.2
volute 380
volution 261.75.1
volva 17.423
Volvo 12
vomer 17.215
vomit 371.20
vomitus 310.64
voodoo 15
Voortrekker 17.31
voracious 310.56
voracity 16.333.25
vortex 496
vorticella 17.163
vortices 513
vorticism 242.35.16
vortiginous 310.33

Vostok 40
votary 16.274
vote 376
voter 17.347
votive 485.14
vouch 71
voucher 17.60
vouchsafe 159
vouge 364
Vouvray 2
vow 13
vowel 228.8
vox 499
vox humana 17.226
vox populi 7.6
voyage 197
voyager 17.150
voyageur 3
voyeur 3
voyeuristic 38.70.5
vraisemblance 315
vroom 241
Vulcan 261
vulcanian 261.3.15
vulcanite 372.6
vulcanize 516.7
vulgar 17.139
vulgarian 261.3.21
vulgarism 242.35.15
vulgarity 16.333.20
vulgarize 516.8
Vulgate 367
vulnerable 228.16.35
Vulpecula 17.174.4
vulpine 253
vulture 17.69
vulturine 253.7
vulva 17.424
vulvitis 300.62

W

WAAF 157
Wabash 349
wacky 16.19
wad 94
wadding 265
waddle 228.34
waddler 17.188
wade 85
wader 17.79
waders 524
wadi 16.65
Wadi Halfa 17.121
wafer 17.111

waffle 228
waft 396
wafter 17.358
wag 178
wage 193
wager 17.146
wages 515
wagga 17.131
Wagga Wagga 17.131
waggish 353
waggle 228.43
Wagner 17
Wagnerian 261.3.22
wagon 261.30
wagoner 17.239
wagonette 368
wagonload 98
wagtail 214
Wahhabi 16.6
waif 159
Waikato 12.73
Waikiki 5
wail 214
wain 247
wainscot 381
wainwright 372
waist 432
waistband 128
waistcoat 376
waisted 91
waistless 300
waistline 253
wait 367
waiter 17.338
waitress 300
waive 482
waiver 17.410
wake 34
Wakefield 115
wakeful 226
waken 261.11
waking 265.9
Walachia 17.3
Waldemar 1.11
Waldenses 513.14
waldgrave 482
Waldorf 166
Wales 536
walk 41
walkabout 377.1
walker 17.37
walkie-talkie 16.28
walking 265.9
walkover 17.417
walkway 2

wall 221
wallaby 16.15
Wallace 300.9
wallah 17.168
wallaroo 15.6
Wallasey 16.307
walled 118
wallet 371
walleye 7
walleyed 92
wallflower 14
Walloon 260
wallop 281.2
walloper 17.260
walloping 265
wallow 12.43
wallpaper 17.249
Wallsend 131
wally 16.122
walnut 378
Walpole 223
walrus 310
Walsall 221
Walsingham 242.17
Walton 261
waltz 312
waltzer 17.310
wampum 242
wan 254
wand 136
wander 17.104
wanderer 17.279
wandering 265.58
wanderlust 443
wanderoo 15.6
Wandsworth 464
wane 247
wangle 228.49
wank 51
Wankel 228
wanna 17.233
want 414
wanting 265
wanton 261
wapentake 34
wapiti 16.333
wappenshaw 9
war 9
waratah 17.352
Warbeck 35
warble 228
ward 95
warden 261.27
warder 17.86
wardrobe 28

wardroom 241
wardship 274
ware 4
warehouse 306
warehouseman 261
wares 512
warfare 4
warfarin 252.20
warhead 86
warhorse 303
wariness 300.23
warison 261.65.1
Warley 16.123
warlike 39
warlock 40
warlord 95
warm 238
warm-blooded 91.11
warmer 17.214
warmish 353
warmness 300
warmonger 17.143
warn 255
warning 265
warp 277
warpath 453
warplane 247
warrant 420.63
warrantable 228.16.57
warrantee 5.24
warrantor 9
warranty 16.360
warren 261
warrigal 212
warring 265.55
Warrington 261
warrior 17.3
Warsaw 9
warship 274
wart 374
wartime 236
warty 16.336
Warwick 38.41
Warwickshire 6
wary 16.264
was 517
wash 354
washable 228.16
washbasin 261.62
washboard 95
washday 2
washer 17.327
washerwoman 261.50
washery 16.274
washing 265

Washington 261
washrag 178
washroom 241
washstand 128
washtub 29
washy 16.323
wasn't 420
wasp 292
waspish 353
wassail 214
wastage 197
waste 432
wasteful 226.12
wasteland 143
wastrel 228
wat 366
watap 269
watch 68
watchcase 295
watchdog 185
watcher 17.57
watchful 226
watchmaker 17.30
watchman 261
watchstrap 268
watchtower 14
watchword 87
water 17.345
waterage 197
waterborne 255.1
waterbuck 43
watercolour 17.173
watercourse 303
watercress 296
waterfall 221
Waterford 103
waterfowl 224
waterfront 419.1
Watergate 367.11
waterlogged 106
Waterloo 15.5
waterman 261.52
watermark 33
watermelon 261.40
waterproof 170
waterscape 270
watershed 86
waterside 92.8
waterspout 377
watertight 372.12
waterway 2.28
waterweed 89
waterworks 497
waterworn 255
watery 16.274

Watford 103
Watson 261
watt 373
wattage 197
Watteau 12.77
wattle 228.104
Watusi 16.402
Watutsi 16.318
Waugh 9
waul 221
wave 482
waveband 128
waveform 238
waveguide 92
wavelength 472
wavelet 371
waver 17.410
wavy 16.379
wax 494
waxbill 218
waxen 261
waxplant 408
waxwing 265
waxwork 36
waxy 16.386
way 2
waybill 218
wayfarer 17.271
Wayland 143
waylay 2
Wayne 247
wayside 92
wayward 103
wayzgoose 309
we 5
weak 37
weaken 261.12
weakling 265
weakly 16.141
weakness 300
weal 217
Weald 115
wealth 465
wealthy 16.374
wean 251
weaner 17.230
weanling 265
weapon 261
weaponry 16.284
wear 4
Wear 6
wearable 228.16.33
wearer 17.271
weariless 300.8
weariness 300.23

wearing 265.52
wearisome 242.24
wearproof 170
weary 16.265
weasand 143.6
weasel 228
weather 17.402
weather-beaten 261.98
weatherboard 95.1
weathercock 40
weatherglass 294
weathering 265.58
weatherman 261.52
weatherproof 170
weatherworn 255
weave 484
weaver 17.413
weaverbird 87
weaving 265.79
web 21
webbed 104
webbing 265
webby 16.8
Weber 17.11
webfoot 379
website 372
wed 86
we'd 89
wedded 91.7
wedding 265.12
wedge 194
Wedgwood 101
wedlock 40
Wednesday 2
wee 5
weed 89
weedkiller 17.166
weedy 16.62
week 37
weekday 2
weekender 17.101
weekly 16.141
weeknight 372
weeny 16.228
weep 273
weeper 17.252
weeping 265.49
weepy 16.247
weever 17.413
weevil 228.119
weft 397
weigela 17.165
weigh 2
weighbridge 197
weight 367

weighting 265.64
weightless 300
weightlessness 300.33
weightlifter 17.359
weightlifting 265
weighty 16.329
Weihai 7
Weill 219
Weimaraner 17.226
weir 6
weird 90
weirdness 300
weka 17.30
welcome 242
weld 113
welder 17.93
welfare 4
well 215
we'll 217
well-aware 4.8
well-behaved 146
wellbeing 265.2
well-built 403
well-dressed 433
well-endowed 99
wellhead 86
well-heeled 115
wellies 515
Wellington 261
well-intentioned 143
well-matched 395
well-oiled 119
well-organized 154
well-paid 85
well-pleased 153
well-preserved 147
well-read 86
well-received 148
Wells 537
well-spent 410
well-timed 126
well-to-do 15.3
well-tried 92
well-wisher 17.326
Welshman 261
welt 402
welter 17.361
welterweight 367.38
Welwyn 252.7
Wembley 16.138
wen 248
Wenceslas 310
wench 79
wend 131
Wendy 16.78

Wensleydale 214
went 410
wentletrap 268
wept 422
were 3
we're 6
weren't 411
werewolf 175
wergild 116
Wesley 16.208
Wesleyan 261.3
Wessex 498
west 433
westbound 139
West Bromwich 197.4
wester 17.382
westerly 16.131
western 261.106
Westerner 17.239
westernism 242.35.14
westernize 516.7
westernmost 441
Westmeath 475
Westminster 17.394
Westmorland 143.4
Weston-super-Mare 4.4
Westphalia 17.3.18
westward 103
westwards 531
wet 368
wether 17.402
wetness 300
we've 484
Wexford 103
Weymouth 464
whack 32
whacking 265
whacko 12.8
whale 214
whaleboat 376
whalebone 257
whaler 17.162
whaling 265.27
wham 229
whang 263
Whangarei 2.17
whangee 5
whare 16.268
wharf 166
wharfinger 17.157
what 373
whatever 17.411
whatnot 373
whatsit 371
whatsoever 17.411

wheat 370
wheatear 6
wheaten 261.98
wheedle 228
wheel 217
wheelbarrow 12.60
wheelbase 295
wheelchair 4
wheeler 17.165
wheelie 16.118
wheelwright 372
wheeze 513
wheezy 16.395
whelk 48
whelp 283
when 248
whence 316
whene'er 4
whenever 17.411
where 4
whereabouts 344
whereas 507
whereat 365
whereby 7
where'er 4
wherefore 9
wherefrom 237
wherein 252
whereinto 15
whereof 487
whereon 254
whereto 15
whereupon 254
wherever 17.411
wherewith 476
wherewithal 221
wherrit 371.31
wherry 16.262
whet 368
whether 17.402
whetstone 257
whey 2
which 67
whichever 17.411
whicker 17.34
whiff 163
whiffle 228.41
whiffler 17.190
whiffletree 5
Whig 184
while 219
whim 235
whimbrel 228
whimper 17.263
whimsical 228.23

whimsicality 16.333.8.3
whimsy 16.403
whin 252
whinchat 365
whine 253
whinge 209
whinny 16.229
whip 274
whipcord 95
whiplash 349
whippersnapper 17.247
whippet 371
whipping 265
whippoorwill 218
whipsaw 9
whipstock 40
whirl 216
whirligig 184
whirlpool 227
whirlwind 134
whirlybird 87
whirr 3
whish 353
whisk 58
whisker 17.48
whiskered 103
whisky 16.41
whisper 17.266
whisperer 17.279
whist 436
whistle 228.85
whistling 265
whit 371
Whit 371
Whitaker 17.42
white 372
whitebait 367
whitebeam 234
whitecap 268
Whitechapel 228.64
whited 91.39
whitedamp 285
whitefish 353
Whitehall 221
whiten 261.100
whitener 17.239
whiteness 300.39
whites 340
whitethroat 376
whitewash 354
whitewood 101
whither 17.405
whiting 265.67
whitish 353
whitlow 12

Whitman 261
Whitsun 261
Whitsuntide 92.12
Whittington 261
whittle 228.102
whittler 17.201
whizz 515
who 15
whoa 12
who'd 102
whodunit 371.27
whoever 17.411
whole 223
wholefood 102
wholehearted 91.33
wholemeal 217
wholesale 214
wholesaler 17.162
wholesome 242
who'll 227
wholly 16.164
whom 241
whomever 17.411
whoop 280
whooper 17.259
whooping cough 165
whoosh 357
whop 276
whopper 17.255
whopping 265
whore 9
whoredom 242
whorehouse 306
whoremonger 17.143
whoreson 261
whortleberry 16.274
who's 523
whose 523
whoso 12
why 7
Whyalla 17.160
whydah 17.83
Wichita 9
wick 38
Wick 38
wicked 91
wickedness 300.28
wicker 17.34
wickerwork 36
wicket 371.9
wicketkeeper 17.252
wickiup 279
wicopy 16.254.1
wide 92
widen 261.25

widespread 86
widget 371
widgie 16.103
Widnes 300.28
widow 12.19
widower 17.6
widowhood 101
widthwise 516
wield 115
wielder 17.94
wieldy 16.74
wiener 17.230
wife 164
wig 184
Wigan 261.32
wigeon 261.37
wigging 265
wiggle 228.46
wiggly 16.160
Wight 372
wigwam 229
Wilberforce 303.1
wilco 12
wild 117
wildcat 365
Wilde 117
wildebeest 435
wilderness 300.26
wildfire 8
wildfowl 224
wildlife 164
wildness 300
wile 219
wilful 226.3
Wilhelm 243
Wilhelmina 17.230
Wilkins 548
will 218
willable 228.16.23
willet 371.16
William 242
Williams 543
Williamsburg 182
Williamson 261
willies 515
willing 265.30
willingness 300.32
will-o'-the-wisp 291
willow 12.42
willowherb 22
willowy 16.3
willpower 14
willy-nilly 16.120
willy-willy 16.120
Wilson 261

wolverine 251.7
woman 261.50
womanhood 101
womanish 353
womanize 516.7
womanizer 17.441
womankind 135
womanly 16.174
womb 241
wombat 365
women 252.14
womenfolk 42
won 254
won 259
wonder 17.108
wonderful 226
wonderland 143.4
wonderment 420.35
wonderwork 36
wonder-worker 17.32
wondrous 310
wonky 16.38
wont 417
won't 417
wonted 91
won ton 254
woo 15
wood 101
woodbine 253
woodborer 17.276
woodchat 365
woodchuck 43
woodcock 40
woodcraft 396
woodcut 378
woodcutter 17.349
wooded 91
wooden 261
woodenhead 86
woodgrouse 306
woodland 143
woodlander 17.109
woodlark 33
woodlouse 306
woodman 261
woodnote 376
woodpecker 17.31
woodpile 219
woodruff 168
woodscrew 15
woodshed 86
woodwind 134
woodwork 36
woodworking 265
woodworm 233

woody 16.70
woof 169
woof 170
woofer 17.119
wool 226
Woolf 175
woolgathering 265.58
woollen 261
woolly 16.129
woolpack 32
woolsack 32
Woomera 17.279
Woop Woop 280
woozy 16.402
Worcester 17.388
Worcestershire 6
word 87
wordage 197
wordbreak 34
wording 265
wordless 300
wordplay 2
Wordsworth 464
wordy 16.61
wore 9
work 36
workable 228.16
workaday 2.8
workbag 178
workbench 79
workbook 44
workday 2
worker 17.32
workfolk 42
workhorse 303
workhouse 306
working 265
workload 98
workman 261
workmanlike 39
workmanly 16.174
workmanship 274.2
workroom 241
workshop 276
workshy 7
Worksop 276
worktable 228.11
world 114
worldliness 300.23
worldling 265
worldly 16.153
worldwide 92
worm 233
wormcast 431
wormwood 101

wormy 16.214
worn 255
worriment 420.31
worrisome 242.24
worrit 371
worry 16.272
worrywart 374
worse 297
worsen 261.64
worship 274
worshipful 226
worshipper 17.253
worst 434
worsted 91
wort 369
worth 456
Worthing 265
worthless 300
worthlessness 300.33
worthwhile 219
worthy 16.375
Wotan 246
would 101
wouldn't 420.12
wound 139
wound 142
wounded 91
woundwort 369
wove 488
woven 261.116
wow 13
wowser 17.443
wrack 32
wraith 454
wrangle 228.49
wrangler 17.194
wrap 268
wrapover 17.417
wrapper 17.247
wrapping 265
wrapping 265.48
wrasse 293
wrath 459
wrathful 226
wreak 37
wreath 457
wreathe 475
wreck 35
wrecker 17.31
Wrekin 252
wren 248
wrench 79
wrest 433
wrestle 228
wrestler 17.197

He just wanted a decent book to read ...

Not too much to ask, is it? It was in 1935 when Allen Lane, Managing Director of Bodley Head Publishers, stood on a platform at Exeter railway station looking for something good to read on his journey back to London. His choice was limited to popular magazines and poor-quality paperbacks – the same choice faced every day by the vast majority of readers, few of whom could afford hardbacks. Lane's disappointment and subsequent anger at the range of books generally available led him to found a company – and change the world.

'We believed in the existence in this country of a vast reading public for intelligent books at a low price, and staked everything on it'
Sir Allen Lane, 1902–1970, founder of Penguin Books

The quality paperback had arrived – and not just in bookshops. Lane was adamant that his Penguins should appear in chain stores and tobacconists, and should cost no more than a packet of cigarettes.

Reading habits (and cigarette prices) have changed since 1935, but Penguin still believes in publishing the best books for everybody to enjoy. We still believe that good design costs no more than bad design, and we still believe that quality books published passionately and responsibly make the world a better place.

So wherever you see the little bird – whether it's on a piece of prize-winning literary fiction or a celebrity autobiography, political tour de force or historical masterpiece, a serial-killer thriller, reference book, world classic or a piece of pure escapism – you can bet that it represents the very best that the genre has to offer.

Whatever you like to read – trust Penguin.